Readings in Intellectual Property
A Selection of Articles from EIPR and Ent. L.R.

Editors
ALISON FIRTH, SHELLEY LANE, YVONNE SMYTH
Faculty of Laws, Queen Mary and Westfield College, University of London

1998
SWEET & MAXWELL
LONDON

Published in 1998 by
Sweet & Maxwell Limited of
100 Avenue Road, London NW3 3PF
(http://www.smlawpub.co.uk)
Typeset by Selwood Systems,
Midsomer Norton
Printed in Great Britain by
MPG Books Ltd, Bodmin

No natural forests were destroyed to make this product;
only farmed timber was used and replanted.

A C.I.P. catalogue record for this book
is available from the British Library.

ISBN 0–421–580–208

Readings in Intellectual Property
A Selection of Articles from EIPR and Ent. L.R.

AUSTRALIA
LBC Information Services Ltd
Sydney

CANADA and USA
Carswell
Toronto

NEW ZEALAND
Brooker's
Auckland

SINGAPORE and MALAYSIA
Thomson Information (S.E. Asia)
Singapore

Preface

This is a selection of articles which we have found useful in teaching at undergraduate and postgraduate levels. Some are old friends: the law may have developed but the authors' analyses and insights have stood the test of time. Others are very recent and give an up-to-the-minute account. There are many other equally valuable pieces which we would have included, had space permitted. We hope that it may be possible to include some of them at a later date.

In making our selection we have drawn on the experience of colleagues in the field. We have tried to strike a balance between the different areas of intellectual property as it appears on the pages of the European Intellectual Property Review and its sister publication, the Entertainment Law Review. Within each category we have tried to include a range of theoretical and practical views, and to give a national and international dimension. After a first chapter on general issues which apply to intellectual property 'across the board', this collection is divided into chapters devoted to the different forms of intellectual property—copyright and designs, passing off and trade marks, patents and breach of confidence. In each of these areas, articles on concepts, context or policy are followed by pieces on substantive principles: subject matter, validity, ownership and transactions, infringement, defences. International aspects are dealt with in the final part of each chapter. Comments and articles on remedies make up the final chapter.

We hope that users will find the collection illuminating and would welcome any comments from readers or librarians. These may be addressed to us at the Faculty of Laws, Queen Mary and Westfield College, or at the publishers.

Our thanks go to the authors for writing the pieces in the first place and for allowing their reproduction in this edition, to editors and publishers of the EIPR and Ent. L.R. who procured their publication the first time round, and to Sweet & Maxwell who have seen the project through to publication.

Alison Firth, Shelley Lane, Yvonne Smyth
August 1997

Table of Contents

Copyright & Designs: Designs

Passing Off and Trade Marks: Passing Off

Passing Off and Trade Marks: Trade Marks

Patents and Related Rights

Breach of Confidence

Remedies

General Aspects of Intellectual Property

Intellectual Property Protection After GATT

[1994] 5 EIPR 195

JOHN WORTHY

Partner, Denton Hall, London

Towards the end of 1993, the commercial world held its breath as international trade negotiators attempted to conclude the discussions on the General Agreement on Tariffs and Trade (GATT) before the 15 December deadline. The major issues under debate at that stage were, of course, the EC/US controversies over agricultural subsidies and the film industry. Nevertheless, one of the important aspects of GATT is the way in which it establishes new multilateral international standards for the protection and enforcement of intellectual property rights. This will have a significant impact on the legal environment for international trade, particularly those operating in, or dealing with, developing countries.

During the previous GATT round, many countries, both industrialised and developing, became increasingly aware of the problem of counterfeiting. As a result, an attempt was made at that stage to lay down common rules for the seizure of counterfeit products by customs authorities. In the event, the proposal ran out of time, but the importance of the issues had been established.

When the Uruguay Round started in 1986, the agenda was extended to cover general issues of intellectual property protection, as well as counterfeiting. Perhaps predictably, there was a tension between the industrialised world and developing countries about the desirability of high levels of protection for intellectual property rights. Industrialised countries saw intellectual property rights as a primary means of promoting technological development by offering inventors and others the chance to gain rewards for their labours. By contrast, many developing countries considered that the purpose of intellectual property was to reinforce the economic power of the Western industrial nations and transfer wealth from the power countries to the richer ones.

During the course of the negotiations, however, a consensus emerged on the need for intellectual property protection. Indeed, while the debates about agricultural subsidies were continuing to rage, progress was made on the proposed text on the trade-related aspects of intellectual property, commonly known as the TRIPS Agreement. Although it received relatively little publicity, it is a major breakthrough in the international protection of intellectual property, both because of its substance and because of the wide measure of international acceptance it achieved.

Essential Principles of the TRIPS Agreement

The TRIPS Agreement is founded on three key principles. The first is to establish minimum standards for the protection and enforcement of intellectual property rights in signatory states. These cover copyright and related rights, trade marks, geographical indications, industrial designs, patents, integrated circuit layouts and trade secrets. The essential point is that these are minimum standards. There is nothing to stop signatory states operating higher standards as long as these do not undermine the effect of the TRIPS Agreement.

The second is that each country should protect nationals of other parties by granting them the rights set out in the Agreement. This principle of national treatment mirrors the provisions in GATT concerned with international trade in goods and the major treaties on intellectual property.

Third, signatories are required to confer on nationals of other parties intellectual property protection no less favourable than is provided to their own nationals. In addition, whatever rights are conferred on nationals of any other country must be granted to nationals of all other countries. This is known as the 'most favoured nation' principle.

In effect, the Agreement requires member countries to protect intellectual property on a basis broadly similar to those set out in the Berne Convention,[1] the Paris Convention,[2] the Rome Convention[3] and the Washington IPIC Treaty (Treaty on Intellectual Property in Respect of Integrated Circuits).[4] The result is (or will be) a system of international protection based on the principle of non-discrimination and backed by a minimum base-line of protection in all 117 signatory countries. The nature of this achievement should not be underestimated.

There was extensive discussion about how far the new regime would be affected by the rules on exhaustion of rights, such as those developed over the years in the EC. However, there was not sufficient consensus to address the issue fully. In the event, the TRIPS Agreement specifies that, subject to the principle of national treatment and the most favoured nation principle, it does not address the issue of exhaustion of intellectual property rights. The outcome leaves the EC free to apply its exhaustion principles as long as it does so on a non-discriminatory basis.

The essential elements of the protection for the various forms of intellectual property can be summarised as follows:

Copyright and related rights

In broad terms, the Agreement follows the principle laid down in the Berne Convention as a starting point but builds on this platform in certain areas. However, in deference to the powerful US lobby, it does not include specific protection for moral rights. This does not, of course, prevent moral rights being recognised, as has been the case in the United Kingdom since 1989 and in most continental European countries for much longer.

There was some debate whether computer programs should be protected as 'literary works' and how far databases should be specifically referred to. In the event, it was accepted that copyright should extend to computer programs in object code or source code form. Moreover, following substantially the proposed EC directive on the subject, databases which, by reason of the selection or arrangement of their contents, constitute intellectual creations are to be protected as compilations. It will remain an issue for debate what level of creativity

---

[1] Berne Convention for the Protection of Literary and Artistic Works.
[2] Paris Convention for the Protection of Industrial Property.
[3] International Convention for the Protection of Performers, Producers of Phonograms and Broadcasting Organisations, adopted at Rome, 26 October 1961.
[4] Adopted 26 May 1989.

this requires, whether that adopted by the US Supreme Court in *Feist v Rural Telephone*[5] or something more akin to the traditional UK test of the 'sweat of the brow'. The point is, however, particularly significant because the TRIPS provisions extend to both manual and electronic databases, by contrast with the draft EC measures which cover only electronic ones.

The Agreement goes beyond the Berne Convention in providing for a rental right. Holders of rights in films, sound recordings, phonographs and computer programs will have the exclusive right to authorise or prohibit commercial rental. This has a number of parallels with the Rental Right Directive in the EC.[6]

In general, signatories will be free to determine the specifics of any exceptions to copyright, such as the United Kingdom's fair dealing defence. The Agreement merely requires any such exceptions to be limited to cases which do not conflict with the normal exploitation of the work and do not unreasonably prejudice the legitimate interests of the copyright owner. The exact effect of this provision is less than crystal clear. While the principle is unobjectionable, it leaves considerable scope for argument about its application in practice. Its value should probably be seen in establishing a platform for persuading countries with unusually wide-ranging, anomalous or arbitrary defences to bring their laws into line with broader international practice.

Trade marks

The Agreement specifies the subject-matter protectable as a trade mark in a similar way to the EC Harmonisation Directive and the UK Trade Marks Bill currently proceeding through Parliament. It includes 'any sign or combination of signs capable of distinguishing goods or services of any undertaking from those of other undertakings'. This would include shapes, personal names, combinations of colours and containers (such as a Coca-Cola bottle).

One of the major debates during negotiations was how far prior use of a mark was to be a requirement for an application for registration. Here the United States and the EC were in opposing camps. The EC wanted to prohibit any requirement for use, which was a problem for the United States—it would then have been forced to change its laws. In the event, a compromise was reached: prior use could be required for registration but not for filing an application for registration.

Specific protection is given to well-known marks by prohibiting registration of the same or similar marks for similar products by someone not connected with the owner. This follows Article 6*bis* of the Paris Convention. There has long been controversy about how to determine whether a mark is well known. However, the TRIPS Agreement goes some way towards clarifying the issue by indicating that account is to be taken of the knowledge of the mark in the relevant sector of the public, including knowledge resulting from promotion. Although far from a comprehensive test, this formula will at least help mark owners who have conducted extensive advertising.

Moreover, protection for well-known marks is extended to give rights against products (or services) which are not similar to the genuine goods (or services) where the use would be likely to indicate a link between those products and the owner of the well-known mark, if this is likely to damage the owner's interests. This is an important safeguard for the owners of well-known marks who wish to extend their operations into new fields (which is increasingly common) or are at risk of having their reputation diluted by cases such as 'Coca-Cola jeans'.

---

[5] 111 S.Ct 1282 (1991).
[6] 92/100/EC, OJ 1992 L346/61.

Geographical indications

As a result of pressure from the EC, a section was included on the protection of geographical indications. These identify a product as originating in a signatory country where a particular quality, reputation or other characteristic of the product is essentially attributable to its geographical origin. Examples include champagne, Harris tweed and scotch. The Agreement establishes protection for geographical indications against misleading the public or unfair competition.

Industrial designs

There are a number of basic rules in the TRIPS Agreement about the way in which industrial designs should be protected. In fact, this area is the least detailed in the Agreement, which may at first sight seem curious given the level of interest in the subject in the United Kingdom and the EC over recent years. The outcome is more a reflection on the degree of controversy at the international level on the most suitable approach. In the absence of a well-established foundation (either through a previous multilateral treaty or by consensus) on the proper basis of protection, it is perhaps surprising that even these principles were agreed.

During the negotiations one of the debates was about the relevance of novelty and originality to protection. Many countries favoured a cumulative test – protection should depend on the design being both new and original. This was opposed by the EC delegation on the grounds that it would be too restrictive. The final text adopts the EC position— designs must be new or original. In either case, they must be independently created (although, of course, this will normally be easy to satisfy if the design is shown to be new or original).

The rights protecting an industrial design are to last for at least ten years and protect against copying for commercial purposes and may be subject to limited exceptions on similar lines to those under the copyright regime.

At a relatively late stage in the negotiations, the US automotive industry became concerned about design protection for spare parts. As a result, signatory countries are permitted to exclude from protection designs 'dictated essentially by technical or functional considerations'.

Patents

Probably the most significant achievement of the TRIPS Agreement is the regime covering patents. This is because in this area, more than in others, the divergent approaches of the industrialised and the less developed countries is particularly apparent. On the one hand, developing countries view patents as restricting their ability to obtain and exploit sophisticated technologies. On the other, developed countries consider an established patent system to be vital to encourage industrial research and development. Faced with such diametrically opposing positions, it is no mean feat to have settled on a formula which both factions felt they could live with.

The two burning questions in the patents field concerned the criteria for patentability and the rules governing the grant of compulsory licences. On the first issue, the criteria broadly reflect the provisions of the European Patent Convention (and hence the UK Patents Act), that is, the invention must be new, involve an inventive step and be capable of industrial application.

The issue of what areas of technology could be excluded from the patent system was a matter of heated debate. There was pressure from many less developed countries to exclude a range of inventions concerned with animal and plant life and extending to pharmaceutical products and processes. This they saw as justified on the grounds of protecting the public interest.

At the other extreme, the United States was in favour of a broad ambit of patent protection in these areas, reflecting its own national system. In the event, the Agreement allows (but does not require) exclusions for, among other things, diagnostic and therapeutic methods (but not pharmaceutical products) for the treatment of humans or animals, plants and animals (other than micro-organisms) and essentially biological processes for the production of plants or animals.

When addressing the issue of compulsory licences, various attempts were made to devise a list of circumstances where the issue of a licence would be justified without the patentee's consent. In the end, the proponents of a comprehensive framework had to accept a compromise once it became clear that agreement on the circumstances in which compulsory licences could be granted was impossible to achieve. Instead, the Agreement specifies that a series of procedural and similar requirements must be followed before a compulsory licence may be granted.

Licences must be granted on the individual merits of the case and, therefore, cannot simply be conditional on a particular event occurring. Licences must be non-exclusive, non-assignable and based on adequate remuneration for the patentee. Significantly, any decision relating to the grant of a compulsory licence is to be subject to judicial review. In addition, a licence is only available if the patentee and the applicant have failed to agree commercial terms within a reasonable period of time.

Integrated circuit layouts

Some time after the United States, the EC and Japan had introduced specific protection for integrated circuit layouts, international delegations concluded the IPIC Treaty in 1989. However, its acceptance, especially by the United States and Japan, was hampered by the fact that it followed lower standards than those countries had already introduced.

In order to overcome this hurdle, the TRIPS Agreement adopts the majority of the IPIC Treaty with a number of enhancements to satisfy the US/Japanese lobby. In particular, minimum protection is extended from eight to ten years from first commercial exploitation or application for registration; innocent purchasers of infringing products are not treated as infringers but, after notice of infringement, must pay reasonable royalties for current stock; and compulsory licences are subject to the same procedural safeguards as apply to patents.

Trade secrets

The protection afforded to trade secrets in different countries is variable in nature and extent. It is therefore particularly significant that trade secret protection is covered by the TRIPS text, since it has not previously been dealt with in detail in a multilateral agreement.

Signatories are required to establish two essential forms of protection. First, trade and business secrets must be protected against use or disclosure 'contrary to honest commercial practices'. This broad concept is defined to include breach of contract and breach of confidence. Each country is free to choose whether this is done through property rights laws of confidentiality or unfair competition. Second, data concerning marketing approval for new pharmaceutical or agro-chemical products is specifically protected against unfair commercial use.

Enforcement

As may have found to their cost in the past, potentially sound protection for intellectual property rights is worthless unless it is backed up by effective methods of enforcement. Indeed, this aspect was one of the driving forces, particularly among developed countries, in the initiative for the TRIPS Agreement. Set against this, a number of developing countries were concerned that they would be forced to establish a separate judicial system in order to deal with intellectual property rights protection or that they would not have adequate resources to provide the appropriate levels of enforcement.

It is therefore notable that a framework for enforcement procedures was agreed. In the context of intellectual property rights, one of the most important provisions is a requirement to establish emergency remedies on an *ex parte* basis to prevent infringement or to preserve evidence. In addition, procedures should be fair and equitable. They must not be unnecessarily complicated or costly or entail unwarranted delays—some would argue that UK High Court procedures fall short of the required standards in these respects. Remedies should cover injunctions, damages, costs and (in most cases) destruction of infringing items. There is also a mechanism for a limited form of discovery where one party has specified evidence relevant to the substantiation of its claims which is in the possession of the other party. This will be helpful as long as the courts do not interpret it as requiring such a level of specificity that it is almost impossible to comply with.

Anti-competitive Practices

The different views of the developing and industrialised world concerning the patent system are symptomatic of their respective approaches to the nature and function of intellectual property itself. These came to the fore again when the developing countries proposed to restrict the freedoms of rightowners in granting licences. According to their view, the ability of a governmental authority to regulate licensing practices is an essential part of technology transfer and a means of ensuring responsible development. In some cases, it goes further in advocating a trade-off between the grant of exclusive rights and a commitment to technology transfer. Not surprisingly, industrialised countries had difficulty with this position, even though most recognise the need for some degree of control over licensing where it has anti-competitive effects.

The Agreement takes account of the first (although not the second) concern of the developing countries. Signatories are allowed to outlaw licensing practices which amount to an abuse of intellectual property rights having an adverse effect on competition (such as exclusive grant-back clauses, no-challenge provisions and coercive package licensing, that is, tie-ins). These principles are familiar to those doing business in the EC. Beyond that, the Agreement recognises that intellectual property rights should contribute to the transfer and dissemination of technology to the mutual benefit of producers and users. At a political level, it appears that this was sufficient to satisfy the developing countries' delegations, even though it is left as simply a statement of principle.

Timetable

It is expected that the TRIPS Agreement will come into force later this year. Once the TRIPS Agreement is in force, industrialised countries will have one year to comply with its provisions. Developing countries have a more relaxed timetable for implementation. As an initial step, within the first year they must introduce national treatment of foreigners and the most favoured nation principle. In the medium term, they have five years to comply with the remaining provisions of the Agreement. Even then, where implementation of the Agreement would entail extending product patent protection to a field of technology not previously protected, an additional five-year grace period is allowed.

Conclusion

The TRIPS Agreement is a welcome development for companies involved in international trading activities, particularly Western companies active in developing countries. It will allow them to have greater confidence that the intellectual property rights which they rely on in the developed world to protect their commercial investment will also be acknowledged in less developed countries. It also means that they will have to consider whether separate steps are required to take advantage of the new forms of protection which will be offered in those countries. Equally importantly, they can look forward to a more uniform and reliable method of enforcing intellectual property rights in developing countries. At a time when many developing countries offer the benefits of low overhead costs and high industrial growth rates, those countries will become even more attractive commercial prospects.

The Increasing Influence of Intellectual Property Cases on the Principles of Statutory Interpretation

[1996] 10 EIPR 526

ABBE E.L. BROWN
Gouldens Solicitors, London

... the court, when acting in its interpretative role ... is doing so as mediator between the state in its exercise of its legislative power and the private citizen ... Elementary justice or ... the need for legal certainty demands that the rules by which a citizen is to be bound should be ascertainable by him (or, more realistically, by a competent lawyer advising him) by reference to identifiable sources that are publicly accessible.[1]

*   *   *

... it would be wrong to apply rules of construction developed during a period when one philosophy of draftsmanship was prevalent to a statute drafted when an entirely different philosophy applied.[2]

Legal advice is sought in the hope that the advice received will be clear and accurate. Solicitors look to statutes and the rules of statutory interpretation to provide such advice. It is therefore of immense practical importance for both solicitors and clients that the rules of statutory interpretation are clearly established. When turning to a new piece of legislation solicitors are faced, however, with an array of potential sources of assistance: English case law; records of Parliamentary debates (*Hansard*); White Papers; Law Commission Reports; decisions of the European Court of Justice ('ECJ'); European Union ('EU') directives and their *travaux préparatoires*; minutes of the EU Council; and decisions of the national courts of other EU Member States. This is particularly so in the field of intellectual property law which has recently seen new legislation (both primary and secondary) enacted in the United Kingdom and is the subject of European directives and regulations as the movement towards harmonisation of intellectual property rights throughout the EU continues. A review of the development of principles of statutory interpretation reveals the different philosophies (which are not confined to the dichotomy between English and European methods) which have been applied by the English courts, the resultant movement away from an extremely narrow principle and arguably the ultimate reversion to a conservative approach.

---

[1] *Fothergill v Monarch Airlines Ltd* [1981] AC 251 at 279 *per* Lord Diplock.
[2] *Wagamama Ltd v City Centre Restaurants plc (1) City Centre Restaurants (UK) Ltd (formerly Garfunkels Restaurants plc) (2)* [1995] FSR 713 at 722 to 723.

Basic Principles

The principle that an English court looks at the actual wording of an Act of Parliament, and cannot look behind those words at what was said in parliamentary debate, is 'judge made' and was first enunciated in 1769.[3] An oft-cited reason for this principle is said to be fear of breach of Article 9 of the Bill of Rights 1689.[4] This accepted constitutional principle continues to govern statutory interpretation. From an early stage, however, it has not been immutable. Since 1898, courts have been able to have regard to White Papers[5] 'for the purpose solely of ascertaining the mischief which the statute is intended to cure'.[6]

There is much which can be said in support of a situation where individuals (and practitioners) can act in reliance on the actual wording of statutes. Possible disadvantages of the alternative are evident: the logistical difficulties of access to *Hansard* and the consequent costs with little likelihood of finding the 'crock of gold'; the fact that the issue in question may not have been anticipated by Parliament; and the potential effect on the willingness of Ministers and Members of Parliament to speak freely in Parliamentary debate.[7]

Impact of European Integration

With the accession of the United Kingdom to the (then) European Economic Community, methods of statutory interpretation changed, as did all facets of UK law.[8] While certain EU instruments are directly applicable,[9] the expansion of accepted rules of interpretation was necessary to encompass legislation implementing a directive. It has been established by ECJ case law that an English court is to have regard to the wording of a directive in interpreting both the implementing statute and in interpreting subsequent and prior national legislation on the subject to ensure that it is not incompatible with Community legislation.[10]

The first significant indication of the effect of European integration on the way statutory interpretation was viewed by the English courts came in 1988 with the decision of the House of Lords in *Pickstone v Freemans plc*.[11] It was held that a court could have regard to what was said by a Minister in Parliament as an aid to interpretation of the intended meaning of the legislation. As this case involved secondary legislation enacted to ensure that the United Kingdom complied with its obligations under a Directive (the ECJ previously having held that the existing legislation was inadequate), it was argued subsequently in England that the

---

[3] *Millar v Taylor* (1769) 4 Burr. 2373 at 2332 *per* Willes J.

[4] Article 9 Bill of Rights 1689 provides 'that the freedome of speech and debate or proceedings in Parlyment ought not to be impeached or questioned in any court or place out of Parlyment'.

[5] For example, *Eastman Photographic Materials Co. Ltd v Comptroller-General of Patents, Designs and Trademarks* [1898] AC 571. This case dealt with a report of a Royal Commission.

[6] *Pepper (Inspector of Taxes) v Hart* [1993] AC 593 at 630 *per* Lord Browne-Wilkinson. Lord Browne-Wilkinson went on to note that in *R v Secretary of State for Transport, ex parte Factortame Ltd* [1990] 2 AC 85, the House of Lords had regard to a Law Commission report to ascertain 'the mischief' but also to draw an inference as to Parliamentary intent.

[7] In 1969 the Law Commissions of England and Scotland in their joint Report on the Interpretation of Statutes, and the Renton Committee on the Preparation of Legislation, advised on such grounds against a movement away from the basic principle.

[8] In *Factortame v Secretary of State for Transport*, Note 6 above, the House of Lords held that any act of Parliament subsequent to the European Communities Act 1972 may be subject to judicial review if it were to contravene the directly enforceable rights conferred by the EC Treaty. The principle that Parliament cannot bind itself does not apply to the European Communities Act 1972.

[9] No national implementing legislation is therefore required to give rise to rights in Member States.

[10] *Marleasing v La Commercial* (Case C-106/8D [1990] ECR 4135).

[11] [1989] AC 66.

effect of this decision should therefore be confined to such circumstances.[12]

Can reference also be made to sources such as statements in minutes of the meetings of the Council? There is a wealth of inconsistency on this point, and it would appear that many of the decisions could arguably be explained on the basis of the particular circumstances in issue.[13] A case frequently cited is *Antonissen*,[14] where the ECJ in its 1991 judgment held that a statement recorded in the minutes of the EC Council which was not referred to in the legislation had no legal significance and could not be used for the purpose of interpreting the legislation. The opinion of Advocate General Darman in this case is, however, of interest: he said that in the light of the decisions available, it could not be said that the Council minutes had no interpretative role.[15] He went on to state that a declaration recorded in the Council minutes regarding the adoption of the relevant item of secondary legislation which the Council had power to adopt could be used as an aid to interpretation; it could not be relied on, however, where it conflicted with or was incompatible with the clear wording of secondary legislation, neither could it be seen as a parallel form of legislation nor used to fill a lacuna in the legislation. Any declaration would also have to be used in conjunction with other sources. Accordingly, in the circumstances in issue, the Advocate General felt that the declaration did not afford useful guidance to interpretation. The general view of the Advocate General was reiterated in *Egle* (1992)[16] in which the ECJ held that it was permissible to refer to a joint declaration of the EC Commission and Council, included in the contemporary (confidential) minutes of the Council, to bolster an interpretation of a Council Directive.[17]

Situation in 1992

A 1992 review of development would have revealed the following principles: an English court could have regard to White Papers, but not to *Hansard*, to interpret a 'home grown' statute; in interpretation of English statutes enacted to implement Directives, an English court could look to the language of the Directive; and the ECJ had indicated that it was

---

[12]   For example, Attorney-General in *Pepper v Hart*, Note 6 above. There had, however, been other, significant developments regarding this principle; *Beswick v Beswick* [1968] AC 58 (reference made to what was said in Parliament regarding the interpretation of a consolidation Act) and *A-G Reference (No. 1 of 1988)* [1989] AC 97. Later, in *Factortame*, Note 6 above, the House of Lords looked at a Law Commission report not only to ascertain the mischief to be cured but also to ascertain Parliament's intention. It has, however, also been said that reference to *Hansard* was unnecessary in that case as the same result would have been achieved in reliance on section 2(2) European Communities Act 1972.

[13]   For example, in *EC Commission v Italy* (Case 38/69), the ECJ said that it was for the Council to adopt decisions which were binding on Member States and any conditions formulated during preparatory discussions of the Council could not be relied on to justify non-compliance. In that case, the exact import of the statement in question could not be determined. In *Vincent Auer* (Case 138/78), reference is made to a declaration recorded in the Minutes of the Meeting of the Council—however, it merely stated that this confirmed the judgment of the ECJ. In *EC Commission v Belgium* (Case 237/84, the ECJ stated that the true meaning of Community rules was to be derived from the rules themselves, and their scope could not be restricted by a declaration of certain Member States. The declaration in question was, however, incompatible with the Treaty of Rome and the wording of the Directive.

[14]   *R v Immigration Appeal Tribunal ex parte Antonissen* (Case C-292/89). The declaration in question had been made pursuant to Rules of Procedure which gave no particular status to Council declarations, but merely confirmed that the Council minutes were themselves confidential.

[15]   Reference was made to, *inter alia*, the decision in *United Kingdom v EC Council* (Case 131/86) that there was scope in interpreting secondary legislation for consideration of documents which were created in preparation of or accompanying the adoption of the measure in question. The ECJ stated in that case that the limits of such scope were, however, to be defined.

[16]   *Conseil National de l'Ordre des Architectes v Egle* (Case C-310/90); Advocate General Darman was also involved in this case.

[17]   Again, the declaration in the minutes served to confirm the interpretation already conferred on the directive by the ECJ. This was noted by Mr Justice Laddie in *Wagamama*, Note 2 above (see further below).

prepared in certain circumstances to look at statements contained in the minutes of Council meetings as an aid to the interpretation of Directives. It is interesting to note the distinction between the methods by which the rights of English citizens are to be ascertained from English statutes, and the sources used by the ECJ in interpreting Directives, particularly as the latter are directly effective and can give rise directly to rights of citizens in EU Member States.[18]

English Developments

The question of *Hansard* as an aid to statutory interpretation was considered by the House of Lords in the case of *Pepper v Hart* (1992). Given the constitutional significance of this case, a second hearing took place before an Appellate Committee of seven Law Lords. Concerns were expressed as to the time and cost implications of the need to review *Hansard* each time advice was to be given. The House of Lords went on to note, however, that these difficulties were not insurmountable (as had been seen in other jurisdictions, for example Commonwealth countries such as New Zealand) and also that practitioners and the public did not appear to be prejudiced by the wealth of secondary legislation which is introduced each year. The suggestion that Article 9 of the Bill of Rights would be breached was rejected. The House of Lords held that reference to Parliamentary material should be permitted as an aid to the construction of legislation which is ambiguous or obscure, or when the literal meaning of legislation leads to absurdity; the material should consist of a statement by a Minister in Parliament promoting the Bill, together with such other Parliamentary material as was necessary to understand the statement and its effect; and the statement relied on should be clear. This is regarded as a landmark decision which lessened the anomaly of methods of interpretation of legislation from different sources.

Pro-European Approach

A new judicial approach to interpretation was seen in the first of three intellectual property cases to influence the area: *Pioneer v Warner*[19] was a patent infringement case involving section 60(1)(c) of the UK Patents Act 1977, which section had not been considered previously by an English court. The preamble to this Act states, *inter alia*, that the Act is to give effect to certain international conventions. Furthermore, section 130(7) states that section 60 (and other sections) are framed so as to have the same effect in the United Kingdom as the corresponding provisions of the European Patent Convention, the Community Patent Convention (which is not yet in force) and the Patent Co-operation Treaty, in the territories to which they apply. Mr Justice Aldous (as he was then) said that, in the light of this, it was appropriate to ascertain how the relevant article of the European Patent Convention[20] was interpreted in other European jurisdictions. The materials subsequently compiled by the parties suggested (and counsel for the defendants submitted) that the European Patent Convention was based on the then laws of Germany, Switzerland and Austria, and that these

---

[18] If they are not implemented by national legislation within the requisite period.

[19] *Pioneer Electronics Capital Inc. (1) Pioneer Electronics (USA) Inc. (2) (t/a 'Discovision Associates') v Warner Music Manufacturing Europe GmbH (1) Warner Music UK Ltd (2)* [1995] RPC 487. This involved two actions between the parties which were dealt with together. This judgment was handed down in respect of the defendants' (successful) application to strike out these actions. This decision has been appealed and is expected to be heard in September 1996.

[20] The relevant article of the Community Patent Convention having virtually the same wording.

laws originated in statements by the Commission of the Reichstag[21] in 1891. Counsel for the plaintiffs did not object to this. Aldous J in his judgment gave particular weight to an article by Dr Karl Bruchhausen[22] which reviewed the position under German law (and whose advocated approach was supported by Swiss, Danish and Austrian law), and interpreted the section 60(1)(c) accordingly.

The decision in *Pioneer v Warner* is an encouraging example of willingness to harmonise English law with the laws of other European states. Although this approach could be distinguished, given section 130(7) of the Patents Act 1977, it could perhaps have been anticipated that this expansion of principle as a result of intellectual property cases would continue, and that a similar approach would be adopted in relation to the Trade Marks Act 1994 ('TMA 1994'), one aim of which was to implement the Trade Mark Harmonisation Directive.[23]

Trade Marks Act 1994

The perception that the basis for much of the Harmonisation Directive was Benelux trade mark law[24] is substantiated by the background to the Harmonisation Directive, in particular in the 'Statements for entry in the minutes of the Council Meeting at which the Directive is adopted' ('Statements'). While there is no provision in the TMA 1994 to the effect of section 130(7) Patents Act 1977, the preamble to the TMA 1994 states, *inter alia*, that it is 'implementing the [Harmonisation Directive] to approximate the laws of Member States relating to trade marks'. The attitude of the English courts to the interpretation of TMA 1994 was awaited with interest against the backdrop of increasing European integration and importance of Directives in all areas of English law; the decision in *Pepper v Hart*; and the *Pioneer v Warner* approach. Texts[25] reviewing TMA 1994 noted that it was likely that the ECJ would be asked to interpret the Harmonisation Directive and that, when it did do so, reference would be made to the Commission's Explanatory Memorandum and to minutes of the meeting of the Council. Although the extent to which English courts would have regard to these documents was noted to be uncertain, the existence of these sources, together with the importance of Benelux trade mark law in framing the wording of the Directive, was considered and seemed generally to be accepted.

Introversion

The first indication of the attitude of the English courts to TMA 1994 came in *Wagamama*. Mr Justice Laddie carried out a detailed review of methods of statutory interpretation and the dichotomy between what he saw as English and European methods. Reference was made to *dicta* of the House of Lords in *Hill v William Hill*[26] that while a Parliamentary enactment is capable of saying the same thing twice without adding anything, such repetition should

---

[21] German Parliament.

[22] *Gewerblicher Rechtsschutz und Urheberrecht*, November 1979, at 743 to 810. Dr Bruchhausen was Presiding Judge at the Regional High Court, Court of Appeal in Dresden and Federal Supreme Court and 'an acknowledged expert' (*per* Aldous J) on patent law.

[23] Council Directive 89/104/EEC of 21 December 1988.

[24] The Benelux countries had formed their own union with a unitary trade mark system and were therefore potentially a model for European harmonisation. Furthermore, as the Benelux trade mark law had been last revised in 1971, it was perceived to be the most modern trade mark law in Europe.

[25] For example, Morcom, *Introduction to the Trade Marks Act 1994*, 1994; Annand and Norman, *Blackstone's Guide to the Trade Marks Act 1994*, 1994; Kitchin and Mellor, *The Trade Marks Act 1994: Text and Commentary*, 1995.

[26] [1949] AC 530.

not be presumed.[27] Counsel in *Wagamama* accordingly sought to argue that in interpreting section 10(2) TMA 1994,[28] the meaning of 'likelihood of association' should be interpreted as having a meaning distinct from 'likelihood of confusion'. Counsel submitted further that the meaning attributed to these words should be taken from Benelux law. Laddie J rejected, however, the argument that English principles of interpretation should be applied to wording of an Act, which wording had been taken from a Directive.[29] This approach clearly has potentially wide consequences for disparity between the interpretation of English statutes and Directives.

Regarding the 'European interpretation route', Laddie J considered three main arguments: (1) that there were sources which supported the proposed interpretation; (2) that it was commonly accepted that the meaning should be taken from Benelux law (this Laddie J referred to as 'Chinese Whispers'); and (3) harmonisation.

(1) First, Laddie J considered whether it was possible to refer back to the Statements as an aid to interpretation of the wording of the Harmonisation Directive. After considering various decisions of the ECJ referred to by counsel,[30] Laddie J held that the burden of authority was against the use of statements recorded in the minutes of the Council,[31] and felt that this was correct given that statements recorded in the minutes of the Council were confidential, whereas the wording of the Harmonisation Directive itself was available to the public. As the Directive was part of the law of all EU Member States, it was important that citizens be able to determine the laws by which they are bound.

Two points should be made in this regard:

(a) In *Carvel*,[32] a decision of the Court of First Instance (delivered shortly after *Wagamama*), reference is made to the 'Code of Conduct Concerning Public Access to Council and Commission Documents',[33] and it is stated that a balancing act must be carried out between the interests of a citizen in gaining access to documents, and the Council's interest in maintaining its deliberations as confidential. While it is clear that it may not be particularly easy to obtain copies of minutes of the Council, it is evident that the minutes of the Council are not *per se* confidential.

(b) A closer review of the documents in issue in *Wagamama* reveals that the *Wagamama* situation, and accordingly the ambit of the decision, may be capable of being distinguished. The documents in question were 'Statements *for entry* in the minutes of the Council meeting at which the Directive is adopted'.[34] No authoritative evidence has been produced that these statements were actually included in the minutes of the Council (despite the evidence of Professor Gielen, the Benelux expert in *Wagamama* and his subsequent writings).[35] Given this lack of certainty, it

---

[27] Laddie J, however, went on to note that Viscount Jowitt had indicated that the legislature sometimes indulged in tautology (*ibid.*, at 543).

[28] The relevant words read: 'A likelihood of confusion on the part of the public, which includes the likelihood of association.'

[29] See Note 2 above and quotation.

[30] Including *Egle* and *Antonissen*, Notes 16 and 14 above (see also Note 13 above).

[31] See also Note 13 above.

[32] Case T-194/94.

[33] (93/731/EC) This was introduced as part of the movement towards transparency within the institutions of the EU.

[34] *Emphasis added.*

[35] Professor Charles Gielen, University of Groningen, expert witness for the plaintiff in *Wagamama*. His subsequent writings on this point include 'European Trade Mark Legislation: The Statements' [1996] 2 EIPR 83.

would not appear in order for the Harmonisation Directive (and ultimately TMA 1994) to be determined by reference to such sources.

It should perhaps be considered, however, that the Statements are in fact widely available, and that until *Wagamama* it was generally accepted that the Statements were likely to be used by the courts as an aid to statutory interpretation. Copies of the relevant Statements were available to intellectual property practitioners, who began familiarising themselves with the relevant principles of Benelux laws.[36]

(2) As regards 'Chinese Whispers', Laddie J would appear to have been greatly influenced by an article on the drafting of the Harmonisation Directive written by two members of the Benelux delegation.[37] Laddie J saw this as a 'fascinating account ... of the manoeuvring which preceded the acceptance of the final version of the directive'.[38] Laddie J noted that while this document could not be used as an aid to interpretation, it gave rise to considerable doubt as to whether the intention of the relevant section of the Harmonisation Directive was in fact to adopt Benelux law. Laddie J also distinguished the approach taken in *Pioneer v Warner*, stating that he did not know what materials had been before the court, whether there had been argument regarding the permissibility of the approach or whether the parties had agreed that the relevant provision was based on German law.

(3) The above reasoning was reflected in the approach to the harmonisation argument. Laddie J acknowledged that English courts should have regard to decisions in courts of other EU Member States in interpretation of the equivalent provisions in English law. Laddie J went on to state, however, that given the possibility (in the light of Fustner and Geuze) that the assumption regarding Benelux law was incorrect it may be that Benelux courts were incorrectly interpreting the Harmonisation Directive—it appeared from Professor Gielen 'that the Benelux court had assumed that the Directive made no alteration to their domestic law'. While noting that the Fustner and Geuze interpretation of events may be incorrect, Laddie J goes on to state that

> the obligation of the English court is to decide what the proper construction is. If that construction differs from that adopted in the Benelux countries, one at least is wrong. It would not be right for an English court to follow the route adopted by the courts of another Member State if it is firmly of a different view simply because the other court expressed a view first. The scope of European legislation is too important to be decided on a first past the post basis.[39]

---

[36] A further example of the regard had generally to this type of Statement is the widespread assumption that for 'use' of a Community Trade Mark ('CTM'), use in one Member State would suffice. This does not come from the Regulation (Council Regulation (EC) 40/94) and can be traced to 'Statements for Entry in the Minutes of the Council at which the Regulation on the Community Trade Mark is Adopted'. Given that the English High Court is to be a CTM court, the potential for widespread inconsistency of interpretation between the High Court and other CTM courts is evident. (Since preparation of this article, both sets of statements have been published in OJ OHIM 5/96. Interestingly, they are there described as 'Joint Statements ... entered in the Minutes'. The publication is without prejudice to interpretation of the text by the ECJ.)

[37] H.R. Furstner and M.C. Gueze, 'Beschermingsomvang van het merk in de Benelux en EEG-harmonisatie' [1988] 10 BIE 215.

[38] See Note 2 above, at 727. This article notes that, outside the Benelux countries, the view was that the protection of the function of origin and prevention of the risk of confusion were the fundamental starting point for any trade mark law, and that suggestions by the Benelux countries for the adoption of the Benelux concept of risk of association as an alternative to risk of confusion were rejected. The ultimate wording was the result of a compromise.

[39] See Note 2 above, at 728.

Rejection of Assistance

TMA 1994 has proven a fruitful source of comment on methods of interpretation. In the Scottish case of *Bravado Merchandising Services Ltd v Mainstream Publishing (Edinburgh) Ltd*,[40] counsel for one party argued that, as the proposed interpretation of the statute was startling and absurd, it would be appropriate to refer to any 'pertinent observations' made by the Government Minister when the legislation was before Parliament, and also to the relevant part of the preamble to the Harmonisation Directive. Counsel for the other party did not object. This approach was rejected, however, by Mr Justice Jacob in *British Sugar v James Robertson*.[41] Jacob J went on to state that the principles of *Pepper v Hart* did not apply to the interpretation of statutory provisions implementing a Directive, as it is the intention of Parliament simply to implement the Directive. An interesting comment, which should be compared with the approach of Aldous J in *Pioneer v Warner*, is that 'Neither the Courts of any other country whose trade mark laws are supposed to implement the Directive, nor the European Court of Justice in interpreting it, would refer to what a British Minister said in Parliament in the course of implementation here. It would be irrelevant'.[42] Accordingly, anything said in Parliament could not assist in resolving an ambiguity which emanated from a Directive. Any comments expressed in parliamentary debate were merely opinion. A similar attitude was adopted with regard to the White Paper.[43] While this reasoning can be followed, the result is seen in the comments of Jacob J in a later part of his judgment (dealing with validity) that '[n]either the Directive nor Act throw any light on this. So I have to use what I at least regard as my common sense'.[44] With the greatest respect to the common sense of Jacob J, it is perhaps somewhat unusual for the harmonisation of trade mark laws throughout the EU to be dependent on the common sense of individual judges.

Further anomalies are revealed by a comparison of *British Sugar v James Robertson* with *Barclays Bank v RBS Advanta*,[45] a comparative advertising case in which the meaning of the 'home-grown' section 10(6) TMA 1994[46] was considered. Although Laddie J looked at section 10(6) in isolation, without reference to sources, he did refer to *Hansard* regarding the background to the introduction of the provision permitting comparative advertising.[47] Laddie J went on to give helpful clarification as to the interpretation of section 10(6) TMA 1994. Elements of section 10(6) TMA 1994 and section 11(2) TMA 1994 are identical.[48] In *British Sugar v James Robertson*, however, Jacob J refers to *Barclays Bank v RBS Advanta* but notes that section 10(6) cannot be used to construe section 11(2), which originates from the Harmonisation Directive. While this distinction is understandable given the reasoning applied by Jacob J, the potential for divergence and inconsistency is concerning where different rules of interpretation apply to identical wording in different sections of the same Act.

---

[40] Decision of the Court of Session: Outer House 11 October 1995 ('Wet, Wet, Wet') *The Times*, 20 December 1995.

[41] *British Sugar plc v James Robertson & Sons Ltd, The Times*, 17 February 1996.

[42] *Ibid.*, at pages 9 and 10 of the judgment.

[43] *Ibid.*, at 10.

[44] *Ibid.*, at 27.

[45] *Barclays Bank plc v RBS Advanta* (sued as RBS Advanta Ltd), *The Times*, 8 February 1996.

[46] The first part of section 10(6) is 'home grown' (*ibid.*, at page 7 of the judgment) and the second part emanates from the Paris Convention 1883 (subsequently also the basis for part of the Harmonisation Directive, and ultimately section 11(2)). The Harmonisation Directive does not deal with comparative advertising. However, the EU Council agreed a Common Position in respect of comparative advertising in late 1995.

[47] Note 45 above, at page 6 of the judgment.

[48] Being the phrase 'In accordance with honest practices in industrial or commercial matters'.

Conclusion

This review would suggest that principles of statutory interpretation may have come full circle. A restricted analysis of *Wagamama* and *British Sugar v James Robertson*, both intellectual property cases, would suggest that, as regards interpretation of statutes implementing directives, no regard can be had to statements included in the minutes of the Council, the position in other Member States, White Papers or *Hansard*. It may be that certain aspects of the *Wagamama* judgment can be distinguished. It would appear, however, that there has been a movement from the Bill of Rights and the principle first enunciated in 1769, through the effects of the European integration, to *Pepper v Hart*, to the pro-European judgment in *Pioneer v Warner*, and ultimately back to this restricted position. While this would give rise to a laudable certainty for clients and solicitors, it would be perhaps unfortunate if the many potential sources for ascertaining the intention of Parliament and the Commission, and achieving the often stated aim of harmonisation, of appropriate laws throughout the European Union, were to be lost. Future intellectual property (and other) decisions are awaited with interest as harmonisation of European law continues.

Harmonising Intellectual Property Laws in the European Union: Past, Present and Future

[1995] 8 EIPR 361

THOMAS C. VINJE
Morrison & Foerster, Brussels*

On the nominal completion of the Single Market on 1 January 1993, there remained significant gaps in European Union[1] (EU) legislation intended to harmonise intellectual property law. A number of key initiatives, including those on biotechnology, databases, design and patents, remain behind schedule. Notwithstanding these delays, the EU institutions,[2] including the European Commission and the European Court of Justice, have recently taken a generally supportive approach to intellectual property protection. This approach is evidenced, *inter alia*, in Single Market legislation (both adopted and proposed) intended to harmonise intellectual property laws, in European Court decisions, and in Commission decisions in competition law cases. Although it would be premature to predict the ultimate outcome of the Union's ambitious plan to harmonise intellectual property law, the final result seems likely to be generally favourable to rightholders, especially to individual creators. Generally speaking, EU institutions are pursuing the goal not only of harmonising intellectual property legislation, but also, and at least as vigorously, of strengthening it at the same time.

This is not to say, however, that either the Commission or the Courts, when faced with claims by intellectual property holders that their rights should prevail over any other considerations (and in particular over EU rules on free movement of goods and freedom of competition), have uniformly decided in favour of intellectual property holders. The European Commission's Decision in the *Magill* case,[3] recently upheld by the European Court of Justice,[4] is perhaps the best-known decision in which EU law was held to prevail over national intellectual property rights.

* The author wishes to acknowledge the valuable assistance of Penny Turner, Beth Bragonier and Tanja Wranik, of Morrison & Foerster's Brussels office, in preparing this article.

1 In the light of the coming into force of the Treaty on the European Union ('Maastricht Treaty') on 1 November 1993, all references in this article to law based on the Treaty Establishing the European Community will be to EU law. For convenience, the term 'EU' will be employed throughout this article to describe the various institutions, even where they might have been called 'EC' institutions at the time in question. However, much existing legislation, such as the Community Patent Convention, continues to refer to 'Community' law.

2 The main EU institutions involved in the legislative process are: the European Commission (which has sole authority to propose legislation), the European Parliament and the Council of the European Union. The process by which legislative measures are adopted in the EU is set forth in Articles 189(a), (b) and (c) of the Treaty Establishing the European Community ('EC Treaty'), as recently amended by the Maastricht Treaty. Under the co-decision procedure introduced through the Maastricht Treaty, the Parliament has considerably greater power than under the old co-operation procedure. Under the co-decision procedure, the Parliament and the Council jointly adopt EU legislation. Conveniently, the Commission has published the Maastricht Treaty in the Official Journal, together with the complete text of the EC Treaty in OJ 1992 C224/1. Figure 1 explains the co-decision procedure (under Article 189(b)); figure 2 shows the co-operation procedure (under Article 189(c)).

3 Commission Decision 89/205/EEC (IV/31.851—*Magill TV Guide/ITP, BBC, and RTE*) OJ 1989 L78/43.

4 Cases C-241/91P and C-242/91P, *Radio Telefís Eireann and Independent Television Publications Ltd v Commission*, Judgment of the Court, 6 April 1995.

Moreover, one cannot say that the various Commission Directorates-General have uniform views on intellectual property protection.[5] Trends show that DGXV, which is primarily responsible for most Commission legislative proposals on intellectual property, tends to promote the broadest possible intellectual property protection without a great deal of consideration for the potential anti-competitive consequences of its proposals. DGIII, DGIV and DGXIII, which often have influence over the Commission's intellectual property policy as so-called 'associated services', tend to be more concerned with the impact on competition and the industrial policy implications of Commission proposals. They are particularly concerned about the potential anti-competitive effects of imposing traditional forms of intellectual property protection on new technologies.

Recently, however, it is fair to say that DGIV has taken a more realistic approach to competition cases involving intellectual property. In particular, DGIV has been more willing to accept provisions in intellectual property licensing agreements that might theoretically restrict competition, but that pose little real risk of anti-competitive dangers. DGIV has also liberated the patent licensing, know-how licensing, specialisation, and research and development block exemptions, and has proposed certain further liberalisations of the patent and know-how block exemptions.

This article first outlines recent EU and international legislative and policy developments, including those already adopted under the Single Market programme as well as those still in the legislative pipeline, and then discusses EU judicial developments in the intellectual property sphere.

European Union Legislative Developments

Software Directive

The Software Directive is perhaps the most significant piece of intellectual property legislation already in place in the EU.[6] Overall, the Software Directive provides an example of the EU's intent to strengthen intellectual property rights. During the debate over the Software Directive, the proponents of open systems and compatibility won a significant victory on the scope of protection for interfaces[7] and on the permissibility of reverse analysis.[8] However, it would be inappropriate to view this victory as having improperly diminished the copyright protection available under the Software Directive to program developers. Indeed, European

---

[5] The Directorates-General with the greatest involvement in intellectual property matters are DGIII (previously Internal Market and Industrial Affairs, but now just Industrial Affairs), DGIV (Competition) DGXIII (Telecommunications, Information Industries and Innovation) and DGXV (Internal Market and Financial Services).

[6] Council Directive 91/250 of 14 May 1991 on the Legal Protection of Computer Programs, OJ 1991 L122/42 ('Software Directive').

[7] Interfaces refer to the aspects of a program that permit its interaction with other components of a computer system. For a more detailed discussion of interfaces, see Alan Palmer and Thomas Vinje, 'The EC Directive on the Legal Protection of Computer Software: The New Law Governing Software Development', 2 Duke J. Comp. & Int'L. 65 (1992), at part I.B.1. See also, Thomas C. Vinje, 'The Legislative History of the EC Software Directive', in M. Lehmann and C.F. Tapper (eds), *A Handbook of European Software Law*, 1993, at 37 to 142.

[8] The term reverse analysis, which is often used interchangeably with reverse engineering, generally refers to a process by which a product is systematically broken down into its component parts to analyse and discover the composition of the product. The US Supreme Court defined reverse engineering in *Kewanee Oil Co. v Bicron Corp.*, 416 US 470 at 476 (1974), as 'starting with the known product and working backward to divine the process which aided in its development or manufacture'. Reverse analysis techniques in the computer context include line traces, test runs, memory dumps and disassembly. For an excellent description of reverse analysis in relation to computer software, see Andy Johnson-Laird, 'Technical Demonstration of "Decompilation" ', 16 Computer L. Rep. 469 (1992).

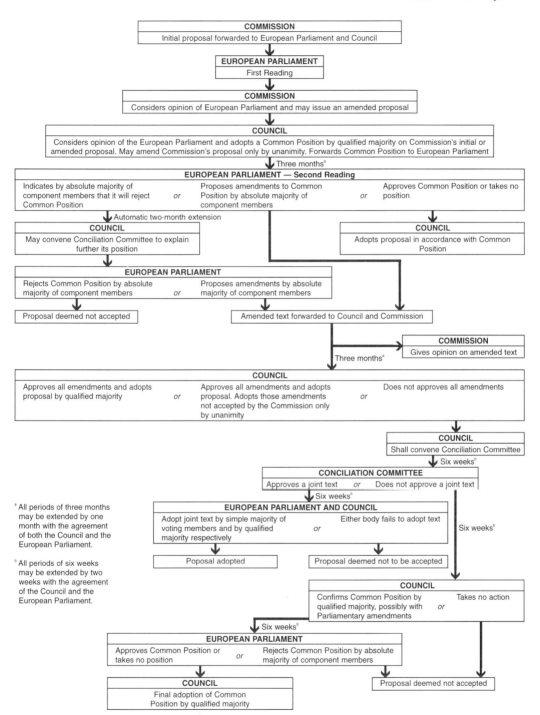

Figure 1 *The Co-decision Procedure (Article 189(b))*

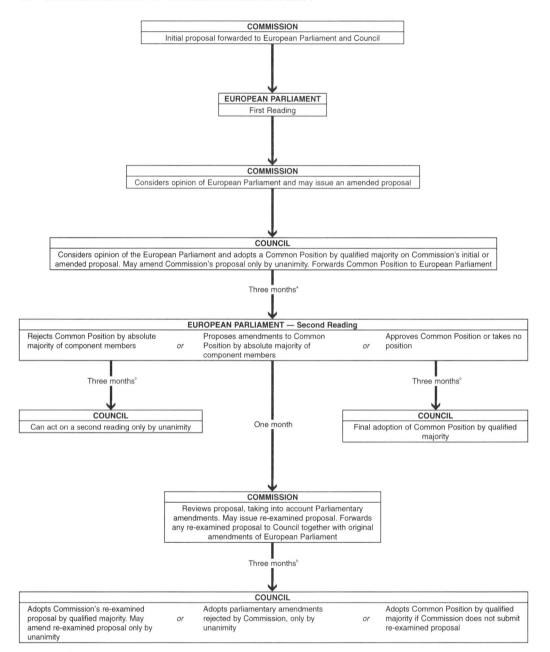

Figure 2 *The Co-operation Procedure (Article 189(c))*

software developers now have an unprecedented and relatively uniform level of protection throughout Europe, and arguably better protection than anywhere else in the world.

Besides providing a broad scope of protection for computer programs (in terms of the restricted acts that are within the exclusive domain of the rightholder),[9] the Software Directive also assures that no special degree of creativity is required for a program to qualify as an original work in the copyright sense.[10] Moreover, the Software Directive ensures the availability of tough enforcement mechanisms.[11] These have been sorely lacking in many places in the world, including some EU Member States, and it is this lack of adequate enforcement mechanisms to which most attention should be devoted in the software protection area.

The Single Market completion date of 1 January 1993 also marked the implementation deadline for the Software Directive.[12] Only three countries (the United Kingdom, Denmark and Italy) managed to meet this deadline. However, all Member States have since finalised their implementing legislation. Generally speaking, little controversy surrounded national implementation of the Software Directive, and it certainly did not approach the battle that raged over the adoption of the Directive itself. Moreover, Member State Governments seem to have little tolerance for continued controversy over software protection. Although the debate over the appropriate balance between protection and competition in the information technology industry has not been fully resolved, further battles in this area appear more likely to occur in courts than in legislatures.

Although apparently decided under pre-Directive law, *John Richardson Computers Ltd v Flanders and Chemtec Ltd*[13] and *IBCOS Computer Ltd v Barclays Mercantile Highland Finance Ltd*[14] are examples of the kinds of cases that are likely to arise in this area. Compared to the United States, the case law in this sphere is in its infancy. *IBCOS* for example, might well be regarded as the equivalent of the *Whelan Associates, Inc. v Jaslow Dental Lab., Inc.*[15] case in the United States. US courts have, after addressing software protection issues for over a decade, become relatively sophisticated in their approach to such cases. The standard for addressing such issues was set in the United States in *Computer Associates International, Inc. v Altai, Inc.*[16] Recently a French court relied heavily on the US decision in *Altai* to hold on virtually identical facts that no infringement existed under French law.[17] The court held that Altai's program does not infringe because (1) it contains no literal (source code) similarities to the Computer Associates program; (2) the non-literal similarities in the program's architecture and organisation are dictated by constraining logic; and (3) interfaces are not subject to copyright protection. However, it remains to be seen to what extent European courts will find useful the experience gained by the US courts in this area.

As far as implementation is concerned, Member States appear generally to have followed

---

[9]   Software Directive, Note 6 above, Article 4.

[10] *Ibid.*, Article 1(3). This will have the greatest impact in Germany, where the *Inkasso* decision established an unusually strict requirement of originality for copyright protection of computer programs. See Judgment of 9 May 1985, Bundesgerichtshof (BGH), CR 22 at 25 to 29 (IZR 52/83, (1986) 17 IIC 681 (English translation)) ('*Inkasso*'). See also Note 23 below and accompanying text.

[11] Software Directive, Note 6 above, Article 7.

[12] *Ibid.*, Article 10.

[13] Chancery Court of the English High Court of Justice, 19 February 1993.

[14] (1989) 1 Ch. 2198.

[15] 797 F.2d 1222 (3d Cir. 1986).

[16] 982 F.2d 693, 23 USPQ 2d 1241 (2d Cir. 1992). See, for example, *Gates Rubber Co. v Bando Chemical Industries Ltd*, 9 F.3d at 832 (10th Cir. 1993), (adopting *Computer Associates* approach to determining software infringement).

[17] *Computer Associates International, Inc. v Faster Sarl*, French Commercial Court of Bobigny, 20 January 1995.

the intent of the Directive, if not its exact language. Two basic approaches to implementation exist. The UK statutory instrument,[18] adopted on 15 December 1992, the French law adopted on 10 May 1994,[19] and the Dutch law,[20] adopted on 7 July 1994, integrate the Directive piece by piece into existing copyright legislation. Other Member States have implemented the Directive as a single 'stand-alone' piece, although few have adopted the Directive word for word.

The UK approach of integrating the Directive's provisions one by one into the Copyright, Designs and Patents Act of 1988, rather than adding the Directive's entire text as an addendum to the existing law, has been the subject of criticism. Some large US software vendors, for example, complained before its adoption that the UK statutory instrument would deprive them of the ability to devise pan-European software licences for use throughout the European Union. However, unlike EU regulations, which are directly incorporated into Member State law, EU directives by their very nature permit some degree of legislative leeway.[21] Moreover, despite its changes to the precise wording of the Directive, the UK implemen- tation appears to be consistent with the meaning of the Directive; indeed, the UK approach would not in practice appear to present any obstacle to the use of EU-wide software licences.

Nonetheless, the Commission (DGXV) expressed its desire that Member States implement the Software Directive as a single piece without significant changes to its language, and at least one DGXV official (now departed) has indicated dissatisfaction with the UK approach. A private party has now filed a complaint with the Commission challenging the UK implementation of Article 4, 5 and 6 of the Directive. It remains to be seen whether the Commission will find merit in the complaint, and seek changes in UK law. If the Commission does so, it will first informally negotiate with the UK Government and, if negotiations fail, the Commission can then initiate formal proceedings by sending the UK Government a 'reasoned opinion' demanding changes to UK law. If the United Kingdom chooses not to make such changes, the Commission can then initiate an action before the European Court. The Commission would, however, appear to be on weak legal ground in challenging the UK means of implementation, and it remains to be seen, especially in these days of 'subsidiarity', whether the Commission will bring an action against the United Kingdom.

As noted, even those countries implementing the Directive as a 'stand-alone' section of their copyright legislation have not adopted the Directive word for word. For example, in implementing the Directive's decompilation provision, several countries exclude Article 6(3) of the Directive from their implementing legislation,[22] and the German legislation seeks to make it clear that the *Inkasso* decision is no longer valid by providing, unlike the text of the Directive, that 'qualitative or aesthetic criteria' may not be applied to determine whether a program is original.[23]

---

[18]   Statutory Instrument 3233, The Copyright (Computer Programs) Regulations 1992 ('UK law').

[19]   Loi 94–361 du 10 mai 1994, Portant Mise en Oeuvre de la Directive 91–250-CEE du Conseil des Communautés Européennes en date du 14 mai 1991 Concernant la Protection Juridique des Programmes d'Ordinateur et Modifiant le Code de la Propriété Intellectuelle ('French law').

[20]   Staatsblad van het Koninkrijk der Nederlanden 521 Wet van 7 Juli 1994 tot wijziging van de auteurswet 1912 in verband met de rechtsbescherming van computerprogramma's ('Dutch law').

[21]   Directives are binding as to the result to be achieved, but they leave to national authorities the choice of methods to be used. EC Treaty, Article 189. Because of this flexibility in implementing Directives into national law in each Member State, Member States' legal regimes may differ with respect to how a directive is implemented.

[22]   Lov 1010 df 19 December 1992, Lov om aendring of ophavsretsloven (Edb-programmer), Article 3 ('Danish law').

[23]   Bundesgesetzblatt (BGBl.), Jahrgang 1993, Teil I, Zweites Gesetz zur Änderung des Urheberrechtsgesetzes, vom 9 Juni 1993 ('German law'), Article 1(3) section 3. In addition, the highest German court has issued a judgment overruling the *Inkasso* decision; *Buchhaltungsprogramm*, CR 1993 at 752 and onward, with comment by M. Lehmann.

Member States have dealt with decompilation, the most controversial of the Directive's provisions, in various ways.[24]

- the Irish law reproduces the text of Article 6 word for word;[25]
- the Greek law basically follows the language of Article 6, but contains certain minor wording changes;[26]
- the Danish law reproduces the text of Article 6(1) and 6(2) word for word, but omits Article 6(3) (the Berne Convention language) altogether;[27]
- the Dutch law introduces relatively minor wording changes to Articles 6(1) and 6(2), and omits Article 6(3);[28]
- the Belgian, French, German and Spanish laws introduce minor wording changes in Articles 6(1) and 6(2). In addition, the German law, in Article 6(3), corrects the Software Directive's incorrectly transposed Berne Convention language;[29]
- the Italian law introduces a number of wording changes to Articles 6(1) and 6(2); however, the changes do not appear to change the meaning intended by the Software Directive. In addition, the Italian law introduces a number of wording changes to Articles 6(1) and 6(2); however, the changes do not appear to change the meaning intended by the Software Directive. In addition, the Italian law adds to its implementation of Article 6 a clause rendering void any contractual provisions contrary to Articles 6(1) or 6(2) of the Directive (rather than including a contractual override in a separate provision, as do other national implementations and as the Directive itself does in Article 9);[30]

---

[24] Article 6, the decompilation provision of the Software Directive, reads:
  1 The authorisation of the rightholder shall not be required where reproduction of the code and translation of its form within the meaning of Article 4(a) and (b) are indispensable to obtain the information necessary to achieve the interoperability of an independently created computer program with other programs, provided that the following conditions are met:
  (a) these acts are performed by the licensee or by another person having a right to use a copy of a program, or on their behalf by a person authorised to do so;
  (b) the information necessary to achieve interoperability has not previously been readily available to the persons referred to in subparagraph (a); and
  (c) these acts are confined to the parts of the original program which are necessary to achieve interoperability.
  2. The provisions of paragraphs 1 shall not permit the information obtained through its application:
  (a) to be used for goals other than to achieve the interoperability of the independently created computer program:
  (b) to be given to others, except when necessary for the interoperability of the independently created computer program; or
  (c) to be used for the development, production or marketing of a computer program substantially similar in its expression, or for any other act which infringes copyright.
  3. In accordance with the provisions of the Berne Convention for the protection of Literary and Artistic Works, the provisions of this Article may not be interpreted in such a way as to allow its application to be used in a manner which unreasonably prejudices the rightholder's legitimate interests or conflicts with a normal exploitation of the computer program.
[25] Statutory Instrument 26, European Communities (Legal Protection of Computer Programs) Regulation 1993 ('Irish law'), Article 7.
[26] Greek Law 2121/4 March 1993 (Official Gazette 25A/4 March 1993).
[27] Danish law, Note 22 above, Article 3.
[28] Dutch law, Note 20 above, Article 45.
[29] Proposition de Loi Transposant en Droit Belge la Directive Européenne du 14 mai 1991 Concernant la Protection Juridique des Programmes d'Ordinateur, Texte Adopté par la Commission de la Justice, 17 mars 1994, Article 7; French law, Note 19 above, Article 5; German law, Note 23 above, Article 1 section 69e; Aprobación por el Pleno, Proyecto de Ley de Incorporación al Derecho Español de la Directiva 91/250/CEE, 14 Mayo de 1991, Sobre la Protección Jurídica de Programas de Ordenador (No. Expediente 121/17), Aprobado por el pleno del Congreso de los Diputados por el Procedimiento Previsto en el Articulo 150 del Reglamento de la Camara, en Sesion Celebrada el Dia 25 de Noviembre de 1993, Article 6.
[30] Decreto Legislativo 29 Dicembre 1992, No 518, Attuazione della Direttiva 91/250/CEE Relativa all Tutela Giuridica dei Programmi per Elaboratore, Article 5.

- the UK Statutory Instrument makes several significant changes to the language of Article 6 to comply with good UK legislative drafting practice. The Statutory Instrument also omits Article 6(3).

Databases

On 15 April 1992, the European Commission issued a formal proposal for a directive on the legal protection of databases,[31] which was amended by the Commission on 4 October 1993.[32] As defined in the Draft Database Directive, as amended, a 'database' is a collection of data, works or other materials arranged, stored and accessed by electronic means, and the materials necessary for the operation of the database such as its thesaurus, index or system for obtaining or presenting information, but does not include 'any computer program used in the making or operation of the database'.[33] Thus, by its terms, the Draft Database Directive in its present form does not cover non-electronic compilations.

The Draft Database Directive proposes two forms of protection for electronic databases. First, it provides for copyright protection for a term equivalent to that for literary works.[34] Under this form of protection, the owner of the rights in a database is granted the exclusive rights generally associated with copyright protection, including the right to reproduce the database, to translate, adapt, arrange, or otherwise alter it, to distribute it to the public, and to communicate or display it to the public.[35] In order to qualify for this form of protection, however, a database must be original in the sense that it is a collection of works that constitutes the author's own intellectual creation by virtue of its 'selection or . . . arrangement'.[36] In requiring this standard of originality, the European Commission has followed the Continental rather than the UK originality standard, and the proposal's copyright approach is consistent with the US Supreme Court's opinion in *Feist Publications v Rural Telephone Service Co.*,[37] which rejected the 'sweat of the brow' theory as a basis for affording copyright protection for compilations.[38]

Second, the Draft Database Directive introduces a *sui generis* 15-year right against 'unauthorised extraction' of the contents of a database for commercial purposes, regardless of whether the database can meet the originality requirements to qualify for copyright protection under the proposed Directive.[39] Currently, among the EU Member States, such a right exists only in Danish law.[40]

---

[31] Proposal for a Council Directive on the Legal Protection of Databases, OJ 1992 C156/4.

[32] Amended Proposal for a Council Directive on the Legal Protection of Databases, OJ 1993 C308/1 ('Draft Database Directive').

[33] *Ibid.*, Article 1(1).

[34] *Ibid.*, Articles 2(1), 9(1).

[35] *Ibid.*, Article 6. When a database is created by an employee during the course of his employment, all economic rights in the database vest in the employer. *Ibid.*, Article 3(4). If a copy of a database is sold anywhere in the EU, the distribution right as to the copy will be exhausted, except for the right to control its rental. *Ibid.*, Article 6(d).

[36] *Ibid.*, Article 9. 'Insubstantial changes' to a database, meaning changes to its contents that are necessary for the database to continue functioning as intended, will not create a new period of copyright protection for databases. However, 'substantial changes' to a database, meaning substantial modifications to the selection or arrangement of its contents that result in a 'new edition' of the database, will give rise to a new term of copyright protection for the new database. *Ibid.*, Article 9(2) to (3).

[37] 499 US 340 (1991).

[38] See Michael Pattison, 'The European Commission's Proposal on the Protection of Computer Databases', [1992] 4 EIPR 113.

[39] Draft Database Directive, Note 32 above, Articles 10, 12(1). Protection under the unfair extraction right actually begins at the creation of the database, and the 15-year period technically will begin to run on 1 January of the year following the date that the database is first made available to the public; Article 12(1). 'Insubstantial changes' to a database which 'taken together, do not substantially modify' its contents will not result in a new period of protection for the database against unauthorised extraction. However, a 'substantial change' to the contents, meaning 'the successive accumulation of insubstantial [changes] resulting in a substantial modification' to the database, will give rise to a new term of unauthorised extraction protection for the new database; Article 12(2) to (3).

[40] Jean Hughes and Elizabeth Weightman, 'EC Database Protection: Fine Tuning the Commission's Proposal', [1992] 5 EIPR 147 to 148.

In tandem with the unfair extraction right, the proposal introduced a compulsory licensing regime, whereby materials contained in a database that cannot be independently created, collected or obtained from any other source may be reproduced against payment of a royalty to the rightholder.[41] In addition 'insubstantial parts' of a database may be extracted and reutilised by a lawful user for commercial purposes, provided acknowledgement is made of their source.[42]

Because the unauthorised extraction right is a *sui generis* form of protection, it does not fall within the scope of the Berne or the Universal Copyright Conventions and, therefore, is not subject to the national treatment requirement expressed in those treaties.[43] As a result, the Draft Database Directive limits the protection of the unauthorised extraction right only to databases that are created by nationals or residents of the EU Member States or by companies formed within the EU and having their registered office, central administration or principal place of business there.[44] Although provision is made in the Draft Database Directive for the European Commission to propose and the EU Council to conclude agreements to extend the unauthorised extraction right to databases created by nationals and companies of non-EU countries,[45] such agreements will most likely require that similar protection be reciprocally provided in the non-EU countries to EU-created databases. This will be problematic for US creators of databases under current US law.

In June 1995, the EU Council reached political agreement on revisions to the Draft Database Directive, but at the time of writing a complete version of the Council's text is unavailable. It is clear, however, that the Council has eliminated the compulsory licensing provisions from the draft, and that a number of other changes will be made in the common position due to be adopted by the Council at the end of June 1996. The common position will then be forwarded to the Parliament for second reading, and although it is difficult to predict the precise outcome of the legislative procedure, it would not be surprising to see the ultimate text of the Directive resemble the Council's common position. Although the original implementation date in the Draft Database Directive of 1 January 1995[46] obviously cannot be retained, the Parliament and Council will remain under considerable pressure from the Commission and industry to give the Directive urgent priority.[47]

Biotechnology Patent Directive

In October 1988 the Commission first proposed a directive on the legal protection of biotechnological inventions in an attempt to harmonise national laws on the patentability of plants and animals and to provide a greater incentive for the development of the biotechnology

---

[41] Draft Database Directive, Note 32 above, Article 11(1). In the light of opposition to the compulsory licensing provision by an apparent majority of Member States at the time of writing, this provision may not survive.

[42] *Ibid.*, Article 11(5).

[43] The national treatment provisions of the Berne and Universal Copyright Conventions generally provide that a country that has acceded to the Conventions must protect the works of nationals of other member countries to the same extent that it protects the works of its own nationals.

[44] Draft Database Directive, Note 32 above, Article 13(1) to (2).

[45] *Ibid.*, Article 13(3), Recital 38.

[46] *Ibid.*, Article 15(1).

[47] Communication from the European Commission (DGXIII) concerning Europe's Way to the Information Society: 'An Action Plan', (17 July 1994) at 5; see also Communication from the European Commission (DGXV) concerning Information Society Services: 'Towards a Coherent Internal Market Regulatory Environment: Completing the Agenda' (1 July 1994) at 11 (not yet adopted or officially published); and 'Europe and the Global Information Society: Recommendations to the European Council' (the so-called Bangemann Task Force Report) (26 May 1994) at 18.

industry in the EU.[48] After languishing in the European Parliament for years owing to disputes over the moral and ethical implications of patenting living matter and over animal testing, the proposed Biotechnology Patent Directive finally received its first reading in Parliament on 29 October 1992. The Parliament proposed 46 amendments to the Commission proposal, a number of which were accepted by the Commission in its amended proposal, issued on 16 December 1992.[49]

On 7 February 1994, the EU Council reached a common position[50] on the proposed Biotechnology Patent Directive. The common position removed the ambiguity concerning the patentability of living matter in the EU by affirming that '[b]iological material, including plants and animals . . . except plant and animal varieties, shall be patentable'.[51] Similarly, the common position would also have provided for the patentability of '[u]ses of plant or animal varieties or of processes for their production, other than essentially biological processes,'[52] and of '[m]icrobiological processes'.[53]

As the European Parliament did not accept the common position text in its entirety, on 23 January 1995 representatives of the European Parliament and the Council met in a Conciliation Committee to agree the contents of this much-debated proposal. As concerns the patentability of the human body it was decided that while the human body itself may not be patented, if elements of the human body form part of an invention, and they have been modified so as no longer to be directly linked to a specific individual, such as invention could be patented. It was also agreed that animals produced by modification of their genetic identity should not be patented if that modification caused the animals disproportionate suffering and physical handicaps. Germinal gene therapy on humans, based for example on *in vitro* fertilisation, would not be patentable.

However, when the compromise text was put before the Parliament for its final approval on 1 March 1995, the Parliament, in an unprecedented move, voted against the text that had been adopted by the Conciliation Committee. This marked the end of the legislative road for the proposal. The only way to breathe new life into the initiative would be for the Commission to issue a new proposal, beginning the entire legislative process from scratch again.

In the light of these legislative developments, a Directive intended to harmonise Member State laws on the legal protection of biotechnological inventions is not to be expected in the near future. Indeed, it is as yet unclear whether the Commission will even seek to reinitiate the legislative process by making a new proposal, although the Commissioner in charge of this subject has indicated that he remains convinced that without a harmonising Directive European research and development is discouraged and placed at a disadvantage compared with third countries, and the EU is left with no legal guarantee concerning the ethical aspects of the protection of the human body.[54]While there has been general disappointment following the failure of this proposal, which has been over six years in the making, the reaction of industry has been mixed. Thus, while many have criticised the Parliament for delivering what they consider a serious blow to investment and employment possibilities in the European

---

[48] Proposal for a Council Directive on the Legal Protection of Biotechnological Inventions, OJ 1989 c10/3.
[49] Amended Proposal for a Council Directive on the Legal Protection of Biotechnological Inventions, OJ 1993 C44/36 ('Biotechnology Patent Directive').
[50] A common position is the Council's preliminary agreement on a Commission proposal, taking into account Parliament's initial proposed amendments on a first reading, but pending parliamentary suggestions on a second reading and, under the co-decision procedure, any negotiations on a final text between the Council and the Parliament within a Conciliation Committee.
[51] Biotechnology Patent Directive, Note 49 above, Article 3.
[52] *Ibid.*, Article 4.
[53] *Ibid.*, Article 5.
[54] Commission Press Release; IP: 25–206, 1 March 1995.

biotechnology sector, others consider that the proposal had, in its final form, been watered down to such an extent that it would anyway have been of limited use to industry.

In any event, it is worth bearing in mind that the proposal's defeat does not affect the present system for awarding European biotechnology patents. Thus the European Patent Office will continue to award patents in the biotechnology field to the extent permitted by the European Patent Convention[55] (as that Convention has been interpreted by the Patent Office) and individual EU Member States will continue to issue patents to the extent permitted by their own national laws, which differ significantly on this issue.

Industrial design

On 3 December 1993 the Commission issued formal proposals for a regulation on a 'Community design'[56] and a directive on the legal protection of industrial design.[57] By harmonising both substantive and formal requirements for protection, these proposals are intended to establish an EU-wide system for industrial designs and models. The Regulation would establish an EU design right and the Directive would harmonise national design laws.[58] At least temporarily, the European Union design system would co-exist with current Member State systems.

These measures would establish protection for the 'features of appearance [of a product] which can be perceived by the human senses as regards sight and tactility'.[59] Irrespective of the 'aesthetic' or 'functional' nature of the design, and irrespective of the nature of the product to which the design is applied, the design can qualify for legal protection. However, protection under both rights would be granted only to products that are distinctive in character.[60] In addition, if the design is dictated solely by the technical function of the product, it will not be protectable under the EU design regime.[61]

The EU design system would establish a two-tier system of protection, introducing on the one hand a registration-based protection and on the other automatic protection that would come into force when the design is made available to the public.[62] 'Registered designs' would enjoy protection throughout the EU for renewable five-year periods (up to a maximum of 25 years) against competing marketing or sales of products deemed to be 'substantially similar'.[63] 'Unregistered designs' would be protected for a non-renewable three-year period against direct copying.[64]

Both the draft Regulation and the draft Directive explicitly exclude from protection

---

[55] The following countries are parties to the European Patent Convention: Austria, Belgium, Switzerland, Liechtenstein, Germany, Denmark, Spain, France, the United Kingdom, Greece, Ireland, Italy, Luxembourg, Monaco, the Netherlands, Portugal and Sweden.

[56] Proposal for a European Parliament and Council Regulation on the Community Design, OJ 1994 C29/20 ('Proposed Community Design Regulation').

[57] Proposal for a European Parliament and Council Directive on the Legal Protection of Designs, OJ 1993 C345/14 ('Proposed Directive on the Legal Protection of Designs').

[58] Proposed Community Design Regulation, Note 56 above, Article 1; Proposed Directive on the Legal Protection of Designs, Note 57 above, Article 2.

[59] Proposal for a European Parliament and Council Regulation on the Community Design, COM (93) 342 final-COD 463 Explanatory Memorandum ('Proposed Community Design Regulation Explanatory Memorandum') at 10.

[60] Proposed Community Design Regulation, Note 56 above, Articles 4, 6; Proposed Directive on the Legal Protection of Designs, Note 57 above, Articles 3, 5.

[61] Such designs may be protectable under patent law or utility model law, provided the requirements for such protection are fulfilled. Proposed Community Design Regulation Explanatory Memorandum, Note 59 above, at 7, § 8.2.

[62] Proposed Community Design Regulation, Note 56 above, Article 1(2).

[63] *Ibid.*, Articles 13, 53.

[64] *Ibid.*, Article 12.

features necessary to permit connection of one product to another, with the exception of features of modular products that are intended to interconnect.[65] In other words, the drafts contain a 'must fit' exception. They do not, however, contain a 'must match' exception that would allow the reproduction of those design features necessary to permit a component of a product to match the overall design of the entire product. Some concession has been made for the absence of the 'must match' exception in these proposals with the introduction of a 'repair clause'.[66] The repair clause allows any party, three years after the marketing of a 'complex product', to reproduce a design applied to part of that product, if the design of the part is dictated by the overall appearance of the complex product. This concession was introduced in order to strike a balance between the conflicting interests of the large automobile manufacturers and the spare parts manufacturers.[67]

Although the EU design system was initially vented as early as 1989 in a Commission Green Paper,[68] the proposed Regulation and Directive remain mired in the EU legislative process. The Commission's formal proposal, finally issued at the end of 1993, is currently under consideration by the Council and the Parliament. The Parliament held its first public hearing on spare parts for automobiles on 1 February 1995. It looks as though the debate over the must fit/must match exceptions is not yet over, and continued lobbying on the proposals is expected. It is hoped the Parliament will finish its first reading and the Council will reach a Common Position by the end of 1995.

Trade marks

On 21 December 1988, the Commission adopted a directive intended to harmonise Member States' trade mark laws.[69] The deadline for national implementation of the Trade Mark Directive was set for 28 December 1991 and subsequently extended to 31 December 1992. At present, all Member States except Ireland, Portugal, and the Benelux are in compliance with the provisions of the Directive. The revisions made to national laws have been substantial, and a good many issues of interpretation will take some time to sort out, providing trade mark practioners with plenty of work to do for some time.

In general, the Trade Mark Directive is aimed at the basic aspects of a system for registration and enforcement of trade marks. The Trade Mark Directive permits a mark to apply to goods and services and to 'consist of any sign capable of being represented graphically'.[70] It also enumerates a number of types of trade marks that cannot be registered or held valid. Such unregistrable or invalid marks include: those that are 'devoid' of any distinctive character'; those that are generic or descriptive or have become 'customary' in the current language or the practices of a trade; those that are identical or confusingly similar to earlier trade marks on identical or similar goods or services; and those that are identical or confusingly similar to earlier EU-wide (or, at the Member State's option, national) trade marks for non-similar goods or services if the earlier trade mark 'has a reputation' in the EU

---

[65] *Ibid.*, Article 9; Proposed Directive on the Legal Protection of Designs, Note 57 above, Article 7.

[66] Proposed Community Design Regulation, Note 56 above, Article 23; Proposed Directive on the Legal Protection of Designs, Note 57 above, Article 14.

[67] See Sarah Faircliffe, 'EC's Adoption of Proposals for Industrial Design Legislation', 7 World Intell. Prop. R. 245 (1993).

[68] Commission of the European Communities, Green Paper on the Legal Protection of Industrial Design, III/F/5131/91-EN (1991) (not officially published).

[69] First Council Directive 89/104 of 21 December 1988 to Approximate the Laws of the Member States Relating to Trade Marks, OJ 1989 L40/1 ('Trade Mark Directive').

[70] *Ibid.*, Article 2.

(or the Member State) that would be taken advantage of or adversely affected by the later trade mark.[71]

The exclusive rights bestowed on a trade mark owner under the Trade Mark Directive allow a trade mark owner to prevent another party from using a mark on identical or similar goods and services that is identical or confusingly similar to the owner's mark.[72] In addition, a Member State may permit an owner to prevent the use of an identical or confusingly similar mark on goods and services that are dissimilar to those of the owner if the owner's trade mark has a 'reputation' in the Member State.[73] These exclusive rights may be licensed as to some or all of the goods or services for which the trade mark is registered and for all or part of a particular Member State.[74] However, if an authorised sale of a particular trade marked good is made in any Member State, the trade mark owner's rights are exhausted as to the good in the entire EU, such that the trade mark owner cannot prevent the resale of the good in another Member State.[75] As does the Software Directive, the Trade Mark Directive opts for EU, rather than international exhaustion. In other words, the placing by a trade mark owner of goods into commerce *outside* the EU will not prevent the resale of those goods in the EU.

The Trade Mark Directive also has a use requirement, which generally provides that a trade mark be used in the Member State in connection with goods or services for which it is registered within five years after the completion of its registration and for any continuous five-year period.[76] If these requirements are not met, the trade mark may be subject to revocation and may not provide a basis for refusing to register or enforce a later mark.[77] Correspondingly, if an earlier-filed trade mark owner acquiesces in the use of a later-registered trade mark by another for a period of five successive years, the trade mark owner may not prevent the further use of the other mark unless registration of the later mark was in bad faith.[78]

In addition to its effort to harmonise the national trade mark laws of the Member States, the Council also has adopted a regulation to create an EU-wide trade mark system that will co-exist with the national systems in the Member States.[79] The Trade Mark Regulation establishes the Office for Harmonisation in the Internal Market (trade marks and designs) (Trade Mark Office)[80] and will permit the filing of a single trade mark application for protection throughout the EU,[81] for renewable ten-year periods,[82] on terms similar to those set forth in the Trade Mark Directive discussed above.

The Trade Mark Regulation has a legislative history dating back to 1976. Several political, rather than substantive, obstacles delayed the adoption of the Trade Mark Regulation. One of these obstacles was resolved when Alicante, Spain was chosen as the location to house the Trade Mark Office. The other main point of contention concerned which of the then-nine official[83] EU languages should be the working languages of the Trade Mark Office. It

---

[71] *Ibid.*, Articles 3 to 4.
[72] *Ibid.*, Article 5.
[73] *Ibid.*
[74] *Ibid.*, Article 8.
[75] *Ibid.*, Article 7.
[76] *Ibid.*, Article 10.
[77] *Ibid.*, Article 12.
[78] *Ibid.*, Article 9.
[79] Council Regulation 40/94 of 20 December 1993 on the Community Trade Mark, OJ 1994 L11/1 ('Trade Mark Regulation').
[80] *Ibid.*, Article 2.
[81] *Ibid.*, Article 16.
[82] *Ibid.*, Articles 46, 47.
[83] With the addition of Sweden, Finland and Austria on 1 January 1995, the EU has increased the official Community languages to 11. Swedish and Finnish are the two new official EU languages.

was finally decided that English, French, German, Italian and Spanish would be the official languages of the Trade Mark Office.[84] Trade mark applications may be submitted in any of the 11 EU languages. However, if an application is submitted in an EU language other than one of the five official Trade Mark Office languages, the Trade Mark Office must arrange to have the application translated into one of the official languages, as chosen by the applicant.[85]

The Trade Mark Office was set up on 1 September 1994 and is currently organising itself and preparing to open on 1 April 1996. If this deadline is met, any application reaching the office between 1 January 1996 and 31 March 1996 will be treated as a 1 April 1996 filing. The extent to which the Trade Mark Office succeeds is likely to depend in large part on its fees, which have not yet been made public. The translation obligations imposed on the Office by the political compromise over its working languages may force the Office to establish fees rendering its services unattractive, a problem that has often been predicted in connection with the still unestablished Community Patent Office.

Supplementary protection certificates

On 18 June 1992, the Council adopted a regulation requiring Member States to issue supplementary protection certificates ('SPCs') extending patent protection of medicinal products to cover the time lost during the product approval process.[86] Specifically, the patent holder can obtain an extension of its patent rights for the lesser of five years or a period equivalent to the time elapsed between the first patent application and first authorisation to market the product in the EU.[87] The Regulation became effective on 2 January 1993.

In *Spain v Council*,[88] filed on 4 September 1992, Spain challenged the SPC Regulation in the ECJ. Spain claims that the EU had no legal competence to create a new category of patent protection and that the new Regulation could only have been established through amendment of the EC Treaty. The outcome of this case is still pending.

On 1 September 1994, the Commission issued a proposal for a regulation establishing similar SPCs for plant protection products (agrochemicals). Despite significant differences between the circumstances in the medicinal and plant protection areas, the Commission has applied the approach embodied in the medicinal products SPC Regulation almost word for word in its agrochemical SPC proposal. A heated debate has begun between the large 'research-based' agrochemical manufacturers and their generic competitors, and European farmers. In the light of this controversy, and in particular the political power of the farmers, the Parliament and Council may consider whether any SPC regime is appropriate in the case of agrochemicals and, if so, whether the medicinal products SPC approach should be applied wholesale in this new context.

Rental rights

On 19 November 1992, the EU Council adopted the controversial Directive on rental rights, lending rights and on certain rights related to copyright.[89] The Directive introduces an

---

[84] Trade Mark Regulation, Note 79 above, Article 115.
[85] *Ibid.*
[86] Council Regulation 1768/92 of 18 June 1992 Concerning the Creation of a Supplementary Protection Certificate for Medicinal Products, OJ 1992 L182/1.
[87] *Ibid.*, Article 13.
[88] Court of Justice, Action Brought on 4 September 1992 by the Kingdom of Spain Against the Council of the European Communities (Case C-350/92), OJ 1992 C260/2.
[89] Council Directive 92/100 of 19 November 1992 on the Rental Right and Lending Right on Certain Rights Related to Copyright in the Field of Intellectual Property, OJ 1992 L346/61.

exclusive right for authors,[90] performers, phonogram producers and film producers to control the rental and the lending of their copyrighted works even after these works are sold or distributed.[91] In order to make rental and lending rights effective in all Member States for all rightholders, the Directive harmonises other rights related to copyrights by providing for exclusive rights of fixation, reproduction, public broadcast and distribution for performers, producers and broadcasters. The deadline for Member State implementation of the Directive was 1 July 1994,[92] and to date Belgium, Greece, France, Italy, Austria and Sweden have complied.

Satellite broadcasting and cable retransmission

On 27 September 1993, the EU Council adopted a directive harmonising copyright and neighbouring rights concerning satellite broadcasting and cable retransmission.[93] This Directive eliminates the need for broadcasting companies and cable operators to negotiate the payment of copyright royalties in every Member State in which their broadcasts may be received. Instead, the Directive requires broadcasters to acquire their pertinent rights only in the Member State in which a broadcast originates.[94] In addition, the Directive requires that cable operators obtain the right for retransmission of broadcasts solely from collecting societies that represent the various rightholders in a broadcast work and that such rightholders will be deemed to be represented by those collecting societies.[95]

The implementation date for the Directive was set for 1 January 1995, although none of the Member States has yet passed the necessary legislation.[96] However, agreements concerning the exploitation of works that are already in effect at that time will not be subject to the provisions of the Directive until 1 January 2000.[97]

Term of protection harmonisation

On 29 October 1993, the Commission adopted a directive to harmonise Member State laws on the duration of protection for copyright and related rights.[98] This Directive harmonises copyright protection at the longest duration provided by any Member State (Germany),[99] a good example of the European Union's effort to provide maximum protection to rightholders when harmonising intellectual property laws. The term of protection for authors runs for the life of the author (or the last surviving author, if more than one) plus 70 years; or, if a work is deemed to have been created by a corporation or other legal person (in those Member States permitting such), 70 years after the work is lawfully made available to the public.[100]

---

[90] With respect to cinematographic or audiovisual works, the principal director will be the author (or one of the authors) of the work; *Ibid.*, Article 2(2).

[91] *Ibid.*, Article 2(1).

[92] *Ibid.*, Article 15(1).

[93] Council Directive 93/83 of 27 September 1993 on the Coordination of Certain Rules Concerning Copyright and Rights Related to Copyright Applicable to Satellite Broadcasting and Cable Retransmission, OJ 1993 L248/15.

[94] *Ibid.*, Articles 1 to 3, 8 to 9.

[95] *Ibid.*, Articles 8 to 9.

[96] *Ibid.*, Article 14(1).

[97] *Ibid.*, Article 7(2).

[98] Council Directive 93/98 of 29 October 1993 Harmonising the Term of Protection of Copyright and Certain Related Rights, OJ 1993 L290/9.

[99] *Ibid.*, Articles 1 to 3.

[100] *Ibid.*, Articles 1 to 3.

Similarly, the term of protection for the related rights of performers, producers, and broadcasters is 50 years after publication of the work.[101]

Regarding cinematographic and audiovisual works specifically, the Directive requires that the principal director of a work be considered as its author or one of its authors, allowing Member States to designate other co-authors.[102] However, the term of protection for the work will expire 70 years after the death of the last remaining among the principal director, the author of the screenplay, the author of the dialogue and the composer of music specifically created for use in the work, regardless of whether these individuals are designated as co-authors.[103] All Member States were required to implement this Directive into their national laws by 1 July 1995, although none has yet done so.[104]

Counterfeit and pirated goods

In December 1994, the Council adopted a new regulation intended to prevent the import, export and transit of counterfeit or pirated goods.[105] The Regulation comes into force on 1 July 1995, and replaces an existing 1986 Regulation on this topic.[106]

The Regulation contains three main innovations intended to combat the counterfeit goods market, which is said to represent over 5 per cent of world trade.[107] First, it sets out the measures to be taken by customs authorities with regard to counterfeit and pirated goods and establishes the conditions under which they should act. Thus, powers are given directly to customs authorities, enabling them to act without first obtaining judicial authority or taking interim protective procedures. Second, the protective rules are extended to cover not only trade marks but also copyright and related rights, and designs and models. Third, the rules are extended to cover a wider range of customs operations, including transit and export.

The Regulation is intended to clamp down on the illegal use of intellectual property rights, and to defend manufacturers and innovators. This it may well do, where goods are clearly counterfeit. However, problems could arise in cases where it is not obvious whether or not goods infringe an intellectual property right. Thus, for example, it may be extremely difficult for a customs official to judge whether particular software contained on a diskette infringes copyright or not, and the Regulation may therefore open the door to unwarranted applications for action that could result in goods that are lawfully being moved within, into or out of the EU being detained at least temporarily.[108]

Home copying

On 22 September 1992, the Commission informally submitted to the Internal Market Council a draft directive on home copying of sound and audiovisual recordings that moves

---

[101] *Ibid.*, Article 3.

[102] *Ibid.*, Article 2(1).

[103] *Ibid.*, Article 2(2).

[104] *Ibid.*, Article 13(1).

[105] Council Regulation (EC) 3295/94 of 22 December 1994 laying down measures to prohibit the release for free circulation, export, re-export or entry for a suspensive procedure of counterfeit and pirated goods, OJ 1994 L341/8.

[106] Council Regulation (EEC) 3842/86 of 1 December 1986 laying down measures to prohibit the release for free circulation of counterfeit goods, OJ 1986 L357/1.

[107] See Commission Information Memo P: 93–31 of 14 July 1993.

[108] Article 7 of the Regulation provides for customs authorities to release goods after ten days (or 20 days in 'appropriate' cases) provided no referral has been made for a substantive decision, and no interim measures have been adopted.

toward the harmonisation of Member State laws concerning compensation for private copying of films, audio and video cassettes, records, and compact discs.[109] The draft proposal would authorise private copying in exchange for a levy of harmonised fees on both tape and recording equipment, to be paid by manufacturers and importers.

Four Member States (the United Kingdom, Italy, Ireland and Luxembourg) immediately voiced opposition to the Commission proposal.[110] Nevertheless, the Commission has continued working on its initiative and recently announced in the context of its work on the European Information Society that a formal proposal for a directive on home copying will be released in the near future.[111] Needless to say, a long and complicated debate can be expected before the ultimate adoption of a directive, especially because this issue is likely to become tied up in the larger debate regarding digital diffusion over the Information Infrastructure.

Reprography

In its 1991–2 working programme in the area of copyright and neighbouring rights, the Commission declared its intent to propose a directive on reprography during 1991.[112] The Commission held a hearing in June 1991 on this topic. No progress has been made since the hearing, and opposition to a proposal on reprography appears to be linked to opposition to the Commission's home copying initiative. In any event, it will be difficult to reconcile the conflicting interests of rightholders with manufacturers and importers of reproduction machines, and there seems little likelihood that the Commission will issue a reprography proposal in the near future.

Utility model

The Commission is working on a Green Paper concerning the possible creation of a European utility model. Publication of this paper is expected soon. Meanwhile, an understanding of the operation of utility model law can be obtained by looking to the national law of Germany. Here the history of utility model law is almost as long as that of patent law.

In short, the utility model is intended to operate alongside patent law to ensure the protection of minor technical inventions that nevertheless have a certain practical value. In theory, this allows small and medium-sized businesses to obtain legal protection quickly and at low cost for innovations that do not justify the time and effort required for an examination for patent eligibility.

In addition, the utility model, being quick to obtain, is increasingly being used in Germany to provide legal protection for inventions that have a patent application pending. However, not every type of invention will be eligible for a utility model. In general, applications are made for inventions related to work appliances or utility items.

---

[109] Because no formal proposal for a home copying directive has yet been submitted by the Commission, this document has not been officially published. All information on this informal proposal has come from Commission sources.

[110] Currently, all EU Member States except the United Kingdom, Ireland, and Luxembourg have blank tape levies.

[111] Communication from the European Commission (DGXIII), Note 47 above, at 6; see also Communication from the European Commission (DGXV), Note 47 above, at 11; and the Bangemann Task Force Report, Note 47 above, at 17.

[112] Working Programme of the Commission in the Field of Copyright and Neighbouring Rights, COM (90) 584 final, chapter 8.4.

Revision of Block Exemptions

With the Patent Licensing Block Exemption scheduled to expire at the end of 1994, in June 1994 the Commission proposed adopting a single Technology Transfer Block Exemption to replace both the existing Patent Licensing Block Exemption and the existing Know-How Licensing Block Exemption. The proposal has met with less than enthusiastic reviews from industry, particularly because of newly introduced market share limitations.[113]

As proposed, the new regulation would provide an exemption from Article 85(1) of the EC Treaty for pure patent, pure know-how and mixed patent and know-how licences, but impose ceilings of market shares above which the exemption would not apply. The draft expands slightly on the existing Patent Block Exemption's 'white list' of conditions that are generally not restrictive of competition.[114] The existing regulations have been further liberalised in the Commission proposal by significantly shortening the 'black list' of provisions that, if contained in licence agreements, currently will render the block exemption inapplicable.[115] Moreover, the proposal would allow the inclusion of 'grey clauses' in an agreement that otherwise qualifies for exemption.

Although industry has welcomed most of the changes to the existing regulations, as well as the general approach of replacing the two existing regulations with one Technology Transfer Block Exemption, the draft has been intensely criticised, mainly because of its introduction of market share criteria. Article 1(5) of the draft requires that for a sole licence to be automatically exempt, the licensee's market share for the licensed product and equivalent products must not be greater than 40 per cent; nor must the parties and one other undertaking together hold a market share of more than 50 per cent. In addition, Article 1(6) allows exemptions of other forms of territorial protection (such as exclusivity) only 'where at least one party holds no more than 20% of the market in all licensed products in the common market'.[116] Observers claim that the market share criteria will increase uncertainty and force companies to undertake expensive market analyses nearly every time a licence agreement is contemplated.

The Technology Transfer Block Exemption was scheduled for adoption at the end of 1994, but the heated (albeit belated) industry objections prevented this from happening. The Commission has therefore extended the existing Patent Licensing Block Exemption by six months, by which time it hopes to have a new regulation in place. It seems likely that the market share criteria will be modified in some way, perhaps by eliminating the oligopoly criteria entirely and by raising the limit to 40 per cent for all purposes.

Global information infrastructure

As in the United States, in the early 1990s the computer, communications and entertainment industries in Europe began to devote attention to the 'Information Infrastructure'. In December 1993, not to be outdone by the Americans, the EU launched its own information infrastructure project in a White Paper issued by the then-President of the European Commission, Jacques Delors. In this White Paper (presented to the Prime Ministers of EU Member States at their Brussels summit in December 1993 and entitled 'Growth, Competitiveness, Employment—The challenges and ways forward into the 21st century'),

---

[113] Draft Commission Regulation (EC) of 19 October 1994 amending Regulation (EEC) 2349/84 on the application of Article 85(3) of the EC Treaty to certain categories of patent licensing, OJ 1994 C313/4.
[114] *Ibid.*, Article 2.
[115] *Ibid.*, Article 3.
[116] *Ibid.*, Article 1(6).

the Commission described its grand vision of a 'European Information Society', (EIS) and heralded the building of the Information Society as one of the major means of re-establishing Europe's global economic competitiveness.

After the December 1993 summit, Commissioner Bangemann took the initiative and established a task force, commonly called the Bangemann Task Force, consisting of prominent private persons, including senior industry representatives, from each Member State. The Task Force presented its report (entitled 'Europe and the Global Information Society— Recommendations to the European Council') to the European Council in May 1994, and the report was approved by the Prime Ministers of the Member States at the European Council summit in Corfu in June 1994. The report concluded that a number of policy and regulatory measures should be taken by the EU to pave the way for the information superhighway. Among other things, the report recommended that (1) inter-connection of networks and interoperability of services and applications should be primary EU objectives; (2) the European standardisation process should be made speedier and more responsive to markets; and (3) EU action should be taken to establish a common regulatory framework for the protection of intellectual property rights, privacy and security of information not only in Europe but globally.

In conjunction with the Bangemann Task Force Report, the Commission has begun a broad consultation process designed to identify how and where intellectual property rights need to be modified to facilitate the growth and development of the EIS. At the beginning of June 1994 the Commission held informal meetings with interested parties to explore some of the intellectual property issues arising in the information infrastructure environment. Further to these meetings, the Commission distributed a questionnaire addressing 'aspects of copyright and related rights in the information infrastructure', which served as the basis for a formal hearing in July 1994.

In many respects the DGXV questionnaire paralleled issues addressed by the US Intellectual Property Working Group;[117] indeed, it is clear that the US Administration's aggressive efforts to set the agenda for multilateral debate over the GII have had considerable success. This is reflected not only in the DGXV questionnaire and subsequent activities, but also in the context of World Intellectual Property Organisation (WIPO) negotiations over a possible protocol to the Berne Convention.

At the Commission hearing last summer, over 50 government officials, academics and a number of organisations and companies (including those active in telecommunications, software, publishing, and the like) participated. Some of the issues discussed included:

- the scope of the concept 'information infrastructure' (should it be limited to digital fixations and transmissions?);
- the best means for identification and clearance of rights (should works on an information superhighway carry some identification of intellectual property rights? Should

---

[117] The US Intellectual Property Working Group (IPWG) is a sub-committee of the Information Infrastructure Task Force (IITF), an inter-agency working group of the Clinton Administration. The IPWG is headed by Bruce Lehmann, Commissioner of Patents and Trademarks, and is made up of representatives from various government agencies, such as, *inter alia*, the White House, the Justice Department, the Office of Management and Budget and the Commerce Department. In the summer of 1994, the IPWG published a Green Paper on the future of various intellectual property issues in the light of the National Information Infrastructure (NII) and received a wave of comments from various corporations, academics and organisations. The US Patent Office is currently drafting the final version of the position paper which will then be circulated to the other members of IPWG for comments. Once the inter-agency review process is completed the paper will be released to the general public as the Government's official position paper on intellectual property issues. The paper is expected to be released in the next few months and is likely to include legislative recommendations.

an identification system be accompanied by a voluntary deposit or registration system?);

● the most appropriate means to regulate the information infrastructure (should existing copyright and neighbouring rights regimes be expanded to accommodate the new technologies or do new *sui generis* rights need to be created?); and

● the best method of adapting legislation to the information infrastructure environment (should it be done piecemeal by amending existing texts or by creating new laws relating specifically to intellectual property rights throughout the EIS?).

Following the hearing, DGXV obtained responses to its questionnaire from many interested parties, and these responses will soon be published by the Commission. Although the submissions have not yet been published, it appears that the majority indicate a preference for leaving European intellectual property laws intact. The majority appear to feel that it would be unwise for the law to race ahead of technology, and that it is too early to reach any conclusions about changes in the law because the ultimate contours of the Information Infrastructure still remain unclear.

Based on the hearing and the responses to the questionnaire, DGXV is now drafting a Green Paper. The Green Paper will outline a work programme and may set forth legislative proposals for future development of the EIS. To this end, both DGXV and DGXIII have prepared communications recommending action plans and setting priorities for areas of work, although only the DGXIII Communication has been adopted.[118]

The Green Paper is now scheduled to be released by summer 1995. It now seems unlikely that the Green Paper will recommend any radical changes to accommodate the Information Society, but it remains possible that certain significant changes to existing law will be recommended.

Community and European Patent Conventions

In 1975, the European Community executed the Community Patent Convention (CPC)[119] that would have created a European patent in much the same way as the EU Trade Mark Regulation created a European trade mark. However, the CPC has never been ratified owing to lack of support from the Member States, and at the time of writing, few believe that it ever will. However, the European Patent Convention[120] entered into force on 7 October 1977.

Under the EPC, the European Patent Office (EPO) applies a uniform system to grant so-called 'European patents'. An applicant can go to the EPO and through one application request a bundle of national patents for any of the 17 countries party to the EPC, including all the EU Member States except Finland.[121] In deciding to grant a European patent, the EPO applies a single set of rules on patentability. If granted, the holder of the European patent then has the option to 'localise' the European patent in any or all of the EPC member countries by asking the European Patent Office to register the patent (and paying the relevant fees to each country). The European patent confers no enforceable rights until it is localised. Moreover, once localised, the patent is treated the same as a national patent and therefore

---

[118] Communication from the European Commission (DGXIII) and Communication from the European Commission (DGXV), Note 47 above.

[119] Convention 76/76/EEC for the European Patent for the Common Market, OJ 1976 L17/1.

[120] Convention on the Grant of European Patents of 5 October 1973 (as amended) ('European Patent Convention' or 'EPC').

[121] See Note 55 above.

must be separately enforced in each country. Thus, although the EPC centralises the application and grant stage of the patent process, it leaves enforcement at the national level. It is this centralised enforcement mechanism that would have been gained within the EU under the CPC system.

Under the CPC, a single patent application would be made to the European Patent Office in the same way it is currently done under the EPC. However, under the CPC, it would be possible to obtain a real European patent valid and enforceable in the national courts of any EU Member State. The CPC would then have established a Common patent Appeal Court in Luxembourg to hear patent appeals from the national courts of the Member States. Once a patent was found to be valid by the Patent Appeal Court, all the Member States would be required to enforce it.

In theory, the system established by the CPC should have resulted in a less costly and more administratively efficient system for obtaining EU patent coverage and enforcement. However, applications for a CPC patent would have had to have been made in English, French or German. Any Member State whose official language is not one of these three would have been entitled to insist that no rights be conferred by a CPC patent in respect of the use of an invention within its territory unless the applicant had supplied a translation of the application in one of that country's own official languages either to the relevant authority of that country or to the person using the invention. Many argue that these translation requirements would have significantly reduced any potential gains in efficiency. For better or worse, it is highly unlikely that the CPC will ever be ratified.

European Telecommunications Standards Institute

After two years of heated debate, members of the European Telecommunications Standards Institute (ETSI) decided to scrap their controversial Interim Intellectual Property Rights Policy and Undertaking.[122] The plan, which was adopted in March 1993, set forth ETSI's policy objectives and included, as an appendix to the policy document, an Undertaking covering principal licensing provisions and intellectual property rights disclosure rules for ETSI members to follow.

The goal of the IPR Policy and Undertaking was to ensure that patented or copyrighted products, equipment or methods incorporated into ETSI standards would be available for licensing to all ETSI members and non-members on non-discriminatory terms. It required members to notify ETSI of any patent that might be covered by a norm within 180 days of an ETSI notification or risk having their patent licensed automatically. This enraged a number of ETSI's members, who complained that the IPR Policy amounted to a form of compulsory licence. Certain US members threatened to leave ETSI rather than sign the IPR Undertaking, and in June 1993 the US trade group, the Computer and Business Equipment Manufacturers Association (CBEMA), filed a formal anti-trust complaint against the IPR Policy with the European Commission.[123] CBEMA claimed that by signing the Undertaking an IPR holder would be forced to sign away present and/or future rights at a forced price.

Although considerable progress was made during the first half of 1994 towards achieving a compromise between the supporters and detractors of the ETSI Policy, the Policy was

---

[122] European Telecommunications Standards Institute (ETSI), Intellectual Property Rights Policy and Undertaking (1993) ('IPR Policy' and 'IPR Undertaking') (not officially published; copies are available from ETSI).

[123] Complaint and Request for Interim Measures Against European Telecommunications Standards Institute (ETSI), submitted to the Commission of the European Communities Directorate-General for Competition by the Computer and Business Equipment Manufacturers Association (CBEMA), (22 June 1993) (not officially published).

rejected by 88.25 per cent of ETSI's members in a General Assembly meeting in August 1994. A slimmed-down Policy, which basically follows the usual licensing policy of international standards organisations, was adopted on 23 November 1994. In several recent US cases,[124] however, a number of interesting issues have arisen concerning intellectual property and standardisation, and these issues may find their way to Europe as well.

Rome and Berne Conventions

The EU Council rejected the Commission's proposed decision requiring Member State accession by 31 December 1992 to the Berne Convention for the Protection of Literary and Artistic Works (as revised by the Paris Act of 1971)[125] and the Rome Convention for the Protection of Performers, Producers of Phonograms and Broadcasting Organisations.[126] The Council rejected the Commission's proposal on the basis that the Commission improperly sought to force Member State ratification of the conventions by means of a decision. The Commission therefore replaced its proposed decision with a non-binding resolution adopted by the Council on 14 May 1992.[127] The resolution notes that EU Member States should undertake to become parties to the Paris Act of the Berne Convention and the Rome Convention by 1 January 1995.[128] Although the resolution is non-binding, EU and EFTA Member States agreed in the Agreement on the European Economic Area (EEA Agreement) to accede to both Conventions by 1 January 1995, and, moreover, to conform their national laws to the substantive provisions of both conventions on entry into force of the EEA Agreement.[129] To date all EU and EFTA Member States have signed the Paris Act of the Berne Convention, and all but Portugal, Belgium, and Liechtenstein have signed the Rome Convention.

EEA Agreement

Apart from the above obligation, the EEA Agreement obligated most EFTA countries to adopt the EU 'acquis communautaire'[130] on intellectual property matters, including judicial decisions such as the *Magill* decision.[131] In addition, the EEA Agreement provided for those EFTA countries to accede to the Community Patent Convention,[132] and required licensing and distribution agreements covering the EFTA members of the EEA to be amended to

---

[124] See *Stryker Corp. v Zimmer, Inc.*, 741 F.Supp. 509 (DND 1990) (estoppel to assert patent rights in *de facto* standard); *Stambler v Diebold*, 11 USPQ 2d 1709 (EDNY 1988) (estoppel to assert patent rights in ANSI standard); and *Potter Instrument Corp. v Storage Technology Corp.*, 207 USPQ 763 (ED Va. 1980) (same).

[125] Berne Convention for the Protection of Literary and Artistic Works, 9 September 1886, revised Paris 24 July 1971, reprinted in Stephen Zamora and Ronald A. Brand (eds), *Basic Documents of International Economic Law*, 1990 715 and 4 David Nimmer and Melville B. Nimmer, *Nimmer on Copyright*, app. 27 (1993).

[126] Rome Convention for the Protection of Performers, Producers of Phonograms and Broadcasting Organisations, 26 October 1961, 496 UNTS 43.

[127] Council Resolution of 14 May 1992 on Increased Protection for Copyright and Neighbouring Rights, OJ 1992 C138/1.

[128] *Ibid.*

[129] Agreement on the European Economic Area ('EEA Agreement') Protocol 28, Article 5.

[130] The term 'acquis communautaire' is used to mean the whole body of rules (whether binding legislation, principles and decisions or non-binding resolutions or guidelines) governing the activities of the EU institutions and the Member States.

[131] Note 129 above, Article 65(2), Protocol 28, Article 2. Now that Austria, Finland and Sweden have joined the EU, Norway and Iceland are the only two non-EU countries party to the EEA Agreement.

[132] *Ibid.*, Protocol 28, Article 3.

conform with EU law (including Article 85 and the various block exemptions), within six months after the EEA Agreement took effect in January 1994.[133]

Association agreements

Agreements were signed in 1992 with Poland, Hungary, and the former Czechoslovakia giving them five years to bring their intellectual property rights into line with a short list of adopted EU legislation, including the Software Directive. Similar agreements have now been signed with the Ukraine, Romania and Bulgaria, as well.[134] Unlike Norway and Iceland, as EEA members, these countries will have no mechanism for providing input on future intellectual property policy-making.

European Union Judicial Developments

Magill

The most significant European intellectual property-related case in recent years has been the European Court of Justice's *Magill* decision, in which provisions of EU competition law were held to override national intellectual property rights.[135] The particular importance of the case lies in its analysis of the balance between intellectual property rights and competition law in the EU.[136]

Magill involved three television broadcasters each of which provided separate television programming in Ireland on their own respective television channels. Each of these broadcasters published a weekly listing containing its own programming schedule for the following week, and under Irish and UK law, these programme listings were protected by copyright. Although the broadcasters granted free licences under their copyrights to newspapers and other third parties to publish these programming schedules on a daily basis, no third party was permitted to publish the listings on a weekly basis. As a result, a single complete listing containing the weekly programming schedule for every television channel in the country was unavailable in both Ireland and the United Kingdom.

Magill TV Guide, Ltd, an Irish publisher, sought a licence from the three broadcasters in order to produce such a comprehensive weekly programme listing for all television channels, but was refused.[137] Thereafter, Magill filed a complaint with the European Commission contending that by refusing to grant a licence, the broadcasters had abused their dominant position in the market in violation of Article 86 of the EC Treaty.[138] The Commission agreed

---

[133] *Ibid.*, Article 53 to 60.

[134] Interim Agreement on Trade and Trade-related Matters Between the European Economic Community and the European Coal and Steel Community, of the one part, and the Republic of Poland, of the other part, OJ 1992 L114/2, Article 36; Interim Agreement on Trade and Trade-related Matters Between the European Economic Community and the European Coal and Steel Community, of the one part, and the Republic of Czechoslovakia, of the other part, OJ 1992 L115/2, Article 36; Interim Agreement on Trade and Trade-related Matters Between the European Economic Community and the European Coal and Steel Community, of the one part, and the Republic of Hungary, of the other part, OJ 1992 L116/2, Article 35.

[135] Cases C241/91P and C242/91P, *Radio Telefis Eireann and Independent Television Publications Ltd v Commission*, Judgment of the Court, 6 April 1995 ('*Magill*').

[136] For more extensive commentary on *Magill*, see Thomas Vinje, 'Magill: Its Impact on the Information Technology Industry', [1992] 11 EIPR 397, and 'The final Word on Magill: The Judgment of the ECJ', [1995] 6 EIPR 297.

[137] Magill actually began producing its television guide but was enjoined by an Irish court, which decision was upheld by the Irish High Court.

[138] Under the EC Treaty, it must be ensured 'that competition in the internal market is not distorted' (EC Treaty Article 3(g)). Article 86 provides that '[a]ny abuse by one or more undertakings of a dominant position within the common market or in a substantial part of it shall be prohibited as incompatible with the common market in so far as it may affect trade between Member States'.

with Magill, finding that the relevant markets consisted of the copyrighted weekly programme listings for each company, that the broadcasters were dominant in these markets, and that in preventing the introduction of a new product, a complete weekly programme listing, and reserving for themselves the derivative market for weekly guides, the broadcasters had abused their dominant position.[139] The Commission, therefore, ordered the broadcasters to provide their programme listings to others on non-discriminatory terms for a reasonable royalty.

The broadcasters appealed the Commission decision to the EU Court of First Instance (CFI), which affirmed the decision on all grounds.[140] In connection with abuse of dominant position, the CFI was required to resolve the conflict between the UK and Irish copyright laws, under which the broadcasters had copyright in their listing, and Article 86 of the EC Treaty. Specifically, the Court had to decide whether the broadcasters' rights to refuse to licence Magill fell within the 'existence' or 'specific subject matter' of their copyright (in which case it would traditionally be outside the reach of Articles 85 and 86), or whether it fell within their 'exercise' of that right (in which case it would be subject to the competition rules). In short, the Court held that the right to refuse licences fell within the existence/specific subject matter of the right, but that, in appropriate circumstances, a rightholder could nonetheless be required to license its rights. As the broadcasters had, in 'using [their] copyright in the [programme] listings which [they] produced as part of [their] broadcasting activity in order to secure a monopoly in the derivative market of weekly television guides', pursued an aim contrary to Article 86, their actions constituted an abuse that could not be safeguarded by the protection conferred by their copyrights.

Two of the broadcasters appealed this decision to the European Court of Justice (ECJ), and on 1 June 1994, Advocate General Gulmann issued his opinion.[141] He reasoned that a dominant company would *not* violate Article 86 by refusing to licence its rights to a third party provided: (i) the products to be produced under the licence would *compete* with the rightholder's products in the sense that they would fulfil roughly equivalent consumer needs, and (ii) the rightholder had not licensed the rights to any other licensee under comparable circumstances. However, a dominant company might violate EU competition laws, depending on the circumstances, if it: (i) refused to license *non-competing* products; (ii) engaged in discriminatory licensing (for example, licensing some but not others under comparable circumstances); or (iii) charged unreasonable royalties.

Applying this reasoning, Advocate General Gulman concluded that the broadcasters were entitled to refuse a licence to Magill, since the Magill TV guide would have competed with the broadcasters' own products.

On 6 April 1995, the ECJ delivered its judgment. Instead of following the opinion of the Advocate General, however, the Court upheld the CFI's decision, and dismissed the broadcasters' appeal. The three most important aspects of the judgment concern the ECJ's findings of dominant position and of abuse of dominant position, and its decision that the Commission has the power to order compulsory licensing as a remedy for Article 86 violations.

While the ECJ found that the broadcasters held a dominant position, it did not come to that conclusion by using traditional economic criteria to test the broadcasters' ability to act independently of competitors and consumers.[142] Instead, it stated that 'mere ownership of

---

[139] Commission Decision 89/205/EEC (IV/31.851—*Magill TV Guide/ITP, BCC, and RTE*) 1989 OJ L78/43.

[140] Case T-69/89, *Radio Telefís Eireann v Commission*, 4 CMLR 586; Case T-70/89, *The British Broadcasting Corp. v Commission*, 4 CMLR 669; and Case T-76/89, *Independent Television Publications Ltd v Commission*, 4 CMLR 745. These cases are collectively referred to as the CFI's decision in *Magill*.

[141] Cases C-241/91P and C-242/91P, *Radio Telefís Eireann and Independent Television Publications Ltd v Commission*, Opinion of Advocate General Gulmann delivered on 1 June 1994.

[142] See *Michelin v Commission* [1983] ECR 3461, point 30.

an intellectual property right cannot confer' a dominant position, but left it unclear why, if this were so, the broadcasters held a dominant position in this case. The problem facing the Court seems to have been that the information over which the broadcasters were found to have had a *de facto* monopoly was the same information which the UK and Irish courts considered protectable by copyright. The Court's cursory explanation of why the broadcasters held a dominant position is less than satisfactory, and some may ask whether the dominance in fact resulted from the legal monopoly granted by the copyright. However, although careful consideration of rightholders' positions will be required in each case in the future, it seems unlikely that the *Magill* decision will be used to support a finding of dominance in cases where no such finding would previously have been made under traditional economic criteria.

As regards abuse of the dominant position, the ECJ held that a refusal to licence an intellectual property right can constitute an abuse under Article 86, in certain circumstances. In short, the broadcasters argued that since their right to refuse permission to reproduce the protected listings constituted part of the 'specific subject matter' of the copyright, their behaviour could not be found to have constituted an abuse. The ECJ was not willing to accept this simple approach. It acknowledged that 'a refusal to grant a licence, even if it is the act of an undertaking holding a dominant position, cannot in itself constitute abuse of a dominant position',[143] but it went on to find that such a refusal might in some circumstances constitute an abuse. In the present case, the Court noted three circumstances that justified a finding of abuse. First, there was 'no actual or potential substitute' for a comprehensive weekly television guide, for which there was a 'specific, constant and regular' consumer demand. Second, 'there was no justification for such refusal either in the activity of television broadcasting or in that of publishing television magazines'. Third, the broadcasters 'reserved to themselves the secondary market of weekly television guides by excluding all competition in that market . . . since they denied access to the basic information which is the raw material indispensable for the compilation of such a guide'.[144] Thus, the ECJ rejected the Advocate General's suggestion (mentioned above) that a refusal to license an intellectual property right to someone intending to create a competing product would not violate Article 86. The ECJ's judgment mentions neither the existence/exercise doctrine nor the specific subject matter concept explicitly. It may be premature, therefore, to pronounce the death of the existence/exercise doctrine. However, it seems likely to have little continuing relevance in determining whether conduct related to an intellectual property right constitutes an abuse under Article 86. Clearly, the Court has moved to a circumstances-based approach to determining whether an abuse exists.

Finally, the ECJ clarified that compulsory licensing was available as a remedy for Article 86 violations by deciding that the Commission was entitled to require the broadcasters to provide the relevant information to Magill. The Court found that 'the imposition of that obligation . . . was the only way of bringing infringement to an end.'[145]

Although Magill involved the atypical issue of copyright protection of purely factual information, which may have a limiting effect on the cope of its application, the underlying principles of the decision could be extended to other situations in which intellectual property rights are asserted to preclude competitive products. Thus, *Magill* may be applied in areas such as information technology and telecommunications, where copyright is now applied in an industrial context far different from that of traditional literary and artistic works. In the context of the global debate concerning the balance between protecting intellectual property

---

[143] *Magill*, point 49 (*emphasis added*).
[144] *Magill*, points 52–56.
[145] *Magill*, point 91.

rights and competition in the information technology industry, the decision in *Magill*, while it does not articulate a bright-line standard as to when national intellectual property rights will be forced to succumb to EU-wide legal standards, nevertheless demonstrates that EU pre-emption of national intellectual property rights may be asserted in certain circumstances, and could be viewed as a blow in favour of those desiring more scope for competition.

Ideal Standard[146]

In the recent *Ideal Standard* case, the European Court of Justice finally killed off the doctrine of common ownership first established in *Hag I* and upheld national intellectual property rights rather than give precedence to the principle of the free movement of goods within the EU.

In *Ideal Standard*, the ECJ held that EC Treaty provisions concerning the free movement of goods[147] did not prevent the owner of a trade mark in one Member State from opposing the importation of goods bearing an identical trade mark from another Member State, where the importing company was not economically linked to the trade mark owner opposing importation, but had been assigned the trade mark by a company affiliated to the opposing trade mark owner.

The basic facts of the case were as follows. Until 1984, the American Standard group owned the trade mark *Ideal Standard* both in France and in Germany for the marketing of sanitary fittings and heating equipment. The trade mark was owned through two different subsidiaries: Ideal-Standard SA in France, and Ideal-Standard GmbH in Germany. In July 1984, following financial difficulties, Ideal-Standard SA assigned to an independent French company (the Société Générale de Fonderie) its trade mark rights in France for the heating equipment sector, and transferred its heating business. Ownership then passed to the Compagnie Internationale du Chauffage (CICH), also a company with which the American Standard group had no economic link. CICH then proceeded to market its heating products under the trade mark *Ideal Standard* in Germany through its subsidiary Internationale Heiztechnik GmbH (IHT). The American Standard group's German subsidiary, Ideal-Standard GmbH, which was itself only marketing sanitary ware under the Trade mark, objected to the importation into Germany of CICH's heating equipment under the same name, and obtained a ruling in the German courts to prevent IHT marketing the equipment. IHT appealed, and the German Higher Regional Court referred the matter to the ECJ.

The ECJ accepted that the prohibition on the use in Germany by IHT of the name 'Ideal Standard' amounted to a measure having equivalent effect to a quantitative restriction under the terms of Article 30 of the EC Treaty. However, it went on to find that the measure was acceptable under Article 36, which allows, *inter alia*, prohibitions on imports that are justified for the protection of industrial and commercial property. In short, the measure was found to be justified for the following reasons:

(1) The object of trade mark law is to protect owners against third parties who might seek, by creating a risk of confusing among consumers, to take advantage of the reputation accruing to the trade mark.[148] The risk of consumer confusion can arise from the use of an identical name for products that are different from those for

---

[146] See Case 9/93, *IHT Internationale Heiztechnik GmbH and Others v Ideal-Standard GmbH and Others*, 3 CMLR 857 (European Court of Justice, 22 June 1994).

[147] EC Treaty, Articles 30 to 36.

[148] See Case 102/77, *Hoffman-La Roche v Centrafarm* [1978] ECR 1139, paragraph 7.

which the trade mark has been acquired, if the products are sufficiently closely related to induce users to believe they come from the same source.[149] Whether the products are sufficiently close is a matter for the national court to decide, and the German court had found this to be the case here.

(2) National trade marks are territorial rights that are independent of each other. Thus a trade mark right can be assigned for one country without at the same time being assigned by its owner in other countries.

(3) In *Hag II*[150] it was held that for a trade mark to fulfil its role it must offer a guarantee that all goods bearing it have been produced under the control of a single undertaking accountable for their quality.[151] Whereas a trade mark owner cannot oppose the marketing of products that have been put into circulation in the exporting state by him or with his consent, this principle (known as 'exhaustion of rights') only applies where the owner of the trade mark in the exporting state is the same as, or economically linked to, the owner opposing importation. Thus, for example, a licensor who has the ability, through contractual agreement, to control the quality of goods imported by a licensee (whether or not it uses that ability) cannot prevent its licensee from importing those goods on the grounds that import would infringe its trade mark. On the other hand, where a trade mark is assigned to a company having no economic link with the assignor, the contract of assignment does not give the assignor any means of controlling the quality of the products to be marketed by the assignee. Therefore, the assignor cannot be said to have given the assignee sufficient implied consent for the doctrine of exhaustion of rights to apply.

In *Hag II*, which concerned a trade mark split as a result of expropriation, the court stressed that the determinant factor was the absence of consent of the trade mark owner in the importing state to the marketing of the products in the exporting state.[152] The court went on to conclude that free movement of the goods in these circumstances would undermine the essential function of the trade mark: consumers would no longer be able to identify for certain the origin of the marked goods, and the owner of the trade mark in the importing state could be held responsible for the poor quality of goods for which he was in no way accountable.[153] In *Ideal Standard*, where the splitting of the trade mark was a result of a voluntary assignment, the same reasoning applied.[154]

Thus the *Ideal Standard* case reinforces the precedence given in *Hag II* to national intellectual property rights over the principles of the free movement of goods. In the words of the German court of first instance, 'there is no longer any foundation for the doctrine of common origin' either in a case of expropriation (as in *Hag II*) or in the case of a voluntary division of ownership of a trade mark originally in single ownership.

Perhaps the most obvious practical implication of this judgment can be seen in the context of acquisitions. Where a company is considering acquiring a business with trade mark rights in one Member State, it should investigate the extent to which that business is able to export, under the trade mark, to other Member States. Thus, where an identical trade mark is owned independently in another Member State, the company acquiring the business may find itself

---

[149] Note that in the *Hag* case, the products were themselves identical (see Cases 192/73 *Van Zuylen v HAG* [1974] ECR 731 (*Hag I*) and C-10/89 *CNL-SUGAL v HAG* [1990] ECR I-3711 (*Hag II*)).

[150] See Note 149 above.

[151] *Ibid.*, paragraph 13.

[152] *Ibid.*, paragraph 15.

[153] *Ibid.*, paragraph 15.

[154] It is interesting to note that IHT's objection that products from different sources could be marketed in France under the same trade mark cut no ice with the ECJ.

prevented from exporting to that other Member State, even if the trade mark rights in both Member States were owned by the same parent company or group of companies prior to the acquisition of the business. This potential restriction on importation should be reflected in the price paid for the business.

Repackaging cases

The European Court of Justice now has before it a number of parallel import cases concerning *Paranova* from Denmark and *Eurimpharm* from Germany. These cases will allow the ECJ to review its 20-year-old decisions on trade mark exhaustion, especially with respect to repackaging, and to examine whether the explicit exhaustion provisions of the Trade Mark Directive have changed the law in this area.

Conclusion

Notwithstanding the pre-emption of intellectual property rights in the particular circumstances surrounding *Magill*, intellectual property developments in the EU are intended to and, for the most part, have resulted in greater and more consistent protection of these rights throughout the EU. National rules will undoubtedly remain relevant in some contexts, but within a few years the EU seems likely to attain its goal of achieving a strong and broadly harmonised European Union-wide intellectual property regime. Moreover, increased protection and more consistent legislation governing intellectual property rights will foster a more attractive business climate for producing and marketing intellectual property in the European Union.

The Final Word on Magill
[1995] 6 EIPR 297

THOMAS C. VINJE
Morrison & Foerster, Brussels

The Judgment of the ECJ

> After *Magill*, it is crystal clear that a refusal to license by a dominant undertaking *can* constitute an abuse under Article 86 and that compulsory licensing is available to remedy such an abuse. Instead of adopting a mechanical approach, holding that a refusal to license falls within the existence/specific subject-matter of the intellectual property right and is hence immune from Article 86, the Court adopted a flexible, *circumstances-based* approach to deciding when a refusal to license constitutes an abuse. By adopting such an approach, and by virtually ignoring the 'existence/exercise' doctrine, the Court appeared to signal a further diminution of the relevance of this doctrine, if not its ultimate demise. Although *Magill* does not mark a revolution in the application of EC competition law to intellectual property licensing, it clearly strengthens the hand of the Commission to attack perceived abuses, and there may be particular scope to apply *Magill* in the information technology sphere.

Finally we have the answer. Six years after the Commission's decision, the European Court of Justice (ECJ) has finally spoken in *Magill*.[1] All doubt has been swept away about the answers to two of the most fundamental questions concerning the application of EC competition law to intellectual property: first, a refusal to license an intellectual property right *can*, in certain circumstances, constitute an abuse of a dominant position under Article 86, and second, compulsory licensing *can* be imposed as a remedy for such an abuse.

Although *Magill* undoubtedly will have a more far-reaching impact on intellectual property practices than any other ECJ judgment in recent years, and many will bemoan the ECJ's failure to hold intellectual property sacrosanct, the ECJ's decision is to be welcomed. Rightholders of traditional intellectual property have little to fear from *Magill*; the Commission is not about to embark on a crusade against common licensing practices. Indeed, the Commission has in recent years come far in grasping the pro-competitive benefits of intellectual property protection and of providing freedom to licensing parties in structuring their relationships.

While no wholesale attacks on traditional and accepted licensing practices are to be expected, the ECJ's judgment in *Magill* preserves the necessary flexibility to apply com-

---

[1] Cases C-241/91 P and C—242/91 P *RTE and ITP v Commission*. Judgment of the Court, 6 April 1995 ('*Magill*').

petition law to situations, such as those that may arise with respect to the 'information superhighway', where the industrial context and new technological constraints make third parties dependent on licensing from dominant undertakings in order to participate in legitimate competitive activities.

Before turning to a discussion of *Magill* and its potential impact, a brief description of the case and its background is in order.

Background to Magill

Facts and Commission Decision

Magill involved the refusal by two UK broadcasters and one Irish broadcaster to license programming information to Magill for inclusion in a new weekly television guide that Magill planned to publish in the United Kingdom and Ireland.

The programming information was created as a natural by-product of the broadcasters' decisions on television programming; those decisions about the channel, date and time of each programme were reflected in what are called 'programme listings'. Because each broadcaster had sole knowledge of its programming decisions and was therefore the only source of the basic information about its programming, they each had a factual monopoly over that information. In addition, the English and Irish courts had held that—unlike in other EU Member States—copyright subsisted in the programme listings (that is, the listings of channels, dates, and times for the programmes).

Each broadcaster published information concerning its own programmes in its own weekly television guide. The broadcasters also allowed newspapers in the United Kingdom and Ireland to publish the comprehensive information for all television channels for one day or for the weekend, and allowed both newspapers and the other broadcasters to publish highlights, but not to publish comprehensive information, on a weekly basis. Therefore, no one had the right to publish comprehensive programme listings on a weekly basis, which meant that the United Kingdom and Ireland were the only two Member States without a comprehensive weekly publication covering all channels.

The Commission held that the broadcasters had abused their dominant position in the market for programme listings by preventing the introduction of a new product, namely a comprehensive weekly television guide, for which there was significant consumer demand.[2] The Commission therefore ordered the broadcasters to license their programme listings to each other and to third parties, subject to a reasonable royalty. This case is the only case to date in which the Commission has held that a refusal to license violates the EC competition rules.

CFI's judgment

The broadcasters appealed the Commission's decision to the Court of First Instance (CFI), which upheld the decision.[3] First, the CFI upheld the Commission's definition of the relevant product markets: the markets for weekly listings and the television magazines in which they are published, which constitute submarkets within the market for television programme information in general. Second, the CFI found that the broadcasters were dominant in those submarkets based both on their factual monopoly over the information necessary to produce

---

[2] Commission Decision 89/205/EEC (IV/31.851—*Magill TV Guide/ITP, BBC and RTE*) OJ 1989 L78/43.
[3] Case T—69/89 *RTE v Commission* [1991] ECR II 485, Case T—70/89 *BBC v Commission* [1991] ECR II 535 and Case T—76/89 *ITP Limited v Commission* [1991] ECR II 575 ('CFI opinion').

weekly television magazines and their legal monopoly based on copyright. Third, the CFI found that the broadcasters had abused their dominant position by refusing to license the programme information.

In connection with this last issue, the CFI was required to resolve the conflict between the UK and Irish copyright laws, under which the broadcasters had copyright in their listings, and Article 86 of the EC Treaty. This is the conflict at the centre of one of the thorniest concepts in EC law: the difference between the 'existence' (or 'specific subject-matter') of a right (which traditionally has been held to be outside the reach of Articles 85 and 86) and the 'exercise' of that right (which *has* been subject to the competition rules).

Specifically, the CFI had to decide whether the broadcasters' right to refuse to licence Magill fell within the existence/specific subject-matter of their copyright. If so, the next question was whether this would *per se* preclude the Treaty's application or rather whether the Treaty could, in some circumstances, nevertheless apply to limit rights falling within the specific subject-matter of the right.

The CFI held that

> in principle, the protection of the specific subject matter of a copyright entitles the copyrightholder to *reserve the exclusive right* to reproduce the protected work ... However, while it is plain that the exercise of the exclusive right to reproduce a protected work is not itself an abuse, that does not apply when, *in light of the details of each individual case,* it is apparent that that right is exercised in such ways and circumstances as in fact to pursue an aim manifestly contrary to Article 86, and in particular if it involves evidence of abusive conduct.[4]

In short, the CFI held that the right to refuse licences fell within the existence/specific subject-matter of the right, but that in appropriate circumstances a rightholder can nonetheless be required to license its rights.

Two of the broadcasters (RTE and ITP) appealed the CFI judgment, supported in intervention by Intellectual Property Owners, a US-based organisation. Overall, the parties relied on five arguments on appeal, namely that the CFI (1) misconstrued the concept of abuse of a dominant position under Article 86; (2) wrongly found an effect on trade between Member States; (3) wrongly refused to hold that the Berne Convention prohibits the Commission from granting the relief ordered; (4) wrongly held that Article 3 of Regulation 17 empowers the Commission to require a proprietor of intellectual property rights to grant compulsory licences; and (5) failed to provide adequate reasons for its decision as required by Article 190 of the EC Treaty. The ECJ's decision on the first and fourth of these questions—the extent to which a refusal to license may constitute an abuse under Article 86 and whether compulsory licensing is available to remedy such issues—are the most important for the future application of Article 86 to intellectual property licensing, and this comment will limit its discussion to the far-reaching consequences of the ECJ's decision on these issues. Before analysing the ECJ's decision, however, it is worth briefly considering the opinion of the Advocate General.

AG's opinion

After an unusually long wait—with the Commission having issued its opinion in 1989 and the CFI in 1991—Advocate General Gulmann (AG) finally rendered his opinion to the ECJ

---

[4] *RTE v Commission* [1991] ECR II 485, points 70 and 71 (*emphasis added*).

in *Magill* in June 1994.[5] The AG's opinion was provocative in the sense that it asked the ECJ expressly to adopt the view that 'it is possible pursuant to Article 86 to interfere with rights within the specific subject-matter'[6] where those rights are exercised in 'special circumstances'.[7] Thus, the specific subject-matter concept would not constitute a bright line, mechanical standard, but rather would involve deciding in each case whether special circumstances exist, justifying application of Article 86. Moreover, the AG asked the ECJ to confirm that it is within the power of the Commission to order compulsory licensing to redress EU competition law violations in appropriate cases.[8]

However, the AG recommended that the ECJ reverse the decisions of the CFI and the Commission and hold that a dominant company generally would not violate the competition laws by refusing to license an intellectual property right provided:

(1) the products to be produced under the licence would *compete* with the rightholder's products in the sense that they would fulfil roughly equivalent consumer needs; and

(2) the rightholder has not licensed the IP rights to any other licensee under comparable circumstances.

As presaged in an earlier comment,[9] the ECJ rejected the AG's suggestion that special circumstances would never justify requiring a dominant company to license others *to produce competing products*, and upheld the CFI decision in all respects.

The ECJ's Judgment

The aspects of the ECJ's judgment[10] with the most far-reaching consequences are those concerning its findings of a dominant position and an abuse and its decision that the Commission has the power under Regulation 17 to order compulsory licensing as a remedy for Article 86 violations.[11]

Dominant position

The court stated clearly that 'mere ownership of an intellectual property right cannot confer' a dominant position. It went on to note that the broadcasters in *Magill* had, as a result of their programming activities, a *de facto* monopoly over the basic information as to the channel, day, time and title of television programmes. The broadcasters are therefore the only sources of information for an undertaking like Magill that wishes to publish it together with commentaries or pictures. The broadcasters were therefore in a position to prevent effective competition on the market in weekly television magazines, and the CFI 'was

---

[5] Opinion of Advocate General Gulmann, *Radio Telefís Eireann and Independent Television Publications Ltd v Commission of the European Communities*, Joined Cases C—241/91 P and C—242/91 P, delivered on 1 June 1994 ('AG opinion').

[6] AG opinion, point 58.

[7] *Ibid.*, point 62.

[8] *Ibid.*, point 84.

[9] Kathleen Paisley and Thomas Vinje, 'Intellectual Property Licensing in Europe at a Crossroads: Advocate General Issues Controversial Opinion in Magill', [1994] 9 ICCLR 297.

[10] Note 1 above.

[11] Surprisingly, the broadcasters did not appeal the CFI's finding of dominance. Only IPO, which as an intervenor was not entitled to raise new issues on appeal, addressed this issue. This may in part explain the ECJ's relatively cursory discussion of this question.

therefore right in confirming the Commission's assessment that the appellants occupied a dominant position'.[12]

The court's cursory explanation of why the broadcasters held a dominant position is less than fully satisfactory—although it may in part be justified by the fact that the broadcasters actually did not appeal the CFI's finding of dominance. Although one might well agree with the court's conclusion, one can still ask why the decision does not mean that 'mere ownership' of an intellectual property right confers a dominant position. The problem for the court, it seems, is that the information over which the court says the broadcasters have a '*de facto* monopoly*' is precisely the same information the English and Irish courts have held protectable by copyright. These courts' findings of copyright protection for basic factual information, and the fact that the programme information is a natural product of establishing the broadcasters' programming schedules, are among the things that made the *Magill* case such a difficult one.

Had the court employed traditional economic criteria to determine dominance, by testing for the broadcasters' ability to act independently of competitors and consumers,[13] the court would have been likely to have found that the broadcasters indeed held a dominant position in the relevant market. Nonetheless, the question remains whether this dominance results from the legal monopoly granted by copyright. Perhaps the provocative answer, but one the court was unwilling to admit, is that in some special circumstances, such as those here, a legal monopoly granted by intellectual property *should* be deemed to confer a dominant position. There may be limits to the extent to which the court is (and should be) willing to accept unusual applications of national intellectual property laws where they run clearly counter to fundamental EC principles.

In any event, the court *did* find a dominant position on the part of the broadcasters, and rightholders will in the future have to examine their positions in the light of the court's holding. Although careful consideration of rightholders' positions will sometimes be required, it seems unlikely that either the Commission or Member State courts will employ the *Magill* decision to find dominance in many if any cases where they previously would not have done so under traditional economic criteria. It also seems unlikely that many future cases will arise where the information necessary for competitors to compete will be co-extensive with writings subject to copyright. As discussed below in the information technology context, usually it will be possible for the competitor to express the information in a manner other than that employed by the rightholder.In this respect, it may well be that *Magill* will be employed more often to justify compulsory disclosure of confidential information rather than compulsory licensing of matter subject to copyright.

Abuse

The second critical aspect of the ECJ's judgment was its finding of abuse. It is now crystal clear that a refusal to license an intellectual property right *can* constitute an abuse under Article 86. Moreover, the judgment appears to have serious consequences, more in what it leaves unsaid than in what it actually says, for the future vitality of the existence/exercise doctrine.

This doctrine, which is far from intuitively obvious, had its origin in a competition law case, *Consten and Grundig v Commission*,[14] in which a trade mark owner argued that applying

---

[12] *Magill*, Note 1 above, point 47.
[13] See *Michelin v Commission* [1983] ECR 3461, point 30.
[14] [1966] ECR 299, 345 (Cases 56/64 and 58/74).

Article 85 to a particular use of a trade mark would violate Article 222 of the EC Treaty (which provides that the 'Treaty shall in no way prejudice the rules in Member States governing the system of property ownership'). In its first statement of the existence/exercise doctrine, the ECJ responded curtly that the challenged decision of the Commission did 'not affect the grant' of the rights under national trade mark law, 'but only limit[ed] their exercise to the extent necessary to give effect to the prohibition under Article 85'.[15]

The appearance of the existence/exercise doctrine was not inevitable. Although most observers seem to take it as an article of faith that the doctrine is required by Article 222 of the Treaty, this uncritical assumption is misplaced. As noted by Marenco and Banks:

> the court could have given a wholly different answer by pointing out that Art. 222 is not a guarantee of property [as is Article 36], but a provision ensuring that the Treaty does not detract from the freedom of Member States to determine the private or public ownership of enterprise.[16]

Thus, the existence/exercise distinction appears to have arisen from a hasty response by the court to *Consten and Grundig's* argument regarding Article 222.

Indeed, the court seems to have been unaware, both in *Consten and Grundig* and later, of the legislative history of Article 222, which indicates that Article 222 was derived from and intended to have the same meaning as Article 83 of the ECSC Treaty.[17] Article 83 clearly has nothing to do with intellectual property rights, and was intended only to ensure that Member States would be free to determine whether enterprises subject to the ECSC Treaty are publicly or privately owned. Thus, neither Article 222 nor any other Article of the EC Treaty appears to provide any basis for applying the existence/exercise doctrine to competition law. Indeed, this appears to be the position taken by the Commission's Legal Service.

Although few commentators have questioned the appropriateness of grounding the existence/exercise doctrine in Article 222, perhaps because the legislative history of the Treaty is not widely available, the existence/exercise distinction has been heavily criticised as unworkable. For example, one of the authors of the IPO intervention in *Magill* said on an earlier occasion that '[t]he distinction between "existence" and "exercise" is easily criticised on the grounds that it is merely a semantic distinction which has no basis in fact'.[18] Similarly, Valentine Korah has said that '[s]ince lawyers tend to define rights in terms of the ways they can be exercised, the distinction between existence and exercise cannot be drawn analytically'.[19]

Moreover, as time has gone by, the emptiness of the existence/exercise doctrine has become ever more apparent. Although its early days were easier, as time went on the court was forced continually to refine the doctrine and to draw lines between the two concepts of a fineness that it plainly did not anticipate when it decided *Consten and Grundig*.[20] The difficulties of

---

[15] *Ibid.*

[16] Marenco and Banks, 'Intellectual Property and the Community Rules on Free Movement: Discrimination Unearthed', (1990) 15 ELR 224 at 226 Note 8 ('Marenco and Banks').

[17] S. Neri and H. Sperl, *Traité instituant la Communauté Economique Européenne—Travaux préparatoires, Déclarations interprétatives des six gouvernements, Documents parlementaires*, Cour de Justice des Communautés Européennes, 1960.

[18] Guy and Leigh, *The EEC and Intellectual Property*, Sweet &Maxwell, 1981, paragraph 1.22.

[19] Valentine Korah, *Know-How Licensing Agreements and the EEC Competition Rules Regulation 556/89*, ESC Publishing Ltd, 1989, at 24.

[20] See Marenco and Banks, Note 16 above, at 224 (the existence/exercise doctrine has 'been subjected to severe strain to a point at which the whole approach appears to be fading and to be giving way to some alternative method of reasoning').

applying the existence/exercise doctrine, especially in Article 86 cases, became particularly apparent in *AB Volvo v Erik Veng (UK) Ltd.*[21]

In *Volvo*, the court held that Volvo's refusal to grant Veng a licence to supply replacement parts, namely body panels, for Volvo automobiles was not an abuse under Article 86. However, while the court found that no evidence of abusive conduct had been presented to the national court, and therefore could not find Volvo to have abused a dominant position by refusing to license its design rights in that particular case,[22] it appears to have acknowledged the limits of the 'specific subject-matter' concept and to have acknowledged that in appropriate circumstances a refusal to license might constitute an abuse. In *Magill*, the court faced even more squarely the rough edges of the existence/exercise dichotomy.

In *Magill*, the broadcasters had effectively urged the court not even to consider whether the individual circumstances gave rise to an abuse, without first establishing that the refusal to permit reproduction of the listings fell outside the 'specific subject-matter' (or existence) of the copyright. Since the right to refuse permission to reproduce the protected listings necessarily constituted part of the 'specific subject-matter' of the copyright, the broadcasters argued their behaviour could not be found to have constituted an abuse.

The ECJ was not willing to accept that things are quite so simple. As stated by the court, 'the arguments of the appellants and IPO wrongly presuppose that where the conduct of an undertaking in a dominant position consists of the exercise of a right classified by national law as "copyright", such conduct can never be reviewed in relation to Article 86'.

Consistently with previous judgments, the court acknowledged that (1) in the absence of EC harmonisation 'the determination of the conditions and procedures for granting protection of an intellectual property right is a matter for national rules' and (2) 'the exclusive right of reproduction forms part of the author's rights, so that a refusal to grant a licence, even if it is the act of an undertaking holding a dominant position, cannot *in itself* constitute abuse of a dominant position'.[23]

For this latter proposition the court relied on *Volvo v Veng*, but it went on to rely on the famous paragraph 9 in *Volvo* for the proposition that in 'exceptional circumstances' a refusal to license can constitute an abuse. Thus, whereas there may previously have been debate about the meaning of *Volvo*, and specifically whether it stood for the proposition that a refusal to license might in some cases constitute an abuse, this controversy appears to have been laid firmly to rest.

Instead of adopting an absolute rule, as some had advocated, that a refusal to license an intellectual property right can never constitute an abuse, the court has, albeit with relatively little discussion, clearly adopted a *circumstances-based* approach to determining when such a refusal may constitute an abuse. Relying on the findings of the CFI, the ECJ pointed to three circumstances justifying a holding that the broadcasters' refusal to license their copyrights constituted an abuse under Article 86.

First the court noted that there were 'no actual or potential substitutes' for a comprehensive weekly television guide and that there was a 'specific, constant and regular' consumer demand for such a guide. According to the court, preventing the appearance of a comprehensive television guide, 'which the appellants did not offer and for which there was a potential consumer demand ... constitutes an abuse under heading (b) of the second paragraph of Article 86 of the Treaty' (which refers to 'limiting production, markets or technical development to the prejudice of consumers').[24]

---

[21] [1988] ECR 6211 (Case 238/87) ('*Volvo*'). The same issues found the same result on the same day in *Consorzio italiano della componentistica di ricambio per autoveicoli and Maxicar v Régie nationale des usines Renault* [1988] ECR 6039 (Case 53/87).

[22] *Ibid.*

Second, 'there was no justification for such refusal either in the activity of television broadcasting or in that of publishing television magazines'.[25] The court did not say why it failed to find any such justification, but this is perhaps not so surprising insofar as the broadcasters themselves took the position that their refusal to license fell within the specific subject-matter of the copyright and they therefore did not need to justify their behaviour. The broadcasters therefore provided no 'justification' for the court to address.

Third, the broadcasters 'reserved to themselves the secondary market of weekly television guides by excluding all competition in that market ... since they denied access to the basic information which is the raw material indispensable for the compilation of such a guide'.[26] Although the court referred to the broadcasters' limitation of competition on the 'secondary market', the court clearly regarded the Magill television guide as a product that would compete with the broadcasters' own guides. As noted above, the ECJ thus rejected the Advocate General's suggestion on this point: after the ECJ's judgment, a refusal to license an intellectual property right to someone who intends to create a competing product *can* constitute an abuse under Article 86.

Perhaps the most striking thing about the judgment is what it does not say: never does the judgment explicitly mention the 'existence/exercise' doctrine or the 'specific subject-matter' concept. The court does not even really address the broadcasters' argument that a refusal to license falls within the specific subject-matter of the right and is therefore automatically immune from Article 86. Thus, although it may be premature to pronounce the death of the doctrine, the existence/exercise doctrine clearly has little if any continuing relevance in determining whether any particular conduct related to an intellectual property right constitutes an abuse under Article 86. Instead, all the circumstances surrounding any particular conduct, including a refusal to license, will be examined and the determination will be made in each individual case whether an abuse exists.

Because the existence/exercise doctrine is fundamentally flawed and has no basis in the Treaty, this development is to be welcomed. Some may argue that a circumstances-based approach offers less legal certainty than a mechanical application of the existence/exercise doctrine, but the fact is that the existence/exercise doctrine has heretofore provided little legal certainty and by its nature is unable to do so. There is little reason to doubt that, as in other Article 86 areas, it will become sufficiently clear over time under what circumstances a dominant undertaking's refusal to license an intellectual property right will constitute an abuse. Such an approach, far from being radical, is completely consistent with the case law: the ECJ has never said that a refusal by a dominant undertaking to license intellectual property is *per se* immune from EC competition law, and a circumstances-based approach is in line with *Volvo* and other Article 86 jurisprudence.[27]

The only way for the court to have created more certainty would have been for it to adopt an absolute rule that a refusal to licence always falls within the specific subject-matter of a right and that such refusals are *per se* immune from EC competition laws. Such a draconian rule would have been likely to have the untoward consequence that the Commission would have been deprived of the ability to bring cases against dominant undertakings along the lines of the case brought against IBM in the 1980s. Such an absolutist approach would also have been contrary to national competition laws on both sides of the Atlantic and would have denied competition authorities any and all flexibility to find that in exceptional circumstances a refusal to license constitutes an abuse.

---

[23] *Magill*, Note 1 above, point 49 (*emphasis added*).
[24] *Ibid.*, point 54.
[25] *Ibid.*, point 55.
[26] *Ibid.*, point 56.

Although the court's bottom line is to be welcomed, it must be acknowledged that the court might have done a better job detailing the reasons why the circumstances in *Magill* justified a finding of abuse. If a circumstances-based approach is to work as it should, the court must provide guidance about the circumstances in which a refusal to license constitutes an abuse. The problem with *Magill* is that rightholders now know that a refusal to license their rights may constitute an abuse, but they can glean relatively little from the judgment about when this will be so.

On the other hand, it was appropriate for the ECJ to avoid creating a straitjacket for itself, the Commission and others. Perhaps it learned a lesson from the famous paragraph 9 in *Volvo v Veng*, where it identified three circumstances in which a refusal to license might constitute an abuse, without indicating that a refusal to license in circumstances other than those three might also constitute an abuse. This left those who had to interpret and apply *Volvo* with the task of trying to match their circumstances with those of the straitjacket imposed by paragraph 9. In *Magill*, the court was careful to preserve flexibility and not unnecessarily to limit the circumstances under which a refusal to license might constitute an abuse.

Compulsory licencing as a remedy

The third aspect of the ECJ's judgment that deserves mention is its response to ITP's argument that Article 3 of Regulation 17 does not empower the Commission to impose compulsory licensing as a remedy for violations of Article 86. Relying on *Keurkoop v Nancy Kean Gifts*, ITP submitted that 'only the Parliaments of Ireland and the United Kingdom may take away or replace the copyrights which they have conferred.'[28] The court unhesitatingly rejected ITP's argument:

> In the present case, after finding that the refusal to provide undertakings such as Magill with the basic information contained in television programme listings was an abuse of a dominant position, the Commission was entitled under Article 3, in order to ensure that its decision was effective, to require the appellants to provide that information. As the Court of First Instance rightly found, the imposition of that obligation—with the possibility of making authorisation of publication dependent on certain conditions, including payment of royalties—was the only way of bringing infringement to an end.[29]

Presumably compulsory licensing will be available as a remedy in national court actions as well.

The Consequences of Magill

So what are the consequences of the *Magill* judgment? Undoubtedly, the Commission's hand has been significantly strengthened in the intellectual property context, and we can expect to see the Commission, which was hesitant to apply the CFI's judgment in *Magill*, now rely on the ECJ judgment to expand its attacks on conduct involving intellectual property. Moreover, competitors will be emboldened by *Magill* to take harder lines in their negotiations with rightholders as well as to make complaints to the Commission (and perhaps to the national courts) about licensing practices. *Magill* is unlikely to be limited strictly to

---

[27] See, for example, *TetraPak Rausing SA v Commission*, Case T—51/89, [1991] CMLR 334 at 384.
[28] *Magill*, Note 1 above, point 88.
[29] *Ibid.*, point 91.

its facts, and it will be necessary for both rightholders and their competitors to review a whole range of conduct involving intellectual property from a new perspective.

On the other hand, *Magill* is unlikely to spark a revolution in the application of EC competition law to intellectual property licensing. The Commission is unlikely to make much use of *Magill* to attack anti-competitive abuses outside situations where the industrial context and technological constraints make third parties dependent on licensing from dominant undertakings in order to participate in legitimate competitive activities. No wholesale attacks on traditional and accepted intellectual property licensing practices are in the offing.

As the Commission noted in its arguments to the ECJ, there is, however, significant scope to apply *Magill* in areas such as information technology and telecommunications, where copyright is now applied in an industrial context for different from that of traditional literary and artistic works. In the great global debate about how to balance protection and competition in the information technology industry, which began in connection with the EC Software Directive,[30] the ECJ has struck a vital blow in favour of those desiring more scope for competition.

The potential application of *Magill* to information technology arises mainly from the 'imperative of interoperability', which was acknowledged by the European Community in the Software Directive.[31] Basically, computer products, such as operating system programs, application programs, CPUs and peripheral devices, interact through 'interfaces', which establish the rules for interaction between such components. For various historical reasons, certain companies' interfaces have become established as *de facto* interface standards with which other companies' products must comply. For example, manufacturers of mainframe computer systems have established interface standards with which companies producing peripheral devices, such as disk drives, must comply. Control over interfaces therefore may allow a dominant vendor to control the ability of competitors to create products that will interoperate with the dominant vendor's products or that will substitute for the dominant vendor's products insofar as they interoperate with other products in the same manner as do the dominant vendor's products—just as in *Magill* the broadcasters' control over information about programme times and dates allowed them to control the market for television guides.

Magill might be applied in a number of ways in the interoperability context. First, *Magill* might be applied, for example, to attempts by dominant vendors of operating systems to limit, by means of their control over the operating system interfaces, the ability of others to create application programs or peripheral equipment that is interoperable with that operating system or to create competing operating systems. Systems vendors often encourage others, at least initially, to develop application programs and peripheral equipment that will run with their operating system. However, especially after achieving dominance in a particular market, such as in operating systems for mainframe computers, a systems vendor may find it economically advantageous to occupy certain market segments itself, excluding competition from other vendors—and it may seek to do so by asserting intellectual property rights in interfaces. This was in part the subject of the Article 86 case the Commission brought against IBM in 1980.

Reverse analysis permitted under the EC Software Directive[32] usually will yield the

---

[30] Council Directive for the Legal Protection of Computer Programs, OJ 1991 L122/42 ('Software Directive').

[31] The Software Directive, as well as other Community actions in the information technology and telecommunications fields, clearly demonstrates the European Community's commitment to the interoperability of computer and telecommunications products—and to the availability of interface information to competitors necessary to create interoperable products. See, for example, Software Directive, Note 30 above, Recitals 19 to 23, 27 and Articles 1(2), 5(3), and 6.

[32] See Software Directive, Note 30 above, Articles 5(3) and 6.

interface information required to create interoperable application programs and peripherals. Sometimes, however, it may not. Moreover, while the interface *specifications* (that is, the rules or methods for interoperability) that must be implemented in application programs or peripherals presumably will not be protected by copyright,[33] on some occasions it may be that only short segments of actual code (that is, 'expression') written by the operating systems vendor will suffice to achieve interoperability. Even if this interface code is not copyrightable by virtue of the merger doctrine, lack of originality, or the like,[34] the only way to gain access to and the ability to use the necessary interface code may be through EC competition law.

The Software Directive explicitly envisions this possibility, by stating that its provisions are 'without prejudice to the application of the competition rules under Articles 85 and 86 of the Treaty if a dominant supplier refuses to make information available which is necessary for interoperability'.[35] The Community thus presaged *Magill* by acknowledging that dominant vendors may be required under EC competition law to provide necessary interface information to competitors, whether it is copyrightable or not. Under *Magill*, the Commission will be in a much stronger position to require dominant undertakings to divulge interface information to competitors on a timely basis and, to the extent that interface specifications or codes required to be used by competitors to achieve compatibility are protected by intellectual property rights such as copyright and patent, to force dominant undertakings to license those rights.

This is not to say that it would be easy to use EC competition law to obtain access to and the ability to use elements required for interoperability. First, small developers usually will not have the resources to mount litigation against a much more powerful company, so the developer would have to convince the Commission to bring an action against the allegedly dominant vendor. While *Magill* tends to confirm the ability of the Commission to bring cases like the one against IBM, the Commission will have neither the inclination nor the wherewithal to attack other than the most egregious of anti-competitive practices. The competition law is a safety net, and is not designed to solve *de minimis* problems.

Second, despite the ECJ's ease in finding dominance in *Magill*, it seems likely to remain difficult to demonstrate dominance—especially dominance on the part of a well-funded and tenacious litigant. If the ECJ is to be believed, the mere existence of the allegedly dominant company's copyright will not demonstrate dominance; rather, dominance will have to be shown by economic criteria demonstrating the ability of the allegedly dominant company to act independently of competitors and consumers.

Third, the Commission would have to demonstrate an abuse, and the bare refusal of the dominant company to license interface code will not, *in itself*, constitute an abuse. The nature of the relevant markets and the entire circumstances of the refusal would have to be examined. While anti-competitive effect is sufficient and abusive intent is not required, nonetheless evidence of the dominant company's intent to defeat competition in the derivative market of application programs and peripherals—as opposed to such permissible objectives as maintaining the integrity of its systems—would be telling. Changes made by the dominant company to its operating system interfaces which are unrelated to technical requirements but which make it more difficult for other companies to achieve or maintain compatibility would be relevant. Granting preferential access to its own application program developers, for example in terms of timing or quality of interface information, may also constitute evidence of abuse.

---

[33] *Ibid.*, at Article 1(2); T. Vinje, 'The Development of Interoperable Products Under the EC Software Directive', [1991] 8 *Computer Lawyer* 1, at 7 to 8 ('Vinje').

[34] Vinje, Note 33 above, at 7 to 8.

[35] Software Directive, Note 30 above, Recital 27.

Another example of an area in which *Magill* might apply is hardware compatibility. There is debate about the extent to which reverse analysis of a computer program is permitted under the Software Directive for purposes of creating interoperable hardware. Contrary to some suggestions,[36] such analysis may be the only way to obtain the relevant interface information if it has not been published. Those who create compatible disk drives, for example, may need to engage in such analysis. If such analysis is in the end not permitted under the Software Directive (or, more accurately, under the national laws implementing the Directive), the compatible hardware developer may have to seek the relevant information from a dominant manufacturer under Article 86.

Magill may also be relevant to maintenance and systems integration. In particular, third party maintenance companies and systems integrators may seek the information they need to operate under Article 86 if a dominant undertaking seeks to use its copyrights in computer software to prevent competition in those derivative markets. In addition, those seeking to compete with a dominant company might have recourse to Article 86 if the dominant company tries to use its software copyright to prohibit alterations to the software necessary for maintenance and systems integration.

In addition, *Magill* may have analogous application to telecommunications. The Commission has indicated that the establishment of telecommunications technical standards over which intellectual property rights are claimed may reinforce a dominant position, and that refusal to licence an intellectual property right in the telecommunications sphere may constitute an abuse under Article 86 when no feasible alternative exists.[37]

Finally, to take a contemporary example of an area where both telecommunications and computing are converging, *Magill* may have considerable relevance to regulation of intellectual property practices employed in connection with the much-vaunted 'information superhighways'. The principles established in *Magill* provide the Commission with a powerful tool to encourage the development of barrier-free interface specifications for critical Global Information Infrastructure (GII) interfaces. In the relatively rare case, for example, that a critical GII interface specification would be subject to patent protection, the Court's reasoning in *Magill* would in certain cases give the Commission the authority to compel the licensing of that specification on fair and reasonable terms.

Conclusion

Even after *Magill*, refusals to licence intellectual property rights will in the vast majority of cases remain immune from attack under Article 86. Fortunately, however, the ECJ has preserved the flexibility to apply Article 86 to special circumstances, such as those sometimes found in information technology, where refusals to license should be deemed abusive and compulsory licensing should be available as a remedy to facilitate legitimate competition. This flexibility is especially important in areas where copyright, which was developed in the context of traditional literary and artistic works that impose no inter-operability constraints on competitors, is applied to industrial contexts such as software. In the end, *Magill* should benefit consumers and the European economy by helping to preserve an appropriate balance between protection and competition.

---

[36] See, for example, B. Czarnota and R. Hart, *Legal Protection of Computer Programs in Europe*, Butterworths, 1991, at 84 to 86.

[37] See 'Green Paper on the Development of European Standardisation', Commission Document COM (90) 456 final (Brussels, 8 October 1990), 2.III.B.iv. point 92, at 46; 'Guidelines on the Application of EEC Competition Rules in the Telecommunications Sector', OJ 1991 C233/2 paragraphs 112 to 114 at 21 to 22.

Copyright & Designs

Copyright

Copyright: Over-strength, Over-regulated, Over-rated?

[1996] 5 EIPR 253

MR JUSTICE LADDIE*
Royal Courts of Justice, London

The purpose of this lecture, given in honour of the memory of a clever and perceptive copyright lawyer, is to consider the current state of copyright law in this country. Does it meet current commercial needs? My purpose this evening is to ask questions and possibly raise doubts. Copyright is one of the quartet of monopolies which form the core of what is not known as intellectual property law. The others, of course, are patents, trade marks and registered designs. I suppose that since the introduction of the unregistered design right in the 1988 legislation, there really is a quintet of such rights. Each, in its own way, places a fetter on the right of others to compete in the market-place with the originator of the right or his employer. Therefore, to some extent, each distorts trade.

If this were all, these monopolies would work against the interests of the public at large. At the simplest level it can be said that the existence of a monopoly enables the monopolist to increase his prices or restrict supply as he pleases. Of course, we know that that is much too superficial a view. It ignores all the benefits to the public at large which can flow from the increased creativity and investment which are the product of a well-balanced monopoly system. But we must always bear in mind that monopoly legislation is the end result of a balancing act: is the restraint on competition justified by the benefits which it gives to society at large? In this lecture I would like to consider this basic balancing act as it applies to copyright.

A Little History

One form or another of restraint on the printing and distribution of books has existed since the early 16th century. Until the 18th century it usually took the form of a monopoly granted by the Crown. It was used for almost 200 years as a form of censorship. The Government used it to suppress or control the distribution of books. Now most of us would say that was quite improper—Government should not control what we think or read. Statutory monopolies in a form recognised by us as copyright has existed in this country since the Statute of Anne in 1709. That legislation was introduced in response to lobbying by the book trade which said it was suffering at the hands of unlicensed copyists and that common law remedies were ineffective. In a style of lobbying which has become common since, it was said that the copyists were always men of straw and that it was impossible to track down even 1 per cent

---

* *This article is a revised text of a Memorial Lecture in honour of Stephen Stewart QC given by Mr Justice Laddie at a seminar organised by the Intellectual Property Institute, November 1995.*

of the copies. That Act created a copyright which lasted for 28 years.

The Statute of Anne sowed the seed of the legislation we now have. Over the years, paintings, engravings, sculptures and other aesthetic creations were brought within the reach of copyright protection. However, it appears that it is in the 20th century that copyright has blossomed into a major monopoly with a commercial importance to match or even exceed that of patents. In this century we have had three major Copyright Acts and their sizes are a crude illustration of the growth of copyright and its reach. The Act of 1911 was a timid little creature. It contained a mere 37 sections. Some believe it was the best Copyright Act we have ever had. The 1956 Act was a more formidable affair. It contained 57 sections. It held sway during a period in which copyright litigation burgeoned. But the 1988 Act puts all of this to shame. It contains over 300 sections, about 280 of which relate to copyright and its new offspring, design right. This increase in size cannot be attributed merely to a trend towards verbosity in modern legislation, although there certainly is some of that present in the 1988 Act. To a large extent it reflects the spread and creation of new copyright-type rights.

Three Sacred Principles

There is nothing inherently wrong in having more legislation. Although we are now a much governed people, no doubt some legislation is worthwhile. The question which I want to consider is whether it is necessary or beneficial to have more of *this* legislation.

The existence of copyright is justified on three principles. The first is the Eighth Commandment: 'Thou shalt not steal'. Why should a trader who has expended nothing be entitled to reap where he has not sown? If Professor Adams were to branch out into writing pop songs so as to augment his paltry academic income or Mr Justice Jacob were to write maudlin poetry (of the sort we all know him to be capable of) to supplement his income as a judge, why should someone else be free to rake in the commercial benefit?

This ties in closely with the second principle. As Laurence Sterne expressed it in Tristram Shandy: 'The sweat of a man's brows, and the exudations of a man's brains, are as much a man's property as the breeches upon his backside'. The concept of owning matter created by the brain is perhaps the most fundamental foundation of copyright law.

But these two principles probably would not have resulted in the awesome width of current copyright legislation were it not for the third principle, namely the principle of reward. When it is suggested that any monopoly, whether it be patent, copyright or registered design, harms the public interest in free and open competition, the answer given usually includes the argument that the rewards furnished by the existence of a temporary monopoly are for the public good since they encourage the investment of time and money in research and development, and allow authors, musicians and the like to support themselves by their creative efforts. The result is that more artistic or inventive creations are made available to the public and the author or creator is encouraged to commercialise his output rather than keep it to himself as a secret.

The most obvious application of this principle is in patent law. Few currently challenge the argument that the existence of a lengthy monopoly period has been the foundation on which modern Western drug developments have been based. No company will put millions of pounds into medical research unless it believes that the product of that research will be protected and thereby offer the possibility of recovering the investment with interest. Comparison of Western drug developments with those in the Communist world have been held up as illustrating the value of the reward principle. However, even here there is a need for balance. It is not infrequently said that the rewards available from aggressively enforced patents have induced some drug companies to patent even non-inventive drugs as a means of keeping up prices.

This same principle of reward applies to copyright as well. Why would a record company spend millions in building, equipping and manning recording studios and pressing records or CDs unless it thought it could recoup the outlay from protected sales?

The Growth of Protection

I like to think of these as the three sacred principles. The question which I will put before you this evening is 'do these principles justify the current width of copyright legislation?' Let us start by considering how these principles have played a part in the development and expansion of copyright protection. Just as lobbying in the late 17th century and early 18th century resulted in the passing of the Statute of Anne, so it has been industry which has pressed and continues to press for greater and more effective protection against commercially damaging competition from copyists. In this century the growth of the entertainment industry has been significant. Entertainment is not now restricted to books and plays as it was in the 19th century. Now creative and artistic skills underpin a network of rich industries. Whether we consider records, computer software, satellite communications or television and films, the picture is the same. Just consider the example of a single large-budget feature film like 'Jurassic Park'. It will have cost tens of millions of dollars to make. It will have been launched with the maximum publicity and merchandising support and it will be expected to generate an income of many millions of dollars. But such riches always attract the attention of those who wish to get rich without the effort of doing it themselves. Multi-million-pound industries selling dreams and pleasure to the public have inevitably attracted the attention of pirates. Similarly, few now will be ignorant of the intellectual, political and legal warfare which is being waged by the record industry against pirate CDs produced in the People's Republic of China—an anti-pirate campaign which has received strong and vocal support here. In the face of this type of unlicensed copying, there has been a persistent and well-received pressure to refine and expand the legal weaponry available both at the national and international level. In fact, there have been very few examples of significant restrictions being imposed on the scope of copyright. Nearly all changes to the law have been to make it wider and more powerful.

The major area of growth in the 1970s and 1980s was associated with the industrial application of copyright. Everyone now knows the basic story. It can be traced back to 1941 and the case of *King Features Syndicate v Kleeman*.[1] That was the case in which it was definitely decided by the House of Lords that the copyright in a two-dimensional drawing could be infringed by copying it directly or indirectly and turning it into a three-dimensional article. In that case, the drawing was a cartoon of Popeye and the infringing three-dimensional article was an unlicensed brooch depicting the cartoon character. Any copyright lawyer worth his salt knew that original drawings were the subject of copyright even if they were functional and non-aesthetic. It followed that copyright subsisted in production drawings of mundane objects such as washers, screws and mechanical parts for cars. Indirect copies of such drawings were infringements of that copyright. The logical consequence of the *King Features* case and its potential commercial impact in the field of industrial design took a long time to sink in. However, a small Act, the Designs Copyright Act, passed in 1968 apparently to broaden copyright protection for jewellery manufacturers, acted as a catalyst. Very soon

---

[1] [1941] AC 417.

our courts and the courts in Commonwealth countries with similar copyright legislation were awash with cases where copyright in production drawings was used to afford proxy protection to industrial articles made to those drawings.

That this could never have been the intention of Parliament was not in doubt, but no court appeared to have the strength or perhaps the will to resist the tide. The first case on this development of the law to reach the House of Lords was *LB Plastics v Swish*,[2] in which the copyright in production drawings for knock-down furniture drawers was used to prevent one company copying the commercial furniture produced by a competitor. The response to criticisms that copyright could not have been intended to go this far was predictable. Copyright is only breached by someone who copies and no one is forced to copy. After all, weren't the defendants pirates? Furthermore, if the minor effort and skill which goes into a Popeye carton can be used to prevent the manufacture of cheap tin-plate brooches, surely no lesser protection should be afforded to the greater effort, skill and precision which went into making production drawings for articles of commerce?

However, the onward progress of copyright appeared to be halted by the *British Leyland*[3] decision, in which the House of Lords discovered the existence of a previously unknown licence at common law which at least enables one trader to copy the spare parts for his competitor's machines. In that case, the House of Lords seemed genuinely shocked at the breadth and power of copyright protection. But, with the exception of the dissenting speech of Lord Griffiths, none of their Lordships felt able to attack the underlying principles as sanctioned in the *Popeye* and *LB Plastics* cases. The result was that industrially applied copyright continued to be used widely to prevent copying of commercial articles. The difficulty the courts experienced in moderating the law is illustrated by the *Lego*[4] case. You may recall that that was the case in which the well-known manufacturers of Lego bricks brought infringement proceedings against some Hong Kong competitors who were making copy bricks. The plaintiff had a number of difficulties in its path, including the fact that virtually all of its brick shapes had been the subject of registered design protection—which should have meant that the equivalent copyrights had expired. Notwithstanding this, both the High Court and the Court of Appeal upheld Lego's claim. It was only in the Privy Council that Lego lost, and then only by some imaginative legal argument.

Pushing Back the Tide

No doubt it was in part because of the *BL* decision and the growing chorus of complaints of those in British industry who were adversely affected by industrial copyright that the subject was dealt with by the 1988 Copyright, Designs and Patents Act. However, the way in which it was dealt with in that legislation is an illuminating illustration of how difficult it is to push back the borders of a monopoly once given.

One of the steps taken in the 1988 Act to overcome the perceived problems thrown up by the *BL* decision was to provide that spare parts were effectively removed from copyright protection. Secondly, copyright in the production drawings for non-aesthetic industrial articles could no longer be used to give proxy protection to the articles themselves. Surely then, at least in this area, copyright had been pushed back. But what about those in industry who complained that no one was forced to copy and that they had sunk time, effort and money into producing drawings and designs? Why shouldn't they be protected by the Eighth

---

[2] [1979] RPC 611.
[3] [1986] AC 577.
[4] [1987] FSR 409; [1988] RPC 343, PC.

Commandment? Was the sweat of their brows and the exudations of their brains to be left to be pirated?

The commercial reality was that from the early 1970s onwards many sectors of British industry had learned the pleasure of being able to prevent their products being copied. Under the protective wings of copyright they were able to fend off the attentions of cheap imitators. Trading without such competition is much more relaxing than having meet the competition on price and quality. Furthermore, it was possible to argue that industrial copyright had protected British-designed products from cheap foreign copies—the xenophobic battle cry which always seems to impress legislators. This argument was never the whole truth. One of the problems with copyright was that it protected not only British production drawings but also, as a result of international conventions, American, Japanese and, in fact, most foreign production drawings too. And those who were stopped included British as well as foreign companies. The truth was that the United Kingdom and other Commonwealth countries became pockets where the normal cut and thrust of competitive copying did not run.

The arguments of those who had benefited from industrial copyright were not ignored. A new right was created called design right. But the new name should not mask the underlying creature. It is, in effect, a ten-year copyright available to protect any design or part of a design which is not 'commonplace'—whatever that may mean. Furthermore, this new quasi-copyright is no longer founded on identifiable drawings. The plaintiff in a design right case can claim monopoly protection for the whole or any part of the design of an article of commerce. The new right is clearly intended to protect designs which have no aesthetic merit or input but are valuable for reasons of functional utility. One of the examples of a suitable candidate for protection given during the parliamentary debates was the design of the upturned end of an aircraft wing now to be found on some larger aircraft. The competitor will not know whether it is the whole or which part is suggested as being protected by the new rights until he receives a writ. I suggest that the creation of design right is an indication of the difficulties the legislature has of removing a monopoly in this field, once given.

The *BL* case highlighted one of the other major peculiarities of copyright law. Under the 1956 Act a copyright owner who sued successfully for infringement was not only entitled to damages, an injunction and delivery up of infringing articles, but also to conversion damages—that is to say, damages which approached the total value of the infringing goods sold by the defendant. Maybe damages on this scale made sense when only a very small percentage of infringements could be traced and where the interests of impecunious authors and composers were at stake, but virtually every legal commentator accepted that conversion damages were now an anachronism which had little justification where commercially exploited copyright was concerned.

Conversion damages were, of course, criticised by the House of Lords in the *BL* case. Such damages were available not only in industrial copyright cases but in all other cases as well, and their size was an enormous deterrent to infringers. I can say from my own experience at the Bar that in many cases defendants would rather settle than fight a doubtful claim for fear of losing and being saddled with a crippling liability to conversion damages. By the same token, the threat of conversion damages was a great benefit to copyright owners. They had a remedy which more than compensated them for any loss they may have suffered by reason of the infringement. Conversion damages were a non-compensatory penalty grafted on top of the copyright owner's right to obtain normal compensatory damages.

Well, with the passing of the 1988 Act, conversion damages disappeared. But did they go completely? I think not. To explain why, I must digress a little into another area of copyright law. In 1952 the Committee considering changes to the law of copyright recommended the introduction of a new head of financial relief in cases where, for example, the infringement had been flagrant. This recommendation was accepted and gave birth to section 17(3) of the 1956 Act. The Committee clearly thought that it was creating a new form of exemplary damages. One may ask the question why exemplary damages should be available against a flagrant infringement of copyright but not a flagrant infringement of patent or act of trespass or breach of contract. Indeed, a person who conspires to steal a consignment of computers will not be amenable to exemplary damages—but flagrantly to copy one of the operation manuals is quite another matter. The copyist of the manual is a pirate, after all, whereas the thief is only a thief.

I suggest that this, too, is an example of the over-sensitivity of the legislature to the interests of copyright owners, a sensitivity no doubt based in part on the belief that copyright is for the benefit of authors, musicians and other worthy people who, as a class, might not be expected to be able to look after themselves. It was to protect them from the predations of those who were and are referred to collectively and pejoratively as 'pirates'. Anyway, section 17(3) provided that such flagrancy damages could only be awarded when the court is 'satisfied that effective relief would not otherwise be available to the plaintiff'. If effective relief was otherwise available, then no flagrancy damages could be awarded. The idea was to ensure that the copyright owner at least got something for the wrong done to him.

If one looks at the 1988 Act one finds that statutory exemplary damages continue to be available, but the drafting of the section has changed. In particular, the requirement that the plaintiff must show that effective relief would not otherwise be available has been removed. It is now easier to qualify for these damages and it is clear that they are designed to give the copyright owner financial relief over and above what is necessary merely to compensate for damage done. Why has this change been introduced? Examination of the parliamentary debates shows that it was intended as a form of *quid pro quo* to copyright owners who were unhappy at the abolition of conversion damages.

Term

These are just two respects in which modern copyright law provides, so some might say, an over-abundance of protection to the monopoly right owner. But there are others. Let me illustrate the point. If a company were to spend millions of pounds on finding and developing a new anti-cancer drug, it could apply for a patent. Securing patent protection would be a costly and time-consuming exercise. It would be necessary to show that the drug was new and inventive. The protection given would be for a maximum of 20 years. A design may be the subject of an application for registered design protection. Once again, some time and effort would need to be expended on the registration procedure and it would be necessary to prove novelty. If registration is achieved, the design will benefit from protection for a maximum of 25 years (increased in 1988, I might mention, from 15 years—an increase of 66 per cent).

What about copyright? We all know that objective novelty is not required. We all know that registration is not required. Like the best things in life—it is free. But what about term? In the Act as passed in 1988, the term of monopoly is specified as life of the author plus 50 full years for literary, dramatic and musical works and a flat 50 years for computer-generated works, films, records and broadcasts. However, as a result of the Term Directive, the copyright in the first category of works, that is to say, literary works and so on, is now life of the author plus 70 full years. This additional 20 years has been imposed throughout the Member States of the European Union to bring us into line with the domestic law of

Germany. As is now familiar in copyright law, the process was one of levelling up the protection rather than levelling down. The result of this new term is that if, for example, a young computer programmer writes a new piece of computer software, he generates a monopoly which will normally last for over 100 years. Depending on his longevity, it may last more than 150 years. Similarly, if a politician writes letters or speeches which are of general historic interest, they also may be protected for a century or more. Indeed, if a modern-day architect were to design a new Albert Memorial, he would have the satisfaction of knowing that his copyright is likely to be sprightly and in the prime of life long after the concrete and steel of his architectural creation have started to crumble.

The question to be asked is: what justification is there for a period of monopoly of such proportions? It surely cannot be based on the principle of encouraging artistic creativity by increasing the size of the carrot. No one is going to be more inclined to write computer programs or speeches, compose music or design buildings because 50, 60 or 70 years after his death a distant relative whom he has never met might still be getting royalties. It is noticeable that this expansion of term is not something which has only occurred in the last decade. On the contrary, it has been a trend which has been in evidence for the whole of this century. Before the 1911 Act, the term of copyright in artistic works extended to seven years after the author's death. In 1911 this was extended to 50 years after death. The growth of term is in fact greater than these figures suggest. Life expectancy in 1910 was far shorter than it is now. The result is that a monopoly which was expected to last about four decades in 1910 should now be expected to last on average more than three times as long.

Indeed, I believe that the same criticism of excessive duration can be levelled at the 50-year flat term which applies to films, recordings and broadcasts. It may be possible to pick out a few creations of exceptional artistic or commercial merit where one could argue for lengthy protection—for example, the recordings of Rostropovich or the Beatles—but is it right that all copyright should be protected on the basis of what might be thought justified for the exceptional few? Furthermore, it is possible to argue that these long copyright terms are not necessary to protect the commercial exploitation of the works themselves. Most works protected by copyright are exploited very rapidly, if at all. This is so whether we are considering films and records or literary works such as computer software. Even books such as those that win the Booker prize are only commercially successful for a short time and then, to all intents and purposes, pass away. Yet the dead hand of copyright lingers on, in most cases serving no useful purpose.

Another of the problems with copyright law is that, unlike inventions protected by patent or designs protected by registration, the requirements for qualification are so low as to be virtually non-existent. Virtually any written material, any sketch and any film footage or sound recording is automatically protected. This has practical consequences. In *Elanco v Mandops*,[5] the Court of Appeal accepted, as it had to, that a label of instructions placed on the side of a barrel of herbicide was a copyright literary work. No doubt depending on the youth of the literary genius who wrote it, the label will be protected for more than a century and perhaps for as long as a century and a half—certainly well beyond the date when for safety or commercial reasons the product has been removed from the market. So one of the troubles with copyright, then, is that it springs up to protect nearly every creation of the human mind, be it ever so trivial. As another member of the judiciary put it, the fact that our system of communication, teaching and entertainment does not grind to a standstill is in large part due to the fact that in most cases infringement of copyright has, historically, been ignored.

---

[5] [1979] FSR 46.

Let me offer you an illustration of the lack of balance in our law. You can libel a dead author to your heart's content, but if you want to honour him by publishing a commemorative edition of his letters, 50, 60 or 69 years after his death, you will infringe copyright, you may have to pay exemplary damages and, as I shall discuss in a moment, you may be prosecuted.

The Bandwagon

Is it surprising that with ever greater monopolies being created and the awareness of them spreading, more and more want to get into the copyright exploitation market? Perhaps the strangest, but most symptomatic, of these is the Government itself. First, many of you will know that the effect of section 301 of the 1988 Act is to grant a perpetual right to royalties in favour of the Great Ormond Street Hospital for Children in respect of the exploitation of J.M. Barrie's play, 'Peter Pan'. It was no doubt thought a good thing that a source of income other than taxation should be found to support that worthy institution, but I suggest that the device of effectively granting permanent copyright in this case illustrates the imbalance when it comes to legislating in this area. Who can lobby against the widening of protection? Those who do are treated as pariahs and parasites Why should they be allowed to exploit J.M. Barrie's creation without paying for it—even if stopping them means extending the copyright not for decades but for centuries?

Perhaps of greater significance is the Government's realisation of the value of the copyright it has bestowed on itself in a vast array of government publications, including Acts of Parliament. This has resulted in the Government seeking a royalty, for example, from those who wish to reproduce legislation—in legal textbooks or in electronic databases. But it does not end there. In *The Times* of 7 November 1995 there was a report, which I believe is accurate, that the Inland Revenue granted an exclusive licence under Crown copyright to one publisher to reproduce its tax manuals. Unfortunately, HMSO appears to have granted a non-exclusive licence to the same material to another publisher. The conflict of licences has been resolved, at least for the moment, by the HMSO terminating the licence to the second publisher and seeking an injunction to restrain it from making further use of the material. Of course, it would not be proper for me to say whether the HMSO is right as a matter of law in its attempts to terminate use of this material. But I do think it is legitimate to point out that the frenzy to get on the copyright bandwagon now extends to the legislature seeking to make money out of the exploitation of the legislation which it passes and which should be available for all of us to see and consult. The Government can now control the dissemination of its laws—does this represent a seed of the problems of censorship which we thought had been abolished 200 years ago?

I should make it clear that it is not just the Government which has been attracted by the ever-widening scope of copyright. Copyright has reached into many other areas. Perhaps the most depressing is the area of pure research. Until quite recently it was seen to be normal and desirable that scientists should share knowledge with their colleagues at symposia at the earliest possible date. New experimental results were disclosed to the community of scientific peers in this way. The plaudits of colleagues were reward enough. This system began to crumble with the realisation of the value of patents. Many senior researchers now no longer publish the results of their work in the scientific press or at meetings with their colleagues at the first opportunity. Now they, and the universities or hospitals they work for, make sure they have applied for patents first.

Copyright has now been harnessed to this desire to acquire proprietary rights in the result of research. As many of you may know, many able scientists are involved in research into gene structure. Some are trying to work out the genetic code of human beings—the fundamental blueprint which determines all of our characteristics. It is, I think, sad that some of them including some of great eminence, are talking in terms of 'copyrighting' that code or parts of it once it has been worked out. The object is to ensure that exploitation of that knowledge can be turned into a money-making exercise. But it is hard to argue that scientists should stand aloof when so many others are using the armoury of intellectual property rights, including copyright, to make money.

Infringement a Crime

So far as I have discussed the width of copyright and two forms of financial relief available in infringement proceedings. But it is wrong to consider only the relief which is available in civil courts. Those of you who have hired video films may have noticed that, when the tape is played, a message comes up on the television screen which says 'VIDEO PIRACY IS A CRIME'. Well it is. Criminal provisions have been found in Copyright Acts for some years but now, apparently for the first time, they are being used in earnest. A recently reported case is illuminating. Criminal proceedings were brought against a book publisher and its directors. I think there were nine directors in all. One of them was the infirm 87-year-old widow of the original founder of the publisher. The publisher had produced a book which contained reproductions of one or more copyright paintings. Difficult questions of fair dealing were raised as a defence. It might be thought that to bring such proceedings with complicated issues of copyright law before a magistrates' court did not make sense. However, I find it difficult to fault the logic of those acting for the private prosecutor. The Copyright Act stipulates that criminal procedures may be invoked against an alleged infringer and, in the case of an infringing company, its directors. Why not use these weapons?

If the proceedings had been brought in civil courts, it is almost certain that the directors would have been struck out of the proceedings since there was no evidence, at least in relation to most of them, that they had any personal involvement in the production of the offensive book. But the criminal provisions relating to directors in the Act are, to say the least, relaxed. And if it is permissible to bring criminal proceedings, why not do so? The threat of a criminal conviction hanging over an alleged infringer's head and the heads of its directors is much more likely to make them sue for peace than the mere risk of losing in civil proceedings. Like the prospect of being hanged, it does concentrate the mind. The fact that these statutory provisions are being used to enforce purely private commercial rights appears to be irrelevant. Furthermore, there is a great incentive to proceed in this way. The costs of the prosecuting copyright owner are usually paid out of central funds, even if the prosecution fails. This little bit of budgetary largesse has escaped critical scrutiny so far.

We have therefore reached the stage where taxpayers' money is being used to enforce private rights which many might think are more than adequately protected by civil remedies. I should also mention that it appears that in most cases it is not the poor and weak who are using these criminal provisions but the rich and well organised.

Fair Use

The reluctance to curtail the copyright monopoly also finds expression in the statutory defences provided by the 1988 Act. In the United States of America, there is, I understand, a statutory defence of fair use. Its limits are not precisely drawn, but it has given the courts the flexibility to prevent copyright from being abused. The absence of precision is, of course, a disadvantage. To some extent, the scope of the defence will be dependent on the personal perspective of the judge. However, I would suggest that a comparison between that system and our own is not flattering to ours. Let us consider this a bit further. The United States Copyright Act of 1976 contains, at section 107, a general statutory defence of fair use. It says that fair use of a copyright work for purposes *such as* criticism, comment, news reporting, teaching, scholarship or research is not infringement. It goes on to indicate some of the factors which the court should take into account in deciding whether use is fair. The factors mentioned are:

(1) the purpose and character of the use, including whether such use is of a commercial nature or is for non-profit educational purposes;
(2) the nature of the copyright work;
(3) the amount and substantiality of the portion used in relation to the copyright work as a whole;
(4) the effect of the use upon the potential market for or value of the copyrighted work.

As the US Supreme Court has said on more than one occasion, this fair use defence 'permits courts to avoid rigid application of the copyright statute when, on occasion, it would stifle the very creativity which that law is designed to foster'.

Compare that with our legislation. Rigidity is the rule. It is as if every tiny exception to the grasp of the copyright monopoly has had to be fought hard for, prized out of the unwilling hand of the legislature and, once conceded, defined precisely and confined within high and immutable walls. This approach also assumes that Parliament can foresee, and therefore legislate for, all possible circumstances in which allowing copyright to be enforced would be unjustified. Based on this approach, we now have an Act in which there are 49 sections of numbingly detailed exceptions to copyright infringement. Let me remind you of one or two examples.

Section 30 provides that fair dealing with a work for the purpose of criticism or review does not infringe copyright, but only provided it is accompanied by a sufficient acknowledgement. Sufficient acknowledgement means that the work has to be identified by title and author. In the absence of the whole acknowledgement, infringement follows even if the review does no harm and all the readers would be aware of both the identity of the work and its author. The requirement for sufficient acknowledgement applies if the criticism or review is in a newspaper, but not if it is in a film, broadcast or cable programme. But if it was not thought necessary for them, why make it a requirement for any other form of criticism or review? Section 32 provides that copyright in a literary, dramatic, musical or artistic work is not infringed by its being copied in the course of instruction or of preparation for instruction and is not by means of a reprographic process. In preparing this lecture, I had to be careful not to photocopy any material. Section 61 contains incredibly detailed provisions permitting the recording of folksongs, but only if it is for certain archival purposes. Apparently, it is permissible to archive folksongs but not any other songs. I am also afraid that archival collection of Mr Justice Jacob's poetry will still be an infringement. Section 63 provides that it is not an infringement of copyright in an artistic work to copy it or to issue copies to the public for the purpose of advertising the sale of the work. No doubt that is of assistance to Sothebys, Christies and other auction houses, but notice that the defence is not available if the work is merely to be hired. I invite the members of this audience to read for themselves the convoluted and essentially self-defeating provisions of section 50B which are concerned with decompilation of copyright computer programs.

These detailed and pedantic exceptions to copyright protection, and their predecessors in the 1956 Act, are not only difficult to understand in some cases, but they also reinforce the perception that virtually all reproductions of copyright works, no matter how innocuous, are infringements. Is it surprising then, that when, for the purposes of advertising the film 'Carry on Cleo', a poster was created which was a harmless but humorous spoof of a similar poster for the Elizabeth Taylor/Richard Burton film 'Cleopatra', it was held to infringe copyright.

It would be possible to go on criticising the width of our copyright laws, but perhaps I have said enough. It might be more useful to inquire why our law has developed as it has. I have mentioned already the value and size of the industries which now believe they need extensive copyright protection to safeguard their income stream. They, quite properly, lobby for their interests. But who lobbies against them? There is no trade union of copyright infringers. Support for any limitation on copyright is easily portrayed as support for pirates— the usual pejorative global expression for infringers. It is depicted as support for the parasites of industry. Is it surprising, then, that the scope of protection gets ever wider? I suggest that the drafting of the legislation bears all the hallmarks of a complacent certainty that wider copyright protection is morally and economically justified. But is it?

A Balanced Future

The whole of human development is derivative. We stand on the shoulders of the scientists, artists and craftsmen who preceded us. We borrow and develop what they have done; not necessarily as parasites, but simply as the next generation. It is at the heart of what we know as progress. When we are asked to remember the Eighth Commandment, 'thou shalt not steal', bear in mind that borrowing and developing have always been acceptable.

I invite you to stand back and imagine that we were not building our copyright law on a foundation of accumulated rights, commercial interests and monetary expectations. Imagine that we have just a blank sheet of paper and are being invited to create a copyright law now from scratch for the new millennium and that the purpose is to give some reasonable measure of protection to those who write books or computer programs or make films for television. Would we really choose to construct a monopoly which might last a century and a half? Would we really make it a crime to copy even quite small parts of the copyright work throughout those many decades? Would we really choose to pick out copyright as the one monopoly where statutory exemplary damages are available? I think not.

But, if we are going to start with a fresh piece of paper, let us do a proper job and really start from first principles. I am sure that all of you here are familiar with the wide variety of materials which are now protected by copyright law. I have already mentioned *Elanco v Mandops*, in which the list of instructions on the side of a tin of herbicide was protected as a literary work. But we also know that it has been suggested, in *British Northrop v Texteam Blackburn*,[6] that a well-drawn straight line or circle would be likely to be protected as artistic works. Indeed, we all know that during the great industrial copyright days of the 1970s and 1980s it was generally accepted that a drawing of, say, a washer—merely two concentric circles on a page—would be protected as an artistic work. In *British Leyland*, some of the drawings sued on, and accepted by a hostile House of Lords as being copyright works, consisted of simple depictions of a short straight length of tube. The law reports of the last 90 years are full of trite and insubstantial works being protected by copyright. How did we get to this position?

Was it always so? I doubt it. Most of us know that although most works have to be 'original', it is now well-accepted law that 'original' means that the work has originated with

---

[6] [1973] FSR 241.

and is the product of at least a small amount of effort of the author. This can be traced back to *Walter v Lane*[7] in 1900, in which the House of Lords held that copyright could exist in the notes of a speech of Lord Roseberry taken down by a shorthand writer in the audience. The original effort involved in transcribing was said to be enough to justify copyright protection. I think it is likely that the current view of originality was not always the law. In *Dicks v Yates*[8] in 1881, the Court of Appeal had to consider whether the words 'Splendid Misery', the title of a book, were covered by copyright. It is quite clear that the then Master of the Rolls, Lord Jessel, thought that a literary work could only be 'original' if it was original in a patent novelty sense when compared with what was already available to the public. The fact that the same words had been used by another author some 80 years previously therefore destroyed originality. Similarly, Lush LJ said:

> I take it to be established law that to be the subject of copyright the matter must be original, it must be a composition of the author, something which has grown up in his mind, the product of something which if it were applied to the patent rights would be called invention.

Whether *Walter v Lane* ever justified the wide scope given to originality now is beside the point. It is the law. But if we were to start again, to mould it closer to the heart's desire, would we really choose to give the full armoury of copyright protection to the trite, the commonplace and the valueless? Whatever the law was in the last century, the costs of reproduction probably went a long way to ensuring that litigation was normally restricted to copyright works of substance—*Dicks v Yates* being one of a handful of exceptions. But we now live in a world where everything is recorded in computers or made available on the Internet. Everything is recorded and the public has begun to learn of the existence of the free and spontaneous monopoly it gets under copyright.

The usual response to this sort of criticism of the breadth of copyright protection is to say that if a work is trite, its copyright is of less value because third parties can get to the same end result by working it out for themselves. But this is just another version of the pernicious refrain: 'You are not forced to copy and what is worth copying is worth protecting'. I suggest that this approach is facile and unconvincing. The fact that a trite subject-matter can be arrived at independently is no reason for giving it a monopoly. We should not be handing out monopolies like confetti while muttering 'this won't hurt'. I suggest we should approach monopolies from the other direction. We should say, as our predecessors did, that the basic rule is that no monopoly should exist unless it is shown to be objectively justified.

Maybe the time has come to look forward, rather than backwards. Perhaps we should consider whether the current law on originality makes sense or serves a useful purpose. To reduce it to its simplest, you can have too much of a good thing and I suggest we have got too much copyright. In the case of copyright, the Eighth Commandment has got out of control. If you go to a restaurant and taste the creation of one of our new breed of flamboyant chefs, say beef with a sauce of mango and pickled parsnips, would you consider it immoral to go home and try to make the same thing? If a friend tells you a good joke, is it immoral to write it down in a letter to a relative? If you read in a newspaper the details of evidence given in a high-profile trial, do you consider it theft to take the essential elements and write a poem about it? Do you know of Mr Robert Fosbery? He was a man who, after much trial, a lot of effort and, no doubt, considerable pain, worked out that it was possible to jump over

---

[7] [1900] AC 539.
[8] (1881) 18 Ch.D. 76.

a higher high jump if he jumped over backwards—the Fosbery Flop. He broke all sorts of records with his new technique. And then along came copyists and did it better. Were they immoral? These examples are meant to be light hearted—but I give them to illustrate the point that not all copying is bad and that, sometimes, copying and developing are to the general good. I should make it clear that I believe copyright has an important role to play in society. I do not advocate an unprincipled free-for-all. But I suggest that the scales are at the moment weighted far too much in favour of would-be copyright owners.

At the beginning of this lecture I referred to the *Popeye* case. It is reported in the 1941 Volume of Appeal Cases. At the beginning of that volume there is another case dealing with another area of law. It contains the well-known statement of Lord Atkin: 'When these ghosts of the past stand in the path of justice clanking their medieval chains, the proper course is for the judge to pass through them undeterred.'[9] In relation to a statutory monopoly like copyright, it is not open to a judge to pass through undeterred. He must apply the law. But it is possible to see that in the case of copyright not only do the medieval chains remain, but they have been reinforced with late 20th century steel. Perhaps the time has come when we should look again at the underlying assumptions on which this monopoly is based.

---

[9] [1941] AC 1 at 29.

The Canker of Reciprocity

[1988] 4 EIPR 99

W.R. CORNISH
London School of Economics

Intellectual property has grown from twin roots. One—idealistic in its thrust—recognises the inherent value of individual creativity. The other—bred from utilitarian stock—looks to the economic and social benefits which are designed to flow from market protection. The tendency of the former is towards universality: its finest flowering was perhaps the French *droit d'auteur*, which offered protection to the authors of the world without distinction of nationality, even in advance of bilateral or multi-national relations with other countries. The tendency of the latter is towards a narrow reciprocity: it sees no reason to give rights to foreigners whose own law does not provide equivalent benefits in return.

Even if one sticks closely to the calculation of national advantage, however, it does not follow that a rule of reciprocity gives a country its optimal return. On the contrary, the main international conventions on industrial property and copyright have adopted the principle of national treatment as their basic tenet, supported to a greater or lesser extent by minimum requisites for the national laws of member states. The measure of obligation between participant countries is not that each must guarantee to the nationals of another country only such degree of protection as that country itself confers within its own borders, but something that is one step more generous and trusting of others.

The United States, however, has recently suffered a notorious relapse into reciprocalism. Its semi-conductor chip enactment imposed on other countries a procrustean demand for precise equivalence if their nationals were to acquire rights under the US law. The contagion soon spread to the EEC, with its directive to Member States to fall in with the US terms for reciprocal rights.

Now the British government appear flushed with the same rabid excitement. In the 'new' rights that will form part of the Copyright Designs and Patents Act 1988, reciprocity has a prominent place. In the Bill, as first presented, the performer's right was to be given only on a reciprocal basis, without recognition of the country's obligation to accord national treatment in respect of countries party to the Rome Convention of 1961. Fortunately this has been corrected by amendment. But the '(unregistered) Design Right' is to be accorded only on a reciprocal basis. Indeed, now that this right is to be confined (more or less) to functional designs for new products but excluding many spare parts, the main reason for creating a wholly new right rather than just limiting the period of protection for copyright in industrial design seems to be in order to keep non-reciprocating foreigners out.

Aflame with zeal, the Government thinks nothing of the suggestion that, in matters of industrial design, it might already be under obligation, by virtue of the Paris Industrial Property Convention, to accord national treatment. Yet that Convention creates a union for the protection of industrial property, an expression to 'be understood in the broadest sense' (see Article 1(3), which indicates that it is to cover not only industry and commerce proper, but likewise agricultural and extractive industries). And among the objects of this industrial property Article 1(2) lists industrial designs.

Convention or no, there is a very real question whether the (unregistered) Design Right ought to be offered to foreigners only on the basis of reciprocity. There is of course the immediate attraction that other industrial countries which produce functional designs on a large scale may be induced to offer protection to the British on our basis or something equivalent. Has the government, one wonders, the Yankee insolence to insist on precise— no more and no less—equivalence: the period must be ten years, there must be compulsory licences in the last five, and anti-monopolistic licences in the first five. If not, it has yet to face some interesting questions about what is to be good enough: Will it suffice to follow Australia's example in protecting functional designs through a mixture of registered design and petty patent? What about unfair competition laws which include rights against slavish imitation? (Fortunately, in Christine Fellner we can boast one informed comparatist capable of resolving these dilemmas). What will we do to our small but perfectly formed 'new' right if some other country says that it is not good enough for them to offer reciprocity? The game is one that each country may play according to its own lights, and that is what led Stephen Ladas long ago to mark it down as dangerously disruptive of good international relations.

There is an even more basic objection. The industrial nations currently seek to draw developing countries into the international nets of intellectual property. To some real extent the latter are being persuaded that, in the longer term interests of their economies, they should introduce or revise the various laws in the field so as to make rights available not only to their nationals but to nationals of other Convention countries. In the case of patents this is not usually a severe task, for a country which is prepared to have patents at all is likely to be interested in their potential for attracting foreign technology. But in the case of other rights—particularly copyright and design—the resistance is likely to be much greater. The country's own industries in need of such protection may appear small indeed beside the large interests of foreigners who are eager for protection. A doubting country is all too likely to think any relations with outsiders are best organised through a series of bilateral arrangements, in which the terms may have to be hammered out industry by industry. There are signs enough that this instinct is currently gaining ground in the Pacific basin.

How can the leading beneficiaries of intellectual property at once proclaim the virtue of national treatment enshrined in the Convention for which they seek new members, and at the same time demand reciprocal provision whenever they begin to extend intellectual property rights to some new (or in the case of 'unregistered' designs, some quasi-novel) subject-matter? Leaving aside high ideals, does not self-interest, when properly estimated, dictate that reciprocity should be used as sparingly as possible, and that the apparently more generous offer of national treatment has much to commend it?

Freedom of expression in copyright law*

[1984] 1 EIPR 3

HERMAN COHEN JEHORAM

Professor of Law, University of Amsterdam

Copyright guarantees the author a share in the marketing of his works, and as such is a means of securing the independence of authors from patronage, and possibly influence, by individuals or the state. In this sense, copyright is one of the oldest means of securing freedom of expression and information.

On the other hand, it is quite obvious that copyright, which is essentially a right to forbid reproduction and publication of works without the consent of the author, constitutes an obstacle to the free flow of information. The information has at least to be paid for and sometimes, for instance when the *droit moral* is involved or when the marketing system of the work would otherwise be threatened, even payment is not enough for the author to waive his right to forbid. This kind of obstacle, however, is acceptable to all civilised nations, which acknowledge that a price should be paid to the creators of works.

One of the best-known documents in the field of human rights, the Universal Declaration of Human Rights of the United Nations, therefore does not only mention the freedom of expression and information (Article 19) but also the eventually conflicting 'right to the protection of the moral and material interests resulting from any scientific, literary or artistic production of which he is the author' (Article 27 section 2). This last right has also been included in the juridically more binding International Covenant on Economic, Social and Cultural Rights of the United Nations of 1966 (Article 15 section 1(c)), not to mention the two more specific worldwide conventions: the Berne Convention and the Universal Copyright Convention.

It should also be recognised that the numerous restrictions in copyright mentioned in the Berne Convention and in national copyright legislation, actually serve to mitigate the impact copyright could have on the freedom of expression and information. Nevertheless, we all know some examples of the perverted use of copyright by state agencies for no other purpose than to curb the author's right to freedom of expression.

Notorious are the censorship clauses in the bilateral treaties the USSR has concluded with some socialist countries,[1] clauses which have not lost any significance by the accession in

---

* This is extracted from an article by Professor Cohen Jehoram entitled 'The Freedom of Expression in Copyright and Media Law' in 'Festschrift für Eugen Ulmer', published in GRUR Int. 1983, 385 to 389.

[1] Hungary, No. 17, 1967, [1968] Dda 64; Bulgaria, 8 October 1971, [1972] Dda 163; DDR, 21 November 1973, [1974] Dda 124. It always concerns Article 2 section 2, of the treaty. To quote the treaty with the DDR:

Les oeuvres non publiées ne peuvent être publiées simultanément dans les deux pays ou rendues accessibles au public pour la première fois sur le territoire de l'autre Partie Contráctante et les oeuvres d'auteurs de l'une des Parties Contractantes ne peuvent être mises en circulation dans des pays tiers par l'intermédiaire des organes de l'autre Partie Contractante qu'après accord, dans chaque cas, entre les organes compétents des deux Parties Contractantes.

May 1973 of the USSR to the multilateral Universal Copyright Convention. The ensuing amendment of the Russian copyright legislation brought the novelty that all international copyright licensing and assignments could only take place via the intermediary of a state agency, in the framework of the state monopoly of foreign trade. Before May 1973, Western publishers had been free to publish Russian works without any (governmental) authorisation, but since then this road is blocked, by the Universal Copyright Convention, and its effect on the USSR legislation.

The worry over this result induced the Dutch Government at the time to put forward a certain proposal for a clause in the Final Act of the Conference on Security and Co-operation in Europe, the Helsinki Declaration of 1 August 1975, which now—in the final form—reads under the heading 'Co-operation and exchanges in the field of Culture':

> The participating States ... Express their intention now to proceed to the implementation of the following: ... To promote fuller mutual access by all to the achievements—works, experiences and performing arts—in the various fields of culture of their countries, and to that end to make the best possible efforts, in accordance with their competence, more particularly—to promote wider dissemination of books and artistic works, in particular by such means as: facilitating, while taking full account of the international copyright conventions to which they are party, international contacts and communications between authors and publishing houses as well as other cultural institutions, with a view to a more complete mutual access to cultural achievements.[2]

It is to be feared that this declaration is as powerless as other texts, binding or not, in the face of such overriding state interests as are involved here, but then lawyers' hopes can only be based on texts.

A most virtuoso abuse of copyright to curb the freedom of expression has been made by the South African Government.

Article 17 of the Berne Convention, since the beginning in 1886 has read:

> The provisions of this Convention cannot in any way affect the right of the Government of each Country of the Union to permit, to control, or to prohibit, by legislation or regulation, the circulation, presentation, or exhibition of any work or production in regard to which the competent authority may find it necessary to exercise that right.

It is generally agreed, in literature[3] as well as by all delegations during the Stockholm Diplomatic Conference[4] in 1967—except the South African delegation—that this—in itself rather superfluous—provision dealt mainly with censorship and that the power to permit or prohibit the dissemination of works could be exercised to that end.

South Africa wanted to interpret Article 17 in a completely different way. This is illustrated by the South African Copyright Act of 1965 and a decision of the South African Copyright

---

[2] See my 'Vrijheid van meningsuiting—auteursrecht—Europese Veiligheidsconferentie', [1975] NJB 1168 and 1169.

[3] Röthlisberger, *Die Berner Übereinkunft*, 1906, at 267; Bappert-Wagner, *Internationales Urheberrecht*, 1956, at 156; Ladas, *The International Protection of Literary and Artistic Property*, 1938, 1, at 611; Baum, GRUR 1950, 476; Nordemann/Vinck/Hertin, *Internationales Urheberrecht*, 1977, at 121; and WIPO *Guide to the Berne Convention*, 1978, at 99.

[4] Records of the Intellectual Property Conference of Stockholm (1967), Geneva 1971, Vol. II, at 806, 911 and 1174/5. See also Rapport sur les travaux de la Commission principale No. 1, n. 262 from Rapports sur les travaux des cinq Commissions principales de la Conférence de Stockholm de la Propriété Intellectuelle 1967, Geneva, 1967, at 66/7.

Tribunal in the years 1968/69.[5] A number of American copyright owners of popular musicals objected to the South African racial policy and in particular to the performing of their works for a racially segregated public. Therefore, they refused to licence their work to South Africa. The musicals involved were *West Side Story, Fiddler on the Roof* and *Man of la Mancha*. The Johannesburg Operatic and Dramatic Society applied in court for a compulsory licence on the basis of the clause in the South African Copyright Act (section 28(3)(a)) 1965 about compulsory licences.

The parliamentary history of this clause indeed reveals that it was meant to put aside refusals of authors to license on 'ideological or unjustified grounds'. One actually thought of refusals because of racial policy. Already at that time reference was made to the term 'to permit' in Article 17 of the Berne Convention. This was not regarded in its censorship context of 'to permit or prohibit'. The word 'permit' was completely taken out of this context and, in isolation, interpreted as a 'permission' by Government overruling the prohibition of the author. This interpretation upsets the whole purpose and structure of the Berne Convention, which, in fact, guarantees the right of the author to forbid and which only allows compulsory licences in very special and narrowly defined cases. No wonder that the English proposal in Stockholm in 1967 to strike the words 'to permit' from Article 17 was vetoed by South Africa. The South African judge, in the case of the musicals, indeed issued the compulsory licences on the basis of section 28(3)(a) of the South African Copyright Act.

On this occasion we witness a governmental measure not in order to suppress an undesirable work but on the contrary to enforce the performance of a highly popular work. The author's political protest, expressed by his refusal to license, was suppressed: a very sophisticated example of infringement of the right to freedom of expression. One is reminded here of the American court decision in *Estate of Hemingway v Random House Inc.* (1968)[6] that freedom of expression not only prohibits 'improper restraints on the *voluntary* public expression of ideas' but that it also entails 'a concomitant freedom not to speak publicly, one which serves the same ultimate end as freedom of speech in its affirmative aspect'. Here a certain *droit moral* aspect of copyright and the freedom of expression fuse.[7]

A few years ago a Danish writer and film-maker, Jens Jørgen Thorsen, wrote a film script entitled 'The many faces of Jesus Christ' and he obtained the promise of financial support for the production from the Danish Film Institute. The script was published and it turned out that Jesus was described in the script as having a number of love-affairs and as taking part in group-sex. In the ensuing alarm and under strong political pressure the Danish Minister of Culture made it known to the Film Institute that the film would constitute an infringement of the Copyright Act and would therefore be illegal, which induced the Film Institute to withdraw its financial support of the film,[8] which resulted in the end of the whole project.

It seems worthwhile to quote that remarkable clause of the Danish Copyright Act which the Minister thought was infringed in this case (section 53): 'Even if copyright has expired, a literary or artistic work may not be altered nor made available to the public contrary to ... section 3 (*droit moral*), if cultural interests are thereby violated.' The Article continues

---

[5] [1972] GRUR Int. at 256, note Dieter Stauder.

[6] 23 NY 2d 341, 348, 244 NE 2d 250, 256 NYS: 2d 771, 778 (1968). Compare Paul Goldstein, 'Copyright and the first amendment', [1970] Colum. LRev., 1002/3.

[7] For a most shocking case of governmental abuse of a Soviet author's *droit moral* in France (Koeznetsov), see my 'Auteursrecht contra vrijheid van meningsuiting?' [1974] NJB 1391 to 1405, which also gives other examples from several countries.

[8] In answer to my inquiry into the matter (I only knew the case from newspapers), Mr Weincke of the Danish Ministry of Cultural Affairs described the case to me in detail in a letter of 21 December 1977.

empowering the Ministry of Education to make statements as to whether this law has been infringed.

In short, Mr Jens Jørgen Thorsen had, with his unusual version of the story of Jesus, infringed the eternal Danish *droit moral* of the Evangelists, the authors of the story.

A few years ago Unesco (independently of WIPO) started a working group on the subject of 'works in the public domain'. The tone is set by paragraph 6 of the final report of a first meeting:[9]

> A large majority of the participants, nevertheless, congratulated Unesco for taking up this difficult question and expressed encouragement for its efforts to guarantee the authenticity of intellectual works in the face of the dangers of distortion, disfiguration and deformation of said works which result from popularisation and commercial exploitation which has become more and more marked, especially in the case of works that have fallen into the public domain.

Examples are given from case law in Belgium (*The Merry Widow*) and France (*Liaisons Dangereuses*). Other countries are mentioned, in particular Denmark. Portugal also could now be mentioned in this context.[10]

In a recent debate within the Executive Committee of ALAI, three members of which had taken part in the Unesco Working Group, further 'scandalous' examples were given: Vermeer's picture *The Milkmaid* being used in a commercial for dairy products and the Venus de Milo clad in Levis.

According to paragraph 23 of the Unesco report, only

> One participant pronouncing himself in favour of a broad interpretation of the notion of free use of works in the public domain, put himself clearly on record against all regulations of adaptation, arrangements, and all other changes of a work in the public domain which could be used as a pretext for intellectual control or permit the State to require an authorisation in each case which it would refuse if the proposed use of a work or a certain type of creation did not please it for any reason whatever.

Evidently, the rest of the working group, enamoured of copyright techniques and eternal respect for works of art, did not let themselves be convinced by this intervention.

Copyright lawyers should show more sensitivity to one of the very functions of copyright: to secure the freedom of expression and information.

---

[9] Unesco Document PRS/CPY/DPR/3, Paris, 7 December 1979. See also the report of the meeting of 17 to 21 January 1983, Unesco Document PRS/CPY/DP/CEG/1/11.

[10] Portuguese Decree-Law No. 150/82 of 29 April 1982, Article 1 section 1:
The Ministry of Culture and Scientific Coordination shall be empowered to defend the integrity and genuine character of intellectual works that have fallen into the public domain.
For full text, see [1982] *Copyright* 253.

The Herchel Smith Lecture 1992: Intellectual Property Rights & Unfair Copying: Old Concepts, New Ideas

[1992] 12 EIPR 428

JAMES LAHORE

Professorial Fellow, University of Melbourne;
Partner, Mallesons Stephen Jaques, Melbourne

When Professor Dworkin invited me to deliver this lecture, I was acting as Chairman of a new Committee which had been established by the Australian Government to examine, once again, the problem of the legal protection of designs.[1] My experience on that Committee suggested that designs law would be an appropriate subject for this lecture, looking at Australian development from the perspective of the new law in the United Kingdom, and the developments in the European Community following the publication of the Green Paper. There have been, however, some recent controversial decisions of the Federal Court and High Court in Australia in intellectual property law which, together, with the issues we have been dealing with in the designs area, illustrate a common problem or theme which I wish to address specifically this evening. It is what Professor Karjala has referred to as the 'anti-piracy policy base' for the creation or recognition of intellectual property rights.[2]

The issue is that the ever-increasing pressure of demands for proprietary rights, both registered and unregistered, to stop unfair copying of industrial or commercial products of one form or another is presenting a challenge to existing intellectual property concepts, to the extent that an attempt is made to satisfy these demands within this existing intellectual property framework, or some new *sui generis* framework analogous to the old. The resulting confusion and uncertainty in how these concepts are to be applied certainly make it difficult for the practitioner to give clear commercial advice to a client. But, more importantly, the basic concepts themselves lose their focus, and the policy justification for granting intellectual property rights in the first place, that is, the reward and incentive to the creator balanced against technological, commercial or cultural development for society, becomes increasingly under challenge. These tensions can be seen most clearly in the pressure for copyright or a copyright-style protection of computer-related technologies. But they are also seen from a rather different point of view in the on-going debate concerning protection for commercial designs. Professor Reichman has referred to '[t]he old puzzle of industrial art (i.e. commercial design) and the new puzzle of industrial literature (i.e. computer programs)'.[3]

I must first disclaim any originality for my remarks this evening. Many commentators have

---

[1] *Inquiry into Intellectual Property Protection for Industrial Designs*, a Report to the Minister for Industry Technology and Commerce, 1991.
[2] Dennis S. Karjala, 'Copyright Protection of Computer Software in the United States and Japan Part 1', [1991] 6 EIPR 195.
[3] 'Legal Hybrids between the Patent and Copyright Paradigms', ATRIP Conference, Salamanca, 1991.

written or spoken on this theme recently. It is not my aim to traverse this ground again; it is a more modest one. It is to examine certain specific issues which have arisen in Australia in these areas of 'industrial art' and 'industrial literature', and seek to draw some lessons from them.

Designs

The first area I wish to address is that of designs. Professor Cohen-Jehoram in his challenging paper presented at the ALAI Congress in 1991 referred to the legal diversity in the protection of designs as 'maybe the most disturbing one in the whole of intellectual property law'.[4] Professor Cornish in a recent Opinion has noted that 'industrial design protection seems these days to provoke a degree of anxiety that is positively neurotic'.[5] I can only say, ladies and gentlemen, that my own experience as Chairman of the Designs Committee in Australia confirms this assessment; the word 'neurotic' is not too strong a word to use in this context. In fact, my task as Chairman of this Committee has been one of the most difficult I have experienced. One is led to question why the issue of protection for designs creates such rancour. And why did we establish another Committee in Australia to look at this problem which has been under examination over a period of more than 20 years and which many thought had been finally solved by legislation in 1989? The answers to these questions are not difficult to find. They go to the heart of the debate as to how, if at all, the claimants for rights to stop unfair copying should be satisfied.

As many of you will know, in 1981 the designs law in Australia was changed, following the recommendations of the Franki Committee. The Franki Committee, in its discussion of the design monopoly system, considered that the distinction between purely utilitarian or functional designs and designs with a visual customer appeal, made in the design law of the United Kingdom, was not appropriate as a basis for determining those designs which were registrable under the Designs Act 1906 in Australia. The Franki Committee therefore recommended the adoption of what is now section 18 of the Designs Act permitting the valid registration of designs the features of which serve, or serve only, a functional purpose. The wide protection which this amendment gives, in theory, under the Designs Act is said to be one of the most generous regimes for the protection of designs in the world.

Subsequently, in 1989, a further set of very comprehensive amendments to the Copyright Act were introduced.[6] These had the effect of depriving all functional designs of copyright protection with the exception of two-dimensional or surface designs, buildings, and works of artistic craftsmanship. The effect was to confine copyright to what were seen to be essentially artistic works of one form or another. The developments in the United Kingdom with the introduction of the unregistered design right had been put forward in an Issues Paper published by the Australian Government, but these developments were never fully examined and were finally rejected as an option by the Australian Government, although I suggest in a rather half-hearted way. In addition, the European Community Green Paper on the Legal Protection of Industrial Designs became available towards the end of the Committee's deliberations.

After the introduction of the 1989 amendments there was an outcry from certain industries which maintained that they had lost the protection they previously had under the Copyright Act, and had been left, in fact, with no protection at all. There was no general perception that

---

4 'Hybrids on the Borderline between Copyright and Industrial Property Law', [1991] *Australian Intellectual Property Journal* 190.
5 W.R. Cornish, 'Designs Again', [1991] 1 EIPR 3.
6 Copyright Amendment Act 1989.

protection under the Designs Act, to the extent that it was available at all, gave any commercially effective protection. Strong lobbying came, in particular, from the pump industry.[7] This produced heated debate in Parliament and the result of that debate was the establishment of the new Committee to which I have referred. The Report has now been published.[8]

The evidence that came before this Committee was interesting for a number of reasons. First, and I think most importantly, it indicated that the Designs Act amendments which had been made in 1981 to protect functional designs did not achieve their purpose. To the extent that wide-ranging protection was intended, that intention was not fulfilled. It also became clear during the course of the inquiry that the definition of design in the Designs Act was itself unsatisfactory and produced great uncertainty and unpredictability.[9] What in fact everyone wanted was something to stop unfair copying.

The inadequate protection given by the Designs Act was the subject of a number of submissions made to the Committee. I suggest that the major reason for this inadequacy is that the scope of the monopoly under the Designs Act with its emphasis on a specific individual appearance which must be novel does not easily accommodate the purely utilitarian or functional design where what is important is not visual appeal, as such. The courts in Australia have been unwilling to extend the design monopoly to include differing appearances, because of the fear that by doing so the monopoly will become a form of product or process patent. It is this patent approach to visual features of functional articles which presents such difficulties.

A clear example is the decision of the High Court of Australia in the *Firmagroup* case.[10] The design was for a recessed garage door handle and lock. Although this lock was described as a commercial breakthrough, it was not protected against a lock with a slightly different configuration although it was admitted that all the salient features of the plaintiff's lock were copied. The High Court stated that general functional features, however novel, useful or commercially significant they may be, are not protected by the Designs Act.

The High Court made the following observations on what was protected:[11]

> The only design features that are susceptible to protection are those features which convey the idea of 'one particular individual and specific appearance' ... No design should be so construed as to give to its proprietor a monopoly in a method or principle of construction. The registration of the appellant's design thus gives no monopoly for the making of an article combining a place in which a keyhole is set and a recessed handgrip; nor in our opinion does it give a monopoly for the making of an article combining a rectangular plate in which a keyhole is set and a recessed rectangular handgrip placed alongside horizontally. The idea of shape or configuration conveyed by those features is altogether too general to attract statutory protection. If the appellant's design was no more precisely specified than that, registration ought to have been refused.

On what the defendant (respondent) had taken the court said:[12]

> What the respondents took from the registered design were not design features sus-

---

[7] It had been held in *Warman International v Envirotech Australia Pty Ltd* [1986] 6 IPR 578 that copyright protected certain drawings for pumps.

[8] On 22 April 1992. See Note 1 above.

[9] The particular problem is the wide interpretation by the courts of the exclusion of a method or principle of construction together with the emphasis on one specific individual appearance as the subject of the monopoly.

[10] *Firmagroup Australia Pty Ltd v Byrne and Davidson Doors (Vic) Pty Ltd* (1987) 9 IPR 353 (Full Court).

[11] At 356.

[12] At 357.

ceptible of protection; they were features which, although intended to make an article to which they were applied more useful than similar articles then in use, were insufficiently precise to convey an idea of unique shape or configuration. Such *general* functional features are not protected by the Act, *however novel, useful and commercially significant they may be. (Emphasis added.)*

It has been argued by one commentator that the result of this decision was that the whole commercial worth of the design was appropriated without redress.[13] The answer is that this may be so, but the system of protection under the Designs Act does not provide an appropriate mechanism to protect what the plaintiffs were claiming in the *Firmagroup* case. In other words, the conceptual basis for the design monopoly under the designs law does not provide an adequate system for protecting modern functional industrial design.

In cases after the *Firmagroup* case the courts have indicated that the statement of monopoly, if properly drawn, might produce a more favourable result for the plaintiff.[14] But this patent-style approach to design protection for functional articles where what is sought is effectively a remedy against unfair copying is not, in my opinion, the path to follow.

On the other hand, in the *Firmagroup* case it is difficult to see how any different result could have been achieved under the present Designs Act. It is understandable that a court, faced with a situation such as that in the *Firmagroup* case, sees the protection of a design which has a slightly different shape or configuration from the registered design, as effectively protecting, not a specific appearance, but the function itself under the guise of a different shape.

There have been a number of decisions since the *Firmagroup* case in relation to products such as pressure spray washers for motorcars,[15] plastic storage containers,[16] and bar chains for use in making concrete slabs,[17] and in not one of those cases did the plaintiff succeed in an infringement action. One reason was, in substance, the reason given in the *Firmagroup* case, that in each case the defendant's design was slightly different from the plaintiff's design; it was not a fraudulent or obvious imitation. The court was not prepared to extend protection to what was seen to be the function of a particular article rather than its specific appearance.

The result of following that particular line of reasoning is that the Designs Act protection loses much of its commercial importance for designs without visual appeal in those cases where a defendant does not make a slavish copy. A design will be adapted in one way or another to produce something which effectively does the same job, but looks slightly different, as was the case of the *Firmagroup* case.

It has been noted that in the Nordic countries, where the position in relation to the registration of functional designs is similar to that under section 18 of the Designs Act in Australia, concern has been expressed as a result of the narrow protection given by the courts to such designs.[18] The reason, it is argued, is that since the right is a monopoly, the courts examine it with a jealousy they often fail to display in copyright actions, and a design which is not virtually a Chinese copy may not be found to infringe. This is similar to the position we have reached in Australia.

The draft design law in the EC Green Paper has been received with considerable interest

---

[13] A.C. Archibald QC, 'The Copyright Amendment Bill as it Affects the Designs Act and Recent Design Case Law', [1989] *Intellectual Property Forum* 4 at 12.

[14] See for example *Turbo Tek Enterprises Pty Ltd v Sperling Enterprises Pty Ltd* (1989) 15 IPR 617.

[15] *Turbo Tek Enterprises Pty Ltd v Sperling Enterprises Pty Ltd* (1989) 15 IPR 617.

[16] *Dart Industries Inc. v Decor Corporation Pty Ltd* (1989) 15 IPR 403.

[17] *Wanem Pty Ltd v John Tekiela* (1990) 19 IPR 435.

[18] Christine Fellner, *The Future of Legal Protection for Industrial Design*, ESC Publishing Limited, 1985 at 106 to 108, 196 to 197.

because it does address the unfair copying issue, although in a somewhat muted form. There are, however, reservations, suggested by our experience in Australia.

First, I agree that a critical defect in the Green Paper is that it envisages the availability of *registered* protection with monopoly effect for functional designs (assuming the design is not dictated *solely* by function).[19]

Second, the proposed system of Community Design Protection clearly shows a 'patent-style' approach. If I may quote Professor Cohen-Jehoram again:[20]

> ... [this] betrays a fundamental misunderstanding of the character of design, and the act of designing, an activity of human imagination and not the inventing of a technical effect ... Designs are quintessentially a subject for copyright protection, though the misunderstanding has a venerable pedigree.

Whether or not one agrees that designs are quintessentially a subject for copyright protection, the essential point is that patent-inspired legislation cannot be an appropriate solution to protect designs where the same or a similar practical or technical functional effect can be achieved with varying shape or configuration.

The other interesting feature of the European draft design law which has attracted us in Australia is the proposal for an unregistered community design. As I said earlier, there has been a strong indication from industry that there needs to be an effective law to prevent unfair copying, but some hesitation in recommending any traditional copyright solution.

I suggest the Australian experience does lead to certain conclusions:

- There is a need for a specifically 'design' approach, as the EC Green Paper recognises.
- The patent-style approach provides no satisfactory solution for many designs.
- The attempt to protect functional designs within the present design registration system is equally misguided.
- If unfair copying is the issue in fact, then that issue must be addressed directly, and maybe with more courage than the European draft design law presently shows.

Computer-related Technologies

I would now like to pass to the second area of law for comment this evening, the protection given to the computer-related technologies of computer software, and semiconductor chips or integrated circuits.

In the last six months there have been a number of critical decisions in Australia from the High Court and the Federal Court which are causing concern in the computer industries and among intellectual property lawyers. I think we are seeing the dangers which many commentators foresaw in bringing the software 'cuckoo' into the copyright nest, but equally the dangers in creating a *sui generis* copyright-style protection for integrated circuits.

As you know, Australia, consistently with world trends, brought computer software into the original 'literary work' pigeonhole in the Copyright Act in 1984. I am not sure that there was any strong conviction that this was the right way to go, but legislation came in very fast in 1984 with strong pressure from the United States and the computer industry.

In retrospect, we may consider the question should have been approached differently.

---

[19] Audrey A. Horton, 'Industrial Design Law: The Future for Europe', [1991] 12 EIPR 442.
[20] Professor Cohen-Jehoram, 'The EC Green Paper on the Legal Protection of Industrial Design', [1992] 3 EIPR 75.

The following comment of Professor Paul Goldstein at the ALAI Quebec Congress, is instructive:[21]

> But, I submit, the interests at stake are far too important to be well-served by the convenience of legislatures and courts. Ten years ago, the correct question that should have been asked was: 'What form of protection will best serve the conditions of authorship in computer programs?' To be sure, the answer may have been copyright. But, *a priori* there is no reason to believe that this would have been the correct answer. The end result is that the question as framed today is: Will copyright and authors' rights survive the computer program? To this my answer is, of course they will . . . The question is not whether copyright will survive the program. The real question is whether the computer program will survive copyright. As to this I have some doubt. Copyright has not expelled computer programs, but rather has consigned them to the margins of protection, margins where protection is thinnest and least supportive of substantial investment—margins where incentives may be insufficient to stimulate the desired level of creativity.

Australian developments indicate that the issue now is not that copyright has consigned software to the margins of protection. Rather, it is that software protection has taken 'centre-stage', although it is not at all clear what the scope of that protection is.

I refer, first, to the recent decision of the High Court in *Autodesk Inc. v Dyason*.[22] The facts, very briefly, were these:

Autodesk owned copyright in a program called the AutoCAD program. This program facilitated architectural and engineering plans and designs. It was sold in Australia for approximately $5,200 with a lock called the AutoCAD lock. The program could not be run without the lock. The AutoCAD program was in fact a compilation of programs and one of these was what was called Widget C. This program operated in conjunction with the lock. Widget C contained a protocol called a 'look-up table'. Challenges were sent to the lock in accordance with instructions in Widget C. The lock responded in the form of binary digital information. The response of the AutoCAD lock to a string of challenges by Widget C was predetermined by the manner in which the lock was wired and was in accordance with the 'look-up table' when read in a particular manner. Widget C compared the response of the lock with the correct response in the 'look-up table'. The response was in fact a 127-bit sequence,known as a pseudo random sequence. The court was careful to point out that in a sequence of 127 binary digits, the possible alternatives would be 2 to the power of 127. It would be virtually impossible to calculate it or duplicate it by accident.

Kelly, the defendant, detected the transitions of the AutoCAD lock with an oscilloscope and constructed a device with the same output as the AutoCAD lock. He did this by storing the sequence in an EPROM incorporated in his autokey lock. Kelly sold his lock for $500. In fact, the two locks had quite different technology to produce the same result.

The court held that Kelly had committed an infringement in making and selling his autokey lock. On what possible basis could the court come to such a conclusion? The basis of the decision was that in programming his EPROM to give the same signals as those sent out by the AutoCAD lock he was in fact copying the 'look-up table', and the 'look-up table' was a substantial part of a literary work, namely Widget C.

---

[21] [1989] *Anuaire* ALAI 541. Quoted by Professor Cohen-Jehoram, see Note 4 above, at 197 to 198.
[22] (1991) 22 IPR 163. See Julian Stephens, 'High Court Protects Computer Lock', [1992] *Australian Intellectual Property Law Bulletin* 9. Note that in the United Kingdom the plaintiff would not have succeeded because of the operation of section 296 of the Copyright, Designs and Patents Act 1988.

Questions relating to basic concepts of copyright are involved in the decision but they are not resolved.

- What is the level of originality required for subsistence of copyright in a program?
- Is reverse engineering possible or not?
- What does it mean to say that only the expression can be copied, not the idea?
- What is a substantial part of a plaintiff's program?

None of these questions is new but their attempted resolution in the context of the protection of computer programs is placing severe strain on the copyright system.

Professor Dworkin has noted: '. . . such questions give the courts scope for flexibility in analysis so that it is possible for them, on a case-by-case basis, to deal with unfair competition and cases where there has been excessive use of monopoly rights'.[23] But should copyright provide the conceptual framework for this analysis?

If one looks at the decision in relation to the traditional principles of copyright law, difficulties immediately arise. First, the court stated that, as a fundamental principle of copyright, copyright does not extend to ideas or schemes or systems or methods. It is confined to their expression and if their expression is not copied, the copyright is not infringed. The court acknowledged the difficulty in distinguishing an idea from its expression in the case of a utilitarian work such as a computer program.

In addition, the court endorsed the principle in the United States case of *Whelan Associates v Jaslow Dental Laboratory* that: '[T]he idea of a utilitarian work is its purpose or function and the method of arriving at that purpose or function is the expression of the idea.'[24] The court also endorsed the 'merger' doctrine, citing the case of *Lotus 1–2–3*[25] without, I might add, adverting to any of the recent criticisms of that case in the courts in the United States and in the US literature. Having said that, the court does not seek to apply the concept other than as one reason for rejecting the decision of the judge at first instance who had adopted a purely functional test in determining infringement.

One commentator has argued that the result, in fact, of the High Court's decision is to protect the function of programs, whatever the court may have said as to the proper scope of copyright protection.[26] I cannot go into this question at length this evening, although it is essential to the copyright debate in this area. What I do suggest is that copyright is not the appropriate vehicle for dealing with what are essentially unfair competition claims. If, as Professor Ricketson argues, the essential nature of a computer program is far removed from the kind of subject-matter usually encompassed by the expressed 'every production in the literary, scientific and artistic domain',[27] then that issue must be addressed in considering the general unfair copying argument.

The second problem raised by the decision is the identification of the work that is copied. The court accepted that a work can exist in a non-sensate form. But what did Widget C contain? It has been asserted that Widget C in fact contained either a copy of the output of the AutoCAD lock or an independently created work.[28] The output of the lock, so the argument runs, was a function purely of its circuit design. 'To suggest that the lock's output

[23] 'The Concept of Reverse Engineering in Intellectual Property Law and its Application to Computer Programs', [1990] *Australian Intellectual Property Journal* 164.
[24] (1991) 22 IPR 163 at 172.
[25] *Lotus Development Corporation v Paperback Software International* (1990) 18 IPR 1.
[26] P.M. Conrick, 'Autodesk—A Response', [1992] *Australian Intellectual Property Law Bulletin* 12.
[27] Sam Ricketson, *The Berne Convention for the Protection of Literary and Artistic Works 1886–1986*, Kluwer, 1987, paragraph 16.12.
[28] Conrick, Note 26 above.

is a copy of some other work is a legal fiction: it is not a copy of anything'.[29]

The High Court considered that the 'look-up table' constituted a substantial part of Widget C and that Kelly's use of an oscilloscope to read the output of a stimulated AutoCAD lock involved an indirect copying of the 'look-up table'. In other words, the 127-bit series embedded in Kelly's EPROM constituted a reproduction in a material form of a substantial part of any 'expression' in binary notation of the set of instructions constituting Widget C.

The fallacy in this line of reasoning is that if the output of the lock is not a copy of the look-up table it cannot be an infringement of copyright to copy the output of the lock.

To put the argument in a different form, the question is whether it would be an infringement of copyright in a railway timetable to stand on a station and observe and write down the times of train arrivals and departures, assuming that those times were the same as those printed in the timetable. This is in essence what Kelly did in relation to the output from the lock. To assert infringement in such a case is to confer a monopoly in the information.

Other concerns are the level of originality and degree of substantiality required respectively, to determine copyright subsistence and infringement. These matters are barely referred to by the High Court and yet they are critical in any assessment of copyright subsistence.

In seeking a solution in favour of the plaintiff the High Court has, with respect, given scant attention to basic copyright principles notwithstanding their ritual incantation by the court. The computer industry itself is now left with great uncertainty as to the extent to which emulation is possible. The reverse engineering issue is significant in the development of the computer software industry. But it has now come to the fore in the present debate because it raises very clearly the problem of defining the proper limits of copyright protection.

Finally, in the area of computer-related technologies, I wish to make a brief reference to a recent decision of the Federal Court on the protection of circuit layouts. The issues are not new, although they are new in the context of the relevant legislation, the Circuit Layouts Act 1989, which is the Australian equivalent of the semiconductor chip legislation in other countries. As this legislation is copyright-style in its concept, the courts have had to ask the same copyright questions they have had to ask in the computer software cases.

How is copying determined? What is the extent of protection against copying? What is the extent of a defence of reverse engineering as far as chip manufacture is concerned? Finally, in any treatment of integrated circuits, how does one deal with the exploitation of products such as video games containing a large number of circuits or circuits manufactured in different ways such as ROMs, EPROMs, OPTROMs, and so on?

The courts have indicated that it is to copyright law that one must look for assistance in determining copying, substantially and infringement. But it is not at all clear how infringement of rights in an integrated circuit can be determined in this way. Is it to be done by comparison of appearance or by comparison of function? Surely not the latter, and yet the former may be a completely inappropriate way of dealing with these technologies. In the *Nintendo* case[30] this distinction was in issue.

The case was concerned with integrated circuits contained in a number of video games which had been brought into Australia without the authority of the Australian distributor. The question was a simple one: were the integrated circuits which were incorporated in these video games unauthorised copies of the circuits the rights in which belonged to the plaintiff?

A major part of the argument of the defendants was what was called dual functionality— that the visible differences were referable to the ability of the defendants' circuit-boards to

---

[29] *Ibid.*
[30] *Nintendo Co. Ltd v Centronics Systems Pty Ltd* (1991) 23 IPR 119 (Federal Court of Australia).

accept and play on a PAL TV receiver cartridges designed to operate on the NTSC system, as well as those designed to operate on the PAL system. The defendants also argued that protection given by the Act was analogous to that afforded to architectural plans by copyright law.

Is infringement, therefore, to be determined by comparing the plaintiff's and defendant's design as one would compare two paintings or two works of art? As I have suggested, the court adopted a dual approach and looked both at the physical manifestation of the layouts and at the question of dual functionality by conducting experiments. Whatever view one takes as to a functionality test, I am not convinced that approaching infringement of circuit layout rights on the basis of a copyright-style analysis provides the appropriate answer. It is not the appearance of a circuit which is relevant in any sense. Another solution is needed.

As I stated at the beginning of this address, the constant theme behind the claims for new rights, whether it be for new rights for the protection of functional designs or for the protection of computer software or circuit layouts, is protection against unfair copying. Should the focus in dealing with this problem be on the creation of more proprietary rights in one form or another?

This leads to my third illustration this evening based on recent Australian case law. As in the United Kingdom, we in Australia have no law of unfair competition as such, but we have something similar in the vast expanding area of liability under section 52 of the Trade Practices Act 1974 which prohibits corporations from engaging, in trade or commerce, in conduct that is misleading or deceptive or likely to mislead or deceive.

A number of commentators in the United Kingdom have written about this action and its advantages.[31] I obviously do not have time tonight, nor would it be appropriate, to discuss this action in any detail. Suffice it to say that recent case law suggests that to sustain the action actual proof of some form of representation may no longer be required. In other words, the action is concerned with misappropriation rather than misrepresentation. To this extent I suggest a section 52 action is becoming in fact, if not in form, an action for unfair competition. Ten years ago Hugh Brett in a perceptive opinion pointed out that a tort of unfair competition would also provide the opportunity for other developments.[32] 'It would mean that statutory monopolies could be drafted and interpreted within recognised disciplined lines'. He continued:

> A new tort of unfair competition would also mean that the courts could adapt more quickly to the needs arising from the rapid development of new technologies—all of which require some protection from unfair exploitation in their growth period in particular. At present far too much time is expended in determining copyright disputes on narrow and artificial grounds of interpretation. Does computer software fall within the meaning of a 'literary work'? Is a film frame a photograph or a part of a film? Is a videogram a record or a film? It cannot be in industry's interest that issues of great commercial importance should rest on technicalities more characteristic of the application of a Taxes Act. A tort or unfair competition would be a useful restraint against plagiarism and would go some way in meeting the needs of new technologies and also in balancing the requirements of their users. It would not prevent the enactment of specific legislation.

---

[31] See for example Anna Booy, 'A Half-way House for Unfair Competition in the United Kingdom—A Practitioner's Plea', [1991] 12 EIPR 439.

[32] 'The Danger of Throwing the Baby Out with the Bathwater—The Reform of UK Copyright Law and the Protection of Designs', [1981] 6 EIPR 163 at 165. See also 'Unfair Competition—Not Merely An Academic Issue?', [1979] 11 EIPR 295.

The case I wish to refer to briefly this evening is *Remy Martin v Carlton Wines & Spirits*.[33] The plaintiffs were companies in the Remy group which were involved in the manufacture and distribution of a range of three liqueurs known as Liquore Galliano, Sambuca Galliano and Amaretto Galliano. The Liquore Galliano is a yellow liqueur with purple and gold lettering on a white label and the Sambuca is clear liqueur with white and silver lettering on a blue label. The Amaretto Galliano is a brown liqueur with white and gold lettering on a brown label. Each of the Galliano labels included a red fortress with green surrounds. The Galliano product was sold in a distinctive elongated bottle with a neck band in the Italian colours of green, white and red.

One of the defendants had been the Australian distributor of the Galliano products. Following termination of the distribution agreement, the defendants launched their own range of three liqueurs under the names Valentino Liqueur, Sambuca from Valentino and Amaretto from Valentino. The combination of colours on the labels of the Valentino products mirrored those of the Galliano range and the colours of the liqueurs themselves were virtually identical, but the shape of the bottles was completely different. The Valentino bottles had a neck band in the Italian colours and each of the labels included a brown castle with green surrounds. The plaintiffs sued the defendants alleging that they had passed off the Valentino liqueurs for the Galliano liqueurs and they also alleged contravention of section 52 of the Trade Practices Act. They succeeded on both grounds.

I am not concerned tonight with the passing off issues, but I think the issues under section 52 are interesting. The court took the view that the use of the castle was a poorly disguised attempt to establish an association or connection with the plaintiffs' products, and it emphasised throughout the improper motives of the defendants: the defendants lacked good faith, their intention was to deceive. The court considered that even if an action in passing off would have failed because there was no actionable misrepresentation, it did not follow that the defendants' conduct was not misleading or deceptive, or likely to mislead or deceive, under section 52. In the words of the court, there are no formal boundaries to the interpretation of the word 'conduct'.

It is clear from the decision that it is erroneous to approach section 52 on the assumption that its application is confined to circumstances which constitute some form of mis-representation. What made the defendants' conduct actionable was improper motive, lack of good faith, and intention to deceive or cause confusion, although there was no direct evidence of this. The defendants, in the opinion of the court, set out to cash in on Galliano's reputation, 'to sail as close to the wind as they could'; it was intentional conduct designed to 'cheat or mislead'.

I do not wish to draw from the *Remy Martin* case any wide-ranging conclusions as to the future direction of section 52 actions in Australia. The fact that the defendant had been the Australian distributor of the Galliano products and that there were breach of contract issues were important factors in the decision. Nor do I suggest that to recognise a tort of unfair competition will in some way be a panacea for the difficulties caused by the pressures on traditional intellectual property rights.

What the Australian experience does suggest is that an action directed against certain conduct, whether it be described as unfair competition or unfair copying or in some other way, can develop effectively within a common law system to provide what is a valuable, flexible and cost-effective remedy as a supplement to those traditional remedies for infringement of intellectual property rights.

My point, simply, is that to recognise and develop a general law of unfair copying is a

---

[33] Federal Court of Australia, O'Loughlin J, 19 February 1992.

preferable method for dealing with many of the claims for protection I have referred to this evening, rather than by the creation of an ever-increasing range of property rights within or analogous to traditional intellectual property. As a learned commentator has written:[34]

> With the dawning of the information age a whole panoply of interests including character merchandisers and sponsors are pressing for the extension of legal protection for an ever-increasing range of information-related 'products'.
>
> How to articulate the mechanism to balance a right to protect labour skill and effort against a right of access to information creates great difficulties but may not be insoluble once a basis for protection outside the traditional concept of property is devised.

I suggest that the task of establishing that basis for protection is one which must now be urgently addressed.

---

[34] Professor Michael Pendleton, 'Character Merchandising and the Proper Scope of Intellectual Property', [1990] *Australian Intellectual Property Journal* 242.

Elanco Products—
The ideas–expression
dichotomy
[1979] 4 EIPR 117

GERALD DWORKIN
*Herchell Smith Professor of Intellectual Property
Law, Queen Mary & Westfield College, University
of London*

There is no copyright in ideas or information as such, only in the form in which such ideas or information are expressed. This, of course, is 'trite law',[1] easy enough to state but frequently difficult to apply.

Elanco Products Ltd v Mandorps (Agrochemical Specialists) Ltd.[2] is a tantalising decision of the Court of Appeal which skirts around, but does not deal satisfyingly with, the problems raised by this dichotomy. The facts can be stated shortly. The plaintiff was the inventor of a patented selective herbicide, Trifluralin, which was marketed in containers under the trade name *Treflan*. In order to obtain the approval of two public bodies, the Pesticide Safety Precautions Scheme and the Agricultural Chemical Approval Scheme, the plaintiff conducted extensive research over a considerable period of time and consulted a wide range of relevant periodical literature. This work was utilised by the plaintiff when compiling its sales literature comprising very detailed information leaflets. The plaintiff's patent expired in August 1977 and the defendant then decided to market its own brand of Trifluralin, undercutting the plaintiff's price by a quarter. The defendant also used sales literature: a leaflet folded and secured to its canisters and a label affixed around the canisters. The defendant's major blunder, it appears, was to prepare labels which were virtually identical copies of the plaintiff's literature. On complaint being made, the defendant withdrew its printed information and replaced it with new sales literature, marks two and three, which this time contained virtually the same data but whose format and language were quite different. The plaintiff sought an interlocutory injunction pending trial of a copyright infringement action. The defendant claimed that an injunction would mean that it would lose the very important autumn market.

Termination of the Patent

A simple commercial view of the situation might be this: The plaintiff could only market its patented product effectively by providing the technical information and instructions which it had prepared. The patent has now expired and, with it, the plaintiff's monopoly. The defendant is now entitled to market the product and it can only do this effectively by providing similar information which, unless the defendant carries out a great deal of work, must be acquired primarily from the plaintiff. Therefore it is entitled to use the plaintiff's

---

[1] See *L.B. Plastics v Swish Products Ltd* [1979] EIPR 56, 58.
[2] [1979] F.S.R. 46.

trade information. Any other view might mean that the plaintiff's enforcement of its copyright rights is protecting not only the copyright work itself but also dealings with the product for which the patent had expired.[3]

This argument, of course, is an oversimplification. The expiry of a patent does not mean that a patentee automatically loses all protection in relation to the patented product. It is common practice for commercial organisations to employ as many intellectual property rights as possible to protect their business activities and adroit use of these can help indirectly to extend basic statutory monopolies. Pharmaceutical companies, for example, frequently attempt to extend the patent life of drugs by use of registered trade marks, passing off actions and registered designs. In *Elanco* the expiry of its patent did not affect the validity of its trade name. In exceptional cases a trade mark may be affected if it is the only practicable name for a product whose patent has expired.[3a]

In some cases efforts have been made to patent instructions or information accompanying products, either because the product itself was unpatentable[4] or in an attempt to obtain more effective protection for a patented product. Thus, in *Ciba-Geigy's App.*[5] the applicants had a patent for a known compound for use as a selective weedkiller but felt unable to police the unlicensed use of the compound unless they could also stop rival manufacturers from selling the compound in containers bearing instructions for its use as a weedkiller. The courts resisted the invitation to grant patent protection to information and instructions and now the Patents Act 1977 expressly precludes the 'presentation of information' from being an invention.[6] Thus, it is the novel idea capable of industrial application which is patentable not the expression of that idea, which is within the province of copyright. To paraphrase a dictum of Bradley J. in the well known U.S. Supreme Court decision *Baker v Selden*,[7] 'the description of the art in a book or other literature, though entitled to the benefit of copyright, lays no foundation for an exclusive claim to the art itself. The object of the one is explanation; the object of the other is use. The former may be secured by copy-right. The latter can be secured, if it can be secured at all, by letters-patent'.

It is arguable, of course, that the limited rights granted by a patent should affect accompanying copyright material. Recently, for example, the *Catnic*[8] case has suggested that the copyright interest in patent drawings may be abandoned after the patent period has expired and this is in line with the thinking of the Whitford Committee which made a similar recommendation.[9] In general, though, it is rare for English courts or legislators to attempt American style fundamental analyses of the interrelationship between competing and some-times theoretically inconsistent intellectual property rights. Hence the difficulties we have got into with industrial designs and copyright law.

To return to the case under review, the defendant raised two substantive legal issues to a copyright action: first, that the plaintiff had no copyright in the compilation; and, secondly, that even if the plaintiff could establish a copyright interest, there had been no infringement. As the court was only concerned with deciding whether the plaintiff had an arguable case the judicial approach was tentative in the extreme and their Lordships demonstrated little confidence in the soundness of their remarks.

---

[3]   Similar problems have been raised in the American doctrine of *Baker v Selden*. See *Nimmer on Copyright* (1978) Vol. 1 para 2.18.
[3a] Trade Marks Act 1938 Section 15(1)(b), Section 15(2).
[4]   *Organon's App.* [1970] R.P.C. 574.
[5]   [1976] F.S.R. 77.
[6]   S.1(2) (d).
[7]   (1870) 101 U.S. 90.
[8]   *Catnic v Hill and Smith* [1978] EIPR December, 25–26.
[9]   Whitford Committee Report on Copyright and Design Law. 1977. Cmnd. 6732 para 868.

Copyright in the Sales Information

As to the first issue, it is a little surprising that there should have been much argument as to whether the plaintiff had copyright in the compilation of its sales information. The Whitford Committee took the view, based on well established authority, that adequate copyright protection already exists for tables and lists in the compilation of which sufficient skill and/or labour has been exercised and thought that no special action was called for.[10] The plaintiff could certainly show far more than the minimum amount of labour, skill and capital usually required to create copyright. It was suggested, though, that in compilation cases skill and labour may be expended in two ways: first, to ascertain information, which is allegedly not relevant for copyright purposes; and, secondly, in the presentation of the information, which is relevant. It may well be that far more labour, skill and energy were used in ascertaining the information; but that cannot disguise the fact that some labour and skill must have gone into the preparation of the sales literature, certainly as much as has been required in earlier cases. Further, a clear distinction can be drawn between a person who expends skill and labour both in ascertaining and presenting information, as here, and the person who uses skill and labour to compile a presentation based upon somebody else's efforts in ascertaining the information.

The defendant also raised a first instance red herring, *Springfield v Thame*[11] to suggest (correctly) that not only is there no copyright in news as such but also (doubtfully) that neither is there copyright in the manner of expressing such news. Thus Goff L.J., while accepting that the plaintiff clearly had an arguable case, stated that it would be for the trial judge to decide whether the plaintiff's literature 'was something in which there could be copyright, or whether it was merely something which gave news or information of which competitors could freely avail themselves'.[12] This is a misleading statement and perhaps may be conveniently forgotten.

Infringement

The second, and more interesting, issue turned on the nature of the defendant's infringement of the plaintiff's copyright in its sales information. The various ways in which the defendant might have prepared its material may be traced from the simple to the not so simple situations.

1 The defendant almost completely copies from the plaintiff's literature. It was alleged that this was the situation with the first version of the defendant's sales literature. If so, there can be no doubt as to infringement. But this literature was withdrawn.
2 The defendant's literature consists of extracts from the plaintiff's copyright material together with 'merely colourable' alterations of language. Here again there is little doubt that this is an infringement of a substantial part of a copyright work. The reference to 'merely colourable'[13] alterations represents a clear, but minor, breach in the theoretical idea-expression division.
3 The defendant obtains its information primarily but not exclusively from the plaintiff's literature but then produces its own literature without consciously copying the plain-

---

[10] *Ibid* para 876.
[11] (1903) 89 L.T. 242. The case is not authority for the doubtful proposition!
[12] [1979] F.S.R. at p. 53.
[13] *Copinger on Copyright*, 11th ed. para 432.

tiff's material. The information-expression distinction would suggest that the defendant's literature does not infringe. The fact that the defendant's version looks very
much the same as that of the plaintiff would seem to be immaterial if, from a marketing
point of view, the defendant can only present its material in a similar way to that of
the plaintiff. This seems to have been accepted by Goff L.J.[14] Of course, it could be
argued that if the two sets of sales literature are similar then the defendant could well
have subconsciously copied the form of expression from the plaintiff. Whether or not
the principle of sub-conscious copying is appropriate for musical works[15] it has not
been applied beyond that and, indeed, one argument raised by the defendant to try
to avoid liability for its first effort, was that if it was a copy it was purely unconscious!

4 The defendant copies the plaintiff's material and form. The defendant withdraws
the infringing literature and independently prepares new literature though based
upon the plaintiff's information. This, in fact, was the problem raised here. Strictly
speaking, on the information-expression distinction, the new literature should be
free from infringement problems. However, the court was considerably influenced
by the fact that the defendant's activities were tainted by the first infringing copy.
The defendant's hands were not clean. Thus Goff L.J. stated that the defendant
'having started off ... by making ... a deliberate copy, did not sufficiently cure
the position by working from that copy instead of going to the whole of the
publicly available information and starting from scratch';[16] and Buckley L.J. asked
whether the defendant 'would still be making use of the skill and judgment of (the
plaintiff), or would they have done their work for themselves?' The defendant
might not have 'done sufficient independent work to eradicate the vice of copying,
if there were such an initial vice'.[17]

These statements require close consideration; further encroachments are being made on
the information-expression distinction. Where this is substantial similarity between the
copyright work and the infringing material there may be liability for both direct and indirect
copying. Thus, if the second and third versions of the defendant's literature had been similar
in form to that of the plaintiff there would have been indirect infringing copying from the
defendant's first version. *Moffatt & Paige Ltd v Gill* was cited by Goff L.J. to support his
statement: there, a first infringing copy was succeeded by a slightly different work and Collins
M.R. stated that the defendant 'was debarred from re-issuing again the same work in the
same language. Being debarred from doing that, he is equally debarred from doing anything
that is a mere colourable alteration.'[18] But in *Elanco* the second and third versions of the
defendant's literature were not simply colourable alterations; they were quite different in
form to the plaintiff's work. It is at this point that the dicta cited above can be seen to be
moving into even more difficult conceptual terrain. It is suggested that the defendant could
only purge itself from its original sins by producing advertising material and instructions
based upon work which the defendant had itself done independently: not only must the form
of the defendant's literature be independent but so also must be the acquisition of the
information.

This proposition is not without considerable support. Thus Copinger states, with regard
to compilations, that 'if it is proved that the defendant has made substantial use of the skill

---

[14] [1979] F.S.R. 46, 54.
[15] *Francis Day & Hunter Ltd v Bron* [1963] Ch. 587.
[16] [1979] F.S.R. at p. 55.
[17] [1979] F.S.R. at p. 57.
[18] (1902) 86L. T.465, 470.

and labour of the compiler, an infringement is committed whether or not there is an exact reproduction of language.';[19] in *Purefoy Engineering Co. Ltd v Sykes Boxall*,[20] Lloyd-Jacob J. said, 'If such substantial identity has resulted from a use of the plaintiff's catalogue, either directly by utilising it as a pattern for the defendant's compilation, or indirectly by utilising the information in it as a guide . . ., thereafter to be illustrated and dimensioned for inclusion in the defendant's catalogue, the copyright would be infringed. If, on the contrary, it springs from the fact that both parties were concerned to describe and illustrate their interest in a common subject matter, the data for which was procured by the defendant, from sources not involving any use of the plaintiff's catalogue, the copyright in such catalogue would not be infringed'; and in *Hogg v Scott*[21] Hal V.C. thought that the 'true principle in all these cases is that the defendant is not at liberty to use or avail himself of the labour which the plaintiff has been at for the purpose of producing his work; that is merely to take away the result of another man's labour, or, in other words, his property.'

There are two major problems in connection with this approach. First, there appears to be a basic misconception, which courts not infrequently show, about the nature of infringement. It may be that some work and skill are required to establish that a copyright interest exists in certain kinds of work. But the test of infringement is whether the defendant has reproduced a substantial part of the plaintiff's work. It should not be necessary for the defendant to be faced with a heavier burden of showing that he has also used his own skill and labour; that may become relevant if the defendant wishes to establish a separate copyright in his work.

The second problem is that of the idea-expression theory. Copyright protection in most countries has, of necessity, moved some way from expression to prohibit broader notions of plagiarism; for example, translations and adaptations of literary works; cartoon versions of novels; three dimensional reproductions of two dimensional works and vice versa.[22] These extensions, though, ought to be balanced carefully against the competing principle that copyright law does not protect the idea or information inherent in the copyright work. Calls have been made for a reconsideration of this concept and, indeed, it has been suggested that there 'appears to be no reason in principle why ideas as well as form should not be recognised as the subject of copyright protection.'[23] That may be so, although it is at least worthy of discussion whether the extension of copyright law is the best way of dealing with all these kinds of unfair competition. It is of interest to note that the recent American Copyright Act has given statutory recognition in restating the principle.

Whatever should be done, it would be desirable for a matter of such consequences to be faced consciously, particularly by examining the issues in the context of all intellectual property rights. There is little in the Whitford Report on this and it is unlikely that, had the courts considered these matters with greater care, they would have been so ready to undermine one of the theoretical pegs of copyright law. As a result of the *Elanco* decision the idea expression principle may have been put in even further disarray. Some of the dicta creeping into the law reports may be unfortunate. Ill considered dicta, repeated too frequently, may give rise to ill considered principles. Part of the blame attaches, perhaps, to the *American Cyanamid*[24] injunction procedure. The need to talk about 'arguable cases' reduces the need to worry about precise legal principles. Injunctions may be granted on tentative and tenuous

---

[19] *Copinger on Copyright*, 11th ed. para 420.
[20] (1954) 71 R.P.C. 227, 231. See also *Kelly v Morris* (1865) L.R. 1 Eq. 697.
[21] (1874) L.R. 18 Eq. 444. See also *Graves v Pocket Publications Ltd* (1938) 159 L.T. 471.
[22] See *L.B. Plastics v Swish*, supra, n.1.
[23] Lahore and Griffith, 'Copyright and the Arts in Australia' Melbourne Univ. Press, 1974, 25.
[24] For a full discussion of American Cyanamid see Cole—Interlocutory Injunctions in UK Patent Cases [1979] EPIR 71.

grounds. The injunction itself may be a powerful weapon in negotiating a settlement of the case. Thus, sometimes *American Cyanamid* injunctions may produce both unsatisfactory law and be unfair on litigants. *Elanco* has been settled and will not come to trial. The opportunity to get to grips here with some of these issues has thus been lost.

CBS Songs Ltd v Amstrad Consumer Electronics PLC

[1988] 11 EIPR 345

IAIN PURVIS
Barrister, London

This decision of the House of Lords has clarified what had been a very confused area of law: the status and scope of the various 'inchoate' torts of incitement, procurement and authorisation, as applied to copyright infringement.

In short, the House of Lords hearing was the climax of two actions: an application by Amstrad for a declaration that their sale of cassette records with a twin-tape, double-recording-speed facility was lawful; and a further application by Amstrad to strike out an action by the BPI against them.

There were several bases for the BPI's action. The House of Lords decided that none of them was sustainable.

Authorisation of Infringing Reproduction

It was not disputed that the sale by Amstrad of their double-speed, twin-tape cassette deck made it much easier for the public to make copies of tapes, and in many cases thereby to infringe copyright. The BPI alleged that by selling their decks Amstrad were themselves liable for authorising infringement.

The House gave this short shrift. They interpreted the word 'authorising' in section 1 of the 1956 Act as meaning 'conferring authority'. No such authority is conferred by the manufacturer of a machine by which one may make copies. 'The purchaser or other operator determines whether he shall copy and what he shall copy. By selling the recorder Amstrad may facilitate copying in breach of copyright but do not authorise it.'

This interpretation of 'authorising' was expanded in the discussion of Amstrad's potential liability through their advertisements. There had previously been a divergence of view on the authorities about the nature of the involvement in the infringing act which was necessary before one could be said to have 'authorised' it.

Lord Templeman's judgment expressly approved a dictum of Atkin LJ in *Falcon v Famous Players Film Co.*:[1] 'To "authorise" means to grant or purport to grant to a third party the right to do the act complained of, whether the intention is that the grantee shall do the act on his own account or only on account of the grantor ...' He also approved a dictum of Whitford J in *CBS Inc. v Ames Records & Tapes Ltd*:[2] 'an act is not authorised by somebody who merely enables or possibly assists or even encourages another to do that act, but does

---

[1] [1926] 2 KB 474.
[2] [1982] Ch 91.

not purport to have any authority which he can grant to justify the doing of the act.'

Thus, a person who sells, supplies or lends articles which may be used for carrying out infringing acts, even if such acts are 'almost inevitable', does not authorise infringement.

Although Lord Templeman held that Amstrad did not 'sanction, approve or countenance' the infringing acts, and seemed to accept those words of Bankes LJ in *Falcon v Famous Players* as representing the law, they are plainly inconsistent with the holding that authorisation in the context of the Copyright Act means a grant or purported grant of the right to do the acts complained of. While the word 'sanction' may be consistent with this, the words 'approve or countenance' are obviously too wide. This was certainly the view of Lawton LJ in the Court of Appeal, with whom Lord Templeman agreed in most respects. It would be better if the 'sanction, approve or countenance' definition were now to be regarded as misleading, and no longer adopted.

Joint Liability

The BPI argued that if the infringing acts were not authorised, then at least Amstrad were jointly liable with the primary infringers for all their acts of infringement. This was rejected by the House of Lords just as shortly. Lord Templeman said 'joint infringers are two or more persons who act in concert with one another pursuant to a common design in the infringement. In the present case there was no common design. Amstrad sold a machine and the purchaser or the operator of the machine decided the purpose for which the machine should from time to time be used. The machine was capable of being used for lawful and unlawful purposes.'

Incitement and Procurement of a Tort

The BPI's case on this was based on the old case of *Lumley v Gye*.[3] Again the House rejected the argument, on the basis that there was no joint or common design to commit the infringing acts. All Amstrad were doing was supplying the means by which the infringing acts could be done. It was an entirely free and unaffected choice on the part of the customers when they decided to infringe. They relied on the dictum of Buckley LJ in *Belegging-en Exploitatiemaatschappij Lavender BV v Witten Industrial Diamonds Ltd*[4] that 'facilitating the doing of an act is obviously different from procuring the doing of an act'.

The guidance was given that 'generally speaking, inducement, incitement or persuasion to infringe must be by a defendant to an individual infringer and must identifiably procure a particular infringement in order to make the defendant liable as a joint infringer.'

Incitement of a Criminal Offence

The BPI's final submissions were rejected even more abruptly. The argument put was that when a purchaser of an Amstrad model has in his possession a record for the purposes of making an infringing copy, the record becomes a 'plate', so that the purchaser then commits the criminal offence under section 21(3) of the Act: having in his possession a plate, knowing that is to be made for making infringing copies.

Lord Templeman's answer was that a record was not a plate, but the product of the master recording which was a plate and from which the record was derived. This seems to be a

---

[3] (1853) 2 E & B 216.
[4] [1979] FSR 59.

reasonable decision. However, it does depart from what was thought to be the law. The definition under section 18(3) of the Act is less than helpful: 'any stereotype, stone, block, mould, matrix, transfer, negative or other appliances'. It had been thought that 'other appliances' could cover in effect any article which could be used and was intended to be used to make infringing copies from. This was based solely on a decision of a magistrate in 1913, reported in *The Times*, and in MacGillivray's *Copyright* cases,[5] to the effect that a defendant who took along a copy of a cinematograph film to a developer and asked him to make copies from it was in possession of a 'plate' within the meaning of the 1911 Copyright Act.

To the extent that this did represent the law, and, in view of the inferiority of the tribunal which decided it, it was only of weak authority, this must be taken to have been overruled. A plate has been given the meaning which the legislature must surely have intended it to have: an article embodying the copyright work which was created for the purpose of making multiple copies of it. The mere fact that it is possible to make copies from it ought not to be relevant. In these days of photocopiers and dual cassette recorders there would otherwise be an awful lot of criminals.

Negligence

The final argument of the BPI which was dismissed by the House of Lords was that Amstrad were liable for negligence through their advertising and in allowing their customers the possession of articles which would facilitate the infringement of copyright. Lord Templeman in his usual colourful style rightly dismissed out of hand the notion that Amstrad could be said to owe a duty of care to copyright owners in this way. As he said:

> The pleading assumes that we are all neighbours now, Pharisees and Samaritans alike, that foreseeability is a reflection of hindsight and that for every mischance in an accident-prone world someone solvent must be liable in damages. In the present proceedings damages and an injunction for negligence are sought against Amstrad for a breach of statutory duty which Amstrad did not commit and in which Amstrad did not participate. The rights of BPI are to be found in the Act of 1956 and nowhere else. Under and by virtue of that Act Amstrad owed a duty not to infringe copyright and not to authorise an infringement of copyright. They did not owe a duty to prevent or discourage or warn against infringement.

Conclusion

The moral of all this, which was explicitly recognised in Lord Templeman's judgment, is that the only way to seek effective relief against rampant and easy home infringement is to change the law. The courts will not step in to prevent entrepreneurs from taking advantage of the ease with which people can infringe and their lack of conscience about doing so.

It is up to the legislature to decide to take action to protect copyright owners. As Lord Templeman suggested, Parliament might well decide that their monopoly protection gave them more than enough rewards as it is. The existence of blank tapes and dual tape recorders may be the only thing which keeps record prices within reasonable bounds. They might well think that restraints on the manufacture of certain kinds of tape recorder would be an

---

[5] 1911 to 1916 at 105.

unwarranted interference with the development of the electronics industry.

The courts are not there to step in to help what they perceive to be needy causes. Where Parliament has codified the law in a statute, the courts are there simply to enforce the statute. They may well feel that the law is being brought into dispute by modern practices, but their role is limited to informing Parliament that this is their opinion.

Demystifying Copyright Infringement of Computer Software

[1994] 5 EIPR 206

LAURENCE JACOBS
Allen & Overy, London

Ibcos Computers v Barclays Mercantile

During the last few years there has been a considerable debate in the United Kingdom about the particular difficulties of applying copyright principles to computer software, but there has been little guidance from the courts. As a result great reliance has been placed on US case law. Earlier this year, in *Ibcos Computers v Barclays Mercantile*, the Court was faced with clear evidence of literal copying of a computer program.[1] The Court took this opportunity to address these difficulties and to reaffirm the importance of applying the basic principles of UK copyright law, which, as the Court emphasised, are different from those of US copyright law.

The difficulties of applying UK copyright law to computer software are well documented. In several interlocutory decisions, notably *Total Information Processing Systems v Daman*, the courts have questioned both whether the general structure of a program could be a copyright work and the scope of protection available to computer programs as functional works.[2] Last year in the *John Richardson* case, the court sought to provide guidelines to resolve these difficulties by utilising the 'abstractions test' set out in the US case, *Computer Associates v Altai*.[3] However these guidelines proved difficult to apply to the facts even of that case. In the recent *Ibcos Computers v Barclays Mercantile* decision, Jacob J returned to these difficulties once again and sought to reaffirm the basic principles of UK copyright law.

The Facts

As with so many disputes regarding the copying of computer programs, the main defendant in the *Ibcos Computers v Barclays Mercantile* case, a Mr Poole, was a former employee of one of the plaintiff companies. Having left the company, he developed a competing program, and it was claimed that this infringed copyright.

---

[1] There were in fact three separate actions, *Ibcos Computers and Another v Barclays Mercantile and Others* and *Ibcos Computers and Another v David Poole and Another*, unreported, Jacob J, 24 February 1994. There was no material difference between the cases by the time they reached trial.

[2] [1992] FSR 171, see also *Thrustcode v W.W. Computing* [1983] FSR 502.

[3] *John Richardson Computers Ltd v Flanders and Another* [1993] FSR 497 and *Computer Associates v Altai*, 775 F. Supp 544, 20 USPQ 2d 1641 (EDNY 1991).

The plaintiffs in the action were PK Computers and Ibcos Computers. PK Computers was established by Mr Clayton and Mr Poole in 1981 and ceased trading in 1988. At that time the assets of PK Computers were transferred to Ibcos Computers. Mr Poole and Mr Clayton had first met in 1978 when Mr Poole sold Mr Clayton an accounts package he had written ('the Mark 3 software'). Subsequently they discussed the possibility of developing a new program based on the Mark 3 software for the particular needs of agricultural machinery dealers. In 1981 they established PK Computers to develop and market the new program which was known as 'Agricultural Dealer System' ('ADS'). Mr Poole had primary responsibility for the programming and over the course of time other programmers joined the company. In 1986 Mr Poole left PK Computers and joined the first defendant, a subsidiary of Barclays Bank, then known as Highland Finances Ltd ('Highland'). Prior to his departure, Mr Poole signed an agreement which provided that:

(1) Mr Poole was to return all PK property;
(2) Mr Poole recognised that all PK software and manuals were the sole property of PK;
(3) for a period of two years from March 1986 Mr Poole would not sell or be employed by a company selling similar software to agricultural dealers (this clause contained an exception for Mr Poole's work for Highland, unless Highland was involved in the sale of similar products specifically for agricultural dealers); and
(4) no confidential information relating to PK was to be passed on to a third party.

In the summer of 1986 Mr Poole decided to write a program for agricultural dealers which would compete with ADS. He worked on this in his spare time and had developed the program by mid-1987, at which point he showed the program to Highland. Highland were aware of the restrictive covenant and were not prepared to market the product until after the two-year period had expired in March 1988. In mid-1988, following the expiration of the two-year period, Highland launched Mr Poole's new program under the name 'Unicorn'. Mr Clayton soon became aware of the existence of the Unicorn program and in June 1989 obtained an *ex parte* Order from Vinelott J requiring the defendants to deliver up all relevant material. The version of Unicorn delivered up in accordance with the Order served as the basis for the comparison with ADS at the trial. Surprisingly no other material, such as design documentation, was delivered up. Nevertheless even the delivery up of this limited material proved vital to the case and demonstrates the value of such orders.

Based on the information obtained following the Order of Vinelott J, the plaintiff claimed for:

(1) breach of the restrictive covenant in the 1986 agreement;
(2) copyright infringement; and
(3) breach of confidence.

The defendants denied these allegations and argued that the 1986 agreement was unenforceable. They also counterclaimed on the grounds that Mr Poole owned the copyright in the Mark 3 software and that ADS infringed this copyright.

The Decision

Clearly the central issue of the case was the plaintiffs' claim of copyright infringement. Before considering this issue, the court dealt briefly with the plaintiffs' claim for breach of the restrictive covenant and the defendants' counterclaim. In relation to the claim for breach of the restrictive covenant, Jacob J held that the agreement prevented the *sale* of a competing program. It did not restrict the *development* of a competing product by Mr Poole. As the program was not marketed until after the two-year period expired, Mr Poole did not therefore breach the restrictive covenant. It might be argued that the clear intention of the restrictive covenant was to stop the development of a competing product, but as Jacob J emphasised, restrictive covenants must be construed narrowly. In reaching this decision he also noted that the scope of the restrictive covenant may have been too wide and may therefore have been unenforceable in any event.

Jacob J went on to dismiss the counterclaim for copyright infringement in the Mark 3 software. On the facts of the case, he held that the reference in the 1986 agreement to the PK software owned by PK had to include the Mark 3 software, as it was an integral part of ADS. As such, the 1986 agreement served as an assignment of copyright in the Mark 3 software. Somewhat more surprisingly Jacob J went on to note that even without the agreement, Mr Poole would be estopped from claiming that ADS infringed copyright in the Mark 3 software. In reaching this conclusion, he noted that it was clear that the Mark 3 software was integral to ADS and that all the work that PK Computers undertook to develop ADS would be rendered useless if Mr Poole could revoke the licence to the Mark 3 software.

A similar argument was in fact advanced in the *John Richardson* case, where independent consultants modified a program in which copyright was owned by the plaintiff. In that case Ferris J held that although there was no formal assignment, such copyright as vested in the independent consultants was held on trust for the plaintiff. The pragmatic approach to the question of copyright ownership in the *John Richardson* and *Ibcos* cases will be welcomed by the computer industry. However, at the same time, these decisions give rise to some concern, as they effectively undermine the statutory requirement that copyright can only be assigned in writing.[4]

Subsistence of copyright

In considering the plaintiffs' claim for copyright infringement, the court first tried to define what were the copyright works in ADS. The plaintiffs claimed copyright in:

(1) the individual programs and sub-routines in ADS;
(2) the general structure of ADS; and
(3) certain general 'design features' of ADS as defined in the plaintiffs' expert's report.

Jacob J had no difficulty in deciding that each of the several hundred programs and sub-routines in ADS were copyright works. With regard to the program as a whole, he was satisfied that the way in which the individual programs and sub-routines were brought together had involved a substantial amount of skill, labour and judgment on the part of the programmer. As such, the general structure of the program was a copyright work as an original compilation.

In reaching this decision, Jacob J was specifically concerned to reject the idea, advanced in particular in *Total Information Processing Systems v Daman*, that because a program has a particular function and that function can only be achieved in one or a limited number of ways, it cannot be a copyright work. As he explained, the fact that a work is functional does not prevent it from being a copyright work if it involves sufficient skill, labour and judgment

---

[4] Copyright, Designs and Patents Act 1988, section 90(3).

on the part of the author. Similarly, it is incorrect to state as a general rule that ideas can never be copyright works. One can distinguish between what Jacob J referred to as 'general ideas' and ideas which involve sufficient skill, labour and judgment to be copyright works.

Jacob J went on to emphasise that, in this important respect, UK copyright law is different from US copyright law. US statute and case law quite clearly excludes protection for functional works and ideas. As a result, the tests developed by the US courts to exclude protection for ideas and functional aspects of computer programs are not relevant when considering the subsistence of copyright in computer programs in the United Kingdom. In the *John Richardson* case, Ferris J had also recognised that there were some differences between the tests for the subsistence of copyright in US and UK law but appears to have been of the view that in practice these differences would not affect the outcome of a case involving computer programs.[5] By contrast in *Ibcos Computers v Barclays Mercantile*, Jacob J was of the opinion that the differences between the approaches of the UK and US courts were substantial and could lead to different results.

Jacob J then considered what were described as the general 'design features' of ADS, which constituted the third category of work in which the plaintiffs claimed copyright. These design features were a disparate group of general program features which were selected by the plaintiffs' expert as they appeared in both the plaintiffs' and defendants' programs. The only evidence regarding these features which was considered in the judgment was of a very general nature. There does not appear to have been any evidence submitted which compared the source code for these features of ADS and Unicorn. Based on the level of generality at which copyright was claimed, Jacob J was not satisfied that copyright subsisted in these general design features. It was held that these design features were simply general ideas which did not require much of the programmer's skill, labour and effort. He went on to note that even if these design features had been copyright works, the copying which had clearly taken place would not have constituted a copyright infringement—it would be the taking of a mere general idea or scheme'.[6]

Infringement of copyright

Jacob J then turned to the questions of:

(1) whether there had been copying of the general structure and the specific programs and sub-routines of ADS; and

(2) whether a substantial part of these copyright works had been copied.

It was clear that there was copying of several sub-routines and programs of ADS. Significantly several idiosyncratic elements of programs and sub-routines of ADS were also present in Unicorn. For example, a program which was part of ADS was referred to on several occasions in Unicorn even though the program itself did not actually form part of Unicorn. It was also clear that the general structure of ADS had been copied, as there were several examples of individual programs in both ADS and Unicorn being put together in both programs' general structure in the same way. The defence did not rally challenge this evidence. They sought to argue that these similarities reflected Mr Poole's phenomenal memory recall or perhaps more plausibly his particular style of programming. The court had little difficulty in rejecting these arguments. Neither Mr Poole's memory nor his particular style of programming could

[5] *John Richardson Computers Ltd v Flanders*, Note 3 above, at 526 to 527.
[6] *Ibcos Computers v Barclays Mercantile*, Note 1 above, at 36.

explain the level of similarity between the programs, particularly the fact that the same spelling mistakes appeared in certain sub-routines but not in other parts of both programs.

The question of whether this copying amounted to a substantial reproduction of the copyright subsisting in ADS was a more difficult issue. It was in relation to this issue that the *John Richardson* judgment has been widely criticised. As noted above, in that case Ferris J had sought to develop an approach based on the 'abstractions test' set out in the *Computer Associates* case. He explained that:

> At the stage at which the substantiality of any copying falls to be assessed in an English case the question which has to be answered, in relation to the originality of the Plaintiff's program and the separation of an idea from its expression, is essentially the same question as the US Court was addressing in *Computer Associates*. In my judgement it would be right to adopt a similar approach in England.[7]

In fact Ferris J found it extremely difficult to apply the 'abstractions test' to the facts of the *John Richardson* case. This was particularly apparent in the difficulties he faced when considering whether there had been a substantial reproduction of the general structure of the plaintiffs' program. He had accepted that the general structure of the plaintiffs' program was protectable as a compilation. However because this compilation was a functional work he was uncertain as to how to apply to the general test for assessing whether a substantial part of a compilation had been taken. As he noted:

> I find some difficulty in applying this to a computer program where the work and skill of the writer of the original program lies in the design of the component parts rather than in the selection of particular components to form part of a composite whole or their arrangement in any particular order.[8]

Faced with these difficulties Ferris J held, in the *John Richardson* case, that only three discrete routines in the defendants' program infringed copyright. Somewhat surprisingly, similarities in many other features which by themselves were not substantial reproductions did not lead Ferris J to the conclusion that there had been copying of a substantial part of the plaintiffs' program as a whole. This could have significant practical ramifications as the defendants could simply amend these three routines and continue to sell their program in competition with the plaintiffs' program.[9]

Jacob J rejected this reliance on US case law:

> For myself I do not find the route of going via US case law particularly helpful. As I have said UK copyright cannot prevent the copying of a mere general idea but can protect the copyright of a detailed 'idea'. It is a question of degree where a good guide is the notion of overborrowing of the skill, labour and judgement which went into the copyright work. Going via the complication of the concept of a 'core of protectable expression' merely complicates the matter so far as our law is concerned. It is likely to lead to overcitation of US authority based on a statute different from ours.[10]

In deciding whether a substantial part of the copyright works in ADS had been copied, he

---

[7] *John Richardson Computers Ltd v Flanders*, Note 3 above, at 527.
[8] *Ibid.* at 559.
[9] See *John Richardson Computers Ltd v Flanders and Another* [1994] FSR 144.
[10] *Ibcos Computers v Barclays Mercantile*, Note 1 above, at 32 to 33.

emphasised that the court should rely on the basic test of how significant the part copied was to the program as a whole. In the words of Jacob J, one should consider whether there had been an 'overborrowing of the skill, labour and judgement which went into the copyright work'. In this case the evidence of literal copying of source code as presented by the plaintiffs' expert was overwhelming and largely undisputed. The court, therefore found that both the general structure and the individual programs and sub-routines of Unicorn infringed copyright in ADS. Obviously it will be more difficult to apply these general principles of UK copyright law, as advocated by Jacob J, to more complex cases, particularly of non-literal copying.

In this regard it is worth noting that while the *Ibcos Computers v Barclays Mercantile* case was a case about literal copying, the issue of non-literal copying was nevertheless considered in passing. In setting out the basic principles for analysing copyright infringement Jacob J endorsed Ferris J's decision that non-literal copying could infringe copyright. In his consideration of copyright in ideas and functional works he further explained that:

> The true position is that where an 'idea' is sufficiently general, then even if an original work embodies it, the mere taking of that idea will not infringe. But if the 'idea' is detailed, then there may be infringement. It is a question of degree. The same applies whether the work is functional or not, and whether visual or literary. In the latter field the taking of a plot (ie the 'idea') of a novel or play can certainly infringe—if that plot is a substantial part of the copyright work.[11]

On the facts of the case, a claim for non-literal copying only arose in relation to the general design features of ADS, and this was not a point which was considered in any detail. Jacob J simply dismissed the claim stating that even if the design features were copyright works, the copying of these features would not constitute copyright infringement, as it would only be the copying of general ideas. It is not surprising that he only dealt with this point very briefly, as he had already held that these design features were not copyright works and there was also clear evidence of direct copying of source code which will always be more persuasive evidence of copyright infringement than non-literal copying. Nevertheless, this part of the judgment is of interest, as it suggests the general approach to be followed in relation to non-literal copying. As he continually stressed, the central question to be considered is whether the non-literal aspects of a work are detailed enough to be copyright works rather than just 'general ideas'. One would then make an assessment of how significant the part copied is to the program as a whole.

The issue of how to assess whether a substantial part of a program has been copied remains the main practical difficulty in cases of this type. As Jacob J made clear in the *Ibcos* case, the courts have to place significant reliance on expert evidence when considering this issue. This itself can create some difficulties. In the *Ibcos Computers v Barclays Mercantile* case, Jacob J was clearly confident that he could rely on the plaintiffs' expert and indeed was quite dismissive of the defendants' experts. By contrast in the *John Richardson* case, Ferris J did not feel able to make such a clear choice between the experts' reports. Moreover, he had great difficulty in understanding what could have been crucial evidence in the experts' reports regarding the copying of source code. If the courts are going to have to rely on experts to this extent, consideration may have to be given as to whether it would not be

---

[11] *Ibid.* at 18. These comments were in particular aimed at the interlocutory judgment in *Total Information Systems v Daman*, Note 2 above, at 179, in which the court had denied copyright protection to the program as a compilation and stressed that when there is only one way of expressing an idea it was not the subject of copyright.

better for the court to appoint its own experts, as increasingly happens in the United States.[12]

Conclusion

There is nothing surprising or novel in the judgment in *Ibcos Computers v Barclays Mercantile*. Jacob J just applied the basic principles of UK copyright law to the facts of the case. This was a relatively straightforward exercise, owing to the overwhelming evidence of substantial copying of the source code of ADS. Nevertheless the decision is of considerable importance. It emphasises the ways in which UK copyright law differs from US copyright law and reaffirms the basic principles of UK copyright law as applied to computer software. In passing it also provides some guidance regarding the analysis of on-literal copying of computer programs. In an area of law which has been dominated by complex and occasionally contradictory judgments this clarity of approach is particularly welcome.

---

[12] The value of a court-appointed expert was particularly clear in *Computer Associates v Altai*. Under Order 40 RSC, the UK courts can appoint an expert to report on questions of fact or opinion, but this rarely occurs in practice. Alternatively, actions can be commenced or transferred from the court to the Official Referees who have greater experience of dealing with technical disputes.

Copyright Protection for Titles, Character Names and Catch-phrases in the Film and Television Industry

[1996] 5 ENT.L.R. 178

REUBEN STONE
University of Wales, Aberystwyth

Few would doubt the marketing potential represented by a well-chosen advertising slogan. In this sense, the entertainment business is no different from any other in the commercial sphere. The popular appeal of most successful films and other works is undoubtedly enhanced by certain key words and phrases which have come to be associated by the public with those works. Indeed, the choice of a title is likely to be a matter of market research even prior to a film's release.[1]

In the motion picture industry, titles have been treated as commodities to be bought and sold like any other. It is unknown for a film company to purchase what it regards as the rights to a title alone quite independent of the work from which it is derived.[2] There is also a long tradition by which song titles have been traded for use in films of the same name. 'Alexander's Ragtime Band' and 'With a Song in my Heart ' are examples among many.[3]

An indication that there may be legal pitfalls associated with the use of titles is provided by the fact that Errors and Omissions ('E & O') insurance policies generally require a producer to conduct a special title search.[4] E & O insurance normally covers intellectual property related risks (among others)[5] encountered during production and exploitation of a film or television programme. Title searches may be conducted at the Library of Congress in Washington DC but it is usual to appoint a specialised research firm for this purpose such as Thompson & Thompson or Brylawski, Cleary & Leeds. A title report should reveal whether there are any US copyright works which utilise the words in question. Such a report may well also reveal the existence of copyright works of non-US origin.[6] Consequently, an indication is provided as to whether the adoption by a producer of a certain title would be

---

[1] See, for instance, Squire (ed.), *The Movie Business Book*, Simon & Schuster, 1992 (2nd edn), at 295; Kurtz, 'Protection for Titles of Literary Works in the Public Domain', (1984) 37 *Rutgers Law Review* 53, at 53. Kurtz mentions as examples how titles were chosen for the films 'Jaws II' and 'The China Syndrome'.

[2] The title 'Heaven can Wait' was sold separately from the play of the same name; and the book *Sex and the Single Girl* was, in effect, purchased for the use of its title by Warner Brothers for $200,000. Refer to Bernstein, 'Who Owns the Audio Visual Work?', [1991] 14 *Copyright World* 40, at 43.

[3] Shemel and Krasilovsky, *This Business of Music*, Billboard Books, 1990 (6th edn), at 152 and 370; Halliwell, *Halliwell's Filmgoers and Video Viewers Companion*, Grafton Books, 1988 (9th edn), also provides a number of examples under 'song titles'.

[4] See, for instance: Baker, *Media Law: A User's Guide for Film and Programme Makers*, Chapman & Hall, 1995 at 196 to 200 and 203 to 204; Angel, 'Legal Protection for Titles in the Entertainment Industry', (1979) 52 *Southern California Law Review* 279, at 307.

[5] Such insurances also cover risks associated with defamation, breach of confidence, passing off, unfair competition and breach of an individual's right of privacy or publicity. These last three heads are not strictly of significance so far as legal action within the United Kingdom is concerned.

[6] See Bernstein, Note 2 above, at 43.

likely to lead to a dispute. If necessary it is also possible to trace the use of particular words or phrases by conducting searches at the trade mark registries of appropriate jurisdictions.

It is therefore recognised that legal disputes may arise if title clearances are not obtained from relevant third parties. For this reason, it is advisable for film and television producers to refer in early production-related documentation to their chosen title as being only tentative or provisional in nature. Such a precaution could serve to defeat any later claim that non-use of the planned title in the final product amounts to a breach of contractual obligations.[7]

Once a potential third party litigant is identified in a search of the kind described, the process of obtaining clearances is a logical next step. It is likely that this procedure will involve dealing directly with rightsholders but there is also the possibility that the rightsholder will have appointed an organisation to act on its behalf. The Licensing Corporation of America ('LCA'), owned by Warner Brothers, is a prominent example of such a concern. It acts as an agent in the licensing of rights to names, photographs, fictional characters, logos and the like.[8]

While on the subject of Warner Brothers, it may be appropriate to mention the legendary dispute which arose over the use of the title 'Casablanca'. During the filming of the Marx Brothers comedy 'A Night in Casablanca' the production team received an ominous letter. Jack L. Warner, the head of Warner Brothers, was threatening to sue over what he regarded as a blatant attempt to capitalise, by the choice of title, on the success of the classic 1942 film starring Humphrey Bogart and Ingrid Bergman. Groucho Marx responded by pointing out that the Marx Brothers had been in business longer than Warners, and that if Warners persisted in using the word 'Brothers' in their company name then Marx would sue *them*. Needless to say, Jack Warner quietly dropped the matter.[9]

The above points and examples would seem to demonstrate a widespread assumption in the business community that there is some kind of property right in titles, phrases or even (as in the last instance) words. In reality, that view is usually at best an exaggeration and at worst a falsity. This article aims to provide an assessment of the copyright status of brief literary phrases[10] in the United Kingdom with an emphasis on the special circumstances applicable to film and television productions. Where appropriate, parallels will be drawn with the position in the United States. It should be noted that protection for literary phrases in the United Kingdom may also be available under the Trade Marks Act 1994 and under the law of passing off.[11]

Titles

It is often stated that there can be no copyright in something so trifling as a mere title. The same strand of reasoning is also deemed to rule out the existence of such a right in short literary phrases and character names; but how accurate a statement of the law is it to say that copyright protection can never extend to cover these circumstances?

The earlier English cases are contradictory. In *Weldon v Dicks*[12] the plaintiffs successfully claimed copyright in the title 'Trial and Triumph'. Lord Malins VC also indicated, *obiter*,

---

[7] See Baker, Note 4 above, at 52.

[8] See Wasko, *Hollywood in the Information Age*, University of Texas Press, 1995, at 51.

[9] The story is noted in Chesterman and Lipman, *The Electronic Pirates—DIY Crime of the Century*, Routledge, 1988, at 3 and by Angel, Note 4 above, at 294.

[10] In this article, the expression 'literary phrase' is taken to mean any sequence of words which exists either by itself or as part of a larger work. It is assumed that literary phrases may appear not only in literary works themselves but also in other types of work such as films and sound recordings.

[11] Readers might wish to refer to the author's further articles to be published on these subjects.

[12] [1878] Ch. 247.

that a similar conclusion might be reached in respect of Thackeray's title 'Vanity Fair'. Despite this decision, it was held in *Dicks v Yates*[13] that no copyright could subsist in the title 'Splendid Misery'. Sir George Jessel MR observed that these words were a 'hackneyed and common combination'[14] which did not merit protection. Since much the same thing could be said of 'Trial and Triumph' and 'Vanity Fair' these two early decisions are difficult to reconcile. In *Francis Day & Hunter Ltd v Twentieth Century Fox Film Corp.*[15] the plaintiffs, who were the copyright owners of the song 'The Man who Broke the Bank at Monte Carlo', objected to the use of the title of their number in a film of the same name. Neither the words nor the lyrics were included in the film. The Privy Council ruled that there was no reason in law why the defendants should not adopt the words for their film because (among other holdings) the title was not protected by copyright. Lord Wright observed that:

> In general a title is not by itself a proper subject matter of copyright. As a rule a title does not involve literary composition, and is not sufficiently substantial to justify a claim to protection. That statement does not mean that in particular cases a title may not be on so extensive a scale, and of so important a character as to be a proper subject of protection against being copied.[16]

The rationale of this judgment, and indeed that of others on this point, is perhaps questionable. First, is it accurate to state that a title does not as a rule involve literary composition? Second, Lord Wright indicates that as a rule a literary title will not be 'sufficiently substantial' to merit protection although allowance is made for particular cases in which a title may be 'on so extensive a scale, and of so important a character, as to be a proper subject of protection'. This seems to describe a standard for protection of a rather demanding order. As shall be seen, it may be argued that such an approach is currently neither necessary in law nor desirable.

It should be noted that *Dicks v Yates* and *Francis Day v Hunter v Twentieth Century Fox* (an appeal to the Privy Council from Canada) were decided on the basis of whether a title was capable of being the subject of copyright under the definition of 'book' given in section 2 of the Copyright Act 1842.[17] Those cases do not therefore directly address the question of whether a title may be regarded as an 'original literary work' which was the expression used in the Copyright Acts of 1911[18] and 1956[19] and which also appears in the current statute, the Copyright, Designs and Patents Act ('CDPA') 1988.[20]

Invented Words

In *Exxon Corporation v Exxon Insurance Ltd*,[21] the plaintiffs sought to restrain the defendant from using in connection with its business the name 'Exxon'. This word had been invented by the plaintiffs to denominate their own business. It was held that, while the defendant was

---

[13] [1881] Ch. 6.
[14] *Ibid.*, at 88.
[15] [1940] AC 112.
[16] *Ibid.*, at 123.
[17] A 'book' is there defined as 'every volume, part or division of volume, pamphlet, sheet of letterpress, sheet of music, map, chart or plan separately published'.
[18] Section 1(1).
[19] Section 2(1).
[20] Section 1(1)(a).
[21] [1982] Ch. 119.

not entitled to engage in passing off, no-one could prevent the name 'Exxon' being used by claiming infringement of copyright alone.

The essential issue in the case was whether an invented word of the kind in question was subject to protection as an 'original literary work' under section 2(1) of the (now repealed) Copyright Act 1956. Graham J, at first instance, whose judgment was quoted at length and with approval in the Court of Appeal, observed that the word 'original' had been given a broad interpretation by the courts.[22] He cited the dictum of Lord Pearce in *Ladbroke (Football) Ltd v William Hill (Football) Ltd*: 'The word "original" does not demand original or inventive thought, but only that the work should not be copied but should originate with the author.'[23] Graham J was of the opinion that 'if a word is invented, it must, for practical purposes, be considered as original'.[24] The plaintiffs had in fact adduced some evidence of the research and effort which had been directed by them towards inventing an effective corporate name.

Perhaps the most contentious issue was whether the word 'Exxon' could be regarded as a 'literary work'. Stephenson LJ, echoing the words of Davey LJ in *Hollinrake v Truswell*,[25] states:

> I would have thought, unaided or unhampered by authority, that unless there is something in the context of the Act which forbids it, a literary work would be something which was intended to afford either information and instruction, or pleasure in the form of literary enjoyment, whatever those last six words may add to the word 'pleasure'.[26]

The Court of Appeal therefore perhaps went further than Graham J who was of the view that the word 'literary should not be read 'in a narrow sense so as to be confined, for example, to material having a high intellectual quality or style of writing'.[27] It could be argued that Stephenson LJ's view is inconsistent with the decision of the House of Lords in *Ladbroke*,[28] a decision which upheld copyright protection for football coupons. In that case, Lord Pearce states that the words 'literary work' are 'used to describe work which is expressed in print or writing irrespective of whether it has any excellence of quality or style of writing'.[29]

The word 'literary' has been defined in the *Shorter Oxford English Dictionary* as that 'pertaining to the letters of the alphabet'.[30] More recently, the word 'literary' has been stated to mean 'of, constituting, occupied with literature or books and written composition especially of the kind valued for quality of form'.[31] In turn, 'literature' has been defined as meaning 'writing whose value lies in beauty of form or emotional effect'.[32] Admittedly, these later definitions imply the existence of some kind of threshold which needs to be reached in order for a collection of words to be regarded as literature or as being literary in nature. However, it is possible to argue that, in law, such a requirement has no relevance.

Section 3(1) of the CDPA 1988 states that a 'literary work' means '*any work*, other than a dramatic or musical work, which is *written*, spoken or sung ...' (*emphasis added*). There is

---

[22] *Ibid.*, at 128.
[23] [1964] 1 WLR 273, at 291.
[24] *Exxon*, Note 21 above, at 128.
[25] [1894] 3 Ch. 420, at 427.
[26] *Exxon*, Note 21 above, at 143.
[27] *Ibid.*, at 129.
[28] Note 23 above.
[29] *Ibid.*, at 291.
[30] *Shorter Oxford English Dictionary*, 1944 (3rd edn).
[31] *Concise Oxford English Dictionary*, 1982 (7th edn).
[32] *Ibid.*

no apparent threshold, either quantitative or qualitative, in the definition. It is therefore tempting to regard this latest provision as a change in the law clearly enabling the protection of titles.[33] However, that interpretation may be inappropriate in view of section 172(2) of the CDPA 1988 which states that provisions of the Act corresponding to provisions of the previous law shall not be construed as departing from the previous law merely because of a change of expression.

The Public Interest in Freedom of Expression

If the courts were to sanction the protection of invented words (or, indeed, short literary phrases and titles) there would be a danger that the public interest might be jeopardised. At first sight, the rights of a copyright owner would appear to be stronger than those possessed by the owner of a registered or unregistered trade mark. A copyright owner has the exclusive right[34] to do a wide range of acts. Those are:

(a) to copy the work in question;
(b) to issue copies of the work to the public;
(c) to perform, show or play the work in public;
(d) to broadcast the work or include it in a cable programme service;
(e) to make an adaptation of the work or to do any of the above in relation to an adaptation.[35]

The owner of a registered or unregistered trade mark, on the other hand, cannot assert rights in the same broad circumstances.[36]

In addition, it may be noted that the statutory fair dealing exceptions of the CDPA 1988[37] could operate unfairly against users of copyright works in these situations. As an initial matter, to suggest that the taking of an entire work could be a 'fair dealing' within the Act seems contrary to authority.[38] This is awkward because it would, in fact, be difficult not to take the entire work if that work was merely a word. Consider section 30(1) of the Act. It states that 'fair dealing with a work for the purpose of criticism or review, of that or another work or of a performance of a work, does not infringe any copyright in the work provided that it is accompanied by a sufficient acknowledgement'. The complication here is that any criticism or review which occurs will not be in connection with the word as a work in itself but, rather, in connection with the larger work in which the word appears. Interestingly, the way in which this section is framed apparently allows for this activity since the criticism or review may be directed at 'another work'. However, the result would still be a strange one since any fair dealing with the word would require a 'sufficient acknowledgement'. This would mean that an acknowledgement would need to be made of the work's 'title or other description' and of the work's 'author'.[39] For a mere word, this is a requirement of a rather high order.

---

[33] Interestingly, artistic works do not necessarily require a demanding standard of artistry in order to fall within the meaning of section 4(1) of the CDPA 1988. The provision defines an 'artistic work' as meaning '(a) a graphic work, photograph, sculpture or collage, irrespective of artistic quality, (b) a work of architecture being a building or a model for a building, or (c) a work of artistic craftsmanship.' Refer to text accompanying notes 116 to 120.
[34] Section 12(1) CDPA 1988.
[35] Section 16(1) CDPA 1988.
[36] See Note 11 above.
[37] Sections 29 and 30.
[38] See, for instance, Lord Denning's judgment in *Hubbard v Vosper* [1972] 2 QB 84.
[39] Section 178 CDPA 1988.

In view of the public policy concerns, Harris J. in the *Exxon* case[40] requested the assistance of the Attorney General. Help was provided in the form of an *amicus curiae*. The case against protection for invented words was, and remains, essentially that such protection would have a chilling effect on freedom of expression. If a word can be regarded in law as an 'original literary work' then it ceases to be part of the public domain and comes within the exclusive control of an individual person (albeit for a limited period of time). It may be argued that this approach, if adopted under English law, would stultify the growth of the language. The fear is that invented words could, in both a metaphorical and literal sense, be barred from the dictionary and that even existing words might, in effect, be rendered unusable through inclusion in newly protected literary phrases.

However, it may be that the dangers of protectionism have been exaggerated. The law of copyright is equipped with other safeguards to insure against abuse by those in whom rights are vested. Even in the absence of an express licence between plaintiff and defendant the courts may deem the activities of a defendant in relation to a copyright work to be permissible on the basis of an *implied* licence. In *Redwood Music Ltd v Chappell & Co. Ltd*[41] it was said that such a licence would exist if 'viewing the facts objectively, the words and conduct of the alleged licensor, as made known to the alleged licensee, in fact indicated that the licensor consented to what the licensee was doing'.[42] It seems that this test might be satisfied in circumstances where a company logo or design is used by a person as a shorthand means of referring to that company.[43] Indeed, even Stephenson LJ in the *Exxon* case hypothesised that, if an invented word were to be the subject of copyright, a company such as *Exxon* would clearly have 'impliedly licensed the world to use this word properly'.[44] However, this rather begs the question as to just what may be regarded as a proper use. In short, how far should an implied licence be deemed to extend? If an organisation is able to suppress adverse criticism of its products or services merely by invoking principles of copyright then there is clearly a serious public policy issue at stake. On the other hand, to suggest that an organisation licenses such criticism simply on the basis of conducting business under its name seems to stretch the established consensual concept of implied licences described in *Redwood Music* (above). A further problem with regard to licences of this kind is that, if they are granted gratuitously and without consideration (which would appear to be the case in these circumstances), they are vulnerable to the risk of being revoked at short notice.[45]

Many of the same considerations would apply to the public's use of invented words originally incorporated in a company's films or other audio-visual products. Perhaps the most controversial issue would be whether such a company could object to uses of its literary property which are regarded by the company as derogatory of its work but which do no discernible damage to the commercial value of the property. Parodies tend to illustrate this conflict rather well.

Unless it were significantly extended by the courts the implied licence theory would evidently not provide the public in these cases with a sufficient buffer against an assertive copyright owner. It is perhaps surprising that more was not made of this specific point in *Exxon*. However, Harris J in that case did state that it would be undesirable if, for instance,

---

[40] Note 21 above.

[41] [1982] RPC 109.

[42] *Ibid.*, at 128.

[43] *Peninsular & Oriental Steam Navigation Co. v Trafalgar House plc*, noted in [1983] 9 EIPR D-188. The plaintiffs were refused summary judgment over their claim that the use of the P & O flag logo in a share capital offer document amounted to an infringement of copyright. The defendants were given leave to defend the action on the basis that their implied licence theory (in particular) amounted to an arguable defence.

[44] Note 21 above, at 144.

[45] *Hart v Hayman* [1911–6] MacGillivray's CC 301.

the Bishop of Exeter could be sued for placing the letters 'Exxon' after his name.[46] It has been observed[47] that this particular example does not take account of the fact that the Bishop could not have copied the letters from the company, a condition which would need to be satisfied in order to establish infringement.[48] Nevertheless, the underlying concern which Harris J articulates here is a legitimate one. The public interest in freedom of expression should not be shackled by the courts unless there is some fair commercial reason, on the part of the copyright owner, for doing so.

As a practical matter, it is worth bearing in mind that the laws relating to registered and unregistered trade marks may well offer a more straightforward means for the originator of a mark to control the uses to which that mark may be put by other persons.[49]

It has in fact been contended that copyright protection for individual words would be inappropriate where those words are registrable as trade or service marks or where the words are capable of forming the subject of a passing off action.[50] The premise is presumably that, if words or literary phrases are subject to these very different legal principles at the same time, the protection afforded will be excessive and therefore damaging to the public interest. This does not necessarily follow. The English courts have never previously insisted that separate doctrines must apply to the facts on a mutually exclusive basis.[51] However, experience in the United States has shown that there is a price to be paid in terms of certainty if the borders between separate intellectual property concepts are allowed to be blurred. The phenomenon has been described as 'convergence'.[52] It has been observed to occur where judges are dealing with copyright, trade mark and unfair competition issues in the same case. For instance there has, in certain instances, been a tendency to reject the copyright test of substantial similarity in favour of the trade mark test of likelihood of confusion as to source in circumstances where the copyright doctrine ought strictly to apply. Despite these possible complications, the answer to the risk of uncertainty in the law should really lie in the exercise of judicial restraint and not in the adoption of the kind of mutually exclusive policies described earlier.

Invented Words in the Context of Film and Television Productions

It may be helpful to mention briefly at this point the American case of *Life Music Inc. v Wonderland Music Co.*[53] The dispute concerned the word 'Supercalafragilisticexpialidocious' which was claimed to be an infringement of the plaintiff's word 'Super-calafajalistickespeealadojus'. Unfortunately, since an interlocutory injunction was denied, the case provides no real guidance on the copyright status of this most interesting example.

---

[46] Note 21 above, at 130.

[47] See, for instance: Cullabine, 'Copyright in Short Phrases and Single Words', [1992] 6 EIPR 205, at 207.

[48] Note, for instance, the comments of Lord Wilberforce in *L.B. (Plastics) Ltd v Swish Products Ltd* [1979] FSR 145, at 149. In terms of section 11(3) of the Trade Marks Act 1994, the Bishop's use of the letters 'Exon' might be excused as the exercise of an 'earlier right'. For the purpose of a passing off action by the owners of the *Exxon* mark, a parallel conclusion might be that the Bishop's continued adoption of the letters 'Exon' would be an honest concurrent use. See, for instance: *Pete Waterman Ltd v CBS (United Kingdom) Ltd* [1993] EMLR 27; *Anheuser Busch Inc. v Budejovicky Budvar NP* [1984] FSR 397.

[49] See Note 11 above.

[50] Refer to the comments of Harris J in *Exxon*. Note 21 above, at 130 and 131 regarding the views of John Mummery as *amicus curiae* for the Attorney General.

[51] *Karo Step Trade Mark* [1977] RPC 255 (trade marks and copyright); *Sobrefina SA's Application* [1974] RPC 672 (registered design and trade mark); *Schweppes Ltd v Wellingtons Ltd* [1984] FSR 210 (trade marks and copyright); see also the comments of Stephenson LJ in *Exxon*, Note 21 above, at 144.

[52] See Helfand, 'When Mickey Mouse is as Strong as Superman: The Convergence of Intellectual Property Laws to Protect Fictional Literary and Pictorial Characters', (1992) 44 Stanford LR 623, at 623.

[53] (1965) 241 Fed. Supp. 653.

However, the court recognised that liability for copyright infringement in the plaintiffs' word would be 'conceivable' on different facts. It is difficult to think of a more deserving candidate for protection than this 14 syllable creation.

Most such words would be far shorter than the one at issue in the above dispute. Apart from their possible application in songs, perhaps a more likely context in which to find created words in the entertainment world is within the genre of science fiction or fantasy stories. Films and television programmes such as those of the *Star Trek®* series, for instance, owe much of their appeal to the imaginary places and alien creatures on which the plots are based. Can the invented names of imaginary places and creatures be protected by copyright? Under English law, such names would appear to fall under the shadow of *Exxon*; that is, they might not be regarded in law as 'literary works'. However, it is just conceivable that the courts might now adopt a more flexible attitude. If the apparently broader definition of literary works given in section 3(1) of the CDPA 1988 (that is, 'any work' ... which is written, spoken or sung') were to be given full effect, as previously described, then the kinds of names in question would be protectible.[54]

Nevertheless, it must strongly be suspected that the courts will continue to insist on some minimum threshold beneath which invented words will not qualify for protection. Even in the case of two or three invented words rather than one, it would probably still be necessary to ask whether those words, taken as a whole, pass a *de minimis* standard. Under English law, the most likely existing source for such a standard is the *Exxon* case. Do the names in question possess 'substance and meaning' as Harris J implied they should?[55] Or can they be said to provide 'pleasure in the form of literary enjoyment' according to Stephenson LJ's more demanding test?[56] Although invented words often have a certain linguistic appeal, it seems likely that they would not satisfy the above criteria.

Character Names

In addition, there are a number of English cases which have indicated that character names both invented and non-invented cannot usually be the subject of copyright. In *Wombles Ltd v Wombles Skips Ltd*,[57] copyright in the word 'Wombles' (describing the television characters of that name) was denied. Similarly, in *Tavener Rutledge Ltd v Trexapalm Ltd*[58] the name 'Kojak' was said to be incapable of copyright protection. However, these particular cases should be viewed with caution. They both, essentially concerned issues of passing off, were decided by the same judge, and the matter of copyright was considered only on a peripheral basis. Having said this, the view that character names, as such, are not protectable under English law has been expressed elsewhere.[59] In the United States, by contrast, it may well be possible to enforce a copyright in a name given favourable circumstances.[60]

---

[54] See, however, the Canadian case of *Preston v Twentieth Century Fox*, 9 November 1990, reported in [1991] 3 EIPR D-41: no copyright in the invented species name 'Ewok'. Nevertheless, it may be noted that the name 'Ewok' is a registered trade mark of Lucasfilm Ltd and is therefore protectible as such.

[55] Exxon, Note 21 above, at 130.

[56] *Ibid.*, at 143.

[57] [1977] RPC 99, at 102.

[58] [1977] RPC 275, at 278.

[59] *Burberrys v J.C. Cording & Co. Ltd* (1909) 26 RPC 693. Parker J, at 701 states: 'apart from the law as to trademarks, no one can claim monopoly rights in the use of a word or name'; *O'Neill v Paramount Pictures Corporation* [1983] Court of Appeal (Civil Division) Transcripts 235, reported in (1984) 134 NLJ 338—no copyright recognised in the name 'James Bond'. See comments of May LJ at 339.

[60] *Universal City Studios Inc. v Kamar Industries Inc.*, 217 USPQ (BNA) 1162 (SD Tex. 1982): character name 'E.T.' protected under copyright; *Edgar Rice Burroughs, Inc. v Manns Theatres*, 195 USPQ (BNA) 159 (CD Cal. 1976): suggests the name 'Tarzan' is protectible.

Existing Words of the Lexicon

Clearly, much of what has been said earlier concerning invented words will equally be applicable to the protection or otherwise of literary phrases containing words which are already defined by existing languages. There are, however, certain distinctions which might be drawn.

First, the policy arguments against allowing the protection of invented words tend to become more compelling still where common dictionary ones are concerned. At least in the former instance the public at large would not be deprived the use of a previously unprotected word. In the latter case, by contrast, there is a clear danger that existing modes of expression could be snatched from the public domain.

Second, the copyright status of a short sequence of this kind could be challenged not only on the grounds that it might not constitute a 'literary work' but also on the basis of a possible lack of 'originality'. While invented words are, by their nature, original, words in common linguistic usage will presumably require a more demanding level of juxtaposition in order to meet the originality standard. In *Ladbroke*,[61] Lord Devlin stated: 'The requirement of originality means that the product must originate from the author in the sense that it is the result of a substantial degree of skill, industry or experience employed by him.' This interpretation appears to be relatively demanding of the author but the originality standard is not generally regarded as difficult to surmount. Lord Hodson, in the same case, suggested that the standard would be met provided that 'more than negligible skill and labour' had been employed.[62] Furthermore, as noted earlier, Lord Pearce stated: 'The word "original" does not demand original or inventive thought, but only that the work should not be copied but should originate from the author.'[63] Considerations of this kind were no doubt behind the older decision of *Broemel v Meyer*[64] in which it was held that there could be no copyright in the expression 'Where there's a will there's a way'. The plaintiff's phrase was copied from the familiar saying.

However, it was suggested by Judge Frank in the American case of *Heim v Universal Pictures Co., Inc.*[65] that the level of originality required for the protection of short phrases should be higher than that for conventional literary works. It has also been said by Professor Nimmer that 'there is a reciprocal relationship between creativity and independent effort. The smaller the effort [in a quantitative sense] the greater must be the degree of creativity in order to claim copyright protection.'[66] These comments are, in a sense, an indirect way of framing the public policy concerns associated with protecting mere words and phrases.

Judicial and academic statements of this kind appear to be at odds with the official line taken by the US Copyright Office which has consistently denied the existence of copyright in 'words and short phrases such as names, titles and slogans.'[67] Although these guidelines do not strictly have the force of law, they have by and large been endorsed by the courts.[68]

---

[61] Note 23 above, at 289.
[62] *Ibid.*, at 287.
[63] *Ibid.*, at 291. In the American decision of *Feist Publications, Inc. v Rural Telephone Service Co.*, 111 S Ct 1282 (1991), the US Supreme Court ruled that some minimal degree of creativity is required for a work of authorship to qualify for protection. A compilation of facts consisting of mere raw data (in this case, a telephone directory) would be insufficient in that respect. The case if of limited persuasive authority in the United Kingdom in view of the fact that the creativity requirement was held to be constitutionally mandated.
[64] [1911–6] MacGillivray's CC 56.
[65] 154 F. 2d 480 (2d Cir. 1946) at 488.
[66] Nimmer, *Nimmer on Copyright*, Matthew Bender & Co., 1994, at 2.01[B].
[67] See, for example, 37 Code of Federal Regulations section 202.1(a)(1994); US Copyright Office Circular 34 (1995).
[68] *Warner Brothers Pictures v Majestic Pictures Corp.*, 70 F. 2d 310 (2d Cir. 1934); *Becker v Loew's Inc.*, 133 F. 2d

Nevertheless, there have been instances where judges have adopted a more flexible line.[69]

As with invented words, however, the question remains whether, under English law, conventional titles or slogans and the like technically can amount to 'literary works'. It is not particularly helpful to read judicial statements to the effect that titles consisting of a whole page of writing would be protected[70] or that elaborate headings written in English, German and Spanish would also qualify.[71] Such titles, if applied to most modern entertainment products, would be hopelessly cumbersome in promotional terms.

If one were to apply the test of whether the words in question are 'intended to afford either information and instruction or pleasure in the form of literary enjoyment'[72] then the scope for titles as literary works would be very limited. However, that test has not been enthusiastically received.[73] If, on the other hand, the correct approach is represented by a literal interpretation of section 3(1) of the CDPA 1988 (a 'literary work' means 'any work ... which is written') then the net is thrown wider.[74] In order to lift a title above the merely trivial or *de minimis* level, a court might take note of the exercise of skill or labour in its creation. For instance, the title 'Green Dolphin Country'[75] falls easily from the lips and has a pleasant, soothing effect on the ear as does 'On Golden Pond'.[76] 'Blame it on the Bell Boy'[77] achieves a certain impact through alliteration as does 'The Wizard of Oz'.[78]

However, it becomes difficult to separate the literary work issue from that of originality when dealing, as above, with quantitatively small groups of words. Many of those qualities which are characteristic of a literary work are also likely to support claims that the work is original. Conversely, those qualities which are not characteristic of literary works will equally tend to undermine a claim of originality. In *Sinanide v La Maison Kosmeo*[79] the court ruled that there was no copyright in the slogan 'Beauty is a social necessity not a luxury'. Although this case could be cited as evidence of what may or may not be regarded as a 'literary work', it is also possible to view it as an instance where the required standard of originality was not met. The court was no doubt influenced by the fact that the similar phrase 'A youthful appearance is a modern necessity' had previously been publicised by other advertisers.[80]

Literary phrases may exist by themselves or as elements of other works. It is even more important to ask what qualifies as 'original' and what qualifies as a 'literary work' in the case of lone phrases since they cannot rely for their protection on the copyright in a larger work. While a catch-phrase can usually be said to be part of the literary work from which it is derived, the same is not necessarily true of an advertising slogan. Where films are concerned, examples of such slogans might include 'Just when You Thought it was Safe to go Back in

---

889 (7th Cir.), *cert. denied*, 319 US 772 (1943); *Tomlin v Walt Disney Productions*, 18 Cal. App. 3d 226, 96 Cal. Rptr 118 (1972); *Arnstein v Porter*, 154 F. 2d 464 (2d Cir. 1946); *Patten v Superior Talking Pictures*, 8 F. Supp. 196 (SDNY 1934).

[69] *Heim v Universal Pictures Co.*, Note 65 above; *Universal City Studios, Inc. v Kamar*, Note 60 above.

[70] *Dicks v Yates* [1881] Ch. 6, at 89 per Sir George Jessel MR.

[71] *Lamb v Evans* [1893] 1 Ch. 218.

[72] *Per* Stephenson LJ in *Exxon*, Note 21 above, at 143.

[73] See, for instance, Dworkin & Taylor, *Blackstone's Guide to the Copyright Designs and Patents Act 1988*, Blackstone Press, 1989, at 21.

[74] See main text accompanying Note 33 above for an explanation of section 3(1) of the CDPA 1988 on this point.

[75] Novel by Elizabeth Goudge, Hodder & Stoughton, 1944; a film called 'Green Dolphin Street', based on the book, was released in 1947.

[76] Best known as the film released in 1981 starring Henry Fonda and Katharine Hepburn (based on a play by Ernest Thompson).

[77] Film released in 1992 starring Dudley Moore and Patsy Kensit.

[78] Written by L. Frank Baum. A well known film based on the story and starring Judy Garland was released in 1939.

[79] (1928) 44 TLR 574.

[80] See also *Broemel v Meyer*, Note 64 above; *Rose v Information Services* [1987] FSR 254 can be interpreted in a similar way. In that case it was held that there could be no copyright in the title 'Lawyers Diary 1986'.

the Water' ('Jaws')[81] and 'In Space no one can Hear You Scream' ('Alien').[82] They form no part of the scripts, as such, but phrases of this kind capture something of the ethos of a film. They also tend, on the whole, to be more substantial than titles in qualitative and quantitative terms and therefore their potential for protection is generally greater.

Words and Phrases as Elements of Larger Works

Up to this point it has been considered whether words and literary phrases are, in and of themselves, capable of being protected by copyright. There is, however, another way of looking at most situations of this kind. Many words and phrases can be regarded as being an element of a larger group of words ('Exxon', being a company name, is an exception). If that larger group of words amounts to a literary work a further possible solution presents itself. The question then becomes whether the complained of use of the words or phrases is an infringement of copyright in the larger work.

In *Exxon*, Harris J, at first instance, provided some helpful guidance on this. He took as an example the poem 'Jabberwocky' appearing in Lewis Carroll's book *Through the Looking Glass*. The title of this poem apparently refers to the invented name of an imaginary monster. Harris J, hypothesising that the work was still in copyright, suggested that it was 'just conceivable' that the use of the words 'Jabberwock' or 'Jabberwocky' in a literary context might be held to be an infringement of copyright in the poem as a whole.[83] However, the judge also indicated that had Lewis Carroll never written the poem but had merely invented the name 'Jabberwocky', no-one could be prevented from copying the word. His reasoning was as follows:

> The word alone and by itself cannot properly be considered as a 'literary work', the subject of copyright under the Act [Copyright Act 1956]. It becomes part of a 'literary work' within the Act when it is embodied in the poem, but it is the poem as a composition which is a work within the Act and not the word itself.[84]

These comments appear to suggest that there may be a tactical advantage to be gained by arguing that individual words are part of a larger work rather than by claiming copyright in the words themselves. In short, it is not necessarily safe to assume that using a group of words cannot amount to an infringement merely because those words, taken alone, are unprotected.

The Copying of a Substantial Part

To refer to the phrasing of the CDPA 1988, it is relevant to ask, for present purposes, whether there has been a breach of the copyright owner's exclusive right to 'copy the work'.[85] 'Copying' in relation to a literary, dramatic, musical or artistic work means reproducing the work in any material form[86] and it is an infringement of copyright to copy, without the

---

[81] Directed by Steven Spielberg and released in 1975.
[82] Directed by Ridley Scott and released in 1979.
[83] *Exxon*, Note 21 above, at 131.
[84] *Ibid.*, at 132.
[85] Section 16(1)(a). It is also possible that there might be a breach of the other exclusive rights of the copyright owner. See generally, section 16.
[86] Section 17(2).

licence of the copyright owner, the work as a whole or any substantial part of it.[87] The determination of exactly what amounts to a substantial part of a work is a complex issue which has been the subject of many disputes.[88] It is a question which will clearly depend very much on the facts of the individual case. The courts have recognised, however, that it would be unreasonable to restrict the test of substantiality to a quantitative measure alone. Accordingly, an assessment will usually also be made of the qualitative significance of the material derived from the plaintiff's work in determining whether a substantial part of that work has been taken.[89]

Despite the existence of a quality test, it is not easy to avoid the conclusion that the larger the work in which copyright is claimed, the more difficult it will be to demonstrate that individual words within that work constitute a substantial part of it. Consider once again Harris J's illustration in *Exxon* involving 'Jabberwocky'.[90] Expanding on that illustration, even if the word 'Jabberwocky' can be regarded as a substantial part of the poem of that title it does not necessarily follow that the word is a substantial part of *Through the Looking Glass*, the book which contains the poem. Therefore, the plaintiff in these cases may face a 'Catch 22' scenario. On the one hand, if copyright is claimed in individual words, those words are likely to be held not to be literary works. On the other hand, if the words are treated as an element of a larger work, they are vulnerable to the charge of insubstantiality.

Public Recognition and its Relevance in Determining Substantiality

It may be that, in determining substantiality, more account should be taken of the wider circumstances in which the alleged copying occurs. In the American case of *Universal City Studios, Inc. v Kamar Industries, Inc.*,[91] it was ruled that the printing of the phrases 'E.T. Phone Home' and 'I Love E.T.' on drinking mugs, pencil sharpeners and other items could be an infringement of copyright. These phrases were protected because they would be 'readily recognisable to the lay observer as being key lines of dialogue from the copyrighted movie'.[92] In addition, it was said that the E.T. character, being central to the story, was itself protected. The name 'E.T.' was highly distinctive and its use would inevitably conjure up the image and appeal of the character.[93] Phrases including that name could therefore, by association, amount to an infringement of copyright in the character. This is a decision of surprising breadth. To protect sequences of this brevity under principles of copyright seems excessive. It may be noted that, in the film, the words used are not 'I Love E.T.' but 'I Love You E.T.'. Even 'E.T. Phone Home' is first heard in the script as 'E.T. Home Phone' although this is subsequently substituted for the familiar line. The fact that the court did not raise these points suggests that it was more concerned with the taking of the letters 'E.T.' than with the remainder of the phrases. Indeed, it seems inconceivable that a court would ever protect under copyright the expressions 'Phone Home' or 'I Love You' alone. That which is being protected here is therefore the association which has been built up in the collective mind of the public between common phrases on the one hand and the E.T. character on the other. This should not strictly be an issue of copyright. It is a matter more appropriate,

---

[87] Section 16(3)(a).
[88] *Francis Day & Hunter v Bron* [1963] Ch. 587; *EMI Music Publishing Ltd v Evangelos Papathanassiou* [1993] EMLR 308; *Ladbroke (Football) Ltd v William Hill (Football) Ltd* [1964] 1 WLR 273; *Ravenscroft v Herbert* [1980] RPC 193; *L.B. (Plastics) Ltd v Swish Products Ltd* [1979] FSR 145.
[89] See *Hawkes & Son*, Note 98 below, at 606; *L.B. (Plastics) Ltd*, Note 88 above, at 145.
[90] Refer to text accompanying notes 83 and 84 above.
[91] 217 USPQ (BNA) 1165 (SD Tex. 1982).
[92] *Ibid.*, at 1166. The film 'E.T.' was released in 1982 and directed by Steven Spielberg.
[93] *Ibid.*, at 1165.

depending on the jurisdiction, to the law of trade marks, passing off or unfair competition.[94]

Also curious is the fact that the court appeared to regard use of the phrases in question as an infringement of copyright in the E.T. character. Even if protection for characters is accepted, either in the form of artistic works or as fictional literary creations, it seems excessive to hold that the taking of a mere name is a breach of copyright in the character.[95]

It is interesting that the court placed such importance on the reputation which the E.T. character had acquired among the public. In a sense, this amounts to treating the level of public recognition as an element of the substantial similarity equation. If the makers of 'E.T.' sue another person for infringement of copyright in the film, they clearly have the advantage of having popularised the story and its elements. On the other hand, if a relatively obscure author were to write a story and sue the makers of a subsequently produced popular film, those same factors might operate to the author's disadvantage.[96]

It is suggested that the public recognition factor should not be accorded this level of importance. The law relating to trade marks is equipped to deal with many of the uses in the course of trade for which such recognition might be relevant.[97] The placing of copyright restrictions on short phrases which consist essentially of mere variations on common expressions therefore seems unnecessary and potentially endangers freedom of expression. This argument perhaps becomes a little less compelling in the case of notably original or ambitious phrases. In these instances public impact considerations may have more legitimacy. This is so because the response of the public is a useful indicator of the qualitative significance of the phrase.[98] Unfortunately, readers and audiences cannot always be trusted to discriminate between original and common expression. For instance, the question 'Who you gonna call?'[99] was, for a time at least, more famous than the proverb 'Once you start down the dark path, forever will it dominate your destiny'.[100] However, the second is clearly more likely to merit copyright protection than the first.

One problem which occasionally presents itself in the case of catch-phrases is that of distortion. The public may, through their own usage and repetition, change the original scripted phrase into something different. For instance, in 'Casablanca',[101] neither Humphrey Bogart nor Ingrid Bergman uttered the words 'Play It again Sam'. The expression actually used was simply 'Play It Sam'. Consider the more recent example of *Star Trek®*. In the original 1968 television series, Captain Kirk did not give the order 'Beam me up Scotty' and yet this quickly became the buzz phrase among fans. In fact, the evidence suggests that the creators of *Star Trek®* incorporated that particular sequence of words only at a later stage.[102]

---

[94] See Note 11 above. For an analysis of a series of hypothetical problems relating to uses of the phrase 'E.T. Phone Home', see Stim, 'E.T. Phone Home: The Protection of Literary Phrases', (1989) University of Miami Ent. & Sports LR 65.

[95] See, for example, Kurtz, 'The Independent Legal Lives of Fictional Characters', (1986) Wisconsin LR 429, at 461; however, see also *Edgar Rice Burroughs, Inc. v Manns Theatres*, 195 USPQ (BNA) 159 (CD Cal. 1976), concerning 'Tarzan', a case which can be read in a similar way to *Universal City Studios v Kamar*.

[96] See *Litchfield v Spielberg*, 736 F.2d 1352 (9th Cir. 1984), *cert. denied*, 470 US 1052 (1985). In that case, the plaintiff failed to persuade the court that the film 'E.T.' was an infringement of copyright in her story 'Lokey from Maldemar'. The story was in the form of a musical adventure featuring two stranded aliens called Lokey and Fudinkle.

[97] Refer to Note 11.

[98] See, for instance, *Hawkes & Son Ltd v Paramount Film Service Ltd* [1934] Ch. 593, at 606 per Slesser LJ concerning the reproduction by the defendant of an extract of 20 seconds from the military march 'Colonel Bogey'; 'anyone hearing it would know that it was the march "Colonel Bogey" and though it may be that it was not very prolonged in its reproduction, it is clearly, in my view, a substantial, a vital and an essential part which is there reproduced'.

[99] The words are derived from 'Ghostbusters', a film released in 1984.

[100] This is the warning given to Luke Skywalker by Yoda, the Jedi Master in the 1983 film 'Return of the Jedi'.

[101] Film released in 1942 and directed by Michael Curtiz.

[102] See Mark Edwards, 'Life as we (almost) Know it', *Sunday Times*, 7 November, 1993, at 11.

It is possible that the kind of distortion mentioned above could, in certain instances, cause some legal difficulty to producers wishing to establish a property right in a phrase.

Public Impact and Market Response under English Law

It has sometimes been recognised that a taking is more likely to be regarded as substantial if the works in question are competing with each other in the relevant market. This view is no doubt aimed primarily at those situations where the works as a whole are strikingly similar and rather less at situations where an isolated phrase has been lifted. Nevertheless, just what is meant by 'competition' in the cases is not entirely clear.[103] The concept would plainly cover the archetypal situation where, for example, two similar songs are vying with each other for the Number One spot in the Charts. However, consider the case of two separately produced films having vaguely similar story lines. Suppose that the later film is released a year after the earlier one and that the earlier film is continuing to earn revenue from its exploitation. If the second film is advertised using a well known catch-phrase from the first, can the makers of the first film sue those of the second for breach of copyright? If the public is misled or is likely to be misled into thinking that the makers of the first film were responsible for the second, then the competition factor could be said to favour the plaintiffs provided that the other criteria relevant to substantiality are also favourable to them.[104] In *Ravenscroft v Herbert*[105] a novel called *The Spear* was found to have infringed copyright in another work entitled *The Spear of Destiny*. Both works were based on the alleged mythical qualities of a lance. There were also other significant resemblances between the two books. In finding that an infringement had occurred, Brightman J took into account factors in addition to those similarities. He was of the view that, although *The Spear* was a work of fiction and *The Spear of Destiny* a semi-historical book, the two publications could be said to be in competition with each other.[106] This seems to be a very broad interpretation of that word. In the context of audio-visual media, it might by analogy be argued that a documentary could compete with a feature film. In the above hypothetical problem one would therefore certainly expect two feature films of the same genre to be capable of competing with each other. This would appear to be consistent with academic opinion in this area: in determining whether a substantial part of a work has been copied, it has been said that account should be taken of 'the degree to which the use may prejudice the sale, or diminish the profits, direct or indirect, or supersede the objects of the original work'.[107]

In *Ravenscroft v Herbert*,[108] Brightman J also mentioned a fourth factor which he regarded as contributing to the substantiality of the taking in that case: *animus furandi*.[109] This has previously been described as an intention on the part of a defendant to take for the purpose of saving himself labour[110] It appears to be aimed at those takings which are performed

---

[103] Contrast, for instance, *Cambridge University Press v University Tutorial Press* [1897] RPC 340 and *Weatherby & Sons v International Horse Agency & Exchange Ltd* [1910] 2 Ch. 297.

[104] This hypothetical scenario is not unlike the facts of the American case, *Dawn Associates v Links*, 203 USPQ (BNA) 831 (ND Ill. 1978). In that case, the plaintiffs were able to obtain a preliminary injunction to stop the defendants using, to promote their film, the phrase 'When there is no room in hell ... the dead will walk the earth.' The words formed a part of the plaintiffs' script for the film 'The Night of the Living Dead' but the defendants' film itself bore no significant resemblances to that of the plaintiffs.

[105] [1980] RPC 193.

[106] *Ibid.*, at 203 and 207.

[107] *Copinger & Skone James on Copyright*, Sweet & Maxwell, 1991 (13th edn), at 175.

[108] Note 105 above.

[109] *Ibid.*, at 203 and 207.

[110] *Per* Lord Page Wood VC in *Jarrold v Houston* (1857) 3 K & J 708. See also, *Copinger & Skone James on Copyright*, Note 107 above, at 175.

deliberately rather than, for instance, by accident or subconsciously.[111] However, most copying would be regarded as deliberate.[112] In the case of literary phrases which are appropriated, the intention is perhaps not so much to save labour as to capitalise on the goodwill in the phrase built up by its originator.

It could be argued that competition and *animus furandi* should be irrelevant to the matter of infringement. They are issues which are, in a sense, external to the question of whether a substantial part, in quantitative and qualitative terms, has been taken. The blatancy of the infringement, in the form of competition, *animus furandi* or other factors, should perhaps properly be taken into account only as to the issue of damages once infringement is established. Otherwise, there is a danger of conceptual uncertainty and convergence:[113] issues, such as goodwill and market impact, which should fall to be considered under the laws relating to trade marks and passing off will become elements of copyright infringement and the scope of protection under these doctrines will become unclear. Against this, it might be noted that many intellectual property disputes are disposed of at the interlocutory level. Since the questions at that stage are likely to be directed towards whether or not to grant injunctions, the issue of damages might never be raised and the flagrancy of the defendant's conduct never accounted for. It is suggested that this is too artificial a reason to justify including competition and *animus furandi* as elements of a substantial taking. Neither the CDPA 1988 nor the Copyright Acts of 1911 or 1956 provide any specific indication that these factors must be considered in determining whether an infringement has occurred.

Similarities Attributable to more than a Single Phrase

In *Ladbroke*, Lord Hodson observed that: 'No doubt [titles] will not as a rule be protected, since alone they would not be regarded as a sufficiently substantial part of the book or other copyright document to justify the prevention of copying by others.'[114] Presumably, His Lordship would also extend those comments to include short literary phrases. Nevertheless, this position must be viewed in the light of what has been said before about the process of determining substantiality. In fact, Lord Hodson's judgment does provide a reminder as to how protection for titles might be secured in a broader sense. If it is too insubstantial to qualify alone, a title's protectability might indirectly be ensured by arguing that it has been copied along with other elements of the plaintiff's work. If, for instance, the title along with catch-phrases have been used by the defendant, then it becomes feasible to argue that these elements, taken as a whole, constitute a substantial part of the plaintiff's work. The approach is reminiscent of Professor Nimmer's term 'fragmented literal similarity' ('FLS'). In the case of literary works, this describes those situations where isolated segments of text in a larger work are appropriated in literal, although not necessarily word for word, fashion.[115]

---

[111] As to whether infringement is possible through subconscious copying, see *Francis Day & Hunter v Bron* and *EMI Music Publishing v Evangelos Papathanassiou*, Note 88 above.

[112] Contrast with the facts of *Hawkes & Son v Paramount Film Service*. Note 98 above, in which the defendants were found to have infringed the copyright in the march 'Colonel Bogey' by including the music incidentally in a newsreel. Section 31(1) of the CDPA 1988 now excludes such incidental inclusions from liability although deliberate inclusions are not excused: section 31(3).

[113] See text accompanying Note 52 above.

[114] Note 23 above, at 286.

[115] Nimmer, Note 66 above, at 13.03[A].

Artistic Works

In addition, if the words for which the protection of the law is sought are incorporated into a design or logo, it will be possible to argue that the words in that particular form are an artistic work. Section 1(1)(a) of the CDPA 1988 confers copyright status on original artistic works. An 'artistic work' is defined by section 4(1)(a) as 'a graphic work, photograph, sculpture or collage, *irrespective of artistic quality*' (*emphasis added*) and a 'graphic work' is stated by section 4(2)(a) to include 'any painting, drawing, diagram, map, chart or plan'. This seems to make it quite clear that even a very simple design or logo incorporating a title or literary phrase would be covered. In *British Northrop Ltd v Texteam Blackburn Ltd*,[116] Megarry J states: 'I do not think that the mere fact that a drawing is of an elementary and commonplace article makes it too simple to be the subject of copyright.' However, Whitford J in *Karo Step Trade Mark*[117] observes that, for instance, a mere straight line or circle would not be so covered. Nevertheless, for the purpose of marketing and promoting a product, it is clear that there are legal advantages to be gained by following a consistent and distinctive artistic plan. For instance, if a specially designed film title were to be copied it would not be easy to argue that a substantial part of that design had not been taken. Indeed, it is not difficult to think of existing film titles which are portrayed in advertising in a highly stylised manner. *Jurassic Park*[118] is a notable example. In fact, the *Jurassic Park* logo, consisting essentially of a circle and bar with other embellishments, was the subject of a recent altercation. London Buses Ltd were threatened with legal action for copyright infringement over a poster of theirs designed to discourage the parking of cars at bus stops. The poster displayed a circle and bar incorporating the words 'Jurassic Parker'. Beneath appeared the caption 'Make parking at a bus stop a thing of the past'. London Buses denied infringement of copyright. They pointed out that a circle and bar design had been used by them since 1985 and that perhaps London Buses should respond by suing the makers of 'Jurassic Park' over their apparent subsequent use of that logo.[119] Although it was settled out of court, the dispute bears a certain resemblance to that which arose between Groucho Marx and Jack L. Warner over the use of the title 'Casablanca'.[120]

---

[116] [1974] RPC 57, at 68.
[117] [1977] RPC 255, at 273.
[118] Film released in 1993 and directed by Steven Spielberg.
[119] See 'Jurassic Parker', [1993] JML & P 121.
[120] Refer to text accompanying Note 9 above.

In Defence of
Originality
[1996] 1 ENT.L.R. 21

GARY LEA
Department of Law, University of Reading

Introduction

This article is intended as a reply to Mark Sherwood-Edwards' bold and interesting attempt in this Review[1] to demonstrate the redundancy of the concept of originality in copyright law (hereinafter 'the Article'): at the risk of gross oversimplification, this author reads the Article as laying down the following propositions:

(1) the present system of copyright and author's rights only offers patchy,[2] indirect protection of fact products through the selection or arrangement of facts in compilations and so on, and better protection of fact products could be achieved by removing the originality requirement from copyright and author's rights altogether.

(2) the abolition of originality would even go so far as to permit facts themselves to be protected but would not create a monopoly since one can distinguish between fact existence and fact availability[3]—independent gathering of facts would still be possible in most cases[4]and, in those situations where monopolisation does occur, anti-trust/competition law can correct any imbalance.

(3) originality would not be missed—one may legitimately compare copyright with tangible property which has no equivalent threshold test for conferral of property rights ('propertisation');[5]

(4) the standard argument that non-propertisation of facts leads to a greater flow of information is incorrect: refusing propertisation will diminish fact produced production because producers' revenue-gathering ability will be worse off by either having to bear the costs of producers' efforts to find alternative forms of protection[6] or, in the worst case scenario, finding that there are no new fact products since

---

[1] Sherwood-Edwards, 'The Redundancy of Originality', [1995] 3 ENT.LR 94.

[2] Patchy because (a) originality will always serve to prevent some fact products from being protected by copyright and (b) there are qualitative tests of (supposedly) varying degrees of severity in the United States (least stringent), France and Germany (most stringent) which could lead to a fact product being protected in one country and not in another; see Article, *ibid.*, (in particular 'Originality as creativity', 'Originality as creation' and 'Originality as labour') at 102 to 104.

[3] *Ibid.*, at 96.

[4] The Article, *ibid.*, suggests two exceptions—where facts are no longer publicly accessible and where source access to a particular sets of facts is restricted; both of these exceptions will be considered below.

[5] *Ibid.*, at 94, note 4, and 95.

[6] Either other legal means (for example unfair competition) or, presumably although not mentioned, technical means (for example anti-copying 'spoilers' in recordings); *ibid.*, at 100.

producers have gone out of business as a result of the unrestrained activity of copiers;[7]

(5) the function that originality performs is not properly part of the concept of property in any event since property is a means to an end (in other words, a mechanism for appropriating economic rewards) and not an end in itself;[8]

(6) on this basis, the traditional treatment of copyright as reward is incorrect—the reward is the value of property when realised in the market-place and not the property itself—and, therefore, the value judgment inherent in originality distorts the market by pre-empting market-based valuation;[9]

(7) the distortion argument holds true whichever variant of the originality value judgment one adopts: even under the low threshold UK originality test, for example, the most efficient a producer is in producing its product,[10] the less 'skill, labour and judgment' will have been deemed to go into the fact product and the less likely that fact product is to gain copyright protection.[11]

In the light of the foregoing, four matters should be considered: the nature of facts, current and near-future trends in fact product protection, the validity of the economic arguments advanced in the Article and a consideration of other non-economic arguments. In connection with the latter, it is important to note that the original Article dealt 'exclusively with economic arguments'[12] and, given that limiting parameter, it may *prima facie* appear unfair to shift the debate to areas not addressed: however, as will be demonstrated below, it is simply not possible to take a narrow, purely 'free market' economic view of the concept of property, given that it has political, social and cultural dimensions as well.

The Nature of Facts

One implicit assumption in the Article is that facts have some inherent utility that would warrant propertisation. However, in order to see whether this is true, one must first consider the nature of facts.

First of all, there is an 'information utilisation' 'hierarchy to be considered with terminology that often becomes conflated: one must distinguish between 'data', the sea of stimuli around us, and 'information' which is that data properly processed and presented in order to help us attain 'knowledge' and, hopefully from that, 'understanding'.[13] Concentrating on the first two terms, the essential difference is one of contextual relevance: to meet a given need for knowledge, the package of information presented to the end user must be (1) a suitably defined subset of data which is (2) qualitatively structured.[14]

The first requirement of a suitable data subset is obvious: if one asks for the time and gets a list of star names, then it is clear that, in the true sense of the word, one has not received information. The second structural requirement is one that can be explained by comparing a randomly shuffled pile of address cards to an address database stored in a computer: the latter has greater information 'utility' since a given address can be found more readily and

---

[7] *Ibid.*, note 45.

[8] *Ibid.*, at 101.

[9] *Ibid.*

[10] For example by automation of fact gathering and collation.

[11] Article, *ibid.*, at 104.

[12] *Ibid.*, at 95.

[13] Benyon, *Information and Data Modelling*, Blackwell Scientific, 1990, at 5 onward.

[14] See, further, Stamper, 'Towards a Theory of Information', 28(3) *Computer Journal* 195 (1985).

the structuring allows more information to be extracted by virtue of the greater number of correlations between data items that the computer can make.

An alternative way of viewing the structure requirement is to consider the following fact— 24°C. What does this mean? What inherent use is it? It has no meaning of use whatsoever until one is told that it was the temperature in Reading on 14 August 1995. This shows the need for collocation of data to create information: even so linked, the two items are of little utility. It is not until a whole sequence of measurements is completed that uses may be found for this weather 'database'.[15]

In short, a single datum has no inherent use without context and, therefore, lacks any potential value: it is during the act of organising subsets of data that fact 'packets' are developed, acquire utility and consequently acquire value. Thus the present copyright/author's right indirect protection scheme which protects the arrangement of facts rather than facts themselves is better modelled on the actual process of information production.

Indeed, it is further arguable that, for reasons of technological change, the originality question is already becoming a 'non-issue' in the United States and will become so elsewhere shortly: the nature of fact products is rapidly altering via the introduction of value added data and organisation schemes[16] on the Internet, on CD ROMs and so on. The result of this change is that new fact products will vault over the originality threshold with ease.

In conjunction with the foregoing, it is quite proper[17] to take account of two more pragmatic considerations: (1) the 'real world' fact product protection situation is not so serious to warrant such a radical change and (2) there would be serious practical problems introducing the same.

Fact Product Protection: Present and Near Future

The US situation

First, the state of play in the United States to recap, in *Rural Telephone v Feist Publishing*[18] the Supreme Court held that the 'White Pages' alphabetical list of subscribers in Rural Telephone's directory (hereinafter 'the listing') was not copyright subject-matter because it lacked originality; while the court was not looking for patent-style novelty, originality meant that the work was both 'independently created' and 'possess[ed] some minimal degree of creativity'.[19]

Facts, such as subscriber names and numbers, were not, and could never be, protected because they were only discovered and not created:[20] it was selection and arrangement of facts that had to be focused on and, even here, the listing failed since a bare A to Z listing pattern lacked the necessary creative spark.

Immediately following *Feist*, producers reacted negatively: it was said that '[the decision in] *Feist* pose[d] a serious problem for the proprietors of . . . [fact products] such as dat-

---

[15] For example for newspapers and television to say that this has been the hottest summer since 1659.

[16] For example hypertext linking of data files, pictures and sounds.

[17] Although the Article asserts that its aim is to look at the possibility of 'copyright in facts (or information) *per se*, irrespective of selection or arrangement [in compilations and so on]' (Note 1 above, at 94 and 95), much space is taken up with coverage of the present indirect protection system debate engendered by the US Supreme Court decision in *Feist v Rural Telephone* and the drafting of the EC Database Directive.

[18] 113 L.Ed. 2nd 385 (1991).

[19] *Ibid.*, at 369.

[20] *Ibid.*, at 370; although for an interesting philosophical argument to the contrary (namely that facts are created and are thus original) see Gordon, 'Reality as Artifact', 18 Rutgers Comp. & Tech. LJ 731 (1992).

abases'[21] since many fact products, like the listing, had no real arrangement by virtue of their simple structures, had no selection pattern as such by virtue of being valued for completeness rather than deliberate exclusion of contents and had contents that were not in themselves capable of garnering copyright protection.

An additional US-specific concern which prospectively compounded the problem was also raised: the possibility of developing alternative systems of rights based either on future state legislation or existing state common law was not possible because of federal pre-emption[22] under section 301(a) of the Copyright Act 1976 which provided that state rights 'within the general scope of copyright' were null and void after 1 January 1978.[23]

Was the instant concern expressed by producers justified? In relation to the basic question of the originality threshold, the answer is clearly 'No'. First of all, if one looks to the situation before *Feist*, while some Circuit Courts of Appeal had adopted a 'sweat of the brow' originality test similar to the UK's 'skill, labour and judgment' test, others had adopted a higher threshold requiring subjective judgment and selectivity in choosing items to list.[24]

On this basis, from the early years of the 20th century onwards[25] the average level of the US originality threshold was higher than that of the United Kingdom and, on the Article's model, should have ultimately resulted in a lower rate of fact product production than in the United Kingdom: yet in 1989, the baseline year that the Article mentions,[26] while the United Kingdom enjoyed an approximate 9 to 13.5 per cent share of the world database fact product subsector that year worth between $1 and 1.5 billion, the United States enjoyed a 56 per cent share worth over $6 billion.[27]

Clearly, therefore, in practical terms the US originality threshold pre-*Feist* did not have any appreciable effect in US fact product production: if anything, the figures underplay the US lead since they do not reflect such factors as the dominance of US corporate subsidiaries in the supposed 'UK' database production figures, the United States' general dominance in the necessary computer hardware/software fields and the ease of adoption of US material in the United Kingdom by virtue of a shared language.

Nor, it must be said, did producers' fears crystallise into significant protection problems after *Feist*. Although the courts have clearly adopted the rule that the key protection issue is 'not whether there is overlap or copying of [factual content] but whether the organising principle is ... substantially similar',[28] the spark of creativity required for fact selection and/or arrangement is not very bright: such dazzling gems as the business categories of a Yellow Pages telephone directory[29] and the average price tables in a 'Red Book' manual of used car price projections[30] have been held to be acceptably 'original'.

---

[21] Schwarz, '*Feist v Rural Telephone*: Case Comment', [1991] 5 EIPR 171, at 181.

[22] The principle whereby if federal law exists and is validly based on a provision of the US Constitution, states cannot validly legislate within the area that federal law covers: see, as a working example in the copyright sphere, *Goldstein v California* (1973) 412 US 546.

[23] See Ginsburg, 'No sweat?': Copyright and Other Protection for Works of Information after *Feist v Rural Telephone*', 92 Col. LR 338 (1992).

[24] The split between Circuits adhering to each standard was approximately half and half: see Ginsburg, 'Creation and Commercial Value: Copyright Protection and Works of Information', 90 Col. LR 1865 (1990).

[25] That is, from the time of initial Supreme Court consideration of the originality threshold in *Bleistein v Donaldson Lithographic* 188 US 239 (1903).

[26] Article, Note 1 above, 105.

[27] Figures collated (or should that be 'pirated'?) from paragraph 2.1.5 to 2.1.24, Explanatory Memorandum (original draft EC Database Directive) and Sandison, 'EC Database Directive', 21 *Copyright World* 22 (1991).

[28] *Key Publications v Chinatown Today Publishing* 945 F.2d 509 (2d Cir. 1991)—directory of Chinese community business contacts held not infringed because, although 75 per cent contents copied, the allegedly infringing KP directory had 260 categories against Chinatown's 28.

[29] *BellSouth Publishing v Donnelly Information* 933 F.2d 952 (11th Cir. 1991), reversed on other grounds 999 F.2d 1436 (1993) it transpired that the defendant had created new directory categories to the point that only the unprotected entries were copied.

Finally, it is noteworthy that the assertion made above of the limited impact of *Feist* is backed up by survey work carried out in late 1992: the trends in post-*Feist* copyright cases have not worried database producers and few changes in operation have occurred save that they are making somewhat more extensive use of contractual and technological access controls.[31] This lack of concern, in turn, has made the federal pre-emption question less important although it appears that the latter point was overstated in any event: as noted by Patry,[32] section 301(1)(b) of the US Copyright Act makes it clear that federal pre-emption does not extend to subject-matter that falls outside the Act and that this restriction on pre-emption was deliberately drafted so that 'state law should be allowed the flexibility [to act against] unauthorised appropriation of facts'.[33] Furthermore, the possibility of a dual regime of federal protection modelled on the European Database Directive with the *sui generis* rights element founded on the Constitution's interstate commerce clause has now also been mooted.[34]

The situation elsewhere: Europe and the draft directive on databases

The Article, like other commentaries before it, draws a distinction between the low threshold of originality of the European common law jurisdictions and the higher standards demanded by author's rights systems in European civil law jurisdictions.[35] However, it is strongly arguable that the degree of difference has been greatly exaggerated: although, as Porter[36] has noted, the degree of difference for 'true' literary and artistic works is supposedly marked as between EC Member States,[37] it can be clearly demonstrated that since the mid-1980s protection for factual products such as collections or compilations has adjusted to provide roughly equivalent and quite broad protection of selection and/or arrangement of fact products.

It is true that there have been problems along the way: French law, for example, provided a vague, open-textured originality test which, in operation, was largely a matter of impression of judges at first instance and not subject to appeal. The practical effect of the system was inconsistent decision-making: a football pools coupon was previously held not to be original while a catalogue of dog grooming accessories was.[38] However, the Court de Cassation's decision in *Microfor v Le Monde*[39] moved the originality cut-off to a more consistent and generous position: it was clear that the necessary 'trace of authorial personality' for French originality could be found in systematic treatment of material to produce indices and other organisational systems.

Even Germany, supposedly the toughest jurisdiction of all on originality, has preserved the effect of a quirky body of inter-War Reichsgericht copyright cases relating to so-called

---

[30] *CCC Information Services v Maclean Hunter Market Reports* 33 USPQ 2d 1183 (2d Cir. 1994).
[31] See Sheils *et al.*, 'What's all the Fuss about *Feist*?', 17 Dayton LR 563 (1992) and Reichman, 'Electronic Information Tools: The Outer Edge of World Intellectual Property Law', 17 Dayton LR 797 (1992) respectively.
[32] 'Copyright in Compilations of Fact or "Why the White Pages are not Copyrightable"', 12(4) Comms. & the Law 37 (1990).
[33] *Ibid.*, quoting HR Rep. 94 132 (1976).
[34] See tentative comments in Samuelson, 'The Originality Standard for Literary Works under US Copyright Law', 42 Am. J Comp. Law (Supp., Part I) 393 (1994)—the Semiconductor Chip Protection Act 1984 is a germane example of prior *sui generis* protection.
[35] Note 1 above, at 102 to 104.
[36] 'Copyright and Information Limits to the Protection of Literary and Pseudo-literary Works in the Member States of the EC', Office for Official Publications of the CEC, Luxembourg, 1992.
[37] *Ibid.*, at 12 to 66.
[38] See *Henault v Puliplast* [1983] RIDA 117 (Cass. Crim.).
[39] Cour Cass., Ass. Plen., 30 October 1987.

'kleine munze' ('small change') works:[40] whereas computer programs were initially exposed to the full blast of 'true' literary and artistic work originality requirements akin to novelty in patent law,[41] fact products such as collections of test questions[42] and trade mark directories[43] have been held to be original under a more relaxed version of the 'personal intellectual creation' test.

Conversely, copyright protection in UK law is not as overarching as commonly portrayed: in the House of Lords decision of *Cramp v Smythson*,[44] both the selection and contents of a diary information section consisting of various tide and sunrise/sunset tables were held to be not original—in relation to contents, Lord Simon LC pointed out that 'one of the essential qualities of such tables is that they be accurate so that there is no question of variation [by way of skill, labour or judgment] in what is selected'.[45]

If protection is roughly equivalent across the EC Member States (and equivalent to that provided in the United States) then why go to the trouble of creating the draft directive on databases at all: The answer appears to be threefold:

(1) a desire to 'lock down' the practical consensus achieved on originality by giving it full legal form,
(2) a desire to harmonise patterns of first and subsequent rights ownership and
(3) a desire to harmonise protection for 'unprotected' selection and/or arrangement schemes and contents.

Turning to the latter point, it must be emphasised that it is mainly on protection of sub-original selection/arrangement and factual content that serious divergences of method and scope emerge:[46] European civil law jurisdictions other than those of Scandinavia rely on unfair competition,[47] European common law countries rely on *ad hoc* selection from various trade torts such as passing off while the Scandinavian legal systems have a *sui generis* neighbouring right known as the 'catalogue rule';[48] this provides carefully limited, copyright-like protection for ten years and, wishing to create a transparent, uniform system of protection, the Commission has clearly taken its inspiration from the latter.[49]

Again, looking at the actual impact on trade, EC originality criteria have not caused a significant problem: while the United Kingdom's position as a major database provider may be questionable, what is clear is that from an 8 per cent share of the world database market in 1985 (worth a mere $400 million), the EC Member States moved up to a 27 per cent share in 1989 (worth some $3 billion).[50]

---

[40] See Hugenholtz, 'Chapter 3: Protection of Compilations of Fact in Germany and the Netherlands' in Dommering and Hugenholtz (eds), *Protecting Works of Fact*, Kluwer, Deventer, 1991.
[41] Although no longer thanks to the EC Software Directive. However, it is interesting to note that the Federal Supreme Court had begun to relax the originality test even before the Directive came into force; Gunter *et al.*, 'The German Implementation of the EC Directive on Software Protection' 9(4) CLSR 197 (1993).
[42] [1981] GRUR 520.
[43] [1987] ZUM 525.
[44] [1944] AC 335.
[45] *Ibid.*, at 339.
[46] The Article incorrectly states that protection is homogeneously achieved other than in the United Kingdom via unfair competition; Note 1 above, at 105.
[47] For example [1963] Rev. Trim. Droit Comm. 578 (Fr.).
[48] See Karnell, 'Chapter 4: The Nordic Catalogue Rule' in Hugenholtz and Dommering (eds), *Protecting Works of Fact*, Kluwer, Deventer, 1991.
[49] Indeed, a ten-year term was stipulated in the original draft.
[50] Figures collated as at Note 27 above.

Practical problems of removing originality

Leaving aside the substantial problems of designing suitable transitional provisions, there are three practical matters to consider. The first (and unavoidable) point is that originality and other copyright concepts are firmly interlaced at root:[51] even if one disposes of originality, it does not automatically follow that a fact or body of facts could be protected as a 'literary work'. If one accepts the definition of that phrase given by Stephenson LJ in *Exxon v Exxon Insurance*,[52] namely that 'a literary work [is] something which was intended to afford either information and instruction, or pleasure in the form of literary enjoyment' then it follows that 'literary' and 'work' will also have to be broadened: if this is done then one rapidly reaches the point where what is left is not copyright law at all but an entirely new form of protection.

Second, the full consequences of propertisation have not been considered: there are hidden costs associated with propertisation that would seriously diminish any economic benefit to either manufacturer or consumer. One important example of this is that, at present, in most circumstances we accept facts at our own risk,[53] in other words people cannot and do not believe that everything that they read is truthful and/or accurate. If facts are propertised, then it would only be reasonable on the part of the consumer to expect that facts supplied are of 'satisfactory accuracy';[54] this could lead to situations where a publisher would be liable for, by way of illustration, faulty information on toxicity of mushrooms[55] which would have 'knock-on' effects such as a need for insurance and product price rises to cover the necessary premiums.

Finally, there is the 'real world' effect of copyright litigation to consider: although the Article argues that, in the absence of originality, independent creation of identical fact products is possible,[56] in practical terms, the marketing of a rival fact product with the same or substantially similar factual content would give rise to an almost irrebuttable presumption of copying.[57] Thus, perversely, removing originality would result in the substitution of *de facto* novelty which, in turn, would lead to the creation of monopolies.

Exceptional products?

Before leaving purely practical considerations, attention needs to be given to two types of fact product that the Article treats as peripheral examples which might cause problems under the new protection scheme: those where the source material is no longer extant and those where the source material itself is protected.[58]

The first problem is that, taken together, these two categories in fact represent a significant portion of the sum total of fact products in both quality and quantity terms: looking at the first category alone, it is clear that, besides purely historic fact products such as the hypothetical

---

[51] *Contra* the Article, Note 1 above, at 95.

[52] [1982] Ch. 119.

[53] An important exception in English law is where misrepresentations are made; see *Derry v Peek* (1889) 14 App. Cas. 337 (fraudulent misrepresentation), *Hedley Byrne v Heller* [1964] AC 465 (negligent misrepresentation) and the Misrepresentation Act 1967.

[54] See Nimmer and Krauthaus, 'Information as a Commodity: New Imperatives, 55(3) Law & Contemp. Probs. 103 (1992), at 125 onward.

[55] See *Winter v G P Putnams & Sons* 938 F.2d 1033 (9th Cir. 1991) (no liability under the present regime).

[56] Note 1 above, at 97.

[57] Avoiding liability would be only possible, it is submitted by keeping detailed and costly logs of fact gathering and organising operations; this would, of itself, create significant barriers to entry in competition.

[58] Note 1 above, at 97.

directory of businesses in London in 1900, census returns, weather statistics, stock market prices and any other fact product with an extended chronological sequence will fall into this supposedly 'exceptional' category.

The second problem is that the justification offered for inclusion of these examples under the umbrella of the new protection scheme are suspect as weak and self-contradictory: in relation to those products where the source material is no longer extant, for example, the Article says that refusing copyright in facts 'serves only to penalise those who by their skill, industry and foresight, have taken the trouble to preserve a version'[59] which is equivalent to saying that those who produce (first) should be rewarded – an argument condemned elsewhere as faulty justification for originality and the conferral of copyright protection.[60]

The final problem is that the solution suggested for these and other problem areas— the application of anti-trust/competition law in the copyright domain[61]—is recognised by economists and others as an unpredictable, difficult and potentially dangerous solution.[62] The danger lies in over-or under-applying anti-trust/competition law, a danger that comes from the enormous complexity of having to decide whether, in each individual case, the nature and/or utilisation of a particular copyright is in fact anti-competitive.[63]

Tackling Economic Theory: Confusion Under Order

All economic arguments rest on assumptions and those contained in the Article, are, like any others, open to question. In tackling the economics of originality removal, three areas must therefore be considered: the assumptions on which the Article is based, the economic model deployed and the conclusions drawn therefrom.

For example, one assumption made is that denying copyright protection increases costs as and when producers are forced to look for product protection under other 'umbrellas' such as unfair competition:[64] it could equally well be argued that producers have always worked under a split system and, given such operational familiarity, any costs associated with it were absorbed long ago with the result that the costs of migrating to a new system would outweigh any residual effects of the old.

However, the most important cost assumption implicit in the 'standard model'[65] adopted is that the cost of copyright protection is lower than the cost incurred through reliance on alternative protection such as trade secrecy or through practical measures such as rapid marketing, technological protection and so on: this has been seriously questioned and has led other 'free market'-oriented law and economics commentators to devise quite a different model.[66] In his seminal article, Breyer[67] argued equally plausibly that there is no need for copyright protection at all: natural features of the fact product market such as publisher lead time, profits derived therefrom and fears of predatory price wars[68] would all suffice to

---

[59] *Ibid.*, at 97.

[60] *Ibid.*, at 101.

[61] *Ibid.*, at 98 and 106.

[62] See the critique of the competition/copyright interaction in Article 6 (decompilation right) of the EC Software Directive in Schmidtchen and Koboldt, 'A Pacemaker that Stops Halfway', 13 Intl. R Law & Econ. 413 (1993).

[63] See the new approach adopted in the ECJ's decision in the *Magill* litigation; Vinje, 'The Final Word on *Magill*', [1995] 6 EIPR 297.

[64] Note 1 above, at 100.

[65] See Palmer, 'Copyright and Computer Databases', 14 IIC 190 (1983).

[66] Of course, socialists and Marxists would argue that one should look away from the market altogether and rely on state provision such as grants or stipends.

[67] 'The Uneasy Case for Copyright: A Study of Copyright in Books, Photocopies and Computer Programs', 84 Harv. LR 281 (1970).

[68] *Ibid.*, at 291 onward.

perform the market maintenance function claimed for copyright. From this it is clear that economics on its own can no more give a single, definitive solution to the problem of fact product protection than the 'soft social sciences' so heartily condemned by Veljanowski.[69]

Turning to model-derived conclusions, the major advantage claimed for fact propertisation is that it will lead to more new facts coming onto the market:[70] while this may be true, the *de facto* monopolisation and hidden costs of propertisation outlined above will lead to higher prices for fact products with the end result that the average consumer will not be able to afford the new products and may even be progressively 'priced out' of the market for updated versions of the older ones.

The Final Assumption: Property as Free Market Mechanism

Another core assumption in the Article is that property is a single, unified and absolute concept which exists as free market component and which is refused or restricted only *in extremis*;[71] this is incorrect in all respects.

First of all, property is not a single concept: adopting Hohfeldian analysis, Gordon[72] has identified five basic attributes which mark out 'property': the right to exclude, the right against harm or interference, the right of benefit yielded from property, the power of transfer and the privilege of use.[73]

Second, property is not a unified concept: taking account of the inherent differences of subject-matter which they have to cover, property laws have evolved separate and specific features relating to identification and delimination of each type of subject-matter, initial and subsequent ownership[74] and so on. The reason for the differences is that each system, once set in motion, has 'autopoesis', a set of policy constraints and internal dynamics unique to it;[75] given this, analogies between different property types should be carefully drawn at a very abstract level (if at all).

Third, property is not an absolute concept: property rights have always been imbued with considerations of morality or public policy since, ultimately, 'property rights serve human values. They are recognised to that end, and are limited by it'.[76] Today numerous market inefficiencies are still tolerated for reasons of social or cultural welfare in many instances such as limitations on free use of land[77] or lack of property in the human body.[78] In truth, there has never been a complete 'web of propertisation and, taking the example of land alone, the tendency in the post-War period has been to favour public non-property interests more not less:[79] one may readily count environmental controls, the massive expansion of planning laws and the imposition of public health and safety measures under this rubric.

In short, it is because of the inclusion of other considerations by virtue of property's relative nature that it is wrong to think of property as a creature of the free market: while it

[69] *The Economics of Law*, IEA, London, 1990.
[70] Note 1 above, at 99.
[71] *Ibid.*, at 102.
[72] 'An Inquiry into the Merits of Copyright', 41 Stan. LR 1343 (1989).
[73] *Ibid.*, at 1354 onward.
[74] Compare rules relating to ownership of rights in commissioned copyright works and commissioned registered designs under UK law; section 11(1) CDP 1988, section 2(1A) RDA 1949 (as amended).
[75] Hamilton, 'Appropriation Art and the Imminent Decline in Authorial Control over Copyrighted Works', 42 J. Copr. Soc'y 93 (1994) at 108 onward.
[76] *State of New Jersey v Shack* 277 A2d 372 (1971) at 374; quoted in Gray, 'Property in Thin Air', [1991] CLJ 252 at 297.
[77] Denman, *The Place of Property*, Geographical Publications Ltd, Berhamstead, 1978.
[78] Munzer, *A Theory of Property*, Cambridge University Press, 1990.
[79] Harris, 'Private and Non-private Property: What is the Difference?', 111 LQR 421 (1995).

is arguably a necessary underpinning for market operation,[80] it does not exist solely or mainly for that purpose. However, that leaves one matter unresolved: what does the property conferred by copyright exist for and what are its constraints?

Leaving the Marketplace Behind: Copyright Redux

Copyright has always provided a limited proprietary interest because it was only ever intended to be one mere stimulus to produce[81] and not a cast-iron guarantee of appropriation of market value: apart from originality there are numerous other cut-offs such as limited duration[82] and permitted or fair uses that cut across copyright operation. Author's rights systems do not even go this far but simply take a 'non-market' view of the property conferred as a species of human right reflecting the dignity of human intellectual labour.

Thus limitations on the property rights conferred under either system are not flaws: they are an integral part of what is offered up. In relation to copyright, 'the primary objective of copyright is . . . [to encourage] others to build freely upon the ideas and information contained in a work'.[83]

The *Feist* quote above makes the point that development in the arts, education and entertainment is accretive rather than revolutionary in nature: copyright and author's rights are loose, quasi-monopolies that allow us to recycle literary, dramatic and artistic motifs in new and exciting ways.

The accretive nature of cultural artefact production also forms a major part of the explanation for non-propertisation of facts: by allowing everybody[84] to copy facts, new information can be created or mistakes corrected.[85] These advantages were recognised by Lord Mansfield CJ as early as 1785: in the case of *Sayre v Moore*,[86] the plaintiff complained that the defendant had copied the contents of four of his maps. The assertion was true but Lord Mansfield rejected the infringement claim as a result of taking account of the fact that the four maps had been condensed to one, depth errors removed and the whole recast in more accurate Mercator projection; these were rightly taken to be 'advancements in knowledge . . . and ship safety' worth more than protecting the basic property right at issue.[87]

A related constraint on copyright derives from the social and cultural facets of human rights law: as Plowman and Hamilton[88] put it:

> In most countries, social and cultural developments have resulted in an increased need to use [material] for public service such as education, research and administration.

---

[80] Although see Breyer's argument at Notes 67 to 68 above.

[81] See the preamble to the Statute of Anne 1709—the Article is somewhat confused on the point of incentive since it both conflates the notion of copyright as incentive and reward and condemns it (Note 1 above, at 101) and endorses the incentive effect of property conferral in tangibles (*ibid.*, at 98).

[82] Despite the recent increase to 'life plus 70' under EC harmonisation measures, the protection is not yet of indefinite duration like chattels; for a good argument that the term should be reduced, see Puri, 'the Term of Copyright: Is it too Long in the Wake of New Technologies?', 12(1) EIPR 12 (1990).

[83] *Feist*, Note 18 above, 369 to 370.

[84] It must be remembered that fact copying is not 'one way traffic' as the Article's allusion to theft implies (Note 1 above, at 99)—the lack of protection for facts means all producers may copy each other's facts and are thus playing 'on a level playing field'.

[85] This explains the supposed oddity of recycling facts alluded to in the Article at page 99.

[86] (1785) 1 East 361 note 1.

[87] For a moment mundane but modern example of property pre-emption in UK copyright law on public policy grounds, see the introduction of the concept of 'non-derogation from grant' in *BL v Armstrong Patents* [1986] RPC 279.

[88] *Copyright: Intellectual Property in the Information Age*, Routledge & Keegan Press, London, 1980.

Policies in the field of intellectual property rights must, therefore, be defined in relation to policies for education, culture, information and communications generally...[89]

The non-binding but influential[90] Universal Declaration of Human Rights 1948 ('UDHR') recognises both public and private interests but, unfortunately, does not actually resolve the problem of the balance between the two[91] since Article 27 simply states:

(1) Everyone has the right freely to participate in the cultural life of the community, to enjoy the arts and share in scientific advancement and its benefits;
(2) Everyone has the right to the protection of the moral and material interests resulting from any scientific, literary or artistic production of which he is the author...

Looking elsewhere in the human rights sphere, two concerns immediately stand out: freedom of expression and rights to education. Looking at the former, it has long been recognised that copyright, if overdeveloped, is a potential enemy to the various species of freedom of expression such as accurate and full news coverage:[92] the First Amendment to the US Constitution and Article 10 of the European Convention on Human Rights[93] both stand to be infringed if copyright is asserted over facts.

Looking at education, it is noteworthy that, although a right to education has not been fully recognised,[94] the copyright conventions have given limited recognition to the need to reproduce protected material for educational purposes: it is submitted that facts are so vital to education that no monopoly or quasi-monopoly should even be contemplated. After all, ignorant, misinformed or propaganda-sated citizens are ultimately the gravest danger to the economic and social well-being of any nation: despite the Article's allusion to the economic failure of the USSR through non-propertisation,[95] it is worth remembering that the free market did not prevent the Bolshevik Revolution occurring in the first place.

---

[89] *Ibid.*, at 35.
[90] The precise status of the UDHR is uncertain—there are some arguments that the UDHR has become binding as international customary law; *The Universal Declaration of Human Rights*, Eide *et al.* (eds), Scandinavian University Press, Oslo, 1992, at 6 to 7.
[91] Although see Davies, 'New Technology and Copyright Reform', [1984] 12 EIPR 335.
[92] Nimmer, 'Does Copyright Abridge the First Amendment Guarantee of Free Speech and Press?', 17 UCLA LR 1180 (1970).
[93] See Robertson *et al.*, *Human Rights in Europe*, Manchester University Press, 1993, at 147 to 157.
[94] Article 26 of the UDHR recognises such a right but it has not been transposed into international conventions on human rights.
[95] Note 1 above, at 99.

Fair Dealing and the Clockwork Orange Case: 'A Thieves' Charter'?

[1994]1 ENT L.R. 6

DAVID BRADSHAW

Barrister-at-Law, formerly Lecturer in Law, Leeds University, and Deputy Dean of Law, University of the West Indies, Barbados

I think the ruling is tragic ... it could become a thieves' charter.

David Putnam (film-maker)[1]

The word 'dealing' does not imply a transaction between two people, but merely use by an individual for the particular purpose (in the US the equivalent exception is known as 'fair use') ...

Terence Prime[2]

The purpose of this article is to examine the very recent decision of the Court of Appeal in *Time Warner Entertainment Company LP v Channel Four Television Corporation plc and Another* (1993)[3] in order to, *inter alia*, assess whether in that copyright infringement action the Court's treatment of the defence of 'fair dealing' under section 30 of the Copyright, Designs and Patents Act 1988 ('the 1988 Act') justified the above-quoted reaction from David Putnam. For the case in question appears to be the very first one in which the English courts have had to rule on the parameters of fair dealing under the 1988 Act when applied to reviews or criticism of broadcast material and it would perhaps be unfortunate for those in the entertainment industry, whose job it is to safeguard the interests of copyright holders, if it was concluded that the Court of Appeal has gotten off to a bad start by opening much too widely the floodgates in relation to what constitutes excusable copyright infringement.

The Facts

The case concerned a film entitled 'A Clockwork Orange' which was produced in 1971 by, *inter alios*, Warner Bros Inc. It was directed by Stanley Kubrick and based on Anthony Burgess' novel of the same name. This award-winning film is described in the plaintiff's own words as: 'A dark, ironic tale of an ultra violent future ... centering on Alex (Malcolm McDowell) who fights, robs, rapes and kills like any conscienceless young predator'.[4] It was exhibited in the United Kingdom during 1972 and 1973 but, owing to the copycat violence

---

[1] Quoted in the *Independent* for Saturday, 23 October 1993 at 3.
[2] *The Law of Copyright*, Fourmat Publishing, London, 1992, at 117.
[3] Judgment of Neill, Farquharson and Henry LJJ, delivered Friday, 22 October 1993, [1994] EMLR 1.
[4] See the typescript of Neill LJ's unreported judgment, at 5 to 6.

which its showing provoked among British teenagers,[5] it was withdrawn on the instructions of the producers.[6] No licence to exhibit the film in the United Kingdom had been granted by the copyright holder since 1974 and, which fact seems to have prompted the independent producers to think about making the television programme that will be referred to shortly, a London cinema was fined for an unlawful screening of the film at the beginning of 1993.

The second defendant in the case was an independent production company which decided to make a 30 minute documentary television programme on the film, to be entitled 'Forbidden Fruit', as part of the first defendant's (Channel 4) 'Without Walls' flagship arts series. Persistent efforts were made, in vain, to get Stanley Kubrick to contribute to the programme either in person or by written statement. When these measures failed the second defendant sent one of its employees on an errand to Paris, where the film evidently was still being exhibited in some cinemas,[7] and in a music and video shop there he bought a NTSC format of the film on laser disc. This was brought back to London where the second defendant had extracts of the film transferred to BETA tape. The programme was duly completed, publicised, previewed and promoted for broadcast by Channel 4 on Tuesday, 5 October 1993 at 9.30 pm.

The plaintiff (Time Warner) was a limited partnership organised under the law of Delaware State, USA and was the undisputed assignee of the copyright in the film. Time Warner found out about Channel 4's proposed broadcast, via some of the journalists who attended the preview screenings, including the fact that the programme in question contained many clips from the 'banned' film. Very quickly Time Warner instructed solicitors to seek an undertaking from Channel 4 that the programme would not go out as planned. When the undertaking failed to materialise, a motion for an injunction was brought before Harman J on the very day that the 'Forbidden Fruit' was due to be broadcast.

At about 4.45 pm on that day Harman J granted the plaintiff an injunction restraining the defendants from, *inter alia*, broadcasting, in any of their programmes, the identified extracts from the film or any substantial part thereof, or otherwise infringing the plaintiff's copyright in the film, without the plaintiff's licence. Channel 4 immediately lodged an appeal to the Court of Appeal against Harman J's order and, in an amazing testament to the speed of English justice, the hearing of the appeal began a mere one and a quarter hours later at 6 pm.[8] There were only three and a half hours to go before the programme's scheduled transmission time and, not surprisingly, in the end it proved not possible to conclude the hearing of the appeal before that deadline. In the result, at 9.30 pm the proceedings were adjourned to the following day and, since the broadcast of the programme had had to be postponed *sine die* in any case, judgment was accordingly reserved.

The Legal Issues

Both before Harman J and in the Court of Appeal the defendants relied on the defence of 'fair dealing' provided by section 30(1) of the Copyright, Designs and Patents Act, 1988. This section provides that:

> Fair dealing with a work for the purpose of criticism or review, of that or another work or of a performance of a work, does not infringe any copyright in the work provided that it is accompanied by a sufficient acknowledgement.

---

[5] See for example the *Independent* and the *Guardian* for Saturday, 23 October 1993 at 3 and 11 respectively; and the *Evening Standard* for Thursday, 30 September 1993 at 22.

[6] See Note 4 above, at 4.

[7] *Ibid.*, at 8.

[8] *Ibid.*, at 3.

The plaintiff conceded that the requirement of a 'sufficient acknowledgement' had been satisfied in this case[9] since Stanley Kubrick, Warner Bros Inc. and the other producer of the film had all been clearly acknowledged, during the programme and at the end thereof before the closing credits.[10] For their part, the defendants accepted that the inclusion of the clips from 'A Clockwork Orange' in 'Forbidden Fruit' represented a 'substantial part' of that film for the purposes of section 16(3) of the 1988 Act[11] (which would thereby render the broadcast of the film *prima facie* an act restricted by copyright under section 16(1)).

In giving the leading judgment in the Court of Appeal in this case, Neill LJ said that there were four principal submissions advanced by Time Warner in support of its contention that the defendants were not entitled to rely on the fair dealing defence in section 30(1).[12] These were that:

(1) the programme did not constitute fair dealing because the laser disc of the film had been obtained in an underhand manner;

(2) the programme did not constitute fair dealing because the scenes depicted in the clips were all scenes of violence and did not accurately represent the film as a whole or give a proper indication of its contents;

(3) the programme did not constitute fair dealing because the clips amounted to over 8 per cent of the film as a whole and about 40 per cent of the programme itself;

(4) the purpose of the programme was not for criticism or review but had the ulterior motive of giving a public viewing of some of the film's most controversial scenes in the interests of sensationalism, as part of a campaign to persuade the plaintiff to re-release the film, and to criticise the plaintiff for declining to do so.

There follows an analysis of how Neill LJ (and his brother judges) dealt with each of these four submissions in turn.

Re (1): the 'underhand' obtaining of the film

It would appear that the main inspiration behind the plaintiff's counsel advancement of this first submission was the case of *Beloff v Pressdram Ltd* (1973).[13] In that case the magazine 'Private Eye' published, in full, an internal memorandum about a cabinet minister which had been written by the political and lobby correspondent of the *Observer* newspaper and sent to her editor. This memorandum had been subsequently 'leaked' to the magazine. Ungoed-Thomas J, in giving judgment for the defendants, *inter alia*, held that the defendants would have had no defence on the ground of fair dealing for the purposes of criticism or review under section 6(2) of the Copyright Act 1956 because publication of information known to have been leaked and which, without the leak, could not have been published, was justifiable for the authorised purposes of criticism or review and constituted dealing which was not 'fair' within section 6(2).

In the present *Clockwork Orange* case, however, Neil LJ was able to rejoice the plaintiff's submission under this first head, as follows:

---

[9] *Ibid.*, at 14.
[10] *Ibid.*, at 12 (quoting from a letter of Mrs Andrew, Channel 4's Legal and Business Affairs Executive).
[11] *Ibid.*, at 13 to 14.
[12] *Ibid.*, at 14 to 15.
[13] [1973] 1 All ER 241.

In my judgment it is important to emphasise that the defence of fair dealing is primarily concerned with the treatment of the copyright material in the publication of which complaint is made.

I do not intend to throw any doubt on the *decision* in the *Beloff* case itself, but it is my present view that criticism of a work *already in the public domain* which would otherwise constitute fair dealing for the purposes of section 30(1) would *seldom if ever* be rendered unfair because of the *method* by which the copyright material had been obtained.

If confidential material is improperly used it can usually be protected by an action for breach of confidence.

... In the present case the laser disc was bought in a shop in Paris. ... I am satisfied that the defence under section 30(1), if otherwise available, is not destroyed by the *method* by which the defendants obtained the clips (*emphasis added*).[14]

Henry LJ in his concurring judgment had this to say:

as the film was once in the public domain in this country and was still so abroad, it is nothing to the point that the process by which the programme makers originally copied the work for public display was a breach of copyright.

If the defence of fair dealing is available, it is capable of covering all dealings with the film.

... So on the facts of this case, there is nothing in this point, as [Harman J] by implication found when he did not refer to it.[15]

Re (2): the 'misrepresentation' of the contents of the film as a whole

The plaintiff in making this second submission tendered evidence (which was disputed by the defendants)[16] to the effect that out of the clips selected for the programme, nine depicted violence, in a context where there were 'only approximately 10 violent scenes in the entire film'.[17] In other words, the plaintiff was alleging that the defendants had given undue emphasis to 'the juicy bits'.[18] On this second submission Neill LJ was prepared to be much more critical of Harman J. The former judge stated that in the light of having seen the programme himself in the course of the hearing, and having read the plaintiff's own description of the film which appeared on the boxes in which videocassettes of the film were produced for the American market, he considered that Harman J 'came to a demonstrably incorrect conclusion'.[19] Neill LJ went on to state that he was not prepared to say that the programme misrepresented the film to any significant extent.

More important for these purposes, however, is the fact that the learned Lord Justice of Appeal continued by making the following point:

it is clear that [Harman J] considered that in order to be able to rely on a defence of fair dealing it was necessary to show that the excerpts were a fair representation of the film *as a whole*.

---

[14] See Note 2 above, at 17 to 18.
[15] See the typescript of Henry LJ's unreported judgment, at 27.
[16] See Note 4 above, at 19 where the evidence of Channel 4's Mrs Andrew is quoted to controvert the plaintiff's contention on this point.
[17] *Ibid.*, at 18.
[18] *Ibid.*, at 19, citing Harman J in the decision below.
[19] *Ibid.*, at 20.

... I am afraid I do not agree with the Judge's approach.

I am satisfied that the Court should be very slow before it rejects a defence of fair dealing on the ground that the criticism covers only one aspect of a film or book or as the case may be.

One can envisage many cases where it *would* be legitimate to select and criticise, for example, a *single* scene of violence even though the rest of the work was free of objectionable material ... (*emphasis added*)[20]

In agreeing with Neill LJ's rejection of the plaintiff's second contention, Henry LJ had this to say:

But even if it is assumed that the infringing excerpts were arguably not fairly representative, would that defeat the fair dealing defence? In my judgment as a matter of law it would not.

... 'Fair dealing' in its statutory context refers to the true purpose (i.e. the good faith, the intention and the genuineness of the critical work—is the programme incorporating the infringing material a genuine piece of criticism or review or is it something else, such as an attempt to dress up the infringement of another's copyright in the guise of criticism, and so profit unfairly from another's work?

... If it is the former, in a genuine criticism of the decision ... to withdraw that work from the public domain, it seems to me that the defence is not lost if the offending excerpts might arguably be thought to be (in relation to the original film) unbalanced or unrepresentative.

If your theme is that either the film should be available for public viewing here or at least that the decision to withdraw the film should be publicly justified, and you are making the point that the violence [in the film] is in fact less violent than many films made since ... then it would not be surprising to me if the excerpts concentrated disproportionately on that violence to make these points.

If satisfied that the theme and *purpose* of the criticism was genuinely as summarised above, I would not regard such imbalance as raising an arguable case that the fair dealing defence was not available ...[21]

Re (3): the total length of the clips

'Forbidden Fruit' used some 12 extracts from 'A Clockwork Orange', which related to 11 separate scenes in the film. The 12 extracts were of varying length from 10 to 115 seconds. In aggregate the extracts were 757 seconds, or just over $12\frac{1}{2}$ minutes, in duration. This fact, as previously stated, enabled the plaintiff to claim that the clips amounted to more than 8 per cent of the entire film and about 40 per cent of the Channel 4 programme itself.

The plaintiff also gave evidence that it was the industry practice that clips of films released for review would normally not exceed one minute's duration per clip and four minutes in length in the aggregate. In the light of this statement of affairs it was no surprise that Neill LJ pronounced that he found the plaintiff's contention under this head 'the most troublesome aspect of the case'.[22]

Despite the gravity with which he characterised this issue, Neill LJ very swiftly ruled that

---

[20] *Ibid.*, at 20 to 21.
[21] See Note 15 above, at 27 to 29.
[22] See Note 4 above, at 22.

there was no unfair dealing by the defendants by reference to the overall length of the film extracts used in 'Forbidden Fruit'. He did so as follows:

(a) he said that he thought that there was 'great force' in the comment made by Channel 4's commissioning editor for arts programmes 'that serious criticism of a film requires you to spend sufficient time showing the film itself';[23]

(b) he reminded himself that although the clips were shown during a substantial part of the programme, 'they were accompanied by voices over which contained comments and criticisms by those taking part in the programme';[24]

(c) he cited Ungoed-Thomas J in *Beloff v Pressdram Limited* (1973) stating that 'fair dealing is a question of fact and impression';[25]

(d) he stated that one 'has to consider whether the allegedly infringing material may amount to an illegitimate exploitation of the copyright holder's work';[26]

(e) he simply concluded by saying that having seen a screening of 'Forbidden Fruit' itself and read the transcript thereof:

In the light of what I have seen and read I have come to the firm conclusion that this programme does not go beyond the bounds of fair dealing by reason of the length of the excerpts from the film.[27]

Unfortunately, Neill LJ's brother judges failed to add to the dearth of learning on this crucial part of the case. For on this point Henry LJ simply said, 'I agree with my lord and have nothing to add',[28] while the third judge, Farquharson LJ, went one better (or worse) and stated that he agreed with both judgments and had nothing to add.[29]

Re (4): purpose of programme not for review or criticism

As seen before, the crux of the plaintiff's argument under this fourth head was that the real motive or purpose of the defendants in making 'Forbidden Fruit' was to start a campaign which would ultimately lead to the plaintiff re-releasing 'A Clockwork Orange' in the United Kingdom. Put another way, the plaintiff was arguing here that it was the decision not to make the film available for release in this country, and not the film itself, that was being reviewed in the programme and that, therefore, section 30(1) did not apply.

Neill LJ accepted that while there *was* some support for the plaintiff's argument contained in the programme itself, nevertheless one had 'to look at the programme as a whole'. In doing so he appeared to accept the evidence of the programme's producers that their (main?) purpose was to seek a re-examination of the film (which he said they 'clearly regard ... as a work of long term significance') and of its social and artistic importance. Accordingly, he was able to hold that in relation to this fourth contention also, and given the interlocutory state of the proceedings, a *prima facie* defence within section 30(1) had been made out by the defendants.[30] Henry LJ's judgment was, however, much more instructive on this point. He said:

---

[23] *Ibid.*, at 22.
[24] *Ibid.*, at 22 to 23.
[25] *Ibid.*, at 23; and Note 13 above at 263.
[26] See Note 2 above, at 23.
[27] *Ibid.*, at 23.
[28] See Note 15 above, at 30.
[29] See the typescript of Farquharson LJ's unreported judgment, at 33.
[30] See Note 4 above, at 24.

It is clear from the wording of [section 30(1)] that the criticism need not be primarily directed at the work infringed, but may be directed at another work.

And *Hubbard v Vosper*[31] makes clear that the criticism relied on need not be directed at the work, but may be directed at the thought and philosophy behind the work.

In these circumstances it seems to me that the fair dealing defence *may* apply equally where the criticism is of the decision to withdraw from circulation a film in the public domain, and not *just* of the film itself. In the present context the two are in my view inseparable.

That decision is clearly a suitable matter for public debate and so for public criticism, and it is clearly highly relevant to that criticism to illustrate by excerpts relevant qualities, whether positive or negative, of the film, so that the public may form a view of the decision criticised and of what they are missing or rightly being spared (*emphasis added*).[32]

Thus in the end the three judges in the Court of Appeal unanimously held that all four of the plaintiff's principal submissions, as to why the section 30(1) fair dealing defence should not be available to the defendants in the present case, had to be rejected. As Henry LJ said, for example: 'I am satisfied that the section 30 defence *would* be available to these defendants, and that there is no serious issue to be tried on that point' (*emphasis added*).[33] Accordingly the defendants' appeal was allowed and the injunction granted by Harman J was discharged on Friday, 22 October 1993. Acting once again with much dispatch, Channel 4 broadcast 'Forbidden Fruit' at 9.30 pm on Tuesday, 26 October 1993—a mere three weeks late!

A Critique of the Court of Appeal's Decision

It is necessary to spend but a short while perusing the Court of Appeal's treatment of the first, second and fourth of the four principal contentions advanced by the plaintiff in the case before swiftly proceeding to a review of the more interesting third contention. For in relation to the former three, Neill LJ (as supported by Henry LJ and concurred with by Farquharson LJ) seems to be saying, in effect, that the adjective 'fair', in the statutorily undefined[34] concept of fair dealing under the 1988 Act, means something other than 'ethical', 'comprehensive' and 'exclusive' respectively.

Thus, in relation to the first contention, although it does not help the cause of those advising copyright holders in the entertainment industry to say so, Neill LJ is to be applauded for refusing to hold that a defence of fair dealing can be defeated by a plaintiff showing that in some way the defendant does not have 'clean hands' in relation to how he first acquired the work with which he has subsequently 'dealt'. For, in this writer's view, copyright infringement problems should be kept conceptually distinct from breach of confidence issues and, accordingly, Neill LJ seems correct in stressing that the issue of the treatment of the copyright material in question by a defendant on the one hand, and the method by which he originally obtained it on the other, should not be confused.[35]

---

[31] [1972] 2 QB 84, at 94f.

[32] See Note 15 above, at 31 to 32.

[33] *Ibid.*, at 32.

[34] See for example Terence Prime, Note 2 above, at 118, for a convincing explanation of why the concept of fair dealing has been left deliberately undefined in the various Copyright Acts passed since 1911.

[35] Indeed, it is arguable that Neill LJ was seeking to confine *Beloff's* case (see Note 13 above) to its own very particular facts by saying that he did not wish to cast doubt on 'the *decision*' (compare 'the *reasoning* of Ungoed-Thomas J') in that case, and by going on to state that fair dealing under section 30(1) would 'seldom *if ever*' be rendered unfair solely because of the *method* by which the copyright material had been obtained. See Note 4 above at 17.

Similarly, in relation to the plaintiff's second principal contention, both Neill and Henry LJ are to be applauded for their convincing reasoning on how section 30(1) is intended to operate and their rejection of the idea that 'fair' in this context means only 'coverage of the work as a whole' or 'comprehensive'. Such a position in fact does assist broadcasters and others in the entertainment industry in that it tells them that they can safely set out to review a part only of a work (subject to what is said on the plaintiff's third contention below) without falling outside the protecting arm of the section. As the editors of *Copinger* have pointed out, however: 'It is only when the court has determined that a *substantial* part has been taken that any question of fair dealing arises'.[36]

Again, in relation to the Court's treatment of the plaintiff's fourth principal contention one must approve of Neill LJ's and, particularly, of Henry LJ's reasoning on this point. As a result thereof, it is now known that fair dealing for the purposes of section 30(1) does not have to mean 'dealing for the *exclusive* purposes of criticism or review' and that mixed motives do not necessarily defeat the defence contained in that provision. However, although Henry LJ's following statement is helpful to copyright holders in suggesting when an infringer might go 'too far', one wonders whether it is not the learned judge himself who is guilty of doing so in relation to the point in question:

> if the intention was to profit from the breach of copyright in ['A Clockwork Orange'] under the pretence of criticism, then no matter how fair or balanced or representative the infringing excerpts might be, the purpose would not be that of criticism or review, and so would not have the protection of the sec. 30 defence.[37]

Turning, finally, to the Court's treatment of what Neill LJ described as 'the most troublesome aspect of the case'[38]—namely the plaintiff's third principal contention concerning the overall length of the clips from 'A Clockwork Orange' used by the defendants in their programme. As intimated before, it is the writer's view that the Court's treatment of this issue, so vitally important for those in the entertainment industry, was woefully inadequate.

It is suggested that, notwithstanding the great time pressure under which the Court of Appeal was originally asked to deal with this case, having taken the decision to reserve judgment following the postponement of the original transmission date of the programme, their Lordships should have taken the opportunity to go back to first principles on the issue in question. For if the case before them was the very first one under section 30(1) of the Act it was not the first to treat of the defence of fair dealing under section 30 generally. That honour goes to *BBC v British Satellite Broadcasting Limited* (1991)[39] in which Scott J admirably went back to the first principles of the defence in question, in relation *inter alia* to the overall length of extracts taken from another's programme, and applied those principles on the facts before him to achieve a reasonably acceptable decision at the end of the day. Needless to say the *BBC* case was not cited by the Court of Appeal in *Time Warner* in relation to the plaintiff's third contention, or at all, so a brief look at that earlier decision will now be taken.

The BBC, in that case, sued British Satellite Broadcasting (BSB) for, *inter alia*, damages for copyright infringement and an injunction arising out of BSB's usage, in its regular sports new programmes, of excerpts from a number of soccer matches in the World Cup 1990

---

[36] E.P. Skone James *et al.*, *Copinger and Skone James on Copyright*, Sweet & Maxwell, 1991 (13th edn), at 250. And see section 16(3) of the 1988 Act, the text above relating to Note 11, and M.F. Flint *et al.*, *Intellectual Property—The New Law*, Butterworths, 1989, at 44.

[37] See Note 15 above, at 29.

[38] See Note 22 above.

[39] [1991] 2 All ER 833.

tournament which the BBC had broadcast live and in which broadcasts the BBC, therefore, owned the copyright. Each excerpt was between 14 and 37 seconds in duration and was shown by BSB up to four times in its sports news programmes during the 24-hour period following each match. Such excerpts concentrated on one or two significant happenings from the related match, such as the scoring of goals or near misses. BSB contended that such *prima facie* infringement of the BBC's copyright was excused under the fair dealing provision in section 30(2) of the 1988 Act. This states that:

> Fair dealing with a work (other than a photograph) for the purpose of reporting current events does not infringe any copyright in the work provided that (subject to subsection (3)) it is accompanied by a sufficient acknowledgement.

In deciding the case Scott J, early in his judgment, pointed out that under section 6 of the Copyright Act 1956 the fair dealing defence only extended to copyright infringement of literary, dramatic and musical works but that, save for photographs in the case of section 30(2), sections 30(1) and 30(2) of the 1988 Act extended the defence to all works including broadcasts.[40] He went on to note, however, that:

> the extension of the fair dealing defence to infringement of copyright in broadcasts had not created a wholly new copyright defence.
> Fair dealing has been a possible defence since the [Copyright] Act of 1911, albeit for a limited class of infringements. Its boundaries have been explored and explained by a number of cases.[41]

Of the cases which Scott J then went on to look at, he clearly found most guidance as to the general approach to be adopted to a fair dealing defence from the following statement of Lord Denning MR in the Court of Appeal's decision in *Hubbard v Vosper* (1972):[42]

> It is impossible to define what is 'fair dealing'. It must be a question of degree.
> You must consider first the *number and extent* of the quotations and extracts. Are they altogether *too many* and *too long* to be fair?
> Then you must consider the use made of them. If they are used as a basis for comment, criticism or review, that may be fair dealing. If they are used to convey the same information as the author, for a rival purpose, that may be unfair.
> Next you must consider the proportions. To take long extracts and attach short comments may be unfair. But, short extracts and long comments may be fair.
> Other considerations may come to mind also.
> But, after all is said and done, *it must be a matter of impression*. As with fair comment in the law of libel, so with fair dealing in the law of copyright. The tribunal of fact must decide *(emphasis added)*.[43]

Having stated Lord Denning's 'matter of impression' formula, and having accepted that the outcome of the application of that formula to the facts before him was *the* question which he had to decide, Scott J eventually made such application as follows:

40 *Ibid.*, at 835h to 836e.
41 *Ibid.*, at 836e.
42 [1972] All ER 1023, at 1027.
43 Cited by Scott J, see Note 39 above, at 836f to j.

The evidence in the present case has ... established ... that the use made by BSB of the BBC material was for the purpose of reporting current events. The question is whether it was fair dealing for that purpose.

Both the quantity and quality of the material used are important. As to duration, the excerpts were very short[44] in relation to the length of the match broadcast in question, 30 seconds or thereabouts of a broadcast lasting, say 90 minutes.

... The number of times each excerpt was shown must be taken into account. The fact that the excerpts were repeated in successive news reports over a 24 hour period is not, in my opinion, a matter of justifiable criticism. The fact that part of each excerpt was repeated up to three times in each news report was also, in my opinion, consistent with fair dealing.

... my *impression*, when I viewed the videos of the [BSB] news programmes was that the use made of the BBC material was fair dealing for the purposes of reporting the results of the World Cup matches. These were news reports.

... The use of the BBC material was short, [and] was pertinent to the news reporting character of the programme.

... The evidence I heard and the arguments addressed to me after my viewing of the videos confirmed my initial *impression* [that] ... the use of the BBC material falls ... fairly and squarely within [the fair dealing defence of] section 30(2) of the 1988 Act (*emphasis added*).[45]

Returning to the 'Clockwork Orange' case, therefore, it can be seen that rather more analysis could have been given by the Court of Appeal to the plaintiff's third contention regarding the length of the extracts from their film which the defendants used in their own programme. 'Forbidden Fruit'. For their Lordships could have looked at Lord Denning's 'matter of impression' formula from *Hubbard v Vosper*[46] as applied in the recent 1988 Act case of *BBC v BSB*.[47] And lest it be thought that while the former test might well be applicable to the section 30(2) news-reporting type of fair dealing, as in the *BBC* case, but not to the section 30(1) criticism or review type of fair dealing, it should be remembered that *Hubbard v Vosper* was in fact an example of the latter type of case, albeit one decided under the 1956 Copyright Act. For had their Lordships applied the Denning formula it is at least highly arguable that a different conclusion would have been reached on the availability of the fair dealing defence for such an extensive usage of the plaintiff's film under the circumstances of that case. Certainly the average film-maker on the Clapham omnibus might well argue that, taking into account the fact that nearly 10 per cent of the film was shown in 'Forbidden Fruit' in a situation where the copyright holders did not want any of it to be seen by the British public at all,[48] when all is said and done as a matter of impression such usage (even for the very highest quality of review or criticism) cannot be said to be 'fair'. But, this writer suggests, not only might someone like David Putnam, say so, but (very likely) so also might the average

---

[44] Were the excerpts so short that there was no 'substantial' part of any BBC broadcast which was re-broadcast by BSB and, therefore, no infringement by virtue of section 16(3)(a) of the 1988 Act? Scott J does not refer to this consideration in his judgment. And see text relating to Note 36 above.

[45] See Note 39 above, at 844g to 845j.

[46] See Note 42 above.

[47] See Note 39 above.

[48] If the moral right known to French Law as the 'droit de divulgation' or right of disclosure (namely the author's right to say whether, and when, publication of his work takes place, or to withdraw such work after publication) had also been given effect to in Chapter IV of Part 1 of the 1988 Act, it would seem that it would have been very difficult, if not impossible, for a court to rule that the defendants' dealing with the film in the particular circumstances of this case was 'fair'. On this French moral right see for example S.M. Stewart, *International Copyright and Neighbouring Rights*, Butterworths, 1989 (2nd edn), at 73.

person, or even the average Lord Justice of Appeal—both of whom would have somewhat less of a professional axe to grind than that leading film-maker.

This writer hopes, therefore, that future courts faced with similar facts to those in the 'Clockwork Orange' case will expressly take all the relevant principles and authorities into account and, by so doing, enable themselves to characterise the decision made in that case as one made particularly on its own facts. By this means such future cases will ensure that, rather than being 'a thieves' charter' whereby, for example, unscrupulous companies could show inordinately long extracts from other peoples' films or broadcasts without paying for them,[49] or a case which opened the 'legal floodgates'[50] for copyright infringers, this first case under section 30(1) of the Copyright, Designs and Patents Act 1988 (and the second under section 30 generally)[51] merely represents the high-water mark of the defence of fair dealing under that new Act.

---

[49] This is a barbarisation of something Waldemar Januszczak, Channel 4's commissioning editor for arts pro-grammes, said in the *Independent* for Saturday, 23 October 1993, at page 3, in commenting on the outcome of the case and in refuting the suggestion in question.

[50] *Per* Claire Dresser in the BBC's in-house newspaper *Ariel* for 26 October 1993, at page 2, basing her statement on what has been predicted in some quarters as being the implications of the decision.

[51] In fact, in addition to the *BBC v BSB* case (see Note 39 above), sub-section 30(2) (as well as sub-section 30(3)) were also pleaded by the defendant recently in *Beggars Banquet Records Ltd (trading as 'XL' Recordings) v Carlton Television Ltd and Another* (1993) (unreported but available on LEXIS). Warner J, in giving his judgment on 4 May 1993 in this interlocutory matter, *inter alia* left this issue for determination at the trial of the action. However, interestingly enough for these purposes, he also had this to say:

> There are questions whether the use of $13\frac{1}{2}$ minutes of the footage in a programme of 25 minutes was fair dealing, whether events that took place in August 1992 can be said to have been 'current' in January 1993 and whether the programme confined itself to 'reporting' them,

see page 13 of the LEXIS transcript of Warner J's judgment.

The Digital Sound Sampler: Weapon of the Technological Pirate or Palette of the Modern Artist?

[1990] 3 ENT L.R. 87

D. PAUL TACKABERRY

*Attorney, Lang Michener Lawrence & Shaw, Toronto**

Introduction

Digital sound sampling is a process by which a natural or pre-recorded sound is reduced to digital messages and later faithfully reproduced with the assistance of a computer. The technology permits the operator of the digital sampler to replicate such sounds as breaking glass and a crying baby with amazing accuracy. One need listen for only a short time to a radio or television station which plays popular music to realise that digital sampling has become standard fare in today's music industries in Canada, the United Kingdom and the United States. However, the technology has not been warmly welcomed by all segments of the industry.

When digital sampling is used to copy sounds which have been recorded by other musicians, the creators of the sampled sounds are often angered at what they believe to be a form of theft. The well-known singer James Brown has stated that '. . . [a]nything that they take off my records is mine. Is it all right if I take some paint off your house and put it on mine?'[1] 'I spent 23 years working on my tone to come up with what sounds good to me, and to have someone take 23 years of work and put it in a sample and use it indiscriminately—well, I think that's wrong.'[2] Nevertheless, record producers '. . . are blatantly stealing from everyone else. Any record is fair game, no matter what it is . . . That's just the way it is done in the '80s.'[3] According to Arthur Blake, proprietor of the Shakedown Studio in New York City, 'the technology has developed to the extent that if you like the sound, you can have it.'[4]

Digital sampling can be used to duplicate a single sound (such as the sound of a person's scream, one note of a pre-recorded saxophone solo or a dog's bark) or a series of sounds (such as a scale or a musical phrase). When used to clone a single sound, the sampler acts simply as a musical instrument. As with a synthesizer, the single sound is 'played' by the musician, usually on the keyboard of an electronic instrument capable of communicating in MID[5] language. In this way, a sample of one note from a pre-recorded trumpet solo by Miles Davis can be used to perform an original musical passage. When the sampler is used to

---

* *Canadian contributor to the* Entertainment Law Review, *the author is an acoustic and electronic musician.*
1 Miller, 'The Questionable Ethics of Modern Creativity', 7 September 1987 Toronto Globe and Mail at B1.
2 Daley, 'Ethically Speaking or Plato, Check Your Messages', November 1988 *Mix* (Volume 12 No 11) at 99.
3 *Ibid.*, quoting the Grammy award winning producer Tom Lord-Alge.
4 *Ibid.*
5 Musical Instrument Digital Interface, discussed in the text accompanying Note 10 below.

replicate a series of sounds, entire sections from pre-recorded musical compositions are often 'copied'. Such sections are sometimes 20 to 30 seconds or more in length. In both situations, various electronic effects are often added to the sample with the final result being quite different in sound and effect from the original.

As an example, *Billboard* magazine reports that the members of the pop group 'The Turtles' have filed suit against the group 'De La Soul' alleging that De La Soul made a loop of the opening four bars of the Turtles' song, 'You Showed Me' and repeated the four bar segment[6] several times in their composition 'Transmitting Live From Mars'. The attorneys for De La Soul state that '. . . because of their diminutive use [of the sample] or because [the sample] had been so substantially modified, it's not a violation of use.' While no sampling cases have gone to trial, a case commenced in 1987 involving the Beastie Boys is expected to receive a trial date shortly.[7]

Most legal commentators who have written on the topic[8] have generally equated digital sampling with copyright infringement and have concluded that it is, to a large extent, an unlawful misappropriation. Under Canadian law,[9] this is not necessarily the case because often only one or two notes are copied. Whether copyright infringement has occurred depends to a large extent on the nature of the particular sample in issue. Generally, the sampling of one or two notes is not copyright infringement.

This paper reviews digital sampling technology and recent developments in the area of electronic musical instruments. The tests for infringement of the copyright in musical works and sound recordings are then examined. The writer's conclusion is that the traditional distinction between the copying of substantial and insubstantial parts is sufficient to differentiate acceptable borrowing of forms of expression on the one hand from copyright infringement on the other. Existing Canadian copyright law ought not to be expanded to give the author of musical works or the owner of a sound recording any more protection in this regard than they currently enjoy.

Digital sampling *per se* is no more undesirable than other less recent technologies affecting the creation and communication of music such as radio and phonograph records. From a public policy point of view, digital sampling is a worthwhile creative tool the use of which should be encouraged and fostered. Any improper use of the digital sampler can be effectively dealt with by traditional copyright concepts. Since very small portions of musical works and sound recordings cannot under usual circumstances represent that portion of an original work which is commercially valuable, musicians should not be restrained from copying and using such small portions in their new musical works.

---

[6] De La Soul has argued that only three bars were actually sampled.

[7] 'Turtles' Flo & Eddie Sue De La Soul Over Sampling', *Billboard*, 26 August 1989, (Vol. 101, No. 34) at 10 and 41. See also 'Singer Sees Red Over Sampling on Black Box's No. 1 UK hit', *Billboard*, 28 October 1989, (Volume 101, No. 43) and 9 and 100.

[8] See Thom, 'Digital Sampling: Old Fashioned Piracy Dressed Up in Sleek New Technology', 8 *Loyola Entertainment Law Review* at 297 (1988); McGivern, 'Digital Sound Sampling, Copyright and Publicity: Protecting Against the Electronic Appropriation of Sounds', 87 *Columbia Law Review* at 873; Fleischmann, 'The Impact of Digital Technology on Copyright Law', 70 *Journal of the Patent and Trademark Office Society* at 5 (1988); Bently, 'Sampling and Copyright: Is the Law on the Right Track?'—*Part I, 1989 Journal of Business Law Review* at 113; *Part II, 1989 Journal of Business Law Review* at 405; Newton, 'Digital Sampling: The Copyright Considerations of a New Technological Use of a Musical Performance', 11 *Hastings Comm/Ent. L J.* at 671 (1989); Wells, You Can't Always Get What You Want But Digital Sampling Can Get What You Need', 22 *Akron L. Rev.* at 691 (1989).

[9] This paper is written from a Canadian perspective. While US and English laws has not been examined in detail, it is submitted that many of the broad copyright principles and policies discussed here are equally applicable in these jurisdictions.

Recent Technological Developments Concerning Electronic Musical Instruments

Synthesizers, MIDI and digital technology

Electronic musical instruments have undergone tremendous development in the last several years. The 1970s saw the emergence of the synthesizer, an electronic component which permits the operator to create sounds by adding and subtracting electronic embellishments and effects. Such devices have been and continue to be used to imitate naturally occurring sounds such as brass and string instruments. However, such imitation has always been somewhat less than accurate.

The 1980s witnessed the development of Musical Instrument Digital Interface (MIDI) which allows synthesizers, computers and a host of other electronic components to communicate with one another regardless of the manufacturer of the components.[10] MIDI technology permits a performer to strike the key of one synthesizer and have the sounds of one or more other synthesizers triggered simultaneously. MIDI also permits synthesizers and computers to communicate with each other so that many of the events of the musical performance (for example, pitch, volume and duration) may be 'recorded' and later triggered by the computer as the keys of a player piano are triggered by a piano roll.

The development and use of the digital sampler must be viewed in this larger context as it is an extension of the technology which has been developing for the last two decades. Digital samplers have been commercially available since the late 1970s,[11] but only in the last few years have they sufficiently decreased in price to the point that a substantial number of musicians can now afford them. Samplers for amateur musicians are currently available for under US $500. Digitally sampled sounds are available on read only memory (ROM) computer chips for use with electronic musical instruments. These instruments are also relatively inexpensive and can produce natural sounds (for example, piano, trumpet or percussion) which are virtually indistinguishable from their sampled source.

Digital sampling technology

Digital technology, the language in which most computers in use today communicate information regardless of the function which they are performing, involves the representation of a quantity expressed in a series of ones and zeros (that is, ons and offs). This is to be contrasted with analogue technology which was, until recently, the only available method to record music and which is used to produce and play phonograph records. Analogue technology uses a continuous scale of values to represent a sound. For example, the value representing the volume of a sound is proportional to the degree of loudness.[12]

By way of basic explanation of a highly technical process, digital sampling may be compared to taking a photograph of an event such as a race.[13] A snapshot captures only a split second of the event but if enough photographs are taken in quick succession, as with a movie camera,

---

[10] See Fleming 'Do Re Midi . . .' Feb/March 1990 *Electronic Composition & Imaging* (Volume 4, Issue 1) at 12 and Dako, 'Mister Music Please . . .' Feb/March 1990 *Electronic Composition & Imaging* (Volume 4, Issue 1) at 15.

[11] Composer and musician Peter Gabriel began using the prototype of the Fairlight, one of the first commercially available samplers, in 1978. See 'Fairlight Instruments, The Phoenix Arises', March 1990 *Keyboard* (Volume 16, No. 3) at 27.

[12] Green, 'A Perspective on Audio Sampling', June 1987 *Electronics Today* at 50.

[13] See Keyt, 'An Improved Framework for Music Plagiarism Litigation', *76 Cal. L. Rev.* 421 at 427 (1998) for a succinct description of digital audio sampling.

the result is a reasonable facsimile of the event. Similarly, when a single digital sample (snapshot) is taken, the sound being produced at that exact instant is reduced to a series of 1s and 0s. To imitate a sound which lasts for one or two seconds, many samples must be taken in a short period of time (the sampling rate). If enough samples are taken, an acceptable reproduction of the original sound results.

The emergence of digital technology as the dominant method of communicating music

It was stated in 1987 that '... digital recording and transmission technology is expected to largely replace analog technology by the end of the 1980s'.[14] The shipment of long-playing records in Canada fell by 55 per cent in 1989 with compact disk shipments increasing by 33 per cent.[15] In addition, *Billboard* reports that 'one-way sales policies by the CBS and WEA labels and A & M Records have accelerated the demise of the [vinyl] format, now widely regarded as being in its death throes.'[16] The format for transmitting recorded music which the experts expect to emerge next, digital audio tape (DAT), employs digital technology, as its name would suggest. Accordingly, it seems that the prophesy is well on its way to coming true: analogue technology appears to be going the way of the eight track cassette tape.

The digital sampler has been embraced by segments of the popular music industry, particularly 'rap' musicians. The sampler is a natural extension of a black American musical form dating back to the 1970s in which disc jockeys, and later musicians, used the *phonograph* as a musical instrument by playing snippets of records repetitively in a rhythmic fashion. Videos of rap groups frequently depict a musician 'performing' a record player much like a guitar, a form of performance sometimes referred to as 'scratching'.

On the other hand, acoustic musicians lament that the availability of their work and the value of their performances are diminishing as the popularity of electronic music (including digital sampling) increases.[17] Such musicians often misunderstand the new technologies. One writer/musician[18] states that:

> Traditional musical ability and training are neither necessary nor sufficient prerequisites for the creation of digital music, as sequences[19] can be programmed in either 'real time' as in actually playing an instrument, or in 'step time', where each component of musical expression is input separately.[20]

This commentator apparently overlooks the fact that computers cannot create pleasing musical sounds if they are not programmed by an operator with musical ability. Digital technology no more negates the requirement for creative talent in musicians than does the word processor in writers.

Another writer states that '[acoustic] musicians have suffered most from the effects of

---

[14] Fleischmann, above Note 8 at 6.

[15] '89 Record-Biz Stats Show CD & Cassette Rise, LP Glide', 17 February 1990 *Billboard* (Volume 102, No. 7), at 68.

[16] 'Vinyl's Demise Accelerated by Label No-Return Policies', 24 February 1990 *Billboard* (Volume 102, No. 8) at 1 and 93. See also, 'CD's Surpass Cassettes in $$ Volume', 17 March 1990 *Billboard* (Volume 102, No. 11) at 8 and 107.

[17] Newton, above Note 8 at 674.

[18] Newton describes himself as a jazz musician (above Note 8 at 671).

[19] A sequencer is computer software and hardware which 'records' MIDI events (for example, pitch, note duration, volume) for playback at a later time. See the articles referred to in Note 10, above.

[20] Newton, above Note 8 at 674.

digital sampling.'[21] But what of the *electronic* musicians who have gained from technology? This commentator continues:

> If left unchecked, digital sampling could have a potentially devastating impact on the livelihoods of musicians in the United States. The issue then becomes *what role copyright law does or should play in protecting musicians from the effects of digital sampling.*[22] (*emphasis added*)

The simple answer to this question is that copyright law should play no special role in protecting the economic interests of a single class of creators (that is, acoustic musicians) but the general principles of copyright law should apply to protect all creators.

The fear of electronic music and the resulting loss of work for acoustic musicians has fostered a hostile critique of such music. It has been suggested that 'perhaps acoustic musicians will suffer unemployment because their instruments will eventually sound bizarre to the listening public.'[23] This critique is an extreme reaction to what is little more than utilisation of a new technology to please the public by adding a new dimension to their musical experience. There will continue to be an audience for acoustic music, an art form which offers the listener something which electronic music cannot: the unique aural experience of sound created by the vibration of such natural elements as wood and string as opposed to the beads and paper of an electric speaker.

The dynamics behind digital sampling

Digital technology has affected much of what we know about music including the way a musical work is composed and arranged, the way a recording is made, reproduced and replayed and the creation of the sounds themselves by musicians. This in turn has created tension in the industry with the big losers being acoustic musicians. However, this is not a new trend. The phonograph caused many musicians to lose work when it replaced them as the form of entertainment at many social functions and drinking establishments. Many of the writers on this topic have extended traditional copyright concepts considerably in an effort to preserve the livelihood of acoustic musicians. These are attempts to maintain the *status quo* while stretching copyright concepts beyond their proper limits. The essence of the problem is not piracy, but competition from a new art form. The purpose of copyright law is to foster creativity, not to frustrate it.

Does Digital Sampling Amount to Infringement of the Copyright In the Sampled Musical Work?

In deciding under what circumstances sampling amounts to infringement of the copyright in the sampled work,[24] it must be remembered that often what is taken by the operator of

---

[21] Wells, above Note 8 at 700.
[22] *Ibid.*
[23] Newton, above Note 8 at 674.
[24] A detailed analysis of the components of the musical copyright infringement action is beyond the scope of the paper. The reader is referred to the following authors on the topic: Sherman, 'Musical Copyright Infringement: The Requirement of Substantiality', 22 *Copyright L. Symp.* (*ASCAP*) 81 (1972); Crowe, 'The Song You Write May Not Be Your Own', *1 Intell.Prop.* J. 29 (1984); Keyt, above Note 13; May, 'So Long As Time is Music' 'When Musical Compositions are Substantially Similar', 60 *Southern Cal L. Rev.* 785 (1987); Raphael Metzger, 'Name That Tune: A Proposal for an Intrinsic Test of Music Plagiarism', 34 *Copyright L. Symp.* (ASCAP) 139 (1984).

the digital sampler is not a unique portion of the sampled work but only a single sound. Another example of a typical sample is the rhythm section of the original work (that is, the bass guitar, drums and piano and/or guitar) without the melody. In analysing at what point *de minimis* copying becomes copyright infringement, the basics of copyright infringement must be reviewed.

Subject matter and access

Copyright in Canada subsists in, among other things, every 'original literary, dramatic, musical and artistic work . . .'.[25] To constitute a protected musical work the 'sounds' must be comprised of a melody (a succession of single notes) or harmony (a succession of chords) or both.[26] A single sound or even three or four successive sounds cannot except in very rare cases be termed a melody and therefore cannot be considered a musical work and enjoy copyright in itself. If such a phrase is to be protected, it must be protected as part of a larger musical work.

Copyright infringement occurs when a substantial part of one musical work (the 'original work') is copied in a tangible form (the 'infringing work'). Because actual evidence of copying is rarely available to a plaintiff, the courts in Canada and the United States have developed a doctrine which provides that copying can be proved if access by the defendant and striking similarity between the original work and the infringing work are established.[27] Access is defined as the actual hearing and knowledge of the work.[28] Once a musical work is recorded and sales of records or compact discs have taken place on a regional or national basis, particularly if the work receives radio air play, access may be inferred.[29]

To reiterate, not all copying amounts to copyright infringement. A substantial part of the original work must be reproduced in the infringing work for infringement to have occurred.[30] Therefore, since copying is assumed in the digital sampling context, the crucial issue is whether a substantial part of the original work has been sampled.

A substantial portion must have been copied

Establishing the extent to which copying must take place before it may be termed substantial is 'one of the most difficult questions in copyright law, and one which is least susceptible to helpful generalisations'.[31] The courts have identified four factors to be considered in determining whether the portion taken from the original work is substantial:[32]

(1) the quality of the portion taken;
(2) the quantity of the portion taken;

---

[25] Canadian Copyright Act, R.S.C. 1985, C-55 (herein 'Copyright Act') section 5(1).
[26] Copyright Act, section 2(p). Timbre and spatial organisation are also important musical elements (Keyt, above Note 13 at 432).
[27] *Gondos v Hardy* (1982), 64 CPR (2d) 145 (Ont. HC); *Fox on Copyright* (2nd edn.) at 374; *Ferguson v National Broadcasting Co.* 584 F. 2d 111 (5th Cir. 1978); *Sid & Marty Kroft Television Products v McDonalds's Corp* 562 F.2d 1157 (9th Cir. 1977).
[28] *Bradbury v Columbia Broadcasting Sys.* 287 F. 2d 478 (9th Cir. 1961).
[29] *Abkco Music, Inc. v Harrisongs Music, Ltd* 722 F. 2d 988 (2nd Cir. 1983).
[30] Copyright Act, sections 3(1), 27(1); *Gondos v Hardy* above Note 27; *Arnstein v Porter*, 154 F. 2d 464 (2d Cir. 1946). This is called the 'substantial similarity' test in the US.
[31] *Warner Bros. Inc. v American Broadcasting Cos.* 654 F.2d 204 (2nd Cir. 1981).
[32] *Ravenscroft v Herbert* [1980] RPC 193 (Ch.).

(3) whether the portion taken competes with the original work; and

(4) the intention of the composer of the infringing work.

How then are these factors to be applied to music?

One broad statement that may be made with certainty is that in order to infringe, one must utilise a substantial portion of the original work.[33] The substantial similarity test as applied in the US cases measures the extent of copying as well as how it is used in the infringing work. The issue is whether enough copying has taken place so that the infringing work is substantially the same as the original work. For the reasons discussed below, when the substantial similarity test is applied to digital sampling, it is submitted that a quantitative threshold must be passed before the court can logically undertake a qualitative analysis.[34] Accordingly, the sampling of one or two notes of a pre-recorded work cannot under usual circumstances amount to copyright infringement.

Where is the line drawn between de minimis and substantial copying?

It is accepted that 'although the amount taken may be small, it may be the unique portion that gives the song *quality*'.[35] In addition, the courts have realised that a unique portion of a musical work can indeed be very small in length.[36] What the courts are concerned with in the final analysis is whether that portion of a work upon which its popular appeal depends, and hence its commercial success, has been copied.[37] Or put differently, has the very part of the work that makes it popular and valuable been taken?[38]

According to one commentator, '. . . a brief sequence of notes can hardly be called an entirety of a performance of any given work, nor can the tonal qualities themselves, without phrasing and sequencing, be called a performance.'[39] Another writer states that the courts do '. . . not wish to enjoin a work simply because a small part of one song [is] similar to a small part of another song. Thus, in order to infringe, one must utilise a substantial amount of the work. This may be standard for musical compositions but it has disastrous effects when applied to sound recordings'.[40]

Nimmer states that '. . . ordinarily, the importance of but one line in the plaintiff's work would be regarded as *de minimis*, not justifying a finding of substantial similarity'[41] and '[i]t is most unusual for infringement to be found on the basis of similarity of a single line, and

---

[33] Copyright Act, sections 3(1), 27(1); *Arnstein v Porter*, above Note 30.

[34] *Maxtone-Graham v Burtchaell* 803 F. 2d 1253 (2d Cir. 1986). This is supported by the commentators McGivern, May and Thom (see the discussion in the following section).

[35] Thom, above Note 8 at 323. 'The more "valuable " the material taken, the more likely that the taking will be found to be "too much". The value of the borrowed material to the defendant's work is ignored in determining liability. As a rule of quantitative analysis, this prevents a defendant from appropriating a five minute song for use in a four hour opera, but would seem, conversely, to allow the defendant to market as his own a five minute aria out of a plaintiff's four hour opera.' (Keyt, above Note 13 at 439). See also Sherman, above Note 24 at 104 to 111: '[I]f the portion copied is the portion of the plaintiff's work that makes it valuable—artistically and commercially—the accused work will be deemed substantially similar to the complaining work' (at 106).

[36] Sherman, above Note 24 at 105.

[37] *Robertson v Batten, Barton, Durstine & Osborn, Inc.* 146 F. Supp. 795 (S.D. Cal. 1956).

[38] *Johns & Johns Printing Co. v Paul-Pioneer Music Corp.* 102 F. 2d 282 (8th Cir. 1930). See also *Northern Music Corp. v King Records Distributing Co.* 105 F. Supp. 393 at 397 (SDNY 1952); *Arnstein v Porter*, above Note 30 at 473.

[39] McGivern, above Note 8 at 1743.

[40] Thom, above Note 8 at 323. In order to avoid the 'disastrous' conclusion that the sampling of one or two notes of a sound recording does not amount to copyright infringement, Thom alters the substantial similarity test as it applies to sound recordings (see text accompanying Notes 92 to 94 below).

[41] Melville B. Nimmer, *Nimmer on Copyright*, Matthew Bender & Co., 1939 at 13 to 46, §13.03[A].

generally the likelihood of copying but a single line of such importance as to warrant a finding of substantial similarity is quite remote.'[42] It is submitted that this statement is applicable to the sampling of a single note in that such a sample could not normally warrant a finding of substantial similarity. However, a substantial portion might well have been copied if the entire chorus (melody and rhythm section) were sampled. It is only in very rare cases that phrases of less than ten notes would constitute the portion of the original work that makes it valuable and then only if the phrase is repeated many times throughout the original work or if it appears in very prominent locations in the original work.[43]

The leading U.K. authority concerning the nature of substantial copying is *Ladbroke (Football) Ltd v William Hill (Football) Ltd.*,[44] where it was stated that the qualitative test is much more important than the quantitative test.[45] However, *Ladbroke* dealt with football betting coupons containing lists of forthcoming matches between teams and the bets offered on those matches and not with a musical composition, a work of an entirely different nature. The essence of a compilation such as betting coupons is a collection of facts which are in the public domain. What is protected in a compilation, therefore, is not the particular pieces of information but the skill and labour required to compile the raw data. Further, *Ladbroke* was not a case of *de minimis* copying at all since the information in 15 out of 16 of the defendant's lists was 'almost identical' to that in the plaintiff's lists.[46] Accordingly, the case is not helpful in determining whether the sampling of a few notes of a musical work is copyright infringement.

Nevertheless, Bently relies heavily upon the *Ladbroke* case when he makes the generalisation that 'it is very difficult to show that anything copied is not an infringement [and that t]his leaves the copyright owner in a strong position, and in our case the sampler in a very weak one'.[47] In making this statement, Bently makes no qualification that the sampling of a single note or sound should be treated differently than the sampling of a series of sounds.[48] Indeed, later in his article, Bently accepts this point when he says 'if a sampler takes only one word from a song, there must be doubt as to whether this would be infringement, even if it were the chorus. Equally the sampler might use only a few notes from the music.'[49] Therefore Bently's statement must be tempered somewhat: it is very difficult to show that anything copied is not an infringement *if what was copied was more than a few notes.* However, this still leaves the important question: what quantity of sounds must be taken for the copying to be substantial?

Writers have attempted to draw the line between *de minimis* and substantial copying in the musical context. For example, one writer states that 'trivial similarities are inconsequential and non-infringing'.[50] This is a particularly critical point in light of the fact that similarity

---

[42] *Ibid.*, at 13 to 47. § 13.03[B].
[43] Sherman, above Note 24 at 109 to 110. Identical combinations of musical elements may appear in compositions which produce strikingly dissimilar value because the value of the original may depend on how the combinations in the piece relate to form an entirety. Substantial similarity should therefore be found to exist, it has been suggested, only 'when a defendant's composition contains an identical or nearly identical combination of elements and the value produced by the defendant's use of the combination is identical or nearly identical to the value produced by the plaintiff's use. Only then has the defendant composer's use of the combination appropriated the value created by the plaintiff. (May, above Note 24 at 788).
[44] *Ladbroke (Football) Ltd v William Hill (Football) Ltd* [1964] 1 WLR 273 (HL).
[45] *Ibid.* at 276, 288, 293.
[46] Above Note 32 at 276.
[47] Bently, above Note 8 at 406.
[48] Other commentators suggest that the sampling of one note amounts to copyright infringement of the sound recording (see the text accompanying Notes 89 to 94, below).
[49] Bently, above Note 8 at 408.
[50] Thom, above Note 8 at 321.

between popular songs is inevitable due to the limited number of elements available to the composer of such musical works.[51]

Another commentator has suggested that:

> An original musical combination must be more than a trivial original use of the common musical elements to sufficiently contribute to the musical and commercial value of a composition to merit protection against unauthorised copying by another composer.[52]

and

> For most listeners, isolated musical elements have no independent significance—like words, but only produce value in relation to, and in combination with, other musical elements.[53]

Significant value may of course exist in very short musical phrases, such as the opening notes of Beethoven's 'Fifth Symphony', Weber's 'Phantom of the Opera' and Gershwin's 'Rhapsody in Blue'.[54] As stated above, this is especially true when the simple figure is repeated many times throughout the original work. In any event, for a succession of notes without words to amount to an artistically and financially important[55] portion of a work, that musical phrase would under usual circumstances, it is submitted, be greater than one or two notes in length.

It is instructive in attempting to delineate the nature of a 'substantial' portion to review the outcomes in actual cases involving musical works (Table I) and literary works (Table II) where what was alleged to have been copied was a comparatively small portion of the original work.

---

[51] '[W]hile there are an enormous number of possible permutations of the musical notes of the scale, only a few are pleasing, and much fewer still suit the infantile demands of the popular ear'. *Darrell v Joe Morris Music Co.*, 113 F. 2d 80 (2nd Cir. 1940). See also A. Schafter, *Musical Copyright* (2nd edn.) Wilmette, Illinois Callagham and Co.) (1939) at 155. Keyt above Note 13 at 427 to 428; May above Note 24 at 790; Sherman, above Note 24 at 124.

[52] May, above Note 24 at 787.

[53] May, above Note 24 at 795.

[54] May, above Note 24 at 793. See accompanying Notes 35 and 36 above.

[55] The relevance of the 'financial importance' of the copied portion has been accepted by some American courts (see the cases referred to in Notes 37 and 38, above) but has apparently not been endorsed by Canadian courts.

Copyright Protection for the Information Superhighway

[1994] 11 EIPR 465

ALLEN N. DIXON AND LAURIE C. SELF
Covington & Burling, London

The Challenges of the Infrastructure

A unique opportunity

The work of the European Community's High Level Group on Europe and the Global Information Society,[1] the National Information Infrastructure initiative in the United States, and other similar developments throughout the world, present a unique opportunity for authors of virtually every kind of literary, artistic, and scientific work; for the publishers, producers, and performers of these works; for the computer and telecommunications industries; and for the public at large.

This information infrastructure, often dubbed the 'information superhighway', offers the potential that every type of work and information could be made available, in digital form, on an electronic network or series of networks that would be accessible world-wide. For authors, publishers, producers and performers, this offers the promise that their works could be disseminated more widely and more efficiently. For the computer, broadcasting, cable, satellite and telecommunications industries, there is great potential for technical innovation and growth. And for virtually every member of the public, this infrastructure could make a wealth of services, data and creative works available, 'on-line', potentially in a form much more useful than is presently available.

Challenges of investment

With this historic opportunity come numerous technical, financial and legal challenges. An information infrastructure as such does not yet exist in a widely available, commercially useful form, and undoubtedly will not involve a monolithic building plan but rather an evolution and convergence of numerous technologies and development efforts.

A substantial amount of innovation will be required to improve and customise existing technology, and to create the new technology that will be required at every juncture of the

---

[1] This EC task force was established in February 1994 by Martin Bangemann, the European Commissioner for Industrial Affairs, Information Technologies and Telecommunications. The task force, commonly known as the Bangemann group, was established to review the European telecommunications industry and recommend steps needed to facilitate the development and operation of the European information superhighway. The Bangemann group presented its report to the European Council last June, which included recommendations for greater openness among national markets and uniformity of regulation.

information infrastructure. From larger and better storage and retrieval devices, to faster and wider data transmission capability, to broader cable and light-fibre coverage, to enhanced wireless networks, to better security for data and other content, to ever more numerous and varied software applications to run the vast selection of equipment that will make up the network – all of these will require tremendous investments of time and money to become a reality.

Moreover, such a network will find success only if it contains high-quality *content*— information, applications, works and services—that consumers find useful. The vast cost and scope of an information infrastructure, which ultimately will be global in its reach, cannot be borne by governments, and will not be borne by the private sector if consumers do not demand it. Consumers will not demand such an information superhighway if it is merely an alternative means of sending messages, playing games or watching television, but only if it is 'application rich'—replete with creative content and services of all kinds that are practical, affordable and valuable to the user.

Intellectual property protection: the key

Strong protection of intellectual property rights is absolutely essential to the promotion and development of such new applications and services, and thus to the creation and success of the information infrastructure itself. The international community has recognised, through the longstanding Berne Convention for the Protection of Literary and Artistic Works, the recent GATT TRIP's treaty,[2] and most national laws, that *protection* rather than *pilfering* of intellectual works is the way to encourage their creation, improvement and dissemination.

It is not through expropriation of intellectual property rights that new works and technology flourish, but rather through the rights granted to authors and other rightholders under the copyright law to license and distribute their works (or to withhold such licensing and distribution) on the terms that they see fit. Not only does this system reward the author's creativity in an abstract and cultural sense, it is the only practical way to ensure that authors and other rightholders receive the appropriate level of economic incentives and rewards to create works in the first place, and to update and improve such works.

In evaluating copyright protections for the information superhighway, this article reviews the basic technical features that would comprise an information infrastructure; evaluates the junctures of the infrastructure that are critical for intellectual property protection; examines the infrastructure in the light of existing copyright laws, including the EC Directive for the Legal Protection of Computer Programs, ('Software Directive'),[3] which will continue to work well for the information infrastructure; and sets forth a statement of principles that should guide copyright protection in the networked age.

Technology Overview of the Information Superhighway

The information infrastructure, at its most basic level, will be much like today's telephone call. On one end of the 'call' will be someone with a receiver, whether that be a personal computer, a television 'set-top' device, a digital telephone, or other similar device that can receive information in digital electronic form. On the other end of the 'call' will be someone with data, applications, works or services that he wants to make available. This content provider may be the rightholder of such content himself, who uses his own personal computer

---

[2] GATT TRIPs refers to the GATT Agreement on Trade-Related Aspects of Intellectual Property Rights.
[3] 91/250/EEC, OJ L122/42 (14 May 1991).

or other digital device to store and upload his content to the network. This provider may instead be a third-party hardware or service company, with whom the rightholder has entered an agreement for storage and upload of his data, applications, works or services to the network on specified conditions.

Such content will flow to the 'caller' only if the provider 'answers the phone', that is, if he willingly makes it available to the caller. This will occur in many instances under specified conditions of the provider, such as a one-time credit-card payment, or per-copy or per-use charges billed to a pre-arranged account. Assuming the content provider's conditions are met, his equipment will transfer or 'upload' the content to the network, the network will transmit it to the authorised user, and the user will either display the content on his equipment as it is received (as with on-line movies) or save or 'download' it to his own computer or other storage device for later use (as with computer programs). The 'call' may also be two-way, as a user's interactive feedback to the provider could change which content he receives.

Various technological protections, many of which have yet to be invented or perfected, will protect content and personal information on the infrastructure from unauthorised access, transfer and use. All manner of encryption devices, access codes and even electronic contracting will become standard features of the infrastructure, supplementing copyright and various other legal regimes that protect the intellectual works on the network.

Equally important, the passive nature of the infrastructure's equipment and operation means that content will not 'float free' on the network for anyone to download or use. Content will only be available if an identifiable person or node purposefully uploads or permits access to it. Content will only be transmitted if someone actively sends it. Transmission or access of content without the rightholder's permission will only take place if someone purposefully engages in such activity. Fundamentally, then, the information infrastructure will be suppliers and users connected by a 'phone call'—a wire or other carrier of electronic signal—rather than through a traditional retail channel or other tangible mechanisms. And the purposeful, human acts at each critical juncture of the infrastructure will continue to be governed by copyright and other legal protections, just as such acts at each stage of traditional distribution and use of intellectual works have been so governed.

Critical Junctions for Copyright Protection on the Infrastructure

There are five critical junctures of the information superhighway for purposes of the copyright law:

Creation of intellectual property

Creation of intellectual property will take place both to develop the content to be made available on the information infrastructure, and to develop the hardware and software that in the aggregate will comprise the infrastructure itself. Creation of content will generally take place 'off-line' by the various traditional means, at the premises of authors, publishers and other service and content providers. Of course, technology will continue to bring new tools to assist this creative process, such as the ability to combine different types of works into 'multimedia' products, to modify works in new ways through digital editing techniques, to provide computer simulations where live action or manual work were once required, and to permit on-line collaboration among authors at great distances and across national borders. Once content is created, it typically will be reproduced and stored in digital form on a computer's hard disk, large storage device, or other digital device ready for approved access through the information infrastructure.

Upload of content

This will typically involve applying an encryption or other access-control device to the content, and then making the content available to approved users by copying or transmission through the network on authorised access. Major publishers and producers would each undoubtedly establish their own upload nodes. The beginning of such a development has already taken place on the CompuServe network, for example, where virtually all major international software publishers already make software utility files and bug fixes available from their own upload nodes to identifiable users. Collection societies could provide online upload services for authors of individual works who did not wish to handle their works directly or through a major publisher, but even this is not a necessary role. The reach of the network, and universal, affordable access by users to network, will give individual authors the unprecedented opportunity to establish their own PC-based nodes for uploading and controlling distribution of their works under terms that they establish—in short, the opportunity for individual authors to become their own publisher—in a way that could never have been possible under existing distribution systems.

Transmission of content

Transmission of content and services from content provider to user would occur through one or a combination of carriers, such as the public telephone or other utilities' networks; cellular, satellite, light fibre, broadcast or cable communications; or local-or wide-area networks. Underlying much of this 'backbone' of the infrastructure will be computers and computer programs. Computer programs created to operate various portions of the infrastructure itself would reside on the transmission computers and other digital equipment throughout the network, and would interact with content suppliers' and users' computer equipment to transmit content between them through the network.

Given that much of this layer of the infrastructure will be developed as an extension to the wide variety of existing systems, it is likely that a multitude of different types of telecommunications and other transmission equipment, computers and software will ultimately comprise the technical delivery means of the infrastructure. This in itself is a good thing, as a competition among such service, equipment and software suppliers will make pricing more affordable for users, will promote investment in systems and improvements that users find worthwhile and easier to use, and will hasten the natural evolution toward 'interoperability'—the ability of different types of systems to send and receive content and services among each other.

Access of content

This juncture of the infrastructure is where the user, manually or automatically, 'signs on' to the network, provides his relevant access authorisation(s), and accesses one or more providers' content and services. This may involve users reproducing content from the provider's equipment onto their own equipment, or accessing a display or other time-sharing use of content on their equipment. In the area of computer software, for example, a user could 'log in' to a software publisher's upload node, review the various software products available, and—on agreeing to the provider's payment and licensing conditions—have a copy of a particular software product transmitted to the hard disk of his own computer, complete with any access codes necessary to decrypt and use the software. The end result here is no different from that with traditional software distribution: a digital copy within the end-user's physical control.

Use of content

Where particular content on the information infrastructure is only useable on-line, the intellectual property issues related to such use are identical to those arising on the access of such content. For example, where a particular software program is accessed and used on-line, a piece of that program is copied into the temporary memory ('random access memory' or 'RAM') of the user's local computer during use; once his use is completed, that portion of the program is erased from his computer's RAM and not saved to his hard disk. The same acts of copying, display and decryption would thus be involved both in accessing and in using the content in such a case. Where a work such as software is reproduced through the network from the supplier onto the user's local storage device for later use, the copyright law is further implicated if any 'off-line' reproduction, alteration or decryption takes place, or if the user himself uploads, transmits or permits access of the work to others through the network. This sequence of events, and the accompanying risk of piracy when a copy is made onto the hard disk of a user's local computer, are not different in kind or implication from the accessing of programs today from the storage devices known as 'file savers' on organisations' existing *internal* networks; the only difference is that programs are now typically loaded onto a file server from a diskette purchased from outside, rather than being downloaded from an external network.

The EC Software Directive: A Good Model for Protection of Digital Works

Existing copyright legislation, particularly the EC Software Directive, already covers the copyright issues that will arise as computer programs become part of the content and 'backbone' of the information infrastructure.

In preparing the Directive, the Commission made a thorough review of copyright issues involved in the software industry, the first major industry built solely on digital works. The Directive expressly recognises the fundamental importance of software for a broad range of industries, and for the Community's industrial development as a whole. The Directive reflects a thorough understanding of the copyright issues surrounding computer programs; and it protects well the intellectual property contained in software, while carefully reconciling various points of view. As such, the Directive as a whole represents the 'state-of-the-art' in software copyright legislation world-wide.

Most significantly here, the Directive already provides the various legal rules and protections governing software at each critical juncture of the infrastructure, and should serve as a good model for other copyright industries as their works become digitised and available on digital networks.

At the stage of software *creation*, the Directive lays out workable rules that clearly define the acts that authors may and may not do. The Directive recognises that creation of software works 'requires the investment of considerable human, technical, and financial resources', and that this process is discouraged where mere copying of other programs takes place, as that can be done 'at a fraction of the cost needed to develop them independently'.[4]

The Directive thus provides that software works which are *original*, and which constitute not mere ideas but *expression*, deserve protection. This protects expression of a program in any form, including interfaces, so long as it is original.[5] Another protected work cannot be *reproduced* into a work as it is being created (or otherwise), in whole or in part in any form, without the rightholder's consent.[6] However, the program of another may be *observed, tested* and *studied* to determine its underlying ideas and principles, if this is done while performing permitted acts of using the program.[7] And the program of another may be *decompiled* in certain cases, to achieve interoperability with other programs under defined conditions.[8] Given that the process of creating computer programs is the same regardless of whether they are used or distributed on a network or on physical storage media such as diskettes, the Directive's rules applicable to software creation will continue to be completely relevant and workable in the networked age.

Uploads of computer programs to the network virtually always involve a *reproduction*—from the provider's computer either to the storage device of a user's computer directly, or temporarily to the memory disk or storage device of another computer along the network in some cases. The rightholder's exclusive right under the Directive to do or authorise reproduction of his work (including the explicit right to control any 'loading' of his work that necessitates reproduction) thus applies to uploads of copyrighted works into the infrastructure. Any uploads that also constitute *distribution* of software works would likewise be covered by the rightholder's exclusive right under the Directive to control 'any form of distribution to the public'.[9]

Similarly, the Directive already covers the area of *transmission* of computer programs via the infrastructure, and the software that makes up any part of the infrastructure itself, in one or more ways. The Directive expressly provides that 'transmission' and 'storage' of software works, to the extent that these involve reproduction, must be authorised by the rightholder.[10] This would cover the situation where software content is temporarily stored or otherwise reproduced by any network equipment between the provider and the user. Software that is incorporated into the 'backbone' equipment running the infrastructure itself is subject to the same reproduction right of the Directive. The copying of such software onto the infrastructure equipment, and any further temporary or permanent copying of that software into the memory of the users' and providers' computers with which it interacts along the network, similarly require the rightholder's authorisation under the Directive.

As the mirror image of uploads, *downloads* of software from the infrastructure are also covered by the Directive's reproduction right. Not only software reproduced onto the user's hard disk or other storage device, but also any program used on-line in 'real time' between the uploader's and the downloader's computer, are covered by the Directive. Given that portions of any program used online are temporarily *copied* into the temporary RAM memory of both the uploader's and the downloader's computer, the Directive's rules prohibiting unauthorised 'temporary' reproduction apply. Moreover, while the Directive does not directly prohibit 'computer crimes', that is, unauthorised access to a computer itself, it does forbid possession or circulation of items designed to remove or bypass technical devices protecting a computer program, which should help to safeguard password-protected upload systems as

---

[4] EC Software Directive, second Recital.
[5] *Ibid.*, Article 1(2)–(3).
[6] *Ibid.*, Article 4(a).
[7] *Ibid.*, Article 5(3).
[8] *Ibid.*, Article 6.
[9] *Ibid.*, Article 4(c).
[10] *Ibid.*, Article 4(a).

well as access-or copy-protected software content distributed on the network.[11]

As for *use* of software downloaded from the network, the Directive confirms traditional copyright rules giving the rightholder the right to do or to authorise reproduction, alteration, and distribution. These apply without distinction to software downloaded from the infrastructure or obtained in other ways, such as by purchase in packaged form from a local shop. This is only logical, as software ultimately exists in the same form and operates in the same way regardless of whether it was obtained via electronic transmission or on diskettes or other physical media.

Consistency with Traditional Copyright Concepts

The copyright and other intellectual property issues implicated by the information infrastructure are thus not fundamentally different from those already faced by authors and rightholders in the pre-networked world, certainly in the software arena. This should not be surprising, as the copyright law establishes intangible rights protecting the *expression of authors' intellectual creation*, over and above the tangible *form* of such expression, the physical media on which the expression is recorded, or the mechanical means by which such expression is delivered.

The information infrastructure simply represents a change in the form but not the substance of authors' intellectual creations. The recording media, the delivery means, and the form of the expression of authors' works may in many cases change. (Most of such changes would not, in fact, take place in the case of software, which has always been created, distributed and used in digital form.) Much of the discussion about the infrastructure so far, however, has fastened onto such potential changes in the tangible aspects of creative works, and has lost sight of the fact that the copyright law fundamentally protects the author's intellectual creation regardless of its form. Some analyses have gone so far as to put the cart before the horse, suggesting that merely because the tangible expression of a work is, for example, digital rather than printed, more easily modified in digital form, or more useful in derivative works than its analogue counterpart, that somehow the intellectual property in that work should receive less or different protection.

Nothing could be further from the mark. As the authors of all types of works enter the networked age, where tangible aspects of their works become even less important, protection of the underlying intellectual property represented in their works becomes even more crucial. The computer software industry, which has dealt with digitised works since its inception, is well-familiar with this need. This industry was built on the foundation of strong copyright laws, and is maintained through vigorous enforcement of such laws. Given that the copyright law fundamentally protects intangible rights in authors' intellectual creations, regardless of their form, it is well-suited to continue protecting software and other types of works that enter the digital age, even though one or more of the following changes in the tangible aspects of such works may take place.

Change in form

Traditional works such as literary, artistic, musical, audio-visual and other works will need to be digitised by the author or rightholder that wants to make them available on the information infrastructure. As in the software area, well-settled rules already set forth the

---

[11] *Ibid.*, Article 7(c).

criteria required for such works to qualify for copyright protection, such as originality and the idea/expression doctrines, and establish the acts of copying and other infringement of other works that must be avoided in creating a work. Works will continue to be 'fixed', albeit in digital form, and any modification required to put such works in digital form would require the rightholder's approval. There would even seem to be little confusion about which copyright label—literary, artistic, musical, audio-visual, computer program—would apply to a work that has been digitised. In short, nothing about the digital form of such works should substantially affect their treatment by the copyright law.

Change in distribution methods

In the networked age, works that were traditionally distributed in printed, cassette, disk, film or other physical form, can simply be distributed and used electronically on the information superhighway. As in the software area, each type of copyrighted work is protected by familiar categories and specialised rules related to reproduction, modification, distribution, performance and other exclusive rights, which appear readily adaptable to the digitised versions of such works in most cases.

Change in ease of access and copying

One important objective of an information infrastructure would be to allow universal access to the network, so that anyone who agrees to the relevant rightholders' terms could enjoy a wide variety of digitised works. Moreover, the nature of digital works is such that in many cases (depending on how a work is developed, encrypted and made available) copies made by users may be completely identical to the original, without any loss of quality. Such broader public access and improvement in copy quality does not mean, however, that unauthorised copying and distribution of protected works will necessarily mushroom in the networked age.

First, numerous new technologies for encrypting, decrypting and otherwise controlling access and copying of protected works are under development. As has been found in the area of certain copy-protected software programs and Digital Audio Tape, technical devices can be developed to reduce or eliminate unauthorised user copying. Similarly, experimental schemes for direct electronic contracting of software are underway, in which the user would agree to legally binding restrictions on copying and other acts as a condition to receiving works electronically. Such encryption and electronic licensing schemes would supplement protections under the copyright law against unauthorised copying. In short, the answer to such technological challenges to copyright very likely will be found in the technology itself.

Second, detection of unauthorised upload, transmission and download of copyrighted works on the infrastructure may well be easier than finding traditional, non-electronic piracy. It will not be technically practical to monitor in Orwellian fashion all 'traffic' on the vast information superhighway as some have suggested, given that the equipment making up the infrastructure will be immensely varied and dispersed and given that the volume of electronic traffic will be staggering. However, anti-piracy organisations, such as the Business Software Alliance, have found that even present-day 'bulletin board' pirates, who engage in systematic copying of software through modems over the existing telephone network, are relatively easy to find and prosecute. In order to do any real damage to the rightholder, they must market themselves in some electronic or other manner, and this generally comes to the attention of an alert rightholder—who, like any other member of the public, can log onto the pirate's bulletin board and see what works he is offering for upload. Latter-day infrastructure pirates, on a public network where works will reside on identifiable upload nodes and can only be uploaded by intentional act, should be no more difficult to detect.

Despite, broader public access and improved copy quality, therefore, the copyright law's protections against unauthorised reproduction will thus continue to be an effective deterrent to uploads, transmissions and downloads of works without the rightholder's consent.

Merger of various types of works

The ability to create digital 'multimedia' works is sometimes hailed as the greatest challenge to established copyright principles. In fact, works like these mark no conceptual change, and relatively little technical advancement, over traditional software works, derivative works, compilations or databases which have been in existence for a long time and which similarly incorporate the works of other authors. A book publisher seeking to publish a collection of essays on a given subject of course must get permission from the author of each included essay. In the software area, 'clip art' drawings that are incorporated into computer programs must be licensed from the artist. The licensing process required for multimedia works is exactly the same as that which the creators of software works, derivative works, compilations and databases have been engaged in for many years, and derives from the same copyright-law requirement that reproduction, modification and distribution of a work remain the exclusive right of the author or other rightholder.

Determining the party from whom a licence should be sought and negotiating a licence may take time and effort, and undoubtedly will require payment to the rightholder. In the case of the computer software that is sought to be included in a multimedia work, identifying the software rightholder is typically easy, given that the software industry is young and the rightholder is virtually always identified in the software itself. Securing a licence is relatively straightforward for software as well; in fact, many packaged software development programs presently *contain* a licence permitting the purchaser to copy and distribute designated useful pieces of the purchased program (sometimes called 'objects', 'class libraries' or 'run-time modules') with programs that the purchaser himself develops. Identifying rightholders and securing licences may be less simple in the case of other types of works, and authors and rightholders do retain the right under the Berne Convention to withhold licences at their discretion. But there is no overriding advantage to multi-media works as such to warrant treating their creators differently from anyone else who might want to incorporate the work of another author or, worse yet, to warrant any weakening of the golden rule of copyright that reproduction, modification and distribution of an author's works may only be done with his permission.

Desire for interoperability

Another aspect of the information infrastructure that will implicate intellectual property law is the drive for various systems on the infrastructure to be able to send and receive content among themselves on a national and international basis. This may involve international standards set by such bodies as telecommunications standards organisations, industry norms that develop naturally in response to user acceptance, or individual efforts to develop products that work with the infrastructure. Though the ever-present temptation in such instances is to *expropriate* whatever works and technology are desired, at no charge or at non-market licence fees, the copyright and other intellectual property laws quite properly protect against involuntary licensing as well as unauthorised copying and distribution, and in fact work well in *encouraging* the development and voluntary licensing of interoperable works and technology.

New terminology

Much of what presently passes for novel about the information infrastructure is little more than jargon. New technical terms, or borrowed or shorthand terms, bandied about in the context of the infrastructure indeed require careful evaluation as to their true meaning. But again, there is nothing inherent in terms such as 'interfaces', 'multimedia', 'interoperability', 'on-line services', or other superhighway jargon that changes the fundamental fact that creative intellectual expression is protected by the copyright law, and cannot and should not be taken without the rightholder's freely given consent.

Statement of Principles for Copyright Protections in the Networked Age

In the light of technology's steady march into the age of the information infrastructure, and the increasing importance of copyright protection for digitised works, the authors offer the following recommended principles for copyright protections in the context of the information infrastructure.

(1) Copyright protections should be maintained at least at present levels in the networked age.

The underlying rationale for protecting authors and other rightholders remains unchanged, regardless of the form of their works or how such works may be distributed. Strong intellectual property protections are the foundation supporting the creation and improvement of works necessary to build the information infrastructure and the content required to make the infrastructure a success, and efficiently and effectively reward the authors and other rightholders for such accomplishments.

(2) The EC Directive on the Legal Protection of Computer Programs works well in providing an appropriate level of protection for software works. The Directive's copyright rules should be maintained in their present form, and should be evaluated as a good model for protection of other types of works that become digitised.

As software was the first major type of digitised work protected by copyright law, the Commission made an exhaustive review of the considerations involved in the creation, distribution, and use of such a digitised work. The Directive has led directly to reductions in software piracy rates in Europe, and to a corresponding growth in the creation of software works and the software industry itself. The Directive's provisions already cover, directly or indirectly, the creation, upload, transmission, access and use of software works on an information infrastructure; its substantive rules thus require no adjustment as Europe enters the networked age.

(3) The author or other rightholder of a digital work should retain the exclusive right to reproduce and modify the work (including the act of digitisation itself), and to incorporate the digitised work, in whole or in part in any form, into other works.

Existing copyright law gives authors and other rightholders the right to control copying and modification of their works, and creation of derivative works. Nothing about digital works, multimedia works, standards setting, or the information infrastructure itself changes this fundamental fact, or the rationale underlying these rules. These protections are vital to encourage the creation, improvement and dissemination of all types of intellectual works for the networked age.

(4) The author or other rightholder in a digital work should retain the exclusive right to upload, transmit, access and download the work electronically.

As has been seen in the software area, such acts are not different in substance from those protected by traditional reproduction, distribution, performance, and other similar rights, and should be protected thereunder.

(5) Exceptions to the exclusive rights of the author or other rightholder of digital works should be few and narrowly drawn.

Given that copies of digital works, such as computer programs, may well be identical to the original, there is even less scope for 'private copying' or other broad copyright exceptions for digital works. The EC Software Directive's narrowly tailored exceptions are on the whole a good model for copyright exceptions in the context of digitised works. Exceptions greater than these could easily swallow the general rule of copyright protection, and violate the Berne Convention rule against unreasonably prejudicing the rightholder's legitimate interests or conflicting with the rightholder's normal exploitation of his work.

(6) The specific exception for decompilation in the EC Software Directive was a hard-fought compromise which does not need adjustment.

Decompilation is, at heart, modifying and reproducing all or part of a computer program that another author has created—acts that would in themselves violate the copyright and possibly even the moral rights of the author. The Commission has recognised that decompilation may be permissible, under a set of detailed conditions, where necessary to achieve the interoperability of an independently created computer program with other programs.[12] Nothing about the information infrastructure, multimedia works or any other recent technological developments have changed the various interests that would seek either to tighten this provision better to protect the author's rights, or to relax it in order to allow more widespread copying of the works of another. The Commission has struck a delicate compromise on the decompilation issue that takes into account all of these interests, and there is no value or reason to re-run this prolonged and difficult debate.[13]

(7) Changes to the copyright law should not be undertaken hastily, and then only to plug gaps found to exist in the current scheme of protection.

The substance of the copyright law is strong and well-established, and has proved flexible enough to deal with new developments as they have arisen. Software developers and other content providers take comfort in the fact that their works are protected under these clear, established rules, and therefore continue to invest in development of new and innovative works which will be of benefit to the information infrastructure. Particularly as the infrastructure is only in its very initial stages of development, and as the technologies and proposals for an infrastructure are not in any way definite, there is little basis on which to

---

[12] *Ibid.*, Article 6(1).
[13] See B. Czarnota and R. Hart, *Legal Protection of Computer Programs in Europe—A Guide to the EC Directive*, Commentary to Article 6: Decompilation at 74 to 76 (1991).

evaluate possible changes to the copyright law, which would only be appropriate as and when gaps in protection begin to appear. Moreover, reducing or otherwise changing intellectual property protections at this time would increase uncertainty and otherwise deter investment of resources in the very works needed for the development and success of the information superhighway itself.

(8) Multimedia works should be created, reproduced and distributed only with the consent of the author or other rightholder of each included work.

Multimedia is, at heart, a high-tech software work, derivative work, compilation, or database which contains a third party's work. There is nothing about multimedia works that warrants a departure from long-established rules requiring the creator of a software work, derivative work, compilation, or database to get third-party authors' or rightholders' consent prior to including their works. Multimedia works should succeed or fail under the market and copyright rules to which all other creators of software works, derivative works, compilations and databases are subject.

(9) Compulsory licensing of any intellectual property right should be avoided.

A fundamental principle of the Berne Convention and the GATT TRIPs agreement is that intellectual property rights are to be licensed and exercised only with the author's or rightholder's consent, which may be freely withheld, and that compulsory licensing is to be avoided except in extreme circumstances.[14] Especially in the context of the information infrastructure, where encryption and other technology will make it easier to protect intellectual property, and where the principal participants who might seek compulsory licensing as a way of increasing their own profits are well able to pay for or develop their own intellectual property, any new forms of compulsory licensing should be avoided. Even indirect encouragement of non-market licensing through such devices as preferential access to information, government contracts or technology—a natural temptation at standards-setting bodies or government-sponsored registration or licence clearance centres—should be prohibited as compulsory licensing schemes.

(10) Rightholders should retain the ultimate decision to determine whether to license their works and enforce their rights collectively or individually.

As pointed out by the World Intellectual Property Organisation at a recent meeting in Paris, 'the freedom of owners of rights to decide what way of exercise of rights they choose and the exclusive nature of the rights involved should be fully respected'.[15] Particularly in an age in which the technology should improve control over unauthorised copying, new collective administration or levy schemes should not be imposed in any case without the voluntary consent of the affected rightholder, given that such schemes typically increase the cost of licence administration, result in reduced or non-market payments to authors and rightholders, and can actually serve as an economic incentive to piracy. Such works as software, which have never been subject to collective licensing or administration, should continue to be licensed only on an individual and contractual basis, whether the software is distributed as a separate work or with other types of works on the infrastructure.

---

[14] See S. Ricketson, *The Berne Convention for the Protection of Literary and Artistic Works: 1886–1986* ¶16.28 (1987). Article 9(1) of GATT TRIPs requires compliance with the Berne Convention as it pertains to the exclusive rights of copyright holders.

[15] Dr Mihály Ficsor, 'New Technologies and Copyright: Need for Change, Need for Continuity', WIPO Worldwide Symposium on the Future of Copyright and Neighboring Rights (May 1994), at 11.

(11) Intellectual property rights should be made part of national or international standards only with the freely given consent of the rightholder.

Established standards bodies have for many years incorporated intellectual property rights into standards only after careful *identification* of affected rights, and voluntary *consent* of the rightholder. The European Commission has recognised that rightholders should have the right in the first instance to grant or refuse licences for use of their intellectual property in standards on whatever bases they wish, and that rightholders choosing to grant such licences should do so on fair, reasonable and non-discriminatory terms. Nothing about the information infrastructure requires variance from this fundamental principle. Indeed, voluntary participation and market-based payments *encourage* rightholders to license their works for use in standards, and thus encourage the very development of better and more up-to-date standards.

(12) Administrative formalities related to copyrighted works should be avoided.

Not only are registration and deposit schemes as a prerequisite to copyright protection prohibited by the Berne Convention,[16] similar administrative schemes should be avoided as counterproductive. Identification numbers should be placed on a work and dealt with in any way only with the full consent of a rightholder; registration of encryption-enabled software should be prohibited. Such administrative requirements are easily enacted, but are difficult to update or eliminate even though a rapidly changing market like the infrastructure makes them obsolete. Voluntary schemes harden into mandatory schemes. And the administrative overhead, cost and delay inherent in such systems in many cases does nothing to serve the primary policy goal of encouraging the creation, improvement and dissemination of copyrighted works.

(13) Copyright, neighbouring rights and any new rights related to intellectual property should be granted and administered on the principle of national treatment.

An underlying requirement of the Berne Convention, as well as the GATT TRIPs text, is that states should grant and protect intellectual property rights on the basis of national treatment, that is, to their own nationals and to foreign nationals without discrimination.[17] This rule has eliminated inequities in national legal schemes, reduced the temptation for international retaliation in the fields of intellectual property and trade, and promoted the improvement and harmonisation of intellectual property rules internationally. The principle of national treatment is equally appropriate for new rights related to intellectual property, such as the unfair extraction right in the proposed EC Database Directive. Closer co-operation among states to harmonise intellectual property norms, rather than discrimination through enactment of reciprocity or other protectionist rules, is necessary to harmonise and strengthen intellectual property and related rights, and thus promote the information infrastructure itself.

(14) Unauthorised access to computers and content through the information infrastructure should be a crime.

Many states have already recognised that not only is the protection of intellectual property vital, protection of computer systems from damage and unauthorised access through the network is necessary to protect personal privacy, personal data, and other confidential data and systems. In addition to good copyright laws, strong laws on computer crimes will be

---

[16] Berne Convention, Article 5(2).
[17] *Ibid.*, Article 5(3); GATT TRIPs, Article 3(1).

necessary to protect against unauthorised access of computers, theft or interruption of computer services, destruction of computer equipment, trafficking in computer passwords or misuse of computer system information that might be attempted on the information infrastructure. It should likewise be a criminal violation to manufacture, import, sell, lease, use or possess a technical device or computer program product, the purpose of which is to circumvent the security of the infrastructure, or any security measures included in the infrastructure or in copyrighted works themselves.

(15) Procedures and remedies to redress violations of intellectual property protection should be effective, efficient and strong.

The principal difficulty in copyright enforcement related to the information infrastructure will be in the legal system, where procedures can be inadequate, cumbersome and slow, and where penalties may be wholly inadequate to redress violations. In many legal systems, procedures and remedies are such that the cost of proving a copyright violation and damages, when compared to the available relief, are a disincentive to the enforcement of authors' and rightholders' rights—and thus an incentive to copyright violations—in even the most obvious cases of piracy. Enforcement procedures and remedies should be modernised and streng- thened, on a national and multi-national basis, to place the full cost of rightholder com- pensation and of copyright enforcement on the infringer, and otherwise to provide true deterrence against the theft of intellectual property.

The Proposed EU
Directive for the Legal
Protection of Databases:
A Cornerstone of the
Information Society?*
[1995] 12 EIPR 583

LAURENCE KAYE
Head of Publishing and New Media
The Simkins Partnership, London

New Legal Framework for Databases

On 10 July 1995, after two and a half years of negotiation, the European Commission's proposal for a directive on the legal protection of databases ('the Directive') formally achieved a Common Position. It is now before the European Parliament for its second Opinion. The Directive will be adopted when (and if) any amendments made by Parliament have been agreed with the European Commission and the Council of Ministers. The target date is December 1995.

The origin of the Directive was the European Commission's 1988 Green Paper on Copyright.[1] At that time, 'databases' were seen primarily as 'business to business', on-line information databases containing share prices, company information and other data. In the meanwhile, the growth (real and potential) of multimedia products and services, the emergence of the Internet and other networks as the means of their 'on-line' delivery have increased the importance of this Directive. To the extent that a multimedia work (such as an interactive encyclopaedia) is a 'collection' of facts, works or other items, and not a single or independent work, then this directive will treat it as a database. The Directive is therefore, in part, the 'Multimedia Directive' in addition to seeking to create a harmonised regime for information databases.

If content is to be king on the superhighway, then the Directive will be of vital importance to content owners, providers and users of information and entertainment products and services in both fixed media and 'on-line' forms. It will harmonise the rules governing copyright in databases and create a new right to protect substantial investment in the contents of databases. For database producers, ranging from directories and encyclopaedias on CD-ROM to on-line providers of information and education products and services, the Directive will be a key element in the intellectual property framework of rights over their databases. These rights, combined with the technology being put in place to monitor and control access and use of databases, will be at the heart of the emerging Information Society. The Directive will introduce a 'two-tier' level of protection for 'databases' (defined below). Copyright will protect the structure of the database and not the contents themselves. A new, 15-year non-

---

[1] Green Paper on copyright and the challenge of technology Copyright Issues requiring immediate action dated 7 June 1988 Catalogue number CB-CO-88-267-EN-C ISSN 0254–1475.

copyright right (the *sui generis* right) will be introduced to prevent the unauthorised taking or re-use of the database's contents provided the database producer (called the 'maker' in the Directive) can show that substantial investment has been made in the obtaining, verifying or presentation of those contents.

The Directive does not take away any subsisting rights in the materials incorporated into the database. For example, in the case of a database which contains films as part of a 'video on demand' service, or sound recordings as part of a 'digital jukebox', the permission of all rightholders in the films, and those in the underlying musical compositions and sound recordings, would still be needed to incorporate those works into the database and then to distribute or transmit them. In fact, the Directive will create a double layer of protection where the database includes contents which are copyright-protected, such as films, photographs or newspaper articles. Those contents will continue to be copyright-protected and, in addition, will be protected by the new *sui generis* right.

What Is a 'Database'?

A database is a '*collection* of works, data or other *independent* materials arranged in a systematic or methodical way and capable of being *individually* accessed by electronic or other means'.[2] The reference to 'other means' is intended to include databases which can be 'accessed' by the human eye. This would apply, for example, to a structured database in paper form. The phrase 'arranged in a systematic or methodical manner' sets a low threshold. It will exclude haphazard collections. In the case of electronic databases, the mere provision of code or other means for identifying one field or record from another will probably be sufficient.

The combined effect of 'collection' and 'independent' is that to qualify as a database there must be the bringing together of a number of separate items (be they copyright works like films, photographs, text, sound recordings or software programs and/or items of mere data like share prices, catalogue details or other factual or statistical data). Also, those items must be capable of being 'individually accessed'. Databases available in fixed formats such as CD-ROM or as part of an 'on-line' service, consisting of data such as directories, share prices, company information, will clearly be capable of falling within this definition. The status of collections of audio-visual materials is more complex.

Although a 'collection' of films may qualify as a database (for example, as part of a video on demand service), an individual film would not. While an individual film consists of a number of constituent underlying works (namely, the film itself, sound recording(s) and musical compositions as part of the soundtrack) those works are not 'independent' in the sense that one frame of the film is not independent from another—they are only meaningful when seen as a series of moving images. The same principles would be true of a collection of computer software programs or video games.

However, there will be interactive audio-visual works which will meet this definition and they will not be confined to databases consisting of image or sound materials or to reference type multimedia works such as *Encarta* and other interactive encyclopaedias, all of which will be protected under the Directive as databases as collections of independent works (photos, videos, literary works and other material).

Sound recordings are capable of falling within the definition as databases because a phonogram is a collection of 'independent' works, that is, the individual musical compositions of individual tracks comprised on a CD or other recorded medium. However, Recital (19) makes it clear that, as a rule, such compilations will not come within the scope of the

---

[2] Article 1.2.

Directive because they will not meet the criteria for copyright and *sui generis* protection as explained later in this article. Each database will therefore be treated on its own merits. For example, a 'page' on the World Wide Web on the Internet will be capable of being a 'database' as a collection of independent works—literary works (such as articles), graphic works (photos, diagrams, illustrations), video, sound and, in some cases, computer software.

In the remaining part of this article, a hypothetical database—'Intercuisine'—will be used to illustrate the protection given to databases by the Directive. 'Intercuisine' is a database available in on-line, CD-ROM and print formats with extensive information about food in Europe. It has details of restaurants classified by price, location, style and theme; details of chefs and their favourite recipes and photo and video material as well.

Copyright in a Database

The Directive follows the 'droit d'auteur' approach to copyright by requiring intellectual creativity on the part of the author(s) of the database. This is also consistent with the approach taken by Article 10.2 of TRIPs[3] to the protection of compilations. Article 3.1 of the Directive provides that 'databases which, by reason of the selection or arrangement of their contents, constitute the author's own intellectual creation shall be protected as such by copyright.' While the Directive will thereby harmonise eligibility criteria for copyright protection, it is silent on what is actually protectable by copyright in the database. This will therefore remain subject to national law. This silence is repeated in the tautological definition in Article 5 that the object of the restricted acts is the 'expression of the database which is protectable by copyright'. However, although not defined, it seems that the use of the word 'expression' is intended to ensure that copyright protection does not extend to ideas and principles such as selection or arrangement criteria.

The rules governing ownership of the copyright in a database will not be harmonised. Ownership will, therefore, be determined under national copyright law. The human author(s) will normally be the first owners. In the case of the United Kingdom, if they are employees of the publisher of Intercuisine, the publishers will be the first owners. In other Member States, copyright ownership, or the scope of any copyright licence, will be determined in accordance with contractual arrangements entered into between the author(s) and the publisher/database producer.

Criteria for Copyright Protection: Intercuisine

If the copyright owner of Intercuisine can show that the individual(s) responsible for the design of the database exercised intellectual creativity in deciding which restaurants and/or chefs to include, then to that extent the database will be protected by copyright. For example, if Intercuisine classifies restaurants which all cook in the style of a particular chef, as against simply listing them in alphabetical order, it may be able to demonstrate the necessary degree of intellectual creativity. The copyright in the database would be infringed if and to the extent that those elements of creativity reflected in the novel classifications were reproduced without authority.

However, if the names and addresses of the restaurants in Intercuisine were reproduced in alphabetical order, it is unlikely that the copyright in the database would be infringed. As already noted, the database copyright owner's rights apply to 'the expression of the database

---

[3] Agreement On Trade-Related Aspects of Intellectual Property Rights, Including Trade In Counterfeit Goods.

which is protectable by copyright' and not the contents themselves. That is why copyright in the database may be regarded as a 'thin' right. Many reference-type databases will not qualify for copyright protection because they will be unable to meet the criterion of intellectual creativity, especially where they are of an exhaustive nature and where the contents are 'self-selecting'. Other databases, particularly those of an 'encyclopaedia' nature, will satisfy the criteria for copyright protection more easily.

In contrast, the *sui generis* right, which protects the contents of the database and not its structure, would be infringed if the contents were taken in that alphabetical form. The protection of the database by copyright is quite separate from the rights in the computer software which enables the user to make use of a range of search strategies. Article 2 states that the Directive is without prejudice to Community provisions relating to the legal protection of computer programs as well as those relating to rental and lending rights and the term of protection of copyright.[4]

Scope of Copyright Protection

Article 5 sets out the 'restricted acts' which the author of a database has the exclusive right to do or authorise others to do. These rights cover all forms of reproduction, distribution and communication of the database to the public. Recital (31) in the Directive makes it clear that the copyright protection of databases includes making them available by means other than the distribution of copies. So on-line transmission of the database clearly requires the consent of the owner of the copyright of the database. It would include on-screen display where (as would normally be the case) a copy of the database was transferred to memory for that purpose.

If Intercuisine is distributed as a CD-ROM, or as a printed directory or guide, the 'exhaustion of rights' principle will apply to each such copy. Following the first sale of a copy of the database in that form, the owner of the copyright in the database cannot control any resale within the Community of that copy (Article 5(c)). In contrast, if Intercuisine is made available as, or as part of, an on-line service, the 'exhaustion' principle will not apply because it does not apply to the provision of a service as distinct from the distribution of goods.[5] Recital (33) states that 'every on-line service is in fact an act which will have to be subject to authorization where the copyright so provides'. Furthermore, the 'exhaustion' principle would not apply to any copy in material form (whether electronic or print) of the database made from an on-line transmission. This means that the copyright owner of the database is able to exercise greater control over the redistribution of the database made available by on-line transmission than over copies which are first distributed in material form. It also means that it will be essential from the database provider's viewpoint that the scope of the user's rights is made clear whenever the database is distributed in material form or made available by on-line transmission.

Intercuisine also contains still images and video material. The producer (referred to as the 'maker' in the Directive from the French 'fabriquant') would need the permission of the owner(s) of the copyright in those materials to incorporate them into the database and to make the database available containing that material.

---

[4] See Council Directive 91/250/EEC of 14 May 1991 on the legal protection of computer programs, Council Directive 92/100/EEC of 19 November 1992 on rental right and lending right and on certain rights related to copyright in the field of intellectual property, and Council Directive 93/98/EEC of 29 October 1993 harmonising the term of protection of copyright and certain related rights.

[5] See *CODITEL v Cine Vog Films*, Judgment of European Court of Justice of 18 March 1980, Case 62/79.

Exceptions to Copyright

The Directive gives Member States the *option* (but not the obligation) to include exceptions to copyright in the database. For example, Member States can allow fair dealing/fair use exceptions for 'the sole purpose of illustration for teaching or scientific research, to the extent justified by the non-commercial purpose' (Article 6.2(b)). 'Scientific research' covers both the natural and the human sciences (Recital 36).

The Directive does *not* allow any exception for home copying of a database in *electronic* form. This means that Member States will not be able to operate levy schemes (such as those currently applying in several Member States for blank audio tapes) for databases.

Duration of Protection of Copyright in the Database

This will be determined in accordance with the Term Directive (Council Directive 93/98/EEC) of 29 October 1993 which is due to be implemented by Member States by 1 July 1995, a deadline which most Member States have already missed!

The New Sui Generis Right: Protecting the Contents of the Database

The rationale behind the introduction of this new right is clearly explained in Recital (40) to the Directive.

> The objective of this sui generis right is to ensure protection of any investment in obtaining, verifying or presenting the contents of a database ...; such investment may consist of the implementation of financial resources and/or expending time, effort and energy.

It is concerned with protecting *investment*. Applied to Intercuisine, that investment may have been made in gathering the contents (for example, by research or sending out questionnaires), and/or by checking the accuracy of the source material and/or in the way in which the contents are presented in the database. It has been observed that 'presenting' resembles the right under current UK copyright law in published editions. 'Presenting' would, for instance, include investment necessary to digitise an existing database.

It is quite possible that different companies will have invested in 'obtaining verifying or presenting the contents'. For example, company A, a data provider, may have invested in collecting the database's contents which are then bought by Company B which publishes the database after either checking the accuracy of the contents and/or designing the way in which the database is presented to the user. Based on the current text of the Directive, in that situation, Company A will own the *sui generis* right in respect of the 'obtaining' of the data and Company B will own the right in respect of the 'verifying' and 'presentation' of the contents. The message for Company B (the publisher) is to make sure it buys the outstanding *sui generis* rights from Company A!

The investment has to be 'substantial'. That will be judged qualitatively and/or quantitatively. So if Intercuisine contains thousands of records and the investment has been principally one of time and money in gathering them together, it will qualify for protection. Equally, if it contains relatively few records, but there has been 'substantial' investment in targeting those records, it will also qualify. The onus is on the 'maker' of the database to show that substantial investment has been made. It will therefore be vital that the necessary records of this investment are kept in order to substantiate any claim for infringement of the *sui generis* right.

What Rights Does the Maker of the Database Have under the Sui Generis Right?

The Directive provides that the maker ('fabriquant' in the French language version) will have the right 'to prevent acts of extraction and/or re-utilization of the whole or a substantial part, evaluated quantitatively and/or qualitatively, of the contents of that database'.[6] 'Extraction' covers any form of transfer (temporary or permanent) of all or a substantial part of the contents to another medium, however achieved. It therefore focuses on the taking of the contents and not any subsequent redistribution. So it would include displaying some of the contents of Intercuisine on screen, assuming that to do so has necessitated making an electronic copy held in RAM.[7] To that extent, the Directive addresses the concerns of those who argue in favour of a new regime—for example, the 'Accessright'—to address the problems for copyright in the digital era.[8] It would also clearly extend to copies made in electronic or paper form as well.

'Re-utilization' involves 'any form of making available to the public all or a substantial part of the contents of a database by the distribution of copies, by renting, by on-line or other forms of transmission'. This clearly focuses on the *distribution* and *transmission* of the database's contents following the act of 'extraction'. Rather than using the copyright language of 'broadcast' or 'communication to the public', this is the first Directive to expressly use the expression 'on-line transmission'. It therefore avoids the problem of whether broadcast or communication to the public extends to point to point transmission.

Extraction and/or re-utilisation of *insubstantial* parts will not infringe the *sui generis* right. That will be judged qualitatively and quantitatively. For example, in the case of Intercuisine, if the 'Top 20' list of restaurants it contains is extracted and re-used without permission, it would in all probability infringe the right. In particular, if those contents reappear in a competing database, the owner of the *sui generis* right in Intercuisine will have a strong argument for infringement based on the potential harm to its commercial exploitation of Intercuisine caused by the competitor's unauthorised action. The cumulative effect of taking of insubstantial parts of the database on a regular basis could also infringe the *sui generis* right.[9]

For owners of rights in a database it is essential that all contracts for databases (whether appearing as printed terms or on-screen) must clearly lay down the scope of the user's rights, particularly with regard to single user versus network access and redistribution. If not, there is a real danger that commercially valuable content will disappear into the ether of the public domain.

---

[6] Article 7.1.

[7] Recital (44) states that 'when on-screen display of the contents of a database necessitates the permanent or temporary transfer of all or a substantial part of such contents to another medium, that act should be subject to authorization by the rightholder'.

[8] See Simon Olswang, 'Accessright: An Evolutionary Path for Copyright into the Digital Era?' Opinion [1995] 5 EIPR 215.

[9] Article 7.5 provides that 'The repeated and systematic extraction and/or re-utilization of insubstantial parts of the contents of the database which would have the result of performing acts which conflict with the normal exploitation of that database or which unnecessarily prejudice the legitimate interests of the maker of the database shall not be permitted'.

Who Obtains Protection under the Sui Generis Right?

In the typical case where the database maker is a corporate entity, the maker (or its successor in title) will only qualify for protection if it has a true business presence in the EU—'its operations must possess an effective and continuous link with the economy of one of the Member States'.[10] So if the 'maker' of Intercuisine (defined as the person who took the initiative and investment risk in producing the database) was a US-based corporation, Intercuisine Inc., it could not transfer the benefit of *sui generis* protection to its French subsidiary, Intercuisine SA. However, there may be scope for the US and French corporations to structure arrangements as between themselves so that Intercuisine SA falls within the definition of 'maker' if it can meet the requirement of being the 'person who takes the initiative and the risk of investing'.[11] It should be noted that sub-contractors are excluded from the definition[12] so a sub-contracting arrangement with an EU entity will not qualify the non-EU database maker for protection under the Directive. The Directive does envisage reciprocal protection for non-EU databases, subject, of course, to negotiating bilateral agreements in the future.[13]

Duration of Sui Generis Right

Despite lobbying from database producers for a longer term, especially in relation to databases with content of an historical nature, the new right will last for 15 years. This runs from 1 January in the year following the date when the database was completed or, if later, the date when it was first published.

Renewing the Sui Generis Right

A fresh 15-year term can be obtained if the contents are 'substantially changed'. This can be achieved by successive additions, deletions or alterations as well as by adding new content. In particular, 'substantive verification' of the contents of a database could qualify. The overriding requirement is that the changes, taken together, amount to 'substantial new investment'.[14] These criteria for renewal of the term of protection appear to be reasonably generous. It should not, therefore, be too difficult for database producers to extend the duration of protection of their databases.

The burden of proof regarding the date of completion of manufacture of the database,[15] and that 'substantial amendment' to the database's contents have been made (so that a fresh term of protection arises)[16] lies with the maker of the database. It will therefore be very important that database producers maintain adequate audit trails so that they can discharge this burden of proof in any action for infringement of copyright and/or the *sui generis* right in their database(s).

If Intercuisine is in CD-ROM or other fixed format, it may be possible to extend protection of the contents in the first edition by including them in the second or subsequent editions, with new content and/or updated original content. However, the contents contained in the

---

[10] Article 11.2.
[11] See Recital (41).
[12] *Ibid.*
[13] See Article 11.3.
[14] See Article 10.
[15] See Recital (53).
[16] See Recital (54).

first edition will fall out of protection and into the public domain at the end of the first 15 years. This means that they can be freely taken from edition one. This is one of the reasons why databases in on-line form, which will be subject to more regular update, will obtain stronger protection under the Directive.

Limits and Exceptions to the Sui Generis Right

The *sui generis* right only gives protection from the taking of the whole or a 'substantial part' of the contents of a database. The Directive therefore makes it clear that a legitimate purchaser of a database (whether delivered 'on-line' or in fixed format such as CD-ROM) cannot be prevented by contract from extracting or re-utilising insubstantial parts of its contents.[17]

However, a database owner can still limit access by contract to some but not all of the levels of a database. Article 8.1 provides that 'The maker of a database which is made available to the public in whatever manner may not prevent a lawful user of the database from extracting and/or re-utilizing insubstantial parts of its contents, evaluated quantitatively and/or qualitatively, for any purposes whatsoever'. For example, this may be the case where there is a tiered pricing structure according to the level(s) of access given to the user. The effect of the second sentence of Article 8.1[18] appears to be that where access to the database is limited in this way, the user cannot claim access to all levels of the database on the ground that a legitimate user cannot be prevented from taking insubstantial parts of a database.

As mentioned earlier, the Directive also gives Member States the option to allow 'fair dealing' style exceptions which would enable legitimate users of a database to 'extract' (that is to take from the database) and/or re-utilise 'substantial' parts without needing permission:

- in the case of extraction for private purposes (namely, home copying) from a *non-electronic* database (that is, home copying of electronic databases would not be allowed);
- in the case of extraction for illustration for teaching and scientific research, as long as the source is indicated and it is for a *non-commercial* purpose;
- in the case of extraction and/or re-utilisation for public security reasons or for administrative and/or judicial procedures.

The battle lines will be drawn when the Directive is implemented into national law. Database producers will try to persuade Government that no exceptions (except the third one mentioned above) should be allowed in view of the limited duration (15 years) of the right and the fact that the *sui generis* right only relates to the taking of substantial parts of the database's contents.

Dealing in the Sui Generis Right

The effect of Article 7.3 of the Directive is that the *sui generis* right is a property right. It states that it can be transferred, assigned or granted under contractual licence.

---

[17] See Article 8.1.
[18] Article 8.1 (second sentence); 'Where the lawful user is authorized to extract and/or re-utilize only part of the database, this paragraph shall apply only to that part.'

Compulsory Licensing

Much to the relief of most database producers, the provisions for compulsory licensing of the contents of databases which cannot be obtained from another source have been dropped. The Directive[19] requires the Commission to prepare a report every three years on various issues, including whether compulsory licensing is needed because of any abuse of a dominant position resulting from the way in which the *sui generis* right has been applied.

Relationship between Copyright and Sui Generis Right in a Database

This is best illustrated by looking at Intercuisine. There are three levels of rights to consider:

(1) Copyright in the material incorporated into Intercuisine (that is, photographs, video clips and text).
(2) The database copyright (if any) in Intercuisine.
(3) The *sui generis* right in the contents of Intercuisine.

The maker of Intercuisine will have obtained licences (probably on a non-exclusive basis) to incorporate the third-party graphic, video or text material into the database and to distribute it in fixed form and/or make it available on-line. Nothing in the Directive affects the third party's rights in that material. In particular, Recital (18) in the Directive expressly states that, where the owner of that material has granted a non-exclusive licence to the database maker, it can license other third parties to use the material without needing the *sui generis* rightholder's consent.

It is quite possible that the owner of Intercuisine will be willing to license a third party to extract or re-utilise the contents (that is, a *sui generis* licence) but not to license any rights in the copyright in the existing database which protect the structure and 'look and feel' of the database. To the extent, therefore, that both copyright and the *sui generis* right subsist in Intercuisine, the two rights will run and can be exploited independently. Obviously, any purchaser of Intercuisine will wish to acquire both copyright and *sui generis* rights unless, in particular deals, only content is being sold.

If the contents of Intercuisine are copied without authority, the infringer could face an action from the database producer for copyright and *sui generis* infringement as well as an action for copyright infringement from the owner of any third party copyright material incorporated in Intercuisine.

Remedies

There will be no harmonisation under the Directive of the remedies for infringement of copyright or the *sui generis* right in a database. Article 12 provides that 'Member States shall provide appropriate remedies in respect of infringement of the rights provided for in this Directive.'

---

[19] See Article 16.3.

Transitional

There are the following transitional arrangements for databases in existence on the date on which the Directive is due to be implemented (currently 1 January 1988):

- *copyright* protection under the Directive will apply if the database meets the criteria for protection as explained above;
- for existing databases in any Member State which do not fulfil the new criteria for *copyright* protection, but which are currently protected under existing copyright laws in that Member State (for example, in the United Kingdom), they will continue to be protected under that existing copyright law;
- existing databases made not earlier than 15 years prior to 1 January 1998 which meet the criteria for *sui generis* protection will enjoy that protection under this new right. This means that a database made more than 15 years before the implementation date will not obtain protection under the Directive. However, if substantial reinvestment in such a database has been made during the 15-year period prior to the Directive, it would appear that it will benefit from a full term of *sui generis* protection. Databases not subject to such reinvestment, which are likely to include databases with historical content, will therefore be at a disadvantage compared to those subject to regular change.

Conclusions

There is still some way to go before this Directive sees the legislative light of day. The European Parliament is likely to look closely at the Directive from the consumer's perspective. This is likely to focus on the inclusion of exceptions to copyright and to the *sui generis* rights being at the option of Member States rather than being mandatory. Also, the Parliament is likely to debate the dropping of the compulsory licensing provisions which were dropped from the latest text of the Directive.

However, now that the European Commission's Green Paper on 'Copyright and Related Rights in the Information Society' has been published, it is likely that pressure will increase to achieve adoption of the Directive. Many interest groups see it as having a pivotal role to play in defining the rights in databases—called by one commentator the 'digital storehouses on the Superhighway'. As such, the continued progress of the Directive needs close scrutiny. In particular, those involved in the database business—an increasingly wide group of players—need to start getting the right strategies in place to maximise protection of their database investments.

Copyright & Designs

Designs

BL v. Armstrong in the House of Lords.
Our Souls Redeemed from the Company Store

[1986] 4 EIPR 117

CHRISTINE FELLNER
Barrister, London

Function design copyright lives—but not for spare parts. Judicial creativity has conjured from the hat a rabbit more familiar with the warrens of real property law—'non-derogation from grant'. This enabled the majority in the House of Lords in *BL v Armstrong*[1] to deliver car owners from after-market bondage to original manufacturers, and competing suppliers into untrammelled enjoyment of that market. But what is the effect and extent of this 'spare parts exception'? And what will be the future of design copyright?

BL v Armstrong is a remarkable decision; remarkable both for the frankness with which various of their Lordships criticised Parliament and the courts for bringing about the protection of functional design by copyright, and for the device which four of them adopted to exclude spare parts from this protection.

Lord Templeman set the scene with customary trenchancy:

> A car has an expectation of life of some 15 years subject to determination by careless driving. A car is a collection of hundreds of components all of which must fit together. From the time that a car is driven out of the factory gates until the day that it is consigned to the scrap heap, there is a risk that the car will be immobilised by the failure of a vital component part as a result of accident or wear and tear.
>
> BL manufacture the Marina car ... The exhaust pipes need replacement at intervals which vary from six months to two years. Armstrong manufacture replacement exhaust pipes for the Marina and in order to do so copy the shape and dimensions of the original. BL claim that the tentacles of copyright have now reached out to prevent Armstrong from manufacturing exhaust pipes for the Marina unless Armstrong pay such royalty as BL think fit to require ... BL have obtained an injunction which effectively prevents Armstrong from manufacturing replacement exhaust pipes for the Marina. If this injunction was rightly granted it follows that any motorist who drives a BL car must buy his spare parts from BL at prices fixed by BL or bear the burden of a royalty payable to BL for the privilege of buying his spare part from somebody else. The purchaser of a BL car sells his soul to the company store.

---

[1] 27 February 1985. The Court of Appeal's decision is reported at [1984] FSR 591; for commentary see C. Fellner and J. Turner [1984] 11 EIPR 317 and 320.

In the course of a hearing lasting 20 days (thought to be a record), their Lordships (Lords Scarman, Edmund-Davies, Bridge of Harwich, Templeman and Griffiths), most of whom had little previous experience of the subject, were given a thorough exposition of the historical development of industrial design and artistic copyright protection and the interrelation between them. They were invited by Armstrong to use their discretion under the 1966 Practice Statement[2] to depart from the House's earlier decision in *LB Plastics v Swish*,[3] which gave the imprimatur to functional design copyright.

The argument which caught their Lordships' attention was that the court should look at the *nature* of the original contribution which confers copyright, and consider whether it is *that* which an alleged infringer has taken. In the case of a drawing of a functional object, the original contribution which confers copyright is the draughtsman's graphic skill and his labour. If the drawing is traced or photocopied, that skill and labour is directly taken. If the drawing is used as a guide to making the object, again that skill and labour is taken. But if it is the object which is copied, then what is taken is not the draughtsman's skill and labour, but that of the designer who designed the object; and no-one suggests that this is entitled to copyright. Indirect reproduction of functional design is therefore not infringement.

Their Lordships were also pressed by Armstrong with the anomalies arising from the giving of a *de facto* monopoly to copyright owners without any of the safeguards (limited term, publicity, compulsory licensing, Crown user) normally provided and with the fact that copyright infringement, unlike patent or design infringement, is a criminal offence, and a tort carrying with it the wholly exceptional remedy of conversion damages. BL argued that there was no monopoly, because anyone was free to copy on payment of a royalty, and they faced competition in the market from their licensees.

Ultimately their Lordships felt able to decide the case purely on the basis of UK law without hearing argument on the Euro-defences; and they unanimously decided in favour of Armstrong.

The Existence of Functional Design Copyright

Lord Templeman

Lord Templeman delivered the leading speech. He traced the history of registered design as well as artistic copyright protection, concluding that until 1912 an exhaust pipe would not have been protected by copyright, nor as a registered design since it lacked novelty and was a mere mechanical device dictated by function. The 1911 Copyright Act introduced the notion of reproduction 'in any material form', but attempted by section 22 to avoid any overlap between copyright and design registration. That this was not entirely successful was shown in the *Popeye* case[4] where copyright in the drawings was not lost because the artist had not originally intended to apply them industrially. The brooches, which were copied from other brooches, were indeed reproductions of the cartoons in a material form; but here what was appropriated was the skill and labour of the artist. A three-dimensional reproduction of an exhaust pipe, on the other hand, owes 'everything to the inventor and designer of the exhaust system and nothing to the original skill and labour of the draughtsman'; and his Lordship held that *Popeye* 'did not extend the ambit of copyright to indirect reproduction

---

[2] Practice Statement (Judicial Precedent) [1966] 1 WLR 1234.
[3] [1979] RPC 551.
[4] *King Features v O & M Kleeman* [1941] AC 417.

of a drawing of a purely functional object'. Thus far, therefore, Armstrong's argument succeeded.

The Gregory Committee favoured 'three-dimensional reproduction', but were adamant that it should not extend to protecting a drawing reproduced as a building, machine or utilitarian article. Nothing functional should be protected by copyright which would not be protectable as a registered design. They therefore recommended the 'lay recognition' test incorporated in the 1956 Copyright Act as section 9(8)—not happily drafted, and almost entirely unsuccessful. In *Dorling v Honnor*[5] and in all cases since 1956, said his Lordship, the courts 'assumed rather than decided' that indirect reproduction of drawings of functional articles was affected by the *Popeye* decision.

However, in *LB Plastics v Swish* Armstrong's argument was raised, albeit obliquely, it being suggested that what had been reproduced was the preliminary work going into the drawing, which was not copyright, and not the drawing itself, which was. But Lord Hailsham dismissed it, as obliquely, by saying he must take copyright law as he found it, which was prohibiting indirect reproduction of functional drawings. Lord Templeman, despite having earlier expressed the view that Parliament had never intended to protect functional objects via artistic copyright, followed this example of judicial humility and 'reluctantly' took the law as he found it.

This appears to involve the curious finding that the House of Lords is bound by judicial law-making indulged in by the lower courts against the intention of Parliament.

Lord Bridge of Harwich and Lord Edmund-Davies

Lord Bridge concentrated on the alleged absurdity of giving functional designs, unprotectable by design registration, a term and quality of protection many times longer and stronger than that accorded to registrable designs. BL attempted to meet this by asking the House to depart from *Amp v Utilux*[6] and rule that the 'dictated solely by function' exclusion in the Registered Designs Act 1949 applied only to those articles whose design was 'mandated' by their function, so that no other shape or configuration could possibly have been adopted. This Lord Bridge declined to do.

He could not accept Armstrong's argument based on what skill and labour was actually taken. This would involve imposing a restriction on the statutory 'three-dimensional repro-duction' definition which would be hard to reconcile with the inclusion of 'diagrams' in the definition of drawings. Section 9(8) also clearly presupposes that three-dimensional reproductions of drawings must be covered by the Act, provided they are recognisable. And all the authorities, including *Swish*, were against Armstrong. Lord Bridge was not prepared to depart from *Swish*, because to do so would cause too much upheaval, the law in its present form having been recognised for more than 20 years.

Lord Edmund-Davies echoed the sentiments of a judge in 1701[7] that 'Parliament can do no wrong, though it may do several things that look pretty odd', and declined to speculate on what Parliament actually intended, feeling bound by *Swish*.

---

[5] [1965] Ch. 1.
[6] [1972] RPC 103.
[7] *City of London v Wood* 12 Mod. Rep. 669, 687.

Lord Griffiths' dissenting speech

Lord Griffiths, like his brethren, was impressed by the absurdity of giving 100 years plus protection to something which was neither patentable, nor design-registrable, nor in itself copyrightable, and felt that Parliament could not possibly have intended to bring this about. Unlike them, he was prepared to do something about it.

He accepted the argument that what Armstrong had taken was the designer's skill and not the draughtsman's. He highlighted the anomaly that if BL had made their pipe from their prototype or had embodied the manufacturing instructions in words or numbers, Armstrong would have been free to copy by reverse engineering. But simply because they had embodied these instructions in the form of a drawing, they could claim a monopoly. This had come about because the courts had construed 'reproducing' as including 'indirect copying' 'in circumstances where it [was] not necessary to do so in order to achieve the purpose of the Act which is to protect the commercial value of the artist's work and labour and not to grant a monopoly to a manufacturer'.

Cases such as *Ex p Beal*[8] which endorsed the concept of indirect copying were readily explicable on that basis. There, Mr Graves owned the copyright in two oil paintings and a photograph, of which he had made engravings. Mr Beal took photographs of these engravings without Mr Graves' consent, and sold them. In the words of Davey L.J. in *Hanfstaengl v Empire Palace* [1894] 3 Ch. 109, 133, protection of indirect copying in such a situation was justified 'both to protect the reputation of the artist ... and also to secure to him the commercial value of his property—to encourage the arts by securing to the artist a monopoly in the sale of an object of attraction'. Where the commercial value of a drawing lies in its aesthetic appeal, it is necessary for its proper protection that 'reproducing' be extended to cover 'indirect copying'.

The 1911 Copyright Act made it clear that reproduction in a different medium ('in any material form') could amount to copying. But the *Popeye* case was one in which the commercial value of the artist's work which had been taken *was* its aesthetic value; while in *Dorling v Honnor* there was a direct taking by the defendants of the labour involved in drawing the plans by using them to construct the boats and kits of parts.

Swish and earlier cases in the lower courts[9] established that indirect copying of functional objects infringed the copyright in the drawings on which they were based; but in none of them was consideration given to why indirect copying was first introduced and why it should be extended to functional design. Lord Griffiths read section 9(8) as indicating Parliament's anxiety not to extend copyright too far, and refused to interpret it as meaning that if the exception did not bite at all there should be universal protection against indirect copying.

Where a draughtsman's work is directly taken by copying the drawing or using it as an instruction to make the object depicted, the commercial value is being expropriated. But he is not 'applying his skill and labour to create an original article from which he may justly expect to reap a reward when it is sold to the public'; he is merely a conduit pipe for communicating the designer's ideas to the shop floor. 'In such circumstances, to construe reproducing as including indirect copying is to transfer the protection of artistic copyright from the draughtsman to the manufacturer which is not the purpose of artistic copyright.'

In applying indirect copying whenever there was a causal link between the drawing and the artefact, without considering why they were doing so, the courts had made 'a false step', and had misconstrued Parliament's intention. This was a suitable case for application of the

---

[8] (1868) LR 2 QB 387.
[9] In particular *British Northrop v Texteam Blackburn* [1974] RPC 57 and *Solar Thomson v Barton* [1977] RPC 537.

1966 Practice Statement so as to depart from *Swish* where the copyright drawing which is indirectly reproduced is of a purely functional object.

One difficulty with this argument is posed by the employee draughtsman producing drawings of a non-functional or only partly functional object, for which 15 years' copyright would be available. His job is the same as the engineering draughtsman's; he does not personally expect to 'reap a reward' for his skill and labour other than his salary; he too is merely a conduit between the designer and the shop floor; his artistic copyright, like his 'functional' counterpart's, is transferred to the manufacturer, not because of indirect copying but simply because he is an employee and section 4(4) gives copyright to his employer. Lord Griffiths said he would not deprive such drawings of indirect copying protection, and papered over the cracks by referring in this instances to the 'designer' rather than the 'draughtsman'. But this is not wholly satisfactory.

The Rabbit

The majority, as well as Lord Griffiths, disapproved of the law in its present form. Lord Edmund-Davies and Lord Bridge of Harwich expressly or impliedly laid the blame on Parliament, Lords Scarman and Templeman on the courts, the latter saying 'the exploitation of copyright law for purposes which were not intended has gone far enough'. Lord Bridge castigated functional design copyright as 'capable of abuse as a means of obtaining many of the advantages conferred by a patent monopoly while circumventing the many stringent conditions and safeguards to which patent protection is subject' and was particularly offended by the availability of conversion damages.

It was accepted that BL had an effective monopoly and, as Lord Templeman observed, 'a monopoly remains a monopoly even if it be benevolently administered and an established monopoly will not necessarily be administered with benevolence'. Was there, then, some way by which the spare parts market, at least, might be freed from a doctrine which it was now too late for the courts alone to change?

The 'implied licence' enjoyed by the owner of a patented or copyright article to repair it with infringing parts was not accepted by the Court of Appeal as permitted a 'third party' like Armstrong to mass-produce such parts ahead of need. This was because it was based, however nebulously, on an implied term in the contract between the manufacturer and (indirectly) the first purchaser. Something wider was needed.

Lord Templeman

Lord Templeman found it in the law of real property. He quoted Bowen L.J. in *Birmingham Dudley and District Banking Co. v Ross*:[10] 'A grantor having given a thing with one hand is not to take away the means of enjoying it with the other'. The principle of non-derogation from grant was well known as between landlord and tenant or vendor and purchaser of land and, as Parker J. said in *Browne v Flower*:[11]

> Under certain circumstances there will be implied on the part of the grantor or lessor obligations which restrict the user of the land retained by him further than can be explained by the implication of any easement known to the law. Thus, if the grant of demise be made for a particular purpose, the grantor or lessor comes under an obligation

---

[10] (1888) 38 Ch. D 295, 313.
[11] [1911] 1 Ch. 219, 225.

not to use the land retained by him in such a way as to render the land granted or demised unfit or materially less fit for the particular purpose for which the grant or demise was made.

And Branson J. in *O'Cedar Ltd v Slough Trading Co. Ltd*[12] extended this principle: 'beyond cases in which the purpose of the grant is frustrated to cases in which that purpose can still be achieved albeit at a greater expense or with less convenience.'

Lord Templeman likened BL to a vendor who sells part of his land but retains the rest and uses it in such a way that the purchaser's land is rendered unfit or materially less fit for the purpose for which it was granted. BL, he said, initially owns a car and a copyright. It sells the car but retains the copyright, and then seeks to exercise that copyright so as to make the car unfit for the purpose for which it was sold—that is, to continue functioning for the whole of its natural life. It cannot do this unless the shorter-lived components can be replaced, and BL seeks to confine such replacement to spares of its own or its licensee's make. Ownership of a car carries with it the right to repair. 'That right', his Lordship said 'would be useless if suppliers of spare parts were not entitled to anticipate the need for repair'.

There appears, with respect, to be a gap between the proposition that the purchaser has a right to repair and the proposition that someone other than the copyright owner has a right to supply him; but his Lordship boldly leaps this and states that the right to repair cannot be withheld from the first or any subsequent purchaser by contract. BL cannot therefore save itself by imposing a condition requiring repair only with its own or licensed spares. (One wonders what effect this will have on warranties.)

The unfettered right to repair would also be enforceable against BL's sub-contractors who manufacture parts, because they would know that these were to be fitted in cars to which the right would attach.

Lord Bridge of Harwich

Lord Bridge, while accepting the use of the non-derogation doctrine, placed his reasoning on a rather broader base. He saw the issue essentially as a conflict between the car owner's right to repair (which, if it is to have any value, must mean to repair with mass-produced, universally available spares) and the manufacturer's right to enforce a monopoly by using his copyright. How far should the latter be allowed to impinge on the former?

He believed BL to have conceded that using copyright to starve the market of spares long before a car was worn out would be 'legally unacceptable'—although he did not say how this could be sanctioned. Given, therefore, that a line could be drawn somewhere, where should this be? Lord Bridge rejected BL's arguments that domestic and European competition law could provide the answer. This would mean that before 1973 (the date of the Fair Trading Act and the coming into effect of the European Communities Act 1972) the law could have done nothing to control abuse of monopoly. He further rejected the suggestion that the courts should decide in each case whether the monopoly was being fairly exercised. This would be unduly onerous, and would leave the manufacturer free to vary his terms as soon as he had received a favourable ruling.

In holding that no halfway house solution was possible, and that the monopoly must not be allowed to prevail, his Lordship had recourse to the exhaustion of rights argument: by selling cars fitted with copyright-protected exhaust popes, BL 'have already enjoyed the

---

[12] [1927] 2 KB 123, 127.

primary benefit which their copyright protects'. Moreover, BL had created a community of car owners enjoying the inherent right to repair as economically as possible. To interfere with this right was 'to a greater or lesser extent, to detract ... at least potentially, [from] the value of their cars'. This might be a novel application of the non-derogation principle, but the common law should be able:

> ... to adapt to changing social and economic conditions to counter the belated emergence of the car manufacturer's attempt to monopolise the spare parts market in reliance on copyright in technical drawings by invoking the necessity to safeguard the position of the car owner.

The Propriety of the Spare Parts Exception

This hitherto unsuspected exception, this principle, as Lord Scarman discreetly puts it, 'latent in our law but not fully discussed or expressed until the present case', is erected on rather flimsy foundations. It depends on the proposition that a car, or other piece of multi-component machinery, is rendered unfit or materially unfit for its purpose (Lord Templeman) or its second-hand value is potentially lessened (Lord Bridge) if the purchaser is tied for spares to the manufacturer or his licensees. This involves the assumptions that the manufacturer may starve the market of spars or keep their prices artificially high. The first of these assumptions is, as Lord Griffiths pointed out in his dissent, commercially dubious. He thought the second was, too, although the Monopolies Commission report[13] on Ford's behaviour in relation to body panels might suggest the contrary. However, expensive spare parts are not particularly good business, since they reduce the second-hand value and increase the insurance premiums for crash repairs, and it is a little fanciful to suggest that even uniformly malevolent exercise of the spares monopoly by all manufacturers selling in the UK would render cars completely unfit for their purpose.

How material does unfitness for purpose have to be to activate the non-derogation doctrine in real property law? Consideration of the cases referred to by Lord Templeman is illuminating. The *Birmingham* case[14] relied on the state of affairs known to both parties at the time the lease was granted as determining the extent of the obligation not to derogate; but a material lessening of the light to the plaintiff's windows was insufficient, their Lordships reserving their position had the light been obstructed completely. In *Browne v Flower*[15] interference with comfort and privacy was held not to amount to a derogation from grant; nor, said Parker J., would activities on the retained land which would 'to a great extent interfere with the comfortable enjoyment and diminish the value of the property sold'.

The derogation found in *Harmer v Jumbil (Nigeria) Tin Areas*[16] consisted in the erection of sheds so close to the plaintiffs' land that their licence to store explosives would be withdrawn, the lessor of both plaintiffs and defendants being fully aware of the position. The plaintiffs' land would therefore be rendered *completely* unfit for the purpose for which it was let. In *Matania v National Provincial Bank*[17] consideration of the derogation point, in connection with a serious but temporary interference with enjoyment of the plaintiffs' property, was not only *obiter*, but fleeting, the matter not even having been pleaded.

---

[13] Cmnd 9437.
[14] See Note 10 above.
[15] See Note 11 above.
[16] [1921] Ch. 200.
[17] [1936] 2 AER 633.

Ungoed-Thomas J. in *Ward v Kirkland*[18] was barely persuaded that the derogation doctrine applied to a refusal to permit occasional entry on to adjoining land for the purposes of maintaining the plaintiff's walls and gutters and cleaning his windows. He inclined to the view that 'derogation ... seems to indicate doing something which defeats in substantial measure the purpose of the grant' and preferred to base his decision on other principles. And in *O'Cedar v Slough Trading Co.*,[19] in the apparently encouraging quotation from Branson J.'s judgment which Lord Templeman cites, the learned judge was asking himself *whether* the principle could apply beyond cases of complete frustration of the purpose of the grant, not stating that it could, but the actual finding was that a sixfold increase in insurance premiums as a result of what was done on the adjoining land was *not* a derogation. He said:

> I should be extending the ... principle into a region quite different from that in which it has hitherto been applied if I were to hold that it applied to anything done by a lessor ... which, while not otherwise affecting the demised premises or their user in any way, merely made it more expensive that it was before for the lessee to carry on his business.

On these authorities, it must be open to doubt whether the possibly increased inconvenience and expense to car owners of purchasing their spares only from the company store can really amount to derogation from grant.

Judicial Restrictions on Statutory Rights

It might have been more satisfactory if the non-derogation principle had been grafted on to the implied licence. The reasoning would be that impliedly to license repair while making it impossible to exercise this licence other than by commissioning one-or two-off manufacture from non-existent blacksmiths (an encouragement to small businesses, perhaps?) amounts to giving with one hand and taking away with the other.

Return to the implied licence, however, raises the problem that it is a licence to *repair*, not to replace. If a part of a car is patented, it can be repaired, but it will be an infringement not only to make a complete replacement but also to use it. Since many modern parts, such as carburettors, are fitted as sealed units not susceptible of repair, only the maker's own part (or one made by his licensees) may lawfully be fitted. Why, as Lord Griffiths asked, should the same rule not apply to replacement parts protected by copyright, if the law does in fact confer a monopoly?

Lord Templeman invoked *Solar Thomson v Barton*, where permitting the exercise of copyright in the whole of a part of a patented article would have stultified the implied patent licence which operated because the patented article was only being repaired. This does not address the principle at issue. He also suggested that a patent protects an article, whereas copyright protects drawings, not the article itself—which appears to endorse the 'indirect copying' argument approved by Lord Griffiths, but already rejected by Lord Templeman. It also applies to functional articles which are not spares. Finally, he adopted the point already made by Lord Bridge and identified the articles sold by BL (thereby exhausting its rights) as cars incorporating exhaust pipes, not exhaust pipes alone. This is neat; but it ignores the economic reality that there are two markets, not one—the original equipment market and the after-market. However, there are respectable precedents for this approach; the European

---

[18] [1967] Ch. 194.
[19] See Note 12 above.

Court has not been shy of defining what it wishes the specific subject-matter of a right to be, whatever may have been the expectation of the parties.

Lord Bridge, faced with the question of whether the court could pick and choose between one statutory monopoly and another, took his stand on patents and registered designs being proper monopolies (with proper safeguards) under which the car owner himself would not be allowed to make or commission a complete infringing part—unlike the copyright position as endorsed by the Court of Appeal.

Lord Griffiths did *not* see how the courts could pick and choose:

> No case has been cited ... in which the courts have refused to enforce a statutory right because it impinged on other freedoms, yet the examples of such a state of affairs must be legion. I regret I feel unable to follow your Lordships down this untrodden path.

Lord Edmund-Davies too, though concurring with the majority, did so with 'substantial and subsisting' doubts. This is the more understandable given his view that Parliament appeared to have granted the monopoly, even if it had been foolish to do so.

Lords Scarman and Templeman, however, need be troubled by no such doubts. Both said that Parliament had never intended to create the monopoly. This being so, it must have been created by the courts, and could therefore be overruled by them. The House of Lords giveth and the House of Lords taketh away.

The Limits of the Spare Parts Exception

It is the spare parts cases which have shown up the law of functional design copyright in its most extreme form. Lord Bridge dealt firmly with the argument that BL had no true monopoly because anyone could design a non-infringing pipe by looking at the underside of the car, without copying BL's:

> I find no substance in this argument for two reasons. First, the evidence stops far short of establishing that a new system designed in the way suggested, which must take full account of the shape and configuration of the underside of the frame, various other parts located beneath it, and of the fixing points provided for the exhaust system, would, even if marginally different in shape from the original pipe, escape the charge of reproduction by copying of a substantial part of BL's drawings. Secondly, we are concerned with economic reality...

Are these reasons cumulative or alternative? Is copying only permitted where it is absolutely necessary if competing spares are to be made at all? Or would it be enough that copying is economically desirable to secure low prices to the consumer, even though technically the part could be redesigned so as not to copy? This may be important where a part only interfaces with the original to a limited extent, and might, technically, but not economically, be largely designed afresh. If the exception applies, it will not be worth the plaintiffs' while to sue at all, even if there is copying of the whole. If it does not, the odds are more favourable. Elsewhere Lord Bridge speaks of products 'of such a nature as to require replacement parts with any degree of frequency, where those parts can, in practice, only be effective if they reproduce the shape or configuration of the originals'. This is a narrower formulation.

Lord Templeman speaks of 'any article which requires replacement parts from time to time', but, as with his other remarks on the point, in the context of a *de facto* monopoly. It seems therefore that such a monopoly must be shown to exist before the exception will apply. But his Lordship seems to introduce some qualification in the form of a 'mass-production requirement'. He refers to the development of 'mass-production of vehicles and other machinery' and stresses the importance of the appeal to 'all manufacturers of mass produced machinery in respect of repairs'. Will the exception apply only to mass-produced goods, and if so, how are these defined? There may be a clue in Lord Scarman's allusion to manufacturers of vehicles or other 'consumer durables'.

Lord Templeman refers to parts which fail 'as a result of accident or wear and tear', and others of their Lordships to parts whose life is bound to be shorter than that of the car (or other machinery). What happens if a part fails, not because of normal wear and tear, nor accident in the sense of a crash, but because of the owner's carelessness—because he does not use antifreeze, or disregards his oil warning light, or fails to maintain his production machinery—or indeed if he chooses to repair with an inferior part which causes damage to other parts of the machinery which would not normally wear out?

Again, part of the justification offered by Lords Templeman and Bridge for the spare parts exception is that the sale which exhausts the right is of the car or machine as a whole. Is replacement limited to the components as originally fitted in which the right has been exhausted? Or is it permissible, if the manufacturer fits improved components to later models, to use these as replacements?

Is Direct Copying Permitted under the Exception?

Lord Griffiths' formulation of the law, while permitting reverse engineering, would have forbidden direct copying from the plaintiffs' drawings, either by tracing or photocopying or by using them to make the object depicted. The remainder of their Lordships rejected this suggested distinction, and some of their language is wide enough to suggest that even reproduction involving direct copying of the plaintiffs' drawings might be permissible. Certainly a superior part might sometimes result from use of the drawings rather than reverse engineering. Oliver L.J. in the Court of Appeal conceded that the implied licence permitted the owner to copy or commission infringing copies of parts, without expressly limiting this to reverse engineering. But Whitford J., in *Weir Pumps v CML Pumps,*[20] stated that the implied licence would only cover reverse engineering, even in the absence of any additional confidential information in the drawings themselves.

Lord Templeman, however, refers more than once to 'indirect' reproduction as that which the exception allows; and it is thought that, against the background of a case where only infringement by reverse engineering was in issue, it is unlikely that any wider permission can be spelled out.

Some Effects of the Decision

Dangerous parts

The decision was predictably greeted with cries of 'Pirates' charter' and horrifying prognostications about the uncontrollable use of defective parts. But 'independent' suppliers, such as Armstrong, sell under their own name and therefore have their own reputation to protect. Real pirates will in many, if not all, cases be attempting to sell their goods as the

---

[20] [1984] FSR 33.

genuine ones, and will therefore be passing off and, commonly, infringing trade marks too. These causes of action have, in the case of imported goods and dealers generally, the immense advantage over copyright actions that they are effective strict liability, actionable without proof of knowledge or intent. In a copyright action, other than against a manufacturer, the plaintiff must *prove* that the defendant knew the goods he was importing or dealing in were infringing copies; and this has often proved difficult or impossible.[21]

Increased use of leasing?

Might the decision lead, in suitable circumstances, to an increase in leasing rather than sale of machinery? Clearly this would not be suitable for consumer durables; but if the spare parts exception does apply to producer goods, would a lease enable the manufacturer to dictate that only his spares should be used?

Lord Templeman makes it clear that he would not permit motor manufacturers to withhold the unfettered right to repair 'by contract with the first purchaser', but this in the context of sale rather than leasing. The doctrine of non-derogation applies to leases as well as conveyances, but is by its nature normally implied rather than expressed, as in the *Birmingham* case.[22] If commercially feasible, leasing may be a way for some manufacturers to avoid the spare parts exception.

Effect on existing actions

'Infringing' manufacturers and dealers currently subject to interlocutory injunctions may now apply to have them discharged pending disposal of the action, and seek to enforce the cross-undertaking in damages—a matter for the court's discretion. What about those unfortunates who gave undertakings, perhaps because of the fear of conversion damages if they continued to manufacture? In *Chanel v Woolworth*[23] the defendants gave undertakings against trade mark infringement and passing off by parallel imports. Then the Court of Appeal in a different action accepted a defence not previously put forward in such cases. The second defendants in *Chanel* obtained evidence suggesting that they might be able to employ this defence, and applied to set aside the undertakings. Foster J. and the Court of Appeal refused, the latter on the basis that the second defendants' advisers should have thought of the defence themselves and obtained the evidence to support it. It is to be hoped that defendants will not now be penalised because their advisers were less learned and creative than Lord Templeman.

The position of existing plaintiffs, apart from any subsisting injunctions, is not an enviable one. Unlike legislation, which may save existing actions, judicial decisions are deemed to declare the law, not change it. Plaintiffs are therefore left with no cause of action and will have to extricate themselves as best they may—at worst, failing agreement to support withdrawal by consent, by discontinuance or striking out, with consequent costs penalties.

The clear statements of some of their Lordships that functional design copyright is the accidental creation of the courts, not Parliament, should help Euro-defences by casting doubt on the authority of aberrant UK law and its ability to 'justify' restrictions on the free movement of goods.

---

[21] For example *Hoover v Hulme* [1982] FSR 565.
[22] Note 10 above.
[23] [1981] 1 WLR 485.

Whither Functional Design Copyright?

One way out of the corner into which the courts have painted themselves might have been by adopting a purposive construction of section 9(8), in line with their Lordships' findings on the purpose of artistic copyright:

—Artistic copyright preserves to the artist the commercial value of his skill and labour (Lord Bridge, Lord Griffiths) which is misappropriated by the reproduction of his work in any medium and dimension (Lord Griffiths and section 48(1)). The *Popeye* case is in line with this, since what made the drawings appealing was reproduced in the brooches (Lord Templeman, Lord Griffiths).

—The Gregory Committee felt that this protection should be extended to maps, plans, etc. (including engineering drawings) because these were 'artistic' in the sense of being depicted in lines and shapes rather than words or numerals. They had previously been protected as literary works. Here the commercial value of the draughtsman's skill and labour is the communication of the designer's ideas to the shop floor (Lord Griffiths) in a way which experienced engineers and manufacturing workers can appreciate and which helps them to produce the object depicted.

—But Gregory realised that the transfer of engineering drawings from literary to artistic protection, coupled with the ban on unlicensed three-dimensional reproduction, could lead to protection for functional objects, of which they disapproved (paragraph 258 quoted by Lord Templeman).

—So they made a suggestion, adopted in section 9(8) which, while designed to preserve to the artist the commercial value of his work as recognised by the ordinary man (the combination of colours and shapes which appeal to the eye), even where reproduced in three-dimensional form, would exclude that commercial value derived from assisting the process of manufacture, which would in any event only be recognisable by persons in the business of manufacturing ('experts in relation to') objects of that description. This would still allow for the eye-appealing aspects of a production drawing to be protected.

—Unfortunately the sub-section has been consistently misunderstood, and mis-interpreted by judges who had, by the time it was applied in any action, after days of instruction by counsel, become 'experts in relation to' the manufacture of objects of that description.

Lord Griffiths was nearly there but mistakenly believed that the sub-section *denied* copy-right to the drawing in question. It does not: it appears in the 'general exceptions' section 9 and provides merely that three-dimensional objects do not *infringe* the copyright if they are not recognisable in the manner stated above.

However, the opportunity was missed; and in the light of the scathing judicial criticism of functional design copyright, the Department of Trade and Industry must now emerge from the woodwork and do its political job of reconciling violently differing interests to produce a fair result. Introducing even a short-term registered design or registered invention/utility model protection for purely functional designs would not, in the light of their Lordships' observations on monopolies, be acceptable—although other factors than these may make it so. Compulsory licensing on the basis of inadequate availability and distribution would not find favour with Lord Bridge, though some simpler machinery for charging a royalty might be devised.

What is needed is for the Government to confront the problem squarely by deciding what *is* to be protected—invention, commercial eye-appeal, artistry, investment—and what public interest safeguards should be built in and provide suitably tailored protection accordingly.

By Accident or Design?
The Meaning of 'Design'
under section 51 CDPA
1988

[1990] EIPR 33

GERALD DWORKIN
*Herchell Smith Professor of Intellectual Property
Law, Queen Mary & Westfield College, University
of London*
RICHARD TAYLOR
Principal Lecturer in Law, Lancashire Polytechnic

Section 51 removes copyright protection from, inter alia, most design documents. The section unfortunately does not make it clear what constitutes design documents or a design, and in particular whether the intention of the maker of the document is relevant. The authors argue strongly that the intention of the maker is not only relevant, but crucial and that designs and design documents are created not by accident but by design.

In an interesting article in last July's issue of EIPR at 253, Andrew Christie examined the scope of the exclusion of certain designs from copyright protection under section 51 CDPA 1988.[1] In the course of that article he expressed the view[2] that the intention of the creator of a record is not relevant in deciding whether that record is a design document, a view which he notes is contrary to that implicit in our discussion[3] of section 51. The purpose of this short note is to explore further the difficult but important question of the precise nature of a 'design' and hence of a 'design document' under section 51.

Christie discusses two examples which we give of the depiction of a vase. In the first, X, an artist, paints a picture of the vase and we conclude that this is not a design document and so the artist's copyright protection is not taken away by section 51. In the second, the vase is drawn as a design for the purposes of industrial exploitation in which case it clearly is a design document and section 51 means that it is not an infringement of copyright for another to make articles to the design or to copy articles made to the design. Although there is no real disagreement in relation to this second example, Christie notes that we assume 'that the vase is not itself an artistic work' (because otherwise section 51 would not be applicable). This point is in itself interesting since it echoes another minor criticism which Christie makes of us[4] in that in paraphrasing section 51 we say[5] that the question is whether the (infringing) article made to the design is an artistic work whereas (we are happy to agree) the true question under section 51 is whether the design is *for* an artistic work. It would seem to follow from this distinction between what the design document is *for* and what article is

---

[1] Section 51 provides 'It is not an infringement of any copyright in a design document or model recording or embodying a design for anything other than an artistic work or a typeface to make an article to the design or to copy an article made to the design'.

[2] 1989 EIPR at 256.

[3] Dworkin & Taylor, *Blackstone's Guide to the Copyright Designs & Patents Act 1988*, 1989, Blackstone Press, at 146 to 147.

[4] 1989 EIPR at 254.

[5] Dworkin & Taylor at 146.

actually made to the design, that the purpose of the creator of the design is indeed in some way relevant because a single design document can be used to create both artistic works and things which do *not* constitute artistic works.

For example, X draws a chair for the purpose of making hand-carved chairs to that design. Assuming the hand carved chairs are works of artistic craftsmanship,[6] then the design document is unaffected by section 51 since it is not a design for something 'other than an artistic work'. Therefore if Y, without permission, markets thousands of mass-produced plastic copies of the hand-made chairs, he will be infringing even though the infringing articles may not themselves be artistic works. Conversely, however, if X drew the chair for the purpose of making thousands of mass produced plastic chairs (assuming that these are not themselves artistic works), it would seem that section 51 would apply to his design document[7] and he would not be able to rely on copyright protection. Thus the purpose of the designer is, to this extent at least, relevant in deciding whether section 51 applies.

This does not of itself prove that the purpose of the designer is relevant in deciding whether something is a design document. It merely shows that if something is accepted to be a design document, the purpose of the designer must be relevant in deciding what it is a design document *for* and therefore whether it is the type of design document caught by section 51. However, once the purpose of the designer is admitted at all in to section 51, it would not be surprising if it were to be found to be relevant to the prior question of whether something is a design document in the first place and it is submitted that it is so relevant for the following reasons.

(1) The dictionary meaning of the word 'design'

The word design itself is not fully defined in the Act. In the absence of a full[8] definition in the Act it is legitimate to turn to the dictionary[9] where we find the following primary definitions of the word as a noun:

    (a) a mental plan, . . .
    (b) a plan in art

The first two subsidiary definitions after these primary definitions are respectively, as follows:

    (a) A plan or scheme conceived in the mind and *intended for subsequent execution*;
    (b) A preliminary sketch for a picture or other work of art: the plan of a building or any part of it, or the outline of a piece of decorative work, *after which the actual structure or texture is to be completed (emphases added)*

---

[6] See *George Hensher Ltd v Restawile Upholstery (Lancs) Ltd* 1976 AC 64.

[7] Because it *is* for something other than an artistic work (or a typeface).

[8] Christie states (at 253) that 'section 51(3) defines "design" as any aspect of the shape or configuration of the whole or part of an article . . .' but in fact section 51(3) merely states that ' "design" means *the design* of any aspect of the shape or configuration . . .' Thus he wrongly treats the design as the same thing as the shape or configuration (which may be what leads him to the conclusion that anything which depicts a shape is therefore a design) whereas the Act treats the design as being something distinct from but related to the shape or configuration, that is, it is the design *of* it. Compare the definition in section 1 of the Registered Designs Act 1949 (under which, significantly, designs are registered in relation to specific articles) which provides that ' "design" means features of shape, configuration pattern or ornament applied to any article . . .' In contrast therefore, section 51(3) is somewhat circular and doesn't so much *define* design as *limit* its meaning (whatever its more general meaning may be) to *the design of any aspect of shape or configuration of an article excluding surface decoration.*

[9] Oxford English Dictionary, 2nd Edn, 1989.

The notion of purpose or plan for future action or execution is clearly central to the natural meaning of design and thus it seems not unreasonable to conclude that the purpose of the creator and whether or not he regards his creation as the blue print for some subsequent work is indeed highly relevant in deciding whether something is a design.[10]

(2) The effect of ignoring the intention of the creator of the record

Let us return to example one, which is the case where there is real disagreement, that is, where X an artist paints a picture of a vase (with no thought of industrially producing vases as depicted in the painting). If this is a design document, (ignoring for the moment the limited period of protection given under the new unregistered design right)[11] then the whole world is free to copy the vase. It is not self-evident why this should be allowed or why someone should wish to do so unless the shape of the vase has some particular functional utility (for example, if it had a very low centre of gravity even when full of water and would thus be difficult to knock over.) Even if this is so, there is nothing to stop someone independently *designing* such a functional vase—the artist will merely want protection against a manufacturer taking the short cut and simply *copying* the attractive shape in his painting. It is different if the artist exploits the shape of the vase himself by licensing the production of copies of the vase. In such a case he should not be allowed to enjoy a longer period of protection than if the shape of the vase were protected as a registered design and accordingly section 52 limits copyright protection to 25 years from the start of such commercial exploitation. But if the artist is not exploiting the shape of the vase then he is not abusing any monopoly position and there is no good reason for restricting his copyright.

The artist's case may seem more compelling perhaps if one considers not a painting of a vase but a drawing of a cartoon character like Popeye.[12] Christie's view would seem to entail that original drawings such as those of Popeye would now be treated as design documents since articles (for example, Popeye figures) can be made to that design and unless those figures are themselves artistic works, the original artist would have no right (at least in copyright) to control the exploitation of his work through the medium of three dimensional figures. Somewhat strangely, his only automatic protection would then seem to be under the new unregistered design right. Surely it would be more sensible to say that there is no design document in such a case and that the copyright continues unimpaired until section 52 curtails it 25 years from such time as the artist licenses the commercial exploitation of Popeye figures. This interpretation has the merit that it makes the minimum change to the law in the *King Features v Kleeman* type case (that is, the *Popeye* case), either as compared with the position under the 1911 Act, under which the case was decided, or as compared with the position under the 1956 Act.[13]

---

[10] Not *every* usage of the word 'design' in the column and a half of significations in the OED involves the connotation of purpose but the majority do and such a connotation is more natural for section 51 which refers to a design *for* something, the word '*for*' itself being suggestive of purpose.

[11] CDPA section 213, which under section 216 lasts for a maximum of 15 years.

[12] See *King Features Syndicate v O and M Kleeman Ltd* 1941 AC 417.

[13] Under the 1911 Act (section 22) copyright protection was never limited if the work was not *initially* used or intended for industrial reproduction, even if it was in fact subsequently so used, whereas under the 1956 Act (section 10 as amended by the Design Copyright Act 1968), copyright protection is restricted for 15 years after *actual* industrial exploitation.

(3) The reasons for restricting infringement by indirect three-dimensional copying of two-dimensional works

This point is related to point (2) above and can perhaps best be summarised by reference to Lord Griffith's judgment in *BL v Armstrong*[14] where he said:

> the original justification for giving reproducing or copying the extended meaning of indirect copying was to achieve the purpose of copyright, namely to give protection to the artist so that he might enjoy the commercial benefit of what he had created ... But what is the purpose to be served by deeming indirect copying to be a breach of copyright in a mechanical drawing or blue print of a purely functional object? The *purpose* of such a drawing is not to use artistic skill to produce an object of attraction to the public. (emphasis added)

By contrast, the purpose of the artist painting the vase or drawing a cartoon figure such as Popeye *is* to produce an object of attraction to the public. Such an artist's copyright should continue unimpaired at least until he himself triggers section 52 by permitting commercial exploitation through industrially produced copies. Until such time, there is no question of *indirect* copying of his original 2—D work because he has not authorised any legitimate 3—D copies which can serve as the link between the original 2—D work and the 3—D indirect copy. The rationale for allowing indirect copying is to allow competition with the authorised 3—D copies (which are not themselves protected by copyright since they are not artistic works and which should not therefore be indirectly protected because they happen to be copies of a 2—D work) but if there are no authorised 3—D copies, there is no need to provide competition. It may be objected that this enables the artist to prevent a market arising in 3—D versions of his work and that this is itself anti-competitive. However, if the work is not functional, there is no real objection to this and if it does have some functional advantage it should be possible to independently design it without reliance on the artist's work. Indeed, the right to prevent a mass market arising in 3—D copies of a 2—D artistic work may be regarded as part of, or at least consistent with, the artist's moral right to object to derogatory treatment under section 80 CDPA. It is otherwise, of course, once the artist has authorised the marketing of industrially produced 3—D copies when, as already mentioned, section 52 comes into play.

(4)The avoidance of an insoluble question

If a picture created purely as a work of art with no thought of manufacturing articles reproducing the picture or part of it is capable of being a design document, this poses the insoluble question of whether or not it is a design document recording a design 'for' an artistic work. The question is insoluble because as has already been demonstrated, some articles reproducing the picture may be artistic works and others may not be, depending on *how* they are made. Virtually any drawing could be reproduced as a work of artistic crafts-manship if enough time, or rather, artistic craftsmanship were lavished on the production of the work.

If, on the other hand, one concludes that something is a design document for an artistic work because it is *capable* of being reproduced as an artistic work, then virtually all design

---

[14] 1986 1 All ER 850 at 882.

documents will fall outside section 51 and that cannot have been intended. Returning to the example of the vase painted with no thought of manufacture, if one treats it as a design document one then has to ask the question, does it record a design for an artistic work? Either the question is insoluble, because it depends on the non-existent intention of the artist as to the nature of the work to be manufactured, or it is absurd because its solution depends on whether the vase is capable of being reproduced as an artistic work on which basis virtually all design documents will escape section 51. On the basis that Parliament didn't intend to pose insoluble or absurd questions, one feels impelled to conclude that the painting is not a design document because the artist did not intend it as such.

(5) Parliamentary intention

Lastly, if only because a court would not be able to take account directly of this point, it is clear from Hansard that section 51 was not intended to apply to objects depicted in paintings, etc. or to 'art for the sake of it'. In the course of discussion of what became section 51, the Under-Secretary of State, Mr John Butcher said:[15]

> The first question that must be asked is whether the copyright work embodies a design for an article—that is, a design intended to be applied to articles. If the answer is no, copyright applies.
> ... In the case of an artist whose painting depicts a vase, or a sculptor's design sketches for a sculpture, it would be clear that copyright applies in both cases. In the first case, the painting would clearly not be a design intended to be applied to articles, but rather the depiction of an article intended to be appreciated for its own sake, as a painting. In the second case, although the sketches would clearly be designs intended to be applied to an article, the article is an artistic work—namely a sculpture.

This re-inforces the point made earlier that there is no evidence of any desire or intention to change the law in relation to drawings etc. not made for the purposes of industrial reproduction.

Conclusion

Section 51, following in the best traditions of statutory provisions on Design Copyright, is not a model of legislative clarity. It is hoped, however, that it has been demonstrated that the more sensible interpretation of 'design' and 'design document' does depend on the purpose (or design) of the person alleged to be 'the designer', that designs do not arise by accident and that paintings and drawings are not design documents merely because it is possible to make the articles which are represented or depicted therein. Having disagreed with some of Mr Christie's opinions, one is more than happy to concur in his conclusion that 'the scope for convoluted legal argument in this area remains as wide as ever'.

---

[15] House of Commons Standing Committee E, 19 May 1988, cols. 245 and 246.

European Design Law and the Spare Parts Dilemma: The Proposed Regulation and Directive
[1994] 2 EIPR 51

AUDREY HORTON
Dallas Brett, Oxford

Following the publication in June 1991 of the Commission's Green Paper on the Legal Protection of Industrial Design, numerous comments were received from various industry organisations and practitioners. Hearings were held on 25 and 26 February 1992 with interested parties and observers. A further meeting was held with government industrial property experts of Member States on 25 March 1992. On 16 October 1992 a hearing was held on the most controversial issue of all, namely legal protection of designs relating to car parts. Preliminary drafts were circulated to interested parties and the controversy and lobbying continued. The resulting redraft of the European Parliament and Council Regulation and Directive is said to take into account many of the observations made by industry and practitioners, although, since the Commission must have been faced with a barrage of contradictory viewpoints, the old adage that not all of the people can be pleased all of the time is particularly apt in this context. This article summarises the major changes in the redraft and analyses the impact of the changes of direction contained in the Regulation and Directive. Although formally adopted on 28 July 1993, the proposals were not officially published until 3 December 1993.[1]

There is no change in the underlying concept of two-tier Community-wide protection for industrial designs consisting of:

(1) informal (unregistered) design protection against unauthorised copying, lasting for three years;

(2) a Community registered design, providing monopoly protection for a maximum of 25 years, renewable in five-year blocks.[1a]

The Major Changes

Article 3: definition of 'design'

'Design' means 'the appearance of the whole or a part of a product resulting from the specific features of the lines, contours, colours, shape and/or materials of the product itself and/or its ornamentation'.

---

[1] Proposed Regulation: COM DOC 93/342 (OJ 1994 C37/20); proposed Directive: COM DOC 93/344 (OJ 1993 C345/14).

[1a] See earlier article, [1991] EIPR 442.

In this definition,

> 'product' means 'any industrial or handicraft item, including parts intended to be assembled into a complex item, set or compositions of items, packaging, get-ups, graphic symbols and typographic typefaces'.

The new definition omits reference to two-and three-dimensional features, and refers only to the appearance of the product or part of a product. The new version also eschews the general and lists a number of features which can constitute the 'appearance'. 'Product' is also defined by a series of specific items. Although the Explanatory Memorandum to the Proposal for a Regulation states that the enumeration of elements of design is not exhaustive, and the list of 'products' is by way of example only, in both cases the lists could perhaps more wisely have been expressed to be non-exhaustive, or have included a sweep-up provision at the end. One of the avowed aims of the Commission, as set out in their Explanatory Memorandum (paragraph 4.5) is to provide a 'fully modern design protection system adapted to the reality of design activities and to the need of the users of the system'. As all IP practitioners know, a recurrent problem is the failure of legislative measures to take into account the continuous development of new technologies. Because of the problems of grappling with old statutes, passed for example before the advent of the computer age, and attempting to apply such laws to issues and products not contemplated when they were originally drafted, perhaps the definitions should be less all-encompassing, allowing the Regulation to be more readily adaptable to new circumstances in modern, fast-changing industries relying on designs.

The omission of the requirement that the design features should be 'capable of being perceived by the human senses' may perhaps have been motivated by such a desire to have a less restrictive definition. However, the Explanatory Memorandum states that the definition of design 'means any feature of appearance which can be perceived by the human senses as regards sight and tactility are features of design'. 'Appearance' certainly covers features perceptible by sight, but not by touch, so the Explanatory Memorandum seems not to be in accord with the draft Regulation. The Explanatory Memorandum also states that weight and flexibility may be design features: again these are not really covered by the umbrella term 'appearance'.

In any event, in both the old and new versions of Article 3, 'computer programs' and 'semiconductor products' are excluded from design protection. This exclusion has been criticised by the relevant industries although both are protected by other regimes.[2] The 'look and feel' of a computer program cannot be supplemented by design protection, although specific graphic designs, such as the icons used in Windows-based applications, may be protected as designs in appropriate cases.

The new definition removes reference to the fact the design should not be 'dictated solely by the technical function of the product', which re-emerges in revised format in the new Article 9. The general principle remains, however, that it is irrelevant whether the design is of an aesthetic character or functional, or whether the appearance of the product is material to the purchaser or the user.

The new definition now includes kits ('parts intended to be assembled into a complex item'), similar to the changes made to the UK's design protection regime by the Copyright Designs and Patents Act 1988.[3]

---

[2] Copyright in the case of computer programs: Council Directive 91/250, OJ L122, 17 May 1991; topography right in the case of semiconductor products: Council Directive 87/54, OJ L24, 27 January 1987.

[3] Section 260(1) of the CDPA 1988 (design right) and new section 7(4) of the Registered Designs Act, as introduced by section 268 of the CDPA 1988.

Colours or materials are not *per se* eligible for protection. The reference to colours and materials is intended to reflect the fact that choice of colour or material can, in combination with other design elements, or as a combination of colours in a graphic design, add to the individual character and therefore be a protectable element of the design.

Prerequisites of protection

The Green Paper's single test of 'distinctive character' (which in effect broke down into a two-stage test of novelty and distinctiveness) has been metamorphosed into the two tests of 'individual character' (Article 6) and 'novelty' (Article 5).

Article 5: absolute worldwide novelty
The novelty test is an objective criterion assessed on a worldwide basis. This is a reversal of the Green Paper's proposal to reject the test of absolute universal objective novelty and limit novelty to 'specialised' business circles operating within the Community. The change is said to be in response to the opinion expressed by a majority of industries. Fears had been expressed that if novelty were Community-based, protection would be conferred on designs created outside but 'imported' into the EU and registered as EU designs. The result might have been that non-EU countries would have enacted similar provisions in their laws which would be to the disadvantage of the Community.

A further change is that only identical or near-identical anticipations destroy novelty. Designs will be deemed to be identical if their specific features differ only in immaterial designs. Gone is the test of 'overall impression of similarity' used in assessing the Green Paper's requirement of 'distinctive character'. Non-identical anticipations might, however, still be relevant in assessing the 'individual character' of the design.

'Made available to the public' is specifically defined: a design is deemed to have been made available to the public if it is published, exhibited, used in trade or otherwise disclosed. Disclosures to third parties under explicit or implicit conditions of confidentiality will not be treated as having been made available to the public.

In response to industry pressure, the revised Regulation has therefore reverted to the patent standard of novelty. This absolute standard applies to both registered Community designs and unregistered Community designs. It is interesting to note that in the first reported case dealing with the UK's new unregistered design right, *C & H Engineering v Klucznik & Sons Ltd*,[4] Aldous J interpreted the requirement that the design in question should not be 'commonplace' as a concept in practice akin to novelty.[5] Previously this has been regarded as a standard lesser than novelty and closer to originality, as used in copyright law, meaning independently created and not copied. Bearing in mind the rationale of the unregistered design right to provide immediate transitional protection pending registration, or shorter protection for more transient designs, such a high standard of novelty seems questionable in this context.

Article 6: individual character
'Individual character' replaces the distinctiveness element of the Green Paper's 'distinctive character'. The assessment is made as against specified prior art only, namely '(a) designs commercialised in the marketplace at the date of reference whether in the Community or elsewhere', or '(b) published following registration as a Registered Community Design or as a

---

[4]   [1992] FSR 421; [1993] 1 EIPR 24.
[5]   See 'Pig Fenders "Commonplace"', Uma Suthersanen Managing Intellectual Property, Jan/Feb 1993.

design right of a Member State, provided that protection has not expired at the date of reference'. Designs applied to products which can no longer be found on the market either inside or outside the EU do not therefore form part of the prior art. Again the test of 'individual character' has been widened out to allow currently commercialised designs outside the Community to negate the individual character of the design under consideration, although the relevant prior art is defined much more restrictively than for the novelty test.

'Individual character' is to be judged according to the 'overall impression' it produces on 'the informed user' and whether this differs from the 'overall impression' produced on such a user by the prior art specified above. The 'informed user' is a new creature of the Commission. Such an 'informed user' in the Explanatory Memorandum is specifically stated not to be a 'designs expert'. The Green Paper had used an assessment by *experts* to determine novelty, and the opinion of *ordinary consumers* to determine the design's distinctiveness. The 'informed user', we are told, will usually be the end consumer. In the case, however, of an internal part of a machine replaced in the course of a repair, where the end consumer of the product is not aware of the appearance of that internal part, the 'informed user' is the person replacing the part.

In a recent UK decision, *Gaskell & Chambers Ltd v Measure Master Limited*,[6] Aldous J's test for determining whether there had been infringement of a registered design was for the court to adopt the mantle 'of a customer who is interested in the design of the articles in question as it is the eye of such an interested person, the interested addressee, which is relevant'. Albeit that the concept is used in determining infringement rather than determining validity, the 'informed user' probably has much in common with 'the interested addressee'. Because 'informed user' tends to suggest an expert or specialist, perhaps the term 'interested addressee' or 'interested user' might more accurately reflect the Commission's intention.

'Informed user' has also been criticised as suggesting a subjective test, giving the impression that the 'informed user' tests 'individual character' only by reference to his own knowledge. The intention is clearly to create an objective test whereby the issue is decided ultimately by the judge with the assistance of expert evidence as necessary.

In assessing individual character, common features are to be given more weight than differences because what counts is the overall impression. The degree of freedom of the designer in developing the design in question is also to be taken into account in assessing individual character, a factor which is relevant also to the question of functionality and interconnections, as covered by new Article 9.

Article 4(2) provides that designs which constitute parts of complex products are not to be considered as having an individual character solely by virtue of the individual character of the complex product but rather by reference to the individual character of the part itself. Thus, for example, a car body part would have to be judged on its own merits, not by reference to the individual character of the whole car.

Overall, the effect of the new provisions relating to novelty and individual character is to raise the threshold of protectability, making it more difficult for a design to meet the required standard of absolute novelty by widening out the scope of prior art.

The Commission cites the risk of an 'abusive search' for anticipations as having been quoted by industry as an argument against the objective novelty requirement. In relation to the test for 'individual character' it believes that it has countered the risk of abuse by restricting the prior designs against which the individual character must be assessed to designs applied to products on the market inside or outside the Community, or national or Community registered designs, published and not yet expired, irrespective of whether the product to which the design is applied is marketed or not. Deigns which have disappeared

---

[6] [1993] RPC 76.

from the market, or are found only in a remote museum, if their registered protection has expired, cannot be cited in the context of 'individual character' assessment, but, if they were to amount to an identical or near-identical anticipation, they would still defeat novelty. The 'abusive search' for anticipations is therefore likely to continue.

The overall restricting of protectability is probably in response to industry opposition, expressed in submissions and hearings, to functional designs being accorded registered design protection, that is, a patent-like monopoly to exclude others, whether the design has been copied or not. What seems odd is that the higher standard of novelty for protection has been applied without distinction to both registered and unregistered Community Designs.

Scope of protection

There has been some criticism of the previous draft Regulation because it protects designs as such, and not by reference to the products on which the designs are applied. The revised draft follows the previous draft Regulation in this respect. By contrast, UK registered design applicants are required to state the article or set of articles to which the design is to be applied. In the case of the monopoly protection accorded to registered Community Designs, this could mean that a third party who had not copied but created a similar design independently would infringe the registration even if he applied it to a different product. On the other hand, requiring the applicant to nominate all possible products to which the design might be applied might also work injustice in the case of a particularly distinctive design if he omitted a product to which the design is later applied.

Article 8: 'non-prejudicial disclosures'

This was previously Article 5 when it was entitled, 'Period of Grace for a Registered Community Design'. The term 'grace period' was dropped, according to the Commission, in order to avoid confusion with the 'different' patent concept of a grace period. The new Article provides, as before, for a 12-month grace period, prior to the filing date (or other priority date), during which disclosures to the public made by the designer or his successor in title, or by third parties on behalf of the designer, will not be taken into account for the purpose of determining novelty/individual character. Missing from the previous draft, but included in the redraft, is a provision that disclosures as a consequence of an abuse (by which is presumably meant a wrongful or unauthorised disclosure of the design) will likewise not be taken into account during the 12-month grace period. However, paragraph 8(2) excludes from the grace period provisions abusive disclosures which have resulted in a Registered Community Design or a registered design right of a Member State. In such a case the person legitimately entitled to the design may apply for a transfer of the registered right resulting from the unauthorised disclosure, using the procedure under new Article 16 (Claims relating to the entitlement of a Community Design).

Disclosures not falling within the definition of Article 8 will have the effect of defeating the novelty of a later design even if, as the Explanatory Memorandum points out, the design is unknown to and could not have been known to the designer of the later design. The Explanation seems otiose since this is the consequence of the absolute worldwide novelty test, already set out. The Commission perhaps wants to justify its *volte-face* on this point by pointing out that in practice the effects will be less dramatic. For example, the holder of an earlier unregistered Community design right may invalidate the later exclusive registered right but he cannot prevent the later designer from commercialising the product to which the design is applied, since the unregistered design confers only a protection against copying. The later independently created design by definition has not copied the earlier design.

Article 9: non-arbitrary functional designs and interconnections

This Article has been one of the most controversial of all the provisions of the draft Regulation. On the one hand, the motor car industry lobbied hard to secure design protection for spare parts. On the other hand, spare parts producers, especially those supplying the motor car industry, lobbied equally hard to open up competition in the spare parts market by excluding 'interconnections' from protection.

Article 9 now consists of three parts.

Functional designs

First, design protection is not available (Article 9(a))

> to the extent that the realisation of a technical function leaves no freedom as regards arbitrary features of appearance.

The Explanatory Memorandum tells us that only in extremely rare cases will form follow function with no possibility of variation, and that it is unlikely that the whole design will be unprotectable: in most cases only specific features will be without possibilities of variations and thus dictated by function.

The question is left open, however, as to the situations in which it can be said there is no freedom as regards arbitrary elements of design. What, for example, about features of form which, although theoretically capable of variation, represent in fact the most efficient or practical choice to perform the technical function of the product concerned?

Interconnections

Article 9 deals with both the issue of functionality and with interconnections, although it does not explicitly link them. The second part is all that remains of the original draft as modified. Article 9(b) provides that there should also be no protection for a design which:

> must necessarily be reproduced in its exact form and dimensions in order to permit the product *in which the design is incorporated* or to which it is applied to be *mechanically* assembled or connected with another product (*portions emphasised represent changes from the earlier wording*).

The Explanatory Memorandum states that designs of interconnections, as defined above, are not eligible for protection even if the design of the interconnecting element is arbitrary in the sense that shape and dimension is not exclusively dictated by the technical function. The purpose of the provision is:

> to enhance the interoperability of products of different make and to prevent manu-facturers of design products from creating captive markets, for example for peripherals, by monopolising the shape and dimensions of interconnections.
>
> Thus for example, the dimensions of the fittings of an exhaust pipe, dictated by the necessity of fitting the exhaust pipe to a specific car model cannot constitute a protectable design element since the dimensions are dictated by those of the underside of the car.

In the shorthand language used by UK practitioners following the CDPA regime, the draft Regulation had a 'must fit' but no 'must match' exception, until, that is, the formulation of the so-called repair clause in relation to spare parts (Article 23), which covers cases where the consumer is concerned with the appearance of a part used for repair purposes.

Some commentators have questioned whether the issue of interconnections would not more widely have been left to be dealt with by EU competition law. Certainly the explicit rationale behind Article 9(2) is the preservation of competition in sub-markets for peripherals or spare parts by ensuring interconnectability or inter-operability. This critical issue touches the heart of the major dichotomy facing the Commission: the perennial struggle between intellectual property rights and freedom of competition in the marketplace, transmuted into the current debate between monopoly or exclusive rights of intellectual property owners and the public interest in standardisation to ensure maximum accessibility to new technology or, in this case, designs.

The Explanatory Memorandum makes the point that, even if variants to the inter-connecting feature were possible, protection will still be excluded in this situation. If variants would have been possible then it might be argued that effectively what has happened is that the particular form and dimensions have become an industry standard, in which case granting design protection would unjustifiably block competition in the sub-market of peripherals and spare parts. An analogy could be drawn with computer interfaces. In the car exhaust example, however, unless the form and dimensions of the interconnecting element of the exhaust pipe have become an industry-wide standard, why should the designer of the interconnecting part, if it is a design which would otherwise have attracted protection as a novel and distinctive creation, be denied protection merely because it mechanically connects with another product?

It is hard to resist the conclusion that this is an area better dealt with openly as a competition law issue. If we bring into play the concerns of the ECJ in *Volvo v Veng*[7] then, if there is no refusal to supply and no blocking of a secondary market by the exercise of intellectual property rights in the primary market, as arguably happened in *Magill*,[8] what is the justification for withdrawing from a designer his finite term of protection?

If the thresholds of novelty/individual character are set at an appropriately high level, and if technical variants for the particular design feature are possible until the particular variant selected has become an industry standard by effluxion of time, or non-enforcement/non-policing of rights, there appears to be little justification for refusing protection, provided that the right holder is willing to supply fairly the relevant market for spare parts or peripherals. At this stage in the analysis one has sympathy for the UK legislators' compromise solution of compulsory licensing in relation to the last five years of the unregistered design right.

Modular products

The final part, Article 9(c), was added later still as a concession to designers to stop misuse or overuse of Article 9(b). Protection *is* available for a design:

> serving the purpose of allowing *simultaneous* and indefinite or multiple assembly or connection of *identical or mutually interchangeable* products within a modular system (*portions emphasised represent changes from earlier drafts*)

This exception is said to be for interconnections of modular products, for example the

---

[7] Case 238/87 [1988] ECR 6211.
[8] Case T-69/89 *RTE v Commission* [1991] CMLR 586; Case T-70/79 *BBC v Commission* [1991] CMLR 669; Case T-76/89 *ITP v Commission* [1991] CMLR 745—collectively known as *Magill*.

fittings for stacking chairs enabling the chairs to be stacked, or Lego bricks ('interconnecting elements of toys designed with a view to being assembled'), provided that such features are eligible for protection in terms of novelty and individual character. Therefore if the innovative character of a design of modular product consists in the design of the interconnecting elements, even if not exclusively, then protection is available.

The original draft of this last section (before the insertion of the additional words in italics) begs the question of how to differentiate between designs which fall to be excluded because of the 'must fit' exception in Article 9(b) (which designs have some degree of innovative character since they are selected from technically arbitrary variants) and innovative interconnections for modular products. The reference to 'identical or mutually interchangeable products' prevents, for example, the fitment of a car exhaust pipe on to a car from being classed as part of a modular product.

The mischief the interconnections exception is seeking to prevent is made explicit in the introduction to the Explanatory Memorandum, in the discussion on 'design protection and competition'. Usually, it is said design protection and competition are compatible, but there can be problems with '*long lasting* complex products', for example motor vehicles where design protection of individual parts of which the complex product is composed could create a 'truly captive market in spare parts'.

The concern ostensibly with the long lasting nature of the product is in reality a concern with the potential duration of intellectual property protection, and the fear of abuse of a monopoly position arising from lack of competition in the spare parts market.

The solution to this problem is complex and the long discussions and debates about design protection for spare parts delayed publication of the proposals by many months. The following elements can theoretically be used to temper the potentially anti-competitive effect of a 'truly captive market in spare parts':

(1) a sufficiently high threshold in determining novelty/individual character;
(2) exclusion of interconnections from the definition of design;
(3) elimination of non-arbitrary technical design features where realisation of the technical functions leaves the designer no freedom to choose between variant features of appearance, but dictates his choice;
(4) a relatively short duration of protection, but sufficiently long to justify the return on the designer's R&D investment. The UK system of providing a lesser form of unregistered protection for essentially functional designs has much to commend it in this context. The problem with the current Community Design, and the reason no doubt that the spare parts pressure groups lobbied so hard for the exclusion for interconnections and spare parts, is that registered monopoly protection lasting up to 25 years is potentially available for essentially functional designs;
(5) as a final check, a system of compulsory licensing, superimposed to deal with abuse of intellectual property rights arising out of, for example, failure to supply spare parts or peripherals, and/or the imposition of discriminatory terms on licensees and so on. Recital 13 to the Regulation does in fact provide that it is 'without prejudice to the application of the competition rules under Articles 85 and 86'.

The Spare Parts Problem Which Remained

The Commission, in response to pressure from the independent spare parts industry, recognised that the exclusion of interconnections *per se* did not solve the spare parts problem.

In UK parlance there was no 'must match' exception. Spare parts for long-lasting goods could only be produced by someone other than the original manufacturer insofar as the consumer was not concerned with visual appearance of the product, for example if the part in question is hidden, as with exhaust pipes fitted under a car. In many cases, however, consumers wishing to purchase spare parts for repair purposes will be concerned with the overall appearance of the product and the part, and the spare parts manufacturer would therefore have to infringe any design rights attaching to the spare part if he is to compete successfully with the original manufacturer. The classic example is a visual design relating to a car body panel such as a door, a wing or a hub-cap.

Article 23: use of a registered community design for repair purposes: the 'repair clause'

The solution to the spare parts problem finally chosen by the Commission, and announced by the official Information Memo released on 28 July 1993, was to insert a specific 'repair clause' which appears as Article 23 in the present draft. Article 23 provides that the rights conferred by a Registered Community Design shall not be exercised against third parties who use the design three years from the first putting on the marking of a product incorporating the design or to which the design is applied provided that:

(a) the product incorporating the design or to which the design is applied is a part of a complex product upon whose appearance the protected design is dependent, and
(b) the purpose of such a use is to permit the repair of the complex product so as to restore its original appearance.

The repair clause therefore gives any third party, three years after the marketing of a 'complex product', the right to reproduce a design applied to a part of the complex product if the design of the part is dictated by the appearance of that complex product. Thus designers of complex products such as motor vehicles will enjoy exclusive rights in the design of spare parts for a period of three years after first marketing, but, when the three year period has expired, independent spare parts manufacturers will be able to compete with the original designer for a share in the after market.

The intention is that consumers will therefore have a choice of sources for spare parts for the greater part of the life of the product. For 'complex product' in practice read 'motor vehicles', although use of this term could lead to disagreement and ultimately litigation as to whether a product is or is not 'complex'. The period of exclusive protection for spare parts was originally proposed at seven years, but shortened to three on the basis that the average life span of a motor vehicle is seven to eight years.

Article 23(c) provides that the right to repair clause has to be exercised in such a way that the public is not misled as to the origin of the product used for the repair.

The repair clause is a very interesting twist to the long-running saga of the spare parts question. It immediately calls to mind for UK lawyers the House of Lords' judicial creation in *British Leyland v Armstrong Patents Co. Ltd*[9] of the right to repair, which it based on the principle of non-derogation from grant, that is, the right of every person to whom a designer/manufacturer sells a motor car to repair that vehicle by replacement of spare parts such as exhaust pipes. This was equally well a response to over-long duration of exclusive

---

[9] *British Leyland Motor Corp. v Armstrong Patents Co. Ltd* [1986] RPC 279.

rights, in that case full copyright protection (life of the author plus 50 years) accorded to functional engineering drawings infringed by the making of three-dimensional objects copied therefrom.

Duration of exclusive rights in spare parts is also seen to be a critical element in the Commission's thinking: the Commission ultimately compromised at three years as representing a sufficient return on the investment of the original designer. The Commission also was at pains to point out that the high threshold for protection means that it should only be exceptionally that a replacement part will be protected by a design right, even if the appearance of the product as a whole is eligible for protection. Nevertheless the danger of some parts of complex products being sufficiently distinctive prompted the Commission to formulate the repair clause as a specific exception to any exclusive design right which would otherwise prevent competition in the spare parts market.

It is interesting to note that the three-year exclusive period of protection given to Community registered designs subject to the 'must match' exception, such as car body panels, equates in duration to the period given for unregistered design protection. Since producers of spare parts will quite clearly be copying the original designs, it must be argued that the monopoly-effect registered protection given to such designs is unnecessary and original designers would have been equally well served by unregistered protection against copying, since the duration of both forms of protection in this context is now only three years.

On the other hand, there are practical advantages to the giving of registered protection to articles without having to decide as a matter of registrability *per se*, whether or not the article concerned is subject to the 'must match' exception. The difficulties of making this decision are amply illustrated by the recent *Ford Motor Company Limited* decision of the Registered Designs Appeals Tribunal, where the court agonised over whether to allow registrations for various vehicle components.[10] The debate centred around whether the 'must match' concept involved a comparison between the part in question and the vehicle as a whole, or between the part and the whole vehicle minus the part in question (the 'n—1' approach). The court in the end held that the comparison to be made is with the vehicle as a whole, unless it can be shown that the items in question (for example steering wheels, wing mirrors, lamps, seats and so on) are sold separately and that manufacturers and owners do in practice fit a wide variety of such parts to the same vehicle.

The spare parts controversy including the viability of the repair clause is likely to follow the draft proposals as they progress to the parliamentary stage.

Proposed European Parliament and Council Directive

As a parallel measure to the draft Regulation the proposed Directive requires Member States by 31 October 1996 to harmonise their national laws as to certain key points, including conditions of protection (novelty/individual character), the one-year grace period for registered protection, the 'interconnections' and 'repair clause' exception, and the duration of protection.

The provisions of the Directive apply only to registered designs and not to unregistered design rights, on the basis that most national design laws of Member States do not provide for such a right. Article 17 (formerly Article 13), which preserves Member States' existing laws of trade marks/distinctive signs, patents and utility models, civil liability and unfair competition, now makes specific reference to unregistered design *rights* and adds protection given to typefaces to the list. The Explanatory Memorandum makes reference to the fact

[10] *Ford Motor Co. Ltd and Iveco Fiat's Design Application* [1993] RPC 399.

that one Member State (the United Kingdom) has introduced unregistered design right protection 'which to a certain extent could be claimed to replace copyright protection in that state'.

Article 18 (formerly Article 14) continues to stipulate that Member States must provide cumulative protection for registered Community designs under copyright law. This will cause problems for the United Kingdom, where the Copyright Designs and Patents Act 1988 provides in practice that there should be no cumulative protection under copyright and design legislation. The extent to which the United Kingdom's unregistered design right will equate with copyright for the purpose of satisfying this provision in the Directive is unclear, but it seems likely that the United Kingdom will nevertheless have to undertake a major overhaul of its new design law in order to comply with the Directive.

The United Kingdom's problem is illustrative of wider diversity problems throughout the EU which will hinder the implementation of a Community Design system. Until the national copyright and unfair competition laws of Member States are harmonised also, in practice the harmonisation of design legislation cannot take effect as planned. There will still be critical differences in the laws of Member States which will impede the free circulation of goods and services with the potential to restrict or distort competition.

The harmonisation of laws within the EU is inevitably proceeding on a piecemeal basis. However, since each harmonisation Directive is really a part of an overall jigsaw puzzle, until all the pieces are in place the whole picture will not materialise and make sense for lawyers and the design industry alike.

Conclusion and Some Thoughts for the Future

The feature of the Regulation and Directive which has caused most controversy throughout its history to date has been the policy decision not to distinguish between functional and aesthetic designs so far as registered protection is concerned. Hard pressed on this point by the spare parts industry lobby, the Commission resisted calls for a visual 'must match' exception, or a compulsory licensing system, in favour of the 'repair right' compromise. It seems to have introduced this concept with some reluctance, recognising that it is a derogation from the primary intellectual property right involved. The Explanatory Memorandum to Article 23 of the Regulation explicitly states that because the provision makes an inroad into the rights of the right holder, 'it should be applicable only under strict conditions'.

The EU's harmonisation Directives have historically been implemented most speedily and successfully when the impetus has been to secure reciprocal protection for EU nationals in the United States (as for example in the case of the semiconductor topography Directive— see footnote 2 above). This catalyst is not at present at work in the industrial design sphere. In fact, the opposite is true, since the United States has dragged its feet for decades in the face of attempts to introduce specific design protection for essentially functional designs. The latest draft US legislation, the Design Innovation and Technology Act of 1991, proposes a form of *registered* protection against copying only, lasting 10 years, for functional designs. The United States also offers design patent protection lasting 14 years for non-functional aesthetic designs as the closest equivalent to registered monopoly-effect design protection. The proposed US and European systems are, as can be seen, at present light years apart.

In view of the ever-increasing importance of international (and not just Community-wide) protection for intellectual property rights, it would seem prudent for the United States and the EU, when framing their respective industrial design law systems, to attempt to reach an agreement at least on key points, so that it is possible for designers to know with a reasonable degree of certainty that reciprocal design protection to that accorded by EU Member States exists also in the United States. At the moment, in the United Kingdom, US companies are frequently unable to avail themselves of the United Kingdom's unregistered design right protection precisely because the United States affords no equivalent protection. Although it is strictly speaking outside the scope of the primary purpose of the Regulation and Directive, perhaps Europe should not miss this golden opportunity, in the context of harmonising its own design laws, of both influencing and taking into account the developing laws of other major trading nations such as the United States.

Passing Off and Trade Marks

Passing Off

A Pervasive But Often Not Explicitly Characterised Aspect of Passing Off

[1987] 6 EIPR 159

ANTHONY WALTON
London

Myself when young went in at every door
Where Dons and Judges talked about the law
Of Passing-Off; nathless for evermore
Could never fathom what a mark was *for*.

'A guarantee of quality' said some.
Others, 'The *distant* rumble of a drum;
Where all you know and all you need to know
Is He that strikes it pockets some small sum'.[1]

It is not the purpose of this article to explore further the inability of English law to make up its mind what a trade mark is for, and to point out the conflicts to which this ambivalent attitude has given rise, but to concentrate on the thoroughly pervasive aspects of one of the two views. These aspects are undoubtedly thoroughly appreciated but seldom collected together and put forward absolutely explicitly. That is what this article will attempt to do.

The view adverted to its quite simply this: one purpose and function of a trade mark is to indicate *quality* and on this aspect of matters, it is only incidentally, in so far as trade origin affects quality, that its purpose is to indicate trade origin.

It is hoped to explore in a later article the conflict between this view and a rival one which will not admit that trade marks are concerned with quality in any aspect of the law. That a case based on the view that quality matters[2] may be followed by a statute negativing its effect[3] is plain enough. But the view to be explored in this article is undoubtedly current and more pervasive than is generally consciously appreciated.

The view is inherent, but hidden, in the classical broad statement of the basis for liability in passing off. This statement is the proposition that 'nobody has any right to represent his goods as the goods of somebody else'.[4] The latest adumbration of broad principle in the *Advocaat* case[5] adds necessary concomitant detail, but does not alter the fundamental basis of the action which this statement propounds.

Of course the principle applies alike to a misrepresentation affecting services rather than

---

[1] From a hitherto unpublished manuscript on industrial property law written by the late Omar Khayyam.
[2] *Starey v The Chilworth Gunpowder Co.* (1890) 24 QBD 90.
[3] Now see Trade Marks Act 1938 section 62.
[4] *Spalding v Gamage* (1915) 32 RPC 273 (HL) at 283.
[5] *Erven Warnink v J. Townend* [1980] RPC 31 (HL) at 93.

goods. And of course the misrepresentation may be made directly (as in the classical case where by supplying B's goods instead of the goods of A which had been demanded by the customer the defendant is saying in effect 'these are A's goods') or indirectly (where the defendant merely applies to his goods some badge of distinctiveness in which the plaintiff has acquired a reputation by user).

But the point of interest for the purposes of this article is *what actually constitutes a misrepresentation that the defendant's goods are the goods of the plaintiff?* By far the commonest cause is where the defendant is in effect saying: 'These goods are the goods of the plaintiff in the sense that they are connected in the course of trade with the plaintiff.' But the principle embraces also the case where the defendant is saying in effect: 'These goods are the plaintiff's goods in the sense that they are similar in all material respects to the goods dealt in by the plaintiff—their *quality* is the same.'

It may not be possible to construct a rigorously logical or historical classification of the types of case in which the view has arisen and played a determinative role in the decision, but the following discussion may perhaps afford a rough preliminary approach to such a classification.

(A) Cases Where the Defendant's Misrepresentation May Also Go To Trade Origin

In cases of this sort, the defendant simply uses the plaintiff's badge of distinctiveness without sufficient qualification. The classical case was where the defendant said in effect: 'My product is *Yorkshire Relish*.'

While this obviously gave rise to the normal case of confusion of trade origin, it is important to remember what was said by the Lord Chancellor (Lord Halsbury) and Lord Herschell:[6]

Lord Halsbury

Now, it is said, on behalf of Defendants as a first proposition of fact, that there is no representation that what they sell is the manufacture of the original inventor by calling it 'Yorkshire Relish', because it has become a well-known commercial article, and calling it by that name merely means that it is that thing. We have had a very long argument on that subject. My Lords, the first objection that can be advanced against that argument is, that it is not true. As a matter of fact, this is not the well-known article. The composition of the well-known commercial article is a secret. The exclusive manufacture of it is by the person who knows the secret, and nobody else can manufacture it because they do not know how it is made. It is obvious, therefore, that the first proposition of fact which is supposed to encounter the Plaintiff's right is displaced by the existing state of the evidence.

Now, the thing that is sold by the Appellants as 'Yorkshire Relish' is not 'Yorkshire Relish' in the sense of its *being the same chemical composition*, in the sense of its having the same taste, in the sense of its being so properly assimilated to the preferences of the persons who take it, either in smell or taste, as the original composition is. If that is so, how can it possibly be contended, as a matter of fact, that a person who is selling this thing as 'Yorkshire Relish' is entitled to do so because it is a well-known commercial

---

[6] *Powell v The Birmingham Vinegar Brewery Company Ltd* (1897) 14 RPC 720 (HL) at 728 and 730.

article, and because he is only selling a well-known commercial article by the only name by which it is known? (*Emphasis added.*)

Lord Herschell

It was said, on behalf of the Appellants, that they had a right to sell what they manufactured, and to call it 'Yorkshire Relish', because 'Yorkshire Relish' had come to be merely the name of a particular sauce with a particular flavour. I do not think that that is an answer which, in point of fact, can be set up in the present case. I do not enter upon the question whether it would have been sufficient in point of law if it had been established in point of fact. But here what they sell and put in the market is not 'Yorkshire Relish' in the sense in which those words had been used down to that time, and would be understood by anybody. It may have been something very like it—a 'good match', and so on; but it was not 'Yorkshire Relish'. When, therefore, they sold their goods as 'Yorkshire Relish', they sold them as the Plaintiff's manufacture when they were not the Plaintiff's manufacture, *nor the article which he manufactured and sold under that name.* (*Emphasis added.*)

In such cases, while undoubtedly questions of misrepresentation as to trade origin do arise, the courts find it relevant to rely on the fact that the plaintiff's and defendant's *products* are not the same.

Also in this category are probably the cases where the defendant falsely attributes to his own goods the awards and prizes actually awarded to the plaintiff's goods.[7] But it is only fair to say that in many such cases the plaintiff has been refused relief. However, it will be found that in many such cases there were highly special circumstances, or that the cases are old, or that the main stream of cases dealt with in this article were not cited.

Another somewhat special case where quality—of a rather meretricious nature—was misrepresented as well as almost certainly trade origin, was where the defendant sold an expurgated autobiography under the same title as the plaintiff's unexpurgated edition of the same work.[8]

But it will be seen that in other classes of case questions of confusion as to trade origin do not even begin to arise for a variety of reasons.

(B) Cases Where the Misrepresentation Manifestly Cannot Go To Trade Origin

(I) Cases where the trade origin is the same

    (a) Cases where the plaintiff himself mislabels his goods
    (b) Cases where the defendant mislabels the plaintiff's goods

In category I(a) are to be found the types of case of which *Starey v Chilworth*[9] is the archetype.

In that case manufacturers of gunpowder had an accident and were unable to manufacture the powder themselves. What they did was to import German manufactured powder and put their own labels on it, and this they supplied in purported fulfilment of their contract

---

[7] *Kerly*, 12th ed. paragraph 16–26 on page 366.
[8] *Allen v Brown Watson* [1965] RPC 191.
[9] See Note 2 above.

with the purchasers. It is fair to say that there was a finding that: 'This powder was as good as the powder which the respondents make themselves',[10] but in finding the manufacturers guilty of using a false description, Lord Coleridge C.J. said: 'The Act is directed against the abuse of trade marks, and the putting off on a purchaser of, not a bad article, but an article different from that which he intends to purchase and believes that he is purchasing.'[11]

For the prosecution, Moulton Q.C. said of the respondents: 'What they did amounted to an attempt to pass off on the Government German powder as being powder of their own manufacture.'[12]

While in cases of category I(a) the question of quality of product may reside only in the question of who was the manufacturer, in cases of category I(b) it is too plain for argument that the quality of the products is different, on whatever basis that question is judged, for what the defendant is doing is selling the plaintiff's own inferior products as and for the plaintiff's own superior products.

These cases alone, without any of the other categories, would show that passing off embraces the offence of misrepresenting quality without there being the least possibility of misrepresenting trade origin, for the trade origin of each of the rival products is the plaintiff and no one else.

The classical case is of course *Spalding v Gamage*.[13] The facts of the case are not as neat as sometimes supposed but for the purpose of understanding what was decided can be paraphrased. It is enough to say that in that case the plaintiffs' *Orb* football proved unsatisfactory and was sold off to waste-rubber merchants. The plaintiffs then brought out their *Improved Orb*. The defendants obtained the discarded balls and sold them under the designation *Improved Orb*. They were duly injuncted and in the leading opinion of the House of Lords, Lord Parker said:[14]

> My Lords, the proposition that no one has a right to represent his goods as the goods of somebody else must, I think, as has been assumed in this case, involve as a corollary the further proposition, that no one, who has in his hands the goods of another of a particular class or quality, has a right to represent these goods to be the goods of that other of a different quality or belonging to a different class. Possibly, therefore, the principle ought to be re-stated as follows: A cannot, without infringing the rights of B, represent goods which are not B's goods or B's goods of a particular class or quality to be B's goods or B's goods of that particular class or quality. The wrong for which relief is sought in a passing-off action consists in every case of a representation of this nature.

But what if the defendants had merely called these discarded balls *Orb*, as the plaintiffs had formerly done? *Spalding v Gamage* itself was a little unclear as to this—although the principle quoted above would undoubtedly catch such behaviour—and in the event that is just what the defendants did do, and were injuncted, but rather on the basis that as they had *started* calling the balls *Improved Orb* it would be thought that plain *Orb* would convey the same representation.

Later cases, however, applied the *Spalding v Gamage* principle quite flatly to cases where the defendant simply continued use of the plaintiff's mark unaltered to goods of the plaintiff on which the plaintiff himself would never have used or continued the use of such mark.

---

[10] *Ibid.* at 94.
[11] *Ibid.* at 96.
[12] *Ibid.* at 93.
[13] See Note 4 above.
[14] *Ibid.* at 284.

Thus, the defendant was injuncted in cases where he continued the use of the plaintiff's mark on deteriorated tins of condensed milk[15] or put the plaintiff's mark on rejected goods obtained from the plaintiff's waste bins[16] or sold a plaintiff's second-hand car as a plaintiff's new car.[17] It can be clearly seen that all these circumstances fall within the *Spalding* principle.

(II) Cases where the trade origin is not the same but there is no misrepresentation about it

(a) Cases where the defendant is explicit
(b) Cases where the defendant cannot be supposed on a fair interpretation of the facts to be making a misrepresentation about trade origin by implication

As to category II(a) we now come to the type of case where the defendant has not the least desire in the world to confuse the public as to trade origin, but wants merely to tell the public that he has a cheaper substitute for the plaintiff's goods.

The classical case is *Irving's Yeast-Vite Ltd v F. A. Horsenail*.[18] In that case the plaintiffs extensively advertised and sold a pharmaceutical preparation under the name and trade mark *Yeast-Vite*.

> The Defendant carried on a retail business at Canterbury dealing in Herbal and other remedies. The Defendant exhibited in his shop windows placards bearing the words 'Do not buy a name—the formula of patent medicines is anyone's property—we have a substitute for the following—Yeast-Vite ...' etc.; 'Why pay fancy prices for Patent Medicines—if you can get the same formulas at a third the price.' Bottles, containing some preparation, were also on sale, labelled 'Yeast Tablets. A substitute for Yeast-Vite.'

Unfortunately the defendant also supplied the substitute in his shop in response to requests for *Yeast-Vite*. Of course that alone would have justified an injunction for passing off. But the plaintiff asked for an injunction in wider terms, and the Court acceded to this in the following manner:

> THIS COURT DOTH ORDER that the Defendant his servants and agents be restrained until Judgment in this Action or until further Order from passing off as the Plaintiffs' goods pharmaceutical preparations not of the Plaintiffs' manufacture or merchandise *and from issuing displaying or distributing printed matter calculated to cause the passing off the Defendant's goods as and for the goods of the Plaintiffs.*[19] (*Emphasis added.*)

This Order of the Court quite plainly regarded the defendant's mere assertions that he had an equivalent substitute as constituting passing off. The case ultimately went to the House of Lords on the question whether there had been an infringement of trade mark, and the House of Lords noted that 'the passing off side of the case has been already dealt with by Mr Justice Bennett and is unappealed'.[20] It was held in that case that the trade mark had not been infringed,

---

[15] *Wilts United Dairies v Robinson* [1958] RPC 94.
[16] *Britains v Morris* [1961] RPC 217.
[17] *Morris Motors v Lilley* [1959] 1 WLR 1184.
[18] (1933) 50 RPC 139.
[19] See page 27 of the appendix to the House of Lords Blue Book.
[20] (1934) 51 RPC 110 at 116.

but in completely analogous circumstances[21] occurring after the alteration of the Act[22] it was held (admittedly controversially) that there was infringement of trade mark.

As to cases in category II(b) the classic modern case is *Combe v Scholl*.[23] In that case the plaintiffs sold shoe insoles containing activated charcoal which they called *Odor-Eaters*. The defendants also sold insoles, containing charcoal, but charcoal which was not activated. Although the defendants' trade name and colours were on their boxes, those boxes were the same shape and size as the plaintiffs' and by stating that the goods were 'Odour Destroying Cushion Insoles' and informing the public that the insoles contained charcoal, the defendants were in effect stating that their goods did the same job as the plaintiffs'. The defendants also gave a guarantee in virtually identical terms to that of the plaintiffs and their insoles were coloured black like those of the plaintiffs.

In these circumstances the judge[24] tout court held the defendants guilty of passing off simply because they were representing their goods as the same as the plaintiffs' in the sense that they were the same in all material respects *qua* goods. He said:

> By reason of the circumstances which I have listed above, the public are, say the plaintiffs, led to believe that the two products are the same. The defendants are, of course, perfectly entitled to say that the products are the same if in fact they are; but it is admitted that they are not; they are quite different products.[25]

It will of course be appreciated that the circumstances he *did* list above, were not the more usual circumstances indicating that the public are confused as to trade origin, but facts and matters relating solely to the quality and function of the goods.

While in that case the judge might have gone further afield for his authorities, as this article hopefully demonstrates, in fact the principal authority he relied on was *Masson Seeley and Co. v Embosotype Mfg Co.*[26]

In that case the judge found that the defendants' conduct was calculated to induce people to believe that the goods offered by them were, contrary to the fact, *the same as* (emphasis added) the goods supplied by the plaintiffs.[27] This statement by itself is ambiguous in that it might have been intended to indicate merely that the defendants were misrepresenting that their goods had the same trade origin. But the judge had adverted earlier to the fact that the defendants' goods 'differed materially' from the goods supplied by the plaintiffs,[28] and it must be taken that he meant 'same' in the sense 'same in all material respects as regards quality', and this is how it was taken by the judge in *Combe v Scholl*.

Spanish Champagne

The acme of generalisation in cases of category II(b) is where all the defendant is doing is merely stating that he too is selling goods similar in all material respects to the *type* of goods sold by the plaintiffs. In the classic case of course these goods were *Champagne*[29] and the defendant called his goods *Spanish Champagne*. No fair-minded person could have thought

---

[21] *Bismag v Amblins* (1940) 57 RPC 209.
[22] Now see Trade Marks Act 1938 section 4.
[23] [1980] RPC 1.
[24] Fox J. as he then was.
[25] Note 23 above at 7.
[26] (1924) 41 RPC 160.
[27] *Ibid.* at 165.
[28] *Ibid.*
[29] *Bollinger v Costa Brava Wine Co.* [1960] RPC 16.

for a moment that the defendant was representing himself as being the Veuve Cliquot or Monsieur Bollinger, or that his goods came from any other trade source known to and loved by the public. But what he was doing was representing that his goods were of such quality as entitled them to be called *Champagne* which was false as they were not made from grapes of the genuine geographical district of that name. This case was notoriously followed in the *Advocaat* case[30] in which the defendant called his drink *Advocaat* when it was not made from spirits. In each of these cases the Courts made no bones about finding that the defendant's conduct constituted passing off.

The principles applicable to this generalised type of case have been expressed as follows:

> I would hold the Champagne case to have been rightly decided and in doing so would adopt the words of Danckwerts J. where he said (at [1960] RPC 31):

>> There seems to be no reason why such licence [sc. to do a deliberate act which causes damage to the property of another person] should be given to a person competing in trade, who seeks to attach to his product a name or description with which it has no natural association, so as to make use of the reputation and goodwill which has been gained by a product genuinely indicated by the name or description. In my view, it ought not to matter that the persons truly entitled to describe their goods by the name and description are a class producing goods in a certain locality, and not merely one individual. The description is part of their goodwill and a right of property. I do not believe that the law of passing off, which arose to prevent unfair trading, is so limited in scope.[31]

> It cannot make any difference in principle whether the recognisable and distinctive qualities by which the reputation of the type of product has been gained are the result of its having been made in, or from, ingredients produced in a particular locality or are the result of its having been made from particular ingredients regardless of their provenance; though a geographical limitation may make it easier (a) to define the type of product; (b) to establish that it has qualities which are recognisable and distinguish it from every other type of product that competes with it in the market and which have gained for it in that market a reputation and goodwill; and (c) to establish that the plaintiff's own business will suffer more than minimal damage to its goodwill by the defendant's misrepresenting his product as being of that type.[32]

But howsoever expressed it is clear that the offence is no more than a generalisation of the more individual case of the *Combe v Scholl* type, and the gist of the offence consists in misrepresenting that the defendant is selling goods which are the plaintiff's goods in the sense only that they are their equivalent.

The Get-up Cases

It only remains to explore a line of cases which, having approached the question from the wrong direction, cannot be considered to afford any guidance as to the application of the above principles.

---

[30] See Note 5 above.
[31] *Advocaat* case, note 5 above, at 95, 96.
[32] *Ibid.* at 98.

These are cases where the plaintiff, being wishful to complain about the defendant's assertions to the effect that he had the same goods as the plaintiff, accuses the defendant of taking his, the plaintiff's, *get-up*.

In so complaining the plaintiff completely misses his way. He is usually told in short order that 'get-up' is something adventitious and cannot possibly be constituted by the goods themselves.[33]

The end of this road is reached in cases like *British American Glass v Winton*[34] where the plaintiff and defendant were both selling identical ceramic ornamental dogs (although the defendant's dogs were made of cheaper material) and the Court (Pennycuick J.) observed:[35]

> *This is not really a passing-off case as regards get-up in any way at all.* It is not a question of getting up; it is a question of the appearance of the actual articles sold. The plaintiff company must, therefore, show that the trade or public on seeing the dogs of this configuration and shape will understand that the dogs are dogs of the plaintiff company's manufacture. Mr Stack, a director of the plaintiff company, states in general terms: 'The shape and configuration of these ornamental dogs are entirely novel and have become associated by members of the trade and public with my company exclusively.' There is no question here of traders being misled and the question is whether members of the public are likely to be misled into believing that the dogs manufactured by the defendant company are manufactured by the plaintiff company. This is on the face of it, it seems to me, improbable since a member of the public buying an ornament trinket of this nature is concerned only with what it looks like and is unlikely to care by whom it is made. (*Emphasis added.*)

Since the plaintiff framed his case as being one of infringing get-up, the judge's reasoning in that case cannot be faulted on the law as it stands. But commenting on the law as it stands, when approaching passing off from the standpoint of get-up, the editors of *Kerly*[36] after setting out the presently made distinction between the goods themselves and the get-up thereof, go on to complain:

> This is hardly a satisfactory approach: it is not easy to see why misleading of the public by close intimation of goods should be any differently treated from misleading of the public in any other way, whilst the distinction between the goods in themselves and features added capriciously to them belongs, perhaps more to the realms of metaphysics than of commercial design.[37]

It is indeed unfortunate that a plaintiff loses merely because he frames his case one way rather than another, when he is entitled to succeed on the facts, but that would appear to be the position. Unless and until *Combe v Scholl* is overruled there can be no doubt whatever that one aspect of passing off consists of the offence of representing that the defendant's goods are the same (that is, the same in all material respects *qua* goods) as those of the plaintiff when this is untrue.

Combe v Scholl is indeed only a particular example of an application of the principle which it is hoped the author has shown is much wider than generally explicitly recognised.

---

[33] *Williams v Bronnley* (1909) 26 RPC 765 at 773.
[34] [1962] RPC 230.
[35] *Ibid.* at 232.
[36] Messrs Blanco White and Jacob.
[37] *Kerly*, 12th ed. paragraph 16–67 on page 403.

That there is often a dim and distant recognition of this truth can perhaps be illustrated by the fact that the plaintiff in the 'China Dogs' case did in fact cite a variety of the *Spanish Champagne* case in his argument.[38]

But the best illustration of all is this, that in *Combe v Scholl* itself, the defendants plainly recognised that if they could only get the case running on the normal 'get-up' lines they would undoubtedly succeed, and that is the Aunt Sally that they skilfully set up. But the judge would have none of it. He said:

> ... the plaintiffs are not saying that the get-up is necessarily distinctive of Combe's product. Until last month Combe's product was, for the present purposes, the only one on the market. Until another product comes along, there is no real question whether something is distinctive of Combe or not; there is nothing to distinguish from. The public simply wants the article. Some of the public may know its name; some may not.
>
> The question is whether the defendants' article is offered in such a way as to lead the public to believe that it is the same as Combe's when in fact it is admittedly different.[39]

Conclusion

The upshot is that a form of passing off, seldom explicitly recognised, consists in misrepresenting that your goods are the same as the plaintiff's in the sense that the nature of the goods themselves is the same, even if you do not misrepresent their trade origin. There is ample and widespread authority for this proposition, but for the common case where the plaintiff introduces a new product and the defendant very shortly thereafter brings out his own copy, *Combe v Scholl* is a direct and explicit authority that this alone may constitute passing off.

---

[38] Actually Brereton sand, *Arthur Smith (S and B Foundry Sands) Ltd v George Fieldhouse Ltd* [1961] RPC 110.
[39] Note 23 above at 8.

Passing Off and Image Marketing in the UK

[1992] 8 EIPR 270

MARK ELMSLIE AND MARGARET LEWIS
Pettman Smith, London

The law of passing off and its application to character merchandising was reviewed and developed by the Vice-Chancellor in *Mirage Studios and Others v Counter-Feat Clothing Co. Ltd and Another*[1] (*Ninja Turtles* case). This was a decision on an interlocutory application concerning the well-known Ninja Turtle cartoon characters. It has generally been considered that the case marked a welcome step forward for the law of passing off in its application to character merchandising. In fact it only served to confuse further the present uncertain state of the law.

The Vice-Chancellor distinguished three earlier decisions, also at first instance, the *Wombles* case,[2] the *Kojak* case[3] and the *ABBA* case[4] in the process of rejecting an argument by Counsel for the defendants that the plaintiffs were not entitled to relief because none of them was involved in the manufacture or marketing of the goods on which the Ninja Turtle characters were affixed.

The issues which invariably arise in character merchandising cases are misrepresentation and damage, the first and fifth limbs of the test laid down by Lord Diplock in the *Advocaat* case.[5] The plaintiff must establish a misrepresentation to ultimate consumers of the goods or services of the defendant and show that this will result in actual or likely damage to the business or goodwill of his trade.

It must always be borne in mind that passing off protects the *goodwill or business of a trader*. In order properly to understand the tort one must define what these terms mean in character merchandising cases. The failure of the courts to do so has resulted in the present confused state of the law.

What is Meant by Character Merchandising?

There are three categories of trader to which those who use this term mean to refer. First, there is the manufacturer and promoter who produces goods and services with which, as part of that business, he associates images of a character or characters, real or fictional, which make the goods more attractive to potential purchasers.

---

[1] [1991] FSR 145.
[2] *Wombles v Womble Skips* [1977] RPC 99.
[3] *Tavener Rutledge v Trexaplam* [1977] RPC 275.
[4] *Lyngstad & Others v Anabas Products Ltd & Another* [1977] FSR 62.
[5] *Warnink v Townend* [1979] AC 731 (HL).

Second, there is the trader engaged in marketing his personality, such as Peter Stringfellow.[6]

Finally there is the image marketer, the trader concerned *solely* with the commercial exploitation of an image, or more often several. The image marketer is usually, but not exclusively, the owner of copyright in drawings or other intellectual property rights of a character (*Ninja Turtles*) or one who trades in a name which he is seeking to market (*ABBA*).

Often these three roles, or two of them, are merged. English law will not recognise any property right in the personality as such, and for this reason anyone who wishes commercially to exploit his personality must seek protection from competitors using the law of passing off. He must therefore establish that he is a trader whose business is marketing his name and that he has goodwill attaching to his trade. He will nearly always be in the business of producing goods or services as a vehicle for the commercial exploitation of his name. However it is of course the *name* which will be of value, and to which the goodwill of his business will attach.

Like the personality marketer, the trade engaged in image marketing may be producing goods and services, although this is less likely. The same considerations apply to image as to personality. It is that which is the valuable asset and to which the goodwill of the business will attach.

The law of passing off should operate as a tool to regulate competition between traders in their local commercial market-place. In character merchandising cases it singularly fails to do so. The reason for this is that the courts have failed properly to distinguish between the three classes of trader referred to above and to ask, in each case, how the law of passing off will apply to the business of that trader. A detailed study of character merchandising is beyond the scope of this paper, which will be principally confined to an examination of the law as it applies to the third category of trader, the image marketer; it was with this category that the *Ninja Turtles* case was concerned. The findings of the Vice-Chancellor in the areas of misrepresentation and damage and concerning the rights of a plaintiff who is merely involved in the marketing of characters such as will be examined. The conclusion which is reached is that the tort, properly understood, should allow the image marketer to exploit and protect his market in an image without the necessity to show that he is the owner of intellectual property rights in it.

The Ninja Turtles Case

There were four plaintiffs. The first was Mirage Studios, a partnership constituted by a Mr Eastman and a Mr Laird, who created the original drawings for the Ninja Turtles. The second plaintiffs, Surge Licensing Inc., were worldwide licensing agents. The third plaintiffs, Copyright Promotions Ltd, were an English company appointed by Surge as licensing agents in the United Kingdom. The fourth plaintiff, Pugh Berry (Imports)/Embesons, had been granted a licence to use reproductions of the Turtles on clothing.

The plaintiffs applied by motion for an interlocutory injunction restraining use by the defendants of cartoon characters on the basis that such use constituted a breach of copyright or unlawful passing off. A working knowledge of the case is assumed and the facts will not be recited again here.

The Vice-Chancellor found that there was an arguable case and, the balance of convenience being equal or nearly equal, looked at the merits. He found (for reasons that need not be gone into) that it would be very difficult to determine what would be the outcome of the copyright infringement case, and turned to the claim in passing off. He recorded that the

---

[6] See *Stringfellow v McCain Foods* [1984] RPC 505 (CA).

plaintiffs had no part in either manufacturing or marketing the goods. It is noted that apparently he was mistaken and the fourth defendant was involved in the marketing of these goods,[7] but that does not matter for present purposes. He recited the five elements of the test laid down by Lord Diplock in the *Advocaat* case and concluded that they were all present. He went on to say that this alone would not suffice to give the plaintiff a cause of action. What concerned the Vice-Chancellor was that:

> In the ordinary case, a passing off action applies to goods which have been manufactured or marketed by the Plaintiff. Here the Plaintiffs have no part in either manufacturing or marketing the goods; they are neither makers nor sellers. The goods, the t-shirts, the jogging bottoms and so on are manufactured by others. The Plaintiffs' only connection with the marketing of these goods is by the affixing of their characters, the Turtles, on to the merchandise of others.[8]

He had already found for the purposes of the fourth test that the first plaintiff's business or goodwill was in creating cartoons, videos and so on of the Turtles and in licensing other merchandising rights. The reasoning in the quoted paragraph is, at first glance, confusing. Whym given that the business or goodwill sought to be protected was licensing and marketing the Turtles, should it make any difference at all whether the plaintiff was involved in creating goods on which the defendant's representations of Turtles happened to appear?

One answer is that the Vice-Chancellor was confusing the requirement that the defendant's misrepresentation be made to customers of his goods and services with the requirement that the plaintiff establish that his goodwill or business is damaged. Hence the reference in the first sentence of the quoted passage to the action applying to goods. It never applies to goods as such, but to business or goodwill.

More probably the Vice-Chancellor was concerned that the customers of the image marketer were not the people who purchased the goods to which they were affixed, but the licensee manufacturers who paid for the right to affix those images to their goods. The defendants were not themselves marketing the Turtle image in competition with the plaintiff: they were manufacturing and selling goods bearing those images. There was therefore no misrepresentation by the defendants to the plaintiffs' trade customers. Hence it was necessary to establish a misrepresentation by the defendants that their goods were connected in some way with the business of the plaintiff.

In order to get round this perceived difficulty the Vice-Chancellor relied on evidence that the public connected the Turtles with the plaintiffs, that they knew that the Turtles were created (by someone) and that they would be licensed for certain goods. He followed two Australian decisions, the *Muppet* case[9] and the *Fido Dido* case.[10] The Vice-Chancellor found that it was crucial that there was evidence that the public was aware that the Turtle characters had been licensed, that is that the public was aware in general terms of character merchandising and, in this particular case, that the owners of the rights in the Turtles would license them. This created a sufficient link between the plaintiff and the goods purchased by the public. It also introduced the requirement that the plaintiff must own the characters; that is, have some proprietary right in them.

The Vice-Chancellor found that the misrepresentation in this case was that the goods were

---

[7] Allan M. Poulter, 'Cowabunga! The English Law of Passing Off in relation to Character Merchandising', *Trade Mark World*, December 1990/January 1991, at page 36.

[8] Note 1 above, at page 156.

[9] *Children's Television Workshop Inc. v Woolworths (New South Wales) Limited* [1981] RPC 187.

[10] *Fido Dido Inc. v Venture Stores (Retailers) Proprietary Limited* 16 IPR 365.

licensed and that the potential damage was loss of royalties. His findings in these areas restricted the application of the tort to those who have rights to license. This affords no protection to a merchandiser or a name or persona, or of a drawing or series of drawings which (for any reason) does not attract copyright protection.

He used this reasoning to distinguish the *Wombles*, *Kojak* and *ABBA* cases. In each of those cases, he said, the plaintiff did not have any relevant intellectual property rights.

Damage, Misrepresentation and Goodwill

The Vice-Chancellor saw the plaintiffs' main hurdle as being to establish a misrepresentation. In order to understand the way in which this requirement should work it is helpful to look again at the facts and reasoning in the three cases analysed by the Lord Chancellor.

ABBA and *Wombles* are similar. In *Wombles* the plaintiff was the creator and merchandiser of the fictitious Wombles characters. They had been commercially exploited. However, the defendant was engaged in the business of providing skips for rubbish collection—not part of the plaintiff's business. There was no reason why the plaintiff should have a remedy in this case because the goodwill of his business was not being attacked by the defendant. To extend the law of passing off to protect the plaintiff in these circumstances would be to give traders in a name in *any field of business* the right to stop other traders from using the name in *all fields of business* no matter whether they were first on that market or not. That would be clearly wrong. The plaintiff was refused relief for two reasons: because there was no common field of activity and because there was no copyright in the name which the Court would protect. The first of these grounds was clearly right, but the second was not. Imagine that the plaintiff and the defendant were competitors in a common field of activity. Why, in these circumstances, should the plaintiff be refused relief because it could not bring home a copyright infringement case?

The *ABBA* case was another example of wrong reasoning and (possibly) right decision. Oliver J refused an application for an interlocutory injunction by the plaintiffs, members of the famous pop group, who were attempting to stop the defendants from marketing goods bearing pictures of members of the group, and the group's name. It was claimed that this amounted to passing the goods off as being associated or connected with the plaintiffs.

The plaintiffs relied on the decision of the Australian High Court in *Henderson v Radio Corp.*[11] in support of the same argument advanced in this article, that the group had developed a local goodwill in the ABBA image which was deserving of protection. Although Oliver J (as he then was) said he had 'very considerable doubt'[12] about the plaintiffs' case he did not find that there was no arguable case. He considered that the offer of the defendant, which had been made before the hearing and was repeated in court, to pay royalties of 7.5 per cent of the wholesale price of goods sold to trial was enough to protect the plaintiffs and dismissed the motion. Although it is difficult to isolate one reason for his decision, the fact that the judge went on to consider balance of convenience means that he must have considered, albeit reluctantly, that the plaintiffs' case may have been sustainable.

Oliver J thought that there was insufficient evidence of confusion (although it is clear that what he really meant was misrepresentation). He considered that the evidence that the public would believe the goods to be licensed or endorsed was insufficient. But it is important that he found (see pages 66–68) that the ABBA group had not established the necessary goodwill in the local market, so the decision may well have been right on the facts.

---

[11]   [1969] RPC 218.
[12]   Note 4 above, at page 68.

In *Ninja Turtles* the Vice-Chancellor relied on *ABBA* to support his proposition that a plaintiff must establish some sort of intellectual property right in the goodwill sought to be protected. He referred (at page 158) to the comments of Oliver J at page 68 of *ABBA*, and relied on them to support the proposition that there was no property in a name which could be protected by English law. What Oliver J in fact said was that 'To suggest that there is some proprietary right in the plaintiff's name which entitles them to sue simply for its use is contrary to all English authorities'. This is axiomatic and cannot be relied on as authority for the proposition that a plaintiff must establish intellectual property rights in the images being marketed to found a case in passing off. Oliver J did not decide the case on this ground, as the Vice-Chancellor's judgment implies.

The decision in *Wombles* (and perhaps *ABBA*) was probably right on the facts, on the common field of activity test. Although the Vice-Chancellor in the *Ninja Turtles* case described this test as being discredited, it is suggested that this is only true so far as it purported to be an absolute bar to relief. The issue is whether the plaintiff can establish loss or likely loss. If the defendant is merchandising in a different area of commerce, it is unlikely that he will be able to do so.

The *Kojak* case is a good illustration of how the law of character merchandising ought not to operate. In this case the plaintiff was an image marketer exploiting the kudos associated with Kojak by selling 'Kojakpops', lollipops of high quality which had extra appeal because of their name. The defendant, claiming to be licensees of the promoters of Kojak in the United Kingdom, went into the same business. It is noted that the Vice-Chancellor in the *Ninja Turtles* case mistakenly reversed the parties and the result in his description of the facts (see page 158).

The defendant argued that because he had been licensed by the owners of the rights in the Kojak series the law of passing off ought to protect his market. However the plaintiff got his interlocutory injunction. He was first on the market for lollipops in which the owners of the rights in the series had no perceived or actual reputation, his goodwill was clearly being hijacked by the defendant, as there was evidence that the lollipop buying public would mistake the new lollipop for his—hence the plaintiff would suffer damage.

The judgment is often cited as a rejection of the argument that the traders defined above as image marketers have rights which the law of passing off will protect. The arguments that found favour with the Court in the *Ninja Turtles* case concerning the public's understanding of the business of character merchandising were rejected by Walton J (at page 280). However on its facts the case was rightly decided. The defendants did not themselves have any local goodwill. They attempted to get round this by relying on a licence for the use of the name from the American creators of the series, who they asserted had a total monopoly right, which they could exercise to prevent the plaintiff from exploiting the persona of Kojak. This was misconceived because the plaintiff had got into this market first and therefore had a better right than the defendant.

The Court characterised the plaintiff (at page 282) as simply a manufacturer with 'a very considerable reputation in their lollies'. This is inaccurate; the plaintiff's reputation resided in both the product as such and in what may be defined as the 'Kojak image'. The image was what the action was all about, the parties being not simply competing manufacturers of lollipops, but of lollipops which sought to exploit the Kojak image. Thus although the Court refused even to recognise character merchandising the injunction was granted to a plaintiff engaged in that very activity or, more accurately, in image marketing.

Having reviewed these cases the Vice-Chancellor distinguished them on the basis that they involved plaintiffs with no intellectual property rights in the name or image sought to be exploited. He concluded that the cases did not prevent him from granting an injunction in the present case as the plaintiff had such rights and there was clearly a misrepresentation by the defendant that it was licensed.

Although there is some support in these cases for this proposition what they best demonstrate is the confusion into which the law has fallen in this area. By distinguishing these earlier cases instead of choosing not to follow them the Vice-Chancellor restricted the application of the relief he clearly (and rightly) felt ought to be given.

Should Intellectual Property Rights be Essential to Qualify for Protection in Passing off?

If the *Ninja Turtles* case is followed, the result will be that the tort will still not apply to protect image marketers as such unless they have intellectual property rights in the images being marketed.

The argument seems to be that to acquire a trade goodwill there must be 'goods' in which trade is carried on. Thus goodwill can be acquired by trading in copyright images because the copyright is a commodity which can be licensed, but trade in a name or non-copyright image, which as a matter of law cannot be the subject of copyright, cannot generate goodwill. The writers believe that this is an artificial distinction. Reputation and goodwill are matters of fact and their existence and extent are determined by the view of the consumer.

The proposition advanced at the beginning of this article was that in its application to image marketers the law of passing off should not require that the plaintiff establish intellectual property rights in the image the subject of the trader's business: in other words intellectual property rights are not what the tort operates to protect.

This is hardly a controversial proposition. There has been no recent House of Lords authority in passing off save for *Reckitt & Colman v Borden*,[13] in which Lord Diplock's *Advocaat* test was approved. The genesis of Lord Diplock's test can be found in *Spalding v Gamage*,[14] in which Lord Parker asked what right the law of passing off protected. He concluded that it was a right in property, went on to ask 'property in what?', and recited the alternative views that it protected intellectual property or property in the business or goodwill of a trader. He concluded that it was the latter that was protected.

> There appears to be considerable diversity of opinion as to the nature of the right, the invasion of which is the subject of what are known as passing-off actions. The more general opinion appears to be that the right is a right of property. This view naturally demands an answer to the question—property in what? Some authorities say property in the mark, name or get-up improperly used by the Defendant. Others say, property in the business or goodwill likely to be injured by the misrepresentation. Lord Hershell in *Reddaway v Banham* ([1896] A.C. 139) expressly dissents from the former view. ... there are, I think, strong reasons for preferring the latter view. ... Even in the case of what are sometimes referred to as Common Law Trade Marks the property, if any, of the so called owner is in its nature transitory, and only exists so long as the mark is distinctive of his goods in the eyes of the public or a class of the public.[15]

In *Star Industrial Co. Ltd v Yap Kwee Kor*,[16] the Judicial Committee of the Privy Council

---

[13] [1990] 1 WLR 491 (HL).
[14] (1915) 32 RPC 273 (HL).
[15] Note 14 above, at page 284.
[16] [1976] FSR 256.

held that a trader who had ceased to use a particular unregistered mark was not entitled in a passing off action to prevent others from using it. The Judicial Committee held that what is entitled to protection in a passing off action is not the right of property in the mark itself, but the '*right of property in the business or goodwill in connection with which the mark is actually being used*'.[17] Thus the plaintiff could not prevent the defendant from exploiting goodwill which it had, in effect, abandoned. Lord Diplock restated the principle first set out in *Spalding v Gamage* with admirable clarity:

> a passing off action is a remedy for the invasion of a right of property not in the mark, name or get-up improperly used, but in the business or goodwill likely to be injured by the misrepresentation made by passing off one person's goods as the goods of another. Goodwill, as the subject of proprietary rights, is incapable of subsisting by itself. It has no independent existence apart from the business to which it is attached. It is local in character and divisible . . .[18]

The reasoning in *Star Industrial* and *Spalding v Gamage* supports the proposition that the existence of intellectual property rights is irrelevant to the question of whether a plaintiff has a cause of action in passing off. Given that the law of passing off does not protect property in a name but in the business or goodwill of a trader, it follows that an absence of intellectual property rights should not disqualify a plaintiff image marketer from relief, and that the reasoning of the Vice-Chancellor is misconceived in this respect.

The plaintiff must, however, go on to establish misrepresentation and damage.

What Misrepresentation and What Damage?

It is helpful in answering this question to look at the other cases involving character merchandising which have been decided in this country. The best examples are *Grundy Television Pty Ltd v Startrain Ltd (trading as Starlight Publication) and Other*[19] (*Neighbours case*) and *Stringfellow v McCain Foods*.[20] In the *Neighbours* case the defendants were engaged in selling magazines which sought to exploit by publicity the TV characters in the well-known Australian television programme. The magazines contained stories about the private lives of the actors in the series. The issues again were misrepresentation and damage. Millet J posed the misrepresentation question thus: 'Is there a misrepresentation that the publication was authorised by or was an official publication of the producer of the television series'.[21] He found, on the facts, that there was not. In the *Ninja Turtles* case the same question would have been posed thus: 'Is there a representation that the t-shirts were "official" Ninja Turtle t-shirts'. This is a more practical way of putting the question than was adopted by the Vice-Chancellor. The t-shirt buying public do not go on to ask what intellectual property rights the creator of the character has in such 'official' t-shirts and whether he might have chosen to license them.

The plaintiffs also failed on damage because they had not sought to exploit this particular area of the market and, consequently, had not and could not foreseeably suffer damage from the defendant's activities. Had they succeeded on the damage point and gone on to show that the publication had purported to be authorised, the injunction might well have been

---

[17] Note 16 above, page 271.
[18] Note 14 above, page 269.
[19] Unreported, High Court Chancery Division, 30 June 1988.
[20] [1984] RPC 501 (CA).
[21] Judgment, page 5.

granted. In considering damage the Court did not address the question of whether the plaintiff had any intellectual property rights.

The *Stringfellow* case, which was cited by Millet J in the *Neighbours* case, is important because it is the only decision of the Court of Appeal on the point. This was an action by the well-known entrepreneur Peter Stringfellow against McCain Foods, who had marketed a long, thin type of chip, which they called 'stringfellow'. This was a descriptive word but was apparently chosen with the plaintiff's famous Disco in mind. The television advertisements of which complaint was made featured two children disco dancing in their mother's kitchen. The plaintiff said this was clearly an attempt to trade off the association with his name.

In addressing the question of misrepresentation the Court of Appeal asked whether the public would be likely reasonably to believe that there was any connection between Mr Stringfellow and the chips. Although this is putting the question somewhat loosely, it is the same question posed in the *Neighbours* case, and raised by the Vice-Chancellor in the *Ninja Turtles* case. The evidence showed that Stringfellow traded in his name; his case was that the defendants were invading his market.

The Court refused relief on the basis that damage was not reasonably foreseeable, in effect a finding that the plaintiff had failed the common field of activity test. Stringfellow was in the business of exploiting his name, but not in the relevant field. As much was admitted by Mr Stringfellow himself in cross-examination. He conceded that the defendants had 'jumped the gun' on him and that he should have been 'making moves' in that direction himself. In other words the plaintiff's business reputation did not extend to the relevant market—the defendants were there first.

As a class of 'product' there is nothing to distinguish Stringfellow's name or the characters in Neighbours from the Ninja Turtles. In neither case when looking at misrepresentation did the Court disqualify the plaintiff at the beginning because no case had been made out that the plaintiff had intellectual property rights in the characters the subject of their business.

The likely damage which the Court found would occur in the *Ninja Turtles* case was the reduction in the value of licensing rights as a consequence of the unauthorised copying. This is of course true, given the finding that the plaintiff had copyright, but unnecessarily restrictive. The first plaintiff was first on the market with the Ninja Turtles. Had it had no copyright, then the business arrangement with the other plaintiffs would undoubtably have been different and probably less profitable; for instance the lack of copyright may have meant that the concept was sold as a package or the drawings were bought piecemeal.

It is also important to remember when considering damage that there need to be no actual loss in a *quia timet* action. All the plaintiff need do is justify an injunction, by showing damage to his business or goodwill. There is no need to establish actual loss of royalties in order to found the action.

In the *Stringfellow* case, had he otherwise qualified for relief the damages would have been the loss of profit to Mr Stringfellow from marketing his name, something no doubt difficult to quantify, a good reason for an injunction.

The Practice of Image Marketing: What Actually Happens?

Dealing in an image occurs each time there is a change in the vehicle through which the character merchandiser exploits his market. What would have been the result in the *Ninja Turtles* case if the first plaintiff had introduced the concept of (non-copyright) Ninja Turtles to this country and advertised them heavily, creating a market? So far as clothing was concerned, imagine he marketed them on some items of clothing only, say jeans, using his own production facilities.

If the defendants had then entered the market and sold jeans which bore copies of the Turtles, the plaintiff could complain in 'traditional' passing off terms. But in fact there would be two misrepresentations, one relating to the jeans and one to the image. The defendant would be representing that his jeans are the plaintiff's or those associated with him, *and he would also be saying something to the consumer about the image appearing on the jeans.* His misrepresentation in this (second) respect was categorised by the Vice-Chancellor in the *Ninja Turtles* case as a representation that the image was affixed with the authority, or licence, of the image marketer.

What happens when the defendant's product is different, say t-shirts? In this case the misrepresentation *must* relate only to the image, because the product has changed. The misrepresentation cannot be that the goods are the plaintiff's or those associated with him, because they are not—the misrepresentation has nowhere to bite. There is no difficulty in these circumstances in accepting that there has been a misrepresentation. It would be nonsense to say otherwise, but the crucial point is that it is a misrepresentation *which relates exclusively to the image.*

What would be the result in such a case? On the authority of the *Ninja Turtles* case, the misrepresentation that the goods were authorised would be insufficient, as the plaintiff would not own copyright. The plaintiff would fail.

Both in terms of the aim of the tort, to protect goodwill, and of the judicial background against which the modern definition of the tort has been framed, the requirement that the plaintiff be the owner of the intellectual property rights cannot be supported.

Reputation

How then to get round the problem of misrepresentation? In most cases the misrepresentation will relate to the goods of the plaintiff. In the case of image marketers there are no goods, but there is goodwill to protect.

It is suggested that the difficulties that have arisen in this area stem from a failure properly to define the nature of the business of an image marketer and the active element of the conduct of which complaint is made. The subject of the image marketer's goodwill is the reputation of the image. What the defendant is representing when he attempts to hijack the plaintiff's market is that he is the proprietor of that reputation; his activities amount to a direct suggestion to that effect. Once the plaintiff establishes his reputation as a fact in the mind of the public or a section thereof, then such activity by the defendant is, by definition, a representation of a connection in the course of trade between the parties. Of course this connection is precisely what the defendant will be seeking to achieve, in order to trade off the plaintiff's goodwill.

It is important to understand that reputation and goodwill have very specific definitions. Passing off does not protect reputation, but goodwill—; the attractive force that brings in the custom'. The plaintiff must satisfy the Court that he has goodwill in his local market-place—his reputation alone is insufficient.[22] But once it is established and defined the next step is to ask what is the subject of that goodwill. The answer will always be the trader's reputation. What the requirement for goodwill does is to limit the application of the tort to a plaintiff's reputation by subjecting it to the test of the market-place, as Budweiser found to its cost.

Because reputation is the subject of goodwill, it makes sense to view the application of the requirements of the tort, such as misrepresentation, in these terms. This is what one does

---

[22] *Anheuser Busch v Budejovicky* [1984] R. 413.

when applying the test to those in the business of producing goods. Of course the question in the latter type of case is—has the defendant falsely represented his goods as those of the plaintiff? It is put this way because the plaintiff's reputation is in the goods it sells. But the reputation of an image marketer resides in the image.

There is therefore no need to go on, as the Vice-Chancellor did, and use the licence to establish a link between the goods with which the image may be associated and the plaintiff. To do that is to misunderstand what the tort is protecting. The link between the plaintiff and the consumer must of course be established, but only in respect of the image, not the goods on which it appears. This can be done by looking to see if there is evidence that the consumer is aware, not of licensing practices or character merchandising, but of *the presence of the image on the market*. The plaintiff will of course have to give evidence about the nature of his business, show that he was first on the local market, and that he has actively sought to create and define that market. If he has intellectual property rights in the image, he should show that he has taken steps to protect them. Of course the absence of intellectual property rights will often make the job harder. Images which are unprotected by intellectual property are fair game until someone establishes a market.

Such is not the case with exploitation of the personality, the second category of character merchandising identified at the beginning of this article. It will be much easier for the plaintiff to establish a market in his personality because the market is usually built up and identified in the public mind only by the plaintiff and over a period of time. He may establish and define his market sufficiently to obtain the benefit of protection under passing off by the time the defendant sees the commercial benefit in exploiting the plaintiff's persona.

Of course the goodwill must exist in the relevant market (in terms of both product and location) to qualify for protection. As far as damage is concerned, all the plaintiff should have to show, as in all cases, is some actual damage or the likelihood of damage to his business.

There is no need for the plaintiff to go on and show that the consumer knows the name of the image marketer. In passing off cases the consumer is frequently aware of the existence of the goods (or image) on the market, but not of the name of the company trading in it.

This analysis avoids the difficulties associated with trying to define the ways in which the defendant in image marketing cases hijacks the plaintiff's goodwill. It is highly artificial to suggest that the purchaser of a Ninja Turtle t-shirt believes that the reproduction of the plaintiff's image is authorised in some way. In fact the reactions of the public depend on particular buying criteria. Some will believe that a t-shirt is licensed and some, because it is cheaper, will be quite aware that it is a fake. Some won't care either way; they just want a Ninja Turtle t-shirt. All the plaintiff should have to prove in this context is that the decision to buy is motivated in substantial part by the presence of the plaintiff's image and that the image is so well known in the context of this category of goods (the common field of activity test will apply here) that it can fairly be regarded as part of the plaintiff's business.

Conclusion

Traditionally, traders who have sought the protection offered by the law of passing off have been engaged in the production and sale of goods in which they have established a market. The law has provided protection from competitors who seek by the use of a misrepresentation to exploit that market unfairly. Until the advent of the character merchandiser, the law had only to deal with plaintiffs who made and sold these goods themselves, or who did so under licence.

The character merchandiser is a new type of trader. He does not seek to exploit the market in a particular type of goods. He sees that money can be made from a fictional character he has created, or the hard won and valuable reputation of his personality, and seeks to gain and protect a market. He has raised fundamental and important questions as to the nature of the protection which the law of passing off provides including the question of what sort of interest or right in the image he must establish in order to qualify for protection, or more particularly whether he must establish that he has intellectual property rights in the image. In their early attempts to deal with this question, the Courts have given inconsistent and inconclusive answers. This article has shown that:

(1) The English law of passing off operates to protect the goodwill of a trader (in whatever he trades in) in his local market-place.

(2) If that trade is in images, there is no need for a plaintiff to establish that he is the owner of intellectual property rights in representations of those images, in order to invoke the protection which the tort will give. Such a restriction is justified neither by principle nor authority.

(3) In fact the way in which the law has developed teaches directly against it. Passing off and 'pure' intellectual property parted company as long ago as *Spalding v Gamage*, when Lord Parker identified business or goodwill as being the subject of the tort's protection.

In marked contrast to the position in Australia, many of the questions which have been addressed in this article have only been examined in passing by the English courts, and there has not yet been an examination of them by an appellate court. This is somewhat curious, given the commercial value of images and the financial strength of those who exploit them. Although it has developed differently from the law in Australia, the English law of passing off is well equipped to meet the challenge posed by the character merchandiser, if properly applied in accordance with the principles of which it is based.

Season of Goodwill: Passing Off and Overseas Traders*

[1996] 6 EIPR 356

DAVID ROSE
S J Berwin & Co, London

Jian Tools

The recent case of *Jian Tools*[1] illustrates the difficulties the English courts have in determining what degree of business activity is sufficient for a foreign plaintiff to establish goodwill in the United Kingdom for the purposes of a passing-off action.[2] The case also demonstrates the underlying tension in the law of passing off in the late 20th century: the requirement that goodwill must be situated within the jurisdiction has to be reconciled with the fact that the reputation of many businesses transcends national boundaries and is international in character. By way of contrast, other common law jurisdictions are now prepared to protect not only locally situated goodwill but also a trader's international reputation even if there are no identifiable customers within the jurisdiction.[3] This comment considers how the courts define, in practical terms, the goodwill requirements that a foreign plaintiff must fulfil under English law. Consideration is also given to whether judges are extending the law of passing off in order to protect foreign plaintiffs from unfair misappropriation in cases where evidence of goodwill within the jurisdiction is questionable.

Background

In the *Jian* case, the plaintiff was an American computer software company based in California. It was not disputed in the action that Jian had established considerable goodwill in the United States in relation to its principal product BizPlan Builder, a software template designed to enable persons engaged in, or proposing to engage in, trading or other business activities to produce a business plan. The first defendant, Roderick Manhattan, had a

---

The views of the author are his personal views and do not necessarily represent the views of his firm, which successfully represented Jian in its reported action.

[1] *Jian Tools for Sales Inc. v Roderick Manhattan Group Ltd and Another* [1995] FSR 924.

[2] Wadlow, *The Law of Passing Off*, 1995 (2nd edn), at 72 to 73, notes that 'the problem of the foreign plaintiff whose goods or business may be known in a particular jurisdiction although he has no business there is one of the most intractable in the law of passing off. It is one of the very few topics where it is impossible to say that the underlying substantive law is essentially uniform throughout the common law world; and now with differences in national case law which are too great to dismiss as the inevitable result of different judges using different factual situations'.

[3] See the decision of the Federal Court of Australia in *Conagra v McCain Goods* [1992] 23 IPR 193. See also the decision of the Court of Appeal of Ontario in *Orkin v Pestco* [1985] 19 DLR (4th) 90 and the decision of the High Court of Calcutta in *Calvin Klein Inc. v International Apparel Syndicate and Others* [1995] FSR 515.

principal business of re-publishing, for use in the United Kingdom, computer software prepared abroad and, because of its expertise in this area, was approached on behalf of Jian in June 1994 with a view to anglicising Jian's BizPlan Builder for marketing in the United Kingdom.

Roderick Manhattan put it to Jian shortly after they had been introduced that they would work on the basis of a full publishing deal with a royalty going to Jian. As negotiations progressed, Roderick Manhattan made it clear to Jian that they reserved the right to create their own product if they wished to. However, at no stage did Roderick Manhattan expressly state that any new product they launched would be called Business Plan Builder. Roderick Manhattan had even been warned in January 1995 by Jian's solicitors (on discovering that Roderick Manhattan had applied for the registration of the *Business Plan Builder* mark pursuant to section 29(1)(a) of the Trade Marks Act 1938) that it owned the rights to the trade marks *BizPlan Builder* and *Business Plan Builder* in the United Kingdom and requested that Roderick Manhattan voluntarily assign their application to Jian.

Negotiations between Jian and Roderick Manhattan continued until about March 1995, but ultimately produced no agreement. In April 1995, Roderick Manhattan in association with the second defendant launched its own business plan software product under the name Business Plan Builder. Jian issued proceedings and by Notice of Motion sought to restrain the defendants (pending trial) from using the *Business Plan Builder* mark.

The first issue considered by the court was whether there was a serious issue to be tried and whether Jian had acquired a protectable goodwill in the name BizPlan Builder. There was no disputing that Jian's business in the United States was substantial: 250,000 copies of BizPlan Builder had been sold and worldwide revenues in 1994 amounted to US$3,750,000. All these sales were of a version made for the US market, denominating US currency and using US terms throughout. Jian had not actively marketed BizPlan Builder in the United Kingdom (hence their approach to Roderick Manhattan to re-publish), but two advertisements had been placed in UK publications. The first of these advertisements had yielded between 7 to 22 sales (depending on the evidence, which was disputed). These figures are not particularly impressive when one considers that the circulation of the publication in question was 110,000. The second UK advertisement placed by Jian had only generated between five and ten sales. It was common ground that BizPlan Builder had also been extensively advertised in various US magazines, some of which circulated in the United Kingdom.

It was submitted by Jian that since the launch of Biz Plan Builder in 1988, 193 units had been sold to 168 customers from the United Kingdom. These figures were criticised by Roderick Manhattan on a number of grounds, including double counting and the erroneous inclusion of Republic of Ireland customers.[4] They also argued that the figures relied on by Jian were inappropriate, as customer figures included deliveries of review copies to magazines on information technology or for research purposes by competitors and academics. In spite of this, Knox J concluded[5] that 'Jian's case on the issue of goodwill was at least seriously arguable'.[6]

While the extent of sales by Jian of BizPlan Builder in the United Kingdom or to UK customers was disputed, the bald facts were not in doubt: a mass-market software product that had sold a quarter of a million copies in the United States had been purchased by approximately 150 customers from the United Kingdom; individual purchasers who swore

---

[4] Roderick Manhattan submitted that these factors reduced the total sales figures to 127 units.

[5] Note 1 above, at 940.

[6] Mr Justice Knox also found in favour of Jian on the issue of distinctiveness and, after considering the balance of convenience, granted Jian an injunction pending trial.

affidavits in the action almost all had a connection with the United States or Canada (for example, from reviewing magazines published in the United States which circulated in the United Kingdom).[7] Jian had made no efforts actively to market BizPlan Builder in the United Kingdom and had retained a consultant with the sole purpose of identifying a re-publisher in the United Kingdom to market BizPlan Builder in an anglicised form in the United Kingdom.

Why, then, did the court find in favour of Jian on the question of whether or not it was seriously arguable that it had goodwill locally situated within the United Kingdom?

Goodwill: An Ongoing Requirement

'A passing off action is a remedy for the invasion of a right of property not in the mark, name or get up improperly used, but in the business or goodwill likely to be injured by the misrepresentation made by passing off one person's goods as the goods of another'.[8]

Whatever other conclusions are drawn from the *Jian* decision, it is not open to doubt that the need to establish goodwill within the jurisdiction remains a fundamental requirement of a passing-off action. Like many judges before him,[9] Knox J in *Jian* quoted the speeches of Lords Fraser and Diplock in the *Advocaat* case,[10] in which their Lordships set out what the plaintiff in a passing-off action needs to show (Lord Fraser) and what the defendant must be shown to have done (Lord Diplock): namely, damage to a business or goodwill of the trader bringing the action. Knox J made it clear that reputation on its own is not enough, noting that 'it is common ground that reputation by itself does not suffice; there must be goodwill which cannot exist as an item of property without a business to which the goodwill is annexed'.[11] He quoted approvingly Lord Diplock in *Star Industrial Co. Ltd v Yap Kwee Koi*:

> Goodwill, as the subject of proprietary rights, is incapable of subsisting by itself. It has no independent existence apart from the business to which it is attached. It is local in character and divisible; if the business is carried on in several countries a separate goodwill attaches to it in each.[12]

---

[7] Jian even put before the court evidence from individual customers who had actually purchased BizPlan Builder while on visits to the United States, although it was never suggested that this was the reason for their visit. Carty states that: 'To be goodwill within the jurisdiction, the attractive force must exist as a reason for travel. If they travel as tourists and happen to experience the plaintiff's goods or services, that should not be sufficient to create goodwill within the jurisdiction' ('Passing Off and the Concept of Goodwill', March 1995, JBL 139, at 148).

[8] Lord Diplock in *Star Industrial Co. Ltd v Yap Kwee Koi* [1976] FSR 256, at 269.

[9] See, for example, Oliver LJ in *Anheuser-Busch v Budejovicky Budvar* ('the *Budweiser* case') [1994] FSR 413, at 463.

[10] *Warnick v Townend* [1979] AC 731.

[11] Note 1 above, at 935. The English court only appears to have deviated from this principle in the decisions of Graham J in *Baskin Robbins v Gutman* [1976] FSR 545 and *Maxims v Dye* [1978] 2 All ER 55. In *Baskin Robbins*, Graham J took an expansive view of the requirement for locally situated goodwill: 'Some businesses are ... truly international in character and reputation, and the reputation and goodwill attaching to them cannot in fact help being international also'. However, Walton J in *Athlete's Foot Marketing Association Inc. v Cobra Sports Ltd* [1980] RPC 343, at 355, noted that Graham J's comments in *Baskin Robbins* were *obiter* and that if the distinction between reputation in the wide sense and goodwill are borne in mind, the decision falls squarely with established authority. With regard to the *Maxims* case, Walton J pointed out that judgment was given in default of defence and the defendants were never heard. Given that the plaintiff had pleaded that their goodwill extended to England it was difficult for the judge to come to any contrary conclusion. Walton J concluded that the persuasive power of *Maxims v Dye* was very small.

[12] Note 8 above, at 269.

Goodwill in Practice: The Customer Connection

Lord Justice Oliver, in *Budweiser*,[13] acknowledged that the principle enunciated by Lord Diplock in *Star Industrial* was in itself sound, but appreciated that it merely begged a further question: what form of activity is required before it can be said that the plaintiff has a 'business' in England to which goodwill can attach? This was considered in depth by Walton J in *Athlete's Foot* and by the then Vice-Chancellor, Sir Nicholas Browne-Wilkinson, in *Pete Waterman Ltd v CBS UK Ltd*.[14]

In *Athlete's Foot*, Walton J concluded:

> It would appear to me that, as a matter of principle, no trader can complain of passing off against him in any territory ... in which he has no customers, nobody who is in a trade relation with him. This will normally shortly be expressed by saying that he does not carry on any trade in that particular country ... but the inwardness of it will be that he has no customers in that country: no people who buy his goods or make use of his services (as the case may be) there.[15]

In *Pete Waterman*, Browne-Wilkinson VC considered this passage to be very important because, among other things, 'it shows that the importance of the plaintiff showing he has a business here is essentially linked to the presence of customers here'.[16] The importance of the passage was heightened, in the Vice-Chancellor's view, by the fact that it had been expressly approved by Lord Justice Oliver LJ in the *Budweiser* case. The Vice-Chancellor summarised his view of the law in the light of his review of the authorities as follows:

> The presence of customers in this country is sufficient to constitute the carrying on of business here whether or not there is otherwise a place of business here and whether or not the services are provided here. Once it is found that there are customers, it is open to find that there is a business here to which the local goodwill is attached.[17]

It is submitted that this interpretation is correct in view of the relevant authorities. However, it is not enough. While Browne-Wilkinson VC accepted that if there are customers it is open to the courts to find that there is a business in the United Kingdom to which local goodwill is attached, he did not go further and state that the presence of customers *per se* constitutes the carrying on of a business. Likewise, while Walton J in *Athlete's Foot* stated that 'if there are no customers there is no goodwill and, if there is no goodwill, it is not there to be harmed', there is no suggestion that the opposite is true, namely, that if there are customers it is axiomatic that goodwill exists.

What can be read into the line of decisions from *Athlete's Foot* to *Budweiser* and more recently *Pete Waterman* is that it is not necessary that foreign plaintiffs must actually have traded within the jurisdiction but they must, as a minimum requirement, have generated

---

[13] Note 9 above, at 465.
[14] [1993] EMLR 27.
[15] Note 11 above, at 350.
[16] Note 14 above, at 56.
[17] *Ibid.*, at 58. The comments made by Vice-Chancellor on the issue of goodwill were in fact *obiter* as he found against the plaintiffs on the issue of whether the name 'the Hit Factory' was distinctive of them. This in itself was enough to dispose of the action.

sales locally.[18] In coming to this conclusion, Browne-Wilkinson VC in *Pete Waterman* criticised the decision of Pennycuick J in *Crazy Horse*.[19] There, Pennycuick J refused to grant an interlocutory injunction in favour of the proprietor of the Crazy Horse Saloon in Paris to restrain the defendant from carrying on business under the same name in London. The judge considered that there had been insufficient business activity by the plaintiff to constitute goodwill, even though the plaintiff had been advertising in England for a number of years. The Vice-Chancellor considered that the *Crazy Horse* decision appeared to establish that, even if the foreign trader had customers in the jurisdiction, he could not protect his reputation unless he had conducted some business in the United Kingdom (although slight evidence of business activity would be sufficient). The problem for Pennycuick J had been that the plaintiffs had at no stage carried out any type of business activity in the United Kingdom. It was acknowledged that the plaintiffs had shown that there were English customers of the Crazy Horse restaurant, but there was no evidence of a causal link between these customers and the carrying on of any type of business activity at all (Pennycuick J was not prepared to accept that advertising on its own constituted business activity). If this causal link could have been established (for example, by evidence that customers had been attracted by virtue of the advertising of the plaintiffs in the United Kingdom), the court would probably have been prepared to find that the plaintiffs did have a locally established goodwill.

The *Crazy Horse* decision in many ways typifies the difficulties faced by the courts in determining what level of customer activity will suffice within the jurisdiction. It is difficult to know precisely why Browne-Wilkinson VC in *Pete Waterman* was so critical of *Crazy Horse* when he himself acknowledged that the existence of customers within the jurisdiction provided an opportunity for the courts to make a finding of goodwill but that this in itself *was not conclusive*. In other words, there must be an additional factor, an 'X Factor' which turns the bare presence of customers into goodwill.

Customers and the 'X Factor': The Requirement of Market Opportunity

In order to appreciate the 'X Factor' it is necessary to revert to first principles and consider how mere purchasers are translated into customers. In the case of *IRC v Muller and Co.'s Margarine Ltd*,[20] Lord McNaghten stated that goodwill 'is the attractive force which brings in custom'. Translating this into a modern international business context appears to require a foreign plaintiff to show that a market opportunity exists within the jurisdiction: an ability on behalf of a consumer to interact with the foreign entity in order to purchase, communicate, receive and react to publicity/advertising materials and other such activities that a trader and consumer ordinarily indulge in. Whether this interaction takes place by phone, fax, e-mail or Internet is irrelevant—what is relevant is the existence of this capability.

---

[18] The *Pete Waterman* case has confirmed the proposition that a business that operates outside England will have goodwill within the jurisdiction to the extent that consumers are prepared to make a special trip to avail themselves of the goods or services in question. Although the *Pete Waterman* case was concerned with the provision of services, there is no reason why the principle should be any different in respect of goods. As the Vice-Chancellor noted (at 51):

> 'The problem is particularly acute with service industries. A first division recording studio is catering to a market which treats crossing the Atlantic as an every day incident. Similar problems arise in relation to professional and other services. For example, an internationally famous hospital in Paris or Boston, Massachusetts has patients from worldwide. Is it unable to protect its goodwill otherwise than in its home country?'

To the extent that anyone is minded to answer the Vice-Chancellor's seemingly rhetorical question, the answer is no.

[19] *Alain Bernardin et CIE v Pavillion Properties* [1967] RPC 581.

[20] [1901] AC 217, at 223.

Taking an extreme example, it is submitted that an individual hot-dog street vendor in Toronto, Canada who may have served many thousands of English customers over a number of years does not have goodwill within the United Kingdom by virtue of these customers alone. These purchasers would not have made a trip to Toronto simply to sample the delights of the hot-dogs and would be in no position to re-order hot-dogs from the United Kingdom on their return.[21] The hot-dog vendor has no 'attractive force' within the United Kingdom; no magnet to draw hot-dog connoisseurs from England to Canada and no capability of catering to repeat customers from within the United Kingdom.

If the requirement for a 'market opportunity' is correct, it is suggested that Knox J in *Jian* should have discounted the evidence of UK residents who purchased BizPlan Builder while they were abroad, given that there was no reason to suggest that this was their only or main reason for travelling to the United States. However, Knox J considered that goodwill is 'local as between jurisdictions, [but] I do not accept that it follows from this that a business should be regarded as divisible in the same way and have apportioned, for the purposes of determining where goodwill is situate, customers according to the historic reason for which they have become customers'.[22]

It is submitted that this is not correct; if historic reasons are not considered, customers *per se* could constitute goodwill even though there is no business activity in the United Kingdom. The tort of passing off does not exist to protect customers of a trader but to protect goodwill, and Browne-Wilkinson VC in *Pete Waterman* (albeit by implication) accepted that customers *per se* are not sufficient.

Interpreting Market Opportunity

The English courts have tended not to be overly concerned about quantitative or qualitative thresholds provided that the market opportunity can be established. In *Metric Resources Corporation v Leasemetrix Ltd*,[23] the then Vice-Chancellor, Sir Robert McGarry, granted an interim injunction, restraining passing off, to a company incorporated in Delaware, United States. The evidence before the court showed that only one customer actually bought equipment hired from the plaintiff in the United Kingdom, although this customer had purchased substantial amounts. This case is clearly not authority for the proposition that one customer in the United Kingdom will, every time, generate the requisite goodwill. In *Budweiser*, O'Connor LJ talked of 'substantial quantities',[24] while Oliver LJ noted that goodwill had been proven in previous cases by 'relatively modest acts'.[25]

Another case in which the actual evidence of business activity in this country was weak is *Sheraton Corporation of America v Sheraton Motels Ltd*.[26] In that case, the plaintiffs were hoteliers; although they had no hotels within the jurisdiction, they did take bookings through a London office (and through travel agents). Nonetheless, Buckley J granted the plaintiffs an injunction pending trial. Very limited trading activity was also enough for the court to find in favour of the foreign plaintiff in *Panhard et Levassor v Panhard Levassor Motor Company*[27] and in *Globelegance v Sarkissian*.[28] In the former case, the foreign plaintiffs were

---

[21] The fact that the British public could not purchase Budweiser beer in Britain even if they wanted to was fatal to the applicants' appeal before the Court of Appeal (see Lord Justice Oliver, at 469).

[22] Note 1 above, at 933.

[23] [1979] FSR 571.

[24] Note 9 above, at 471.

[25] *Ibid.*, at 470.

[26] [1964] RPC 202.

[27] [1901] 2 Ch. 513.

[28] [1974] RPC 603.

a French car manufacturer who deliberately refrained from selling their Panhard automobiles directly to England, but nonetheless English agents and individuals had imported their cars from France into England. In *Globelegance*, the plaintiff fashion designer was based in Rome, although his fashion shows had been held in England and limited sales of his branded clothes had occurred in the United Kingdom.

The jurisprudence of the courts shows that foreign plaintiffs are much more likely to establish goodwill in the United Kingdom in respect of goods and services at the luxury end of the market such as in high fashion (*Globelegance*) and cars (*Panhard Levassor*). By contrast, everyday inexpensive goods and high turnover goods and services are less likely to generate goodwill for a foreign trader in the United Kingdom, not because they are incapable of generating a protectable goodwill, but merely because the nature of such businesses (such as overseas fast-foot restaurants) makes them essentially local in nature: the hot-dog vendor in Toronto is unlikely actively to seek British customers from within the United Kingdom and, likewise, British customers are unlikely to go to Toronto specifically to get their fill of hot-dogs. Such a factor was acknowledged by Knox J in *Jian*:

> The nature of the goods sold or services rendered is something which should, in my view, be taken into account and it may well be that it is significant that the eating, drinking and making merry involved in the Crazy Horse Saloon is essentially a local activity, as compared with the rather more durable enjoyment of the Panhard Car.[29]

There is, however, the customary cautionary note that the circumstances of each case are different and must be duly considered. For example, a pizza company trading out of New York's Broadway (named Jerusalem Pizza) has, according to press reports,[30] been doing a swift trade in global pizza deliveries. From Manchester and Paris to Canada, kosher Jews, vegetarians and those who apparently appreciate natural ingredients, are prepared to spend more than £60 for a ten-inch pizza delivered to their homes. Putting to one side the issue of whether or not the name 'Jerusalem Pizza' is distinctive enough of the company to be protectable, it is submitted that Jerusalem Pizza may well have a protectable goodwill in the United Kingdom. There is an attractive force: an ability to make repeat purchases, an ability to interact with the supplier and, crucially, from within the jurisdiction.

The Goodwill Factor: Right or Wrong?

Consideration has been given, in both the English courts and other jurisdictions, to extending the law of passing off to protect foreign traders, in circumstances where these traders conduct no business activities in the United Kingdom which would ordinarily be required to bring a passing-off action. The rationale appears to be that the requirement of local goodwill is seen as formalistic and a barrier to overseas traders obtaining relief in obvious cases of 'unfair' trading.

In *Pete Waterman*, the Vice-Chancellor gave detailed consideration to the issue of whether an English court should protect the trade connection with the UK customers of non-UK traders. He recognised that the second half of the 20th century had produced worldwide marks, worldwide goodwill and brought separate markets into competition with one another:

> radio and television with their attendant advertising across national frontiers. Electronic communication via satellite produces virtually instant communication between all

---

[29] Note 1 above, at 937.
[30] *London Evening Standard*, 31 January 1996, at 17.

markets ... In my view, the law will fail if it does not try to meet the challenge thrown out by trading patterns which cross national and jurisdictional boundaries due to a change in technical achievement.[31]

As a matter of legal principle, the Vice-Chancellor saw no reason why the English courts should not protect the trading relationship between a foreign trader and his UK customers by restraining anyone in the United Kingdom from passing himself off as the foreign trader:

> The essence of the claim in passing off is that the defendant is interfering with the goodwill of the plaintiff. The essence of the goodwill is the ability to attract customers and potential customers to do business with the owner of the goodwill. Therefore, any interference with the trader's customers is an interference with his goodwill. The rules under which for certain purposes a certain local situation is attributed to such goodwill appeared to me to be irrelevant. Even if under such rules the situ of the goodwill is not in England, any representation made to customers in England is an interference with that goodwill wherever it may be situate.[32]

The only problem standing between the Vice-Chancellor and his legal principle was authority to the contrary[33] that the basis of a plaintiff's claim in passing off must be a goodwill locally situate within England.

The Federal Court of Australia in *Conagra v McCain Foods*[34] considered whether a foreign trader could rely on reputation alone in a passing-off action. In *Conagra*, the plaintiff manufactured and marketed in the United States a range of frozen food products under the name 'Healthy Choice'. Between 1986 and 1991, Conagra distributed its frozen food in Australia and New Zealand through a licensee. Shortly after the expiry of this licence, the defendants launched a McCain's Healthy Choice range of products. The packaging, get-up and obvious use of the name were almost identical to that used in the United States by the plaintiff. At first instance, the court dismissed the passing-off claim, as precedent dictated that without the existence of a business in Australia and actual or probable damage, the plaintiffs had no cause of action. On appeal, it was held to be sufficient in a passing-off action if the foreign plaintiffs 'could have a reputation in this country amongst persons here, whether residents or otherwise, of a sufficient degree to establish that there is a likelihood of deception among consumers and potential consumers and of damage to his reputation'.[35]

In the Canadian case of *Orkin v Pestco*,[36] the plaintiffs were an American pest control company with no business in Canada but, given the inevitability of cross-border trade between the United States and Canada, there had been some Canadian customers (or at least Canadian citizens) of the plaintiff who owned properties in the United States. The defendant blatantly adopted the plaintiff's name in the telephone directory and the plaintiff's logo on its invoices, and ended up on the receiving end of a permanent injunction from the Ontario Court of Appeal.

In *Calvin Klein Inc. v International Apparel Syndicate and Others*,[37] the internationally renowned American design house, Calvin Klein, successfully injuncted an Indian trader who

---

[31] Note 14 above, at 51.
[32] *Ibid.*
[33] Notably, Lord Justice Oliver in *Budweiser* and Lord Diplock in *Star Industrial*.
[34] Note 3 above.
[35] On the facts it was held that the plaintiffs did not have a sufficient reputation in Australia.
[36] Note 3 above.
[37] Note 3 above.

had been advertising jeans which adopted marks virtually identical to *Calvin Klein*. One of the advertisements even stated that 'Calvin Klein jeans will shortly be available at the best stores in town; a product of International Apparel Syndicate (the official brand owner)'. Despite the fact that Calvin Klein did not trade in India, Mrs Justice Rumau Pal in the High Court of Calcutta determined that Calvin Klein was entitled to an injunction.[38] The judge took an expansive view of the requirement of goodwill in a passing-off action and noted that 'the basis of the action [for passing off] is deception or the persuasion of the public to purchase goods of one in the belief that it is another's. It should not matter whether that other carries on business in the country'.[39] The judge also acknowledged that the use of the mark *Calvin Klein* by the respondents was a clear attempt to 'cash in' on the reputation of Calvin Klein. As in *Conagra* and *Orkin*, the court in *Calvin Klein* seemed to be prepared to override the requirement of damage to goodwill in the face of clear evidence of a local trader taking advantage of the international reputation of an overseas trader who had no presence within the particular jurisdiction.

In *Pete Waterman*, the Vice-Chancellor seemed to be championing a cause of action for foreign plaintiffs that could be labelled (for want of a better expression) 'unlawful interference with customers', while the Federal Court of Australia in *Conagra* acknowledged the existence of reputation as a protectable business interest in itself. Relief for both interference with customers and damage to reputation could conceivably come under the umbrella of a general tort of unfair competition: a legal remedy that would entitle a foreign plaintiff to prevent another from reaping what he has not sown in circumstances where the foreign plaintiff has no business activity in the local jurisdiction (or even customers, incidental or otherwise).

The problem with this approach (as Wadlow points out[40]) is that damage to goodwill is the essence of a passing-off action. The removal of the goodwill requirement as it is currently understood would require the courts to go into the murky waters of assessing damage by reference to injury to the overseas plaintiff's reputation. Theoretically at least, this involves a quantum leap for the courts: passing off protects a trader's property right, namely goodwill. Whether reputation exists or not is, however, treated by the courts as a question of fact.[41]

Passing off, with its requirement of goodwill, does present a problem to the courts in cases where a trader's name has been usurped by another in a jurisdiction where the trader has no business activity. Trade may be international and global communications instantaneous, but passing off requires that each jurisdiction be considered separately. Reputations (good or bad) can spread quicker than wildfire. And where the reputation goes the business may follow, but in many industries a time lag is inevitable while the infrastructure to create 'market opportunities' is put in place. In the interim, the potential for local traders to hijack a foreign trader's name and reputation is considerable.

Some overseas traders will be in a position to avail themselves of section 56 of the Trade Marks Act 1994 which gives protection to marks well-known in the United Kingdom, regardless of whether the foreign trader carries on business or has goodwill in the United Kingdom. It is submitted that this is a considerable step in the right direction, but the point of reference of section 56 is whether the mark is 'well-known', not whether there has been misappropriation. This may lead to two-tier protection which prejudices foreign traders whose reputations within the United Kingdom have not been transformed into well-known marks for the purposes of section 56.

---

[38]   Calvin Klein also brought an action for trade mark infringement, but this was not heavily relied on at the hearing.
[39]   Note 3 above, at 523.
[40]   Note 2 above, at 101.
[41]   Graham J, in *Baskin Robbins*, Note 11 above, at 547, took the view that the existence and extent of both reputation and goodwill was a question of fact.

Goodwill and the Unfair Trader

While there is no law of unfair competition in the United Kingdom, foreign plaintiffs have frequently succeeded in proving the existence of goodwill here, even though the evidence of customers within the jurisdiction was very thin.[42] One interpretation for this is that the courts are more willing to find goodwill in favour of a foreign plaintiff where defendants have entered the markets with their 'eyes open' and made a deliberate effort to take advantage of a foreign business's distinctive name. This can be inferred in *Jian* by looking not only at Knox J's consideration of the question of goodwill, but also the balance of convenience.

In determining the balance of convenience, Knox J noted that the balance was about equal, but continued that there were two matters which tipped the scale in Jian's favour. Knox J noted:

> the defendants adopted the name *Business Plan Builder* in the face of very clear and explicit opposition from Jian ... In contrast, the defendants never gave any indication, other than inferentially, of their intention to use a name indistinguishable in meaning from Jian's established name in connection with the defendants' own product. ...
>
> This is, in my view, a legitimate fact to take into account [in considering the balance of convenience]. An important feature of, if not a better name for, what the Court is called upon to do at this stage is to strike the appropriate balance between the *injustice* involved in denying the plaintiffs an injunction at this stage, should they turn out at trial to be entitled to a permanent injunction, and the *injustice* involved in granting the injunction against the defendants at this stage should they succeed in showing at trial that no injunction should be granted. *The conception [sic] of justice should, in my view, include considerations outside those which can be measured in economic terms.*[43]

In this regard, Knox J approved the decision in *Highmac Ltd v Priestman Brothers Ltd*,[44] where Walton J stated:

> I think that there is a special reason connected with convenience which it is necessary I ought to take into account and that is this. I cannot believe that this is a case where the defendants have not acted with their eyes fully opened throughout. I cannot think that with an organisation of their size and reputation somebody on their side must not have said when names of this new machine were being discussed 'if we use 580, will not the plaintiffs object?'. If that question was asked, as I think it must have been, the defendants must thereafter have gone on knowing the risks involved. They therefore, in my view, cannot complain if they play with fire in that way and get burned.[45]

The serious question to be considered here is whether 'non-economic' factors should be considered by the court in determining the existence of a foreign plaintiff's goodwill in the United Kingdom.[46] There is nothing in *Jian* (nor, indeed, in the *Sheraton* and *Poiret* cases)

---

[42] Notably, *Sheraton Corporation of America v Sheraton Motels Ltd*, Note 26 above, and *Jian* itself.

[43] Note 1 above, at 943 (*emphasis added*).

[44] [1978] RPC 495.

[45] *Ibid.*, at 500. The other fact which Mr Justice Knox took into account was the preservation of the status quo which he also found in Jian's favour.

[46] It is acknowledged that both the *Jian* and *Sheraton* cases were interlocutory injunction applications where the balance of convenience had to be considered. However, given that interlocutory applications often dispose of the action one way or another, this factor should not be ignored.

to suggest that the 'eyes open' factor was used by the courts to compensate for evidence which did not strongly support the finding of goodwill in the United Kingdom. However, where a plaintiff is seeking to invoke an equitable discretionary remedy, defendants who do not come to the court with 'clean hands' may find that in borderline cases the courts are more likely to infer goodwill (at least until trial in interlocutory applications) in an effort to provide a remedy to the foreign trader.[47]

Conclusion

Looking at the *Jian* case in the light of the authorities reviewed by Knox J, it does not necessarily follow that the court was correct in finding that there was an arguable case on the question of goodwill. Certainly, there was no evidence that consumers would consciously cross the Atlantic in order to avail themselves of BizPlan Builder; indeed, the sales to UK residents in the United States appear to have been merely incidental to those individuals who happened to be in the United States at the time. Quantitatively, there was nothing to suggest that the number of sales were anything other than insubstantial.

On balance, it would appear that Jian were fortunate to persuade the court that they had a protectable goodwill in the United Kingdom. The case quite clearly illustrates the fundamental requirement of proving goodwill within the jurisdiction and that such goodwill is defined by reference to business activity which has led to a customer base. However, the court was generous in finding that such a small number of customers (several of whom had not even purchased the product) for a business plan software product was sufficient to constitute a customer base. This is compounded by the fact that the court was prepared to accept (albeit as an arguable case)[48] that UK residents who had purchased BizPlan Builder while in the United States could constitute the relevant customer base for the purposes of determining the question of goodwill.

What *Jian* does show is that where defendants have failed to show a 'clean pair of hands' the courts appear to be more inclined to make a finding in favour of the foreign plaintiff by liberally interpreting the requirement of goodwill. However, damage to goodwill is the essence of a passing-off action, not damage to reputation or interference with customers. Ultimately, foreign plaintiffs with no customer connection within the jurisdiction whose names have been blatantly taken by opportunistic traders can only seek redress by reference to section 56 (if their mark is 'well-known') or an unfair competition law which at present does not exist in the United Kingdom. The type of activities that the defendant traders undertook in cases like *Conagra*, *Orkin* and *Calvin Klein* should, it is submitted, not be beyond remedy on the basis of a formal requirement that the overseas trader have customers within the jurisdiction. Foreign plaintiffs should be able to avail themselves of a remedy in unfair competition where customer confusion or deception will result from the defendant's activities or where the defendant has acted in bad faith. This will also carry with it the advantage that the law of passing off need not be artificially stretched by the courts to accommodate the victim of unfair competition. The subject of unfair competition is explored

---

[47] Even in the *Crazy Horse* case, the judge was alert to the fact that the defendants had taken the name from the plaintiff and his finding against the foreign plaintiff had been made 'with regret'.

[48] Laddie J in *Series Five Software Ltd v Philip Clarke and Others* (unreported, 18 December 1995) revisited *American Cyanamid v Ethicon* [1975] AC 396 and concluded that courts should, at the interlocutory injunction stage, not be afraid to come to a non-binding view of the merits of the case. This may, if followed, lead to foreign plaintiffs with only questionable goodwill in the United Kingdom being unsuccessful at the interlocutory stage, even if they show that there is a serious issue to be tried.

frequently and in great depth elsewhere,[49] and it is not proposed that this issue be dealt with further here. However, it is suggested that in the meantime the law of passing off should not be used as a poor relation to help deserving cases.

---

[49] For example, *Robertson v Horton*: 'Does the United Kingdom or the European Community Need an Unfair Competition Law?' [1995] 12 EIPR 568.

Passing Off and Trade Marks

Trade Marks

A Consumer Trade Mark: Protection Based on Origin and Quality*

[1993] 11 EAPR 406

ANSELM KAMPERMAN SANDERS
Former EC Human Capital Mobility Research Fellow at QMWC, presently Senior Lecturer at Maastricht University

AND SPYROS M. MANIATIS
I.P. Law Unit, Queen Mary and Westfield College, London

Introduction

Trade marks made up of either words or signs are a traditional form of expression and are valuable conveyers of information. Enabling man to convey a message to his fellow man about the products or services that he owns or wants to trade in allows a multiplicity of functions to be satisfied. This information can be categorised in many forms depending on the perception of the exchanged message.

Anthropological and historical findings on trade marks indicate that they fulfil a universal and perpetual role,[1] the merit of which is appraised by the legal recognition attached to them. Different legal traditions, reflecting specific cultural and economic variations, find ways to characterise the above-mentioned perception.

Since trade marks are a monopoly conferred by the state, their regulation should vary depending on the social needs justifying the monopoly's existence. To prove this, in this article, the link between unfair competition and trade marks will be shown and some of the contrasting perceptions of the functions of a trade mark will be discussed. It will be suggested that the combined use of unfair competition, consumer protection and trade mark law would satisfy more effectively the common underlying theme of fair and efficient competition. This is a target for which state intervention through market regulation is generally accepted, even in the most deregulated markets.

The categorisation of the functions of trade marks that is being increasingly accepted will be used in this article: first they can be indicators of origin, incorporating their aptness to distinguish and identify varying products and numerous traders. Second they can suggest a guarantee of consistent quality, albeit rarely legally enforceable. And finally they are a factor in the advertising and sales of the marked products manifesting the goodwill that they enjoy in the market-place. The trade mark incorporating all three functions will be referred to as a consumer trade mark, qualifying its monopolistic character.

* *The authors wish to thank Alison Firth, Professor G. Dworkin and Professor B. Keating for their comments and remarks, which have been invaluable in the preparation of this article.*

[1] From the bibliography on trade mark history, it is worthwhile, and also fun, to read the visionary early work of F.I. Schechter, *The Historical Foundations of the Law Relating to Trade-Marks*, 1925, and for a shorter authoritative review, S.A. Diamond, 'The Historical Developments of Trademarks', [1975] 65 TMR 265 to 290. M. Vukmir offers the latest review in 'The Roots of Anglo-American Intellectual Property Law in Roman Law', [1992] 32 IDEA 123 to 154.

Functions of a Trade Mark

Although trade marks primarily and traditionally denote origin in both civil and common law jurisdictions,[2] the slight definitional differences and the contradistinction of unfair competition in civil law with passing off in common law, create an infinite series of variations on the same theme.

Indicators of origin

We live in a world of symbols, where we have learned, through social interaction, to overlook everything that does not confer a symbolic meaning.[3] Another characteristic of this consumer society is the overabundance of products in the market-place. Thus the consumer has the freedom to choose, an ability inherent in a free market economy. But the exercise of that freedom would be impossible without the interaction between symbols and products. Thus trade marks come into play.

A trade mark first of all enhances the ability to conceptualise the abstract notion of a product and consequently enables the individualisation of the product by creating the tie between a product and its mark. This is a notion of a new product as such, completely different from the previous unmarked product. The natural consequence of this process is the identification of the product. If one decides to purchase a product, the mark, if generic, helps to recollect the product itself or puts next to the notion of the product the marks/names of all these similar products. A television, for example, is something which brings sound and vision into our living room and is made by Philips or Sony. The conceptualisation of the product has taken place. The consumer then goes to his dealer, individualises between the Philips, Sony and ITT sets and identifies his preference.[4]

---

[2] F.K. Beier, 'Basic Features of Anglo-American, French and German Trademark Law', [1975] 3 IIC 285 to 303 at 285 and 286 with a historical overview of the relevant systems. With reference to the *Hag* decision, which raised doubts about the classical function of the trade mark as the indicator of the commercial origin of the marked goods, he expresses his feelings: 'I don't like coffee without caffeine, nor, I may add, trademarks without origin. So much for Kaffee Hag...'.

[3] On the symbolic value of goods, see for example A.S. Oddi, 'Consumer Motivation in Trade Mark and Unfair Competition Law: on the Importance of Source', [1986] 31 *Villanova Law Review* 1 to 79, describing at 42 to 63 the affective functionality of goods and the resultant impulse buying and the emotional buying caused by the symbolic functionality.

It is therefore true that: 'Some products are presented as the symbols by which people achieve financial, professional, or personal power over others: the equation for success.' S. Ewen, 'Advertising and the Development of Consumer Society', in I.H. Angus and S. Jhally (eds), *Cultural Politics in Contemporary America*, Routledge, 1989, at 82. Finally, see M. Douglas and B. Isherwood, *The World of Goods*, Norton, 1979, at 57, asserting that all material possessions carry 'social meanings'.

[4] This last process is subject to later remarks in this article on trade marks as indicators of quality.

Initially, trade marks enable the consumer to identify the unobservable qualities of the product. See N.S. Economides, 'The Economics of Trademarks', [1988] 78 TMR 523 to 539 at 526 to 527:

> The economic role of the trademark is to help the consumer identify the unobservable features of the trade-marked product. This information is not provided to the consumer in an analytic form, such as an indication of the size of a listing of ingredients, but rather in summary form, through a symbol which the consumer identifies with a specific combination of features. Information in analytic form is a complement to, rather than a substitute for, trademarks.

See also G. Kelly, *The Psychology of Personal Constructs*, Norton, 1955, quoted by D. Edwards and S. Johnson, 'The Meanings of Products in Consumers' Lives: The Grid Approach', in J. Olson and K. Senties (eds), *Advertising and Consumer Psychology*, Proreger, 1986, at 259:

> Grid Research proposes that consumers are trying to understand their experiences with products by building models of the experiences. Then they use their models to make the decisions that they believe will allow them to maximise their opportunities to fulfil their 'needs and desires'.

What are the variations in origin that the trade mark can denote?

(1) *Concrete origin*
— the trade mark equals the firm's or producer's identity;
— the trade mark denotes a certain conglomerate, or group of producers (collective marks);
— the trade mark contains information about its owner;
— the trade mark does not make a direct preference to its owner, but the producer is traceable.

(2) *Abstract origin*
The fact that a product exists denotes that it has been produced somewhere. The mere occurrence that a mark has been affixed to the product is immaterial in the sense that it may influence the consumer's choice. It is through referring to previous occurrences of the mark, creating a new connection between this product and consistently similar products, that influence is exerted. This flows into the second function of the trade mark, guarantee of quality.

Guarantees of quality

To return to the consumer faced with the task of making a rational purchase decision about a television. Like most of us, he is not an expert in the field of television and lives in a world of immense imbalances of access to information.[5] His direct contact with the product takes place in the environment of the dealer's room, where he can check image, sound, style and feel of the TV set in that instant, but he has no way of checking durability, or the state of technology and so on. The only thing he can rely on, apart from the personal contact, is his previous experience with the product, or indirect information through experience of his social surroundings, consumer guides and advertising about the product or its maker. Trade marks enable him to fill in some missing pieces of the product's jigsaw. He hopes that the goods of each maker will be of consistent quality, similar to the one previously experienced, or portrayed.[6] Thus the trade mark becomes an indicator of consistent quality,[7] be it good or bad.

---

[5] G.A. Akerlof, 'The Market for "Lemons": Quality Uncertainty and the Market Mechanism', [1970] 84 *Quarterly Journal of Economics* 488 to 500. Akerlof succinctly depicts the breakdown in the market when the consumer cannot trust the information about the product he wishes to purchase. Then he will prefer to buy goods of lower quality until—as in a vicious circle—the only goods available will be those of the lowest quality.
 On the value of information see also W.R. Landes and R.A. Posner, 'A Positive Economic Analysis of Products Liability', [1985] 24 *Journal of Legal Studies* 535 to 567 at 543 and 547 to 551. In arguing for a strict liability doctrine on products liability law they show the high costs of consumers absorbing additional information.
 For a contrary view see P.M. Danzon, 'Comments on Landes and Posner: A Positive Economic Analysis of Products Liability', [1985] 24 *Journal of Legal Studies* 569 to 583 at 571 to 573.
[6] W.R. Cornish and J. Phillips, 'The Economic Function of Trade Marks: An Analysis with Special Reference to Developing Countries', [1982] 13 IIC 41 to 64 at 43. After referring to the modern practice of licensing trade marks and the consistent use of brand names in advertising, they state that: 'If he [the consumer] is interested in origin, it is normally because origin imports an expectation about some quality.'
 L. Akazaki, 'Source Theory and Guarantee Theory in Anglo-American Trade Mark Policy: A Critical Legal Study', [1990] 3 JPTOS 225 to 278 at 258, concludes that source theory is not the only theory in trade mark law, because that would be contrary to the market and legal practice. Specific reference is made to the licensing of certification marks, which would be illegal if one were to follow a strict origin theory.
[7] For example in legal terms this proposition stands at the basis of the 'unclean hands doctrine'. A change in the quality or nature of the product bearing a trade mark may result in a forfeiture of rights to protection vested in the mark. See E.W. Hanak III, 'The Quality Assurance Function of Trademarks', [1975] 65 TMR 318 to 335 at 320 and onward and I.P. Cooper, '"Unclean Hands" and "Unlawful Use in Commerce": Trademarks Adrift on the Regulatory Tide', [1981] 71 TMR 38 to 58.

But here things get complicated. Despite the fact that the trade mark partially fulfils the role of a guarantee of quality, this function is not a legally binding warranty.[8] If consumers had in their hands such a strong weapon, then the floodgates of litigation would be opened. The imbalance of access to information between the consumer and the marketeer and their relatively unequal footing can create confusion or deception. It is questionable whether the origin-orientated forms of protection are sufficient to address their particular imbalance. There is, of course, a strong argument that market rules themselves will oblige the marketeers to keep a consistent quality in their products as this is the only way to retain consumer loyalty,[9] but the market is not a place for angels and the consumer demand for legislative supra-market intervention may be desirable.[10]

It should not be forgotten that one can play with taste, but not with quality. Even that is questionable when one considers taste in foods, or fashion-dictated designs.

It is acceptable to have different product characteristics in various countries. In the obscure and complicated business world of multinational enterprises, licensees and licensors, supra-national traders and fly-by-night marketeers, goods may be traceable up to a name origin, but one may never be able to trace the actual originator. Even when the name used points to a multinational enterprise, the consumer is not capable of distinguishing between the multitude of arms of the enterprise and the resulting differences in product quality.[11] In the European Community (for example), despite the harmonisation procedure and the creation of an internal market, it is still conceivable to have differing tastes or qualities of products marketed under the same banner. Goods stem from various national markets, yet operate

---

[8] See Beier who, in explaining why the guarantee function of the trade mark cannot be the basis for an autonomous legal doctrine, also uncovers the reason why no legal backing can be given to the mark as a warranty. F.K. Beier and U. Krieger, 'Wirtschaftliche Bedeutung, Functionen und Zweck der Marke', [1976] 3 GRUR Int. 125 to 128 at 127:

> Were one to focus only on the quality function and the protection of the public against quality disappointment, the logical consequence would be that the markowner would never be allowed to change the quality of his marked product, because then every competitor that produces goods of the same nature and quality should be allowed to use the same mark. Therefore the mark would lose its individuality and adopt the character of a common indicator of attribution or certification of quality that everybody should be allowed to use for the same good (*translation*).

[9] R.S. Brown, 'Advertising and the Public Interest: Legal Protection of Trade Symbols', [1948] 57 Yale LJ 1165 to 1206 at 1187:

> Since the user of a symbol probably guarantees by it nothing more than his hope that the buyer will come back for more, the term smacks strongly of the ad-man's desire to create the illusion of a guarantee without in fact making more than the minimum warranty of merchantable quality.

[9] R.A. Posner and W.M. Landes, 'Trademark Law: An Economic Perspective', [1989] IP Law Rev. 229 to 273 at 233:

> The benefits of trademarks in reducing consumer search costs, require that the producer of a trademarked good maintain a consistent quality over time and across consumers. Hence trademark protection encourages expenditures on quality.

C. Shapiro, 'Premiums for High Quality Products as Returns to Reputations', [1983] 98 *Quarterly Journal of Economics* 659 to 679, argues that a firm owning a valuable trade mark would not endanger the investment in the mark by lowering its inherent quality. This argument is also found in the White Paper, *Reform of Trade Marks Law*, HMSO, 1990, Cm 1203, 4.36, at 25 to 26.

[10] Up till now and especially after the demise of the socialist bloc, market rules are a taboo that nobody can touch. Recent economic events, however, put the question of eligibility of state regulation on the agenda.

[11] In *Colgate I (Colgate Palmolive Ltd v Markwell Finance Ltd* [1988] RPC 283), for example, the Court held that it was in the interest of the consumer and the UK trade mark owner to stop the importation of genuine Brazilian Colgate toothpaste into the United Kingdom, where the quality standards were higher. Falconer J in his judgment paid considerable attention to the mark's message of quality. See also *Colgate II (Colgate Palmolive Ltd v Markwell Finance Ltd* [1989] RPC 497 (CA)).

within the same marketplace, cater for different national tastes[12] and cause tremors on the legal foundations of a single market where, despite the advanced state of harmonisation procedures, trade mark laws are in essence territorial[13] and therefore give rise to confusion and controversy.[14] Similarly controversial is the practice of parallel importation, causing debates on the extent of the monopoly conferred by a trade mark and the conflicting interests of producers and consumers, even *inter se*.[15] The bibliography on the subject is vast and cannot possibly be dealt with here.[16]

Advertising and sales

The advertising function of the trade mark can be seen as a cumulative result of its origin and quality connotations in all of their guises. The factor that gives it its unique character is the additional advertising tool.[17] It is obvious that without names, goods could not be advertised as easily,[18] and it is true that '[t]he protection of trade-marks is the law's recognition

---

[12] In *Cinzano v Java Kaffeegeschäfte* [1974] 2 CMLR 21 (West German Supreme Court), where the makers of Campari attempted to partition the market, because of the different liquors used to make Campari in each market and accordingly different tastes. The German Supreme Court made it clear that the function of registered marks to show origin was fulfilled and the makers of Campari had to find another way to inform the consumers about the diverging tastes.

[13] F.K. Beier, 'Territoriality of Trademark Law and International Trade', [1970] 1 IIC 45 to 72 at 66:

> It is my opinion, however that trademark law does not give a trademark owner the power to prevent importation of genuine goods of a different quality into a given country. Only that function of the trademark is legally protected which guarantees the origin of the goods; the mark fulfils a quality function to the extent only that it guarantees to the consumer a constant source of origin.

For an analysis of the impact of European Community law, see W.R. Cornish, *Intellectual Property*, Sweet & Maxwell, 1989, at 485 to 494 and T.A. Larkin, 'Harmony in Disarray: The European Community Trademark System', [1992] 82 TMR 634 to 650.

[14] The notorious contradictory decisions of the European Court of Justice in *Hag I*, Case 129/73 *Van Zuylen Frères v Hag* [1974] ECR 731, and *Hag II*, Case 10/89 *SA CNL-Sucal NV v Hag GF AG*, exemplify the tricky character of trade marks. For an analysis of the cases and the underlying doctrines, see W.R. Rothnie, '*Hag II*: Putting the Common Origin Doctrine to Sleep', [1991] 13 EIPR 24 to 31. For some criticism on *Hag I*, see S.P. Ladas, 'The Court of Justice of the European Community and the *Hag* Case', [1974] 5 IIC 302 to 313.

[15] For the history of parallel imports, see Vandenburgh, 'The Problem of Importation of Genuinely Marked Goods Is Not a Trademark Problem', [1959] 49 TMR 707. For a comparative survey see K. Takamatsu, 'Parallel Importation of Trademarked Goods: A Comparative Analysis', [1982] 57 *Washington Law Review* 433 to 459.

[16] On the vast market for grey market goods, its boom during the 1980s and the interrelation of law and economics on that matter, see R.J. Staaf, 'The Law and Economics of the International Gray Market: Quality Assurance, Free Riding and Passing Off', [1988] 4 *Intellectual Property Journal* 191 to 235.

[17] Despite uncertainty on the actual power of advertising and the difficulty of measuring its effects most of the commentators—adversaries and advocates alike—agree that advertising can be a barrier to entry, does affect consumers' taste and is able to decrease the elasticity of the product's price. M.S. Albion and P.W. Farris, *The Advertising Controversy: Evidence on Advertising's Economic Effect*, Auburn House Publishing, 1981, at 32 to 34, 'Advertising and Market Power', chapters 3 and 4, at 45 to 87. For those without scientific economic knowledge, it is almost impossible to obtain a clear overview of the real advantages and disadvantages of advertising. Everything seems to be black and white depending on the fervour with which each commentator is taking part in the crusade, for or against, advertising. Most convincing is the argument of F.M. Scherer and D. Ross, *Industrial Market Structure and Economic Performance*, 1990, Chapter 6 at 571—although made in a different context—that:

> It is easy to be fervent in advancing simplistic theories of economic behavior. It is much more difficult to work up passion over the view, held by the authors of this work, that the industrial world is quite diverse and complex, requiring complex theories if it is to be understood.

Nevertheless W.S. Comanor and T.A. Wilson, 'The Effect of Advertising on Competition: A Survey', [1979] 17 *Journal of Economic Literature* 453 to 476, offer a review of the contrasting theories on advertising.

[18] Above the symbolic value of goods was noted, and:

> If goods have a symbolic aspect it is largely because advertising gives them one. They plainly do not spring from the factory fully possessed of their ability to communicate. It is advertising that enables them to

of the psychological function of symbols. If it is true that we live by symbols, it is no less true that we purchase goods by them.'[19]

Recognition of advertising as a separate function of a trade mark merely acknowledges the goodwill which the trade mark can attract to itself independently of the goodwill of the product or its maker. Good branding is a prerequisite to successful marketing. The example of Coca Cola and the value of the brand independently of the soda drink itself demonstrates that.[20] The reasons behind the loyalty stemming from brand attractiveness are hotly debated.[21]

It is true that advertising conveys information.[22] It relates a new product to an existing product that consumers recognise from the shelves of the stores. It facilitates comparison and undermines loyalty to other brands. It creates a package product: that of the advertised marked good, the net worth of which may be higher than the worth of the non-advertised marked good which in turn may be higher than that of the generic good. Some people may even enjoy watching advertisements and many gain some added pleasure from identifying themselves with 'a new generation'.[23] But advertising can be misleading, or it may reallocate

---

assume this ability ... It is part of the process with which we endow objects with certain meaningful properties. It is advertising that makes goods 'communicators'.

G. McCracken and R. Pollay in 'Anthropology and the Study of Advertising', 1981, unpublished paper of the University of British Columbia at 2 as quoted by S. Jhally, *The Codes of Advertising*, Routledge, 1990, at 11.

[19] Frankfurter J, in *Mishawaka Rubber & Wooden Mfg Co. v S.S. Kresge Co.* 316 US 203, at 205 (1942).

[20] See for example T. Blackett, 'The Nature of Brands', in J. Murphy (ed.), *Brand Valuation*, Hutchinson Business Books, 1989 at 1 to 12, and G. Duckworth, 'Brands and the Role of Advertising', in D. Cowley (ed.) *Understanding Brands*, Kogan Page, 1991, at 57 to 83, and J.P. Jones, *What's in a Name?: Advertising and the Concept of Brands*, Gower, 1986, at chapter 2, where at 29 he defines a brand as: 'a product that provides functional benefits plus added values that some consumers value enough to buy', and categorises these added values as: (a) added values that come from experience of the brand; (b) added values that come from the sorts of people who use the brand; (c) added values that come from a belief that the brand is effective; and (d) added values which come from the appearance of the brand. It is interesting to note that trade marks have found their way onto the balance sheet, in addition to the evaluation of goodwill: J. Hall, 'The Valuation of Intellectual Property and Intangible Assets', [1990] IPJ, 11 to 22.

[21] The beer examples described by D.F. Greer, *Industrial Organization and Public Policy*, Macmillan, 1990, at 87 to 91, are fascinating. Although the consumers could not identify their brand in blind tests, they overwhelmingly preferred their brand when compared with others even when the bottled beer did not correspond with the brand label.

[22] As to how much of advertising is informative or merely persuasive, one should refer to the opinion survey conducted by R.A. Bauer and S.A. Greyser in *Advertising in America: The Consumer View*, Harvard University, 1968, at 175 to 183 as quoted by Greer, Note 21 above, at 72. Seventy-three per cent of the respondents agree that advertising often persuades people to buy things they should not buy. After all: 'The purpose of advertising is not to inform buyers—not in a purely cognitive, unbiased sense anyway. The idea is to sell goods by influencing buyers.' For a classic advocate's view, see P. Nelson, 'Advertising as Information', [1974] 82 *Journal of Political Economy* 729 to 754, who concludes that highly advertised goods are in fact the best buys. See also R.E. Kihlstrom and M.H. Riordan, 'Advertising as a Signal', [1984] 92 *Journal of Political Economy* 426 to 450. However, different levels of advertising do not necessarily convey the right information abut the quality of a product. For a more qualified view, see R. Schmalensee, 'A Model of Advertising and Product Quality', [1978] 86 *Journal of Political Economy* 485 to 503, who establishes that under certain conditions poor quality brands may advertise as heavily as high quality brands.

[23] Part of the Pepsi advertising strategy is to make the consumer part of the conveyed message, using the symbolic function of the mark to its maximum effect. After all advertising wants us to familiarise with the product and then, by reminding us of its existence and by spreading the news of the new product, attempts to overcome our inertia and add the value not in the product, creating real, but subjective values. This is where the advertising controversy lies. This is how Albion and Farris present the teachings of J.W. Young in *The Advertising Controversy: Evidence on Advertising's Economic Effect*, Note 17 above, referring further to a lecture by J.A.P. Treasure, contained at 2 to 3 in Y. Brozen (ed.) *Advertising and Society*, New York University Press, 1974, at 149 to 168, summarising the teachings of J.W. Young.

On the Cola wars see—fascinating for the uninitiated—J.J. Tharp, 'Raising Rivals' Costs: of Bottlenecks, Bottled Wine, and Bottled Soda', [1990] 84 *Northwestern University Law Review* 321 to 374. For the latest episode in the Cola saga, we refer to the quick reaction of Coke to the misfortunes of the Pepsi sponsored Michael Jackson, with the launch of the slogan 'Dehydrated? There's always Coke!'

resources to uses that are not efficient at all.[24] Advertising is an activity that will never cease to exist and it requires regulation[25] to make it work as effectively and as beneficially to society[26] as possible.

What trade marks offer to advertising, in addition to the ability to identify a product, is the automatic initialisation of the advertising process.[27]

Three Sets of Rules

Consumer protection and trade marks

It is clear that trade marks already serve as an instrument of consumer protection. This is achieved despite the fact that most of the principles of trade mark and unfair competition laws are based on the interests of the competing business concerns.[28] But the requirement of distinctiveness, the exclusion of generic marks, the protection against trade mark infringement, the prohibition of deceptive marks and the provisions on parallel importation, protect the consumer, in an indirect[29] rather than a

---

[24] It may be that advertising channels the rivalry of price competition, something too dangerous to compete over, into another strategy for winning customers. Paraphrasing J.K. Galbraith, *The New Industrial State*, Penguin Books, 1978, at 209.

[25] There is evidence to suggest that the complete lack of advertising may raise prices. This is shown in the US market for eyeglasses, where in states where advertising was permitted, consumers had the choice between less thorough but much less expensive service and more thorough, higher priced service. For similar quality, however, the average price was lower on average, when compared to those states in which advertising was prohibited. See F.H. Scherer and D. Ross, *Industrial Market Structure and Economic Performance*, Houghton Mifflin, 1990 (3rd edn), chapter 16 at 574 with his appreciation of J.E. Kwoka Jr, 'Advertising and the Price of Quality of Optometric Services', [1984] 74 *American Economic Review* at 211 to 216.

[26] It must not be forgotten that we live in a consumerist society, closely interlinked with advertising, the social effects of which are part of people's general attitude towards life. Advertising has the dual role of creating social values and being the mirror of people's social values. On advertising's social role, see T.H. Qualter, *Advertising and Democracy in the Mass Age*, Macmillan, 1991, at 56 to 84.

[27] In essence medium and message are one and indivisible and by the use of the message in any connotation, the process of circulating the name is self-initiated. See the visionary Marshall MacLuhan, *Understanding Media, The Extensions of Man*, Routledge & Kegan Paul, 1964, 'The medium is the message', at 7 to 21 and 226 to 233. Therefore an additional advantage of trade mark ownership, in a world where symbols dominate and manifest people's social standings, is the ability of the owner to fix the signifier by owning the sign. One can use a mark outside its original connotation and connection with the product only insofar as the owner of the mark does not object. This has been enhanced by the anti-dilution statutes in the US and an ever-expanding passing off and unfair competition doctrine in the rest of the world. See the challenging analysis of R.J. Combe, 'Objects of Property and Subject of Politics: Intellectual Property Laws and Democratic Dialogue', [1991] 69 *Texas Law Review* 1853 to 1880 at 1864 to 1877.

[28] Protection of consumers, somewhat anathema in the heyday of *caveat emptor*, was merely the device for applying the misrepresentation test for infringement and ensuring the purity of a trader's rights, that is, where the relevant public in various contexts is deceived and/or confused by a mark which is the subject of complaint. The interest of mark holders remains the driving force for enhanced trade mark protection in the GATT TRIPS Draft Convention

M.D. Pendleton, 'Excising Consumer Protection—The Key to Reforming Trade Mark Law', [1992] 3 AIPJ at 110.

[29] See *The Role of Industrial Property in the Protection of Consumers*, WIPO, 1983, at 9, to find a description of the reasons underlining the connection of trade mark laws and consumer protection:

Those laws also serve against the deceit of consumers:
—because the law on marks helps to establish the link between the product or service that the consumer is about to choose and the enterprise which produces or markets the product and service; thus, it helps the consumer to choose, among the countless variety of products and services, those which he trusts and wants, rather than those which he does not trust or want;
—because the law on trade names identifies a given enterprise; thus, it helps the consumer to deal, among the many available enterprises, with that enterprise with which he wants to deal, rather than with one with which he does not want to deal;
—because the law on geographical indications requires that there be a true link between a given product and

direct[30] manner. The ever-increasing call for more extensive consumer protection, a result of the consumerist 1970s and 1980s, and the alleged need to elevate the citizen to the core of the political argument and transform him to a participant in the decision-making process,[31] may lead to closer and more effective blending of trade mark and consumer protection laws.

Unfair competition and trade marks

The industrial revolution brought with it a huge increase in trade, but this time at a massive international level, and with a corresponding boom in the retail trade.[32] Transportation of goods between trading nations far apart was now feasible, advertising flourished and encouraged the creation of a global market. International players-traders pressed for national and international protection of their investment, enhancement of their prominence and fortification of the new establishment. In the power struggle for a post in the market-place: 'Trade marks and trade names have become nothing more nor less than the fundament of most market place competition.'[33] Unfair competition rules were conceptualised at their birth as rules governing relations between competitors.[34]

But somewhere along the line of their historical development,[35] together with the gradual

---

a given country or region or locality; thus, it helps the consumer in choosing a product from that country or region or locality which he wants, rather than one that comes from somewhere else;

—because the law of unfair competition prohibits, among other things, in the marketing of products and services, untrue allegations or insinuations; thus, it helps the consumer to be correctly informed rather than misled.

[30] Even the EC Directive of 25 July 1985 (5/374/EC) on Product Liability sets out a system in which a producer is liable for damage caused by the defect of his product. The defectiveness of a product lies in the lack of safety which the consumer is entitled to expect. The presentation of the product is one of the circumstances that is expressly taken into account in order to determine to what use the product could reasonably be expected to be put. P. Kelly and R. Attree (eds), *European Product Liability*, Butterworths, 1992.

[31] All the pre-and post-Maastricht debate is focused on the democratisation of the European Community and the need for openness and participation. President Clinton was elected on a liberal platform which could easily be a watered-down version, as to the end, of the one described by Ronald Dworkin, who perceives liberals as those who:

believe that government should intervene in the economy to promote economic stability, to control inflation, to reduce unemployment, and to provide services that would not otherwise be provided, but they favor a pragmatic and selective intervention over a dramatic change from free enterprise to wholly collective decisions about investment, production, prices and wages.

The politics of democracies, according to this answer, [to the question of what a government should be] recognises several independent constitutive political ideals, the most important of which are the ideals of liberty and equality.

R. Dworkin, 'Liberalism', in *Philosophy of Law*, Cambridge University Press, 1978 at 122 and 123.

On the ambiguity of a Clinton administration's 'cautious activism' see page 5 of the *Financial Times* of 26 November 1992.

[32] P.A. Samuelson and W.D. Nordhaus, *Economics*, 1989, at 640 to 641, 852 to 853 provide a brief, to the point description.

[33] Cornish, Note 13 above, at 392. See 392 to 399 for the complete historical sketch.

[34] See E.S. Rogers, 'Unfair Competition', [1919] 17 *Michigan Law Review* 490 to 494 at 492: 'Unfair trade was perilously close to being crystallized and limited to mere passing off.' See also K.F. Beier, 'The Law of Unfair Competition in the European Community—Its Development and Present Status', [1985] 16 IIC 139 to 164.

[35] G. Schricker, 'Unfair Competition and Consumer Protection—New Developments', [1977] 3 IIC 185 to 227 at 188, notes why unfair competition best serves the balance of several interests:

The conclusion seems to be justified that the law of unfair competition may exercise a central and integrating function in the law of consumer protection. The law of unfair competition leads particularly to balanced solutions: Where it is necessary, as in the framework of the German general clause of Sec. 1 of the Unfair Competition Act (UWG), to balance the interests of competitors and purchasers in view of the needs of the community at large, it may be expected that consumer protection may acquire a level which is desirable with respect to the interest of consumers, but nevertheless acceptable under general economic policies.

At 186 he chronologically positions the initiation of consumer protection:

democratisation of politics and economy,[36] and in order to support the expansion of the economy and the crucial sector of retail trade, unfair competition laws have also been acknowledged as means for the active involvement of the consumer in the competitive process.[37] The flexibility of the general doctrine of unfair competition could satisfy two separate requirements. First it is adaptable to address diverse social and economic needs and second it is capable of becoming an approximating agent of common and civil law jurisdictions: expanded common sense common law doctrines can be equated to general and flexible civil codes' unfair competition provisions, quantified by extensive case law.[38] Unfair competition can also serve as the medium to extend the regulation of monopolies from their horizontal nature (that is, between market competitors) to a concept that incorporates vertical competition leading ultimately to the inclusion of the consumer in the definition of a commercial competitor.[39]

Monopolies and trade marks

It is apparent that the strength of a trade mark to a trader lies in the creation and the enforcement of a monopoly[40] on the use of a name[41] and its connection with specific types of goods. If I were able to use the name of my competitor on the same goods, then the confidence of the consumers on the meaning—whatever that may be—of the mark would collapse.[42]

It took many decades before consumer interests were consciously and purposefully recognized in the law of unfair competition. Indeed, it is only the consumer movement, which started in the early sixties, that has led to decisive statutory and case law development of unfair competition law in the direction of improved consumer protection.

[36] Personal freedom is now synonymous with economic freedom. Competition laws are there to protect individual and economic freedom and maintain an equilibrium in a market comprised by a multitude of buyers and sellers. See for example M. Freedman, *Capitalism and Freedom*, University of Chicago, 1962, at 1415.

Accordingly legal doctrines and institutions are there to balance the interests of: 'People [who] are rational maximizers of their satisfactions—all people in all of their activities that involve choice.' R.A. Posner, *The Problems of Jurisprudence*, Cambridge, 1990, at 353. Although unconditional as an argument, the maximisation of satisfaction is a valid guide.

[37] By prohibiting dishonesty in trade, unfair competition law can provide consumers with protection even in cases in which other branches of industrial property law do not provide for protection. What is unfair or dishonest largely depends on the economic and social realities at a given time and place. *The Role of Industrial Property in the Protection of Consumers*, WIPO, 1983, at 59.

[38] It must be noted, however, that a general theory of a tort of unfair competition is mainly established in civil law jurisdictions. In the United Kingdom, it is only 'passing off' that constitutes a tort and in the United States, despite the existence of a general provision in the Lanham Act, in reality it is an extension of passing off.

[39] In *Colligan v Activities Club of New York Ltd*, US Court of Appeals, 2d Circuit, 1971, 422 F. 2d 686, *cert. denied*, 404 US 1004, 92 S. Ct 559, 30 L. Ed. 2d 557, it was held that section 43(a) Lanham Act, despite its general reference to 'any person', provided for an action only available to competitors. See B. Morris, Note 54, below.

[40] Keeping always in mind that:

Even a mark used in furtherance of a monopoly scheme is *an instrument only, not an incarnation, of the monopoly*. We should, therefore, be on guard that 'the tendency of a principle to expand itself to the limit of its logic' (Cardozo, The Nature of the judicial process [1922] at 51) does not leave us with a theorem of trademarks as vehicles of monopoly power which has no foundation in the concepts of our modern law, no matter how closely trademarks may have been linked in their early history to the then existing, differently constituted monopolies (*emphasis added*)

P.H. Behrendt, 'Trademarks and Monopolies—Historical and Conceptual Foundations', [1961] 51 TMR 853 to 865 at 862.

[41] On the linguistic approach towards the monopoly on parts of language, see R.C. Dreyfuss, 'Expressive Genericity: Trademarks As Language in the Pepsi Generation', [1990] 65 *Notre Dame Law Review* 397 to 424 at 412 to 424.

[42] Consumers would not economise by trusting a mark and finally one would arrive to a point where massive state intervention would be needed to establish some minimal standards. This argument is strengthened by the result of dilution of a mark. The basis for this doctrine was formulated by F.I. Schechter in 1927: 'The Rational Basis of Trademark Protection', in 40 Harv. LRev. 813, 22 TM Bulletin at 152, or 60 TMR at 342 and has found its way in developed form into the Trade Mark Acts of numerous countries.

Without the monopoly power granted to them, trade marks could not fulfil any of their functions.[43]

The desirability of product differentiation and monopoly protection of trade marks was challenged a couple of decades ago.[44] Here, there will be no argument for or against product differentiation, because it is apparent that in real terms today such a discussion is futile, given (western) economic reality and consumer demand, real or provoked.[45] The validity of this question for developing countries is undermined by other, more basic, economic and political arguments. But trade marks and industrial property rights in general became a banner on the debate on economic development and trade relations.[46]

Given the need for monopoly protection, the argument today has shifted from the fundamental question of the existence of a monopoly to its extent and scope of protection and therefore accordingly to its regulation.[47]

From the outset monopolies are a state-given entity and their extent can vary according to the corresponding social and economic requirements. Controversy stems from the effort to strike a balance between free, deregulated or self-regulated markets and the urge to intervene and regulate.[48] In the long run economic rules can themselves heal market ills, but the state in its role as a regulator of economic activities—public expenditures and taxes being the other two interventionist weapons—has the primary duty to create the legal framework of a market economy. The extent and the fine-tuning of the trade mark monopoly is therefore a rightful objective.

The anti-dilution doctrine enables the trade mark proprietor to protect his mark against forms of use where the traditional requirement of likelihood of confusion is absent. It is not the deception or confusion as to origin of goods against which the doctrine provides protection, but the detrimental effect to the distinctive character and unique quality of the mark. That is brought about by the association of the mark used by the defendant in a commercial context with the plaintiff's trade mark.

The value of the registered mark here lies in the ability to carve out a niche in the market through the persuasive message which the trade mark conveys to the public: the mark's selling power.

The trade mark can only perform this function properly if it is unique to a single proprietor. As a consequence, confrontation with the mark or sign by someone else, whether used on similar or dissimilar goods, conveys a different message and does not spark off the immediate conscious or unconscious association in the minds of the public with the trade mark proprietor's product. The message becomes ambiguous.

[43] D. Shanahan, 'The Trademark Right: Consumer Protection or Monopoly?' [1982] 72 TMR 233 to 251 at 234 to 235: 'It is true that the law confers a limited monopoly on the trademark owner, but this is but a necessary consequence of the public interest in excluding rival traders from the field in question.'

[44] Reference here will only be made to E.H. Chamberlin, *The Theory of Monopolistic Competition*, Harvard University Press, 1933, who devised a theory of monopolistic competition, somewhere between extreme monopoly and extreme competition, stating at 61 that: 'If a trademark marks offers one product as different from another, it gives the seller of that product a monopoly, from which we might argue that there is no competition.' Therefore at 270 he argues that the protection of trade marks is the protection of monopoly. If goods were *perfectly standardised*, then there would be no need for a monopoly since the consumers would have no reason to discriminate between products. So by defining high quality standards, the only necessary protection afforded to a producer would be against the forging of his name. As far as product differentiation is concerned, Chamberlin limited its desirability, describing it at 273 as: 'A question of weighing variety at a higher price against a more uniform product at a lower one.'

[45] On this, see Scherer and Ross, Note 25 above at 600 to 608.

[46] One only needs to look at the current round of GATT negotiations and trade related issues of intellectual property. B. Pretnar, 'Industrial Property and Related Trade Policy in Less-Developed Countries: Economic Appraisal of Legal Concepts', [1990] 21 IIC 782 to 799.

[47] R.S. Brown, *Advertising and the Public Interest: Legal Protection of Trade Symbols*, at 1206: 'In an acquisitive society, the drive for monopoly advantage is a very powerful pressure. Unchecked, it would no doubt patent the wheel, copyright the alphabet, and register the sun and moon as exclusive trade-marks.'

[48] The monopoly to the use of a name, enforced by the state, already is an intervention in an ideally free market.

Synthesis of the Three: A Consumer Trade Mark?

For the present purposes, a minimalistic definition of a trade mark is chosen that only indirectly acknowledges the multitude of functions mentioned above. Nevertheless it opens the door to a flexible origin function, easily expandable in order to accommodate all the modern attributes of trade marks. Thus trade marks are: 'indicating source of origin of the goods bearing such. The word origin denotes at least that the goods are issued as vendible goods under the aegis of the proprietor of the trade mark who thus assumes responsibility for them'.[49]

If fair play rules are to be set and enforced, the state, in its legislative and law-enforcing task, is the most suitable actor to provide them.[50]

In practice and for the present purposes, this means that trade mark, consumer protection and unfair competition—or passing off—rules can become the tools to create a level playing-field for all participants in the economic game, traders and consumers alike.

The reigning trend[51] is that these are three separate sets of rules, developed concurrently, but independently.

In reality, though, markets do not consist of sealed compartments. They are places where fair traders, fly-by-night marketeers, rational and naive consumers co-exist.[52] Consumers themselves cannot obtain complete protection because they are not able to participate directly in the rules that govern competition.[53]

One of the key aspects of consumer emancipation is to take away their dependence on competitors to bring proceedings[54] and acquire their own legal standing.[55] It is to be hoped

---

[49] S.P. Ladas, 'Trademark Licensing and the Antitrust Law', [1973] 63 TMR 245 to 266, at 248.

[50] Besides, the state has the role of the guardian of people's pursuit of welfare, the reallocator of resources—targeting an improvement in economic efficiency—and the redistributor of wealth—fulfilling its social purposes. This economic approach to state intervention is simplistic, being more the result of observation than concrete economic knowledge.

Part 6 of P.A. Samuelson and W.D. Nordhaus, *Economics*, McGraw Hill Book Co., 1989, offers a basic, but excellent and unbiased, review of the different economists' approaches to state intervention and the economic role of modern government. See Dworkin in Note 31 above.

[31] Worldwide separate provisions govern anti-trust, trade mark, unfair competition and consumer protection. Directly, but mostly indirectly, one common rationale of these laws is the protection of the consumer.

[52] F.I. Schechter in 'Trade Morals and Regulation: The American Scene', [1937] 6 *Fordham Law Review*, commentating on what is the ordinary course of business sanctioned by the court as fair competition, refers to the answer given to Robert Louis Stevenson by Old Tembinok, a trader of the South Seas who classified people who did business with him under three heads: ' "He cheat a litty"—"He cheat aplenty"—and "I think he cheat too much." "For the first two classes," says Stevenson, "he expressed perfect toleration; sometimes, but not always, for the third." '

[53] For the situation in the United Kingdom, see for example A. Booy, 'A Half-way House for Unfair Competition in the United Kingdom—A Practitioner's Plea', [1991] 12 EIPR 439, who argues that passing off for example does not protect consumers directly, because only competitors, or potential competitors of the defendant can sue to obtain redress for a tort based on a misrepresentation practised on consumers. Similar problems exist when the consumer wants to sue for deceit.

For another, American, aspect of restrictive interpretation of unfair competition provisions, see D.B. Wolf, 'Effective Protection Against Unfair Competition Under S. 44 of the Lanham Act', [1992] 82 TMR 33 to 57, where it is noted that some significant rights, described in section 44(h) and (i), could carry section 43(a) even further. Section 44(h) provides that certain foreign nationals are entitled to 'effective protection against unfair competition' and that US citizens have 'the same benefits'. These provisions are, however, not enforced, being largely ignored in domestic and international cases.

[54] In the United States section 43(a) of the Lanham Trademark Act does—in theory—give any person who believes he is likely to be damaged by the use of a false description or representation, a form of action. A strong case for consumer class action has therefore been made by B. Morris, 'Consumer Standing to Sue for False and Misleading Advertising Under Section 43(a) of the Lanham Trademark Act', [1987] 17 *Memphis State University Law Review* 417 to 438.

In the European Community, the process towards emancipation of the consumer has found legal recognition, indirectly via the Commission's interventions through the Social Charter, Product Standardisation and its present

that this evolution will come, where it is not already present, with further integration of consumer and unfair competition laws, although there are authoritative advocates of the opposite view.[56]

The field of trade marks, however, has generally escaped from being engulfed in this process. It is still considered to be an unmitigated monopoly. Many commentators argue that the main function of a trade mark is the origin function. By shifting the emphasis to the quality function alone, one may inadvertently become a supporter of fragmented markets, where the principle of international exhaustion is neutralised.[57]

Two suggestions can be made in connection with the trade mark functions debate. First, that the emphasis has to be shifted once more: this time from the false dilemma of origin or quality trade marks to the need for a consumer trade mark or better, a notion of a trade mark that incorporates both protection of industrial property and the consumer.

Second, in a similar vein, it would be much more productive and efficacious to strengthen the relation between trade mark and unfair competition laws, since unfair competition is the most appropriate mechanism for the integration of the diverging interests of competitors and consumers.

The result of these proposals can be termed: the 'consumer trade mark'.

In reality both suggestions stem from the existence of a common denominator which has shaped the three sets of rules: the need to regulate the market fairly and efficiently.

The difficulties in such an endeavour may appear huge, but it seems that certain, variable,

---

quest for a reapproachment of the citizen to the core of the European Community, and directly via the community Trade Mark Regulation. Articles 33 and 46 allow consumer group action for revocation on the grounds contained in Article 6.

See also Professor Vito M. Mangini, 'Advertising, Consumer Protection and the New Italian Law of January 25, 1992', WIPO, 1992 Annual meeting of the International Association for the advancement of teaching and research in intellectual property, who at page 5 states that under the new Italian law individuals are entitled to bring an action before the anti-trust authority on advertising matters.

[55] On the question of conflicts between identical or confusingly similar marks arising during the filing of an application to register, opposition proceedings, actions of cancellation or rectification of a registration and finally during infringement proceedings, WIPO states:

> It is in the interest of consumers that their concerns should be taken into account in such proceedings, since one of the main purposes of the system of marks is to protect the consumer against deception and confusion in connection with the use of marks ... One possible approach may be for the relevant law, as a general rule, to allow any 'interested party' to initiate and participate in opposition, infringement and cancellation proceedings.

The Role of Industrial Property in the Protection of Consumers, WIPO 1983, at 19.

[56] See for example E.K. Beier, 'The Law of Unfair Competition in the European Community—Its Development and Present Status', [1985]. 16 IIC 139 to 164 at 164, who concludes:

> The future unfair competition law of the Community should not lean too strongly towards consumer interests. It must give equal effect to the interests of all market participants ... for the European Economic Community a model of an integrated unfair competition and consumer protection law with a neutral position on goals of structural policy would seem even more appropriate than for individual member states.

[57] See Cornish, Note 13 above, who at 402 presents the recent apologia for trade marks as indicators of origin as a result of the reaction of the courts against the attempt to use the quality function as means to: 'erect trade marks into barriers against the international movement of an enterprise's products'. It appears that all this, as Cornish says, 'is a theoretical concern with "function" that is essentially defensive'.

See *Revlon v Cripps & Lee* [1980] FSR 85, where Revlon was not able to establish that the sale of a shampoo independently imported into the United Kingdom amounted to passing off. See *Cinzano v Java Kaffeegeschäfte* [1974] 2 CMLR 21. For the results of existing differences in quality, see *Colgate-Palmolive v Markwell Finance* [1988] RPC 283, where it seems that a multinational enterprise may partition the international market simply by marketing goods of different qualities in different national markets. Can this lead to unjustifiable dumping practices into economies where the consumer is not well protected? What is a 'good' branded product must be good for all. For qualified differences in climate for example—and the resulting partitioning, see *Castrol v Automotive Oil* [1983] RPC 315.

For a recent comment on the US perspective, see also H. Hahm, 'Gray Market Goods: Has a Resolution Been Found?', [1991] 81 TMR 58 to 94.

combinations are viable and that the nucleus for such changes already exists.[58] For the consumer trade mark to take practical effect, major changes in legislation are not needed. Slight adjustments are enough, since one could merely superimpose consumer participation over the existing legislation.

The result of these suggestions would be a further liberalisation of the market, only this time in a new direction. The consumer would be able to have his own legal standing and act according to his economic interest. The practical result would be that in addition to the Ombudsman or Commissioner of Fair Trading power, there would be the unpatronising exercise of the consumer's right. In the future, if consumers were able to defend their rights directly and efficiently, either individually or through associations, the need for state intervention would decrease.

Viability of the Consumer Trade Mark

As seen above, advertising has increased the value of a trade mark. A brand now epitomises the perceived quality of a product. Therefore misrepresentation or deceit through improper use of a trade mark also addresses quality. Forms of deceit are double-faced.

When a trade mark is not genuine, the deceit lies in its supposed connection to the origin of the goods. This creates no special problems. Registered trade marks are strong enough in most jurisdictions to protect consumer and original trade mark owner against an infringer. There are also attempts through international co-operation to combat counterfeiting.[59] In the absence of a registered trade mark or in the grey area surrounding trade mark infringement, unfair competition or the law of passing off can provide sufficient relief.[60] When the competitor does not take any measure, then the state or the consumer can undertake some form of action.[61]

Problems begin to appear when a trade mark is used by its owner so as to take unfair advantage[62] of its perceived 'quality'. In this case the deceit lies in the mismatch of justified consumer expectations, arising from the trade mark, and the product reality. It should be

---

[58] In some European countries consumer associations were able to bring actions. In Germany section 13(2)(3) of the Act Against Unfair Competition allows consumer organisations to bring action under section 1 of the same Act, thus for example addressing telephone advertising: *Telephone Advertising II*, Bundesgerichtshof, 8 June 1988, Case I ZR 178/87, [1991] 22 IIC 112. And in France the Cour de Cassation upheld a trial court decision, imposing on a restaurateur an administrative fine and awarding damages to a general interest organisation (Association Générale des Usages de la Langue Française), because contrary to the requirement for the use of French in all matters of commerce (Article 1 Statute 12 December 1975), the restaurant issued only menus in English, [1987] 18 IIC at 575. Unfortunately in 1987 a US attempt to introduce a consumer right to sue on false and deceptive advertising under s. 43A of the Lanham Act was dropped as a trade off against the introduction of a federal dilution statute. See J. Gilson, 'A Federal Dilution Statute: Is It Time?', [1993] 83 TMR 108 to 122 at 115.

[59] R. Knaak, 'National and International Efforts Against Trademark Counterfeiting. A Progress Report', [1988] 19 IIC 581 to 606.

[60] On the expectancy for passing off to develop to a doctrine of unfair competition in common law jurisdictions, see J. Adams, 'Is There a Tort of Unfair Competition', [1985] JBL 26 to 33, G. Dworkin, 'Unfair Competition: Is the Common Law Developing a New Tort?', [1979] 2 EIPR 241 to 247 and W.R. Cornish, 'Unfair Competition: A Progress Report', [1972] 12 JSPTL 126 to 147, and 'Unfair Competition and the Consumer in England', [1974] 5 IIC 73 to 87 at 74:

> In comparison with many continental systems, English law on the subject appears to be a set of isolated instances. The justification for the English approach has been that every new imposition of liability is a potential restraint upon competition, which accordingly requires a special case to be made for the protection of a particular interest.

[61] See for example the UK 1968 Trade Descriptions Act.

[62] On what may constitute a false trade description, see R.J. Bragg, *Trade Descriptions*, Clarendon Press, 1991, at 22 to 48.

stressed here that the perception of quality is not necessarily the result of prior experience or rational decisions, but of marketing techniques and excessive advertising.[63]

The power of trade marks can be exercised in order to diversify products, to license the mark, or even to get a quick profit by lowering the quality of a product marketed under a reputable mark.

In the case of product diversification, problems will arise when it coincides with a deterioration of quality.

Problems also exist in the case of licensing and of possible consumer deception as to the consistency of quality. Trade mark licensing, however, is a regulated activity and in most cases there are provisions which insist on quality controls on behalf of the licensor. But, in many cases the statutory provisions regarding quality control are not enforceable. The legislators tend to disregard or abolish them.[64] Even in the case where contractual quality clauses exist, the consumer has no standing to invoke them. One would wish to enable the consumer to initiate some form of proceedings to enforce such clauses despite the fact that he is not a party to the agreement. His power to intervene could be based on his direct interest in the enforcement of quality control clauses.

Thus although competition between traders and consumers is acknowledged in general economic and political terms, in the question of trade marks that are regulated as between competitors, consumers have no legal standing, despite the fact that they are the only valid yardstick as to the existence and the extent of infringement. Competition, in conventional terms, only describes the relationship between producers trying to gain entry to and maintain a position on a market, or the relationship between consumers *inter se* trying to get the best buy on the market.[65]

Rules addressing this form of relationship basically regulate the behaviour of parties of similar status[66] but could also be used to mitigate the differences in status between competitors and consumers.

---

[63] As shown above.

[64] It is questionable even if such controls suffice. 'Violators of the trade mark licensing rules are not always, or indeed often, subjected to retribution or penalized by losing the trade mark.' A.M. Marks, 'Trademark Licensing—Towards a More Flexible Standard', [1988] 78 TMR 641 to 658 at 641.

In the United Kingdom it seems that the new Trade Mark Law will not contain such provisions. See White Paper, *Reform of Trade Marks Law*, HMSO, 1990, Cm 1203, 4.37, at 26.

In a perverse way English judges' reluctance to extend passing off in character merchandising cases, not recognising the licensing tactics of industry, was a limitation on the monopoly conferred by the ownership of a symbol:

> It was not established by the evidence that [the growth of merchandising had] yet arisen ... but there may come a time when the system of character merchandising will have become so well known to the man in the street that immediately he sees 'Kojakpops' he will say to himself: 'They must have a licence from the person who owns the rights in the television series'.

Per Walton J in *Tavener Rutledge Ltd v Trexapalm Ltd* [1977] RPC 275 at 280. An anachronistic approach in economic terms, but interesting in its distrust towards the people in industry. See also Note 30 above.

The time came in *Mirage Studios v Counter Feat Clothing Co.* [1991] FSR 145.

[65] Competition rules are either a game-like book of rules of the competitive struggle, or in their anti-trust capacity, laws preventing the unnatural 'peace' in the competitive game. R. Callmann, 'What is Unfair Competition', [1940] 28 *Georgetown Law Journal* 585 to 607 at 604.

When reference is made to buyers, reference is being made to them as consumers and not as strong industrial buyers who could exercise monopsony power. This falls in the regulation of vertical restraints.

[66] D.M. McClure, 'Trademarks and Unfair Competition: A Critical History of Legal Thought', [1979] 69 TMR 305 to 356 at 305 to 306:

> The broader area of business regulation proscribes such behavior as false advertising, defamation or disparagement of a competitor, inducing breach of contract and refusals to deal, and theft of trade secrets and customer lists, and predatory pricing. Separate from this law of unfair practices is a body of antitrust law and economics which is on a collision course with the law recognising exclusive rights in intellectual property.

Having established the ratio for an independent consumer, the authors submit that the ultimate penalty for using a trade mark as a tool for deceit should be the expunction of that mark from the register,[67] making sure at the same time that the mark will not re-enter the market unless confusion and deception can be avoided. Analogies could be drawn from the 'unclean hands' theory, under which it is possible indirectly to consider trade marks as guarantees of quality. Courts have not hesitated to refuse protection for their owners, stripping them of their monopoly because of their 'unclean hands'. In *Independent Baking Powder Co. v Boorman*,[68] for example, the owner of the trade mark, who had secretly substituted one of the ingredients of the marked product, was denied relief when a competitor took on the same mark. A similar result was reached in *Mulhens & Kropff, Inc. v Ferd Meulhens, Inc.*,[69] where the question was the change of the formula of '4711'. It was held that the continuation of trade mark protection could not be justified when a variation of the formula resulted in an inferior or different product. In the similar facts of *Reuter (R.J.) Co. Ltd v Muhlens*,[70] in the United Kingdom, the opposite result was reached. Despite the fact that the courts later avoided such solutions, fearing that the result would be even more confusion for the consumers and an erosion of the trade mark—*Ames Publishing Co. v Walker Davis Publications, Inc.*[71] and *US Jaycees v Philadelphia Jaycees*[72]—the approach was reaffirmed in *Menendez v Faber, Coe & Gregg, Inc.*[73] and *Urecal Corp. v Masters*[74] where the misrepresentation had to do with the core of the trade mark.

It is also the territorial character of intellectual property laws that, even when harmonised, urges the development of a coherent and broad basis of a tort of unfair competition,[75] which would encompass all the interests involved in commerce.[76]

The harmonisation and expansion of consumer protection laws, as welcome as it may be, is not sufficient, because it only sets minimum standards. As has been stated above, consumers themselves are handicapped by the fact that information is not readily available to them. It is also true that legal action available to consumer organisations or individual consumers is money-and time-consuming.[77] What is needed is more information, more access to it, more

---

Unfair competition, even when not recognised as a separate tort, as in some common law jurisdictions, is covering the above-mentioned subjects. As to the second question: 'the compatibility of the trade mark monopoly and the anti-trust laws': although this does not feature in the core of the present discussion, it is hoped that it has been shown above that the only workable trade mark would be one protected by monopoly. It is the extent of the monopoly that is underlined by controversy.

[67] This could only occur in extreme cases of intentional behaviour.

[68] 175 F. 448 (CC NJ 1910).

[69] 38 F. 2d 287 (SDNY 1929).

[70] [1953] 70 RPC 102.

[71] 372 F. Supp. 1 (ED Pa. 1974).

[72] 639 F. 2d 134 (3d Cir. 1981).

[73] 345 F. Supp. 527 (SDNY 1972).

[74] 413 F. Supp. 873 (ND Ill. 1976).

[75] ... by prohibiting dishonest trade, unfair competition law can provide consumers with protection even in cases in which other branches of industrial property law do not provide for protection. What is unfair or dishonest largely depends on the economic and social realities at a given time and place. This is what makes unfair competition law particularly adaptable to changing circumstances and realities and therefore, a potential powerful instrument in protecting consumers. Unfair competition law can furnish a solid legal framework and yet provide a sufficiently flexible standard for formulating and applying measures which can be at the same time sensitive to the particular and ever-changing social and economic conditions of consumers in a particular country and effective to combat the specific types of dishonest trade practices which give rise to concern.
The Role of Industrial Property in the Protection of Consumers, WIPO, 1983, at 59.

[76] On the difficulties of harmonisation of unfair competition law, even in the European Community, see G. Schricker, 'European Harmonisation of Unfair Competition Law—A Futile Venture?', [1991] 22 IIC 788 to 801 at 798 to 801.

[77] J. Hughes, 'The Philosophy of Intellectual Property', [1988] 77 Geo LJ 287 at 306: 'People rarely go to court

consumer education, and an open mind to class action which could become the fiat for consumer action in the cases where any individual remuneration would be minimal.

Even a small change to the courts' attitude[78] can, by expanding the doctrine of unfair competition[79] and by demolishing revered barriers, create a broad theoretical basis for a tort of unfair competition and serve as a catalyst for the approximation of trade mark and consumer protection rules. The examples of the dormant[80] provisions in Australian Trade Practices Act 1974, where in section 52(1) it is provided that: 'A corporation shall not, in trade or commerce, engage in conduct that is misleading or deceptive or is likely to mislead or deceive', the uncertainty about the expansion or constraint of passing off in the United Kingdom,[81] and the lasting debate on the legal and social standing of the consumer in the European Community and the United States, strengthen the argument that the nucleus for change exists.

---

unless something valuable is at stake. When intellectual property is created more systematically, such as through legislation, the resulting property doctrines seem less singularly oriented towards rewarding social value.'

[78] The approach towards unfair competition as displayed by Deane J, baptising unfair competition 'idiosyncratic' in *Moorgate Tobacco Co. Ltd v Phillip Morris Ltd and Another*, at 88 (1984) 59 ALJR 77, displays a fundamental unwillingness even to consider unfair competition as a viable option for conflict resolution. His comment reflects the general fear that by allowing cross-breeding or wild growth of diverse rules, the lid on growth of monopolistic protection would be lifted with unforeseen results.

International News Service v Associated Press, 248 US 215 (1918) had given unfair competition its independent doctrinal base, recognising a quasi-property interest in news, where the value of it as the fruit of someone's labour was in danger of being usurped by another, or in the words of M. Pitney J (63 L. ed 211 (1918) at 219 to 221):

> The fault in reasoning lies in applying as a test the right of the complainant as against the public, instead of considering the right of complainant and defendant, competitors in business, as between themselves. The right of the purchaser of a single newspaper to spread knowledge of its contents gratuitously, for any legitimate purpose not unreasonably interfering with complainant's right to make merchandise of it, may be admitted; but to transmit that news for commercial use, in competition with complainant which is what defendant has done and seeks to justify,is a very different matter. In doing this, defendant, by its very act, admits that it is taking material that has been acquired by complainant as the result of organisation and the expenditure of labour, skill and money and which is saleable by complainant for money, and that defendant in appropriating it and selling it as its own, is endeavouring to reap where it has not sown, and by disposing of it to newspapers that are competitors of complainant's members is appropriating to itself the harvest of those who have sown. Stripped of all disguises, the process amounts to an unauthorised interference with the normal operation of complainant's legitimate business precisely at the point where the profit is to be reaped, in order to divert a material proportion of the profit from those who have earned it to those who have not; with special advantage to defendant in the competition because of the fact that it is not burdened with any part of the expense of gathering news. The transaction speaks for itself, and a court of equity ought not to hesitate long in characterizing it as unfair competition in business ... Regarding the news, therefore, as but the material out of which both parties are seeking to make profits at the same time and in the same field, we hardly can fail to recognise that for this purpose, and as between them, it must be regarded as quasi-property, irrespective of the rights of either as against the public.

Some US courts have been keen to pick up on and develop this rationale and recognise the flexibility of unfair competition, stating that:

> The theoretic basis [of the law of unfair competition] is obscure, but the birth and growth of this branch of the law is clear. It is a persuasive example of the law's capacity for growth in response to the ethical, as well as the economic needs of society. As a result of this broad background, the legal concept of unfair competition has evolved as broad and flexible doctrine with a capacity for further growth to meet changing conditions. There is no complete list of the activities which constitute unfair competition.

Dior v Milton (1956) 9 Misc 2d 425, as quoted by J.T. McCarthy, *Trademarks and Unfair Competition*, Bancroft-Whitney, 1984, at 21, Note 4.

[79] See R. Callman, 'He Who Reaps Where He has not Sown: Unjust Enrichment in the Law of Unfair Competition', [1942] 55 HLR 595 to 614, who demonstrates that through the incorporation of the doctrine of unjust enrichment into the law of unfair competition, its theoretical base has been expanded.

[80] For the definitions and restrictions see J. McKeough and A. Stewart, *Intellectual Property in Australia*, Butterworths, 1991, at 293 to 295 and for the connection of passing off and unfair competition, at 285 to 293.

[81] The principles of *Erven Warnink v Townend (Advocaat)* [1980] RPC 31, as perceived in later contradictory cases, can go either way.

Conclusion

It is clear that a re-establishing of the *locus standi* of the consumer in the legitimisation of trade mark monopolies faces difficulties that seem insurmountable. For example: what are justified consumer expectations? How does one define deceit in the case of consumer disappointment? What is the strength of the mark in question? Are there not enough existing consumer protection laws? Do we want to open the floodgates of litigation? It was not the purpose of this article to answer these questions in detail. It has been shown above that it would only be in strong cases of deceit that the propositions contained in this article would take effect. It is also clear that the courts and the legislators already face such problems. Difficulties in tackling them cannot serve as an excuse to avoid facing them, but should only serve as a strong initiative for a fresh approach, questioning the opposite extreme belief: that trade marks are there and the monopoly will be an ever-expanding one. Something is worth protecting, not only because it is worth stealing, but also because it is worthy of protection. The economics of the judicial system will then decide as to the viability and the efficiency of protection.

The approach maintained in this article may also make it easier to consider an expansion of the doctrine of unfair competition and the affiliated monopoly regulation. One of the strongest arguments against expansion is that monopolies will become uncontainable. The approach of giving an additional right to common folks, who are after all the recipients of trade mark communication, may allow one safely to strengthen the trade mark monopoly of the broadcasters of trade mark communication.

The 'consumer trade mark' also allows protection by adjusting existing rules and proceedings. As shown, these rules, dealing with regulating competition in the market-place, already address consumer protection in an indirect manner. By allowing the consumer to participate directly in application, opposition, cancellation and infringement proceedings, there will be no need for major new legislation.

As far as judicial and administrative procedures to accommodate consumer action are concerned, much depends on the legal system of any particular country. Consumers should be able to bring action individually or collectively, by *amicus curiae*, consumer associations or semi-public organisations, and they should be able to enforce their rights through speedy and inexpensive proceedings. Small claims, market courts and intervention in proceedings spring to mind here.

This will lead to a comprehensive system in which one is safely adding value to the medium of communication, but at the same time demanding that the message had better be correct.

Does the United Kingdom or the European Community Need an Unfair Competition Law?

[1995] 12 EIPR 568

AIDAN ROBERTSON AND AUDREY HORTON

Aidan Robertson, Wadham College, Oxford and 4 Raymond Buildings, Gray's Inn, London; Audrey Horton, Bird & Bird, London

> The countries of the Union are bound to assure to nationals of such countries effective protection against unfair competition.[1]

> To draw a line between fair and unfair competition, between what is reasonable and unreasonable, passes the power of the courts.[2]

English law does not have a tort of unfair competition.[3] Nor has such a tort been imposed on the United Kingdom by the European Community.[4] English law remains sceptical about the value of a law against unfair competition, despite the United Kingdom's international obligations.[5] As Gerald Dworkin has said, the very term 'unfair competition' is paradoxical:

> law and business morality overlap and the courts must apply their own standards to determine which unethical (and in that non-legal sense unfair), must remain legally permissible. There are those who would argue that such tasks should not be undertaken lightly by the courts.[6]

English law has traditionally refused to deal in concepts such as fairness or good faith in business,[7] leaving the market-place to determine its own morality without the force of legal

---

[1] Article 10*bis* Paris Convention for the Protection of Industrial Property.

[2] *Mogul Steamship Co v McGregor* (1889) 23 QBD 598, 626, *per* Fry LJ.

[3] For analysis of the position under common law, see W.R. Cornish, 'Unfair Competition? A progress report' (1972) 12 JSPTL 126; G. Dworkin, 'Unfair competition: is the common law developing a new tort?' [1979] EIPR 241; Burns, 'Unfair competition: a compelling need unmet' [1981] EIPR 311; A. Terry, 'Unfair competition and the misappropriation of a competitor's trade values' (1988) 51 MLR 296. See also the Report issued by the Association Internationale pour la Protection de la Propriété Industrielle, 1993/III, on 'Effective protection against unfair competition', at 125 to 132. For opinions on the debate, see A. Booy, 'A half-way house for unfair competition in the United Kingdom—a practitioner's plea' [1991] EIPR 439; J. Adams, 'Unfair competition: why a need is unmet' [1992] EIPR 259; and subsequent correspondence between L.T.C. Harms and J. Adams at [1993] EIPR 74.

[4] For a European perspective see F. Beier, 'The law of unfair competition in the European Community—its development and present status' [1985] EIPR 284; Schricker, 'European harmonisation of unfair competition law—a futile venture?' (1991) 22 IIC 788.

[5] See Compatibility of UK Law with International Treaty Obligations, below.

[6] [1979] EIPR 241.

[7] See, for example, *Walford v Miles* [1992] 2 AC 128 (*per* Lord Ackner, delivering the only reasoned judgment, at 138: 'A duty to negotiate in good faith is as unworkable in practice as it is inherently inconsistent with the position of a negotiating party.') This, however, has been questioned extra-judicially by Steyn J in his Royal Bank of Scotland Law Lecture 1991, delivered at Oxford University, 'The role of good faith in contract law: a hairshirt philosophy?'. Now Article 4(1) Unfair Terms in Consumer Contracts Regulations, I 1994/3159, requires the application of a test of good faith as a test of enforceability of certain contractual terms.

sanction. However, during the passage of the Trade Marks Act 1994 there was much lobbying from certain sections of industry to create new rights against unfair competition.[8] This was resisted by the Government and the new Act does not explicitly create any general right to restrain unfair competition.[9] That lobbying can be expected to continue in an attempt to keep unfair competition high on the law reform agenda.

This article examines whether the United Kingdom needs a specific unfair competition law, and, if so, what form it should take. To do so the article first examines the extent to which the Trade Marks Act 1994 gives additional protection beyond that currently available in English law against what would, both under international law and in other jurisdictions, be regarded as unfair competition. In doing so, the article provides a brief survey of unfair competition law in the United States and in continental European jurisdictions. It then considers the extent of interaction between European Community and national unfair competition laws, determining the extent to which civil unfair competition law provides greater protection than that available under English law, and whether there is a need for European harmonisation of unfair competition laws. Finally the article concludes by considering the extent of the need to introduce a new UK or EC law against unfair competition. It is suggested that there may be need for such a law harmonising unfair competition laws within the EC, but not by wholesale adoption of the civil model. Rather, the authors would propose that reform be restricted to certain problem areas specifically relating to trade marks currently not satisfactorily dealt with by UK or EC law, and that it take as its conceptual basis the doctrine of misappropriation developed under US law.

UK Law

It is accepted that there is at present no general right to restrain unfair competition. An attempt to persuade the Privy Council to develop such a concept in *Pub Squash* was met with judicial indifference.[10] English law is difficult to summarise succinctly, as it depends on the interaction of a number of torts, each of which has been developed in largely piecemeal fashion. As a *broad* generalisation,[11] it could be said that English law prevents unfair competition in three principal ways.

(1) *Passing off.* A may be restrained from misappropriating B's reputation in its goods by misleading B's customers, for example, by suggesting a connection or association with B's business. This is done by B bringing an action for passing off against A. The essence of this action is customer confusion. Unless B can show that its customers have been or are likely to be misled into confusing A's for B's goods or into making a false connection or association with B's business, it will not succeed.[12]

(2) *Inducing breach of contract and unlawful interference with contractual relations.* A may

---

[8] Consumer groups lobbied against new rights. The Consumers' Association magazine, *Which*, (March 1995, at 30), carried a survey which concluded that 'the overwhelming majority of shoppers are not confused by lookalike products'.

[9] The White Paper preceding the Trade Mark Act, 'Reform of Trade Marks Law' (Cm 1203, 1990), did not address the issue of a more general prohibition on unfair competition.

[10] [1981] RPC 429. The Privy Council chose to state that their Lordships expressed no opinion on the development of a tort of unfair competition by the US Supreme Court in *International News Service v Associated Press* (1918) 248 US 215. See further Unfair Competition Law in the United States, below.

[11] It is emphasised that this classification is necessarily general. The multiplicity of different tort actions, summarised by G. Dworkin, Note 3 above, makes it difficult to be completely comprehensive, but the authors believe that these categories cover the vast majority of cases.

[12] Most recently emphasised by Jacob J in *Hodgkinson and Corby Ltd v Wards Mobility Services Ltd* [1994] 1 WLR 1564.

be restrained from acquiring B's customers through unlawful means. This applies where A induces B's customers to break their contracts with B or otherwise unlawfully interferes with B's contractual relations.[13]

(3) *Defamation and injurious falsehood.* A may be restrained from acquiring B's customers by telling lies to B's customers about B or B's goods. In the case of lies about B, there is an action for defamation. In the case of lies about B's goods, there are actions for slander of goods and injurious falsehood.[14]

Seen in this way, the law emphasises the role of the customer. It is unfair competition to acquire customers by causing them to transfer their custom by (1) confusing them as to with whom they are doing business; (2) inducing them to break existing contracts with competitors, or (3) lying to them about competitors. Beyond these limits, attempts to attract customers from other competitors are considered legal.[15]

Indeed these categories may be further rationalised, and it may be seen that there are two underlying assumptions at work here. First, lying is a means of confusing customers as to reality. Hence, the essence of the law is that customers should not be confused. Secondly, the prohibition against inducing breach of contract should be seen as part of English law's regard for the 'sanctity' of contract.

The focus of English law relevant to unfair competition (as distinct from contract law) is to prevent customers being confused. Provided customers have available correct information about what and with whom they are dealing, and that bargains once struck are adhered to, the law is prepared to leave the proper functioning of the market to the free play of market forces. A similar attitude is taken by US federal and state laws.[16]

In continental Europe, while civil law jurisdictions also prevent customer confusion,[17] unfair competition law starts from the basis that its rationale is to enforce the 'honest usages' of the market-place. Beier summarises this as meaning that a trader was granted 'the right to restrain his competitors from causing him injury by unfair conduct'.[18] Thus the focus is not just on customer confusion, but on what is fair or ethical[19] commercial conduct. English law has eschewed this approach, and continues to focus on customer confusion, as two recent decisions of the English courts demonstrate.

(1) *Teenage Mutant Hero Turtles*

In *Mirage Studios v Counter-Feat Clothing*[20] (the *Teenage Mutant Hero [sic]*[21] *Turtles* case), an interlocutory injunction to restrain passing off was granted against the defendants, who had induced customers to believe that their clothes featuring cartoon characters were produced under licence from the plaintiff. This conclusion was based on the finding that the public would normally expect such clothing to be produced under licence, notwithstanding that the defendants had gone to some lengths to design clothing that would not require a licence

---

[13] See generally *Winfield and Jolowicz on Tort*, 1994 (14th edn) Chapter 18.

[14] See, for example, *Compaq Computers v Dell* [1991] FSR 93, noted by Cornish [1992] CLJ 231.

[15] There is some voluntary self-regulation of the content of advertising, through the Advertising Standards Authority's Code of Practice, the application of which is subject to judicial review: see *R v Advertising Standards Authority Ltd ex parte Vernons Organisation Ltd* [1993] 2 All ER 202.

[16] See Unfair Competition Law in the United States, below.

[17] Although some, notably German law, have an exaggerated view of what will confuse customers: see for criticism of German law in this respect, Shricker (1991) 22 IIC 788 at 794.

[18] See Beier [1985] EIPR 284.

[19] See P.J. Kaufmann, 'Passing Off and Misappropriation' (1986) IIC Studies, Vol. 9, at 7 to 16.

[20] [1991] FSR 145, Chancery Division (Browne-Wilkinson VC).

[21] The name was changed from the original US 'Ninja' Turtles at the insistence of the BBC, which broadcast the cartoon series on children's TV.

under any intellectual property right. By applying an extensive notion of what would cause customer confusion, based on the public's misapprehension of the legal niceties of intellectual property licensing (known in this field as character licensing), the court thus restrained commercial conduct which was arguably unfair, but did not actually involve the breach of any intellectual property right.[22] The fundamental requirement of customer confusion is stressed even as it is stretched further than previously before.

(2) *Elderflower Champagne*

Taittinger v Albev[23] (the *Elderflower Champagne* case) also displays this emphasis on the requirement of customer confusion. The plaintiffs brought an action in effect on behalf the French Champagne industry[24] seeking an injunction[25] to restrain the defendant, a small English producer of traditional fruit wines and cordials, from calling one of its products, a non-alcoholic sparkling fruit drink, 'Elderflower Champagne'. The Court of Appeal, overturning Sir Mervyn Davies' judgment at first instance, granted the injunction. It did so because there was sufficient evidence of a likelihood of confusion as the trial judge had held,[26] but also found, contrary to what had been held previously, that there was sufficient likelihood of damage, both in loss of sales of champagne and in loss of distinctiveness leading to loss of reputation in the name 'Champagne'.[27] What is important to stress is that the loss of distinctiveness is relevant only to assessing the likelihood of damage caused by the defendant. It would not be sufficient in itself to form the basis for an action. That is why the court was so concerned to find that there were consumers capable of being confused into thinking 'Elderflower Champagne' was in fact real French Champagne, Sir Mervyn Davies' 'simple unworldly man' proving a more appealing prospect for this purpose than the 'moron in a hurry',[28] despite the fact that no evidence of actual confusion was adduced at trial.[29]

Both the *Teenage Mutant Hero Turtles* and *Elderflower Champagne* cases push at the boundaries of the tort of passing off, while remaining firmly wedded to the necessity of showing customer confusion. The courts have as yet not seen the need to break free from that

---

[22] Arguably there was a breach of the plaintiff's copyright by the defendants, who had however attempted to avoid substantially reproducing the artistic works in question. Browne-Wilkinson VC (as he then was) stated that he 'would not like to say [at interlocutory stage] what the final outcome of any case based in copyright would be', Note 20 above, at 154.

[23] [1993] FSR 641, Chancery Division (Sir Mervyn Davies) and Court of Appeal.

[24] The first plaintiff should not require introduction to the readers of this up-market publication; the second and third plaintiffs, the Comité Interprofessionnelle du Vin de Champagne and the Institut National des Appellations d'Origine, regulated the Champagne industry and wine appellations of origin respectively.

[25] Robert Reid QC, sitting as a deputy judge of the Chancery Division, had accepted an undertaking from the defendant at the interlocutory stage and would, if necessary, have granted an interlocutory injunction, [1992] FSR 647.

[26] *Per* Sir Mervyn Davies at first instance: 'There is the simple unworldly man who has in mind a family celebration and knows that champagne is a drink for celebrations. He may know nothing of elderflower champagne as an old cottage drink. Seeing "Elderflower" on the label with below the name "Champagne" he may well suppose that he is buying champagne. Since the simple man I have in mind will know little of champagne prices, he is likely to suppose that he has found champagne at a price of £2.45. I do not mean that I now refer to any majority part of the public or even to any substantial section of the public, but to my mind there must be many members of the public who would suppose that the defendant's "Elderflower" is champagne. Thus it is that I find it established that the defendants' misrepresentation is a misrepresentation that is calculated to deceive', Note 23 above, at 654.

[27] *Per* Peter Gibson LJ, *ibid.*, at 670, Mann LJ at 674 and Sir Thomas Bingham MR at 678.

[28] *Per* Peter Gibson LJ: 'It is not right to base any test on whether a moron in a hurry would be confused, but it is proper to take into account the ignorant and unwary' *Ibid.*, at 667.

[29] It should be added that a second ground for the decision was that the use of the name 'Champagne' by Allbev infringed Community rules on wine names, discussed below.

conceptual basis and establish a separate right against unfair competition.[30] If one then turns to look at the statutory provisions in the new Trade Marks Act 1994, however, one can see the emergence of some limited degree of protection against unfair competition not involving consumer confusion.

The UK Trade Marks Act 1994

The United Kingdom's Trade Marks Act 1994 was passed as a result of the adoption by the EC of the First Trade Marks Directive.[31] The Act has two main and two subsidiary purposes. Its main purposes are:

(1) to implement the Trade Marks Directive; and
(2) to enable the United Kingdom to ratify the Madrid Protocol, signed by the United Kingdom on 28 June 1989.

Its subsidiary purposes are:

(3) to enable the Secretary of State to make regulations consequent on the introduction of the Community Trade Mark Regulation; and
(4) to provide protection for well-known trade marks under Article 6 Paris Convention for the Protection of Industrial Property of 20 March 1883.

For present purposes, this article will concentrate on those aspects of the Act which are relevant to unfair competition. Nothing in the Act introduces a law of unfair competition *eo nomine*, but the Act does increase protection for trade mark owners, in four principal ways, which on analysis go some way to creating additional rights against unfair competition:

(1) a wider range of marks is now registrable;
(2) the scope of infringement of registered marks has been both expanded and restricted;
(3) 'anti-dilution' protection has been introduced; and
(4) protection is introduced for internationally well-known marks.

However, there are also two principal ways in which trade mark owners' rights have been limited by the Act, in addition to limitations on the scope of infringement:

(5) comparative advertising is now allowed; and
(6) the exhaustion of rights principle has been specifically introduced.

These will now be considered in turn.

---

[30] *Cadbury Schweppes v Pub Squash*, Note 10 above.
[31] First Council Directive (89/104) of 21 December 1988 to approximate the laws of the Member States relating to trade marks OJ 1989 L40/1. See White Paper on Reform of Trade Marks Law, Cm 1203, September 1990. Most provisions of the Act came into force on 31 October 1994. There was a delay in implementation of the Directive of 22 months, the deadline being 31 December 1992 under Article 16 Directive 89/104, 1989 OJ L40/1, as amended by Council Decision 92/10, 1992 OJ L6/35.

Registrable marks

Since a wider range of marks are registrable, a trade mark owner needs less recourse to the tort of passing off. Shapes,[32] sounds and even smells[33] are now registrable.

Expansion of scope of infringement of registered marks

The scope of registered trade mark infringement has been expanded by widening the concept of what constitutes infringement to include non-graphic use, and by increasing the range of infringing acts. These include, for example, oral infringement.[34]

On the other hand, the Act can be said to have limited trade mark owners rights to bring infringement proceedings in one important way. Sections 9 and 10 set out the rights conferred by a registered trade mark. The registered trade mark confers the right to stop use of a mark if there is a likelihood of confusion on the part of the public because the mark is identical or similar to the registered trade mark and is being used in relation to similar goods or services. This requirement of likelihood of confusion seems to equate registered trade mark law with what is currently the position, as has been seen, under passing off.

Likelihood of confusion includes 'the likelihood of association with the trade mark'.[35] Gielen[36] discusses the problems encountered with this definition of infringement. The problem is that likelihood of association is a wider concept in Benelux trade mark law than that of likelihood of confusion. Marks can be associated even if not confused. However, the Council Minutes for the meeting at which the Directive was adopted state that 'the Council and the Commission note that "likelihood of association" is a concept which in particular has been developed by Benelux case law', so the intent seems clear.

Association as interpreted by the Benelux court has been used to indicate similarity between marks, confusion not being used as a test. In *Union v Union Soleure*,[37] the Benelux Court of Justice decided that similarity was to be determined by all the circumstances of the case, including the distinctive power of the mark and auditory, visual or conceptual similarity in order to determine whether associations are evoked between the two marks. In *Anti-Monopoly*,[38] the owners of the *Monopoly* board game trade mark successfully enjoined the use of the name 'Anti-Monopoly' for an anti-capitalist board game, on the ground of association, not confusion.

It seems that this provision allows the development within the sphere of registered trade mark law of a similar anti-dilution concept as has been used in some, though not all, English passing-off cases (contrast *Lego*[39] with *Stringfellows*[40]). However, such a development under section 10(2) is restricted by the requirement that the marks be used for similar goods or services.

---

[32] The opposite position to that under the Trade Marks Act 1938: see *Re Coca Cola Trade Mark* [1985] FSR 315.
[33] Thus providing simpler protection against 'smell alike' copycat fragrances than under the Trade Marks Act 1938, *Chanel v Triton Packaging* (1993) IPD 16002.
[34] Section 103(2) Trade Marks Act 1994.
[35] Section 10(2) Trade Marks Act 1994.
[36] C. Gielen, 'Harmonisation of trade mark law in Europe' [1992] EIPR 262 at 266 to 267. See also A.W.J. Kamperman Sanders, 'Some frequently ask questions about the Trade Mark Act 1994' [1995] EIPR 67.
[37] Case A82/5, Decision of 20 May 1983, cited in footnote 22, [1992] EIPR 262, 266.
[38] Decision of 24 June 1977, cited in footnote 23, [1992] EIPR 262, 267.
[39] [1983] FSR 155.
[40] [1984] RPC 501.

Anti-dilution rights

Anti-dilution may be introduced, on the other hand, by section 10(3). This clause provides that infringement occurs where an identical or similar trade mark is used for different goods or services 'where the trade mark has a reputation in the United Kingdom and the use of the sign, being without due cause, takes unfair advantage of, or is detrimental to, the distinctive character of the repute of the trade mark'.

This concept also has its roots in Benelux trade mark law. Gielen cites the *Claeryn/Klarein*[41] decision of the Benelux Court of Justice, in which the use of the trade mark *Klarein* for toilet cleaner was successfully challenged by the owners of the mark *Claeryn* for Dutch gin. The court acknowledged that similar marks can affect the demand for unrelated products, for example where the loss of exclusivity in the mark means that the mark no longer immediately conjures up the immediate association with the goods for which it is registered, or where the appealing nature of the registered mark is affected by the infringing mark. Thus thinking of toilet cleaner at the same time as gin would affect the market for that gin.

Internationally well-known marks

Section 56 grants protection to the proprietor of a well-known trade mark, as that term is used under Article 6*bis* Paris Convention. A well-known trade mark is defined under section 56(1) as being the mark of a person who is a national, domiciled or has real and effective industrial or commercial presence in a member state of the Paris Convention, where that mark is well-known in the United Kingdom as being the mark of that person. This is whether or not that person carries on business or has any goodwill in the United Kingdom. The requirement that the mark be well-known in the United Kingdom seems to be narrower than provided in Article 6*bis*, which refers to the mark being well-known in the country of registration or use.

Section 56(2) gives such a person the right to restrain the use in the United Kingdom of an identical or similar trade mark for identical or similar goods or services, where such use is likely to cause confusion.[42] This might be applicable in cases such as *Budweiser*.[43]

However, there are two main ways in which trade mark owners' rights have been limited by comparison with the 1938 Act.

Comparative advertising

Use of a registered trade mark in comparative advertising will no longer be prohibited under section 10(6), provided:

(1) it is done for the purpose of identifying the goods or services as those of the proprietor or a licensee;

(2) it is use which is in accordance with honest practices in industrial or commercial matters; and

(3) does not without due cause take unfair advantage of or be detrimental to the distinctive character or repute of the trade mark.

---

[41] Decision of Benelux Court of Justice of 1 March 1975, referred to at [1992] EIPR 262 to 267. Other similar examples are cited in the text on that page.

[42] The owner of a well-known mark may also oppose registration of a later mark, under sections 5(3) and 61(1)(c) Trade Marks Act 1994.

[43] [1984] FSR 413.

The requirement that such use be in accordance with honest practices in industrial or commercial matters is an addition to what is specified in the Directive[44] and to that extent seems to be an incompatible restriction. However, it may be regarded as merely an articulation of the difference between 'due cause' and 'unfair advantage' and to that extent may be permissible.

Exhaustion of rights

The principle of exhaustion of rights is embodied by section 12, which removes the right of the proprietor to prohibit the use of a mark which it has applied itself or has been applied with its consent to goods put on the market in the European Economic Area (not just EC[45]). This principle does not apply where there are 'legitimate reasons' to oppose further dealings. An example is specified in the Act: where the condition of goods has been changed or impaired after first marketing. Gielen suggests[46] that *Colgate v Markwell Finance*[47] would be an example of this, but the authors would suggest that the difference in quality in that case occurred through the action of the trade mark owner. The Directive and the Act's examples both refer to changes being made after marketing, not before, that is, to events outside the trade mark owner's control. To allow different qualities to justify an exception to exhaustion of rights would go against the idea of free circulation of goods within the EEA.

Overall, therefore, the Directive as it has been implemented in the United Kingdom gives a greater degree of protection for registered trade marks than was previously the case. Some of the provisions do give protection against unfair competition, particularly those concerning the scope of infringement, anti-dilution and protection for internationally well-known marks. Others, in particular that relating to comparative advertising, are more restrictive than typical unfair competition laws. Moreover, as far as providing protection against unfair competition is concerned, the Act does nothing outside the field of registered trade marks. Whether more extensive registered trade mark protection would lead the English courts to conclude that there should be more extensive protection in tort for unregistered marks or more generally against unfair business practices seems doubtful.

Compatibility of UK Law with International Treaty Obligations

The United Kingdom is bound under international law by Article 10*bis* Paris Convention, which states:

(1) The countries of the Union are bound to assure to nationals of such countries effective protection against unfair competition.
(2) Any act of competition contrary to honest practices in industrial or commercial matters constitutes an act of unfair competition.
(3) The following in particular shall be prohibited:
   1. all acts of such a nature as to create confusion by any means whatever with the establishment, the goods, or the industrial or commercial activities, of a competitor;

---

[44] See Article 5(5) Trade Marks Directive.
[45] In addition to the 15 Member States of the EC, the EEA also comprises Iceland, Norway and Liechtenstein.
[46] [1992] EIPR 262 to 268.
[47] [1989] RPC 497.

2. false allegations in the course of trade of such a nature as to discredit the establishment, the goods, or the industrial or commercial activities, of a competitor;
3. indications or allegations the use of which in the course of trade is liable to mislead the public as to the nature, the manufacturing process, the characteristics, the suitability for their purpose, or the quantity, of the goods.

Broadly speaking (again), English law provides the protection required by Article 10(3). Passing off deals with paragraph 1, injurious falsehood or slander of goods with paragraph 2 and paragraph 3 is implemented through the Trade Descriptions Act 1968.

The main issue is whether Article 10(2) requires a wider degree of protection beyond the specifically enumerated examples in Article 10(3). That depends on what view is to be taken of the interpretation of the phrase 'honest practices in industrial or commercial matters', but in the absence of court with jurisdiction to decide such a point conclusively, it remains open to doubt whether the United Kingdom does comply with its international obligations on this point.

In summary, therefore, one can say that UK law does not recognise a specific law of unfair competition. However, there are difficulties in making this statement, not least (as has just been noted) that there is no conclusive definition of an unfair competition law. Instead, the UK lawyer must study other jurisdictions for evidence of what constitutes a law on unfair competition. Accordingly, the next two sections will summarise the principal features of US and European laws on unfair competition.

Unfair Competition Law in the United States

International News Service v Associated Press and the misappropriation doctrine

Unfair competition, in the form of a general tort of misappropriation separate from copyright or trade mark law, or any other specific form of intellectual property, first arose in the celebrated Supreme Court case of *International News Service v Associated Press*.[48] What was 'taken' in that case was 'hot news' relating to events in the First World War, gathered by Associated Press (AP) using its transmission facilities from the front line and sold to newspaper subscribers in the United States. International News Service (INS) telegraphed these 'hot stories' to the West Coast after they had been published in East Coast newspapers which subscribed to AP. In some cases Hearst newspapers on the West Coast, which subscribed to INS, were published before newspapers which subscribed to AP and thus took away AP's commercial advantage. The US Supreme Court, in a majority decision, held that although there was no copyright infringement (the 'hot stories' were not copied verbatim but generally rewritten on the underlying news idea) no breach of contract, or appropriation of confidential information, no violation of trade mark law, no attempt to palm off the goods of one party as those of another (there was no misrepresentation as to the source of the stories); nevertheless what had occurred was a wrong requiring a remedy. The mis-

---

[48] 248 US 215 (1918).

appropriation was famously characterised by the Supreme Court as INS 'endeavouring to reap where it has not sown'.[49]

Hence the elements of the US common law tort of misappropriation can be summarised as follows: (1) the plaintiff has expended time and effort in gathering news stories; (2) this work had transitory commercial value; and (3) INS had misappropriated this work, depriving AP of its anticipated profit. This doctrine involved no customer confusion, only unfair commercial advantage which did not involve violation of any intellectual property right. Were the misappropriation doctrine to be applied in the United Kingdom today, it could be utilised by brand owners against lookalike products to protect transient commercial advantages such as that given by new product packaging. However, it could be of more general application. It could take into account surrounding circumstances, such as deliberate positioning of a lookalike product on a supermarket shelf next to the branded product it resembles or even the ultimate delisting of the branded product after a period of time by a supermarket.

The misappropriation doctrine has had a rather chequered history since *AP v INS*. This is tied up with its status as a state-based doctrine and its interaction with the concept of federal pre-emption. The US Constitution's Supremacy Clause provides that state law must yield to any conflicting federal law, including, in this context, federal patent, design, copyright and trade mark laws.[50] After a period of uncertainty as to whether the misappropriation doctrine was pre-empted for matters which could have been, but which were in fact not, protected under federal laws, it seems to have been accepted in *Bonito Boats Inc. v Thunder Craft Boats Inc.*[51] that state laws against unfair trade practices are not pre-empted by federal statutes as long as they are not in direct conflict.

Statutory protection

That said, unfair competition, as the term is generally understood, is of course heavily regulated by US federal laws. In particular, section 43(a)[52] Lanham Act gives federal statutory protection against unfair competition consisting of false designations of origin and false descriptions. This section has therefore been frequently used in the United States to protect unregistered trade dress[53] and is broadly similar to the UK law of passing off.

---

[49] *Ibid.*, at 239. There were two dissents. Holmes J, concurred with by McKenna J, stated that there had been a misrepresentation: namely, that on the West Coast it would appear that AP had copied INS's 'hot stories'. Brandeis J's dissent was more fundamental, in that he argued that since INS's acts were not prohibited by any specific common law right of a third party, they should be allowed as part of the public interest in dissemination of information.

[50] See *Sears Roebuck & Co. v Stiffel Co.* 376 US 225 (1965); *Compco Corp. v Day Bright Lighting Inc.* 376 US 234 (1964).

[51] 489 US 141 (1989).

[52] Section 43(a) states:

'Any person who, on or in connection with any goods or services, or any container for goods, uses in commerce any works, term, name, symbol or device, or any combination thereof, or any false designation of origin, false or misleading description of fact, or false or misleading description of fact which

(1) is likely to cause confusion or to cause mistake or to deceive as to the affiliation, connection, or association of such person with another person, or as to the origin, sponsorship, or approval of his or her goods, services or commercial activities by another person or

(2) in commercial advertising or promotion misrepresents the nature, characteristics, qualities or geographic origin of his or her or another person's goods, services or commercial activities

shall be liable in a civil action by any person who believes that he or she is likely to be damaged by such act.'

[53] For example, interior decor of a restaurant in *Two Pesos Inc. v Taco Cabana* US 112 S.Ct 2753 (1992); exterior appearance of a restaurant, *White Tower Systems Inc. v White Castle System of Eating House Corp.* 90 F.2d 67 (6th Cir.) *cert denied* 302 US 720 (1937).

Further statutory unfair competition protection derives in the United States from other federal statutes such as federal anti-trust laws, the Copyright Act, federal and state trade mark registration statutes and state unfair competition statutes.

Common law of unfair competition

The common law of unfair competition varies from state to state but is reasonably uniform, despite the Supreme Court decision in *Erie Railroad Co. v Tomkins*[54] in which the then developing federal common law of unfair competition was eliminated as a result of the federal courts being required to apply state unfair competition law.

The key features of section 43(a) Lanham Act and the other forms of unfair competition protection, with the notable exception of the misappropriation doctrine, may be summarised as an element of customer confusion or of false allegations disparaging another's business. As already noted above, this is similar to the development of UK law.

Anti-dilution laws

There are specific legislative provisions which, as in the United Kingdom, go some way to giving protection against unfair competition. Although there is no federal trade mark anti-dilution law, approximately 26 states have adopted anti-dilution statutes. These operate in situations involving no likelihood of confusion, but where there has been dilution in the sense of taking advantage of the exclusive nature of a trade mark, by either:

(1) blurring, weakening the senior mark's unique significance, distinctive character or ability to identify a particular source or quality; or
(2) tarnishment, by creating a negative association such as 'Enjoy Cocaine' instead of 'Enjoy Coke'.[55]

The long-standing debate in the United States about whether a federal anti-dilution statute should be enacted centres on the difficulty of preserving freedom of speech, especially in the form of parody, in circumstances where there is no confusion and/or the parties may not be in competition with one another. Generally speaking it is accepted that anti-dilution laws are for the protection primarily if not exclusively of 'famous marks'.

The Model State Trademark Bill (1992 Revision) and INTA's proposed factors for a federal anti-dilution statute would limit protection given to famous marks by considering whether the mark in question:

(1) is inherently distinctive (as opposed to having acquired secondary meaning through use);
(2) has substantial duration and extent of use;
(3) has substantial duration and extent of advertising;
(4) has substantial geographical extent of trading area;
(5) has substantial renown;
(6) has been used by third parties.

---

[54] 304 US 64 at 78 (1938): 'There is no federal general common law'.
[55] Compare *Claeryn/Klarein* Decision of Benelux Court of Justice of 1 March 1975, Note 41 above.

Slavish copying

Except insofar as it might amount to the tort of misappropriation and avoid the federal pre-emption doctrine, there is no protection in the United States for 'slavish copying' as such, in the absence of a likelihood of confusion or deception. Under state unfair competition laws, the functionality doctrine, as its name suggests, prevents protection being given to the functional features of a product or packaging or presentation of a service.

Trade secrets

Finally, it is worth mentioning for the sake of completeness that trade secrets, both commercial and technical, are protected by various common laws and state statutes, and such protection is not pre-empted by federal patent laws.[56]

It is hard to resist the conclusion that the current move in the United States for strengthening or federalisation of trade mark anti-dilution laws is an attempt to fill the gap to provide protection where goodwill or reputation associated with a trade mark has been taken or 'misappropriated', but where there has been no customer confusion and hence traditional remedies are inadequate. Recent US commentators have analysed the problem using the language of misappropriation, echoing the *AP/INS* case. It has been argued[57] that the positive associations that comprise a brand have risen to the level of a quasi-property right, maintained by considerable investment of time and money and so a brand should be entitled to protection irrespective of confusion or dilution. If trade marks are merely regarded as an indication of source, then it makes sense to consider their infringement in terms of likelihood of confusion. However, it is now generally accepted that a trade mark or brand is in modern industrial society not just an indication of source but also a valuable business asset, into which considerable time and effort will have been invested. For such asset or property right, likelihood of confusion is not an adequate measure of infringement of that right. Since it is a property right, it is argued, 'taking' it without permission is misappropriation, and, in particular, the likelihood of a 'free ride' or negative associations with a mark should equate with likelihood of confusion in determining whether infringement has occurred. It is therefore possible to see signs that some in the United States are moving towards the idea that dilution is not a wide enough concept and that there is a need for a broader concept to cover generally the taking of something developed by another thereby giving the taker an unfair advantage.

While the United States does not provide a model for Europe to adopt, owing to different tensions in the development of federal and state laws leading to its own particular structure, it does provide an examination of the doctrinal basis for such laws which, it is argued, should be taken into account when deciding what direction European unfair competition law should take. It is thus to European laws that this article now turns to assess their development to date, and the impact of EC law.

Unfair Competition Laws in Europe

European unfair competition laws must be considered at two levels. First, there are national laws in most states, and, secondly, laws in those states which are now members of the European Union must be examined for their compatibility with European Community laws.

---

[56] *Kewanee Oil Co. v Bicron Corp.* 416 USPQ 470 (1974).
[57] J.B. Swan and T.H. Davis, 'Dilution, an Idea Whose Time Has Gone: Brand Equity as Protectible Property, the New/Old Paradigm' (1994) 84 TMR 267.

While there is no EC law specifically addressing substantive unfair competition law,[58] certain aspects of EC law can alter national unfair competition laws. Accordingly, this article will first summarise national laws before going on to consider the impact of EC law.

National unfair competition laws in Europe

It is not proposed to present a comprehensive survey of national unfair competition laws.[59] Rather the authors seek to present some general observations about civil unfair competition laws, illustrated by case law examples, as a means of giving common lawyers a flavour of what they typically involve. They then seek to draw a contrast with English law.

A survey of unfair competition cases reported in English[60] reveals much apparent activity in most jurisdictions under this name.[61] Most attention in the literature available on this topic in English is focused on German unfair competition law, owing principally to the fact that it is seemingly often the most strict and rigid[62] and therefore is the most eye-catching, not to say startling, for a common lawyer. However, it is possible to summarise more generally the content of civil unfair competition laws.

Ulmer[63] identified a coherent body of unfair competition law across Europe, which despite national differences, could be said to have a unifying objective. This is described by Beier as being the interest

> of the honest trader in having the right to restrain his competitors from causing him injury by unfair conduct. The test was whether a competitor's conduct complied with 'honest usages' of the trade, the 'usages honnêtes' (Article 10*bis* Paris Convention), the 'correttezza professionale' (Article 2598 Codice Civile) or the 'bonos mores' ('gute Sitten') in the course of trade (Article 1, German Law against Unfair Competition 1909)'.[64]

Beier takes the view that this 'classical' unfair competition law has, in more recent times, been 'shattered [as u]nfair competition law has become a playground for special interests and competences, unco-ordinated and lacking any clear vision'.[65] However, from a common law perspective the similarities in the civil law approach remain more striking than the differences and while there are undeniably very distinct national differences, the following common elements of unfair competition law can be identified:

---

[58] See Schricker, 'European harmonisation of unfair competition law—a futile venture?' (1991) 22 IIC 788.

[59] For such a survey, now somewhat out of date, see Ulmer *et al.*'s six-volume opinion referred to by Schricker, *ibid.*, footnote 3, and by Beier [1985] EIPR 284, footnote 6. See also P.J. Kaufmann, 'Passing Off and Misappropriation' (1986) IIC Studies, Vol. 9, which covers France, Germany, the Netherlands and the United States; R.J. Plaisant, 'The Action for Unfair Competition in French Law' [1979] JBL 83; and, for a summary of German Law, Böcker, Märzheuser, Nusser and Scheja, *Germany—Practical Commercial Law*, 1992, at 27 to 35, and G. Dannenmann, *An Introduction to German Civil and Commercial Law*, BIICL, 1993, at 83 to 88. In particular, the authors have not covered those unfair competition laws which relate to trade secret protection.

[60] The EIPR contains an excellent digest of recent cases from across Europe, and the IIC also reports unfair competition cases on a less frequent though usually fuller basis.

[61] For the purposes of illustration only, cases reported in the EIPR under unfair competition can be found from every civil law jurisdiction currently comprising the EU except for Portugal and Luxembourg (which nevertheless does have unfair competition laws along Belgian lines).

[62] See Fammler, 'Important changes in German Unfair Competition Law' [1994] EIPR 448. The research conducted in this area by the Max Planck Institute is, of course, another reason why there is much available in English on German law.

[63] Referred to in F. Beier, 'The law of unfair competition in the European Community—its development and present status' [1985] EIPR 284.

[64] *Ibid.*

[65] *Ibid.*, at 289.

Prohibition on unfair conduct

This includes laws regulating comparative advertising, special offers, low prices (including loss-leading), prohibiting disparaging competitors,[66] and a general prohibition on discriminatory sales conditions, including price discounting.

In France, it was held that a supermarket is permitted to advertise its prices as against those of competitors only in relation to identical products and under precisely similar conditions. Thus it would not be possible to have a price comparison between a supermarket and a small shop.[67] In Germany, Ford was held to have contravened unfair competition law by inviting Opel drivers to trade in their 'good old Opels' for a 'well-designed Sierra, a sports Capri or a comfortable Granada'.[68] This was regarded as comparative advertising, implicitly denigrating a competitor's products.

Low prices were condemned as unfair competition in Italy, where a court held that sale is not fair if the seller does not charge all costs plus a reasonable profit.[69] Similarly, the Hague Appeal Court condemned as unfair competition an attempt by Dutch daily newspapers to queer the pitch of a new weekly sports newspaper which was to come out on Monday mornings by distributing free their normal Monday evening sports sections some hours earlier on Monday mornings. Such sports sections, it was held, could only be legitimately distributed at a reasonable price.

Its capacity for novel applications is illustrated by a case in France in which a software company were restrained from selling software which would enable users to evade anti-copying protection included in other software. Enabling infringement of copyright was considered an act of unfair competition.[70] Similarly, a Dutch court held that sales of pirate decoders for subscription television was an act of unfair competition, even though not an infringement of any intellectual property right.[71] Importing bootleg compact discs into the Netherlands, though not an infringement under Dutch intellectual property law nor in the country of manufacture, was held to be unfair competition.[72]

An example of the German courts' extensive interpretation of what contravenes 'bonos mores' is afforded by the Federal Supreme Court's condemnation on this ground of telephone solicitation, without prior approval from the person concerned to be phoned.[73] Similar condemnation has also been made of telex or fax solicitation methods.[74]

Prohibition on deceptive advertising and marketing

A classic example of deceptive marketing of goods was condemned as unfair competition by a Swedish court which ordered a spaghetti importer not to sell its product in a packet larger than was necessary for its contents.[75] Beier notes that the suppression of deceptive advertising

---

[66] See Italian Supreme Court Case 10704, 28 October 1993 [1994] EIPR D—30.

[67] *Société Carrefour v SRGL* [1987] EIPR D—28.

[68] *Opel v Ford* [1985] EIPR D—135.

[69] *Peg Perego Pines v Doveri* [1988] EIPR D—134. Contrast, on predatory pricing under EC law, with the European Court of Justice's decision in *AKZO* [1993] 5 CMLR 215.

[70] *LCE v Artware* [1989] EIPR D—161. Contrast with the position under UK copyright law in *Amstrad Consumer Electronics plc v BPI Ltd* [1986] FSR 159.

[71] *Esselte Abonee TV v Ten Electronics NV* [1992] EIPR D—181. Contrast with *Holland Nautic v Racal Decca* [1987] EIPR D—50.

[72] *EMI Bovema BV v Kierke Amsterdam BV* [1989] EIPR D—199.

[73] Case I ZR 178/87 *Wine Tasting* [1990] EIPR D—23.

[74] *Telex and Fax Solicitation* [1989] EIPR D—6.

[75] *Di Luca v Buitoni Perugina* [1983] EIPR D—228. Buitoni had put only 400g of spaghetti in 500g sized packages, since Swedish spaghetti was marketed in 400g packs.

still poses great difficulties in Italy, as courts refer to the principle of Roman law *omnis mercator mendax*, viewing the Italian consumer as suspicious and vigilant enough to exclude the possibility of deception. The Italian judiciary's view of its consumers is to be contrasted with that of the German judges with their concern to protect, in Schricker's words, 'purchasers with below average talent'.[76]

The German Federal Supreme Court has condemned, for example, the sort of promotional advertising which requires returning a lucky winning ticket for a prize, if potential participants are excessively enticed by being misled as to the chances of winning a prize.[77] Indeed, it was held in the same case that the distribution of money-off coupons as a promotional tool can infringe the law on rebates which forbids discounts on goods and services of more than 3 per cent.[78] The Federal Supreme Court regarded as unfair competition anything that tied a prize to the purchase of a product. In another case, it was held that a promotional game which required contestants to enter the defendant's shops to collect a sticker required to play the game would make them feel morally obliged to buy something and thus was contrary to unfair competition.[79] Similar promotional devices such as restaurant guides including vouchers for two main courses for the price of one[80] and American Express card air miles points in return for expenditure charged to the card account[81] have also been held to be in contravention of this law.

An advertising description of a mineral water as 'A Champagne among Mineral Waters' was condemned by the German Federal Supreme Court as *contra bonos mores*, since the defendant was devaluing the plaintiff champagne producers' product by comparing champagne to water (the ultimate in trade mark dilution perhaps?[82]), unless the slogan was permitted under French law, since this was the country of origin of both products.[83] This can be compared with an Italian Supreme Court decision[84] in which a Champagne producer failed to prevent a bath foam producer using champagne shaped bottles, on the basis that it had not shown either that there would be confusion between customers nor that use of the same type of bottle would cause customers to think less of the Champagne producer's product. Similarly, in France, the same producer failed[85] to stop a publicity campaign

---

[76] Schricker (1991) 22 IIC 788 at 791. Though one can see impatience with the rather strained arguments of confusion put before them in some cases: see for example *Rheingau Riesling* [1989] EIPR D—81.

[77] *Lucky Number/Winning Ticket promotions* [1989] D—182.

[78] See Fammler [1994] EIPR 448, 451. An attempt at repeal failed: Schroeder [1994] ECLR R—191. Similar prohibitions existed under Austrian law [1985] EIPR D—188, but are now repealed: see Poch, 'Deregulation of Austrian Unfair Competition Law' [1993] EIPR 132. Swiss law seems to retain this prohibition [1993] EIPR D—15.

[79] *Everything Fresh?* [1987] EIPR D—160. More recently, the *Financial Times* reported on 7 July 1995 that an appeals court had ruled a Benetton advertisement depicting an HIV positive man published in *Stern* magazine in 1992 as being in unfair competition, because it sought to link human compassion for others' suffering with Benetton's name and products.

[80] *Frankfurt restaurant vouchers* [1986] EIPR D—93.

[81] *Financial Times*, 23 June 1994, at 16.

[82] Perhaps not. In *D&D Scotch Whisky mit zusätzlichem Wasser* [1987] EIPR D—48, the Federal Supreme Court upheld a finding of unfair competition against a firm marketing blended Scotch diluted to a 21 per cent alcoholic strength, since it was insufficiently clear from the label that this was not the usual strength Scotch normally available on the market. The purpose of this blend appears to have been to circumvent Danish customs regulations which prohibited day trippers from Germany from returning to Denmark with alcoholic beverages exceeding 22 per cent alcoholic strength.

[83] Case 1 ZR 109/85 *Perrier: A Champagne Among Mineral Waters* (1988) 19 IIC 682. See also for similar cases preventing the use of well known names on dissimilar products: *Quattro* [1986] EIPR D—113, where Audi successfully prevented the use on skis of its trade mark for cars; and *Dimple*, where the Federal Supreme Court refused to allow the brand name of a whisky be used by another trader for mens' cosmetic preparations, but did permit its use on washing, cleaning, bleaching and polishing agents [1985] EIPR D—188.

[84] *Moet et Chandon v F. Zani* [1990] EIPR D—5; (1991) 22 IIC 552.

[85] *Moet et Chandon v Borel* [1984] EIPR D—6.

advertising its product as a prize to winners of a draw, on the basis that it was disparagement of their trade mark.

Prohibition on false indications of origin

In Belgium, a Scotch whisky producer was able to obtain an injunction preventing a Belgian blend of Scotch whisky and Belgian alcohol from using a name and get-up suggestive of Scottish origin.[86]

In France, a perfume company was restrained by injunction from calling its perfume 'Champagne', the action being brought by two French state-controlled organisations, the Institut National des Appellations d'Origine and the Comité Interprofessionel du Vin de Champagne.[87]

Prohibition on slavish copying

In Denmark, slavish copying of an item not protected by copyright or patent may be an act of unfair competition.[88]

In Italy, protection against slavish copying has been granted to protect colours used in packaging a product in circumstances which might well not amount to passing off under English law,[89] although it was stressed that protection depended on evidence of customer confusion. Confusingly similar packaging (*in casu* a petroleum additive packaged in a way similar to beer and soft drinks cans) was condemned as unfair competition in a German court on the grounds of consumer protection.[90] However, in another Italian case, an injunction was granted to prevent slavish copying (*in casu* an opera libretto copied from the original score, now out of copyright) even though it was specifically found that there was no risk of customer confusion.[91]

In the Netherlands, the style of a particular artist in illustrating children's books was protected under unfair competition even in the absence of copyright infringement.[92]

Protection for distribution networks

This is illustrated by two Greek cases. In one, an injunction was ordered against an unauthorised trader refilling the plaintiff's butane gas cylinders, this being held to give an unfair advantage over the appointed agent who had to bear costs of repairing damaged cylinders.[93] In the second, an injunction was granted to the exclusive distributor of 'Lacoste' products in Greece preventing parallel imports of genuine Dutch Lacoste goods.[94] However, the Italian courts reached the opposite conclusion in a case involving parallel imports of

---

[86] *George Ballantine & Sons Ltd v Rubbens Gebroeders pvba* [1986] EIPR D—159. The name involved was 'Mac Rose' and the get-up involved a picture of a guard wearing a bearskin hat and a tartan strip.

[87] *Yves Saint Laurent* [1994] EIPR D—74.

[88] Contrast *Nomadic v Medicare* [1986] EIPR D—192, where it was, with the Supreme Court case of *BR-Legetøj v Jeva* [1989] EIPR D—91, where it was held that the copy did not sufficiently reproduce all of the plaintiff's product.

[89] *Farmaceutici Dr Ciccarelli SpA v Lidl Italia Srl* [1992] EIPR D—238; contrast with *Sainsbury's Classic Cola* [1994] EIPR D—182.

[90] *LM . . . amx* [1987] EIPR D—5.

[91] *Casa Musicale Sonzogno v Bianchi* [1990] EIPR D—132.

[92] *HM Bruna & Mercis BV v Rolf BV* [1982] EIPR D—53.

[93] *Application de Gaz* [1987] EIPR D—70.

[94] *Sportsman SA* [1994] ECLR R—80.

'Christian Dior' perfumes,[95] applying notions of privity of contract familiar to the common law.

However, German unfair competition law did not prevent a German importer of computer games from Japan selling them in the absence of an authorised German distributor.[96]

German law seemingly goes further than other civil laws in two principal ways.[97] First, it allows a wider class of plaintiffs to enforce unfair competition laws. Competitors and trade associations may sue even without proof of direct injury.[98] Secondly, in assessing deceptiveness, German courts place great reliance on the public's opinion of whether something would be false or misleading, rather than judging such issues on the basis of legislative intent or on an assessment of competing interests.[99]

Conclusions on the relationship between UK law and European unfair competition laws

It appears that European unfair competition laws go further than English and federal US laws in the following areas by including:

(1) general prohibitions on unfair conduct, such as disparagement of competitors;
(2) prohibitions on making special offers, low prices (including loss-leading) and discounting;
(3) prohibitions on slavish copying; and
(4) protection for distribution networks.

Moreover, the rules on who may sue frequently allow competitors to bring actions to restrain unfair competition in the civil courts. Therefore, while applying a false trade description is a criminal offence in the United Kingdom, it may be restrained by way of an action brought by a competitor in many continental European systems.

EC Law and Unfair Competition Law

There is no Community law on unfair competition. Rather, national laws have to be reconciled with the Community rules on free movement of goods contained in Articles 30 to 36 and the equivalent rules on services in Articles 59 to 66 of the Treaty of Rome. The competition rules set out in Articles 85 and 86, when read in conjunction with Articles 3(g) and 5(2) and/or 90, may also be relevant.[100] In addition, there is now some specific legislation which is relevant. The impact of the Treaty and the specific legislation will be considered in

---

[95] *Dior Italia SpA v Servetti Profumi SpA* [1989] EIPR D—24.
[96] *Parodius* [1993] EIPR D—105.
[97] The principal features of German law appear to have been reproduced in Austrian law, but Austria's law has now been substantially altered; see Pöch, 'Deregulation of Austrian Unfair Competition Law' [1993] EIPR 132. German law has also been changed, though to a rather lesser extent: see Fammler, 'Important changes in German Unfair Competition Law', [1994] EIPR 448 and Schroeder [1994] ECLR R—191.
[98] Fammler states [1994] EIPR 448 at 449 that some trade associations indulge in litigation purely for their own financial interest in obtaining damages. Contrast, for example, with Italy where it has been held that only businessmen may sue: see note by Franzosi on *Collegio dei Ragioneri e Periti Commerciali v Associazione Commercianti* [1993] EIPR D—107.
[99] Beier describes this as a judicial 'adulation of public opinion', [1985] EIPR 284 at 286.
[100] See Rose, 'Passing Off, Unfair Competition and Community Law' [1990] EIPR 123. As an example, the compatibility of French anti-loss leading legislation with Articles 3(g), 5, 85 and 86 of the Treaty of Rome has been referred to the Court of Justice in Case C—211/94 *Luback* [1994] OJ C275/13.

turn. But first some cases will illustrate the way in which the application of national laws may raise problems for Community law.

The scope for conflict between EC law and national laws

In Greece, an injunction was granted to the exclusive distributor of 'Lacoste' products in Greece preventing parallel imports of genuine Dutch Lacoste goods.[101] No such injunction would be available under English law. In Italy, the Supreme Court held that it did have jurisdiction under the Brussels Convention (1968) to hear an unfair competition case against a British company alleged to be spreading false information on foreign markets about an Italian manufacturer's products.[102] It is likely that the same result would be achieved were an injurious falsehood or slander of goods case to be brought in equivalent circumstances before an English court. In Germany, an injunction was ordered against a German company distributing advertising pamphlets in the United States making false statements as to its circulation, in an attempt to attract advertising from the United States.[103] On its facts, this case did not raise any wider issues for EC law, but now that Austria has acceded to the Community, it would be possible that this magazine would also circulate in Austria and thus the German court's prohibition would have an impact on the circulation of goods within the Community.

In considering the impact of Community law on national unfair competition laws, it is convenient to look first at the application of the Treaty rules on free movement of goods, then at Community competition law, before finally considering the legislative developments that have taken place.

EC law on free movement of goods

Article 30 EC ensures free movement of goods within the EC. The Court of Justice has developed this Article into a means of ensuring that Member States' trading rules do not place disproportionate restrictions on trading goods across borders.[104] Hence in *Cassis de Dijon* itself, minimum alcoholic content rules were declared to be contrary to Article 30, since equivalent consumer protection could be achieved through labelling requirements.[105] In *Prantl*,[106] German law restricting use of a traditional shape of wine bottle was held not to comply with Article 30, since it prevented imports of another wine also traditionally produced in this shape of bottle.

On the other hand a Dutch law restricting promotional gifts was held to be compatible with Article 30 since it pursued legitimate objectives of consumer protection and fair trading.[107]

The *Cassis de Dijon* principle has been qualified by the Court of Justice in *Keck*[108] to

---

[101] *Sportsman SA* [1994] ECLR R—80. This ruling would seem incompatible with Community law as the result of the case is to enforce partition of the market: see 22/71 *Béguelin* [1971] ECR 949, [1972] CMLR 81.

[102] Case 10704, Italian Supreme Court 28 October 1993 [1994] EIPR D—30.

[103] *PC Professional* [1993] EIPR D—7.

[104] 8/74 *Dassonville* [1974] ECR 837, [1974] 2 CMLR 436; 120/78 *Cassis de Dijon* [1979] ECR 649, [1979] 3 CMLR 337; 60 & 61/84 *Cinetheque* [1985] ECR 2605, [1986] 1 CMLR 365; C—267 & 268/91. The Court of Justice ruled in 6/81 *Beele* [1982] ECR 707, [1982] 3 CMLR 102, that Article 36 did not apply to unfair competition rules, and that these therefore required assessment only under Article 30.

[105] See *Grand Marnier* [1993] 2 CMLR 123 and *Hellebrekers Advocaat* [1993] 2 CMLR 61.

[106] 16/83 *Prantl* [1984] ECR 1299, [1985] 2 CMLR 238.

[107] 286/81 *Oosthoek* [1982] ECR 4575, [1983] 3 CMLR 428. See also 382/87 *Buet* [1989] ECR 1235; [1993] 3 CMLR 659.

[108] C—267 & 268/91 *Keck* [1995] 1 CMLR 101.

provide an exception to this principle that selling arrangements are not caught by Article 30 EC, provided they apply equally as between domestically produced and imported products:

> In *Cassis de Dijon* it was held that, in the absence of harmonisation of legislation, measures of equivalent effect prohibited by Article 30 included obstacles to the free movement of goods where they were the consequence of applying rules that laid down requirements to be met by such goods (such as requirements as to designation, form, size, weight, composition, presentation, labelling, packaging) to goods from other Member States where they were lawfully manufactured and marketed, even if those rules applied without distinction to all products unless their application could be justified by a public interest objective taking precedence over the free movement of goods.
>
> However, contrary to what had previously been decided, the application to products from other Member States of national provisions restricting or prohibiting certain selling arrangements was not such as to hinder directly or indirectly, actually or potentially trade between Member states within the meaning of the *Dassonville* judgment, provided that those provisions applied to all affected traders operating within the national territory and provided that they affected in fact, the marketing of domestic products and of those from other Member States.

It is not clear how this ruling applies to unfair competition law. Do such rules constitute marketing arrangements, potentially within the ambit of Article 30, or are they selling arrangements falling beyond Article 30's jurisdictional scope? Some guidance may be obtained from the Court of Justice's judgment in *Clinique*.[109]

German law on packaging of goods prevented *Clinique* being used by Estée Lauder as a trade mark for cosmetics on ground that it could mislead consumers into thinking that the products had medicinal qualities. Estée Lauder wanted to relaunch the product in Germany and to cease repacking it as 'Linique' (*sic*) in Germany.

On an Article 177 reference, the court cited *Keck* as support for the proposition that a rule relating to requirements such as presentation and labelling was prohibited by Article 30 unless justified by a 'public interest objective taking precedence over free movement of goods'. It was held that as the products were not presented as medicinal, were not sold in pharmacies but in cosmetic and perfume departments and the use of the name *Clinique* had not apparently misled other consumers in the EC, the German law could not be enforced. Thus provisions of national unfair competition laws relating to the packaging of goods would seem not to be classified as selling arrangements.

This may be contrasted with the *Yves Rocher* case.[110] In this case, detached prior to *Keck*, a German law prohibiting eye-catching advertisements on price, even where the price information was correct, was struck down as being contrary to Article 30 EC. Advertising can now be seen as a selling arrangement falling outside Article 30 and thus German controls on what is permitted in advertisements would remain a matter exclusively for German unfair competition law. The only way of escaping this conclusion would be to recognise that advertising price is a way of promoting cross-border trade and therefore while advertisements may be seen as selling arrangements, they should not be included in the class of 'certain' selling arrangements referred to by the court in *Keck*. The goal of the single market should

---

[109]   C—315/92 *Clinique* [1994] ECR I—317.
[110]   C—126/91 *Yves Rocher* [1993] ECR I—236.

enable some selling arrangements necessary to make the market function to remain within the ambit of Article 30. However, this argument appears not to have succeeded in *Leclerc-Siplec*,[111] where the Court of Justice held that Article 30 did not apply to a restriction on television advertisements which affected all products and distributors in the same way.

Thus a case like *Yves Rocher* could be contrasted with the *American Express Air Miles* case. German unfair competition law prevented American Express from granting air miles as a reward for use of their card. American Express' promotional exercise was designed to promote use of their charge card within Germany, but did not form part of a wider plan to encourage cross-border trade, and therefore remained a matter for German regulation. It seems, following the *Keck* judgment, that American Express would now find it more difficult to invoke Article 30 to challenge the German law.

More generally, one can hazard a classification of unfair competition laws into those involving selling arrangements outside Article 30 and those to which Article 30, as interpreted by *Cassis de Dijon*, still applies:

(1) *Selling arrangements outside Article 30*
 —general prohibitions on unfair conduct;
 —laws regulating comparative advertising;[112]
 —prohibitions on making special offers, low prices (including loss-leading)[113] and discounting;
 —prohibitions on disparaging competitors; and
 —prohibitions on deceptive advertising.
(2) *Unfair competition laws subject to Article 30 (ceteris paribus)*
 —prohibitions on deceptive packaging;[114]
 —prohibitions on false indications of origin;[115]
 —prohibitions on slavish copying; and
 —rules on distribution networks.

Despite the attempt at clarification in *Keck*, the classification suggested above is difficult to make and the authors are not confident that it would be followed by the court. It seems that the overall picture remains confused and in need of rationalisation specifically addressed to the problem of unfair competition law.

EC Competition Law

A further question to consider is whether it is possible to argue that the application of EC competition law may preclude the application of national unfair competition laws.[116] It could be argued that Articles 3(g), 5, 85 and/or 86 preclude Member States from introducing or maintaining in force measures which may render ineffective the competition rules applicable to undertakings. Therefore unfair competition laws, since they restrain undertakings from engaging in certain types of competitive activity, inherently provide a mechanism whereby a

---

[111] Case C—412/93 *Leclerc-Siplec v TFI and M6 Publicité*, judgment of 9 February 1995.
[112] Community law on comparative advertising is dealt with below.
[113] Such as *Keck* Note 108 above.
[114] Note 109 above.
[115] 286/86 *Deserbais* [1988] ECR 4907, Edam cheese not to be made subject to Dutch minimum fat content rules when imported from another Member State. See now the designation of foodstuffs legislation referred to below.
[116] The compatibility of French anti-loss leading legislation with Articles 3(g), 5, 85 and 86 of the Treaty of Rome has been referred to the Court of Justice in Case C—211/94 *Luback* [1994] OJ C275/13.

state, in breach of its obligations under Articles 3(g) and 5 of the Treaty, enabling undertakings to impose restrictions which could not be permitted under Articles 85 or 86. Such an argument would have to satisfy the Court of Justice's ruling in *Van Eycke*[117] that this depends on showing that the measures in question 'require or favour the adoption of agreements, decisions or concerted practices contrary to Article 85'. As regards Article 86, such an argument would depend on showing that the measure in question required the undertaking to abuse its dominant position.[118]

This is an illustration of the tension that has historically existed between unfair competition law and anti-trust or competition law,[119] and which has yet to be dealt with specifically by the Court of Justice.

As with the case law on the interaction between unfair competition law and Articles 30 to 36 EC, the compatibility of unfair competition laws with Articles 85 and 86 EC is unclear. While many aspects of unfair competition law, such as trade secret protection or prohibitions on slavish copying, may well not raise clear competition issues, others, such as limits on ability to compete on price, do. For example, a state law limiting discounts to 3 per cent may restrict the ability of smaller undertakings to compete, especially in an oligopolistic market where there are other barriers to entry and the ability to be able to enter as a cut-price competitor is the most important way of attracting new custom. The limited case law to date has only given the most general guidance, and a more specific approach is needed to deal with the particular problems raised by unfair competition laws.

EC legislation

As Schricker has noted, 'in the field of unfair competition law many have doubted whether legal harmonisation [is] necessary at all',[120] though he concludes that it 'in no way appears to be a lost cause, but a real chance to consolidate the internal market'.[121] It appears that the sceptics held sway, and as a result, although there have been studies made about the law in this area,[122] there has not been any legislative attempt at harmonisation. Instead, particular measures have been adopted which affect certain aspects of unfair competition laws, most importantly in the areas of trade marks, indications of origin and advertising.

Trade marks

The impact of the first Trade Marks Directive[123] has already been considered. The Community Trade Mark Regulation[124] also contains equivalent provisions to those discussed above in relation to the new Community trade Mark,[125] through the wide range of registrable marks, the wide concept of infringement, the existence of 'anti-dilution' protection, and the protection for internationally well-known marks. As with the Directive, there are also two principal ways in which trade mark owners' rights have been limited by the Regulation, in

---

[117]   267/86 *Van Eycke v ASPA NV* [1988] ECR 4769, [1989] 4 CMLR 330.
[118]   C—41/90 *Höfner v Macrotron GmbH* [1991] ECR 1—1979, [1993] 4 CMLR 306.
[119]   P.J. Kaufmann, Note 19 above, at 16 to 30.
[120]   Note 4 above, at 789.
[121]   *Ibid.*, at 801.
[122]   See Ulmer *et al.*'s six-volume opinion commissioned by the European Commission referred to by Schricker, *ibid.*, at 788, footnote 3, and by Beier, Note 4 above, at 284, footnote 6.
[123]   First Council Directive (89/104) of 21 December 1988 to approximate the laws of the Member States relating to trade marks OJ 1989 L40/1.
[124]   The Council Regulation on the Community Trade Mark, Regulation 40/94 OJ 1994 L11/1.
[125]   At the time of writing, the CTM is expected to come into operation in 1996, the CTM Office being located in Alicante, Spain.

that comparative advertising is allowed[126] and the exhaustion of rights principle has been specifically incorporated.[127] However, the Regulation does specifically preserve the right to bring actions under Member States' unfair competition laws.[128]

Indications of origin for food and drink

A Community regime has been set up which governs descriptions of food and drink. There are two principal EC regulations relating to names of foodstuffs: the Regulation on Protection of Designations of Geographical Origin[129] and the Regulation of Certificates of Specific Character of Foodstuffs.[130] There are separate regimes for wine,[131] sparkling wine,[132] aromatised wines[133] and spirits.[134] The former regime was applied by the Court of Appeal in *Elderflower Champagne*,[135] in holding that the name 'Champagne' was protected and not available for use other than by French champagne producers.

Advertising

So far the only legislation which has been adopted is the Misleading Advertising Directive,[136] which provides for Member States to enable action to be taken against false advertising. In the United Kingdom this was implemented by granting additional powers to the Director General of Fair Trading to seek court orders to put a stop to such advertisements, but it did not give any civil remedies to other third parties.[137] A proposed Comparative Advertising Directive[138] is seemingly stalled, and it may be doubted whether it is needed in view of the provisions of the Trade Marks Directive.

Conclusions on the relationship between EC law and national unfair competition laws

Although EC law has not confronted the unfair competition law debate head on, both case law and legislation has shaped national law to a considerable extent. Although the *Keck* judgment has greatly increased the uncertainty over the extent to which rules on free

---

[126] Trade Marks Regulation, Article 9(1)(c).

[127] *Ibid.*, Article 13.

[128] *Ibid.*, Article 14.

[129] Regulation 2081/92, OJ 1992 L208/1.

[130] Regulation 2082/92, OJ 1992 L208/9. Both Regulations are discussed by Kolia, 'Monopolising Names: EEC Proposals on the Protection of Trade Descriptions of Foodstuffs' [1992] EIPR 233, updated at [1992] EIPR 333.

[131] Regulation 823/87, OJ 1987 L84/59, laying down special provisions relating to quality wines produced in specified regions, as amended by Regulation 2043/89, OJ 1989 L202/1.

[132] Regulation 2333/92, OJ 1992 L231/9, laying down general rules for the description and presentation of sparkling wines and aerated sparkling wines. See C—306/93 *Firma SMW Wintersekt GmbH v Land Rheinland-Pfalz* [1994] ECR I-5555. See also C—309/89 *Codorniu v Council* [1994] ECR I-1853, noted by Usher (1994) 19 ELRev 636, in which the Court of Justice quashed, at the suit of a Spanish producer, that part of the amended Regulation which purported to reserve the term 'crémant' for French and Luxembourg producers.

[133] Regulation 1601/91, OJ 1991 L149/1, laying down general rules on the definition, description and presentation of aromatised wines, aromatised wine-based drinks and aromatised wine-product cocktails. In case this wording is less than clear, what is meant is products like Sangria, Glühwein and Vermouth.

[134] Regulation 1576/89, OJ 1989 L160/1, laying down general rules on the definition, description and presentation of spirit drinks. This is now due to be amended.

[135] *Taittinger v Allbev*, Note 23 above.

[136] OJ 1984 L250/17.

[137] The Directive was implemented in the United Kingdom by the Control of Misleading Advertisements Regulations 1988, SI 1988/915. Only one case has been reported concerning the implementation of the Regulations: *Director General of Fair Trading v Tobyward Ltd* [1989] 2 All ER 266.

[138] OJ 1991 C180/14.

movement override national unfair competition laws as they relate to selling arrangements, other areas have been rationalised and even harmonised to an extent, in particular those involving:

— comparative advertising;
— indications of origin;
— deceptive packaging;
— slavish copying; and
— distribution networks.

The areas of greatest uncertainty remain:

— general prohibitions on unfair conduct, such as disparagement of competitors; and
— prohibitions on making special offers, low prices (including loss-leading) and dis-counting.

Indeed, the interaction of EC with national laws in all of these areas where there has not been specific harmonisation remains unclear and open to doubt in many situations. Furthermore, even where there has been specific harmonisation, as in trade marks, the lack of harmonisation of unfair competition laws remains a problem. This is because the harmonised areas are affected by the lack of harmonisation in the neighbouring area of unfair competition. For example, the First Council Trade Marks Directive is stated to be without prejudice to the application of unfair competition laws,[139] as is the Software Directive[140] and the proposed Database Directive.[141] In each of these areas, it is or will be impossible to advise fully on the application of the law to the business activities of brand name, software, database or design[142] protection without taking into account the existence of national unfair competition laws. The lack of harmonisation of unfair competition law is not only a problem in its own right, but it also detracts from attempts to harmonise neighbouring areas of law.

The authors therefore submit that the need for harmonisation of unfair competition laws by Directive exists. The Court of Justice has touched on the problems of reconciling EC law with national unfair competition provisions, but its attempts to do so speak eloquently, if silently, for the need to approach this by way of legislation. The next question is to determine what should the content of such harmonising legislation be? To give some guidance as to how this should be answered, this article needs to return to English law, in order to determine what practical problems have arisen.

Reform of English and EC law

The need for reform

In assessing the problem areas under English law, this article will be restricted to considering unfair competition law as it applies to trade mark protection. It is beyond the article's present

---

[139] OJ 1989 L40/1, Recital 6.
[140] Council Directive of 14 May 1991 on the legal protection of computer programs, OJ 1991 L122/42, Recital 26. This Directive was implemented into UK law by the Copyright (Computer Programs) Regulations 1992 (SI 1992/3233).
[141] OJ 1993 C308/1, Recital 5, which refers to the 'absence *as yet* of a harmonised system of unfair competition' [*emphasis added*].
[142] Under the proposed Community Design Right Regulation OJ 1994 C37/20 and Harmonisation Directive OJ 1993 C345/14.

scope to consider the need for a common approach to unfair competition law as it applies to software or may apply to databases and design rights, though it is acknowledged that these are issues which would also confront any body charged with producing a proposal for a harmonising Directive.

The restriction to trade mark issues has four principal reasons. First, full harmonisation of registered trade marks law has still to be implemented. The Trade Marks Directive itself is only a measure of approximation, not harmonisation. Until the Community Trade Mark has come into full operation and it is seen how it interacts with national trade mark laws at whatever degree of harmonisation then exists, creation of wide-ranging as opposed to specific new rules on unfair competition may well simply create only further uncertainty in the legislative regime for the marketing of goods.

Secondly, it is unclear the extent to which unfair competition laws are properly a matter for EC law at all. The Court of Justice's *Keck* judgment creates considerable uncertainty as to the extent to which Article 30 is applicable to unfair competition laws. To the extent that EC law does not apply, because of a lack of effect on trade between Member States, then this is an area which is not subject to EC law, and hence may not be harmonised. Further elaboration on this aspect of *Keck* by the Court of Justice is required. Trade marks on the other hand are clearly within the ambit of EC law.

Thirdly, some will remain unconvinced that there is a political or economic need for a uniform Community unfair competition law. Single market integration does not require the same marketing law throughout the Community, as the *Keck* judgment illustrates. Those elements of unfair competition laws which are capable of discriminating against imported products are subject to Article 30 in any case, or may be dealt with by specific legislation. While one can understand the natural desire for uniformity through codification felt by those from jurisdictions in which this has taken place, the objectives of the Community do not permit the luxury of law reform for its own sake.

Finally, it should not be assumed that harmonisation must be along civil law rather than common law lines.[143] As should have been shown by now, civil unfair competition law covers a multiplicity of different issues, not all of which by any means are suitable for transplant into the more stony soil of the common law. It is possible to identify certain specific problems which have arisen in the area of trade marks arising out of the implementation of the Trade Marks Directive in the United Kingdom which would be capable of remedy by an unfair competition law. While these problems could be remedied simply by introducing an unfair competition law for the United Kingdom, this could also form the basis for EC-wide harmonisation.

Problems in practice

In the authors' experience, there are three main criticisms about UK law in support of the need for an additional unfair competition law. First there is the 'timing' problem, relating to the problems of obtaining quick relief in trade mark and passing-off cases. Secondly, and related to the first point, is the 'point of sale' problem relating to the fact of when the passing off is said to occur. Thirdly is the 'decor' problem, relating to the difficulty of protecting a combination of design elements under trade mark law.

---

[143] This is particularly the case given that both Germany and Austria have recently considered it necessary to reform their domestic unfair competition laws along more liberal, though still far from common law, lines. See for Austria, see Pöch, 'Deregulation of Austrian Unfair Competition Law' [1993] EIPR 132. For Germany, see Fammler, 'Important changes in German Unfair Competition Law' [1994] EIPR 448, and Schroeder [1994] ECLR R—191.

(1) *The 'timing' problem.* Both passing off and registered trade mark infringement have a built-in time factor which prevents instantaneous relief.[144] As soon as a new product packaging or container appears on the market, 'lookalikes' can appear almost immediately. An application to register the product shape or packaging as a trade mark can be made immediately, but no action for infringement will lie until registration is granted in approximately 12 to 18 months' time. Damages can be backdated to the date of the application, but no immediate injunctive relief is possible. Passing off is not available until goodwill and reputation can be established, impossible in practice without a period of use. In the interim, there is usually no protection against even the most blatant slavish copying.

(2) *The 'point of sale' problem.* If the trade mark is not seen by consumers at the point of sale, then it may be impossible to establish that there has been passing off. In *Bostik Ltd v Sellotape GB Ltd*[145] customers did not see the plaintiff's 'Blu-tak' product until they had already purchased it. The packaging was opaque and the similarity related to the particular colour of reusable adhesive putty rather than to the packaging *per se*. Passing off by the defendant's similarly coloured product was held not to have taken place, owing to the fact that only the packaging was visible at point of sale. Many confectionery and food products are made in distinctive shapes or with distinctive patterns which are not seen by the customer until the outer protective wrapping is removed. The 'Blu-tak' problem may pose a barrier to establishing passing off if the 'hidden' shape or pattern is copied, but the packaging, seen at the point of sale, is not. Registration of the shape or pattern should be possible under the new Act since the shape or pattern is presumably capable of distinguishing the goods (the *Unilever*[146] striped toothpaste problem where the trade mark is not seen at point of sale should no longer be relevant under the new law). However, again there will be a gap in the crucial first stages before registration is obtained when no protection is available and copying is possible.

(3) *The 'decor' problem.* This problem stems from the difficulty of using either registered trade marks or passing off to protect a combination of design elements such as those found in a restaurant or the interior or exterior design of, for example a department store or restaurant. Such elements might include signage, layout, interior decoration, positioning and design of furniture or shelving, overall colour schemes and a myriad of other factors which, considered singly and out of context, would perhaps not themselves attract any form of protection but which nevertheless form a distinctive whole. Even if passing off did provide a remedy in a case where substantially the whole decor were copied, the 'timing problem' would mean that protection might only be available, despite a substantial outlay of expenditure, after perhaps a few years of use, by which time the copier can cheerfully point to co-existence and rely on it as negating any customer confusion.

These three problems have a common theme, in that timing affects obtaining registered trade mark and passing-off protection. Since the United Kingdom (at least for the present)[147] does not operate a deposit-based system and instead examines the registrability of a mark

---

[144] Hazel Carty, 'Passing Off and the Concept of Goodwill' [1995] JBL 139 at 154 concludes that '[a]lthough it can be confidently predicted that for the foreseeable future, passing off will not develop into a tort of unfair competition, the importance of the judicial debate over international reputations and pre-launch publicity is that it called into question the adherence to a strict definition of goodwill'.

[145] [1994] RPC 556.

[146] [1987] RPC 13.

[147] See Section 8 Trade Marks Act 1994, which gives the Secretary of State the power to abandon the *ex officio* search procedure and to require relative grounds of objection to be raised only in opposition proceedings, this power only, however, coming into effect ten years after the Community Trade Mark has been in force.

before granting registration, there seems little that can be done in the context of registered trade mark protection, short of moving to quicker examination based on absolute rather than relative grounds for registrability.

One change enacted by the Trade Marks Act 1994 is that a requirement of likelihood of confusion[148] has been introduced in the case of infringement by a non-identical (that is, similar) mark on identical or similar goods. The classic difference between registered trade mark infringement and passing off under the 1938 Act was that the former required a straightforward comparison of the two marks to determine whether one 'nearly resembled' the other without reference to any extraneous factors (for example, other distinguishing features which might negate confusion). On the other hand, passing off (and registered trade mark infringement which requires a showing of confusion or association) brings into play the whole of the surrounding circumstances to determine whether a misrepresentation or confusion/association has occurred. The result is that co-existence for a period of time might well serve to negate any finding of confusion or association.

Some of these problems could be dealt with in a piecemeal fashion. The timing problem could be ameliorated with a different system of examination and the decor problem could be said to be partially dealt with under existing passing-off law. However, it seems to us that a more fundamental rethinking of the basis for protection is preferable, and that inspiration for this can be drawn from US law.

Adopting the misappropriation doctrine

It is argued that consideration should be given, either by Parliament or by the courts in the United Kingdom or, less parochially, by those responsible for drafting a harmonising Directive for unfair competition, to adopting the Supreme Court's misappropriation doctrine from *INS v AP*. Applying this to each case above:

(1) time and effort had been expended in developing a new product, shape or container, or a new 'look' for a store or restaurant;
(2) the result of the work was something which had (or would in the future have) commercial value against competitors; and
(3) misappropriating it gave the copier an unfair advantage because it prevented the person who developed it from becoming exclusively associated with it, as he has planned to do, and it thus deprives him of the return on his investment.

An unfair competition law based on these elements would thus venture where UK passing-off law currently fears to tread. Moreover, by adopting the misappropriation doctrine, the law would be put on a sound doctrinal basis, and moreover, one which would be consistent with modern competition or anti-trust law, in that it effectively would be allowing protection against those who seek to 'free-ride' on others' investments.[149] There would remain the need to ensure that such a law would safeguard competition. This could be achieved by adopting the functionality doctrine developed in the United States for this purpose.[150] It has been argued that certain elements of product shape or packaging must be reproduced by any

---

[148] Section 10(2)(b) Trade Marks Act 1994. See above.
[149] For an analysis of the free rider doctrine, see N. Green, *Commercial Agreements and Competition Law*, 1986, at 464 to 465; F. Scherer and D. Ross *Industrial Market Structure and Economic Performance*, 1991 (3rd edn), at 550 to 555.
[150] See Horton, 'Designs, Shapes and Colours: A Comparison of Trade Mark Law in the UK and the US', [1989] EIPR 311.

competitor who wishes to compete in the market for goods of that type. In other words, certain design features or colours or shapes have become industry standard or generic. They operate as 'visual signposts' or a type of shorthand to denote a type of product or perhaps characteristics of a product. Supermarket own brands give a good example of this across a range of products. For example, red-topped coffee jars indicate decaffeinated instant coffee.

Alternatively, the shape of the product or its packaging may be in practice the only economically feasible way of producing such goods. The question is whether there can be effective competition using variant designs for the product shape or packaging, or whether preventing use of a particular shape, colour or design would be a barrier to entry into that particular market.

What an unfair competition law, based on the concept of misappropriation subject to a functionality exception, would protect would be the ability of brand owners who have developed a potentially distinctive get-up for their products to reach 'first base' without being copied. It would also provide a remedy, in later stages, if confusion sufficient to establish passing off cannot be easily established, typically where the copier has taken the get-up but adopted a different word mark.

This proposal is limited to dealing with the problem of brand name protection, but it has wider implications. An unfair competition law of misappropriation tempered by functionality could provide solutions to other areas where intellectual property rights sits uncomfortably besides competition law principles or interoperability requirements, as in computer software. Perhaps the infringement complexities of software infringement could be reduced by analysing the problem in terms of misappropriation. This is beyond the scope of the present article, but should not be left out of consideration in any EC harmonisation of this question.

Ultimately the question to be answered is whether there is a need for a more general law to protect work or 'creations' which are not specifically protected by particular intellectual property rights. Should everything not specifically protected be freely available in the public domain? To those who argue the need for certainty and fear the ill-defined ambit of an unfair competition law, it can be answered that the existing UK laws of passing off is fluid and constantly developing. It has not, however, crossed the Rubicon of misappropriation. It may well be that it will take EC harmonisation to bridge this gap.

If this is to happen, it is argued that there is a role for an unfair competition law within the United Kingdom and that it would reduce the confusion evident from the EC case law if this were done by way of harmonisation from the EC. However, such a law should not simply replicate what is currently the case in many civil law jurisdictions. The problems to be tackled must be clearly identified and the solutions proposed must be based on a sound conceptual basis. In the area with which this article is concerned, trade mark law, the authors have identified what they regard as the main problem areas. It may be that both UK and continental European law can use the US misappropriation doctrine as a model for a modern, harmonised unfair competition law. Rather than dealing in vague notions of good faith[151] or honest business practices, the authors advocate making the doctrine of misappropriation central to such a law. This doctrine requires the identification of specific interests which deserve protection. This would not only make harmonisation more likely to be achieved by converging common and civil law, but would also be in line with much of modern EC competition law, making sure that the two laws were striving to achieve the same ends.

---

[151] As the Unfair Terms in Consumer Contracts Directive OJ 1993 L95/29 (implemented in the United Kingdom by the Unfair Terms in Consumer Contracts Regulations SI 1994/3159) rather unfortunately, in the authors' opinion, attempts in the field of contract law.

Trade Marks Invisible at Point of Sale: Some Corking Cases

[1990] 7 EIPR 241

PETER PRESCOTT
Barrister, London

In this note I propose to consider this question: to what extent must a mark be visible in the course of trade for it to count as trade mark use? And I wish, in particular, to consider the validity of the *Striped Toothpaste* cases[1] from that point of view.

Suppose a trade-marked product is supplied in an opaque container such that the consumer has no opportunity for inspection before acquisition.

At first sight this might appear to happen so rarely in practice as to make the question of academic interest only. It might also seem that the trade mark proprietor deserves little sympathy if he chooses to hide his light under a bushel in this way. But neither proposition is necessarily correct. For instance, it is possible to envisage a trade mark for pen nibs, or a watermark for writing-paper, or a trade mark consisting of a two-colour pattern or a pharmaceutical capsule, and so on; in each case the product being supplied in an opaque container.

The legal question is, is this use of the trade mark? If not: (1) use by a usurper is not infringement and (2) use by the registered proprietor is not 'use' sufficient to satisfy section 26 of the Trade Marks Act 1938 and the mark may have to come off the register.

I shall simply review the cases (so far as I know, all of them) and conclude with some general observations.

In *Ponsardin v Peto* (1862)[2] Sir John Romilly M.R., and again in *Moet v Clybouw* (1877)[3] Sir George Jessel M.R., granted an injunction to restrain the defendants from selling their champagne in bottles whose corks bore counterfeit brands. Then as now, the marks were branded on the bottom and sides of the corks and so could not be inspected before opening.

The same kind of infringement was restrained in *Moet v Pickering*.[4] As in the forementioned cases, it was taken for granted that this was conduct the Court ought to restrain, so much so that it is probable that none of these would have been reported if other, more debatable points, had not been involved.

These cases were about so-called common law trade marks. *The Army and Navy Co-operative Society Ltd v The Army, Navy and Civil Service Co-operative Society of India Ltd* (1891)[5] was a passing-off case. The defendants had a name similar to the plaintiffs' which

---

[1] *Unilever's (Striped Toothpaste) TM* [1980] FSR 280; *Unilever plc's TM* [1984] RPC 155; *Unilever Ltd's (Striped Toothpaste) No. 2) TM* [1987] RPC 13.
[2] 33 Beav 642.
[3] Sebastian's Digest at 533. The point is particularly apparent from this report.
[4] (1878) 8 Ch.D. 372—CA.
[5] 8 RPC 426.

they were entitled to use provided they did not abbreviate it. They caused an abbreviated version to be stamped on a large number of corks which were sent out to India, where they were used in bottles of wine. Kekewich J said: 'They probably will be looked at by persons who use those bottles in the sense of taking out the corks with the intention of drinking the wine which they are protecting.' He granted an injunction restraining the defendants from selling the wine, even though the bottles were not only labelled with the full version of their name, but also had capsules (covering the necks) similarly marked. The learned judge said that the label and capsule diminished the risk of confusion but did not obviate it altogether; but the principal ground of his decision was that it would be dangerous to create a precedent facilitating the practice of fraud. He expressly acquitted the defendants themselves of fraudulent intent; so in the context the danger of fraud can only have referred to the practice of label switching at the retail level.

It is here, perhaps, that we arrive at the heart of the matter. The practice of branding champagne corks had two objects in Victorian times. One (which may or may not have been known to Mr Justice Kekewich) was so that the wine waiter could claim his commission on delivering up used corks. The other was so that the consumer could verify that he had not been cheated. It is easy to switch labels; it is much harder to switch corks.

Ten years later the same practice came up before the same judge in *Findlater, Mackie, Todd & Co. v Henry Newman & Co.*[6] The defendant, a Bournemouth wine merchant, had been accustomed to buy his wines from the plaintiffs, a London firm, and to use their name in connection therewith. There was a falling off in their business and it was proved that the defendant had ordered, and had used, a great many wine corks branded with the plaintiffs' name but which had not been applied to bottles of the plaintiffs' wine. The plaintiffs sued for passing off. Kekewich J said he had no doubt about the following: 'The object of putting the cork with the brand on it into the bottle is that when the cork is drawn and seen by the customer he may connect the contents of the bottle with the brand.' He added that if the customer was satisfied he would thereupon attribute importance to the brand. The defendant's object was to encourage his customers to believe that what was in the bottle had been supplied by the plaintiffs. He ordered an account of profits.

In *Singer Manufacturing Co. v Wilson*[7] Sir George Jessel M.R., in the course of expounding the principles of common law trade marks, said:

> Sometimes you do not find anything put on the goods themselves, the reason often being that the goods are not capable of it; for instance, when they are liquids, upon which of course you cannot put a mark, and therefore a mark is put on the bottle containing the liquid, or on the cork which is in the bottle and helps to retain the liquid. *These are again true trade-marks*, whether affixed in the shape of a label on a bottle of liquid or in the shape of a device on the cork ... they ... go along with the goods on sale.

It is therefore apparent that by the end of the 19th century the Chancery judges had no difficulty with the idea of a trade mark which is not visible until after the container has been opened and which, therefore, cannot be inspected before the moment of purchase. Such marks perform two functions. They serve the function of verification and make it harder to counterfeit. And, if the consumer comes across goods, for example at a dinner party, and likes them, he may repose confidence in the brand and order it next time.

---

[6] (1902) 19 RPC 235.
[7] (1876) 2 Ch.D. 434, 441.

Those were unregistered trade marks. Although we should not expect to find any different principle in the case of registered marks, we cannot rule out *a priori* because the matter is governed by statute; and so it is necessary to consult the statutory language.

There was no functional definition of 'trade mark' until the Trade Marks Act 1905. Section 3 said:

> A 'trade mark' shall mean a mark used or proposed to be used upon or in connexion with goods *for the purpose of indicating that they are the goods of the proprietor* of such trade mark whether by virtue of manufacture, selection, certification, dealing with, or offering for sale.

There was, therefore, nothing in that definition which required that the 'indicating' had to be performed at the moment of sale. A branded champagne cork could have satisfied it. The definition in the current Act[8] so far as relevant is:

> 'trade mark' means ... a mark used or proposed to be used in relation to goods *for the purpose of indicating, or so as to indicate, a connection in the course of trade* between the goods and some person having the right ... as proprietor ... to use the mark...[9]

This definition is, if anything, wider; but the point to notice is that 'connection in the course of trade' refers to the message the trade mark must convey, and is a generalisation of the earlier expression 'manufacture, selection', etc. So branded champagne corks could also satisfy the current definition.

In two early registration cases the practice of branding corks was before the courts but the present point was not decided.

In *Richard v Butcher* (1891)[10] the plaintiffs had registered as trade marks the words MONOPOLE and DRY MONOPOLE. The marks had been registered under the 1875 Act. This Act did not permit the registration of a word mark unless the proprietor had used it before 1875. Moreover, the courts in interpreting the Act required in practice that the pre-1875 use must have been of the mark alone, not accompanied by other matter.[11] The purpose of this judicial device was to prevent people from acquiring monopolies in non-distinctive matter. The proprietors of MONOPOLE and DRY MONOPOLE could not prove use of these words alone. The best they could do was to show use on the sides of the corks (different trade mark matter appearing on the bottle), and even then the cork bottoms were impressed with a distinctive device including the firm name. The Court of Appeal held that the proprietors had never used the registered words *solus* and ordered them to be expunged from the register.

In *Kinahan's Application* (1893)[12] there was an application to register the word KINAHAN in an oval for spirits. This was an application under the 1883 Act as amended. By this law the applicants could not register KINAHAN except on proof of use before 1875.[13] The

---

[8]   Trade Marks Act 1938, section 68(1).
[9]   By the same subsection it is provided that:

> References in this Act to the use of a mark shall be construed as references to the use of a printed or other visual representation of the mark, and references therein to the use of a mark in relation to goods shall be construed as references to the use thereof upon, or in physical or other relation to, goods.

[10]   8 RPC 249.
[11]   Kerly on Trade Marks, 1908 edition at 205.
[12]   10 RPC 393.
[13]   Patents, Designs and Trade Marks Act 1883, as amended in 1888, section 64.

applicants proved use of the mark on the circumference of their corks for a great many years; but unfortunately, it was always accompanied by other trade mark matter, for example on wax seals or capsules on the necks or on labels on the bottles. Other parties claimed to have used the name 'Kinahan' concurrently. Chitty J held that the mark had not been used exclusively as a trade mark before the relevant date. The judge left open the question whether hidden use on a cork could ever be trade mark use. The 'champagne cork' cases, however, were not cited to him.

Neither of those two cases is authority for the proposition that trade mark user does not count unless it takes place at the point of sale.

In *Re TM of Crompton & Co. Ltd* (1902)[14] a party had registered as a single trade mark a collection of three different labels. These were used for cotton yarn, as follows. Two of the labels were placed on the outside of the packages of yarn, but the third was always placed on the inside, in fact on the cardboard backing about which the yarn was wound, and was invisible to the purchaser. An application was made to expunge the registration on the ground that the composite mark had never been used; Mr Kerly, the applicants' counsel, argued that 'the concealed mark was not used as a Trade Mark . . . A Trade Mark must sell the goods to the purchaser before he opens the package.' Mr Sebastian for the registered proprietors denied this and cited the champagne cork cases. Swinfen Eady J rejected Mr Kerly's argument. This is, therefore, an express judicial determination of the point.

Charles Goodall & Son Ltd v John Waddington Ltd (1924)[15] was a case about playing cards. The plaintiffs had registered a highly distinctive representation of the ace of spades. The defendants' playing cards had an ace of spades which the plaintiffs claimed was too similar, but this contention was rejected by Eve J and the Court of Appeal; this was the actual ground of their decisions. The unusual aspect of the case was that the ace of spades card was, with rare exceptions, not seen by the purchaser of the deck until after the sealed pack was opened and, therefore, not until after purchase. The defendants argued that this was not trade mark use at all. Different views were expressed by the judges. Eve J, noted that 'the distinctive mark is rarely, if ever, used to effect a sale':

> but those members of the public who play cards, and thereby become acquainted with the distinguishing mark adopted by the manufacturer whose goods they prefer, do, of course, identify and, it may be, look for the mark they desire, in order to satisfy them that the origin is that which they have been accustomed to know.

In the Court of Appeal, Pollock M.R. doubted whether the parties had used the ace of spades as a trade mark; but this was because it had not been shown that the public had come to recognise the ace as an indicium of origin.[16] Warrington LJ expressed no opinion on the question. Sargant LJ doubted whether the plaintiffs had used the ace as a trade mark, but he treated the fact that the ace was not seen before purchase merely as part of the factual matrix, the real point being whether the public relied on the ace as an indication of origin or simply as an attractive design.[17] He pointed out that the plaintiffs used a special heart device as 'their regular Trade Mark'.

The real point of the *Charles Goodall* case, therefore, was not whether a mark did not count because invisible until after purchase; but whether it performed the function of a trade mark at all, even when inspected. The relevant public might just have considered it as a

---

[14] 19 RPC 265.
[15] 41 RPC 465; on appeal 41 RPC 658.
[16] 41 RPC at 663.
[17] 41 RPC at 671 to 672.

pretty design: a question of fact. That the ace was not visible before purchase was evidence as to this, but nothing more. In the event all opinions were *obiter* because the judges decided the case on the ground that the defendants' ace was not close enough to the plaintiffs'.

In *Unic SA v Lyndeau Products Ltd*[18] (better known as *Everglide TM*) the defendants supplied a large number of ball-point pens bearing the plaintiffs' registered trade mark. The mark was printed around the push-button on the end in lettering so small as to be scarcely visible. The mark was not there to brand the pens but to comply with a marking requirement in a patent licence. However, Ungoed-Thomas J held that the defendants' purpose was irrelevant since the test was objective, and the small size of the mark did not prevent it from being a trade mark. However, there it was possible for the purchaser to examine the mark at the point of sale. It is submitted that the fact (if it was a fact) that few purchasers would have noticed this tiny mark was a matter going to mitigation of damages, not an answer to liability. However, the case is of some limited assistance in this sense, that it tends to show that it is not an essential function of a trade mark that it makes you want to purchase the goods at the point of sale.

It is possible no doubt to find some *obiter dicta* explaining the functions of a trade mark in terms narrow enough to exclude the kind of use we are considering. Such have no normative value unless one can see that the judge had our point in mind. Thus, in *Powell's TM* (1893)[19] Bowen LJ said:

> The function of a trade mark is to give an indication to the purchaser or possible purchaser as to the manufacture or quality of goods, to give an indication to his eye of the trade source from which they come … It is obvious that if it is to be an indication to the purchaser's eye of what I have stated, it must either be impressed on the goods or so accompany the goods as to produce that effect on the purchaser.

This, however, is not to be treated as statutory language: there is a perfectly good definition in the statute itself. Moreover, Bowen LJ in referring to the 'purchaser' seems merely to have been referring to the customer, not necessarily the moment of purchase. The person who buys a bottle of champagne and spots the wrong brand on the cork when he has his dinner is a purchaser for all that. The context of the *Powell* case was that Bowen LJ was concerned with the presence of the words 'Yorkshire Relish' on the rough packing cases holding the sauce bottles (which themselves bore a much more detailed trade mark):

> [It] may be that its object is not to indicate anything at all to the purchaser, but to indicate something to those who are handling the packing case either for the purpose of carriage of storage.

★   ★   ★   ★   ★

We may pause there. It is apparent that from an early date the courts took it for granted that a mark, branded on wine corks and hence invisible before opening, performed the function of a trade mark; that no less an authority than Sir George Jessel regarded such marks as 'true trade marks'; that such marks fall within the statutory definition of 'trade mark'; that there was no contrary authority decided under the registration system; and that

---

[18] [1964] RPC 37.
[19] 10 RPC 195, 200.

it was judicially determined in the *Crompton* case that trade mark use may be performed although the mark is invisible at the point of purchase.

The *Striped Toothpaste* cases all concern the well-known dentifrice sold under the brand name *Signal*. The tube is so constructed that, when squeezed, red stripes are formed along the length of the extruded strip of paste. In the past it was advertised as 'The toothpaste with the mouthwash in the stripes'; more recently, fluoride was put in the stripes, which fact was advertised.

In the first of these[20] the proprietors of the brand sought to register the stripes themselves. The application defined the mark as 'the colour red applied in five evenly spaced longitudinal stripes to white toothpaste on extrusion in circular cross-section from the container in which the toothpaste is sold'. This was rejected by the Registry and (on appeal) by Whitford J. It is submitted that this was one of those cases where the objectors instinctively felt that it was not a valid trade mark but incorrectly articulated the reasons for saying so.

Surely the proper objection to this mark was that the applicants (upon whom the onus lay) had failed to show that the preponderant function of the stripes in the mind of consumers was to indicate trade source. Perhaps they attached importance to these because they indicated the presence of a mouthwash, or fluoride, or simply because it was a pretty gimmick which they liked for its own sake. It would not be enough, of course, merely to show that consumers associated the stripes with *Signal* toothpaste. (Many a functional device is associated with a particular manufacturer, because nobody else makes it.) It would have to be shown that consumers relied on the stripes as an assurance of origin (source motivation). This was a pure question of fact with which we are not concerned.

The Registry is reported to have objected because the mark was never in existence in the course of trade. It is respectfully submitted that if that is what they said, their objection was misconceived.

Suppose that, instead of stripes, the tube incorporated an ingenious device such that, when squeezed, the word SIGNAL was printed on the emergent toothpaste strip in a repeat motif.

Why would that not be trade mark use? The printed message would surely satisfy the statutory definition since it would serve 'to indicate a connection in the course of trade' between the goods and the proprietors. It would serve its purpose in commerce in two ways. First, it would perform the function of verification. Consumers accustomed to relying on the print motif would notice its absence in a counterfeit (or, shall we say, a Brazilian parallel import?) and could take it back to the shop. Secondly, it would serve as an excellent advertisement. Other members of the households where this toothpaste was used, would have the brand name impressed on their minds and would be likely to order it in future if satisfied with the product.

The reported Registry objection seems to be predicated on the supposition that 'trade' is something which ceases the moment goods are sold. Not so.[21] One of the most important functions of a trader is to seek repeat orders. This is best done by supplying goods which satisfy the consumer—and arranging that she is reminded of the source of her satisfaction, preferably at the very moment of use. If his goods do satisfy in use, and at the same time he is able to send a message attached to the goods into the consumer's home saying 'And I am the man responsible for bringing you this satisfaction—please remember my name', it is at least inaccurate to deny that the mark is being used in trade. Why else is he doing it? Besides, the objection is not based on the Act. This does not require that the mark enunciate a

---

[20] [1984] FSR 280.
[21] Most prescription pharmaceuticals are not *sold* to the public at all: see *Pfizer v Ministry of Health* [1965] AC 512, 535.

message *in the course of trading*, that is buying and selling, but that the message, when perceived, should indicate *a connection in the course of trade*, for example 'These are the goods of the SIGNAL people'; not quite the same thing, after all.

Besides, under the current Act a trade mark need not be physically attached to goods at all. It can be used in advertisements. Why should not a SIGNAL motif printed on the paste extrusion, viewed every time the consumer cleans his teeth, be regarded as an advertisement?

The learned judge relied on the *Smith Kline and French Laboratories* coloured capsule case[22] (in which a distinctive pattern applied to pharmaceutical capsules was admitted to registration as a 'mark'). Referring to Lord Diplock's speech in that case, Whitford J said:

> [It] refers to the fact that, whatever else a trade mark may consist of, it must consist essentially of some sort of visual representation which is applied either to the goods themselves, which may in fact include incorporation of the mark in the goods as well as the application of the mark to containers or its use in advertising matter upon tags and labels, so that the mark is used in the course of trade, *that is, at a representation which can be seen by the purchaser at the time when he buys the goods.*[23]

That Lord Diplock said that a mark must be present in a visual representation is undeniable—he was merely citing section 68(2) of the Act. It is harder to discover where Lord Diplock is supposed to have laid down the proposition that a mark *must* be visible to the purchaser at the time of purchase. Perhaps the learned judge was referring to the following passage:[24]

> The [Smith Kline and French] colour combinations have thus been shown by undisputed evidence [which led the opponents to concede that a passing-off action could have been brought] to serve the business purpose of a trade mark. They do precisely what a trade mark is meant to do: they indicate to potential buyers that the goods were made by SSKF and not by any other manufacturer. To the ordinary business man it would, I think, appear a strange anomaly in the law of trade marks if these colour combinations applied to the capsules and their pellets were disentitled to the protection conferred by registration.

With great respect, this was not a statutory definition, and it is submitted that Lord Diplock (who, if anyone, was strong on 'purposive construction') would have been the first to object if told that in using these words he was implicitly overruling the champagne cork line of cases. To paraphrase his own words,[25] 'Nobody has been able to point to any business purpose that would be served by drawing a distinction between marks' that are relied on to make sure of having got the right goods at the moment of purchase, and at some later opportunity convenient for observation. The sense of the indented passage is clear enough. Here we have SKF with a colour combination which serves to distinguish their capsules from those of other traders. They do precisely what a trade mark usually does.

The tendency to treat passages in speeches in the House of Lords as if they were to be construed as an Act of Parliament ought to be guarded against. It is inadmissible when the

---

[22] [1976] RPC 511, House of Lords.
[23] *Emphasis supplied.*
[24] *Ibid.,* at 533.
[25] *Ibid.,* at 534 to 535.

House is expounding the common law,[26] and more so when considering a statutory definition. The point about marks appearing after purchase simply was not before the House.

The learned judge rather encouraged the applicants to come back with a fresh application for a two-dimensional picture mark showing the product. This they did, and it gave rise to the second *Striped Toothpaste* case.[27] Here the applicants failed before Falconer J who held that the picture mark was a descriptive device, being a mere representation of their goods! However, given that the coloured stripes on the goods were taken to be unregistrable (the Whitford J decision not being challenged) the decision seems correct on its facts.

In the third *Striped Toothpaste* case[28] (confusingly, reported under the reference '*Striped Toothpaste No. 2*'), the applicants came back again with stronger evidence and slightly different picture marks. The application was rejected by Hoffman J, essentially on what I have called the 'proper' ground, namely, that the marks were not inherently distinctive, because their true function was not so much to indicate origin as to be inherently attractive to children and others. With this ground we have nothing to do in this note. What is of present concern are certain observations of the learned judge delivered *en passant*. He supported the correctness of the original decision on the basis that the stripes were not used 'to distinguish the product in the course of trade'. He added:

> If the evidence in *Smith Kline & French* had shown that the capsules were invariably sold in sealed opaque packages, the registration of their three-dimensional appearance would have been open to the same objection as the appearance of the toothpaste in this case.

This is rather a far-reaching proposition. Opinions differ, of course, about whether capsule colour registrations should be allowed for pharmaceuticals at all, but that aside, it would seem rather a strong result to deny registration to marks *a priori* because the products bearing them are sold in opaque sealed containers. For example, it is common for two different trade marks to be used in relation to goods. One mark may be applied to the opaque container where space is not at a premium and the other may consist of a small device (for example the maker's logo) applied to the goods themselves, for example pills. Or the goods might consist of writing-paper, with a water-mark worked into the material, and with a second, probably more elaborate mark printed on the wrappers. If one is right in supposing that the concealed mark may perform the valid function of verification, making counterfeiting difficult, it is hard to see why this should not qualify as trade mark use. However, these observations do not seem to form part of the *ratio decidendi*.

It should be added that there is no evidence that in any of the *Striped Toothpaste* cases but the first was the present point in issue; nor that there was an adequate citation of authority in the first.

In summary, it is submitted that:

(1) The fact that a mark is not capable of being seen until after purchase does not *ipso lege* prevent its use from qualifying as trade mark use.
(2) But in such cases the facts may require careful examination to see that the mark is really performing a trade mark function, that is, serving to indicate a connection in the course of trade.

---

[26] See Slade LJ's observations in *My Kinda Bones v Dr Pepper's Stove* [1984] FSR at 297; in *Chelsea Man Menswear v Chelsea Girl* at [1987] RPC 206.
[27] [1984] RPC 155.
[28] [1987] RPC 13.

(3) The language of the Act, and the weight of the authorities, are consistent with the above propositions.

(4) The first *Striped Toothpaste* case was wrongly decided, or at any rate decided on the wrong ground.

Think Before You Waga Finger

[1996] 6 EIPR 317

PETER PRESCOTT

8 New Square, Lincoln's Inn, London

In the January issue of this journal Mr Kamperman Sanders[1] takes Mr Justice Laddie to task for getting it wrong in *Wagamama*. The title says it all: 'Back to the Dark Ages of Trade Mark Law'. And it ends: 'The decision undermines the legitimate interests of trade mark owners and furthermore frustrates the objective of the Directive to approximate the laws of the Member States. Clarification by the European Court of Justice is now in order.'

A person may do a valuable service, not by being right, but by being wrong. Kamperman Sanders' article is particularly valuable because not only does he embrace a series of propositions, every one of which is wrong, but he does so with great clarity. This is a combination which is rare, and very instructive. Let us examine this reasoning, and thus benefit from it.

In *Wagamama*, of course, Mr Justice Laddie held that *Rajamama* was an infringement of *Wagamama*, because the names were close enough to cause confusion. But this is not enough for Mr Kamperman Sanders. He wants the judge to have held that there was infringement even if nobody was confused at all.

The test under the Act is whether, because of the similarity, 'there exists a likelihood of confusion on the part of the public, which includes the likelihood of association with the trade mark'. (The relevant sections of the Act are reproduced on page 321 below.) In rejecting the contention that association without confusion is not enough under section 10(2), Mr Justice Laddie has apparently taken us back to the Dark Ages, which I take to be an era when views prevailed which the Netherlands school of trade mark writers does not happen to share.

I should have thought that where a statute says that confusion *includes* a likelihood of association, then the latter must be a subset of the former. It must be that sort of association which involves confusion. Mr Justice Laddie held that to embrace the Benelux philosophy, as it were, would be to introduce a new kind of monopoly for which he was unable to discern any clear legislative intent. However, Kamperman Sanders thinks that Mr Justice Laddie's anti-monopolistic arguments are too 'one-sided', because a trade mark is more than an indicator of origin, a proposition which he claims to derive partly from the writings of the legal school to which he belongs.

Well, in one sense it is true that a trade mark is more than an indicator of origin. As he points out, it can be an investment, or an asset in a balance sheet; but why stop there? It may also be a corporate totem pole; a Pavlovian stimulator; a cultural icon; a nostalgia-

---

[1] [1996] 1 EIPR 3.

provoker; an expropriator of surplus value; a repository of illusions; a disfigurer of the visual environment; and so forth.

But all this does not address Mr Justice Laddie's point. Because it is also a monopoly, some outward limit has to be set on its scope. I shall argue, first, that valid monopolies cannot derive from anywhere but the will of the legislators, *clearly expressed*. I do not mean this just as a legal proposition (for that would be trivial enough) but as a moral and logical one. I shall argue that no coherent alternative view can be entertained. It is worth emphasising this point even beyond the limits of the present controversy since, increasingly and not least in this journal, political contention is purveyed as legal discourse.

A monopoly is that which constrains the freedom of action of others and restrains the cleansing effect of competition. Thus it cannot be supported save and insofar as those evils are felt to be outweighed by other considerations, for example, distributive justice or superior efficiency.

The first objection (much the less serious one, but enough to be fatal in itself) is that the court has no way of measuring the alleged superior efficiency conferred by the wider monopoly. It is indeterminate. Kamperman Sanders writes that 'the decision undermines the legitimate interests of trade mark owners'. How do we know this to be so? A trader may dislike the possibility of trade mark dilution, but I suspect that possibility is heavily outweighed by a consideration infinitely more persuasive in practice, which is that widening the monopoly makes it more difficult for him to choose a safe trade mark to use in the first place. In real life, corporations do not spend too much time worrying about association without confusion, but they spend an awful lot of their time selecting marks which can be used without conflicting with other registrations. If they are large corporations, like Exxon, the cost of selecting a corporate mark may run into millions. This is a *real* burden, actually cast on industry, and not one that exists merely in the imaginations of trade mark writers. If they are small enterprises it may prove impossible to select a safe mark at all—they just have to hope for the best. Not always can they afford to wait for their application to register their trade mark to grind its way through the system.

In parentheses, a real European trade mark law aimed at completing the internal market would address this topic as the top priority. Needless to say there is no such law, and never can be, unless we presuppose that local cultural differences can be abolished. But local cultural differences have a way of being resistant to institutional integration. That which is not confusing in Maastricht may be so in Montpellier, and may continue to be so no matter what laws are passed or treaties entered into.

More fundamental than indeterminacy, however, is the objection of value-incommensurability. Suppose the Benelux solution promoted superior efficiency, a proposition which cannot be shown, which I strongly doubt, but which I shall assume for the sake of argument. It would still remain to compare this value against the others, namely, liberty of action and distributive justice, and perhaps other values we might be able to identify. But as a court of law how do you perform this exercise?

The answer, of course, is that you cannot. They are incommensurables, and cannot be weighed against each other according to any rational process which would command general support. But the point is that to decide *how far the monopoly shall go* requires precisely that: a comparison of incommensurables. A choice between incommensurables involves the giving up of a benefit different in kind from that which one acquires,[2] and cannot be a matter for legal deduction or reasoning.

[2] Joseph Raz, *Ethics in the Public Domain: Essays in the Morality of Law and Politics*, Oxford, Clarendon Press, 1994, Chapter 6.

Of course, individual citizens may have their private preferences. They are not required to reason at all. They may legitimately say: 'The supermarkets are thieves and I would *like* trade mark owners to be able to stop lookalike brands even though nobody is confused'; but they cannot *show* that this has to be so. They cannot logically refute the opponent who says, with equal legitimacy: 'I dislike trade mark owners because I believe they peddle illusions without actually lying, thus tending to expropriate the most vulnerable sections of the community; they are rip-off merchants; I hope the supermarkets take them to the cleaners'. Neither can refute the other.

The answer to the problem, therefore, cannot be obtained by any process of ratiocination. It is not a task for lawyers at all, or any other sort of self-elected *nomenklatura*. It is a task for political compromise. In short, it is a task for legislators.[3]

Now, if legislators wish to introduce new monopolies, it is open for them to do so, incurring whatever degree of public odium as may arise, but they ought to say so sufficiently clearly. Clarity as such costs them nothing. Why, by the way, did they not say 'confusion on the part of the public *or* the likelihood of association'?

Having failed to persuade the Community to adopt the Benelux solution; having failed to persuade the English courts, at any rate, that the Community *had* adopted the Benelux solution (and had signified its intention to do so, not by writing it into the Directive, but by the curious device of the leaking of Council minutes, certainly a rather unorthodox method of legislative fiat); it remains for the school of writers to which Kamperman Sanders belongs—perhaps it would be unkind to call it the Dutch Spin College—to arrive at their chosen goal by interpretation of the legislation.

Let us then, with Kamperman Sanders, consider further what the legislators actually said, with the object of elucidating their will. He has a particular affection for section 10(3), of which he writes: 'It is almost impossible to find a clearer legislative statement of intent on the expansion of the confusion rationale to the non-origin dilution rationale'. This may be so, but helps us not at all if section 10(3) is *sui generis*. For then it does not throw any further light on the meaning of section 10(2).

Section 10(3) concerns marks which have a reputation, and covers the use of similar marks on dissimilar goods where such use takes unfair advantage or is detrimental. The first thing to notice is that *section 10(3) is not mandated by European Community law*. Article 5(2) of the Directive[4] expressly states that Member States 'may' make a law to that effect. They do not have to. This is foreshadowed by the two Recitals which say:

> Whereas it does not appear to be necessary at present to undertake full-scale approximation of the trade mark laws of the Member States and it will be sufficient if approximation is limited to those national provisions of law which most directly affect the functioning of the internal market,

and

> Whereas it is fundamental, in order to facilitate the free circulation of goods and services, to ensure that henceforth registered trade marks enjoy the same protection under the legal systems of all Member States; whereas this should however not prevent the Member States from granting at their option extensive protection to those trade marks which have a reputation.

---

[3] John Gray, *Enlightenment's Wake*, London and New York, Routledge, 1995, Chapter 6.
[4] 89/104/EEC.

Thus section 10(3) is permitted as a derogation from the general principle, nay, the 'funda-mental' principle, that Member States may not create wider trade mark monopolies than are prescribed by the Directive.

It is therefore rather hard to see from whence Kamperman Sanders obtains the confidence to write that the *Wagamama* decision 'frustrates the objective of the Directive to approximate the laws of the Member States'. His point, if he has one, must be the lesser one that Mr Justice Laddie misinterpreted the domestic legislation of the United Kingdom. His school is now reduced to arguing that the English courts do not understand their own Act of Parliament. This is always a possibility of course, so we must examine his reasoning to see if it carries conviction. It is worth remarking, however, that his undertaking is a bold one indeed, seeing that he is writing from Maastricht to do battle with the judge on the latter's native ground. As it turns out, it is not much of a contest.

Here is his argument in a nutshell:

- According to section 10(3), you can have infringement even where there is no confusion.
- But section 10(3) is confined to the case where, although the two trade marks are the same or similar, the respective goods are not at all similar.
- However, if there may be infringement without confusion where the goods are dissimilar, *a fortiori* it ought to be possible for there to be infringement without confusion where the goods are similar.
- Since this situation is not catered for by section 10(3), it must be catered for by section 10(2).
- It follows that under section 10(2) there may be infringement without confusion. Hence, 'likelihood of association' must include non-confusing association.

The attentive reader will at once spot that there is something rather suspect about this reasoning, because sections 10(2) and 10(3) are themselves incommensurable. Thus, under 10(3) you have to have a reputation and the test is unfair advantage or detriment. But under 10(2) there is no requirement for reputation at all and nothing is said about unfair advantage or detriment. It does not at all follow from the *mere* fact that the public associates two trade marks without confusing them that the one is taking an unfair advantage of, or causing a detriment to, the other.

We may paraphrase the marks/goods relationships required by section 10 as follows:

10(1): Marks and goods identical.
10(2): Marks and goods too close.
10(3): Marks too close but goods not too close.

Of these, 10(1) is trivial and need not detain us further. There is automatically infringement and the court does not need to evaluate anything. (This would prohibit honest comparative advertising, were it not for section 10(6).)

Under 10(2) the court cannot decide whether the combination of marks/goods is 'too close' as a mere abstract proposition, for such a test would be meaningless. The test must be that they are 'too close' for something. Close enough for what? Close enough for confusion (which includes the likelihood of association) to occur. The test is therefore functional. That is what the Act says. It uses the word 'because'.

Despite this, it is possible for confusion to occur where the goods are completely dissimilar. Thus, if a party were to sell watches branded *Rolls-Royce*, a sector of the public would (one easily imagines) buy these in the belief that they were put on the market with the authority of Rolls-Royce, trusting to that name as an assurance that the watches were of sound manufacture. Such persons would not just be confused, they would be deceived, and on discovering the truth could bring an action for fraud. Yet the case does not fall within 10(2). (If watches are objected to as an example, on the ground that they are not different enough from cars, substitute goods which are even more dissimilar, for example, medicines.)

However, there would be no confusion at all if it were not for the fact that *Rolls-Royce* is not just an entry in some register, it is a superlatively well-known brand of motor car. This is where 10(3) comes in. It requires the plaintiff's mark to have a reputation. Then, if the defendant has used a mark which is identical or too similar, and *in such a way as to take unfair advantage or cause detriment*, it does not matter that the goods are dissimilar. There may be detriment or unfair advantage arising out of origin-confusion, as in my watch example, or it may arise even though there is no confusion.[5] That there is a likelihood of confusion, or even the likelihood of bare association without any confusion, may supply the likelihood of unfair advantage or detriment, but it is not automatic. Perhaps many people thought that SKF (the pharmaceuticals group) was somehow connected with SKF (the ball bearings group). I confess that I did so myself once, when a youth. But if the confusion/association does no harm, and is not unfair, it is not prohibited by 10(3).

The reason 10(3) is confined to cases where the goods are dissimilar is that, if the marks are close enough to cause unfair advantage/detriment even where the goods are dissimilar, then the marks will be close enough to cause more than that; they will cause confusion, if the goods are similar. There will be confusion anyway within 10(2). For instance, suppose the mark *Rolls* when applied to T-shirts is thought to take unfair advantage of the mark *Rolls-Royce*, here assumed to be registered for cars alone, but is not thought to be confusing. That would be within 10(3). But if that is so, *Rolls* will surely cause confusion when applied to goods which *are* similar, for example, lorries, which is within 10(2) anyway.

Is it possible to think of a relevant and convincing counter-example, that is, one where the registered mark has a reputation, the goods are similar, the defendant's mark is close enough to the plaintiff's to cause detriment or take an unfair advantage—close enough to do so even if the goods were *not* similar—yet there is no likelihood of origin confusion? I do not believe that it is. Of course, such confusion could be avoided, theoretically, by the defendant always issuing prominent disclaimers. Even if that were successful it would not be legally relevant, because the comparison is between mark and mark, external added matter being discounted.[6] He would infringe all the same.

For that reason, a party who uses a similar but non-identical mark on similar goods by way of comparative advertising (as in 'More leg-room than a Rolls'), or to supply spare parts (as in 'Use our replacement windscreens on your Rolls'), falls within 10(2). The reason he does not infringe, if he behaves honestly and so forth, is not that the mark fails to be confusingly similar when subjected to the mark versus mark test, but that he is exempted by 10(6) or 11(2).

Even if I am wrong and a convincing counter-example can be found, the legislator may well have thought otherwise. That, which is at the very least plausible, is quite sufficient to account for the absence of a 10(3) extended to similar goods, without having to invent a

---

[5] This may be somewhat rare in practice, however, because the public are rather more robust than some trade mark writers give them credit for. Thus not only is there the well-known brand of lemon juice *Jif*, there is also a floor cleaner (lemon-scented, for good measure) which is also called *Jif*. Although presumably the public 'associated' the floor cleaner with the lemon juice, when it first came out anyway, it is rather difficult to believe that it has done anyone any harm. The contents of use are so disparate and mutually irrelevant that the human mind soon learns to ignore the cross-reference. The public have not been put off enjoying Jif lemon juice with their pancakes.

[6] *Origins Natural Resources Inc. v Origin Clothing Ltd* [1995] FSR 280, 284, Jacob J.

Benelux doctrine. Thus, 10(3) was not extended to similar goods because it was not thought to be necessary to do so. Hence Kamperman Sanders' proposition, that 'it is almost impossible to find a clearer legislative statement of intent on the expansion of the confusion rationale', by which he means expansion within 10(2), not 10(3), is built on sand.

Sections 10(1) to (3) Trade Marks Act 1994

Infringement of A Registered Trade Mark
10(1) A person infringes a registered trade mark if he uses in the course of trade a sign which is identical with the trade mark in relation to goods or services which are identical with those for which it is registered.

(2) A person infringes a registered trade mark if he uses in the course of trade a sign where because—

(a) the sign is identical with the trade mark and is used in relation to goods or services similar to those for which the trade mark is registered, or
(b) the sign is similar to the trade mark and is used in relation to goods or services identical with or similar to those for which the trade mark is registered.

there exists a likelihood of confusion on the part of the public, which includes the likelihood of association with the trade mark.

(3) A person infringes a registered trade mark if he uses in the course of trade a sign which—

(a) is identical with or similar to the trade mark, and
(b) is used in relation to goods or services which are not similar to those for which the trade mark is registered.

where the trade mark has a reputation in the United Kingdom and the use of the sign, being without due cause, takes unfair advantage of, or is detrimental to, the distinctive character of the repute of the trade mark.

The Return to Wagamama

[1996] 10 EIPR 521

ANSELM KAMPERMAN SANDERS

Former EC Human Capital and Mobility Research Fellow at QMWC, presently Senior Lecturer at Maastricht University

In the June issue of this journal, Mr Prescott QC[1] gives his barristerial reply to my opinion[2] on the *Wagamama* case.[3] According to Prescott my assessment of the case is wrong, as are the propositions on which my argument is based.

In short, the bone of contention is whether the concept of trade mark dilution is incorporated in section 10(2) of the Trade Marks Act 1994. This controversy is induced by the fact that the wording of section 10(2)[4] is ambiguous. The relevant question to ask here is whether association is to be seen as a subset of confusion, or if it has to be seen as a separate entity, based on the fact that the association criterion is wider in scope than the confusion rationale. My position is that, by the inclusion of the wording 'likelihood of association', the origin-based confusion rationale has not only been widened, but has also been appended by non-origin association, or the dilution doctrine. The justification for this argument is that, since subsection (3) of the same section 10 caters for this latter type of protection where dissimilar products are concerned, the same must be true for similar products. Mr Prescott's principal argument is that section 10(3) is *sui generis*, so that it cannot be used to shed light on section 10(2).

Before I discuss this point, however, I would like to address some of the minor points raised by Mr Prescott. In order to do so, I shall return to the *Wagamama* case and my reasons for writing a critical piece[5] with that intentionally provocative title 'Back to the Dark Ages of Trade Mark Law'. The *Wagamama* decision remains a case which, albeit correct in outcome as to the likelihood of confusion, displays unsatisfactory characteristics.

Obiter

The first factor is that Laddie J's statements about the association criterion were *obiter*, when the case could have been and indeed was decided on the basis of likelihood of confusion between signs used by the restaurants in question. It would have been better to wait for a

---

[1] P. Prescott, 'Think Before You Waga Finger' [1996] 6 EIPR 317.

[2] 'The Wagamama Decision: Back to the Dark Ages of Trade Mark Law' [1996] 1 EIPR 3.

[3] *Wagamama Ltd v City Centre Restaurants plc and City Centre Restaurants (UK) Ltd (formerly Garfunkels Restaurants plc)* [1995] FSR 713.

[4] See the extract from section 10 overleaf.

[5] See J. White, 'What's an Opinion For?', 62 [1995] U. Chicago LR 1363 on judicial opinions at 1368: The criticism of opinions ... —rational, political, moral—is an essential part of the activity of law. It is crucial to legal practice, for it is on the basis of such criticism that one will argue for or against the continued authority of a particular opinion or line of opinions.

case in which non-origin-based protection was sought against the use of identical or similar signs on similar goods or services. If it is indeed so that such a case is not conceivable, as Mr Prescott seems to infer,[6] it prompts the question whether Laddie J's exercise was one in futility.

Tautology

The second factor is that Laddie J dismissed[7] the association criterion as a tautology, as repetitive or unnecessary.[8] If this is so, then what is the scope of the confusion doctrine? Is it confined to origin-based confusion—in which case 'back to the dark ages' is an apt description—or is it at least interchangeable with origin-based association, which would mean that the association criterion is not an irrelevancy after all? In this latter case association is certainly not a tautology, as it has the effect of widening the scope of the confusion doctrine to those cases where the likelihood of confusion can only be demonstrated tentatively, by inference that affiliation in the mind of the consumer must ultimately lead to confusion, however minor.[9] Furthermore, the association criterion would have provided the courts with an excellent opportunity to infuse trade mark law with the law of passing off.[10]

Sections 10(1) to (3) Trade Marks Act 1994

Infringement of A Registered Trade Mark

(1) A person infringes a registered trade mark if he uses in the course of trade a sign which is identical with the trade mark in relation to goods or services which are identical with those for which it is registered.

(2) A person infringes a registered trade mark if he uses in the course of trade a sign where because—

(a) the sign is identical with the trade mark and is used in relation to goods or services similar to those for which the trade mark is registered, or

(b) the sign is similar to the trade mark and is used in relation to goods or services identical with or similar to those for which the trade mark is registered.

---

[6] Note 1 above, at 320: 'Is it possible to think of a relevant and convincing counter-example, that is, one where the registered mark has a reputation, the goods are similar, the defendant's mark is close enough to the plaintiff's to cause detriment or take an unfair advantage—close enough to do so even if the goods were *not* similar—yet there is no likelihood of confusion? ... Even if I am wrong and a convincing counter-example can be found, the legislators may very well have thought otherwise.'

[7] Laddie J: 'In particular it is quite artificial for the court to pretend that each word of a modern statute which has been lifted more or less verbatim from an EC directive was chosen with the economy which was believed to have been applied to the drafting of British statutes of purely domestic origin. There is no basis upon which the court can assume the original directive was drafted so as to avoid tautology.'

[8] Reference was made to the view of Lord Greene in the *Hill* case [1949] AC at 552.

[9] The inclusion of the risk of confusion in the broader sense in Community law is supported by *Deutsche Renault AG v Audi AG* [1995] 1 CMLR 461, which was indeed, paradoxically, referred to by Mr Justice Laddie in the *Wagamama* case.

[10] One can think of the *Elderflower Champagne case, Taittinger v Allbev Ltd* [1993] 20 FRS 641. The rich tradition of the law of passing off may also prove invaluable when it comes to measuring the reputation, the distinctive character and the repute in Article 10(3). See A. Kamperman Sanders, 'Some frequently ask questions about the 1994 UK Trade Marks Act' [1995] 2 EIPR 67 at 72 to 74.

there exists a likelihood of confusion on the part of the public, which includes the likelihood of association with the trade mark.

(3) A person infringes a registered trade mark if he uses in the course of trade a sign which—

(a) is identical with or similar to the trade mark, and
(b) is used in relation to goods or services which are not similar to those for which the trade mark is registered.

where the trade mark has a reputation in the United Kingdom and the use of the sign, being without due cause, takes unfair advantage of, or is detrimental to, the distinctive character of the repute of the trade mark.

Council Minutes

The third factor is that Laddie J has chosen, acknowledging the possibility that it may create barriers to inter-state trade,[11] to put the protection of a competitor trader at a higher level than the approximation of judgments on this point. According to the judge, the recognition of non-origin-based protection would amount to the creation of a new quasi-copyright in trade marks,[12] which requires an unequivocal statement of legislative intent to do so. The judge dismissed the statements for entry in the minutes of the Council meeting at which the Directive was adopted as a valid reference. Even if one were to accept that the Council minutes are confidential,[13] the fact remains that they were circulated and available for inspection. In keeping with British tradition[14] the result was that this search for the expression of intent had to be constrained to the legislative text itself. The judge then made a value judgment about the clarity of the expression of the will of the legislature to grant a monopoly.[15] In this light the judge came to the conclusion that 'If it had been the intention to make the directive identical with Benelux law on this important issue it [the preamble to the directive] should have said so.'[16]

---

[11] Note 3 above, at 731.
[12] Ibid.
[13] The fact is that minutes do now not appear to be confidential. See C. Gielen, 'European Trade Mark Legislation: The Statements' [1996] 2 EIPR 83 (to which the minutes are provided as an annex at 87), who concludes at 85 that, on the basis of the Council Decision of 20 December 1993 on public access to Council documents, OJ 1993 L340/43, minutes of Council meetings should be kept confidential in particular circumstances, only if disclosure undermines certain specific interests. In other instances broadest public disclosure is presumed to be favoured.
[14] See however *Pepper v Hart* [1992] 3 WLR 1032 (HL), [1993] 1 All ER 42 and *Warwickshire County Council v Johnson* [1993] 2 WLR 1, [1993] 1 All ER 299.
[15] We must, however, not forget that the lack of unequivocal clarity is quite often a welcome omission, which enables the courts to develop the law. See R. Nozick, *The Nature of Rationality*, Princeton University Press, 1993 at 5:

'Lawlike statements do not contain terms for particular individual objects, dates, or temporal periods—or if they do, these statements can be derived from more general lawlike statements that do not. Lawlike statements contain purely qualitative predicates: stating the meaning of these does not require reference to any *particular* object or spatio-temporal location. Lawlike statements have an unrestricted universality; they are not simply a finite conjunction that was established by examining all cases. Lawlike statements are supported not just by instances falling under them but also by a linkage of indirect evidence. These very same features might be what enables a normative principle to license derivation of new judgments from previously accepted ones.'

[16] Note 3 above, at 731.

Prescott argues that any other position would amount to a choice between incommensurables. The choice of the recognition of non-origin-based protection would negate other values such as liberty of action, distributive action and others.[17] In his view this is a value judgment which the court is not equipped to make, since it cannot be a matter for legal deduction or reasoning. While I accept that monopolies are not to be created frivolously, it is also a fact that judges make value judgments all the time, even when there is no unequivocal legislative imperative or boundary to do so.[18] Judges can make value judgments on the basis of legal reasoning, provided that all relevant socio-economic data are taken into account.[19] In the *Wagamama* case, however, certain data were expressly discarded when they should not have been.

This again leads us to the references in the *Wagamama* case to the Council minutes, stating that the association criterion is a concept which in particular has been developed by Benelux case law, and the article by Furtner and Geuze,[20] who were members of the Dutch delegation in the Working Party on Intellectual Property for the—then—draft Directive on trade marks. Their account of the discussions that shaped Article 5 of the 1988 Directive may be an account from the perspective of one delegation only, but it does give an insight into the way in which the Benelux managed to have the association criterion included in the Directive in the face of opposition from other Member States.[21] The reason remains as valid now as it was then and is contained in Article 233 of the Treaty of Rome, which precludes the impairment of the completion of the regional union between Belgium, Luxembourg and the Netherlands insofar as the completion has not been achieved by the implementation of the Treaty. Within the Benelux a uniform trade marks act has been in effect since 1971, under which both the classical origin-based confusion rationale and elements of common civil law, such as passing off and non-confusion-based protection against dilution of a mark, are operational. The resulting harmonisation of trade mark and common law of the Benelux countries is therefore at a more advanced level than the harmonisation that was envisaged by the trade marks Directive and could therefore not be reduced by it. If the scope of protection of Benelux trade mark law had been reduced, the result would have been that non-origin-based protection against dilution would still have been available under common law. The alternative, namely reduction of protection available under common law in the Benelux states, would have amounted to interference with the law of tort, which clearly fell

---

[17] Note 1 above, at 318.

[18] As a far-reaching example see in this respect A. van Aswegen, 'Policy considerations in the law of delict' [1993] 56 *Tydshrif vir Hedendaagse Romeins-Hollanse Reg* 171, who describes the way in which South African judges deal with policy considerations in deciding unfair competition cases.

[19] Nozick, Note 15 above, at 6 to 7:

'Of course, a judge is a figure in an institutional structure, and principled decisions that fit past cases have a particular point within that institution. ... Principled decision making might be desired to constrain a judge's basis for decision. To be excluded are her personal preferences or prejudices, moods of the moment, partiality for one side of a dispute, or even thought-through moral and political principles that are personal to her. It might be held that a judge's own views, preferences, or even considered views should have no more effect than anybody else's—the judge was not given that institutional position to put her own preferences into effect. A requirement that decisions be principled fittings to past precedents might be a device to constrain the effect of such personal factors, limiting their play or crowding them out altogether.

However, the analogy to science, where the aim is truth and correctness, casts doubt on the last strong claim. Fitting the scientific data is a requirement, but this does not uniquely determine one lawlike statement. An indefinite number of curves can fit any finite set of data points; more than one will be lawlike. Hence additional criteria will be necessary to select which lawlike statement to accept tentatively and use in predicting. These criteria include simplicity, analogy to supported lawlike statements in related areas, fit with other accepted theories, explanatory power, theoretical fruitfulness, and perhaps ease of computation.'

[20] H.R. Furstner and M.C. Geuze, 'Beschermingsomvang van het merk in de Benelux en EEG-harmonisatie' [1988] 10 BIE 215.

[21] Note 20 above, at 216.

outside the mandate to approximate trade mark laws. Owing to the fact that the Treaty of Rome itself stood in the way of a requirement for the Benelux countries to undo the efforts of harmonisation, a compromise was forged. The wording of optional Article 5(2) was changed to reflect that the mark need not be famous to qualify for protection, but merely needs to have a reputation, and the optional Article 5(5)[22] was also appended to reflect Benelux practice. It follows that Benelux practice does not have to be altered in this respect.[23] It is, however, true that Benelux practice will have to change in that a mark must possess a reputation in order to qualify for protection under the Benelux equivalent of Article 10(3) of the UK Act, where before this was not a fixed legal requirement.[24]

So does this mean that just because the Benelux countries harmonised their common law by means of the inclusion of the association criterion in their trade mark law, by means of a precedent, enforced through the Treaty of Rome and acknowledged in the Council minutes, the association criterion has become the norm for the community? Leaving aside arguments of the need for approximation, which are sufficiently clear, not all commentators are convinced. A German commentator[25] observed that the association criterion came into existence because the Benelux states did not have a general law of unfair competition.[26] From this German point of view, the trade mark system need not be pervaded with notions of unfair competition law, because Germany does have an Unfair Competition Act. In fact the Unfair Competition Act serves as a safety net,[27] so that compliance with the Paris Convention is secured. However, the fact that a national provision is capable of supplying a similar type of protection does not mean dilution is not included in Community law where similar products are concerned, especially now that Article 5 of the Directive includes protection against dilution.

Sui Generis

Now let us turn to Mr Prescott's main argument, that Article 5(3) of the Directive is *sui generis*. My submission is that this cannot be so. It is true that Article 5(3) was optional and that Member States are under no obligation to implement this provision.[28] This does, however, not mean that it is merely a derogation from the principle that Member States may not create wider trade mark monopolies than are prescribed by the Directive. It is equally true that Article 5(2) sets out the minimum criteria for protection from which the Member States may not derogate and lower the scope of trade mark protection. Thus Article 5(3)

---

[22] Article 5(5), which deals with protection against use of a sign other than for the purpose of distinguishing goods or services, has been incorporated into Article 13A(1)(d) of the new Benelux trade mark law.

[23] Confirmation of this position at a judicial level was given in the case *Regina v Procter & Gamble*, Court of Appeal, Brussels 27 May 1993 [1993] IER 122 (*Always/Regina*).

[24] In practice, however, the strength of the mark (namely, a combination of distinctiveness and reputation) was often decisive. For an excessive judgment in this respect see *Hessels v Muelhens*, President of the Court of Justice The Hague 11 December 1991 [1992] IER 49 (*Sabatini*), where an unknown shoe manufacturer and owner of the mark *Sabatini* for footwear managed to stop Gabriela Sabatini from launching her own range of perfumes and cosmetics. The court accepted that Gabriela Sabatini's fame would easily lead to dilution of the shoe manufacturer's mark. The case was settled before an appeal decision could be handed down.

[25] See F. Albert's supportive comment on the *Wagamama* decision in [1996] GRUR Int. 735 at 739.

[26] The truth is that the Benelux countries did not have an Act of unfair competition, but that the law of unfair competition was, and still predominantly is, based on tortious liability, codified in a general clause in the respective civil codes. For practical purposes this general provision is very similar to the German custom of relying on the general clause contained in §1 of the Unfair Competition Act ('Gesetz gegen den unlauteren Wettbewerb' of 1909 as amended).

[27] Protection against dilution was already available on the basis of the law of unfair competition. See D. Ohlgart, 'Gebrauch der Marke eines Dritten ohne Verwechslungsgefahr' [1989] GRUR Int. 211.

[28] Austria chose in fact not to adopt it.

and its UK equivalent, section 10(3), equally form a natural and sanctioned evolution from these minimum criteria. This natural progression is emphasised by the drafting of Article 5 of the Directive (section 10 of the 1994 Trade Marks Act), which describes the rights conferred by a trade mark from its minimal application to its maximum effect, each with its specific boundary. It does so in an internally coherent way where the onus of proof increases disproportionately to the level of similarity of both goods or services and the marks.[29]

How then does Mr Prescott arrive at his conclusion that Article 5(3) is *sui generis* when there is nothing in the Directive, nor the preamble, nor the working papers, nor the Council minutes to support this position? He does so by leaving the factor of onus of proof out of the equation of the mark/goods relationship required by section 10.[30] He argues that sections 10(2) and 10(3) are incommensurable, because unlike Article 10(3) Article 10(2) does not require the unfair advantage or detriment test to the reputation of the mark and that therefore section 10(2) cannot extent to non-origin-based protection.

The fallacy is now easy to see. Section 10(2) simply does not require the plaintiff to show that the mark has a reputation, because the goods or services are too close. The plaintiff then does not have to prove that unfair advantage is being taken of the distinctive character or the repute of his mark or that use of the same/similar sign is detrimental to it. The plaintiff merely has to show a likelihood of confusion or association on the part of the public. And there, in section 10(2), the test is a different one, namely that of the strength of the mark.[31] The conclusion can only be that the test may be different, but that sections 10(2) and 10(3) are not incommensurable, since this fits within the conceptual progression of the single section. The extra requirements in terms of proof contained in section 10(3) may very well be the reason for the narrow definition of similarity of goods that was contained in *British Sugar plc v James Robertson and Sons*.[32] The result will be that more cases will have to be tried on the basis of section 10(3), placing plaintiffs under a higher onus of proof, while on the other hand allowing for a wider absolute scope of protection.

Examples

Let us now turn to the practical examples. From the above it is now clear that the convincing counter-example Mr Prescott asks for[33] already comprises more elements than are required under section 10(2). He wants the mark to have a reputation, where the strength of the mark is the only requirement. While it is true that the strength of a mark may depend on its reputation, distinctiveness is the more important criterion. Also the detriment and unfair advantage test is not part of section 10(2), although these are criteria which can be used in order to assess the *likelihood* of confusion or association.

The relevant question to ask, therefore, is whether there are cases in which there is a mark with sufficient strength, where the goods are similar, but where the use of a similar/identical sign does not cause confusion as to the origin of the goods. These cases come in various guises. In the category of look-alikes or product configuration cases, likelihood of confusion

---

[29] It is easy to picture this as a progression to the framework that can be found in A. Firth, *Trade Marks, The New Law*, Jordans, 1995 at 75 to 76.

[30] Note 1 above at 319 to 320.

[31] To emphasise that procedural rules of proof may also influence the operation of the association criterion—weak marks may still cause confusion, but are not likely to cause association—the Benelux negotiators insisted that a statement be included in the preamble to the Directive indicating that national procedural rules are not prejudiced by the Directive. See Note 20 above at 220 on Recital 10 of the preamble to the Directive.

[32] 7 February 1996, [1996] 9 RPC 281, Ch.D. *per* Jacob J.

[33] Note 6 above.

is not always likely,[34] but this category covers an area which the UK legislator has meant to leave for another day.[35]

In the category of comparative advertising a similar situation occurs, as the Directive on comparative advertising will apply.[36] It is, however, interesting to look at the US deer logo case.[37] The case involved two rival lawn tractor manufacturers. MTD used an animated version of John Deere's deer logo in a comparative TV commercial. The animal's appearance was small in comparison to a small dog and a lawn tractor, from which the animal scampers away, looking over its shoulder in apparent fear. The court held that this was a case of dilution.[38] A closely related category of cases where confusion is often absent[39] involves trade mark parody and parody advertising. Yet also in this area dilution may perform a function, even when the goods or services are similar.[40]

From the abundance of US examples,[41] it is a small step to the German *Springende Raubkatze* case,[42] in which the German Supreme Court has put a prejudicial question to the European Court of Justice as to the interpretation of Article 4(1)(b) of the Directive.[43] The Bundesgerichtshof asked two questions:

(1) Is it sufficient for the confirmation of the likelihood of confusion of a sign, comprised of a word and an image, with a sign that is merely registered as an image for the same and similar goods and which does not enjoy any particular reputation in the market, that both images are similar in spirit?

(2) In this correlation, which meaning needs to be attributed to the wording of the Directive, where the likelihood of confusion includes the likelihood of association with the earlier trade mark?

---

[34] For relevant recent US examples see [1995] 85 TMR, Annual Review at 704 to 707, where the cases *Versa Products Co. v Bifold Co. (Mfg) Ltd*, 33 USPQ 2d 1801 (CA 3 1995) and *Conopco Inc. v May Department Stores Co.* 32 USPQ 2d 1225 (CAFC 1994) are referred to. The former case dealt with the appearance of directional control valves for offshore oil drilling rigs and the latter dealt with skin care lotion. In both cases consumer confusion was not held to be likely in view of the clarity of labelling in packaging and advertising. On the tremors the *Conopco* case sent through the 'community charged with enjoining trademark rights', see S. Rosen and L. Gigliotti, 'Conopco-Kaputco for Trade Dress Plaintiffs?' [1995] 85 TMR 135.

[35] See Note 1 above, at 320. This is also what I indicated in my original opinion, Note 2 at 4. See in this respect HC Debs 16 May 1994 c. 301.

[36] See 84/450/EEC.

[37] *Deere & Co. v MTD Products Inc.*, 32 USPQ2d 1936 (CA 2 1994), [1995] 85 TMR Annual Review at 755 to 756.

[38] See in this respect also the examples given by S. Rosen and L. Gigliotti, Note 34 above, at 141 to 143 and the description of the 'foot in the door' theory of infringement in *Playboy Enterprises, Inc. v Chuckleberry Publishing Inc.*, 206 USPQ 70 (SDNY 1980), where an injunction against the use of the mark *Playmen* for adult magazines was granted on the basis of subliminal association, and *Grotrian, Helfferich Schultz, Th. Steinweg Nachf. v Steinway & Sons*, 186 USPQ 436 (CA 2 1975), where an injunction was granted for infringement of the *Steinway* trade mark for pianos, notwithstanding the absence of any likelihood of confusion. See in this respect also J. Garcia, 'Trademark Dilution: Eliminating Confusion' [1995] 85 TMR 489 at 508 to 511.

[39] See *Jordache Enterprises v Hogg Wyld Ltd*, 4 USPQ 2d 1216 (CA 10 1987), involving parody logos on jeans, where the likelihood of confusion in the wider sense was dismissed.

[40] See B. Keller and D. Bernstein, 'As Satiric as they Wanna Be: Parody Lawsuits under Copyright, Trademark, Dilution and Publicity Laws' [1995] 85 TMR 239, at 248 to 256.

[41] Dilution is now contained in section 43(c) of the Lanham Act. For a full exposé of the dilution theory see T. Martino, *Trademark Dilution*, Clarendon Press, Oxford, 1996.

[42] BGH 29 June 1995 [1996] 1 GRUR Int. 60, a case in which a refusal to register a mark comprising of the mark *Sabèl* with the image of a jumping feline for jewellery, leather goods and clothing, because of a conflict with a (not so similar) image mark of jumping feline.

[43] Article 4(1): 'A trade mark shall not be registered or, if registered, shall be liable to be declared invalid:
(b) if because of its similarity with, or similarity to, the earlier mark and the identity or similarity of the goods or services covered by the trade mark, there exists a likelihood of confusion on the part of the public, which included the likelihood of association with the earlier mark.

It would seem that some clarification on the association criterion may be forthcoming. It is, however, important to note that the second question is instrumental to the first question of determining the similarity of the signs and may therefore not lead to any clarification on the meaning of the association criterion itself in an infringement setting. We must also recognise that if it is meant that the criterion of likelihood of association can determine whether the signs are similar in spirit, the question is surely misplaced. The wording of Article 4(1)(b) indicates that the similarity of the signs may lead to the likelihood of confusion or association, not the other way around. Recital 10 of the Directive furthermore indicates that interpretation has to be given 'of the concept of similarity in relation to the likelihood of confusion; whereas the likelihood of confusion ... depends on numerous elements ...'. The controversy may therefore be with us for some time to come.

In revisiting the *Wagamama* case, however, I have given even more rock-solid arguments to support my original proposition that the association or dilution doctrine has a role to play in non-confusion cases involving similar goods. I therefore respectfully disagree with Mr Prescott that the expansion within section 10(2) is built on sand.[44] The only *faux pas*, therefore, was to write from abroad,[45] from the ancient Roman-medieval city of Maastricht, backdrop for the Treaty that means many things to many people. It may mean that we can all look forward to relying on more well-reasoned European doctrines in future.

---

[44] Note 1 above at 321.
[45] *Ibid.*, at 319.

Has the Benelux Trade Mark Law Been Written into the Directive?

[1997] 3 EIPR 99

PETER PRESCOTT Q.C.
8 New Square, Lincoln's Inn

The Controversy

Mr Kamperman Sanders[1] continues to maintain that 'the Benelux [delegation] managed to have the association criterion included in the Directive in the face of opposition from Member States'.

All arguments are futile unless we know what we are arguing about. First, what is the 'association criterion'? I believe the Benelux position was clearly stated by Professor Gielen in cross-examination in the *Wagamama* case:

> A. If Company A has a registered trademark, and Company B comes on to the market with another trademark where the marks have similarities, but no member of the public would be confused as to origin, but some members of the public say "Well that has a passing similarity. It brings to mind the company A's mark, but I know that they are nothing to do with each other." Would that be infringement?
> A. That is an infringement, yes ... If the relevant part of the public thinks of trademark A when seeing trademark B, the effect of that is, in fact, loss of exclusivity and dilution. So, I think the Benelux concept of association includes that danger.[2]

Secondly, avoidance of false controversy. Is it possible to infringe a registered trade mark under section 10(2) even though nobody is confused in fact? Certainly. Such has been the law in England for at least 90 years. In the first place, the plaintiff need not have used his mark at all; in which case nobody will have heard of it and nobody will be confused. In the second place, because comparison is between registered mark and defendant's sign, extraneous added matter being irrelevant. Hence a clear and prominent disclaimer, sufficient to avoid the public being confused, while it will avoid passing off, will not avoid trade mark infringement if the defendant's sign is similar to the plaintiff's mark—similar enough for confusion to occur in the absence of that disclaimer. Thus, in *Origins Natural Resources Inc. v Origin Clothing Ltd*,[3] Mr Justice Jacob said, apropos of section 10(2):

> [It] requires the court to assume the mark of the plaintiff is used in a fair and normal manner in relation to the goods for which it is registered and then to assess a likelihood of confusion in relation to the way the defendant uses its mark, discounting external added matter. The comparison is mark for mark.

---

[1] 'The Return to Wagamama' [1996] 10 EIPR 521.
[2] *Wagamama Ltd v City Centre Restaurants plc*]1995] FSR 713 at 724.

The same judge made the same point in *British Sugar plc v. James Robertson & Sons Ltd.*[4] The law was the same under the Trade Mark Acts 1905[5] and 1938,[6] and in a case under the latter statute Lord Greene M.R. said:

> The statutory protection is absolute in the sense that once a mark has been shown to offend, the user of it cannot escape by showing that by something outside the actual mark itself he has distinguished the goods from those of the registered proprietor.[7]

Incidentally, one effect of such a law is that it tends to protect marks against dilution. And why not? We try not to live in the Dark Ages here.

The Key Point

Where we differ from the Benelux law of 'association', therefore, is not that we require actual confusion while they do not. Nor is it that they protect against dilution while we never do. Rather, it is that in making the crucial mark v sign comparison we require more than a 'passing similarity' which 'brings to mind' the plaintiff's mark, although everyone can tell that they are 'nothing to do with each other'. Otherwise, we think it is likely to bring more loss than benefit. As I pointed out in my June 1996 Opinion[8] it would make it harder for a trader to choose a safe trade mark to use in the first place. Not a wholly irrelevant consideration, after all, if one wants to have a properly functioning internal market.

Council Minutes

Despite Mr Kamperman Sanders' reference to Council minutes, in the end he does not feel able to place any secure reliance on these. Here he is being consistent.[9] That a mature democracy should be ruled by minutes, the complete text of which nobody is able to produce in court,[10] would be an abomination, and more appropriate to a novel by Kafka. The idea

---

[3] [1995] FSR 280 at 284.

[4] [1996] RPC 281 at 293–294.

[5] *JB Stone & Co. Ltd v Steelace Manufacturing Co. Ltd* (1929) 46 RPC 406 at 418: 'I ask myself: why should the owner of the Registered Trade Mark "Alligator" be mixed up with such questions as those? It seems to me that directly a rival manufacturer makes use of the Plaintiffs' Trade Mark in connection with the manufacture and sale of his steel belt lacing, he is violating the right conferred by the Statute on the Plaintiffs as the registered owner of that Trade Mark' (*per* Lawrence L.J.).

[6] For Part A marks. For Part B marks it was a defence to prove nobody would be confused.

[7] *Saville Perfumery Ltd v June Perfect Ltd* (1941) 58 RPC 147 at 161, CA.

[8] 'Think Before You Waga Finger' [1996] 6 EIPR 317 at 318.

[9] In his January 1996 Opinion ('The *Wagamama* Decision: Back to the Dark Ages of Trade Mark Law' [1996] 1 EIPR 3), he said: 'The judge's considerations in the rejection of this "European interpretation route" are sound as far as the isolated points of the inference of meaning for section 10(2) on the basis of the Benelux law and perhaps even the Council minutes are concerned.'

[10] I am amazed that anyone continues to dispute this. In *Wagamama*, it was in the interests of the plaintiffs to produce these minutes, if they could. The best they could manage was Professor Gielen's document, on which he gave evidence and was cross-examined. Mr Justice Laddie was (pp. 725–726):

> 'The Gielen document not only has the word "Annex" typed at its top, but also begins at page numbered 3. Professor Gielen was cross-examined as to its provenance. He did not know what it was an annex to, he did not know who wrote it and he did not know what was on the other pages. He did not claim to have attended the relevant Council meeting or to have seen the minutes of it. However, he said that he believed from a source of his that the statement as recorded above was in fact entered on the Council minutes ... The Council minutes are confidential. The Gielen document is not a copy of them. In my view it would be wrong for the court to draw any conclusions as to the meaning of a directive on the basis of suggestions as to what is said in the minutes when the minutes themselves are closed for inspection.'

In 'The Increasing Influence of Intellectual Property Cases on the Principles of Statutory Interpretation' [1996]

was exploded in *Wagamama* and, incidentally, the decision on this point was not *obiter* according to well-established English rules. When a court arrives at a reasoned decision, each reason it gives is part of the *ratio decidendi*.

A more accurate formulation, therefore, would be that Benelux lawyers *claim* that they managed to do it. As far as I can tell, it rests on sheer assertion. But saying something, however repeatedly, does not make it come true.

The world is full of lobbyists of all sorts seeking to put their imprint on pending legislation or, if that fails, bringing themselves to believe that they have and going around saying so. Their best hope, if their cause be unpopular, is to try to get the legislators to include, by a sort of passing reference, something so obscure that the latter, busy men and women, do not understand its implications. For this reason the legal systems of mature democracies demand certain elementary safeguards.

The first of these is that the primary document is always the text of the legislation itself. Here, the Directive. (I notice that Mr Kamperman Sanders has not responded to my challenge: 'Why, by the way, did they not say "confusion on the part of the public *or* the likelihood of association"?')[11] Only if this text—after all, the only one the legislators saw fit to promulgate in order to inform the public what is the law they must henceforth obey—is ambiguous is it permissible to have recourse to secondary aids to interpretation, such as the *travaux préparatoires*. The second of these is that all such sources must be freely accessible to the public. Manifestly, the official Council minutes are not. If they had been, they would have been produced to the court in the *Wagamama* case without difficulty.

Article 233

Accordingly, Mr Kamperman Sanders now adopts a rather more sophisticated approach. He relies on Article 233 of the Treaty of Rome which, he says, 'precludes the impairment of the completion of the regional union between Belgium, Luxembourg and the Netherlands insofar as the completion has not been achieved by the implementation of the Treaty'. Apparently, the harmonisation of the Benelux trade mark law is 'at a more advanced level than the harmonisation that was envisaged by the Trade Marks Directive and could therefore not be reduced by it'.

---

10 EIPR 526 at 529, Mr Brown complains that 'Copies of the relevant Statements were available to intellectual property practitioners, who began familiarising themselves with the relevant principles of Benelux law'. Or so they thought, anyway.

[11] Prescott, 'Think Before You Waga Finger', Note 8 above. This is strongly reinforced by the text of Recital 10 of the Directive:

> '*Whereas* the protection afforded by the registered trade mark, the function of which is in particular to guarantee the trade mark as an indication of origin, is absolute in the case of identity between the mark and the sign and the goods or services;
> *whereas* the protection applies also in case of similarity between the mark and the sign and the goods or services;
> *whereas* it is indispensable to give an interpretation of the concept of similarity in relation to the likelihood of confusion;
> *whereas* the likelihood of confusion, the appreciation of which depends on numerous elements and, in particular, on the recognition of the trade mark on the market, of the association which can be made with the used or registered sign, of the degree of similarity between the trade mark and the sign and between the goods or services identified, constitutes the specific condition for such protection;
> *whereas* the ways in which likelihood of confusion may be established, and in particular the onus of proof, are a matter for national procedural rules which are not prejudiced by this Directive.'

Here it is plain that 'association' is merely an element to be taken into account when addressing the question of confusion. It is not a replacement.

But Article 233 of the Treaty of Rome does not say that the detailed provisions of Benelux treaties are sacrosanct. It merely says:

> The provisions of this Treaty shall not preclude the *existence or completion of* regional unions between ... Belgium, Luxembourg and the Netherlands, to the extent that the objectives of these regional unions are not attained by the application of this Treaty.

Why should a harmonisation of European trade mark law preclude the 'existence or completion' of a regional union between Belgium, Luxembourg and the Netherlands? If those countries change their trade mark law to conform with the Directive, their regional union will continue to exist, or be capable of completion, as before.

His argument is weakened in any case by his admission that 'not all commentators[12] are convinced'; and destroyed by his further admission that: 'It is, however, true that Benelux practice will have to change in that a mark must possess a reputation in order to qualify for protection under the Benelux equivalent of Article 10(3)[13] of the UK Act, where before this was not a fixed legal requirement'.[14] Precisely so. Except that 'Benelux practice' and 'not a fixed legal requirement' seem rather grudging. What he means is that Benelux *law* will have to be changed. Yet, according to Mr Kamperman Sanders' reasoning, what we have here is an element of 'harmonisation' which can and will be 'reduced'. If one element, why not others?

Section 10(3) is sui generis

Section 10(3) admits of the concept of detriment/unfair advantage without requiring confusion, which (thinks Mr Kamperman Sanders) is a clear indication that confusion is not a necessary requirement of section 10(2) either. I say that the two subsections are so mutually different that the one is hardly any guide to the interpretation of the other.

We have eyes to read the text of the Directive. For convenience I refer to sections 10(2) and 10(3), since these are copied verbatim from the Directive. If we do so, we are in a position to tabulate the differences:

	s. 10(2)	s. 10(3)
Mandatory in Community law?	True	False
Requires reputation?	False	True
Requires unfairness/detriment?	False	True
Extraneous added matter relevant	False	True[15]
Goods must be dissimilar?	False	True
Goods may be dissimilar?	False	True
Confusing similarity an explicit requirement	True	False

---

[12] He means German commentators.

[13] *sc.* s. 10(3).

[14] Note 1 above, p. 523.

[15] Extraneous added matter is not relevant under s. 10(2), see above, but it may be so under s. 10(3). This is because under 10(2) the language is '*where because ... the sign is* similar to the trade mark *and is used in relation to goods or services ... similar* to those for which the mark is registered, there exists a likelihood of confusion ...'. But under s. 10(3) the language is 'where ... the *use* of the sign ... is detrimental to the ... repute of the trade mark', etc. Thus, *how* he uses the sign—the whole context of use—is relevant. This figures. Clearly, if the defendant uses it in a derogatory context it may make quite a difference.

We can also tabulate the similarities—such as they are:

	s. 10(2)	*s. 10(3)*
Mark/sign must be similar?	True	False
There must always be passing off?	False	True

It may have crossed the reader's mind that these subsections would seem to belong to remarkably different genera. Only a relentless deconstructor of the text, a Derrida of the trade marks world, could contend otherwise.

No Lacuna in the Act or Directive

The most commonly used argument for saying that 'association' in the Benelux sense must be imported into section 10(2) is that confusion is not required by section 10(3). If, therefore, there can be infringement without confusion under 10(3) where the goods are completely different, *a fortiori* it can happen under 10(2) where the goods are the same of similar. Hence, if *Wagamama* is correct, there must be a lacuna in the Act.

That argument can be turned round against itself. It can be said that, if that is so, section 10(3) requires confusion too. Thus, an English deputy judge[16] has now given effect to that thought.[17] The judge's opinion was strictly *obiter* and the deputy judge could perfectly well have decided the case on other grounds.

I respectfully disagree with those judges. While I accept that in many cases, perhaps most, confusion will be part of the element of unfair advantage/detriment, I see nothing in the Directive or the Act that makes it an absolute juridical requirement. If it was, it would be incredible to use the word 'confusion' in section 10(2) but omit it from 10(3). So here I agree with Mr Kamperman Sanders.

I say, rather, that there never was any lacuna in the first place. If a sign is so similar that it can help to take unfair advantage/cause detriment *even when used on dissimilar goods* (10(3)), then it is bound to be close enough to cause origin confusion when used on similar goods (as assessed by the mark v sign comparison test) (10(2)). In my June 1996 Opinion in this journal, I gave the example of 'Rolls' used for jeans, assumed to take unfair advantage of 'Rolls-Royce' registered for cars alone. That would be section 10(3). If we now assume 'Rolls' is used for similar goods, *e.g.* lorries, there will be confusion. That is section 10(2).

One Good Counter-example Would Have Been Enough

If there were a lacuna, it would be possible to think of a practical counter-example. In my June 1996 Opinion in this journal, I challenged anyone to come up with one. The only person who has responded is Mr Kamperman Sanders but, with respect, his examples are not examples at all.

What we are looking for is very simple. We want a sign close enough to the plaintiff's registered mark so that it can cause detriment (or take unfair advantage) when used on completely dissimilar goods. Then we have to imagine exactly that same sign, this time being used on similar goods, which fails to cause confusion—extraneous (added matter being ignored).

Now, Mr Kamperman Sanders appreciated that he must face this challenge. He could

---

[16] Mr Crystal Q.C. in *Baywatch Production Co. Ltd v The Home Video Channel*, July 31, 1996.
[17] Supposedly (but mistakenly) founding on Knox J. in *BASF plc v CEP (UK) plc*, October 26, 1995.

have given any example that he liked, taken from case law anywhere in the world or drawn from his own imagination. I think I have looked at his October 1996 article pretty carefully, but I have not seen any that fits the bill.

I shall just take his best example. (At least, I believe he thought it was the best, because it is the only one discussed in the text of his Opinion.) This is *Deere & Co. v MTD Products Inc.*[18] This was a case under the New York anti-dilution law.[19] The facts of that case were that:

> The plaintiff Deere was the owner of the well-known logo consisting of a representation of a leaping male deer. The defendant put out a TV commercial by way of accurate comparative advertising: the message was that the defendant's tractor was better and cheaper than the plaintiff's. In order to purvey this message the defendant took the Deere logo, animated it and somewhat distorted it. The sting of the advertisement was that the plaintiff's deer ran away from the defendant's tractor, and was made to look small. The court granted an injunction under the anti-dilution law.

Suppose that claim had been brought in England. Since the goods were similar, section 10(3) could not arise and the case would be pleaded under section 10(2). *It would fall squarely within 10(2)*. The defendant might or might not successfully plead the defence of honest comparative advertising,[20] but that is another question. It would fall squarely within the terms of section 10(2) because the goods were similar and so was the defendant's deer. So similar, that its use by a competitor as his own trade mark without a clear and prominent disclaimer would be bound to result in good, old-fashioned, confusion.

It is true that in the *Deere* case there was no passing off, because of the extraneous added matter. But, as I have been at pains to point out, that is not the test under registered trade marks law, nor has it been, in England at least, for many years. Matter external to the trade mark or sign itself does not count. The comparison is a straight mark v sign. I was under the impression that I had made precisely that point in my June 1996 Opinion.[21] So this is not a counter-example at all. It was a case of a confusingly similar mark.

I believe that all of the 'practical examples' he gives are merely cases where there were disclaimers or other extraneous added matter. I am now all the more persuaded that no such example can be given. The reason is fairly easy to see. For section 10(3) to bite, the defendant's sign must be close enough to the plaintiff's mark even to override the awkward fact that the goods are completely different. It is hard to see how such a sign could fail to be confusing—judged by Mr Justice Jacob's mark v sign test—if the goods were similar.

---

[18]   41 F.3d 39 (1994, U.S. Court of Appeal for the Second Circuit). The first instance decision (860 F.Supp. 113) contains a rather fuller recital of the facts.

[19]   Section 368-d of Article 24 of the New York General Business Law states:

> 'Likelihood of injury to business reputation or of dilution of the distinctive character of a mark or trade mark shall be a ground for injunctive relief in cases of infringement of a mark registered or not registered or in cases of unfair competition, notwithstanding the absence of competition between the parties or the absence of confusion as to the source of the goods or services.'

[20]   Section 10(6). I express no opinion about this.
[21]   Note 8 above, at 320, last complete paragraph.

The 'Threats' Section in the UK Trade Marks Act 1994: Can a Person still Wound without Striking?*

[1995] 3 EIPR 138

LIM HENG GEE
Queen Mary and Westfield College, London

The purpose of the Trade Marks Act 1994 ('the Act') is to implement EC Council Directive 89/104. Although the Directive does not require any provision regarding unjustified threats, section 21 of this Act contains a provision entitling a person threatened with legal proceedings for infringement of a registered trade mark[1] to bring an action against the person issuing the threats, claiming certain remedies. It thus brings trade marks law into line with that for patents and designs and implements a commitment made in the White Paper.[2] This article attempts to analyse the provisions and to see whether the section will in effect safeguard the competitors by providing a comprehensive and effective protection against unjustified threats in relation to allegations of trade marks infringement. First, the harm occasioned by ground-less threats will be demonstrated by references to cases decided. The available common law remedy will then be examined. This will be followed by a brief analysis of the section and the perceived weaknesses of the section.

Threats as Intimidatory Tactics

Underlying the harmful effects of a threat of infringement action is the fear of getting involved in one. In relation to patent infringement action, Whitford J aptly explained why threats are so effective. He said that 'the expense and the waste of time and money which is involved in patent litigation is likely to mean that the mere threat of proceedings is going to be a very effective deterrent calculated to ensure that anybody who might have embarked upon a course which could bring him into conflict with a patentee will decide that it is better to abandon it'.[3] He then went on to explain that threats in relation to allegations of infringement of patent did not stand in the same position in relation to their potential damage as did any question of trade libel. It was true that in a trade libel case damage may be caused by loss of business through the activities of the defendant. This however was not the same or as serious as when potential customers of one manufacturer were told by another manufacturer that if they were to continue buying from the first manufacturer they would be sued for patent

---

* *The author is on study leave from the School of Administration and Law, MARA Institute of Technology, Selangor, Malaysia, at the Intellectual Property Law Unit, Queen Mary and Westfield College, University of London. The author's thanks go to Alison Firth for her valuable time and helpful comments on an early draft.*

[1] Note that under the 1994 Act, there is no distinction between a trade mark for goods and a trade mark for services—see for example, section 1(1).

[2] 'Reform of Trade Marks Law'—Cmnd 1203, see Chapter 3, paragraph 3.31.

[3] *Johnson Electric Industrial Manufactory Ltd v Mabuchi Motor KK* [1986] FSR 280 at 284.

infringement.[4] Although this explanation was made in relation to patents, the same applies, although to a lesser degree, to other intellectual property rights, the common thread being the fear of being sued for infringement of an intellectual property right.

Tactics

Intimidatory tactics adopted by patentees are many and varied. They range from:

— direct or indirect threat of infringement proceedings against the competitor;
— direct or indirect threats made to customers of the competitor;
— communication to customers of the competitor, intimating to them that they may be dealing with infringing products, but at the same time assuring them that they would not be sued.

While a threat made to the competitor may be damaging, he is nevertheless in a better position to assess the validity of the threats. The effect is worse if the threats are made to customers of the competitor, who may be reluctant to get involved in what is essentially a dispute between the rights owner and the competitor, in other words, it is 'not their fight'. Therefore the customer is easily persuaded into not dealing with the competitor of the patent owner. The third tactic listed above is especially effective when both are competing for supply of products or competing for the same supply contract.[5] Even if the customers are not put in fear of being sued directly, there is still the problem of being cut off from supplies in the future if there are actions against their suppliers, resulting in disruption of their production or services to their own clients.[6]

Consequence

Drawing from examples in the reported cases on threats in relation mainly to patents, the serious consequences of such threats to the business of competitors can be demonstrated. Threats of legal proceedings could lead to the threatened competitor being inconvenienced by having to waste the time and effort of taking expert advice about his patent position,[7] or being forced to give an indemnity to his customers to safeguard against any risk before they would be willing to purchase his products.[8] Financing arrangements with a financial institution could be temporarily derailed or aborted.[9] Threats could deter customers from dealing with him or lead to a cessation of negotiation of purchase contract by his customer

---

[4] See Whitford J, *ibid.*, at 287, in relation to infringement of patent rights.
[5] See for example *Johnson Electric*, Note 3 above.
[6] *Bowden Controls Ltd v Acco Cable Controls Ltd and Another* [1990] RPC 427, *per* Aldous J, at 434.
[7] *Benmax v Austin Motor Co. Ltd* (1953) 70 RPC 143; (1953) 70 RPC 284 (CA) *per* Evershed MR for the Court of Appeal at 295: 'It also seems open to serious doubt whether on any inquiry as to damages they could prove any damage at all, and whether taking expert advice about their patent position and the costs thereby involved could be regarded in any event as damages within the meaning of this section.'
[8] As in *Wren v Weild* (1868–69) 4 LR QB 730 and *Howson (W.H.) Ltd v Algraphy Ltd* [1965] RPC 183. See also *The Royal Baking Powder Co. v Wright, Crossley & Co.* (1898) 15 RPC 677; (1899) 16 RPC 217; (1901) 18 RPC 95.
[9] As happened in *Berkeley & Young Ltd & Goodman Ltd v Stillwell Darby & Co. Ltd & Konig* (1940) 57 RPC 291, where the Finance Corporation were not prepared to find any further moneys for financing the schemes of the second plaintiffs until they could be satisfied that there was no question of infringement of the patent.

who feared getting involved in a patent litigation with the patent owner,[10] or the competitor's retailer ceasing to advertise or carry the competitor's products.[11] Even when there was already a contractual relationship between the competitor and his client, the threats could result in countermanding of orders made to the competitors.[12] In the case of a pending patent, threats from another patentee could lead to abandonment of negotiation for the sale or licence of the recipient's patent rights.[13] Last but not least, in one case it led to the customers insisting on a deduction from the contracted price, amounting to the sum which they had paid the patentee in consideration of the patentee waiving any rights which he might have in the patent.[14] According to the British Science Guild, 'hardship from this cause is most frequently incurred by makers of seasonal goods, who sometimes lose the market for a year in consequence of threats addressed to their customers by some person claiming an interest in a patent'.[15]

Finally, it is not only the business of the competitors which is affected or ruined; the public at large is also affected. The closing down of a competitor's business or the resultant impairment in competition results in the consumers having fewer sources of supply or alternative choices. This would have the undesirable anti-competitive effects on the supply of the particular product in question. Ultimately, assuring fair competition among enterprises will benefit the economic development of the country.

The Common Law Remedy for Threats

Unfair tactics used to get a competitive edge over rivals in the trade involve many different forms of activity. Imputation could be made, questioning title to deal with property. Disparaging remarks could be made of a competitor's goods or business. Of relevance to this article, however, are the use of threats of legal action to frighten either the competitors away, or more commonly, to frighten off competitors' customers. The essence in all these tactics is the use of false assertions which cause damage to a person's commercial interest.

The main remedy available under common law in these situations is the action for the tort of injurious falsehood. Two particular forms of injurious falsehood are slander of title and slander of goods (sometimes referred to as trade libel). Until the 1994 Trade Marks Act came into force, a person unfairly threatened with action for infringement of a registered trade mark had to rely on these common law actions. To establish his cause of action in an action for slander of title or goods or malicious falsehood, the plaintiff must prove that the words were uttered, that they were false, that they were published maliciously and, that they caused him special damage. This doctrine originated from the case of *Pitt v Donovan*,[16] which involved an action for slander of title relating to land. It was extended to threats in

---

[10] A good example is in *Neild v Rockley and Another* [1986] FSR 3, *per* Falconer J at 5 to 6: 'the threats had and have frustrated the two sets of negotiations ... She has had several years delay in marketing her existing stock ... she had not been able to obtain some return on her capital expenditure ... and had lost a possible opportunity to obtain a niche in the market ...'. See also *Halsey v Brotherhood* (1880) 15 Ch. D. 514; (1881) 19 Ch. D. 386; *Wren v Weild*, Note 8 above; and *Skinner & Co. v Perry* (1893) 10 RPC 1; *Solanite Signs Ltd v Wood* (1933) 50 RPC 315—negotiation for an amalgamation of businesses broke off, also loss in investment of capital in the proposed venture.

[11] As in *Berkeley & Young Ltd* Note 9 above; see also *Craig v Dowding* (1908) 25 RPC 1 at 259.

[12] As in *The National School of Salesmanship Ltd v The Plomien Fuel Economiser Ltd* (1942) 59 RPC 95.

[13] As in *Horne v Johnston Brothers* (1921) 38 RPC 366.

[14] See *Speedcranes Ltd v Thomson and Another* [1978] RPC 221.

[15] Report of the Departmental Committee on the Patents and Designs Acts and Practices of the Patent Office, Cmnd 3829 (1931) (Sargent Committee), paragraph 47 of the submission of the Committee of the British Science Guild, see paragraph 164 of the Report. See also *Mentmore v Fomento* (1955) 72 RPC 157 (CA): threats which stopped 'Christmas trade'.

[16] (1813) 1 M. & S. 639; 105 ER 238.

relation to patent infringement by the case of *Wren v Weild*,[17] where the judge applied the rule in *Pitt v Donovan*[18] and directed the jury accordingly. On appeal, Blackburn J, while acknowledging that no action precisely like this had ever been brought, nevertheless referred to the action for slander of title in relation to real property. He then made the fateful statement, which was to set the approach of later judges in similar cases, that there was no reason 'why a similar rule should not apply where the false and malicious assertion relate to goods, and the damage arises from the loss of a bargain to sell them'.[19] The same approach was adopted by the Court of Appeal in *Halsey v Brotherhood*.[20]

In relation to threats for trade marks infringement, *Colley v Hart*[21] was the first case where the plaintiff tried to maintain an action to restrain, *inter alia*, threats relating to allegations of trade mark infringement issued to his customers. North J hesitantly conceded that an analogous right of action with respect to a threat about a trade mark might be available as under common law with respect to a threat about a patent. However, relying on the case of *Wren v Weild*, he held that since there was not a malicious threat there was no cause of action.[22] The Court of Appeal in *Ratcliffe v Evans*[23] had to deal with an action for false and malicious publication, and followed the line of approach adopted in *Wren v Weild*, holding that 'that an action would lie for written or oral falsehood, not actionable *per se* nor even defamatory, where they were maliciously published, where they were calculated in the ordinary course of things to produce, and where they did produce, actual damage, was established law.'[24] Interestingly, the presence of malice does not usually render an otherwise lawful conduct tortious.[25]

More relevant for present discussion was the case of *The Royal Baking Powder Co. v Wright, Crossley & Co.*,[26] which involved an action to prevent the defendants from maliciously threatening the customers of the plaintiffs with legal proceedings in respect of their sales of the plaintiffs' baking powder.[27] In his oft-quoted speech Lord Davey said:

> My Lords, I am of opinion that this is not an action for libel or defamation of character. I think it can only be maintained as an action for what is called slander of title—i.e., an action on the case for maliciously damaging the plaintiffs in their trade by denying their title to the use of a certain label and threatening to sue their customers. To support such an action it is necessary for the plaintiffs to prove (1) that the statements complained

---

[17] Note 8 above.

[18] Note 16 above; see also *Greeen v Button* (1835) 2 Cromp. M. & R. 707.

[19] Note 8 above, at 735, *per* Blackburn J.

[20] Note 10 above; the threats action was treated as founded on a right of action for slander of title and hence the required elements of malice and special damage must be present. *Wren v Weild* was expressly adopted by the Court of Appeal—*per* Lord Coleridge, LCJ, at 388. See the concurring opinions of Baggallay LJ, at 389 to 390 and Lindley LJ, at 392.

[21] (1890) 7 RPC 101.

[22] See *ibid.*, *per* North J, at 113 to 114.

[23] [1892] 2 QB 524.

[24] *Ibid.*, *per* Bowen LJ, at 527 to 528. The same approach was applied in *Nahmaschinen Fabrik Vormals Frister und Rossman Actiengesellschaft and Siegmund Loewe v The Singer Manufacturing Co.* (1893) 10 RPC 310, although the case was finally decided on a finding that the advertisement in issue was not libellous. The House of Lords in *White v Mellin* [1895] AC 154, an action for disparagement of goods (interestingly also referred to in the opinions variously as action for slander of title and trade libel), stressed that an action will not lie for a false statement disparaging a trader's goods where no special damage is proved—*per* Lord Macnaghten at 169.

[25] See *Allen v Flood* [1898] AC 1.

[26] Note 8 above.

[27] Variously referred to in the opinion as trade libel and slander of title.

of were untrue; (2) that they were made maliciously, i.e., without just cause and excuse; (3) that the plaintiffs have suffered special damage thereby . . .[28]

Therefore, starting from its origin in relation to slanders of title to land, this form of tort has been extended to apply to and cover other mis-statements relating to other forms of property and business until any falsehood was encompassed. However, remedy is only available if the aggrieved person could prove the two key elements of malice[29] and special damage.[30] Therefore it was with justification that Cornish observed that 'this formulation, which encapsulates the tort in its modern form, is broad so far as types of falsehood are concerned, but narrow on its requirement of malice and special damage.[31]

The Legislative Response

Malice being such a nebulous concept, its requirement before relief can be obtained severely

---

[28] (1901) 18 RPC 95 at 99. See also Lord James (with Lord Morris concurring) at 101; Lord Robertson at 102 to 103. *White v Mellin* and *Wren v Weild* were referred to and applied. One of the very few successful cases where the plaintiff was able to obtain the assistance of the court to prevent the issuance of unjustified threats of proceedings for an infringement of a registered trade mark was in *Greers Ltd v Pearman & Corder Ltd* (1922) 39 RPC 406. It has to be noted again that in giving judgment for the plaintiff, all the judges involved stressed the need to prove malice and special damage, see Bray J, at 410 to 411; Bankes LJ, at 417; Scrutton LJ, at 417 and Atkin LJ, at 418. See also *R. J. Reuter Co. Ltd v Mulhens* (1953) 70 RPC 102 and 235 and *Wilts United Dairies Ltd v Thomas Robinson Sons & Co. Ltd* (1957) 74 RPC 220. For an unsuccessful attempt to rely on the common law remedy to prevent the sending of letters warning against infringement of copyright to the defendants' customers, see *Polydor Ltd and Another v Harlequin Record Shops Ltd and Another* [1980] FSR 26.

[29] Although in actions for slander of goods and malicious or injurious falsehood, malice is an essential element, the definition of malice in the content of malicious falsehood remains uncertain. It had been said that 'there is a regrettable exuberance of definition'—*British Railway Traffic and Electric Co. Ltd v CRC Co. Ltd and LCC* [1922] 2 KB 260 at 268, *per* McCardie J. Various definitions have been adopted—see, for example, *Royal Baking Powder Co. v Wright, Crossley & Co.* (1901) 18 RPC 95, HL where 'maliciously' was said to mean 'without just cause and excuse . . . the threat to sue must be shown to have been made for the purpose of injuring the plaintiffs, and not for the *bona fide* protection of the defendants' rights, and without any real intention to follow it up by action or other legal proceedings', *per* Lord Davey at 99; *Halsey v Brotherhood*, Note 10 above, 'reasonable and probable cause' is necessary—*per* Baggallay LJ, at 390; there is no evidence of malice if all that is shown is that the defendant wrote or spoke honestly, even though wrongly, in defence of a real or supposed right or title to the property, or carelessly, believing the words to be true, or merely for the purpose of advancing the sale of his own goods—*White v Mellin*, Note 24 above, at 160, HL, *per* Lord Herschell; in *Dunlop Pneumatic Tyre Co. Ltd v Maison Talbot* (1904) 20 TLR 579 (CA), Collins Mr was reported to have said, at 581, that 'It was not malice if the object of the writer was to push his own business, though at the same time it might incidentally injure another person's business. To make the act malicious it must be done with the direct object of injuring that other person's business. Therefore, the mere fact that it could injure another person's business was no evidence of malice.'; *Olin Mathieson Chemical Co. v Biorex Laboratories Ltd* [1970] RPC 157, *per* Graham J at 196: 'Malice in this context means improper motive . . .'; *Household and Rosher v Fairburn and Hall* (1884) 1 RPC 109 at 113: 'That it is not *mala fide* for a man to issue circulars in defence of his own right, if he *bona fide* believes that what is being done is an infringement of that right'. See also *Pratt and Others v British Medical Association and Others* [1919] 1 KB 244 at 276, where McCardie J reviewed the cases and pointed out the various and wide meanings to the word 'malice'.

[30] The words 'special damage' were clarified in *Ratcliffe v Evans* Note 23 above, at 527 to 528, *per* Bowen LJ, where the various meanings of special damage were discussed and explained. He further added that to support a case for malicious prosecution, special damage in the sense of actual damage must be shown. See also *Farr v Weatherhead & Harding* (1932) 49 RPC 262, *per* Luxmoore J at 267: 'I think that so far as this type of case is concerned that means that the plaintiff must prove that he has suffered some actual loss which is directly attributable to the threats of which he is making complaint.' Note that it is not necessary to prove special damage where section 3, Defamation Act 1952 applies—that is, if (1) the words on which the action is founded are calculated to cause pecuniary damage to the plaintiff and are published in writing or other permanent form; or (2) the words are calculated to cause pecuniary damage to the plaintiff in respect of any office, profession, calling, trade or business held or carried on by him at the time of the publication.

[31] See W.R. Cornish, *Intellectual Property: Patents, Copyright, Trade Marks and Allied Rights*, Sweet and Maxwell, 1989 (2nd edn) at 427.

limits this common law action. It was because of the inadequacy of the common law remedy that the threats provision for patents was introduced.[32] Partly in response to *Halsey v Brotherhood*, the UK legislature introduced a statutory remedy for persons who were aggrieved by the issuance of unjustified threats of proceedings for patent infringement.[33]

The above-mentioned section was aimed at 'a patentee who causes damage by disseminating threats which he dares not or will not justify by an action, who is willing to wound, but yet afraid to strike'.[34] Bowen LJ said that it was the outcome of the legislature's desire that 'threats of patent actions shall not hang over a man's head'; that the Sword of Damocles, in such a case, 'shall either not be suspended or should fall at once'.[35] The provision therefore provides statutory protection against a patentee seeking to end competitive activities without putting his patent and claim for infringement to the test of court proceedings. The need for such protection is to obviate the possibility of the patentee seeking to coerce the customers of a competitor not to purchase the competitor's goods. The object of the section was to give the person threatened an entirely new right of action in which malice is not an issue.[36]

That the statutory mechanism has been effective to control abuse of the competitive process by the unjustified use of threats can be illustrated by the statistics showing the

---

[32] By section 32 of the Patents, Designs and Trade Marks Act, 1883. See for example the following comments: *Halsey v Brotherhood*, Note 10 above, *per* Lord Coleridge LCJ, at 389: 'I feel strongly that there is great force in what Mr Ince has said about the difficulty in which a plaintiff may be placed by the conduct of a person in the position of the defendant. I do not pretend to be able to answer his observation on that head, but unless there is *mala fide*, it is one of those instances in which the law, in the interest of society, permits an injury to be done without any remedy commensurate with it'; *Crampton v The Patents Investment Co. Ltd* (1888) 5 RPC 382, *per* Field J at 392: 'Before this enactment, if a person maliciously and without reasonable and probable cause, threatened to interfere with another man's rights in that way, it might be made the subject of an action. But it was thought by the legislature that this did not afford sufficient protection to persons who were using patented inventions ... There were ... several cases which were considered to be very oppressive. People in possession of rights apparently covered by patents were in the habit of threatening the customers of persons claiming to be patentees, destroying the sale by them of the subject of their patents, and then never proceeding any further'; *Benmax v Austin Motor Co Ltd*, Note 7 above; *per* Evershed, MR for the Court of Appeal (Jenkins LJ and Morris LJ concurring) at 294 to 295: 'I can well understand that a business which receives what are commonly called 'threatening' letters from persons who have a somewhat similar business may suffer serious business damage, and to rely upon the common law action for slander of goods may be a wholly ineffective remedy, having regard to the necessity of proving malice...'.

[33] *Skinner & Co. v Perry* Note 10 above, *per* Lindley LJ at 5; 'this section in the Patent Act was introduced after, and partly in consequence of the decision of the court in *Halsey v Brotherhood* (1880) 15 Ch.D. 514 ... Now the object of this Act was to cure two blots—first of all to give an action for damages where there was not one before; and secondly, to enable an action to be brought against who uses threats unless he will or does follow up his threats by commencing an action himself. That is the key note.' It is not clear who exactly originated the threats provision in the 1883 Act. It did not appear in the original Bill, nor was it mentioned by Mr Chamberlain, President of the Board of Trade, nor was it mentioned by Mr Chamberlain, President of the Board of Trade, when he presented it during the Second Reading (Hansard Set 3, CCLXXVIII, 1883). It seems to have been introduced during the committee stage (see A.J. Davies, 'On Threats of Legal Proceedings and the 32nd Section of the Patents, Designs, and Trade Marks Act, 1833', Transactions of the Institute of Patents Agents, Vol. V Session 1886–7, 218). According to Daniel, section 32 was introduced by Sir George Jessel who decided the case of *Halsey v Brotherhood*: see E.M. Daniel, 'On the Proviso to Section 32 of the Patents Act 1883'. Transactions of the Institute of Patents Agents, Vol. VIII, Session 1889–90, 241, at 242.

[34] *Day v Foster* (1890) RPC 54 *per* North J at 60.

[35] *Skinner & Co. v Perry* Note 10 above, at 8; see also Lindley LJ, *ibid.*, at 5, quoted in Note 33 above; *Norbert Steinhardt and Son Ltd v Meth and Another* [1960–1961] 105 CR 440 *per* Fullagar J, in the High Court of Australia, in relation to an equivalent provision in the Patents Act 1952–1955 (Cth) at page 447: 'It is intended, I think, to have a strict and dramatic effect to supplement a less effective common law remedy ...'; see also *Townsend Controls Pty Ltd v Gilead and Another* (1988–1989) 14 IPR 443, *per* von Doussa J at 448.

[36] See *Skinner & Co. v Perry* Note 10 above, *bona fide* of defendant is irrelevant—what matters is what he said not what he intended; *Craig v Dowding* Note 11 above, *per* Cozens-Hardy MR, at 262: 'section 32 does not ... merely relieve a plaintiff from the obligation of establishing malice in the old common law action, but it confers an entirely new right of action and one in which malice is not an issue between the parties ...'; see also *Alpi v Wright* [1972] RPC 125, *per* Whitford J, at 129.

number of threats actions in relation to patents since its introduction in 1883.[37]

This statutory right of action was soon extended to registered designs in 1907. The present provision is now contained in section 26 of the Registered Designs Act 1949. When the Copyright Designs and Patents Act 1988 was enacted, an equivalent provision was provided for unregistered designs in section 253.

Analysis of Section 21[38]

After a lapse of 100 years since it was first introduced for patents, the statutory mechanism has finally been extended to trade marks. This is timely in view of the fact that acts which would not previously have been a registered trade mark infringement (for example, use of the mark on similar goods or services and use of well-known marks) would now be.[39] Owing to the enhanced infringement rights of a trade mark owner, there is greater danger of infringement and hence greater opportunity for threats to be issued. By and large, the section has drawn heavily from the experience gained from the working of the threats provisions in the Patents Act, from its inception to its present form. How some of the provisions are to be construed could safely be predicted with guidance from cases decided under the existing threats provisions since they are *in pari materia*. Reference will be mainly be made to the case law of the patents threats provision since this is the area most litigated and a considerable body of case law has been developed. However, owing to the particular characteristics of a registered trade mark, the construction of other aspects of the section will of necessity be a matter of conjecture until the matter has been adjudicated on and construed by the courts.

Who may be liable for making threats?

The section starts with the words, 'Where a *person* threatens ...'. There is no qualification to the word 'person', so it is potentially of wide import. This would imply that any person threatening could be liable under this section. It therefore need not be the registered proprietor himself or a co-owner. It could be the exclusive licensee, a sub-licensee, an authorised user, or in fact anyone else.

What kinds of threat are actionable?

Here the operative word is 'threatens'. An expressed and direct threat would obviously fall within the meaning of the word 'threat' in the section. However, the cases have shown that there is no need to prove that the defendants had actually threatened proceedings in order to constitute a threat. The test that is to be applied is that enunciated by Clauson J in *Luna Advertising Co. Ltd v Burnham & Co.*,[40] where he held that it was a question which entirely depended on the inferences which an ordinary man would draw from the words used. This approach was applied in *Willis & Bates Ltd v Tilley Lamp Co.*,[41] where Bennett J held that the terms of the act were satisfied if the defendant in the action was proved to have asserted

---

[37] The figures culled from the Report of Patent Cases and Fleet Street Report on the number of reported threats actions for every ten-year period from the years 1884 to 1993 is illuminating: 1884 to 1893 = 28; 1894 to 1903 = 26; 1904 to 1913 = 9; 1914 to 1923 = 5; 1924 to 1933 = 7; 1934 to 1943 = 12; 1944 to 1953 = 7; 1954 to 1963 = 6; 1964 to 1973 = 6; 1974 to 1983 = 3; 1984 to 1993 = 2.
[38] Please refer to appendix for the provisions of section 21.
[39] See section 10 of the Act.
[40] (1928) 45 RPC 258 and 260.
[41] (1944) 61 RPC 8.

that he had legal rights in respect of letters patent and that he intended as against the plaintiff to enforce those rights.[42] Since a threat of action for infringement could thus be made indirectly or by implication, regard has to be had to the background in which the alleged threat was made.[43]

Where must the threat be made?

It has been held that threats of patent infringement need to have been made within jurisdiction.[44] Whether this will hold true once the first community trade mark has been registered is uncertain. Under section 52(3)(a)(i) of the Act, regulations may be made applying in relation to a Community trade mark the provisions of section 21. When the regulations are eventually made, would a threat made outside the United Kingdom, but within one of the Member States, be actionable in the United Kingdom?

Is a general warning a threat?

It would appear that a general warning to the trade that the trade mark proprietor intends to enforce such rights as he has may avoid being an actionable threat so long as it points no warning finger against any specific trader.[45] However, should such warning amount by implication to a suggestion that the manufactures of a certain person are infringements, an action will lie.[46]

There is also a departure from the usual formulation in the threats section in the patents and also the registered designs statutes. For example, in section 70 of the Patents Act 1977, the phrase 'by circular, advertisements, or otherwise' is utilised.[47] The section is, however, similar to the provisions of section 253 of the CDPA 1988. This is, anyway, a more logical formulation, for in whatever form the threat is clothed, it should be actionable. So an oral threat could be actionable, as it should well be.[48]

---

[42] *Ibid.*, *per* Bennett J, at 11; *Desiderio v Currus Ltd* (1935) 52 RPC 201, *per* Crossman J, at 205; also followed by the Court of Appeal in *H. V. E. (Electric) Ltd and Others v Cufflin Holdings Ltd* [1964] RPC 149, *per* Salmon LJ, at 158 and *Reymes-Cole v Elite Hosiery Co. Ltd* [1965] RPC 102 at 112, 119 to 120 (CA). The same approach was applied in *John Summers & Sons Ltd v The Cold Metal Process Co.* (1948) 65 RPC 75; *C. & P. Development Co. v Sisabro Novelty Co. Ltd* (1953) 70 RPC 277 (CA); *Speedcranes Ltd v Thomson and Another*, Note 14 above; *Bowden Controls Ltd v Acco Cable Controls Ltd and Another*, *per* Mr Justice Aldous, at 431; 'The letter does not explicitly threaten patent proceedings, but states that the first defendant will enforce its rights. The fact that it is not explicit that patent proceedings will be taken is in no way conclusive as a threat can be veiled or implied just as much as it can be explicit. . . . (applying the approach of Clauson J in *Luna Advertising Co. Ltd v Burnham & Co.* (1928) 45 RPC 258).'

[43] See *Surridge's Patents Ltd v Trico-Folberth Ltd* (1936) 53 RPC 420 at 423, 424; and *Bowden Controls Ltd v Acco Cable Controls Ltd and Another*, Note 6 above, *per* Aldous J at 432.

[44] See *Egg Fillers & Containers (Aust) Proprietary Ltd v Holed-Tite Packing Corp. & Packing Products Corp.* (1934) 51 RPC 9: this case was followed by the High Court of Australia in *Norbert Steinhardt and Son Ltd v Meth and Another*, Note 35 above; see also *Townsend Controls Pty Ltd v Gilead and Another*, Note 35 above.

[45] See *Johnson v Edge* (1892) 9 RPC 142, *per* Lindley LJ, at 148: 'I cannot suppose that the section prevents a patentee from saying that which the patent itself implies—that anybody infringing must expect legal proceedings to be taken against him. I do not think it can mean that. That is merely saying what everybody knows already. That is not a threat against anybody in particular.'

[46] See *Johnson v Edge*, *ibid.*, at 148 to 149; Kay LJ at 149, after referring to *Challender v Royce* (1887) 4 RPC 363, held that 'a general warning . . . not pointed against any particular person, which would not be by the public understood to apply to any particular person, might not be within this 32nd section at all . . .'; see also *Boneham & Hart v Hirst Bros & Co. Ltd* (1917) 34 RPC 209; *Alpi v Wright* Note 36 above; *The Selsdon Fountain Pen Co. Ltd v Miles Martin Pen Co. Ltd* (1948) 65 RPC 365.

[47] Though the Court of Appeal in *Skinner & Co. v Perry*, Note 10 above, unanimously agreed that the term 'or otherwise' was not to be construed *ejusdem generis* with the words, 'circular' or 'advertisement'. The words 'circulars or advertisements' was rather to enlarge the words 'or otherwise' than to cut them down—*per* Lindley LJ at 5 to 6 and Bowen LJ, at 7 to 8; followed in subsequent cases, see *Douglass v Pintsch's Patent Lighting Company* (1896) 13 RPC 673; *Benmax v Austin Motor Co. Ltd* Note 7 above.

[48] *Driffield & Co. v Waterloo & Co.* (1886) 3 RPC 46, *per* Bacon, VC, at 48. See also: *Crampton v The Patents Investment Co. Ltd* (1888) 5 RPC 382; *The Combined Weighing Machine Co v The Automatic Weighing Machine Co.* (1889) 6 RPC 502; *Barrett & Elers, Ltd v Day* (1890) 7 RPC 54.

May 'threats' be made in response to inquiries?

From the cases it would seem that a threat is not necessarily confined to volunteered threats. In some situations an answer to an inquiry may be construed as a threat. One of the issues in *Beven & Alexander v Welsbach Incandescent Gas Light Co. Ltd*[49] was whether an answer in response to an inquiry from the customer of the plaintiff who sued for unjustified threats could amount to a threat. Byrne J, after discussing the difficulties in such a situation, held that although in principle it could amount to a threat, the circumstances in the present case were different.[50] In *Alpi v Wright*[51] the decision on this point was reserved. It is difficult to see how the section could have been framed to provide a satisfactory answer to fit all situations. In the final analysis, the issue seems best to be determined by the court according to the circumstances of the case.

Who can be the recipient of an actionable threat?

Where a person threatens 'another' with trade marks proceedings, it is clear from the section that the person threatened need not be the one suing under the section. The threats could be directed against the manufacturer who applies the mark to goods manufactured by him or it could also be directed against the secondary infringers, that is, the retailers or customers of the manufacturer (subject to the proviso). Furthermore, it is not necessary in order that the threat should be actionable that it should have been communicated either directly or through an agent to the person threatened. An interesting point was raised by the defendant in *John Summers & Sons Ltd v The Cold Metal Process Co.*,[52] where it was argued that the provisions of the section were not brought into play unless the threatener communicated a threat of proceedings to the person threatened, either directly or through an agent. This question was first alluded to by Bowen LJ, in *Skinner & Co. v Perry*,[53] where he said in general terms, 'If I threaten a man that I will bring an action against him, I threaten him none the less because I address that intimation to himself, and I threaten him none the less because I address the intimation to a third person.' Romer J, in line with the views expressed above, held that the words in section 36, 'threatens any person', read in its proper context, did not only mean 'communicate a threat to any person' but included also the expression of a threat, by circulars, advertisements or otherwise, in relation to any person. Therefore, a person who had expressed a threat to sue another person, although the threat was not communicated to the person threatened but to a third party, would be liable under the section.[54]

What kind of infringement must be alleged in the threat?

The section states that 'where a person threatens another *with proceedings for infringement of a registered trade mark* ... any person aggrieved may bring proceedings for relief under the section'. The words being general, it would appear that any threat of an action for infringe-

---

[49] (1903) 20 RPC 69.

[50] *Ibid.*, Byrne J at 73 to 74, after referring to *Douglass v Pintsch's Patent Lighting Company*, Note 47 above and *Skinner & Co. v Perry* Note 10 above.

[51] Note 36 above, *per* Whitford J, at 132.

[52] Note 42 above.

[53] Note 10 above, at 7.

[54] See Romer J's discussion on this issue in *John Summers & Sons Ltd v The Cold Metal Process Co.*, Note 42 above, at 96 to 97; followed in *Speedcranes Ltd v Thomson and Another*, Note 14 above; see also the facts in *Olin Mathieson Chemical Co. v Biorex Laboratories Ltd*, Note 29 above.

ment of a registered trade mark, even though no particular trade mark was mentioned, would fall within the section. It would seem that, as section 10(5) of the Act has extended the meaning of infringement to include 'the application of a registered trade mark to materials intended to be used for labelling or packaging goods, as a business paper, or for advertising goods or services', a threat against such a person would fall within the section too.

Persons exempted from bringing threats actions

Threats relating to certain types of infringement are specifically exempted from the section. Where a person threatens another with proceedings for infringement of a registered trade mark, in relation to *the application of the marks to goods or their packaging, the importation of goods to which, or to the packaging of which, the mark has been applied, or the supply of services* under the mark, the person threatened has no recourse to the section.

The primary infringers

Like the existing threats provision, the effect of the first two provisos is generally to categorise the alleged infringers into two main classes, the often-called 'primary infringers' and 'secondary infringers'. Persons involved in the application of the marks to goods or their packaging, normally the manufacturers of the goods and those involved in the importation of goods to which, or to the packaging of which, the mark has been applied, will fall under the first category. The second infringers will generally be those persons involved in activities down the distribution chain, who are one step removed from the originating source of the alleged infringing activities. The scheme of the proviso in the section is to allow threats to be made with impunity against the primary infringers. Liability for groundless threats would only lie if the threats were made to the secondary infringers.

Supplier of services under the mark

Another category of person included are all those involved in the supply of services under the mark. There is, however, no differentiation here between a primary and secondary supplier of services. Thus any person involved in the supply of services under the allegedly infringing mark has no recourse to the threats provision, save insofar as they also supply materials under the mark. It would seem, therefore, that a franchisee of, say, a car rental business has no protection from threats.

Who may bring a threats action?

'Any person aggrieved' may bring proceedings for relief under the section. Any person who is actually threatened is a person aggrieved.[55] However, the statutory right of action is not merely limited to the person to whom the threats are directly made; any person to whom damage was occasioned by the issue of the threats should be entitled to relief as a person aggrieved. Thus in *Johnson v Edge*,[56] where circulars were issued to the trade intimating that the articles manufactured and sold by the plaintiff were infringements of the defendant's patent and that proceedings would then be taken against any person dealing with such articles, it was held that the plaintiff was a person aggrieved and could maintain an action, although no threats were made to him personally. However, in *Reymes-Cole v Elite Hosiery*

---

[55] *Challender v Royce* Note 46 above, *per* Cotton LJ at 371; *John Summers & Sons Ltd v The Cold Metal Process Co.*, Note 42 above, *per* Romer J at 98.

[56] Note 45 above.

Co. Ltd,[57] the defendants were held not to be persons aggrieved as they had ceased production of the type of stocking prior to the threat being made.[58]

What if the threat is justified?

The section provides that 'the plaintiff is entitled to such relief *unless* the defendant shows that the acts in respect of which proceedings were threatened constitute (or if done would constitute) an infringement of the registered trade mark concerned'. This clearly indicates that the whole basis of the section, like the existing provisions, is that the threats are groundless. If the defendant can show that the acts in respect of which the threats are made constituted an infringement, he will escape liability. Further, the phrase 'or if done' shows that the threats could relate to a threatened infringement. So the threats of proceedings could be in respect of past, present or future infringement.[59] In all cases, it is only when it is groundless that the statutory remedy is available to the person aggrieved. The burden of proving that the threats were not groundless is on the person who issued the threats. The question of whether interlocutory injunction is available if threats are to be justified was argued in *Johnson Electric Industrial Manufactory Ltd v Mabuchi Motor K.K.*[60] The plaintiffs sought interlocutory relief to restrain threats. The defendants, however, contended that infringement had occurred, that the patents in issue were valid, and that accordingly the threats were justified. This being so, they sought further to argue, by analogy to the practice with respect to justification in libel and trade libel cases, that interlocutory relief should not be granted. The judge held that 'threats in relation to allegations of infringement of patent do not stand in the same position in relation to their potential damage as does a question of trade libel. Threats in the context of allegations of patent infringement represented a very grave mischief. To accede to this application would effectively mean that the threats section in the Act would be of no real use to persons who were aggrieved by activities of this kind'.[61]

What if the registration is successfully attacked?

Even if the person threatening legal proceedings could prove that the act complained of amounted or would amount to an infringement, 'the plaintiff is nevertheless entitled to relief if he shows that the registration of the trade mark is invalid or liable to be revoked in a relevant respect'. In other words, the plaintiff could still make out a case for groundless threats if he could show invalidity of the mark or some grounds for revocation of the mark.[62]

Does notifying registration of the mark amount to a threat?

It is specifically provided that 'the mere notification that a trade mark is registered, or that an application for registration has been made, does not constitute a threat of proceedings

---

[57] Note 42 above, *per* Wilmer LJ at 111 to 112 and Diplock LJ at 120.

[58] In *Hart & Co. Pty Ltd v Edwards Hot Water System* (1979–80) 30 ALR 657, Lavan SPJ, following the case of *Johnson v Edge*, held that 'The statutory right of action conferred by s. 202(1) is not limited merely to the person to whom the threats are made but may be exercised by any person to whom damage may be occasioned by the issue of the threats: see *Johnson v Edge* [1892] 9 RPC 142 ...'; see also *Townsend Controls Pty Ltd v Gilead and Another*, Note 35 above.

[59] See *Kurtz v Spence* (1888) 5 RPC 161, *per* Kekewich J, at 171 to 173; see also *Johnson v Edge*, Note 45 above; *Desiderio v Currus Ltd*, Note 42 above; *Reymes-Cole v Elite Hosiery Co. Ltd.*, Note 42 above.

[60] Note 3 above.

[61] *Ibid.*, see Whitford J at 284 to 289.

[62] For revocation, see section 46 of the Act and for invalidity, see section 47 of the Act.

for the purposes of this section'. This provision is self-explanatory and is a feature common in all the existing equivalent provisions for patents and design rights. A mere notification of the existence of a registered trade mark will not constitutes a threat. If, however, words are added to the effect that what was complained of constitutes an infringement of the mark, this will constitute a threat. The same applies if the notification is accompanied by threats to sue in passing off.[63]

Weaknesses of the Section

The threats section did not arouse as intense a debate as that directed to the issue of lookalikes. As all sections of both Houses were keen that the progress of the Bill should not be delayed, it is understandable that a rigid time-table was imposed on the debates. However, the Government had three years to draft the Bill, and it is regrettable that the draftsmen had chosen to simply model the section on the existing provisions instead of trying to improve it. It is feared that the legislators may have left a loophole which would render the provisions otiose. There are also shortcomings in the section which may be exploited.

Pending registrations

First, the section refers to a situation 'where a person threatens another with proceedings for infringement of a registered trade mark'. Would the section apply if the threats are made during the interval between application and grant? It could be argued that since the person threatening is not in a position to sue for a registered trade mark infringement in the interim, the section does not apply to him.[64] Furthermore, what if the application for registration is refused? Would the defendant be liable? There seems to be room for the argument that since there is no registered trade mark in existence, he would never have been able to sue for a registered trade mark infringement. This was a problem in relation to the application of the threats provision for patent under the Patents and Designs Act 1907, as amended by the Patents and Designs Act 1919.[65]

Admittedly, it is also arguable that this phrase could be construed differently, and is applicable even where the person concerned has no registered trade mark in existence at the time the threats are made. In this connection, it may be argued that since section 21(4) specifically provides that a mere notification that an application for registration has been made does not constitute a threat, this would by implication mean that threats in relation to a pending registration are encompassed by the section. However, for the purpose of clari-

---

[63] A good example is found in *Finkelstein v Billig* (1930) 47 RPC 516, *per* Bennett J, at 518 (threats in relation to a registered design, Patents and Designs Acts, 1907 to 1919, sections 36 and 61). See also *Jaybeam Ltd v Abru Aluminium Ltd* [1975] FSR 334; [1976] RPC 308.

[64] Section 9(3) provides that the rights of the proprietor have effect from the date of the registration (which in accordance with section 40(3) is the date of filing of the application for registration). However, by virtue of section 9(3)(a), no infringement proceedings may be begun before the date on which the trade mark is in fact registered.

[65] In *Ellis and Sons Limited v Pogson*, (1923) 40 RPC 62; (1923) 40 RPC 179, the Court of Appeal (see PO Lawrence J at 66 to 68, and Warrington LJ, at 182) held that although it had been proved that the defendant had threatened the plaintiffs' customers as alleged and that in consequence, the plaintiffs had suffered damage, the defendant was not liable. This was because the then section 36 of the Patents and Designs Act 1907, as amended by the Patents and Designs Act 1919, presupposed the existence of a patent, and did not apply to the case in which there never had been in existence a patent in respect of which the threats had been made.

This defect was cured by section 36 of the Patents and Designs Act 1932, which repealed the former section 36 of the 1907–28 Acts and enacted a new section 36 in its place, which gave a remedy for groundless threats irrespective of whether the person making the threat did or did not have any interest in a patent.

fication, would it not have been prudent to state specifically that the defendant will be liable irrespective of whether he is or is not entitled to, or interested in a, registered trade mark or an application for one?

Threats in passing off only

Secondly, section 21(1) specifically mentions threats in relation to a registered trade mark infringement. This raises the question 'what if the defendant side-steps the prohibition by threatening to sue for passing off only?' Is it covered by the section? This problem was alluded to by Lord Cawley when the Bill was at the Public Bill Committee stage but no answer was forthcoming.[66] If a person threatening action for trade marks infringement is careful to confine his threats to a passing-off action and is careful to omit any reference to his registered trade mark, it would appear that he could threaten with impunity.[67] Is it really the intention of Parliament to keep threats relating to passing-off actions from the ambit of the section? It has been said that passing-off action is more difficult to institute successfully and therefore threats relating to such action may not have such an adverse impact on the person threatened. With respect it must be pointed out that this distinction is only appreciated by intellectual property lawyers. A tradesman is unlikely to feel happier just because he is threatened with such an action and not a registered trade mark action.

Allegations of 'mixed' infringement

Under the section, a threat against a primary infringer, namely, a person who is the originating source of the alleged infringing products, is not actionable. The trade mark owner is, therefore, allowed to threaten at 'source', that is, against a manufacturer or packer, and importer and a service provider. This is justifiable for various reasons. In the first place, the primary infringer may be in a better position to face the threats. Secondly, in certain situations the issuing of threats may be beneficial because it could lead to negotiations for the settlement of the trade mark disputes and thus avoid the necessity for the needless issuing of court proceedings.[68] This exception will provide a proper balance between practical expediency and the potential for abuse when the threats are issued against people involved in the alleged secondary infringing act.

There is, however, a need to have clarified in the section that the exception applies even against the manufacturer in his retail activities, because he is not, in the true sense of the word, involved in the secondary activities of retailing the products.[69] In *Bowden Controls Ltd*

---

[66] PBC 19/1/1994 c. 67.

[67] Compare the situation in *Jaybeam Ltd v Abru Aluminium Ltd*, Note 63 above.

[68] See the justifiable disquiet of North J in *Barrett & Elers Ltd v Day; Day v Foster*, Note 48 above, at 59: 'It has been held ... that such a letter by a patentee's solicitor to an alleged infringer or his solicitor, threatening an action for infringement, does give a cause of action under this section, and I fear this will have the effect of preventing a patentee from adopting the course thus pointed out to be fair and reasonable, and that for the future the warning letter will only accompany instead of preceding the writ, and will consequently be useless ...'; see also *Alpi v Wright*, Note 36 above, *per* Whitford J, at 132: 'Section 65 has presented great difficulties in the past in a number of cases. It does very often stand in the way of the initiation of negotiations for settlement of patent actions, because people are afraid to say anything to potential defendants lest they be faced with a threats action. It is no doubt a very useful weapon against a patentee who makes a habit of going round and threatening purchasers so as to impede the arrangement for distribution and sale by their competitors. It is probably of more doubtful value for its relation to direct dealings between competing manufacturers or distributors.' (But see now section 70(4) of the Patents Act, 1977.)

[69] See the views expressed by Aldous J in *Bowden Controls Ltd v Acco Cable Controls Ltd and Another*, Note 6 above, at 434.

v Acco Cable Controls Ltd and Another,[70] the plaintiff, manufacturer of the allegedly infringing parts, submitted that subsection (4) of section 70 of the Patents Act 1977 only prevented proceedings being brought in respect of threats alleged to consist of making or importing a product for disposal and that the statements made in the defendants' letter went wider and included threats in respect of sales by the plaintiffs. Thus, the subsection did not provide a defence in respect of the particular threats that were made. Aldous J held that the plaintiff had a reasonably arguable case that the threats did go wider than threats to enforce the patent to restrain the manufacturer since the letter could be read as seeking to enforce all rights given under section 60 of the Patents Act 1977.[71] Though admittedly at interlocutory level, it is submitted that this decision could not stand in view of the purpose for the introduction of the subsection. Since every manufacturer of articles or parts of articles would ultimately have to sell them to third parties, it would leave the subsection inoperative if Aldous J's argument were to be accepted. However, be that as it may, the section should have clarified that a manufacturer or importer or supplier of services in such a situation is still subject to the exceptions under section 21(1) (a), (b) and (c).

Indirect communication of threats

It should have been expressly stated that the exemption from liability for threats under section 21(1)(a) to (c) applies only if the threats were directly communicated to the persons exempted under the section. It should not be applicable if such threats are communicated to the customers of the alleged primary infringer. This is to prevent possible abuse of this exception by the communication of threats against the primary infringer, not to him directly, but to customers. One possible scenario where there could be an attempted evasion if there is no such condition is when the trade mark owner issues circulars to customers of the alleged infringing manufacturer. The circular will contain allegations that the manufacturer is infringing certain trade marks rights and that actions will be taken against him. However, the circular is careful to assure the customers that the owner will not in any circumstances proceed against them for infringement. In this scenario, there are no threats against the retailers. If the aggrieved manufacturer sues for threats, he will be met by the defence of merely issuing a threat against the primary infringer. However, despite the assurance of being told that they will not be sued, the manufacturer's customers may be reluctant to deal further with the manufacturer, who will then suffer damage without a remedy.[72] It is also unfortunate that Parliament did not state that a person not entitled to sue for a trade mark infringement cannot rely on this proviso.[73]

---

[70] *Ibid.*

[71] *Ibid.*, *per* Aldous J, at 434.

[72] The potential for harm is neatly illustrated by the case of *Strix Ltd v Otter Controls Ltd* [1991] FSR 163, though the case was on a different issue, being concerned with an application by the defendants for costs on the indemnity basis. The plaintiffs had written to some ten customers of the defendants, drawing their attention to the existence of litigation for patent infringement between the plaintiffs and the defendants. However, these letters made it clear that the customers themselves would not be sued. There was evidence that at least one contract which the defendants believed they were certain to obtain was put on hold pending disposal of the action. Aldous J, in the Patents Court, commented that a party who had been damaged by the action of another must look to his legal remedies to recover them; whether it be by way of a threats action or by way of an action for malicious falsehood, or otherwise, depending on the facts. But it has to be noted that on the facts he was unlikely to get a remedy for either cause of action. As regards the possibility of a threats action, it is likely that the plaintiff could shelter behind the section 70(4) defence since the threats were made against the defendants and not against their customers.

[73] This point was raised in *Bowden Controls Ltd v Acco Cable Controls Ltd and Another*, Note 6 above. However, Aldous J declined to rule on it since it was unnecessary to his decision—see page 434.

Conclusion

The right to sue for infringement, that is, the right to exclude others from the exclusive territory encompassed by the rights obtained by registration or otherwise, is the basic right or essence of the intellectual property systems. However, unfair coercion and anti-competitive practices lead to an unwarranted and unjustified extension of this right. There is therefore a need to achieve a proper balance between the right of a registered proprietor to notify the public and to issue general warnings against infringement of his rights and the need to ensure that such warnings do not exceed the boundary of fair practices to the detriment of his rivals. Ensuring that the threats provision only applies when the threats are directed against persons involved in activities down the distribution chain, who are one step removed from the originating source of the alleged infringing activities, will ensure that the rights holder is not unduly restricted in enforcing his monopoly rights. At the same time, the alleged secondary infringers would be spared being harassed by 'legal thunderbolts in the shape of lawyers' letters warning them of the awful consequences that will ensue if they continue to infringe'.[74] The harmful effects of threats in relation to infringement proceedings against the receiver have already been shown. When the threats are issued against the customers of a competing manufacturer, it is easy to ensure their capitulation because it is not their battle. The weakness of common law remedies is that there is no liability unless malice is shown. Therefore the introduction of the threats provision to the trade marks regime is to be welcomed. Despite some initial misgiving by certain members of the legislature, all are agreed on the utility of the provision. The provision will impose accountability in the exercise of the rights. However, it would seem that the legislature has taken the easy way out and adopted wholesale the existing models without any attempt to see how they could be improved. It may perhaps be regrettable that the legislators have not deemed it fit to take the opportunity to address some of the issues that had troubled the court in equivalent provisions under the existing threats provision of the patents and design legislation. The wisdom of omitting or failing to provide a remedy for unjustified threats in relation to passing off may also be questioned. An opportunity seems to have been missed to provide a more comprehensive model to cater for some of the apparent shortcomings and uncertainties of the existing models as revealed by the cases. Is it too much to hope that the concerns raised here will be addressed in a future revision of the law?

Section 21 Trade Marks Act 1994

21(1) Where a person threatens another with proceedings for infringement of a registered trade mark other than:

- (a) the application of the marks to goods or their packaging;
- (b) the importation of goods to which, or to the packaging of which, the mark has been applied; or
- (c) the supply of services under the mark;

any person aggrieved may bring proceedings for relief under this section.

21(2) The relief which may be applied for is any of the following:

---

[74] A.J. Davies, 'On Threats of Legal Proceedings and the 32nd Section of the Patents, Designs, and Trade Marks Act, 1833', Transactions of the Institute of Patents Agents, Vol. V Session 1886–7, at 174.

(a) a declaration that the threats are unjustifiable;
(b) an injunction against the continuance of the threats;
(c) damages in respect of any loss he has sustained by the threats;

and the plaintiff is entitled to such relief unless the defendant shows that the acts in respect of which proceedings were threatened constitute (or if done would constitute) an infringement of the registered trade mark concerned.

21(3) If that is shown by the defendant, the plaintiff is nevertheless entitled to relief if he shows that the registration of the trade mark is invalid or liable to be revoked in a relevant respect.

21(4) The mere notification that a trade mark is registered, or that an application for registration has been made, does not constitute a threat of proceedings for the purposes of this section.

Trade Mark Agreements and EC Law

[1996] 5 EIPR 271

ELIZABETH MCKNIGHT
Herbert Smith, London

There has been much written recently about new EC-based legislation on trade marks: the Community trade mark is a right created by a Community Regulation which automatically forms part of national law without the need for further enactment; the new rules governing national registrations contained in the UK's Trade Marks Act 1994 were enacted by the UK Parliament to give effect to requirements laid down in the First Council Directive on Trade Marks for harmonisation of Member States' trade mark laws.

But even while the legislative institutions of the European Community were working on these legal instruments, the European Court of Justice (ECJ) has been establishing a whole body of case law affecting the way in which companies can exercise and enforce their trade mark rights in the Community, and it is that case law that is examined in this article.

There are numerous ways in which the ECJ can be called on to adjudicate on matters relating to trade marks. But, in practice, there have been two distinct lines of case law relating to trade marks: the majority of cases concern either:

— exhaustion of rights; or
— anti-competitive agreements.

Exhaustion of Rights

The rules as to exhaustion of rights are not central to the subject-matter of this article; however, some explanation of them is required by way of background to the points which arise in the competition cases which are discussed in more detail below.

The trade mark cases on exhaustion of rights have arisen under Article 30 EC. Article 30 is one of the central provisions of the EC Treaty dealing with free movement of goods. It is intended to ensure that Member States' national laws do not operate in such a way as to pose obstacles to the free movement of goods between Member States. In principle, a product which has been lawfully marketed in one Member State should be capable of being exported to another Member State and should be capable of being traded in that second Member State without confronting legal obstacles to such trade.

However, some Member States' laws have traditionally been capable of being used to impede the free movement of goods: for example, if a company sells its trade marked product in one Member State with the intention that it should be traded within that Member State, the company could well have compelling commercial reasons for wanting to keep the product out of other Member States: for example, the company could be selling its products at a higher price in other Member States, so that parallel imports of the cheaper products from the first Member State could undermine its pricing structure in those other Member States. On its face, it would appear that the invoking of trade mark rights would be a good lawful way to obstruct parallel imports. The company would take infringement proceedings against the parallel importer or subsequent dealers for infringing the trade mark right in the Member State of importation. The company would argue that the acts of importation and sale of trade marked products without the consent of the trade mark proprietor constitute acts of infringement of the trade mark right in the Member State of importation.

A long line of case law in the ECJ has established that, in principle, a Member State may not permit companies to invoke their trade mark rights in a manner which poses such obstacles to inter-State trade. But Article 30 does not prohibit *all* attempts to exercise trade mark rights, just because the enforcement of the trade mark right will inhibit inter-State trade: it will be compatible with Article 30 EC, and therefore permissible, for companies to enforce trade marks rights where the enforcement of the right is justified as being a means of protecting the very essence, the so-called 'specific subject-matter', of the trade mark right.

Over the years the ECJ has reluctantly, it seems, offered guidance as to what are the 'specific subject-matter' and 'essential function' of a trade mark. The case law is complex and its details fall outside the scope of this article, but it is fair to say that, for the most part, a trade mark owner will not be permitted to enforce his trade mark rights to inhibit the marketing of his trade marked product anywhere in the Community if (*inter alia*) the product in question was first marketed under the relevant mark by him or with his consent somewhere in the Community. After the first such sale, the trade mark owner's rights are said to be exhausted.

Hag II and Ideal Standard

For a long time, one important question remained unresolved: imagine that a company owns registrations for the same mark in Member States A and B; if the company assigns to a third party the mark rights for Member State A, but retains the rights to the mark in Member State B, can the company later restrain the importation into Member State B of products marketed under the relevant mark by the assignee in Member State A—that is, can it be said that the assignor company has, by making the assignment, 'consented' to all subsequent uses of the trade mark in Member State A, so that he cannot block the importation of goods which are effectively 'franked' by that consent?

After a period of considerable uncertainty, the position has been resolved, apparently to the satisfaction of most trade mark owners. In two recent cases (*Hag II*[1] and *Ideal Standard*[2]), the ECJ has held that a trade mark owner does not, by assigning his trade mark registration in Member State A, consent to all subsequent uses of the trade mark in Member State A; nor does he therefore deprive himself of the right to object to the importation of goods bearing the relevant mark from Member State A into other Member States where he continues to hold rights in respect of the same mark.

This is clearly a very important point: the value of the retained trade mark right is clearly greater if the rights holder enjoys protection under trade mark law against leakage into his territory of branded products first marketed by the assignee in Member State A.

Although the legal profession and trade mark owners heaved a collective sigh of relief

---

[1] *CNL-SUCAL v Hag GF AG* (C-10/89) I ECR 3711.
[2] *IHT Internationale Heiztechnik v Ideal Standard* (C-9/93) (judgment delivered 22 June 1994).

when the ECJ gave judgment in *Hag II* and *Ideal Standard*, the judgments are not without difficulty for trade mark owners: the reasons why this is so are explained in more detail below.

Cases under Articles 85 and 86 EC

Cases involving trade marks tend to come before the ECJ in one of two ways: either as cases on exhaustion of rights or as cases under the competition rules of the EC Treaty, and, in particular, Article 85 EC. Article 85 EC is potentially applicable where a trade mark owner seeks to realise the value of his trade mark by dealing in the mark, for example, by entering into some kind of agreement for the exploitation by a third party—most usually an assignment or licence.

These kinds of agreement are extremely important: although the use of a trade mark in the course of the proprietor's trade is the most obvious means of obtaining value from a trade mark, many trade mark proprietors prefer instead (or as well) to obtain value from their marks by entering into some kind of contractual arrangement relating to the trade mark.

The remainder of this article, therefore, examines some of the commonest kinds of contract and how EC competition rules can affect those kinds of contract. The commonest trade mark agreements fall into three categories:

— agreements for the licensing of trade marks, whereby a licensee is authorised to use the mark in accordance with a licence contract;
— assignments of the trade mark rights (for example, as part of a business sale agreement); and
— so-called 'delimitation agreements' whereby a trade mark owner agrees with another party as to the manner in which, and extent to which, each will use specific trade marks as a means of resolving a dispute as to the entitlement of each party to use the marks. In some cases, the value of a mark can be secured only by resolving in this way a dispute which could, if not resolved, threaten the validity of the proprietor's right to his mark, or diminish the value of his rights even if they are valid.

All these kinds of agreement can raise issues under EC competition law. Licensing agreements often form part of a franchising agreement and raise numerous issues of competition law. (The principles applied by the EC Commission are explained, in part, in the block exemption for franchise agreements.) This article concentrates instead on trade mark assignments and delimitation agreements.

Why is Competition Law Relevant?

Before one looks in detail at the relevant law, a preliminary question arises: why is competition law relevant at all to trade marks? One can readily understand that, if a company owns patents protecting a method of manufacturing a particular kind of product, the patents could well confer on the patentee an effective monopoly over the manufacture of the products in question. So competition law would clearly be relevant to regulate the exploitation of the patents. Similarly, ownership of a copyright for an important computer program could confer on the copyright holder a dominant position in a market for the supply of certain kinds of computer software, so one would expect the competition authorities to be concerned to ensure that the copyright is not used to create barriers to entry in a manner which restricts competition.

But it is not obvious that ownership of a trade mark creates the same kinds of problems. A company which enjoys an exclusive right to sell products of a particular kind under a particular trade mark does not thereby monopolise the market for those products: the company's branded goods will compete with similar unbranded goods or with similar goods marketed under a different trade mark.

One would, therefore, expect the EC and national competition authorities to look on trade mark rights with less suspicion than is reserved for other kinds of intellectual property rights. In fact, the recent case law under Article 85 EC demonstrates a dawning realisation that trade mark rights do not raise the same issues of competition law as are raised by other intellectual property rights.

Nonetheless, agreements for the licensing or assignment of trade marks, and for delimitation of trade mark rights, may display anti-competitive features, and the EC Commission will intervene under EC competition rules in appropriate cases. The remainder of this article examines what are the anti-competitive features of trade mark agreements which the EC Commission and the ECJ are likely to find objectionable. This article also examines how trade mark owners may avoid some of the potential pitfalls.

Article 85 EC

By way of background, it is necessary first to outline the substantive provisions of Article 85 of the EC Treaty.

Article 85(1) EC

Article 85 EC is the principal provision of EC competition law dealing with anti-competitive agreements. It prohibits, as being incompatible with the common market, agreements between undertakings and concerted practices which have the object or effect of preventing, restricting or distorting competition in the common market and which are capable of affecting trade between Member States.

First, '*agreements*': Article 85 applies to contractually binding agreements and to less formal arrangements. The assignment and delimitation agreements discussed in this article are invariably of a contractual nature.

Second, '*undertakings*': Article 85 applies to agreements between undertakings: for this purpose, an undertaking is a legal person carrying on business on its own account—most commonly a company—or a collection of persons carrying on such businesses but forming a single economic unit—for example, a corporate group or a private company together with its sole principal proprietor. The ECJ has held that an agreement between a company and its wholly-owned subsidiary which simply allocates tasks and responsibilities between them is not an agreement between two different undertakings and will not, therefore, infringe Article 85 EC. So an agreement whereby one group company licenses another group company to use a trade mark, even if recorded formally, will generally not infringe Article 85(1) EC.

The next point to consider is the kinds of agreements which are prohibited: 'agreements which have as their *object or effect* the *prevention, restriction or distortion* of competition in the common market'.[3] Some agreements are regarded as having the object of infringing Article

---

[3] *Emphasis added.*

85 EC: for example, naked non-competition covenants between actual or potential com-petitors. In contrast, an agreement for the sale of a business by one firm to another may include, as an ancillary provision, an obligation on the vendor not to compete with the business which is being sold for a period of, say, two years after the sale. Such a non-competition covenant is regarded as being part of an agreement which has the legitimate object of enabling a business to be sold, so the non-competition covenant will not infringe Article 85 EC so long as it is not excessive in duration or scope.

In some cases, such as those mentioned above, it is quite easy to say what is the object of an agreement. But, in other cases, the question is more difficult. It may be difficult to articulate what is the object of an agreement or to decide whether that object is anti-competitive. Trade mark delimitation agreements provide a good example. Early case law of the EC Commission and the ECJ reveals their uncertainty as to what is to be regarded as the object of a trade mark delimitation agreement and this is a point which is discussed in more detail below, in looking at the substantive application of Article 85 EC to this kind of agreement.

A question also arises as to what is meant by the terms 'preventing', 'restricting' and 'distorting' competition. At this stage, it is to be noted that the EC authorities are interested in promoting intra-brand competition as well as inter-brand competition. Thus, if a franchise agreement confers on a franchisee an exclusive right to market certain goods under the franchisor's trade mark in a specific territory, the parties could well argue that the agreement has the effect of promoting inter-brand competition: the franchisee, knowing that there will be no free riders in his territory, is motivated to advertise his franchisor's brand and to invest in facilities dedicated to the promotion of the franchisor's goods. This arrangement could well lead to enhanced competition with similar goods produced by rival brand owners, but it effectively removes any possibility of competition among different franchisees all dealing in the franchisor's branded goods. In principle, the EC Commission will regard such a franchise agreement as being restrictive of competition unless it is altogether insignificant or unless it can be demonstrated that the franchisee *needs* exclusive rights (including an exclusive trade mark licence) in order to induce it to participate in selling the franchisor's goods. Thus, often, this kind of agreement will infringe Article 85(1) EC, but will merit exemption under Article 85(3), which is discussed below.

The next point to be considered is the phrase 'incompatible with the common market'. The text of Article 85 EC makes clear that the anti-competitive agreements which it covers are prohibited as being incompatible with the common market. This wording reveals the priorities of the draftsmen of the EC Treaty: the fundamental objective of the Treaty is to establish a single market, comprising the territories of all Member States, in which goods may be traded without obstacles between Member States; the draftsmen of the Treaty considered that, if a single market of that sort could be achieved, then competition could flourish among manufacturers and suppliers throughout that common market. It is therefore not surprising that the EC competition authorities have traditionally considered export bans, prohibiting one party from exporting goods from one Member State to another, to be one of the gravest infringements of Article 85 EC: the EC Commission considers the cross-border movement of goods as being instrumental to the creation of a single market.

The final point to be examined is the application of Article 85 EC to agreements which may 'affect *trade between Member States*':[4] an agreement will affect trade between Member States within the meaning of Article 85 EC only if it is such as to affect trade between Member States to an appreciable extent. In its early case law, the EC Commission and the

---

[4] *Emphasis added.*

ECJ were keen to establish jurisdiction to review agreements under Article 85 EC and would find, on the slightest of facts, that an agreement was capable of affecting trade between Member States. More recently, national courts applying EC competition rules have shown more caution: the English High Court, in the *George Michael*[5] case, has recently suggested that, for Article 85 EC to apply, it must be shown that an agreement is such as to cause an appreciable change in the pattern of trade between Member States. If the EC authorities were to adopt that view, it is possible that fewer trade mark agreements would fall to be reviewed under Article 85 EC. At present, it is probably premature to expect that to happen, and trade mark owners should probably assume that any agreement for the assignment or licensing of a trade mark right in one Member State but not another will be such as to affect trade between Member States within the meaning of Article 85 EC, provided that the goods sold under the relevant mark are sufficiently significant in volume to make the agreement of more than minimal significance in terms of competition.

So far, this article has examined the substantive elements of an infringement of Article 85 EC. It is appropriate next to consider the consequences for a company of being party to an infringing agreement.

Article 85(2) EC

Article 85(2) EC provides that an agreement which infringes Article 85(1) EC is void. In its case law, the ECJ has made clear that Article 85 EC has the effect of rendering void only those provisions of an agreement which actually prevent, restrict or distort competition. It is then a question of national law, to be determined by a national court, what is the consequence of that voidness on other provisions of the agreement. Slightly different consequences may ensue under different legal systems of different Member States.

There are other sanctions for infringement of Article 85 EC: the EC Commission has power to levy substantial fines on persons who are party to an agreement which infringes Article 85 EC: the quantum of fines is based on the gravity of the infringement and the parties' annual turnover. Fines may be levied of up to 10 per cent of the undertaking's previous year's turnover; and, of course, the undertaking may include other members of the corporate group of the company which is party to the infringing agreement.

It is also often argued that a third party who is injured by the operation of an infringing agreement may claim damages against the parties to the agreement to compensate him for his loss. In English law, such a claim would constitute a form of action for breach of statutory duty because Article 85 EC is incorporated into English law via an English statute, the European Communities Act 1972. There is, however, no case decided to date in which the court has awarded damages for breach of Article 85 EC and there remains scope for argument that Article 85 EC is not a statutory duty owed to a specific class of persons who are entitled to damages. Instead, Article 85 EC may be regarded as a measure enacted for the public benefit, to promote competition but not to protect specific competitors. On that basis (and subject to general principles of Community law), no damages would be available to injured parties.

Article 85(3) EC

Article 85(3) EC sets out the circumstances in which an agreement which infringes Article 85(1) EC may be exempted from the consequences of infringement.

---

[5] *Panayiotou v Sony Music Entertainment (UK) Ltd* [1994] 1 All ER 755.

An agreement will be eligible for exemption under Article 85(3) EC only if it fulfils four criteria:

(1) it must contribute to improving the production or distribution of goods or to promoting technical or economic progress;
(2) it must allow consumers a fair share of the resulting benefit;
(3) it must not impose on the undertakings concerned restrictions which are not indispensable to the attainment of those objectives; and
(4) it must not afford the undertakings concerned the possibility of eliminating competition in respect of a substantial part of the products in question.

Under the implementating regulations for Article 85 EC, the EC Commission is exclusively entitled to grant exemptions under Article 85(3) EC. For the most part, parties to an infringing agreement need to notify their agreement to the EC Commission to obtain an exemption. The EC Commission will issue an exemption by decision, and its decisions are subject to review by the Court of Justice. Notification generally brings with it an immunity from fines in respect of the performance of the agreement from the date of notification.

Application of Article 85 EC to Trade Mark Agreements

The following part of this article examines the substantive application of Article 85 EC to various kinds of trade mark agreements.

Substantive application of Article 85 EC

In this regard, it is useful to look at some of the decided cases and see what principles can be deduced from them.

Trade mark assignments
First, trade mark assignment agreements. The leading case in this area is *Sirena v Eda*:[6] in that case, a trade mark proprietor had registered the mark *Prep good morning* for a medicinal cosmetic cream in Germany and Italy. Before the coming into force of the EC Treaty, the proprietor assigned the Italian trade mark rights to an Italian company, Sirena, while selling (at some later stage) the German trade mark rights to a German company, Eda. From then on, Sirena sold the cosmetic cream under the *Prep* mark in Italy, while Eda sold similar products under the same mark in Germany. The case before the ECJ arose when Sirena took infringement proceedings in Italy to restrain the sale of Eda's products in Italy.

The Italian court referred a question of Community law to the ECJ for a response, so that it could take account of the ECJ's judgment in assessing the questions before it. The ECJ was asked to decide whether the agreement for the assignment of the *Prep* mark to Sirena infringed Article 85 EC and, if so, whether that affected Sirena's entitlement to bring infringement proceedings in reliance on its trade mark registration.

The questions placed before the ECJ admitted of no obvious answers: in one sense, the assignment agreement in question was fully performed and, hence, spent: once the original proprietor had assigned the marks, and the assignment had been perfected by the entry of Sirena's name on the trade mark register as proprietor of the mark, the parties could no

---

[6] Case 40/70 [1971] ECR 69.

longer be said to be 'performing' the agreement pursuant to which the assignment was made. On the other hand, the ECJ had held, in an earlier case, that the apparently unilateral exercise of a trade mark right may infringe Article 85 EC if it is to be regarded as a manifestation of an agreement which has the object or effect of restricting or distorting competition.

In the event, the ECJ held that, where a trade proprietor has acquired his rights to a trade mark pursuant to an agreement, then Article 85 may apply to prohibit him from exercising his trade mark rights to prevent importation of a competitor's goods if, by exercising these rights, he achieves an anti-competitive effect contemplated by the agreement. Moreover, the ECJ held that, even if some considerable time has passed between the date of the agreement for assignment and the later infringement proceedings, the enforcement of the trade mark rights through the infringement proceedings will continue to infringe Article 85 EC insofar as the agreement is thereby continuing to produce its effects.

It is important to note that the ECJ was not invited to consider whether the agreement in question between the original proprietor and Sirena did, in fact, prevent, restrict or distort competition and hence infringe Article 85 EC: the ECJ was simply asked to decide whether, in principle, an agreement for the assignment of a trade mark and the subsequent exercise of the trade mark rights by the assignee are capable of infringing Article 85 EC. In the event, the Italian court, taking account of the answer provided by the ECJ, held that, in all the circumstances, the agreement in question was not an infringing agreement.

Nonetheless, the case of *Sirena v Eda* is very important: if a company carries on business in two or more Member States using the same trade mark and wishes to sell the business as carried on in one Member State, while retaining the business as carried on in the other Member State, it must think carefully about how to deal with the relevant trade mark rights.

It was noted earlier that the case of *Ideal Standard* has finally established that, if the vendor assigns the trade mark rights for Member State A, he can, purely as a matter of trade mark law and under Article 30 EC, restrain the importation into Member State B of goods originally marketed in Member State A by the purchaser of the business in Member State A. The doctrine of exhaustion of rights will not, on its own, operate to prevent him from exercising his trade mark rights for that purpose. But it is precisely because *Ideal Standard* allows such an exercise of trade mark rights that a business sale agreement which simply assigns the trade mark rights for Member State A will (if it is of any significance) be likely to infringe Article 85 EC.

In order to assess whether an agreement infringes Article 85 EC, the EC Commission and the ECJ examine whether the agreement is such as to prevent, restrict or distort competition. *Prima facie*, an agreement which provides for one company to sell its business in Member State A to another company, with an assignment of the related trade mark rights in Member State A, does not do any of these things. It simply substitutes the purchaser company, in place of the vendor, as a participant in the relevant market in Member State A.

However, the test which the EC authorities apply to determine whether there is a restriction or distortion of competition is more complex. The EC authorities ask themselves the question: could the parties to this transaction reasonably have been expected to effect the transaction on terms which would have allowed the market to operate more competitively? If so, then, by failing to do so, the parties' agreement will prevent, restrict or distort competition.

In assessing the competitive position which the parties have created by their agreement, the EC authorities will take account of the legal and factual circumstances in which the agreement was made and is to operate and, since the judgment of the ECJ in *Ideal Standard*, one aspect of the legal context is that the business sale agreement could, if valid and enforceable, have the effect of permanently preventing the vendor's products from being sold under the common trade mark in the purchaser's territory, and of permanently preventing the purchaser's products from being sold in the vendor's territory under the common trade mark.

In most cases relating to a significant trade mark, the EC authorities are likely to view this kind of arrangement with disapproval. They will start from the premise that, *prima facie*, the vendor and the purchaser are potential competitors in each other's territories: after a transitional period during which the parties may agree not to compete in each other's territory, to enable each to enjoy the goodwill of the business which it has retained or acquired, each should be free, at least indirectly, to extend the geographic area of its sales into the other's territory. So, if the purchaser, operating from Member State A, produces goods bearing the common trade mark, it should be able to sell them to its distributors in Member State A to be on-sold to customers throughout the Community (including Member State B). If this cannot happen (because the vendor can invoke its trade mark rights in Member State B), and if the parties in question have more than a minimal market presence, then the EC authorities are likely to conclude that the vendor's attempt to enforce his trade mark rights infringes Article 85 EC, so that a national court should not assist in his efforts at enforcement. Thus, enforcement of those rights is prohibited under Article 85 EC as being a manifestation of the agreement. So much for *Ideal Standard*!

As a result, the vendor's trade mark rights are devalued, because they no longer confer on him an exclusive right to use the registered mark in Member State B, but allow the mark also to be used on goods originating from his assignee in Member State A, over which the vendor has no control. Indeed, his registration could become liable to expungement, on the grounds that the mark is not distinctive of his goods or is deceptive. The only consolation is that, whereas Article 30 EC and the rules as to exhaustion of rights apply *automatically* where they apply at all, Article 85 applies only to agreements which are such as to prevent, restrict or distort competition to more than a minimal extent, thereby allowing agreements in respect of very minor brands to slip through untainted.

This is, in the writer's view, a logical result of the judgments in *Ideal Standard* and *Sirena v Eda*. It is a possibility which is acknowledged and accepted by the ECJ in *Ideal Standard* and which a trade mark owner should certainly take seriously if it proposes to sell off one geographic division of its business, while retaining other geographic divisions carried on under the same mark. Ideally, the trade mark owner should avoid creating a permanent division of the Community market; instead, it should create only a transitional division, after which each party should be permitted to compete in the other's territory, possibly using different marks.

Delimitation agreements

The next category of agreements to be considered is delimitation agreements—that is, contractual agreements whereby two or more companies agree to settle a dispute about their entitlement to use a particular trade mark, or particular trade marks, as an alternative to proceeding to trial to determine the rights and wrongs of their dispute.

(1) *Sirdar/Phildar.* The first case of any interest in this area is *Sirdar/Phildar*,[7] a case considered by the EC Commission in 1975. In that case, two competing manufacturers of knitting yarns sold their goods under the marks *Sirdar* and *Phildar* respectively in various Member States of the Community. It was notable that in some Member States (and in some non-Member

---

[7] OJ 1975 L125/27.

States) both parties were content to allow the marks to co-exist, each using its own mark without any apparent concern as to confusion or deception. However, disputes arose when Sirdar attempted to block Phildar's efforts to register the *Phildar* mark for knitting yarns in the United Kingdom, even though Sirdar had not objected to a previous registration by Phildar in a different class.

Ultimately, the two companies entered into a delimitation agreement whereby they agreed that Sirdar would not attempt to register or use its *Sirdar* mark in France, while Phildar would not attempt to register or use its *Phildar* mark in the United Kingdom. In all other territories of the Community, each would allow the other's registration and use of its mark to continue unchallenged.

When the United Kingdom acceded to the Community, Sirdar notified this agreement to the EC Commission to seek, if necessary, an exemption for it under Article 85(3) EC. By the time the EC Commission looked at the agreement, Sirdar was attempting to enforce it in the English courts, to restrain the importation of Phildar's product bearing the *Phildar* mark into the United Kingdom.

The EC Commission issued a preliminary decision, holding that, in its preliminary view, the agreement infringed Article 85(1) and could not merit exemption, because it had the object of restricting competition. The EC Commission put it as follows:[8]

> the object of the agreement is to restrict competition in the common market, since it reflects the stated intent of the parties to prevent Sirdar ... and other firms, particularly dealers and importers, from selling knitting yarn in France under the *Sirdar* trade mark, and to prevent [Phildar] and other firms from selling knitting yarn in the United Kingdom under the *Phildar* trade mark. The significance of the bar to imports from France to the United Kingdom is underlined by the fact that Sirdar ... is seeking through the courts, on the grounds of the agreement in question, to oblige [Phildar] to cease importing.
>
> It cannot be said that, because, under the agreement, [Phildar] may import knitting yarn to the United Kingdom under a trade mark other than *Phildar*, there is, in effect, no restriction of competition, the use of a different trade mark would deprive [Phildar] of the impact of the advertising under its trade mark.
>
> It would in any case be financially impossible for other undertakings (for example, dealers, importers or mail order firms) to separate the 50 gramme packs of knitting yarn from the larger packages in which they are put and to replace each individual wrapper bearing the *Phildar* trade mark with a different wrapper.
>
> Nor can the existence of a restriction of competition be denied on the ground that the trade marks *Sirdar* and *Phildar* are similar and therefore likely to be confused. Even if this were so, it would not justify market sharing among the parties.

This part of the EC Commission's decision merits quotation because it sets out quite clearly how a trade mark delimitation agreement will be assessed for compatibility with Article 85 EC.

First, the competition authorities will ask whether there is a genuine dispute to be settled. It is clear that the EC Commission appeared not to accept that the *Phildar* and *Sirdar* marks were confusingly similar (and hence concluded that there were no grounds for a genuine dispute). While the decision is very brief, it seems that Sirdar could not establish that the object of the agreement was to settle a genuine dispute, because, in the vast majority of

---

[8] *Ibid.*, at 29.

territories, the parties used their respective marks without any apparent concern as to confusion and without any dispute.

The moral to be drawn is that a trade mark owner should intervene as soon as it sees another company using a confusingly similar mark to its own mark. If the trade mark owner lets it slip by, on the basis that the market in question is unimportant, and possibly outside the Community, it could well have difficulty persuading the courts that any later dispute is genuine when it relates to use of the marks in a larger, more important market.

The next point to emerge from the decision is this: an agreement which restrains one party (Phildar) from using in the United Kingdom a trade mark which it uses in France will not automatically restrict or prevent competition in the United Kingdom: there may be nothing to stop the party so restrained from using a different trade mark in the United Kingdom from the one he uses in France, and he may be able to compete equally effectively by using a different mark from the one in dispute. But whether this is possible (and whether he will be so disadvantaged by doing so that competition will be distorted) will be judged by reference to the factual context: in this case, Phildar had, it appears, already started using its *Phildar* mark in the United Kingdom for different kinds of goods pursuant to its earlier registration, and it would have lost the benefit of the goodwill which it had established there if it could not utilise that goodwill by selling additional products (namely, knitting yarns) under the same mark.

If the EC Commission had accepted that, owing to Sirdar's earlier registration of its *Sirdar* mark in the United Kingdom for knitting yarns, Phildar could not have registered or used its *Phildar* mark for such goods in the United Kingdom, the disadvantage to Phildar of not being able to capitalise on its goodwill should not have mattered: the disadvantage would have flowed not from the contractual restriction undertaken by Phildar, but from the proper application of trade mark law. But, as mentioned above, the EC Commission clearly considered that Sirdar would not have succeeded in excluding Phildar's trade marked goods if it had relied only on its rights in the *Sirdar* registration.

Another point to be noted is that, as well as commenting on the disadvantage to Phildar of not being able to use on its knitting yarns in the United Kingdom the same mark as it used in its advertising, the EC Commission took note of the particular manner in which trade marks are generally applied to the wrappers of knitting yarn: each ball of wool is enclosed in a paper band bearing the trade mark, as well as having the trade mark appear on each larger bag which contains some ten or more balls of wool. Given that market practice, it would have been particularly expensive and impractical for Phildar or its distributors to re-label goods destined for the United Kingdom. The message is that, if a trade mark owner proposes to enter into this kind of delimitation agreement, it is not enough to argue to the EC Commission that competition is not distorted because the restricted party remains free to sell his goods however he likes under a different trade mark: the EC Commission will want to examine whether the restricted party suffers a loss of competitive edge by being force to do so.

Finally, in the *Sirdar/Phildar* case, the EC Commission made another very telling point: even if it had been satisfied that there was a genuine risk of confusion of the *Sirdar* and *Phildar* marks in the United Kingdom, it still would not have considered it acceptable under Article 85 EC for the parties to dispose of their dispute by Sirdar's agreeing not to sell *Sirdar*-marked goods in France, while Phildar agreed not to sell *Phildar*-marked goods in the United Kingdom. This point was not decisive in the *Sirdar* case, but it is one of the most important points to emerge from the entire line of case law on delimitation agreements: a delimitation agreement which is capable of affecting trade between Member States will be compatible with Article 85 EC only if it constitutes the least restrictive means by which the parties can resolve their dispute: it is clear from other cases that the EC Commission will expect parties first to consider settling their dispute on terms which leave both parties free to market their products freely, and without being subjected to any competitive disadvantage, throughout the entire Community: often, this will entail the adoption of distinctive forms of marks which would otherwise run the risk of confusion (for example, the *Persil*[9] case). Alternatively, the EC Commission will expect any restraints on one party's freedom to market his goods in part of the Community to be limited to a transitional period, during which one party can phase out use of the disputed mark.

(2) *Penney's Trade Mark.* Other cases raise similar points. For example, in the case of *Penney's Trade Mark*,[10] a delimitation agreement in respect of the trade mark *Penney's* was held to merit a negative clearance (that is, a decision confirming that it is compatible with Article 85(1) EC), because it left one party free to use the *Penney's* trade mark throughout the Community while allowing the other party to adopt a different mark in which it had already invested significant sums, so that it was not disadvantaged by having to use that mark instead of *Penney's* mark.

(3) *BAT Cigarettes v EC Commission.* The case of *BAT Cigarettes*[11] raised a multitude of different points, not least because the contracting parties disputed the terms and effect of their delimitation agreement. Probably the most important point to emerge from that case is that: in the dispute which preceded the delimitation agreement, the first party, Segers, could have taken proceedings for expungement of BAT's German registration of its mark *Dorcet*, on grounds of non-use, but Segers did not raise this point in the proceedings between the parties. The EC Commission considered that he had not done so because he could not face the prospect of expensive litigation against a company as large as BAT. But, because the EC Commission considered that an application for cancellation of the BAT registration could have succeeded, the Commission concluded that the delimitation agreement could not be regarded as a reasonable and proportionate means of settling the parties' dispute: it imposed on Segers restrictions to which he would not have been subject had the proceedings reached 'the right' result, because BAT's trade mark registration would have been struck out, leaving Segers free to register his own mark and use it without constraint.

This illustrates again the fact that, in considering whether a particular delimitation agreement has the unlawful object of restricting competition or the legitimate object of resolving a genuine dispute, the EC Commission will seek to form a view as to the merits of the dispute: this could well pose difficulties for parties who wish to compromise proceedings by concluding a delimitation agreement but who genuinely do not agree as to the rights and wrongs of the matters in dispute between them. It is unfortunate that, in assessing the legality of a settlement agreement, the EC Commission seeks to work out what would have been the outcome of their litigation had the parties proceeded, since it is the inevitable consequence of their settlement that the competent national court will not be invited to rule on the matters in dispute.

The requirement that a delimitation agreement should be no more restrictive than necessary to achieve its legitimate purpose of settling a genuine dispute is pertinent to the EC Commission's examination of whether the delimitation agreement infringes Article 85(1) EC at all and, if so, whether the restrictions which it contained are indispensable, as is required if an exemption is to be available under Article 85(3) EC.

---

[9] EC Commission's Seventh Report on Competition Policy, point 138.
[10] OJ 1978 L60/19.
[11] Case 35/83 [1985] ECR 363.

For the same reason, the EC Commission will assess rigorously the scope of any no-challenge clause: in the *Penney's* case (and in the *BAT Cigarettes* case), the EC Commission appeared to expect the parties to limit any 'no-challenge' clauses to the specific subject-matter of their dispute: thus, even though Penney's Ireland agreed, in effect, that Penney's America should be exclusively entitled to the *Penney's* trade mark rights, it was important that Penney's Ireland should be free, after a number of years, to challenge Penney's America's entitlement to the marks, because new circumstances could arise which would entitle Penney's Ireland to make a new challenge, on different grounds from the ones giving rise to the dispute to be settled by the delimitation agreement. Thus, contracting parties will be permitted effectively to settle the very dispute in question, but they will not be entitled to use their settlement as a means of gagging a potential challenger in perpetuity.

(4) *Apple Corps/Apple Computer.*[12] Before leaving the subject of delimitation agreements, it is worthwhile to note one further point which emerges from some of the cases and, in particular, a case between the Apple computer company and the Apple record company as to the use of the *Apple* trade mark on computers having music-related applications.

It is not only restrictions which limit the territories in which a company may use its established mark which will be capable of infringing Article 85 EC. An agreement may also infringe Article 85 EC if it restrains a company, to a greater extent than is necessary, from using on one kind of product the trade mark which it has established for other kinds of product. Thus, in the *Apple* case, one of the points in dispute was whether a delimitation agreement infringed Article 85 EC by precluding the Apple computer company from capitalising on its goodwill in its *Apple* mark for computers, by restraining it from using that mark in connection with 'musical computers'. The argument in such a case runs as follows: a company which makes computers of one kind is likely to be a potential entrant into the market for making other kinds of computers; customers who are familiar with the company's original product range and with the company's trade mark for that range will be attracted to any products of a new kind which the company later introduces; if the company is unable to use its established trade mark for new ranges of products, it may lose the competitive edge which it ought properly to enjoy, thereby causing a distortion of competition in the market for those new products.

The message for trade mark owners is that any delimitation agreement must be reviewed for compatibility with Article 85 EC not only by reference to any geographic restrictions which it imposes on the use of specific trade marks, but also by reference to any 'field of use' restrictions.

Clearly, if a contracting party is restricted from using a trade mark on certain classes of goods, it may be possible to argue that the party in question was not, in any event, likely to enter the market to provide such goods, so that the provision does not, in fact, have any effect on competition. This argument will often succeed and should certainly be put forward in appropriate cases where a delimitation agreement is to be notified to the EC Commission for approval or is under attack in the courts.

It is, however, to be noted that the competition authorities will sometimes take a relatively long-term view in assessing whether a company is a potential entrant to a market: in the *BAT Cigarettes* case, the EC Commission noted a possible argument that there was no effect on competition arising from the contractual restriction on Segers' using his trade mark on certain kinds of tobacco since there was no evidence that he had any significant presence in the market for the supply of such tobacco; the EC Commission rejected that argument on

---

[12] *Apple Corps Ltd & Another v Apple Computer Inc. and Others* [1992] FSR 431.

the basis that a trade importer with experience of such matters had expressed the opinion that new market entrants often took many years to establish a significant market share in the tobacco markets and it should not be ruled out that, in the absence of the contractual constraint, Segers could *ultimately* have done so.

Does the First Trade Mark Directive[1] Allow International Exhaustion of Rights?

[1995] 10 EIPR 463

NICHOLAS SHEA
Barrister, London

According to the principle of exhaustion of rights, a trade mark proprietor cannot use his right to prevent the resale of goods bearing his trade mark, which he has himself put on the market, or which have been put on the market with his consent. A trade mark right is granted and applies only in the territory of one country.[2] Exhaustion applies primarily to goods put on the market in that territory. However, the European Court of Justice has developed case law to prevent trade marks from being used to stop the sale in one Member State of goods put on the market by a connected trade mark proprietor in another Member State. These cases, based on the rules on free movement of goods in Articles 30 and 36 of the Treaty of Rome, have led to a principle of Community-wide exhaustion of trade mark rights in certain circumstances.[3] If a company tries to charge markedly different prices for the same product in different Member States, then so-called parallel importers can rely on the principle of Community-wide exhaustion to resell throughout the Community goods brought in the Member State where their price is lowest.

Article 7 of the directive confirms the principle of Community-wide exhaustion, building on the case law of the Court of Justice and arguably extending the scope of the principle of exhaustion beyond that which was previously required in order to comply with Articles 30 and 36 of the Treaty. The agreement on the European Economic Area has extended the principle of exhaustion in Article 7 to EEA countries.[4] Article 7(1) is in the following terms:

> The trade mark shall not entitle the proprietor to prohibit its use in relation to goods which have been put on the market in the Community under that trade mark by the proprietor or with his consent.

Article 7(2) provides an exception which will, among other things, allow the proprietor to prevent the use of his trade mark on his goods if they have been damaged or altered.

Before the directive entered in force, some Member States had a wider principle—that a trade mark proprietor cannot use his right to stop the sale of goods which have been put on

---

[1] Directive 89/104/EEC, OJ 1989 L40/1.

[2] With the exception of cases where a unitary right is granted in several states, for example Benelux trade marks, or a Community Trade Mark under Regulation 40/94, once the Community Trade Mark Office comes into operation.

[3] See for example *Centrafarm v Winthrop* [1974] ECR 1147; *Hoffman-La Roche v Centrafarm* [1978] ECR 1139; *Centrafarm v American Home Products* [1978] ECR 183; *Pfizer v Eurim-Pharm* [1981] ECR 2913.

[4] Annex XVII, point 4. EEA countries are presently only Norway and Iceland, with Liechtenstein due to join.

the market bearing his trade mark by him or by a connected company anywhere in the world. This is known as international exhaustion. Some commentators have argued that Article 7 does not allow Member States to maintain a principle of international exhaustion.[5] Others maintain that Article 7 lays down only a minimum requirement of EEA-wide exhaustion, permitting individual Member States to extend the principle.[6] The question becomes important in Member States such as the United Kingdom which previously had a principle of international exhaustion in their case law, and have implemented Article 7 of the directive by incorporating the words of Article 7 directly into national law, without explicitly saving or quashing the principle of international exhaustion.[7]

The directive clearly harmonises national provisions as to EEA-wide exhaustion, insofar as the case law based on Articles 30 and 36 of the Treaty permitted national differences. The question is, therefore, whether the directive intends tacitly to harmonise national provisions as to international exhaustion. If so, any national provision conflicting with the harmonised provision will be illegal.[8] If not, national measures are permissible provided they are compatible with the Treaty.

The Commission's original proposal did intend to harmonise international exhaustion by imposing a principle of international exhaustion on all Member States.[9] However, it is strongly arguable that by restricting the ambit of Article 7 to EEA-wide exhaustion, the Council[10] intended not to harmonise international exhaustion, leaving the Member States to make or retain their own provisions.

Such a partial harmonisation of the law of exhaustion is understandable in the context of a directive which expressly undertakes only a partial harmonisation of national law:

> Whereas it does not appear to be necessary at present to undertake full-scale approximation of the trade mark laws of the Member States and it will be sufficient if approximation is limited to those national provisions of law which most directly affect the functioning of the internal market.[11]

Therefore, it is submitted that the directive did not carry out a complete harmonisation of the principle of exhaustion, from which it follows that Member States are free to make their own provisions.

If the directive does indeed allow Member States to preserve a principle of international exhaustion in their domestic law, then there will be barriers to the free movement within the

---

[5] Lars Kjølbye, *Ugeskrift for Restvæsen*, 1994.B., at 58 to 50; Jens Fejø, *Vennebog til Mogens Koktvedgaard*, 1993, at 261 to 274; and Hans Peter Kunz-Hallstein, *GRUR Int.* (1992) at 90. All quoted by Rasmussen, 'Exhaustion of Trade Mark Rights Pursuant to Directive 89/104', [1995] 4 EIPR 174, in which he identifies some circumstances in which international exhaustion should survive.

[6] Anders J. Andersen and Kund Wallberg, *Juristen*, 1992, at 36 to 37; and Annette Kur, *GRUR Int.* (1991) at 788; both quoted by Rasmussen, Note 5 above.

[7] Denmark and the Benelux countries may similarly be in this position. France and Italy have also used a similar wording to Article 7 of the directive.

[8] Case 65/75 *Tasca* [1976] ECR 291; Case 5/77 *Tedeschi v Denkavit Commerciale Srl* [1977] ECR 1555; Case 148/77 *Pubblico Ministero v Ratti* [1979] ECR 1629; and Case 227/82 *Van Bennekom* [1983] ECR 3883; as recently confirmed in the opinion of Advocate General Léger in Case C-5/94 *ex parte Hedley Lomas*, delivered 20 June 1995. Member States retain the right to take national measures based on the grounds in Article 100a(4) of the Treaty if the procedure there is followed.

[9] Article 6(1) of the proposed directive at OJ 1980 C351/80, p. 1.

[10] The term 'Council' is used throughout as shorthand for 'Community Legislator'. The proposal to restrict the ambit of Article 7 to Community-wide exhaustion was endorsed by the Council, but originated in the Economic and Social Committee.

[11] 7th recital to the directive. This is why it is called the 'First' Council Directive in the field of trade marks.

EEA of goods which have been imported from third countries[12] without the consent of the trade mark proprietor. Such goods will only be free to circulate in the Member States which decide to preserve or adopt a principle of international exhaustion.[13] On the other hand, the directive will have succeeded in its main aim of preventing a trade mark proprietor from partitioning the Common Market. Thus, on this interpretation of Article 7, the directive has arguably harmonised those national provisions which most directly affect the functioning of the *internal* market (free movement of goods produced within the Community) leaving a margin of discretion to the Member States as to the interaction of their domestic markets with external markets.

The barriers to the free movement of goods created by differing national provisions on international exhaustion are clearly unwelcome. However, they are the direct result of the Council's decision not to impose a rule of international exhaustion throughout the Community, and thus to allow a multinational to use trade marks to isolate the Community market from other markets, at least in some circumstances. In the absence of agreement in the Council to international exhaustion, it was better to allow some Member States to take advantage of international exhaustion, hampering free movement, than to prevent all Member States from doing so. Any Member State which considers that its consumers are having to pay higher prices for goods because of these barriers is, it is submitted, free to introduce a principle of international exhaustion.

The Court of Justice has confirmed in its Opinion on the signing of the Uruguay Round of the GATT[14] that Member States retain competence in conjunction with the Community in matters of international intellectual property.[15] If the directive does indeed allow international exhaustion, then Member States are free to negotiate or maintain agreements with third countries allowing mutual exhaustion of trade mark rights. The TRIPs agreement leaves open the possibility of any of the signatory countries unilaterally adopting a principle of international exhaustion.[16]

The Commission has expressed the view that the present version of Article 7 gives scope to national courts to extend the principle of EEA-wide exhaustion to third countries:

> The restriction to Community-wide exhaustion, however, *does not prevent the national courts from extending this principle*, in cases of a special nature, in particular where, even in the absence of a formal agreement, reciprocity is guaranteed.[17]

If national courts may recognise a principle of international exhaustion in some circumstances without further Community legislation, it follows that the Commission must be of the opinion that a national principle of international exhaustion is compatible with Article 7 of the directive. Of course, the Commission's view on the matter is not binding.

---

[12] 'Third countries' is EC-speak for countries outside the European Community; it is used here to mean outside the EEA.

[13] Article 36 of the Treaty allows imports into other Member States to be prevented in order to protect intellectual property rights.

[14] Opinion 1/94 [1994] ECR I-5267.

[15] Thus requiring each Member State individually to ratify the TRIPs agreement.

[16] Article 6 of TRIPs even provides that the issue of exhaustion cannot be the subject of dispute settlement under the agreement, unless a country applies the exhaustion principle in violation of the TRIPs non-discrimination rules of most favoured nation and national treatment.

[17] COM(84) 470 final (*emphasis added*). The Commission was commenting on Article 11 of the proposed Council regulation (now Article 13 of Regulation 40/94) which is in identical terms, and underwent an identical amendment, to Article 7 of the directive. The explanatory memorandum on the amended proposal for the directive, COM (85) 793 final, explicitly refers back to the explanatory comment on Article 11 of the proposed regulation.

The English Law of International Exhaustion

The limited principle of international exhaustion of trade mark rights in English law prior to the implementation of the directive by the Trade Marks Act 1994 was based on implied consent. If any branch of an enterprise of which the UK trade mark proprietor forms part had put goods on the market abroad bearing its trade mark, the trade mark proprietor was held to have impliedly consented to the goods being exported from the country where they are put on the market, and sold in the United Kingdom.[18] This is a limited principle of international exhaustion, and would apparently not apply, for example, if the goods were sold abroad subject to an export restriction and were of a markedly different quality.[19]

The directive retains the defence of consent. Article 5 only allows the proprietor to prevent all third parties 'not having his consent' from using the trade mark.[20] Thus, however Article 7 of the directive is interpreted by the English courts,[21] the limited principle of international exhaustion in English law would appear to survive on the basis of Article 5 of the directive. That is, unless the European Court of Justice were to rule that Article 7 of the directive prevents Member States from adopting or retaining any principle of international exhaustion, and that such a definition of consent is incompatible with Article 7 of the directive.

In a recent case, Jacob J conjectured that the Trade Marks Act 1994 might prevent a multinational from using trade marks in order to divide markets.[22] He was of the view that the detailed reasoning in the *Revlon* and *Colgate* cases would no longer be of assistance in cases of parallel imports. Certainly, for marketing within the EEA, Article 7 of the directive[23] has superseded this case law; but the defence of consent based on *Revlon* arguably still survives in cases of international exhaustion from outside the EEA. It would perhaps be surprising if the Trade Marks Act 1994 in fact made it easier for a multinational to divide the UK market (as part of the EEA) from its markets in third countries.[24]

Conclusion

The directive arguably imposes on Member States only a minimum requirement of enacting a principle of EEA-wide exhaustion of trade mark rights, leaving the national legislatures and courts to decide whether to adopt or maintain a principle of international exhaustion. However, the directive does not provide a plan answer to the issue, and the questions will probably have to be conclusively determined by the European Court of Justice.

---

[18] *Revlon v Cripps & Lee* [1980] FSR 85. The defence is probably based on implied consent of the registered proprietor, rather than by regarding the use on the imported goods as use by the registered proprietor, see *Kerly*, para. 14–30.

[19] *Colgate Palmolive Ltd v Markwell Finance Ltd* [1989] RPC 497.

[20] Implemented in sections 9 and 10 of the Trade Marks Act 1994.

[21] Article 7 of the directive is repeated *verbatim* in section 12 of the Trade Marks Act 1994.

[22] *Northern & Shell plc v Condé Nast & National Magazines Distributors Ltd* [1995] RPC 117 at 124.

[23] Section 12 of the Trade Marks Act 1994.

[24] 'The question of parallel imports under the Trade Marks Act will probably have to be considered in due course, but the detailed reasoning of *Revlon* and *Colgate* will not assist. It may well be that the result reached is that trade marks will not be a machinery whereby a multinational can divide markets. Lloyd LJ recognised the system under the 1938 Act was "perhaps underdeveloped" and that a sensible view would be that it is the same mark applied by any member of a group of companies forming a multinational whole. Certainly Joe Soap seeing a trade mark on the goods of a multinational is not concerned with the fine detail of the multi-company structure of the group', *per* Jacob J in *Northern & Shell*, Note 22 above, at 124.

Benelux: A Guide to the Validity of Three-dimensional Trade Marks in Europe

[1995] 3 EIPR 154

BENOÎT STROWEL
Nauta Dutilh, Brussels

European harmonisation measures in the field of trade mark law have brought new legal concepts to various EU Member States. The registration of shapes as trade marks is one of these. If all signs capable of distinguishing can be valid trade marks, some of them must be denied protection for reasons of public policy. What is at stake in refusing protection under trade mark law to certain shapes is not a question of overlap of intellectual property rights but rather the defence of a free trade. This comment analyses the exceptions to the validity of three-dimensional trade marks in the light of Benelux trade mark law.

The Council Directive ('the Directive') of 21 December 1988 to harmonise the laws of Member States with respect to trade marks should have been implemented by each national government by 31 December 1992. Several governments have, however, failed to do so. At the time of writing only France, Greece, Denmark, Spain, Italy and the United Kingdom had adapted their legislation accordingly. Although the three Benelux Governments agreed to the text of the new Trade Mark Bill in 1992, ratification by the respective Parliaments and subsequent enactment is not expected before mid-1995. The Benelux legislatures did not deem it necessary to diverge from the existing provisions of the Uniform Benelux Trade Mark Act ('the Act') on the validity of three-dimensional trade marks, in the new Bill since, in their opinion, the Act reflects the essential teaching of the Directive in this respect.[1]

Indeed, the Directive is so closely inspired by Benelux trade mark law that its provisions on the grounds for refusal of three-dimensional trade marks must be interpreted in the light of Benelux case law. This comment will therefore examine those provisions in the Directive which deal with the signs of which a trade mark may consist and the grounds for refusal and invalidity of a three-dimensional trade mark (Articles 2 and 3 section 1(3)), and try to interpret them in a manner which is consistent with the Benelux experience of such marks.

These provisions give rise to an interpretation problem which is of considerable interest to any owner of marks which either cannot be registered under the existing national laws or

---

[1] See the Common Commentary of the three Benelux Governments to the protocol for the modification of the Act (Ing.-Cons., 1992, at 370, § 4):

> The principle on which the adaptations to the (Harmonisation) Directive have been suggested, was to modify the Act only when necessary, that is, when Benelux trade mark law is not compatible with the Directive or when doubts could arise in that respect; as a result, only a limited number of modifications to the Act were needed, thanks to the relatively new and modern character of this Act. It should be recalled that a directive does not impose a systematic and literal adaptation of the national legislation, but contents itself with specifying the objective to achieve under national law (*unofficial translation from French*).

whose validity is under scrutiny. Although the principle of registrability of three-dimensional signs has been largely welcomed by industry and trade in various Member States, the owners of such potentially registrable signs remain bewildered as to the exact meaning to be given to the exceptions to this principle in practice.

Definition of a Trade Mark

Article 2 of the Directive lays down an illustrative list of signs of which a trade mark may consist 'provided the sign is capable of distinguishing the goods or services of one undertaking from those of another undertaking'. Shapes of goods or of their packaging are included in this list.

Likewise, Article 1 of the Act contains a similar list of signs which can be considered as trade marks. Article 1 of the Act reads:

> Are considered as individual trade marks: denominations, designs, prints, stamps, letters, numbers, shapes of goods or of their packaging and all other signs used to distinguish the products (or services) of an undertaking.

The Directive uses the same wording: 'shapes of goods or of their packaging'; the list of signs in Article 1 of the Act is also non-exhaustive, the only prerequisite being that the sign *must be used for distinguishing* the goods of an undertaking. Hence, the Act stresses from the outset the importance of distinctiveness acquired by way of intensive use.

On the other hand, the Directive indicates that the sign *must be capable of distinguishing* the goods of an undertaking; although such wording apparently departs from that of the Act, Article 3 of the Directive refers to the theory of 'secondary meaning' by way of intensive use.

The distinctive character of a three-dimensional sign

In assessing the validity of a three-dimensional trade mark, it is important to separate the issue of distinctiveness and that of whether such a mark falls within the exceptions laid down in Article 3 section 1(e) of the Directive. Numerous three-dimensional trade marks will not be distinctive *ab initio* and will only eventually acquire their necessary distinctive power after long usage.

The use in the Directive of the wording 'capable of distinguishing' combined with the exclusion of three-dimensional trade marks from the benefit of 'secondary meaning' (Article 3 section 3 of the Directive), throw both questions into confusion. An illustration of such confusion can be found in Article 711–2 of the French Intellectual Property Code which provides that:

> are deprived from any distinctive character:
>
> . . .
>
>> signs made exclusively of a shape which is imposed by the nature or the function of the product, or which gives to the latter its substantial value.
>
> The distinctive character can, with the exception of (c), be acquired by means of usage (*unofficial translation*).

By directing that such three-dimensional signs are deprived from the outset and cannot acquire distinctiveness, the French legislature has, with respect to such signs, wrongly interpreted and applied the overriding principle according to which all signs capable of distinguishing are valid trade marks. The question of whether the three-dimensional sign at stake in practice distinguishes the goods of an undertaking must indeed be isolated from that of whether a potentially valid trade mark, and henceforth a distinctive sign, must be denied protection for reasons which in essence are foreign to the fundamental principle of distinctiveness governing trade mark law.

Although any sign used to identify the products or services of an undertaking is probably capable of becoming distinctive, some are refused registration as valid trade marks for the sake of public policy. It is the monopolisation of certain shapes which is considered as abusive in the case of shapes which are so important for the public and/or traders that they cannot be the subject of exclusive rights and which consequently justifies their refusal for registration as valid trade marks.

While the question of whether a three-dimensional trade mark falls within the exceptions of Article 3 section 1(e) of the Directive (or of Article 1 section 2 of the Act) should be assessed at the time of application or registration, the appreciation of its distinctive power must be determined *hic and nunc*, when the question arises, which might be after extended use. A three-dimensional trade mark cannot be declared invalid or refused registration simply because at the time of application or registration its shape is not considered 'as being capable of distinguishing the products of an undertaking' (a straight-forward bottle, for example), and because further to Article 3 section 3 of the Directive, such an inherent lack of distinctive power cannot be cured by the means of intensive use. It is not the shape's alleged original lack of distinctiveness which cannot be put right by extensive use of such a shape as a trade mark, but the intrinsic characteristics of such a shape which have rendered it unavailable for appropriation under trade mark law: this is the prevalent reason for excluding certain shapes falling within the exceptions of Article 3 section 1(e) from the benefit of Article 3 section 3 of the Directive.

Legal writers in the Benelux have expressed the above idea, as has the Benelux Court of Justice, in a rather abridged manner: although three-dimensional signs which fall within the exceptions to their validity as trade marks, are *capable* of distinguishing, these *may not* be used to distinguish the products of an undertaking.[2] However, such wording does little to reduce the current confusion between distinctiveness and 'intrinsic' validity.

When is a sign distinctive?

The Benelux Court of Justice ruled that the sole fact that the public (or a sufficiently representative percentage of it) recognises the product, thanks to its 'aspect', as emanating from a certain undertaking, meets the requirement of the sign's distinctive power;[3] accordingly, it is not necessary that the sign used as a mark discloses the identity of the producer as long as it distinguishes the producer's product from those of his competitors by virtue of its very 'aspect'. In other words, the sign will be considered a mark provided the public could (reasonably) perceive such sign or aspect as being distinctive of a product of an undertaking.[4]

A three-dimensional trade mark, the distinctive character of which is established in accordance with case law from the Benelux Court of Justice, may, however, be declared

---

[2] Benelux Court of Justice, 23 December 1985, Case 83/4, *Adidas*, Rec., 1985, at 38 to 86. Ch. Gielen and L. Wichers Hoeth, *Merkenrecht*, W.E.J. Tjeenk Willink Zwolle, 1992, at 165.

[3] Benelux Court of Justice, 16 December 1991, Case 90/4, *Burberrys II*, IER 1992, at 57.

[4] Benelux Court of Justice, 7 November 1988, Case 87/3, *Omnisport*, Rec. 1988, at 90.

invalid if its shape falls within one or more of the three exceptions laid down in the Directive and the Act.

The Exceptions to a Three-dimensional Trade Mark's Validity

The grounds for refusal or invalidity of a trade mark are listed exhaustively in Articles 3 and 4 of the Directive. Member States thus have no latitude to add further grounds for refusal or invalidity other than, for example, for procedural reasons, which are not provided for in the Directive.

Some of these grounds for refusal or invalidity and, *inter alia*, Article 3 section 1(e), are also mandatory: Member States must transpose into national law the following exceptions to the validity of three-dimensional trade marks.

Article 3 section 1(e) of the Directive reads:

The following shall not be registered or if registered shall be liable to be declared invalid:

. . .

signs which consist exclusively of:
— the shape which results from the nature of the goods themselves; or
— the shape of goods which is necessary to obtain a technical result; or
— the shape which gives substantial value to the goods.

It has already been mentioned that the Benelux legislatures did not deem it necessary to diverge in the new Bill from the existing provisions in the Act with respect to the above exceptions.[5]

Article 1 section 2 of the Act reads:

However, cannot be considered as trade marks, the shapes which are imposed by the nature of the products, which affect their essential value or which produce industrial results.

Broadly speaking, the wording of both provisions is very similar, the main literal difference lies in the expression in the Directive, of ground (2) ('necessary to obtain a technical result'): if anything, the Directive appears to be more restrictive than the Act with respect to the scope of the grounds for refusal or invalidity. This is evident from the use of the words 'exclusively' (signs which consist exclusively of), 'necessary' (necessary to obtain a technical result) and 'substantial' (gives substantial value to the goods).

It is interesting to note that the initial wording of the second ground for refusal in the Directive (and in the Regulation for a Community Trade Mark), that is, 'the shape which has some technical consequence' was abandoned in early December 1986 for the final formulation referred to above. This is the fruit of pressure from, *inter alia*, the Benelux delegation to have the scope of the initial draft of the second exception to the validity of trade marks (which was deemed too broad and not in conformity with its rather liberal trade

---

[5] See Note 1 above.

mark law ideal), narrowed down. Unfortunately, no material or document is readily to hand to provide an explanation of the rationale behind this amendment.[6]

The abusive monopolisation of a shape

In excluding some signs from the benefit of trade mark protection, the legislatures in Europe and the Benelux were concerned that indefinitely renewable monopolistic rights could be granted to the owner of a mark 'which would provide him with abnormal advantages or impose on his competitors unjustified and extraordinary restrictions and burdens'.[7] The same idea was expressed in the Proposal for a Community Trade Mark of 25 November 1980 with respect to Article 6 of the proposed Regulation:

> Moreover, the shape of a product shall not be allowed to be registered if the registration of such a shape would enable an undertaking to monopolise this shape to the detriment of its competitors and the consumers (*unofficial translation from French*).

The above concern goes largely beyond a simple will to avoid the overlapping of monopolistic protection resulting from the various intellectual property rights such as copyrights, designs or patents. Its general character means that the validity of the three-dimensional trade mark must be assessed by referring to the trade mark's finality.[8]

The Three Grounds for Refusal and Invalidity

The 'synthesising' analysis of a three-dimensional trade mark

It has already been emphasised that although the wording of Article 3 section 1(e) in the Directive is very similar to that of Article 1 section 2 of the Benelux Act, the former marks an apparent departure from the Act in requiring that in order for a three-dimensional trade mark to be declared invalid, *all its elements* must fall within one or more of the three exceptions to the mark's validity discussed below.

Indeed, Article 3 section 1(e) states very clearly:

> The following shall not be registered or if registered shall be liable to be declared invalid:
> . . .
> signs which consist *exclusively* of: . . .

Pursuant to the Directive, only signs *made exclusively of shapes* which cannot be monopolised for fear of granting the owner of such three-dimensional signs a special advantage in the manufacture, design or packaging of a product, are to be denied protection under trade mark law.

---

[6] It has not been possible to find any document, whether from the Council of Ministers or from the Commission, with an explanation as to the reasons behind such an amendment. Likewise, the questions and amendments in the European Parliament do not shed any more light on the rationale behind the change of wording. The almost complete dearth of official preliminary works in the legislative process in use in the European Union should be deplored.

[7] Unofficial translation from French—Chavanne, RIPIA, 1972, 391 in A. Braun, *Précis des marques de produits et de services*, Larcier, 1987 (2nd edn) No. 75, at 70.

[8] See Chavanne, *ibid.*, and B. Michaux, note under Court of Appeal, Liège, *Unica v Lego*, 30 June 1993, Ing.-Cons., 1993, at 217.

Likewise, the same rule is expressed in Article 3 section 1(c) and (d) of the Directive in relation to descriptive, deceptive and common trade marks.[9] This reference to marks made *exclusively* of signs which cannot be registered is, in our opinion, nothing other than the confirmation that a mark must be analysed in a synthesising manner rather than being dissected in its various elements. This is a governing principle as to the analysis of a trade mark's validity, at least in France and in the Benelux.[10]

In practice, a mark will often be made of various separate elements which taken in isolation are not distinctive or which have fallen into the public domain. Such elements cannot be used as trade marks.

Their combination or the shape given to that combination might, however, earn protection as an indivisible whole under trade mark law. It is therefore the mark seen globally which must be considered.

The same idea has been expressed by the European legislature, while the Directive provides that, for the mark to be declared invalid or refused registration, all parts of a sign must be descriptive, insufficiently distinctive or must have fallen into the public domain. It is indeed the sign as a whole which must fall into the above categories for trade mark protection to be denied.

Reference will be made below to this principle of synthesising analysis with respect to each ground for refusal or invalidity of a three-dimensional trade mark.

In extreme cases, the shape will be imposed by its function without any possibility of variation. Nonetheless, in most instances only a limited number of characteristics or elements will be determined by the shape's function without any room for varying them. In such cases, the shape taken as an indivisible whole will not have excluded the introduction of arbitrary elements which are independent from the function of the shape.

It is the combination of these various elements—functional and arbitrary—which constitutes the sign seen by the public as a distinctive trade mark. Provided the functional elements are used as non-autonomous parts of a larger combination, the sign as a whole can be protected under trade mark law. Conversely, if the functional elements are used in an autonomous manner and are perceived by the public as independent distinctive signs, trade mark protection of the same must be denied.

The excluded shapes

'The shape which results from the nature of the goods themselves'
The Benelux Act refers to 'the shapes which are imposed by the nature of the products'. The legislative history of the Act makes it clear that 'one cannot impose on the industry or the trade, restrictions on the sue of a shape which is indispensable to the manufacture or the distribution of a product'.[11] Indeed, such a monopolisation would lead to a monopolisation of the products themselves. An umbrella, a carrier bag or an eggbox immediately spring to mind as examples of such shapes. Only basic shapes will be imposed by the nature of the goods.

In practice, indispensable shapes seem to be largely determined by the extent of their use,

---

[9] It can be informed from the wording of the Directive regarding the other mandatory grounds for refusal of a trade mark (Article 3 section 1(c) and (d)), that a mark which does not consist *exclusively* of signs which are descriptive or common is, however, valid. The intention of the legislature was clearly to restrict the possibilities for refusal or invalidity of a trade mark. The use of the word 'exclusively' in relation to the above grounds for refusal (Article 3 section 1(c) and (d)) marks a departure from the wording of Article 6 *quinqies* B.2° of the Paris Convention which inspired the text of the Directive in that respect.

[10] P. Mathely, 'Le droit français des signes distinctifs', Paris, 1984, in A. Braun, Note 7 above, at 291.

[11] Unofficial translation from French.

and because of their extensive use, indispensable shapes are rarely distinctive.[12]

However, additional three-dimensional elements could be attached to that indispensable shape, which, taken individually or in combination, can work as distinctive trade marks. Although the screw-top of a bottle is necessarily round, other three-dimensional elements can be added (a peculiar rim, grooves, specific proportions, and so on) which will be seen by the public as being distinctive either on their own or in combination.[13] The Tribunal of The Hague held that the general shape of a bottle of olive oil is indispensable; of the presence of grooves and a purposefully designed handle in the body of the bottle itself, however, it concluded that the bottle with all its additional characteristics had merged into a distinctive trade mark[14].

This is a perfect illustration of the principle of synthesising analysis discussed above. The Tribunal upheld the principle provided for in the Directive, namely that the shape of the bottle was not exclusively made of three-dimensional elements resulting from the nature of the product itself and that its general shape in combination with other characteristics worked as a distinctive whole.

'The shape of goods which is necessary to obtain a technical result'

Although it is referred to in the Benelux as 'the shape which produces industrial results', the exception laid down in the Directive should be read along the same lines as those developed in the Benelux.

Pursuant to the legislative history of the Act, all shapes of products and packaging the effect of which is technical should be excluded from protection. Such shapes will therefore be refused as trade marks as soon as their use provides their owner 'with a concrete advantage in the manufacture and packaging of the goods'.[15] The Act also provides that the reference to 'industrial results' marks a departure from any mere aesthetical or intellectual advantage.[16]

The above comment is, however, not very helpful since in the creation of a shape for a product or a packaging, there will always be a mixture of technical, conceptual, aesthetic and other elements which cannot be separated; if interpreted extensively the above ground for refusal would exclude most shapes from the benefit of protection under trade mark law since all shapes have a technical effect in one way or another.[17]

This was not the aim of the legislature which indeed, made it very clear in Article 2 of the Directive (and in Article 1 of the Act) that all signs which are capable of distinguishing can be valid trade marks. As exceptions to this paramount principle, the various grounds for refusal and invalidity must be interpreted restrictively.

---

[12] Court of Appeal, Amsterdam, 4 April 1984, BIE 1896, at 77, regarding an octagonal cheese box which had been filed as a trade mark.

[13] See Ch. Gielen and L. Wichers Hoeth, Note 2 above, at 166.

[14] Pres. Tribunal, The Hague, 4 February 1992, IER 1992, at 115.

[15] The legislative history of the Act also confirms that the concept of a shape producing industrial results is wider than that of an invention under patent law. Accordingly, evidence that a shape is not patentable does not establish that the same shape can be protected under trade mark law. This reference to another system of protection under intellectual property law is perhaps rather unfortunate and misleading. Indeed, it is often interpreted *a contrario*, in order to say that any shape which is protectable under patent law must therefore be declared invalid. This was not, in the author's opinion, the aim of the legislature; see also, although *obiter dicta*, the submissions of the Advocate General in the *Burberrys I* case, Note 29 below.

[16] Which might however, be caught under the third exception (see below).

[17] For example, the shape of any bottle produces industrial results. A hole must necessarily be designed in its upper part while its base must also be sufficiently wide for it to stand. These essential characteristics can obviously never be monopolised, whereas nothing prevents a trader from filing the unusual shape given to a bottle as a trade mark; see in connection with a copy of the Cointreau bottle, Tribunal of Commerce, Brussels, 5 February 1985, Ing.-Cons., 1985, at 102 or in connection with the bottle of olive oil, see Note 14 above.

The author believes, as do many others, that 'it is the finality of the trade mark right which must serve as the criterion for assessing the validity of three-dimensional trade marks'.[18]

It has already been emphasised that the legislature's concern in excluding from protection certain types of shape was to avoid indefinitely renewable monopolistic rights granting the owner of a three-dimensional trade mark 'abnormal advantages or imposing unjustified and extraordinary restrictions and burdens on its competitors'. It is, accordingly, the abusive monopolisation of a shape which is unlawful. This will occur whenever the shape in question is *necessary* to produce industrial results and consequently cannot fulfil an indicator of origin or advertising function.[19] The Directive clarifies the present situation by referring to the criterion of 'necessity' of the shape for the sought-after result as being the test for determining whether the same shape can work as a valid trade mark.

To be disqualified from protection the shape must be more than merely useful in order to produce the same industrial effect: it must be *necessary*. No *hic et nunc* usable alternatives must exist. Evidence that a multiplicity of workable forms exists at any given moment in time to perform the same technical function necessarily excludes the application of the above ground for refusal. The existence of feasible alternatives to reach the same technical result ensures that the owner of the three-dimensional trade marks does not enjoy 'a concrete advantage in the manufacture or the packaging of the goods'.[20]

If a shape, notwithstanding its evident technical effect or the fact that it serves a function, is arbitrarily determined or fanciful, it deserves protection. The existence of that distinctive character of a trade mark and the evidence that it serves, *inter alia*, a function of indicator of origin or as a means of communication, can only be adduced by applying the criterion of necessity of the shape for the intended technical result while apprehending the mark as a whole in a synthesising manner.

It is interesting to note that the same principle of necessity likewise governs the validity of registered designs for similar reasons. The wording ultimately adopted in the Directive is also identical to that of the Benelux Registered Design Right Act which excludes from protection 'the shape which is necessary (essential) to obtain a technical result'.[21] Application

---

[18] Unofficial translation from French   A. Braun, Note 7 above, at 70; some authors have recommended that the main function of the mark at stake be identified. If the main function of the mark is that of distinguishing the products as opposed to, for instance, a technical function, then the three-dimensional mark is valid. Such a criterion is, however, not workable in practice as it implies the impossible task of assessing whether the public is primarily attracted in buying the product by technical (or aesthetic) reasons; see Ch. Gielen and L. Wichers Hoeth, Note 2 above, at 170.

[19] In accordance with a modern theory of trade mark law, the function of the mark is not exclusively to serve as indicator of origin, but also, to an increasing extent, to represent a means of identification and communication in relation to the product or service for the producer or the retailer. A sign fulfilling such a function facilitates the choice of the product in the market-place and is used for promotion and advertising purposes. The legislative history of the Act specifies, in relation to the shape which produces an industrial result, that the advertising function of a mark cannot be taken into consideration in order to deprive such a mark from protection under the Act.

[20] For an application of such a reasoning see Unreported, Court of Appeal, Brussels, 21 January 1993, *Kortman Intradal v Benckiser*, referring to a kind of packaging for shoe polish, namely a cylindrical box with a particular closing device which had benefited from patent protection.

[21] Article 2 section 1 of the Benelux Registered Design Right Act; see also D.W.F. Verkade, *Bescherming van heet Uiterlijk van Produkten*, Kluwer, 1985, at 170. The legislative history of this Act specifies that:

> The first paragraph of this article does not prevent the protection of useful devices which have an aesthetical value independent from their technical merit. As such this technical value is not protected under the present Act.
>
> Accordingly, it is, for example, possible to obtain protection for the new shape given to a shoe with a reinforced type of heel; the protection granted under the present Act shall extend to the shape of the shoe as a whole but not to the reinforced heel as such. In certain cases the system of strengthening of the heel could also be patentable.
>
> On the other hand, if the shape given to the heel is exclusively dictated by technical imperatives, in other

of the criterion of necessity is constant in Benelux case law on registered designs.[22]

A similar exception, expressed in a most explicit manner, is to be found in the Commission's proposals for a Directive on the legal protection of designs and a Regulation on the Community Design.[23] Article 9 of the draft Regulation makes it clear that:

> A Community Design right shall not subsist in a design to the extent that the realisation of a technical function leaves no freedom as regards arbitrary features of appearance.

And the Explanatory Memorandum to the draft Regulation specifies with regard to Article 9:

> It is unlikely, however, that the whole design will be unprotectable. In most cases, only specific features will, without possibilities of variations, be dictated by function. Therefore, the provision provides for unprotectability to the extent that there is no freedom as regards arbitrary elements of design.

In practice, it is the existence of different shapes allowing the achievement of the same effects or results as those obtained via the shape at stake which determine the 'non-necessary' character of such a shape. Although Benelux case law on this ground for invalidity is rather sparse, the case of *Lego*, the well-known manufacturer of building bricks, versus *Blomson*, a Dutch counterfeiter, merits mention, Lego had filed various trade marks in the Benelux for the three-dimensional representation of its building brick, which in the case in question, was slavishly copied by Blomson.

In summary proceedings initiated by Lego, Blomson raised as a defence the nullity of Lego's trade mark on the basis of Article 1 section 2 of the Act; in particular, Blomson relied on the first ground for invalidity and argued that Lego's shape trade mark No. 401.801 was imposed by the nature of the bricks.[24]

The District Court of Haarlem dismissed Blomson's defence as follows:

> Blomson's defence that no protection can be derived from the registered form trade marks because the form of the goods is determined by its nature ... misses its mark for it cannot be seen that Blomson could not indeed, have opted for some other form and design for its toy building blocks than those which it chose. It is true that it cannot be denied that by their nature, building blocks usually have a three-dimensional rectangular

---

words, if the peculiar shape is only meant to reinforce the heel, the same shall not be protectable under the present Act (*unofficial translation from French*).

[22] See case law in D.W.F. Verkade, Note 21 above, at 40 and onward; in particular see a case regarding a roof covering profile for which several types of profiled shapes were available: Court of Appeal, Leeuwarden, 6 April 1983, BIE 1984, at 323; see another case concerning crates for the transport of bulbs: Pres. Tribunal, Utrecht, 18 September 1979 and Court of Appeal, Amsterdam, 21 March 1980, BIE 1980, at 205. See also Pres. Tribunal, Hertogenbosh, *Unilever & Iglo-Ola v Campina*, 8 November 1993, IER 1994, at 16 (the *Viennetta* case). The same argument as to the technical effect of the shape of a cake was put forward by the defendant in order to claim the nullity of the plaintiffs' design right and trade mark; after having rejected this argument with regard to the plaintiffs' design, the tribunal indicated that the same reasoning must be applied in relation to the trade mark.

[23] COM(93) 344 final—COD 464, 3 December 1993 and COM(93) 342 final—COD 463, 3 December 1993.

[24] In practice this first ground for exclusion is not fundamentally different from the one under discussion, bar the fact that the first exception of Article 1 section 2 of the Act does not cover packaging. Article 711-1 of the French Code for Intellectual Property refers, for instance, to the shape imposed by the nature or the function of the goods, and the explanatory memorandum to the Benelux Act specifies that 'one cannot impose on the industry or the trade, restrictions on the use of a shape which is *indispensable* to the manufacture or the distribution of a product'.

and/or cubic form which makes this form only natural for a toy building system, but this is not to say that no other forms could have been added to this form, which would have put more distance between the design in its entirety and the building blocks of the Lego building system. This is all the more obvious since the list of toy building systems found in the trade and tolerated by Lego, produced in court by the latter, sufficiently establishes that even while preserving the basic brick shape, it is possible to develop a building system which will not infringe Lego's form trade marks.[25]

If protection under trade mark law ought to be granted to all distinctive forms seen as a whole and which are not necessary for achieving a specific technical result, such protection must however, be limited in its scope: generally, the reproduction of one or a few elements only, or even of the basic shape, provided all or most of the other arbitrary features of the shape under scrutiny are different, will not constitute an infringement of the mark.

'Shape which gives substantial value to the goods'

Although the Act makes provision for the shape which 'does not affect the essential value of the goods', the respective wording found in the Act and in the Directive are equivalent.

Pursuant to the legislative history of the Act, the last ground for refusal aims, apparently, at limiting the possibilities of an owner of a three-dimensional sign of invoking the protection of both trade mark law and copyright and/or registered design law. The said legislative history indicates that the shape which can be protected under such legal systems lends an element of attractiveness to the utilitarian value of the product. An example could be the shape given to a set of miniature china houses, the essential value of which derives largely from the beauty of their shape.[26]

Conversely, the shape given to chocolates or cakes is unlikely to have a decisive influence on the intrinsic value of the product since these products are bought primarily for their taste and comestible value[27].

The same reasoning applies in the case of the crisps with an unusual twirled shape.[28]

Case law from the Benelux Court of Justice on the validity of shapes with an attractive appearance is very clear.

The court held that the above exception to the validity of a three-dimensional trade mark must be considered irrespective of whether the shape under scrutiny is protected or is protectable by a registered design right or under copyright and the court made it clear that the wording of the exception was not intended to govern the concurrence of protections resulting from trade mark law and from other intellectual property rights.[29]

In the *Adidas* case of 23 December 1985,[30] the court addressed the question of whether the shape affects the essential value of a product by stating that:

---

[25] Unreported, District Court, Haarlem, *Lego v Blomson*, 14 December 1993 (*unofficial translation*). *Contra*, see in an interlocutory proceeding, Court of Appeal of Liège, *Lego v Unica*, 30 June 1993, Ing.-Cons., 1993, at 217; in this case the court held that 'the Act does not require for the exception to be applied that the technical result cannot be achieved by using another form; even if alternative solutions exist, a technical system which is not [?] or not any more protected under a patent must be made available to the public (see decision of the Swedish Supreme Court of 17 December 1987)'. The report of this case is followed by a critical note from B. Michaux.

[26] See Pres. Tribunal, Rotterdam, 29 April 1982, BIE, 1984, at 193.

[27] See Pres. Tribunal, Brussels, 7 April 1983, Ing.-Cons., 1983, at 143. See also the *Viennetta* case, Note 22 above.

[28] See, for example, Dutch Supreme Court, *Smiths Food v Red Mill*, 21 April 1989, IER, 1989, at 58.

[29] Benelux Court of Justice, *Burberrys I*, 14 April 1989, Rec. 1989, at 23 to 24. See also the submissions of the Advocate General who stated that although the exceptions of Article 1 section 2 of the Act are meant to limit to a certain extent the concurrence of protections under intellectual property law, such a concurrence is not to be excluded; *ibid.*, at 30 to 31.

[30] See Note 2 above.

it depends on the nature of the products in question; if the product is of such nature that its aspect and its shape determine strongly its trade value, the answer must be affirmative; in the opposite case, the answer must be negative (*unofficial translation*).

In the *Burberrys I* case of 14 April 1989,[31] the court was more explicit:

> The fact that the distinctive shape of a product affects its essential value should only preclude protection as a trade if the product is of such a nature that its aspect and its form, because of their beauty or their originality, determine largely the commercial value of the product, with however, the reservation that the influence on the commercial value which would not result from the aesthetic attraction of its shape but from the advertising effect attached to its goodwill as a distinctive sign, must be excluded (*unofficial translation*).

The first question to be asked is whether the shape of the product possesses such an attractiveness that it constitutes the determining factor in the consumer's decision to buy. The second question is whether or not that determining influence of the shape on the public's behaviour is the result of the shape's beauty or originality rather than the consequence of an acquired goodwill or notoriety.

Accordingly, the Coca-Cola bottle, for example, would not fall within the above exception since (should it be decided that it is not (anymore?) for its taste that the famous soft drink is drunk), the influence of the bottle's shape on the public's decision to buy a bottle of Coke results predominantly from the large goodwill existing in the worldwide famous bottle's shape.

Some have argued, with regard to crisps with an unusual shape, that because nearly all crisps on the market-place have a similar kind of taste, it is precisely the shape given to the product which determines its commercial success. The Dutch Supreme Court rightly considered that the added commercial value of a product resulting from the goodwill attached to its shape was not the consequence of a shape affecting the essential value of the product.[32]

In most instances, only the shapes of the goods themselves, rather than the shape of the goods' container or packaging, can affect their value. In the *Lego v Blomson* case,[33] the District Court of Haarlem held also that the shape given to a building brick cannot favourably influence the commercial value of the product and hence its price.[34] On the other hand, it has been held that a children's bath in the form of scallop's shell could not constitute a valid trade mark.[35]

Conclusion

The cornerstone of the three exceptions to the validity of three-dimensional trade marks lies in the risk of witnessing an abusive monopolisation of some shapes.[36]

Some argue that the protection of certain three-dimensional signs under trade mark law would grant their owner an illegitimate monopoly of that shape—trade mark protection can be renewed and extended without limitation in time—which is detrimental to both the

---

[31] See Note 29 above.
[32] Dutch Supreme Court, 11 November 1983, NJ, 1984, at 203.
[33] See Note 25 above.
[34] See also Court of Appeal, Liège, *Lego v Unica, ibid.*
[35] Court of Appeal, Bois-le-Duc, 12 January 1993, Ing.-Cons., 1993, at 238.
[36] See the Proposal for a Community Trade Mark and Note 7 above.

competitors and the public. Such a detrimental effect would in particular occur whenever the shape used as a distinctive sign is or was protected or protectable under patent law, registered design law or copyright law.

A trade mark does not require novelty, inventiveness or originality—but a lower requirement, distinctiveness. Protection granted under trade mark law is accordingly limited to protection from competitors who would attempt to misappropriate, for their own benefits, the goodwill attached to such a mark. It is only the amount of goodwill, which might vary through the years, which will determine the scope of protection enjoyed by the sign.

The European Court of Justice (ECJ), albeit in different circumstances, defined what might constitute an abusive monopolisation of trade mark; in doing so, the Court had to refer to the specific object of a trade mark and its essential function.

> For the trade mark to be able to fulfil its role, it must offer a guarantee that all goods bearing it have been produced under the control of a single undertaking which is accountable for their quality.[37]

According to the ECJ, the specific object of a trade mark is, *inter alia*, to guarantee to its owner the right to use the mark for the first marketing of his products and consequently to protect his products from competitors who would attempt to benefit from the goodwill in the mark by selling their products under the same mark.

In the trade, there are many designs which are not registered trade marks because they are not used to distinguish the products as originating from a given source. The same applies to patents and copyrighted works. These works can, however, be used as trade marks and become distinctive of a product, irrespective of the fact that they are/were protected under another intellectual property right or that they could have been. The Rolls Royce radiator grille or the Phillipshave razor's head[38] come to mind.

Any use of a three-dimensional sign, whether it is or can be protected under patent, design right or copyright law in accordance with the function defined above, grants its owner a relatively legitimate monopolisation of a shape which is highly distinctive of its products. The general interest of the public and of a free trade might, however, direct that some of these signs are not exclusively appropriable.

---

[37] Case C—10/89, *CNL-Sucal v Hag*, 1990, ECR I—3711 (*Hag II*).
[38] See the Canadian Federal Court's decision of 8 October 199, *Remington Rand Corp. v Phillips Electronics NY*, [1994] 3 EIPR D48.

Patents and Related Rights

An 'Investment Patent'

[1981] 7 EIPR 207

WILLIAM KINGSTON
Lecturer in Innovation, Trinity College, Dublin

The first point to be made about the following proposals for adding to the patent system's capacity to stimulate investment is that they do not affect existing patent arrangements at all. The latter are specifically directed towards A-phase, or originative, innovation, whereas what is now needed is a means of granting monopolies that will make a rational activity out of investment in B-phase, or incremental innovation.

This means protection for 'combinations' that are 'obvious to one skilled in the art', and therefore unpatentable under present arrangements. Amongst these would be most of the improvements to products and processes which are individually small, but cumulatively of supreme economic importance. The managements of large numbers of firms see perfectly clearly what the next stage of incremental development of the products in their field must be. But they are paralysed by the fear that if they do design and tool up for the improved product, they will find themselves submerged by the capability market power of a competitor long before any kind of return on the investment has been earned. If this fear is removed by extending the patent system appropriately, such firms are immediately enabled, not merely to match, but to leapfrog the very best of the present international competition. The consequent freeing of resources of men and money that are currently frustrated could have dramatic consequences for both investment and employment.

The primary characteristic of the extension to the patent system which is proposed is that the monopoly granted should be explicitly linked to the making of an investment, thus pulling the system back towards its original objective of underwriting 'new manufacture'. For this reason, it can be called an 'investment patent' (IP).

Secondly, money is introduced as a measure of the monopoly that is granted. It is an indication of how poorly all patent systems have kept up with changing circumstances that their measure is still only time—substantially the two terms of apprenticeship of the early grants which were thought necessary for new technology to take root. But the true measure of any monopoly cannot be anything except money. In the early days of patents, there was obviously no practical alternative to time as a measure, but never to change from it has meant ignoring all the achievements of accountancy in the interim.

Money as Measure

In the IP, therefore, while time would still define the lower limit of the monopoly granted, money, as expressed by profits earned, would measure the upper limit. The new type of patent would be granted subject to the investment specified in the application being made by a prescribed date. Once made, this investment would be protected on a win or lose basis for an initial period, the length of which would reflect a balance between giving time for innovations to be carried through, and ensuring that no firm can use the system to prevent others from trying where it has manifestly failed. If a firm *is* successful, however, the patent would continue in force until aggregate profits earned from the innovation reached a prescribed multiple of the investment.

Not only do the techniques for measuring monopoly by money in this way already exist, they are readily accessible. Because Government support of R&D in the US has characteristically been through development contracts to private firms, several Government departments there have had to develop exceptional expertise in monitoring complex investments in innovation. It would not be difficult for this expertise to be transferred to any Patent Office as pump-priming for its own development of techniques.

Other Characteristics

Next, the criterion of what is patentable under the extended system would cut through all abstract questions of novelty or obviousness, and be strictly commercial, as befits a device which has no other object than generating investment and employment in viable manufacturing industry. This criterion would depend upon the answer to one simple question. Can a product with this particular new feature or combination of features actually be bought in the ordinary course of trade for the type of goods in question, at the present time? If it can, then the product is not patentable under either the existing or the extended system, but if it cannot, then investment to put such a product on the market would be a candidate for the new type of patent protection. For example, the hybrid petrol/electric motor for cars is widely regarded as very promising. It is not patentable now because it is no more than a combination of known elements which would be held to be obvious 'to one skilled in the art'. But because no one can go out and buy a car with such an engine, investment to change this situation would be able to be protected by an IP, and the existence of this protection, which is a new type of specific market power, would be a powerful countervailing force against the capability market power of the giant US and Japanese firms, in the race to put such a car on the world market.

Fourthly, an IP, once granted, would be irrevocable. Who would prospect for minerals if the geographical limits of his claim could be called into question at any time? Yet this is the position of every present patentee, which goes far to explain why other forms of market power have so largely replaced patents as the means whereby the risks of innovation are justified.

Fifthly, the burden of policing the monopoly would be removed from the patentee. There seems to be no good reason why it should be a crime to rob a firm of its cash in hand, but not of the value and fruits of its investment in new technology. Or why it should only be intellectual property that is excluded from the care of the Fraud Squad. A minor corollary would be removal of the protection of limited liability from patent infringers.

Beneficial Monopoly

Clearly the IP as proposed would be vastly stronger than a patent of the present type, and this is necessary if it is to provide an adequate basis for investment at relatively high risk. But the use of money as its measure draws the sting from monopoly and ensures that this serves the public interest. There have been many calls over the years for the strengthening of patents, but the decisive objection against these has always been the quite excessive profits which might then be earned from the (admittedly few) successful innovations. This objection loses its force once money, rather than time, is made the measure of the monopoly. The more valuable the development that is protected by an IP, the quicker its profits will reach the ceiling prescribed by the 'multiple', and the sooner it will therefore come into the public domain and be open to all comers. Profits from the monopoly cannot exceed the statutory multiple of the investment which has had to be made to earn them. The size of this multiple would be decided by the authorities according to publicly debated investment and employment objectives, and the system would be administered with the same impartiality by Patent Offices as patents of the traditional type have been.

International Arrangements

Although there are now several international agreements relating to patents, the only one that is relevant to the IP is the International Convention for the Protection of Industrial Property. This does not bind a country to have any particular kind of patent system, or indeed to have one at all, only to treat foreigners, if they are citizens of member states, on exactly the same basis as nationals, under whatever system there is. Not only would extending the patent system to include IP's be permitted by the Convention, therefore, it would actually shift the balance of its effect in the direction of generating investment and employment locally instead of abroad. Patents for invention, as currently defined, are of greatest value to those firms which are in the vanguard of technical progress, and reciprocal international agreements therefore benefit those countries which possess most such firms at the expense of those in the second or lower ranks of technology. Patents granted in the less advanced countries are monopolies within their boundaries which actually intensify import penetration. In contrast, making IP's available to foreign firms on the same basis as local ones would have the opposite tendency, since to gain most advantage from an IP these firms would have to make an investment, not only in the B-phase development work, but also in local production facilities.

Industrial Policy

To the extent that the cause of unemployment is foreign competition, it is inevitable that the case for import controls will be argued strongly as a means of alleviating the problem. Comparison of the effect of IP's with such controls is instructive, and shows that the advantages are all with the new type of patent. By protecting industry that has become uncompetitive with foreign rivals, import controls ossify it, and ensure that it will never again be a force in export markets. Since B-phase innovation will continue to forge ahead abroad while the pressure for it has been relaxed at home, not only must the protection become permanent, it must be made progressively stronger as the quality gap between home produced and foreign products widens. In contrast the IP, by definition, protects industry only to the extent that its products are judged to be better than the foreign competition by the market; this protection is strictly temporary (and the stronger and more valuable it is, the shorter time it will last); and it is explicitly linked to investment of the type that can lead to penetration of export markets with these improved products on the basis of capability market power.

Regional Possibilities

For both science and regional policy, the 'multiple' of the IP could be an instrument of the greatest flexibility. The United States Patent Office already discriminates in practice in favour of certain types of invention (for example those relating to energy or genetic engineering) by advancing them ahead of their turn for examination. As a means of encouraging particular developments, however, this device is trivial in comparison with that of offering a higher multiple than average for appropriate IP's. Regional industrial policy based upon different multiples could be highly sophisticated and capable of rapid adaptation to changing circumstances. The need to find alternative employment quickly for a town where a steel mill has to close, for example, could result, under the IP system, in an exceptionally high multiple for investment there for a limited period. None of these policies would require a penny in subsidy from either national or local Government; they would be virtually costless to administer; and the distortions and misdirection of energy that are inseparable from present regional incentive schemes would be eliminated. The industrial developments thus encouraged would be as organic and as soundly based as possible, because they would be undertaken and carried on throughout under the discipline of the market. Large differential advantages would indeed be offered to firms to invest in certain types of industry or in certain places, but actually realising these advantages would depend upon the new products being bought in preference to those offered by competitors, so that profits are earned. If IP's resulted in comparable flexibility on the part of the trade unions, not only would their power to redress regional imbalance be enhanced, but they would be contributing to the solution of the longer term structural problems of the economy.

'The Multiple'

The question of what the 'multiple' should be is a pragmatic one, and it might with advantage be capable of being changed in the light of circumstances by ministerial order rather than by statute. There are four reasons why error should be on the side of generosity:

— the urgency of the need for investment in B-phase innovation;
— the strength of well-founded conviction amongst businessmen and financiers that 'pioneering doesn't pay', which it will take very attractive terms indeed to overcome;
— the extent to which it is only when firms with IP's are actually seen to be making money out of them that others will be drawn in large numbers to invest in incremental innovation; and, above all,
— the fact that innovatory managements will not stop with one success, so that a large part of any IP profits is certain to be re-invested in developing further new products.

The attractions of the IP to the managements of manufacturing firms and those who finance them are obvious. A firm which faces annihilation in both home and export markets from the quality and price of competitors' products can now develop an investment plan, not only for improving on existing products, but also for manufacturing by the very latest techniques. Because the improved product is not yet available on the market, the project would be eligible for an IP, and once this is granted, the investment can be made in the secure knowledge that if technical success is achieved, then commensurate profits will follow. Every resource can then be devoted to achieving this technical success, without the fear of sowing for others to reap, or having to provide for the expense and distraction of litigation.

Although the IP would only cover the home market, the capability resulting from the new investment would also give an advantage in lead-time in export markets, and the concentration on technical success, also made possible by the IP, could only reinforce this advantage. Exports might be further encouraged by only counting home market profits against the IP 'multiple'.

Cultural Factors

The industrial structures of the West depend upon a complex of positive law which dates from the middle of the last century. To the extent that they are now unable to cope with pressures emanating from the Middle and Far East, new types of market power must be called into being to redress the balance of the old. The obvious source for these is within the patent system, since it must be clearly understood that absence of a particular kind of market power will not prevent innovation happening: it merely ensures that the innovation takes place elsewhere, modified by, and under the protection of, whatever market power there is. The fact that there are as yet no patents to cover incremental innovation in manufacturing, therefore, simply means that such innovation will be what can be underwritten by capability or persuasive market power. The stark reality which must be faced by every one of the second—and third—rank countries is that they are now at an overwhelming disadvantage in both—to the Americans especially in persuasive or marketing power, and to the Japanese in capability. It is impossible to overstress, for example, how effective for B-phase innovation Japan's Zaibatsu-Keiretsu institutions are. No matter how inventive Western countries have shown themselves to be, none of them, even the US, now matches Japan in the ability to produce 'the second invention that every invention needs—how to mass produce it at an affordable cost'.

   This ability cannot be equalled, let alone surpassed, by Western attempts to copy Japanese methods, because our cultural tradition does not include the required degree of social cohesion. Our tradition is individualistic (which is why it has led to so much innovation in the past) and the patent is the classic social invention for fostering individual creative effort in the economic sphere. This is why modernising the patent system is so promising. It could produce a flood of energy innovations that would cut OPEC down to size. It also offers a means of meeting the competition from Japan and the Confucian world, which, fierce as we feel it to be, is yet only at an early stage in its momentum. As a powerful and flexible instrument of specific market power, expressly directed towards increasing employment, the investment patent has strong claims to be considered urgently. The cost of trying it out is trivial, and it could have surprisingly quick and valuable results for the survival, and revival, of 'manufacture within these realms'.

Recession and Intellectual Property—'Innovation Warrants'

[1981] 12 EIPR 367

Letter from William Kingston
Lecturer in Innovation, Trinity College, Dublin

May I refer to my Opinion and article on the need and means for providing specific protection for incremental innovation ([1981] 5 and 7 EIPR). These were written in terms of extending the scope of existing Patent Offices. This may not be appropriate everywhere, and there is a case for calling the new type of protection by a name which does not include the word 'patent', so that thinking about having it administered in radically different ways is not impeded.

The objective is to ensure that those who innovate can obtain a protection which is appropriate to the far above average risk which attaches to their investment. 'Innovation safeguard' is an accurate description, if not an inspiring one. A far better candidate is 'innovation warrant', because the original meaning of 'warrant', coming from the old High German root 'Gewähren', was *guarantee*. Reversion to this meaning in the present case would therefore cause no difficulty in the languages of any of the countries likely to develop the proposed new system.

Of the dozen senses of 'warrant' in the Oxford English Dictionary, the first is 'protector' and the second 'safeguard'. Another reference in the Dictionary which is interesting in the present context is to land grants in Colonial America, some of which were patented, but others *warranted*.

The main advantage of using the term 'innovation warrant' is that vested interests and inertia will have less power to stifle the emergence of the new kind of protection. If a Patent Office, or the Government department which is responsible for it, does not wish to extend the Office's scope, progress need not be blocked because the word 'patent' is in the title. Innovation warrants could issue from another source—which could be in a completely different department. On the other hand, a dynamic institution in any country might turn itself into a Patent, Trade Mark *and Warrant* Office.

Is the United States Right about 'First-to-Invent'?

[1992] 7 EIPR 223

WILLIAM KINGSTON

Associate Professor (Innovation) Trinity College, Dublin

The United States is currently under considerable pressure from the rest of the world to abandon its traditional 'first-to-invent' system in favour of the 'first-to-file' arrangements of every other country which subscribes to the Paris Convention except the Philippines. Apparently missing from the discussions so far is awareness of the fact that 'first-to-invent' has a valuable inherent advantage over 'first-to-file' as a means of underwriting innovation. This indeed is so strong as even to suggest that countries other than the United States should consider adopting 'first-to-invent' *in their own economic interest.*

Simultaneous Invention

When patentable inventions are the result of large-scale, purposive research programmes, often initiated as the result of independently forecast market demand, it is hardly surprising that two (or even more) firms will sometimes reach a particular goal at much the same time. This phenomenon of simultaneous invention is not taken into account by the system of granting patents to the applicant who first files his application in any Member State of the Paris Convention.

The contrasting procedure in the United States is that when it is found that two (or more) applications which seem to be claiming the same inventive entity have been filed, an 'Interference' is declared.[1] All parties must then provide evidence as to their respective dates of 'conception of the invention' and their efforts to reduce it to practice. The evidence submitted may include laboratory notebooks, internal test reports, even the classic envelope with an idea scribbled on the back. Filing of a patent application is considered to be 'constructive reduction to practice'. The case law prescribes very stringent tests of performance for 'diligence' in reducing a conception to practice, and these apply not just to the inventing firm, but also to its professional advisers. In a by no means exceptional case, for example, an unexplained delay of three weeks in an attorney's office between receiving instructions and actually filing a patent application was held to be fatal lack of diligence.[2] There are about 200 such interferences each year, and the probability of an applicant for a patent becoming involved in this procedure is about three per thousand.[3] All interferences are dealt with by the Board of Patent Appeals and Interferences, which is composed of the

---

[1] United States Code, Title 35, section 135.
[2] Interference No. 101235, relating to holders for drill bits. Kennametal Inc. filed on 27 March 1981, Mining Tools Inc. on 4 April 1981.
[3] Report of the Commissioner of Patents and Trademarks, 1991.

most experienced examiners in the Patent Office, but there is of course the possibility of appeal to the courts. However, only about four per cent of the Board's final decisions are even partially reversed on appeal.[4]

Discrimination by the United States

There are two reasons why the United States has come under pressure from other countries in recent years to change to a 'first-to-file' system. Firstly, as it is operated at present, 'first-to-invent' discriminates against applicants from abroad; secondly, even if the foreign party wins, its application will have been involved in considerable delay (the average time for interference proceedings is a year) and expense (in a typical 1990 case, attorney's fees ran at $7,000 a month); and third, the holder of an earlier patent can impose this delay and cost upon a competitor by filing an application for re-issue of his patent, even if he does not expect this to succeed.

Discrimination exists because in interference proceedings unless it is being claimed that one or more of the parties 'derived' the invention from another, the United States Patent and Trademark Office only recognises evidence that relates either to invention and reduction to practice within the United States or to 'introduction' of an invention from abroad into the United States and its reduction to practice there. To illustrate, consider an interference between, say, a German firm and a US firm, in which the former was actually the first to make the invention, and there is no question that either firm 'derived' the invention from the other. The US firm would nevertheless be granted the patent if the only evidence that the German firm could adduce for its earlier invention date and reduction to practice related to what happened *in Germany*.

Another, though less important way in which discrimination occurs is that interferences are not declared when there is a gap between effective filing dates of more than three months for minor inventions and of six months for inventions thought to be important, 'except in exceptional situations'. Such a situation is considered to exist if the earlier effective filing date is the result of claiming Convention priority.

Mitigatory Provisions

This discrimination can be mitigated in two ways, both of which 'introduce' an invention from abroad into the United States before a patent application is filed for it there or in any other Paris Convention country. Evidence of invention and steps to reduce it to practice can be communicated in confidence by a foreign firm to its subsidiary or to some other party in the United States, such as its patent attorney. Alternatively, the US Patent Office's own 'Disclosure Document' service can be used. For a small fee, the Office will hold information submitted to it in sealed envelopes for two years. If no patent application related to the information contained in these envelopes is filed within the period, the envelopes are destroyed; if such an application is filed, then their contents become part of the file, and are available as evidence of 'date of introduction of the invention into the United States' if needed for interference purposes. For foreigners, 'introduction' of all their new information into the United States in either of these ways would be troublesome, especially since only a small part of it is ever likely to emerge into a patent application. In spite of the mitigatory

---

[4] I.A Calvert and M. Sofocleous, 'Interference Statistics for Fiscal Years 1986 to 1988' (1989) *Journal of the Patent and Trademark Office Society*, 71, at 399–410.

provisions, therefore, 'first-to-invent' as at present administered by the United States, remains discriminatory against non-US applicants, as is illustrated in Figure 1.

Interference Decisions

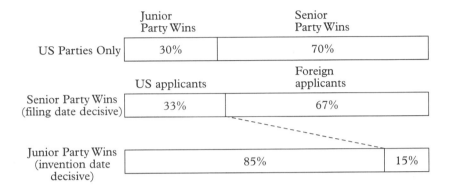

Figure 1

US and Foreign Parties

The senior party is the one with the earliest effective patent application filing date, and the onus is therefore on the junior party to prove that it had made the invention earlier than this. In about eight per cent of cases the Board of Appeals and Interferences gives a 'split' decision, awarding patents to both parties or to neither party. Calvert and Sofocleous have shown that, leaving these exceptional decisions aside, in cases which only involve US firms, the junior party succeeds in proving earlier invention only 30 per cent of the time. In 70 per cent of cases, therefore, the outcome is just the same as it would be under a 'first-to-file' patent system. Where interferences are between US and foreign applicants, however, foreigners win two-thirds of the cases where the decision is in favour of the senior party—that is, where filing date is the determining factor. But where this factor is not filing date, but evidence of earlier invention, US firms win no less than 85 per cent of the interferences.[5] This difference can only reflect the inability of foreign firms to adduce evidence of inventive activity in their own country.

From the standpoint of national treatment, therefore, which is the fundamental principle of the Paris Convention, other countries do indeed have a strong case for urging the United States to move from 'first-to-invent' to 'first-to-file'. The strength of this case has been recognised by the United States, which offered in the harmonisation discussions of June 1991 to change its system so as to accept evidence of invention abroad. This offer was rejected by other countries, presumably because it leaves the cost aspect of interference procedures unchanged. It should be noted that this aspect is not discriminatory, since attorneys' costs are presumably much the same for both foreign and US firms. American industry was also unhappy at one prospect of losing its advantage over foreign firms. These negotiations are now stalled, awaiting the outcome of the Uruguay Round of the GATT.

---

[5] *Ibid.*

Empirical Research Results

There is another side to this whole question, however, which has emerged, quite unexpectedly, as a by-product of the author's empirical research into simultaneous invention. The US interference files are a uniquely valuable mine of information for the study of this phenomenon.

It is perhaps inevitable that those who are professionally involved in the patent system will tend to see its function simply as the granting of patents. This, however, is only a means to an end, which is successful technological innovation. Any particular patent system must ultimately be judged by its contribution to this, rather than on how well it processes documents and how smoothly it runs in administrative terms.

As a means of encouraging innovation, the great value of 'first-to-invent', reflected in the empirical evidence, is the pressure it puts on the parties involved in simultaneous invention to come to an early agreement. When two (or more) firms have arrived at a particular technical goal at around the same time and find themselves involved in interference, they naturally consider why they should incur the expense and delay of the proceedings, with the risk of a third party actually getting the new technology to the market first. The equally natural conclusion is that it is in their interest instead to agree that each will be able to use whatever patent or patents may issue, in its own way.

One of the most striking aspects of interference procedures is the high proportion of cases which are settled voluntarily. Fully three-fifths of all interferences are now terminated in this way, and an important reason is that the parties have come to agreement.[6] Out of 90 voluntarily settled cases which the author has examined so far, no less than 24 ended in agreement between the parties. For such an agreement to be legally enforceable, a copy must be filed in the Patent Office, but any party to it may ask for it to be kept separately from the main interference file and the public denied access to it. As might be expected, most applicants use this facility, so that it is not possible to be absolutely certain of the conditions which generally apply in such agreements. However, some cases where agreements have been found in the files suggest that, as one might expect, the parties do cross-licence their inventions. The result is that any new technology arising from these inventions will reflect competitive development effort by at least two firms.

Innovation Benefits from Multiple Sources

The importance of this is that there is now considerable empirical evidence that economic innovation is encouraged by competition even at the earliest stages, as is illustrated by the following summary of a recent authoritative survey:

> Our general conclusion is that multiple and competitive sources of invention are socially preferable to a structure where there is only one or a few sources. Public policy, including patent law, ought to encourage inventive rivalry, and not hinder it. As the 'race to invent' models show, a rivalrous structure surely has its inefficiencies. But such a structure does tend to generate rapid technical progress and seems a much better social bet than a regime where only one or a few organizations control the development of any given technology.[7]

---

[6] *Ibid.*
[7] Richard R. Nelson and Robert P. Morges 'On the Complex Economics of Patent Scope' (1990) *Columbia Law Review* 90, at 908. See also R.M. Isaac and S.S. Reynolds 'Schumpeterian Competition in Experimental Markets' (1992) *Journal of Economic Behavior and Organization* 17:1, at 59–100.

Compared with 'first-to-invent', a 'first-to-file' patent system is less likely to result in multiple sources of development of an invention. This is because under it whichever firm first reaches a Patent Office in a Paris Convention country with its application has the opportunity to pre-empt all its competitors, everywhere. All other things being equal, it must get the patent monopolies in whichever countries it chooses, and it is under no pressure at all from the international patent system to share them with rivals. This slows down innovation.

Obviously, 'first-to-invent' has costs that 'first-to-file' does not, but if the multiple sources it encourages are better for innovation, this cost is certainly justified. To avoid it for the sake of administrative convenience seems to be to sacrifice correspondingly the reason for existence of the patent system. Also, since the chances of becoming involved in the procedures associated with 'first-to-invent' are low and actuarially calculable, applicants for patents should be able to buy relatively inexpensive insurance against the extra costs.

The Need for Objective Analysis

At the very least, therefore, there is a case for the countries which have been pressing the United States to change its system, to widen the perspective from which they have been considering the balance of advantage between 'first-to-file' and 'first-to-invent'. Within such a wider perspective, the emphasis should then be on *what a patent system is supposed to do*. It is also important to disentangle the issue of which system is intrinsically better, from that of the discrimination currently practised by the United States in its administration of 'first-to-invent'. Acceptance of its offer to take evidence of invention and reduction to practice abroad into account in future would appear to deal satisfactorily with the latter point. Canada operated a 'first-to-invent' system until 1990, and the author has carried out parallel research on simultaneous invention in the 'conflict' records of that country's Patent Office. This did not reveal any difficulty, either to applicants or to examiners, as a result of accepting evidence of actual invention date from outside Canada.

With the discrimination aspect disposed of, then if 'first-to-invent' is indeed an intrinsically better component of a system for encouraging innovation, continuing pressure on the United States to abandon 'first-to-invent' seems to be trying to move the international patent system in the wrong direction. It is equally likely that as an economic policy, persistence with 'first-to-file', in spite of the greater costs of the alternative, is short-sighted and self-defeating in a world where competitive advantage increasingly depends upon the capacity to innovate.

The Patent System—What Future Role in the Creation of Wealth?

[1983] 4 EIPR 83

HUGH BRETT
Editor

This year marks the centenary of the first international patent convention—the Paris Convention. It was signed in 1883, and established the principle of the mutual recognition of national patent rights. Most countries of the world have now ratified the Convention; but the principle of the patent monopoly and public policy considerations behind the patent system are being increasingly questioned.[1] In this centenary year it is perhaps not inopportune to consider whether the original justification for the granting of patents remains as valid today as when the system was first established on a modern footing.

It is tempting to take a complacent attitude towards the future of the patent system. Many thousands of applications are filed each year and the system provides a good living for professionals throughout the world. Substantial institutions like the European Patent Office and the World Intellectual Property Organization with their large infrastructures indicate an assured future for the system. But on the other hand it is salutary to recall that when the modern patent system was established some hundred years ago it was not received with universal acclaim. In 1869 a United Kingdom Member of Parliament, Mr McFie, wrote 'Under this system authority and opportunity are given for tyrannical and cruel acts, exorbitant demands, unfair practices and severe wrongs, detrimental to British manufacturers . . . as well as consumers'. At the same time Pierre Vermier writing in Belgium said that 'the abolition of the patents system would be an immense benefit to the country and not less to that unfortunate class of men called inventors'; Michel Chevalier echoed the same sentiments in France when he said that 'the patent system was an infringement of free industry, independence and liberty, which is the most precious, necessary and salutary result of the Revolution of 1789'.

The warnings and appeals of McFie, Chevalier and Vermier were overruled by those who foresaw public benefits in the patent system. The majority argued that an individual had a natural right to own the products of his mind, and that patents were justified because it was in the public interest that inventors should be encouraged to develop and disclose their inventions. The basic rationale still remains the primary objective of the patent system today. But to what extent does the patent system support the public interest today and take account of the economic changes that have taken place during the last 100 years?

In the late nineteenth and early twentieth centuries the structure of industry was very different from today. Industries were small and were managed mostly by entrepreneurial

---

[1] For example the Nairobi and Geneva Conferences on the Paris Convention, [1983] 2 EIPR D—40; also contributions made at European Commission Conference on 'Patent Protection and Innovation'. Proceedings are obtainable from DG Information, Market and Innovation, European Commission, Luxembourg.

owners; it was an era of expansion, foreign competition was non-existent, and it was possible to conceive of the patent system as a means whereby individuals could found new industries. But since the turn of the century the influence of the private company has gradually been overtaken by the dominance of large corporations.[2] Today the great majority of patents are owned by such corporations, their inventions originating either from employee inventors or from inventors whose funding is conditional on the ownership of all patent rights belonging to the corporation. But those who manage large corporations do not have any significant stake in their ownership, and the individual qualities required to manage differ from the entrepreneurial outlook associated with innovators. The financial strength of the corporations gives them power to use the patent system to claim ownership in many inventions, some of which may never be exploited; patents are filed sometimes to confuse competitors, and even to defeat innovation!

Unquestionably, the growth of the corporation has encouraged the increase of patent applications; the filing of some 600 patents a year does not impinge significantly on the corporate budget. But this development has changed what was originally regarded as an individual right to a corporate weapon. This is not to say that the patent system does not play a role in encouraging corporations to invest and to undertake research; but the original vision of the patent as being an entrepreneurial and individual right can no longer be so forcefully maintained.

The shift towards the corporate influence also makes the patent system more vulnerable, since those whose seek to control corporate power will see the patent system as a part of the corporate system which needs to be curtailed. Anti-trust laws are sometimes criticised as being anti-patent; but in fact their sanctions are directed more to the economic dominance of the corporation itself. Also of serious concern is the fact that some corporations may become disaffected with the unreliability of the patent system and may decide to establish their influence on the market through other forces.

Even if the original justification of the system is accepted as still being relevant in theory, to what extent is the patent system significant in practical terms? The costs of patent litigation are such that very few small companies can undertake the enforcement of their patents, or indeed fight the threat of an infringement action. If the patent system is to play a more meaningful role, then the legal system and its costs must be reformed.[3] Why should, for example, small companies *per se* often be outside legal aid provisions? And is it desirable that interim injunctions should be more readily available to large corporations merely because they are able to give a more secure 'cross undertaking' in damages?

The cost of patenting is high, and it must be of concern that a study on innovation and smaller companies concluded that 'Mechanical inventions were difficult to protect ... and in all the cost and time were deterrents'.[4] There are of course instances where the patent system has provided the individual inventor with substantial rewards, but there is a growing impression that the system is not relevant to the small inventor.

Another important factor is that public policy considerations have changed in the course of the century. The political cry is not for new inventions, but for more investment to produce more employment. If unemployment is to be reduced then new industries need to be established; but the patent system cannot meet today's demands fully because the concept of novelty is a strict condition for the grant of a patent. The standard of novelty and the problem of 'mosaicing' can create unsuspected hurdles for the patent attorney and inventor. Thus the patent application for the CT Scanner—invented by Dr Hounsfield, who was

---

[2] See Adolf Berle and Gardiner Means, *The Modern Corporation and Private Property*.
[3] See Peter Prescott's Opinion at [1982] 11 EIPR 297.
[4] See CBI Report 'Innovation and Competitiveness in Smaller Companies'.

awarded the Nobel Prize for his achievement—was met with resistance and delay from the national Patent Offices sometimes exceeding ten years. The requirement of 'novelty' may be contrasted with the public policy consideration behind the mediaeval concept of patents, with its emphasis on investment. Patents then were royal privileges granted to those who introduced an industry into the realm. The grant of the monopolies was conditional on the new industry being established in the country, and was often conditional on terms being imposed to ensure that local inhabitants were educated on the techniques of the new industry.[5]

The danger for the future of the present patent system is that it will not be able to meet criticism, if its proponents argue that it is the only system relevant to innovation. It has an undoubted role to fulfil; but it must be recognised that fundamental reforms would be very difficult to achieve because of the international infrastructure of the patent system. Reform and improvement can best be achieved if the patent system is seen as one of many tools of innovation, and as part of a cumulative system of encouragement and protection for invention. If such an approach were adopted, it would be possible to consider specific proposals to encourage economic investment and assist in making invention profitable.

A cumulative approach would enable patent practitioners to expand their expertise to meet requirements and demands of new fields of technology. To an outside observer it must appear curious that the two most prolific areas of technological expansion—biotechnology and computer software—are both on the borderlines of patentable activities. There is no reason why these important industries should not have their own system, as with that provided for the plant breeders.

No system can survive which does not revitalise itself by self-questioning—and those who argue that the patent system is efficient because it is used and because no alternative exists put the future of the system at risk. At no time has industry or technology so urgently required an effective legal system for encouraging investment and innovation. Criticisms are being made;[6] the opportunities for the patent and legal professions to consider fruitful reforms are exciting and imperative if indeed economic prosperity and the patent system are not to remain illusory.

---

[5] Thus Stephen Croyett was granted a patent in 1561 to make a new soap. Some of the conditions of the grant of the patent were that the soap had to be manufactured within two years, at least two employees had to be educated, and the soap had to be as good as that in Seville.
[6] For example William Kingston's proposals on an 'Investment Patent'—see [1981] 7 EIPR 207; and Leslie Melville's arguments for a law of activities—see [1982] 3 EIPR 61.

The Patentability of Computer-related Inventions in the United Kingdom and the European Patent Office*
[1991] EIPR 85

BRAD SHERMAN
London School of Economics and Political Science

Introduction

One of the most noticeable features of the 1977 Patents Act and the 1973 European Patent Convention (EPC), upon which it is based, is that the patentability of information does not depend upon any express definition of the invention.[1] Despite the absence of any formal requirement to show the existence of an invention, a number of recent decisions in the UK and by the Technical Boards of Appeal at the European Patent Office (EPO) have focused on the way in which the invention should be conceptualised. It is the intention of this article to examine the way the concept of the invention has been approached in these decisions. In particular it will highlight the growing importance of the idea of the invention in patent law and, in turn, show how this concept has been instrumental in the increasingly liberal attitude towards the patentability of inventions.[2]

Part 1

While the 1977 Patents Act and the EPC contain no express definition of the invention, patentable inventions are defined in a negative sense in section 1(2) of the 1977 Patents Act and Article 52 of the EPC (hereinafter section 1(2) and Article 52).

Section 1(2), which is the same as Article 52, reads:

> It is hereby declared that the following (among other things) are not inventions for the purposes of this Act, that is to say, anything which consists of:
>> (a) a discovery, scientific theory or mathematical method;
>> (b) a literary, dramatic, musical or artistic work or any other aesthetic creation whatsoever;
>> (c) a scheme, rule or method for performing a mental act, playing a game or doing business, or a program for a computer;
>> (d) the presentation of information;

* The author would like to thank E. Van der Graaf and F. Kaganas for their comments.

---

1. This is particularly so in the United Kingdom and where prior to the 1977 Patents Act inventions were defined by the phrase 'manner or manufacture' (1949 Patents Act section 101).
2. The scope of inventions covered in the text includes inventions which relate to text processing, presentations of information/aesthetic creations and computer programs.

but the foregoing provisions shall not prevent anything from being treated as an invention for the purposes of this Act only to the extent that a patent or application for a patent relates to that thing as such.

Not surprisingly it was in relation to section 1(2)/Article 52 that the first problems regarding the nature of the invention arose. One problem in this context was the question of the way in which the invention as described in the application should be interpreted for the purposes of section 1(2)/Article 52. In answering this question, a number of different and sometimes conflicting styles of interpretation have been proposed: responses which, broadly speaking, fall into four main categories:

(1) Advocates of the first style of interpretation maintain that section 1(2)/Article 52 requires that the application be examined without reference to any of the excluded categories. That is, when determining whether an invention falls within section 1(2)/Article 52, the task of the court is to separate the excluded and non-excluded elements of the application and to focus only upon the non-excluded components.[3]

(2) The second style of interpretation is often referred to as the 'point of novelty' approach.[4] This is the idea that, when the court is determining whether an invention falls within one of the excluded categories, only the novel or inventive elements of the invention are to be examined—an approach which requires the court to exorcise or ignore those features of the invention which are non-inventive.

(3) The third style of interpretation is the 'kernel theory'.[5] The kernel theory is based on the idea that when determining whether an invention falls within the excluded categories, the court should focus only upon the essence or core of the invention (which is often expressed as the substance of the main teaching or the field involved).

(4) The final style of interpretation is the 'whole contents' approach. Proponents of this style of interpretation argue that, when assessing whether an invention falls within section 1(2)/Article 52, instead of looking only to the novel or non-excluded elements in an invention, the role of the court is to examine the claims as a whole. Only after this step is successfully completed should the court examine the invention for novelty and non-obviousness.

The first three styles of interpretation share a number of points in common. First, all three approaches require the court to evaluate and prioritise elements or parts of the invention. This can be seen, for example, with the first approach where the court is required to separate its excluded and non-excluded elements. Likewise according to the point of novelty approach one of the first tasks for the court is to identify the inventive components of the invention.[6] By contrast, one of the features of the whole contents approach is that the court is not

---

[3] That is, the first task for the court is to examine the application and determine whether it contains any excluded elements listed in section 1(2)/Article 52 (for example a computer program). If the application does contain a computer program, this should be excluded from the examination. This was the approach proposed by Falconer J in *Merrill Lynch Inc.'s Application* [1988] RPC 1.

[4] For an example of this approach in the UK (albeit in an extended form), see Falconer J in *Merrill Lynch Inc.'s Application* [1988] RPC 1. Perhaps the best example of this approach can be seen in the US decisions concerning the patentability of computer-related inventions. For example see the majority decision in *Parker v Flook* 437 US 584 (1978) and the minority in *Diamond v Diehr* 450 US 175 (1981).

[5] The kernel theory is most often associated with the German patent system. For a recent application of this concept in relation to computer programs see *Dispositions Programm*, GRUR no 2, 96 (177) (Federal Supreme Court). In two recent decisions of the German Federal Court, however, the courts rejected the kernel *Transformationsanordnung*, GRUR no. 5, 336 (1989), and *Elektronisches Ubersetzungsgerat* GRUR no. 5, 338 (1989).

[6] The kernel theory requires the court to identify the core or essence of the invention.

required to weigh up or categorise elements of the invention. The second feature shared by the first three styles of interpretation is that they greatly reduce the scope of protection available for computer-related inventions. The reason for this is that each of the different approaches would, if adopted, invariably lead to the exclusion from examination of computer programs. For example, if the point of novelty test were applied to inventions which have as one of their components a computer program, this would first mean examining the invention to determine which elements were novel (which in practice would often be the computer program) and then excluding the non-novel elements from the examination. Given the nature of Article 52(3)/section 1(2)c, this approach would greatly reduce the scope of protection for inventions which relate to computer programs.

The question of the way in which the invention should be interpreted was one of the central issues before the Technical Board of Appeal in *Vicom*[7] and *Kock & Sterzel*.[8] In these decisions, the Board of Appeal rejected the first three responses, preferring instead the whole contents approach to the interpretation of the invention. Thus, in relation to computer-related inventions the Board said that one should disregard the fact that the invention has as one of its elements a computer program and focus, instead, on the invention as a whole. In reaching this conclusion the Board said that it was irrelevant that an invention is made up of a mixture of technical and non-technical means.[9] In turn the Board of Appeal also made it clear that the test of whether an invention falls within the excluded categories of Article 52 is separate and distinct from the question of whether the subject-matter is new and involves an inventive step.[10]

Despite initial doubts, the UK Court of Appeal has in recent decisions followed the approach of the Board of Appeal in *Vicom* and *Kock & Sterzel* and held that when an invention is interpreted for the purposes of section 1(2), it should be examined as a whole.[11] In reaching this conclusion the Court of Appeal ended any doubts about inconsistencies between courts in the UK and the EPO.[12]

The harmony between courts in the UK and the EPO has to some extent, however, been disturbed by the Board of Appeal in its recent *IBM decision*.[13] While reaffirming the whole contents approach,[14] the decision differs from *Vicom* and *Kock & Sterzel* in that it reintroduces the need to evaluate and balance the different elements of the invention. This can be seen in the comment of the Board that 'while it follows [from *Kock & Sterzel*] that the EPC does not prohibit the patenting of inventions consisting of a mix of excluded and non-excluded

---

[7] T208/84, OJ EPO (1987) 14; 2 EPOR 74.

[8] T26/86, of OJ EPO (1988) 19; [1988] 2 EPOR 72.

[9] For example the Board said the 'European Patent Convention does not ask that a patentable invention be exclusively or largely of a technical nature; in other words it does not prohibit the patenting of inventions consisting of a mix of technical and non-technical elements', *Kock & Sterzel* T26/86, above Note 7, paragraph 3.4. By adopting the whole contents approach the Board avoided the problematic task of having to evaluate and categorise the elements of an invention.

[10] Thus following the *Guidelines for Examination in the EPO* (1985 and Supp. 1989), hereinafter *Guidelines*. The amended *Guidelines* to Article 52(2) state that 'the basic test for patentability, that is whether there is an "invention" is completely separate and distinct from the question of whether there is an inventive step'. Part C, chapter iv, 2.2. While the *Guidelines* are not binding upon the Board of Appeal, as will be seen they have been endorsed again and again in the decisions of the Technical Board of Appeal.

[11] *Merrill Lynch Inc.'s Application* (1989) RPC 561 (CA), *Genentech v Wellcome* (1989) RPC 147 (CA). An interesting comparison can be drawn here with the developments in the USA. For example see *Parker v Flook* 437 US 584 (1978), where a point of novelty approach was adopted, and *Diamond v Diehr* 450 US 175 (1981) where the majority adopted a whole comments approach.

[12] For an example of the inconsistencies that existed as a result of the *Merrill Lynch* decision at first instance, see Hart, 'Application of Patents to Computer Technology—UK and the European Patent Office Harmonisation' (1989) EIPR 42.

[13] T38/86, 14 February 1989, to be published in the OJ of the EPO.

[14] *Ibid.*, paragraphs 15 and 16.

features ... it does not necessarily follow that *all* such mixes are patentable'.[15] What the Board did not explain, however, was what type of mix was to be patentable. That is, they did not explain whether the patenting of inventions was to be limited by the novelty of the elements, by the fact of whether the elements fell within Article 52, by the notion of the core of the invention, or by some *de minimus* principle. Until the Board rules clearly on this matter, the *IBM* decision should be seen as introducing some yet to be determined qualitative limit upon the idea of the invention.[16]

The adoption of the whole contents approach brought with it a number of important changes to patent law. As in the United States, the dominance of the whole contents approach marked an important move towards the liberalisation of the patentability of computer-related inventions.[17] In turn, the adoption of the whole contents approach signalled an important change in the legal attitude towards information technology. The reason for this is that for many years computer programs were, in the rhetoric of patent law, despairingly referred to as mere tools or as non-technical information which excluded them from patent protection.[18] Despite this, when computer programs were incorporated into an industrial process, they were still singled out for special attention. It seems as if reality has finally met with the rhetoric with the adoption of the 'whole contents' approach, however, as computer programs are now treated as a standard part of the modern technical process. This new approach towards computer programs can be seen in *Vicom* where it was said 'an invention which would be patentable in accordance with conventional patentability criteria should not be excluded from protection by the mere fact that for its implementation modern technical means in the form of a computer program are used'.[19]

In addition to shaping the way the inventions are to be interpreted, the first three styles of interpretation also function as internal constraints which filter out inventions not deserving of patent protection. With the acceptance of the whole contents approach, however, this internal mode of regulation is absent. The fact that this internal constraint is absent generates a new type of problem. This problem arises because in practice the patent application will always attempt to establish links with substantive technical features.[20] That is, the applicant will attempt to describe the *form* of the invention in a manner so that it extends beyond the scope of the excluded categories in section 1(2) and Article 52. The task for the court,

---

[15] *Ibid.*, paragraph 12.

[16] While the introduction of a qualitative limit changes the way the invention is interpreted from that outlined in *Vicom*, it is incorrect to suggest that this decision amounts to an acceptance of the kernel theory as Meijboom argued (the author agrees with Meijboom that if the kernel theory is adopted this will greatly reduce the scope of protection for computer-related inventions.) Meijboom, 'Software Protection in "Europe 1992"' [1990] Rutgers Computer & Technology Law Journal 407, 417. There are a number of reasons why the author cannot agree with Meijboom's interpretation of the *IBM* decision. First, there is no indication of what exactly an 'acceptable mix' is. Certainly there is no indication that the court looked to the kernel of the invention. Second, the Board spoke of and applied a whole contents approach. Third, when one examines the way the Board examined the application, as distinct from the comments about how this should be done, it is apparent that the Board used the same approach as in *Vicom*. It is important to realise in this context, that the whole contents (and indeed the kernel theory) are only preliminary questions in the reasoning process. There is nothing contradictory in the Board initially looking to the invention as a whole and then looking to the elements of the invention to determine whether any of these elements are 'technical'.

[17] *Diamond v Diehr* 450 US 175 (1981) where the majority adopted a whole contents approach and granted patent protection for a computer-related invention.

[18] The pre-1977 case law on this in the UK is not conclusive, however even in those cases where patents were granted, computers and computer programs were often treated as alien objects.

[19] T208/84, OJ EPO (1987) 14, paragraph 15. Given that for many practising and academic lawyers, the computer and computer program still remains the most alien and exotic aspect of the invention, one can expect inventions which include computer programs to be treated, for some time at least, as technical oddities

[20] That is, a computer program in its pure form will rarely be the subject-matter of a patent application. Given this, where someone invents something which is *prima facie* unpatentable often the response to this will be to attempt to describe the invention in a manner so that it falls outside the scope of the excluded categories.

however, is to ignore the *form* of the claims and focus, instead, upon the *substance* of the invention.[21] To do otherwise would, in the language of the US courts, mean exalting form over substance. Fox LJ took up this problem in the UK Court of Appeal when he said:

> it cannot be permissible to patent an item excluded by section 1(2) under the guise of an article which contains that item—that is to say, in the case of a computer program, the patenting of a conventional computer containing that program.[22]

A similar comment was made by the Board of Appeal:

> it cannot have been intended by the Contracting States to the EPC that express exclusions from patentability could be circumvented simply by the manner in which the invention is expressed in a claim.[23]

So when the invention has as one of its elements a forbidden matter (for example a computer program), the question arises whether the invention is 'in reality' or 'in truth'[24] a claim to a computer program as such, or whether the invention as a whole, although based on a computer program, falls outside the scope of the excluded categories. The problem created by the adoption of the whole contents approach is, in short, how to determine whether the invention as claimed relates to a disqualified matter. That is, how should the courts distinguish inventions which are composed solely of excluded matter, and are therefore unpatentable, from inventions which only happen to include as one of their components, say, a computer program, and are therefore *prima facie* patentable. It is this question that is now addressed, looking forward to the approach of the Technical Board of Appeal and then to that adopted in the UK.

Part 2

Technical Board of Appeal

The method used by the Technical Board of Appeal to determine whether an invention falls within Article 52 has been to ignore the question of whether the invention relates exclusively to a computer program or a mathematical method and ask, instead, whether the invention-as-claimed exhibits the 'technical character' necessary for a patentable invention.[25] Rather than focusing on the specific question of whether the invention relates exclusively to a computer program or to a mathematical method, the Technical Board of Appeal has focused on the more abstract question of whether the invention exhibits the technical character necessary for patentability. This is despite the fact that the formula 'technical character' does

---

[21] Dillon LJ summed up the root of this problem when he said: 'It would be nonsense for the [Patent] Act to forbid the patenting of a computer program, and yet permit the patenting of a floppy disc containing a computer program, or an ordinary computer when programmed with the program; it can well be said ... that a patent for a computer when programmed or the disc containing the program is no more than a patent for a program as such.' *Genentech v Wellcome* [1989] RPC 147, 240 (CA).

[22] *Merrill Lynch Inc.'s Application* (1989) RPC 561, 569 (CA), emphasis added.

[23] T22/85, OJ EPO (1990) 12, paragraph 10; [1990] EPOR 98, 105.

[24] This is the language used by Aldous J in *Norman Henry Gale* unreported; (delivered on 22 January 1990 by Aldous J in the Patents Court); at 14 to 15 of the court transcript.

[25] For example see T22/85, OJ EPO (1990) 12. On this point, compare the distinction between 'conventional' post-solution activity (unpatentable) and 'significant' post-solution activity (patentable) in the reasoning used in the USA. See *Parker v Flook* 437 US 584 (1978); *Diamond v Diehr* 450 US 175 (1981).

not appear in the provisions of Article 52 nor elsewhere in the EPC.[26]

One of the main advantages of this way of approaching Article 52(2) is that by shifting attention towards the idea of 'technical character', the Board of Appeal is able to avoid having to formulate a workable definition of 'computer program', a task which is not only technically problematic but also one that changes in technology are likely to render obsolete. Indeed one of the major problems with specific formulations such as Article 52(2) is that because they are drafted in the light of contemporary technology they are prone to obsolescence or, at least, convoluted interpretations.[27] Whatever advantages this approach to Article 52 may have, it still leaves the Board of Appeal with two further questions: first, the need to characterise the invention; second, the task of having to formulate and understand what is meant by the term 'technical'. It is to these questions that we now turn.

Characterisation of the invention

The first task that confronts the court when deciding whether an invention falls within one of the excluded categories is that the claims must be interpreted or, to put it another way, the invention must be characterised.[28] One of the interesting features of the way in which the invention has been interpreted under Article 52 is that the Board of Appeal has focused not so much upon the 'invention' as outlined in the claims, as upon the tangible manifestation of the invention.[29] While there are a number of different ways in which the tangible nature of the invention has been interpreted—ranging from effect, contribution to the art and the resolution or solution of a problem—in practice, the Technical Board of Appeal has focused upon the effect or contribution of the invention. That is, when determining whether the invention falls within Article 52 the Technical Board of Appeal has concentrated not so much upon the invention as outlined in the claims, as upon the contribution or effect that the invention has upon the known art.

This shift away from a pure examination of the claims is in line with the general move towards objective reasoning that is occurring at the EPO.[30] More specifically, the focus upon the effect of the invention arises because of the way the claims in question are drafted. While the technical nature of an invention can exist either in the effect or the structure of an invention, given the exclusionary nature of Article 52(2) most applications will be formulated in terms of effect rather than structure. As such, the most common question will relate to the nature of technical effect rather than the structure of the invention itself.[31]

---

[26] For an examination of the justifications for this approach see Part 3.

[27] The Technical Board of Appeal said in relation to Article 53(b) of the EPC (the exception in relation to essentially biological inventions) that 'at the time when the exception is drafted, the knowledge of the potential development in the field of biotechnology was rather limited'. *Lubrizol Genetics Inc.* T320/87, OJ EPO (1988) 71, paragraph 5. The Australian High Court warned of a similar problem when they said the 'truth is that any attempt to state the ambit of s.6 of the Statute of Monopolies by precisely defining "manufacture" is bound to fail ... To attempt to place upon the idea the fetters of an exact verbal formula could never have been sound'. NRDC (1961) RPC 134, 142.

[28] The term 'characterised' has been used here in an attempt to differentiate the act of interpretation that occurs in infringement cases from that which occurs in cases where the question is as to the patentability (in a European sense) of an invention—that is, whether the application falls within Article 52/section 1(2).

[29] For an examination of some of the potential problems (and their solution) with this approach in relation to substance claims see Szabo 'The Problem and Solution Approach to the Inventive Step' [1986] EPIR 293.

[30] Nowhere is this more apparent than in relation to the problem and solution approach to obviousness which has been adopted, in part, in the EPO. See Szabo, *ibid.*

[31] It seems that 'effect' is a term which is much favoured in the language of science for, as Hacking said, when 'physicists got their hands and minds on a truly instructive phenomenon, they came to call it an effect'. Ian Hacking, *Representing and Intervening*, Cambridge University Press, 1983, at 224.

Meaning of 'technical'

Once the invention has been characterised, the next task is to decide whether this effect or contribution is technical. Such an analysis clearly requires that a definition or meaning be given to the term 'technical'. The problem with this, however, is that providing an acceptable definition of technology is a very difficult if not impossible task. The difficulty of this task was borne out by the fact that while the legal studies which prompted the revision of the EPO guidelines[32] were able to propose 'technical character' as one of the criteria for determining whether subject-matter was excluded from patentability, they were unable to provide a precise definition of what was meant by the term 'technical'.[33]

Ultimately, providing a definition of 'technology' is a question of interpretation and, as such, one that warrants the attention of theory (for want of a better word). Broadly speaking two approaches to this question could have been adopted. One was to adopt a style of interpretation known as 'definition *per genus et differentiam*'. This is an approach which attempts to define things genus-species, in an analytical and precise manner. Alternatively, one can move away from this approach and attempt to define the object in 'use'.[34] Such an approach attempts to move away from specific formulations into the meaning of particular words and adopt the definition which is currently in use.

Recognition of the limits of language and, more specifically, the inability to define technology in any helpful way, led the Working Group of the EPO to adopt an approach that has much in common with the definition in use approach. This can be seen, for example, in the comment by the Working Group that the EPO examiners did not find the concept of technical character difficult to apply in practice, but very difficult to define precisely in words. Because of this they abandoned any attempt to define technology in terms of genus/species and suggested, instead, that the task of defining 'technical' was best left to the jurisprudence of the Board of Appeal.[35] While numerous arguments have been put forward in support of such approach to the problem of defining words, the merits of the definition in use approach were implicitly referred to in the comment that:

> While the German Courts traditionally lose themselves in extremely problematic disquisitions concerning the relations of mind, nature and technology, the guidelines abandon completely such considerations and express an extremely pragmatic viewpoint. No abstract definition is adduced to mark the boundary line between technical and non-technical inventions, but attention is essentially drawn to examples.[36]

---

[32] The Working Group on Computer Programs was set up in 1984 by the EPO to examine, *inter alia*, the question of the patentability of computer-related inventions in the EPC. The Working Group led to the amendment of the *Guidelines for Examination at the EPO* in 1985.

[33] WG/CP/I/1. The difficulty of defining 'technical' was highlighted in the comment that 'a technical intervention seems to be rather like a camel; it is more easily recognised than described'. Wallace, 'The Patentability of Software-Related Inventions Under the European Patent Convention' (1986) Software Law Journal 249, 252.

[34] Perhaps the most well-known example of this is Wittgenstein's analysis of 'family resemblances'. See Wittgenstein, *Philosophical Investigations*, Basil Blackwell, Oxford, 1958, paragraphs 64 onward.

[35] The working group said that the question of defining 'technical' was best illustrated by examples. WG/CP/I/1 paragraph 5, at 13. This approach ties in with those who decided when drafting the EPC not to define computer programs 'so as not to tie the hands of the EPO and of the national courts which would have to settle these questions'. Doc. BR/135/71, no. 96. Quoted in M. Van Empel, *The Granting of European Patents*, Sijthoft, Leyden, 1975, at 35.

[36] Axel von Hellfeld, 'Protection of Inventions Comprising Computer Programs by the European and German Patent Offices—A Confrontation' (1986) Computer Law and Practice, 182, 186. As will be seen the approach that the Board of Appeal has built around these examples has its roots in the traditional practice of German patent law.

The approach adopted in the Technical Board of Appeal follows the spirit of the *Guidelines* in that there have been no attempts to explain in any detail what is meant by 'technology'.[37] Despite this, it is possible to glean from the cases a particular approach to the interpretation of 'technology'. This approach is best described as an artefact-based view of technology. The reason for this is that the Board of Appeal has said that an invention is technical if it provides or leads to a concrete, causal or non-abstract result or change in things. That is, if the effect or results of the invention lead to a tangible physical change, this acts as virtual proof that the invention is technical and therefore falls outside the scope of the excluded categories. The use of physical change to determine whether an invention is of a technical character can be seen, for example, in *Vicom* where the Board of Appeal explained how to differentiate unpatentable mathematical methods and algorithms from patentable inventions:

> the fact that a mathematical method or a mathematical algorithm is carried out on numbers ... and provides a result also in numerical form, the mathematical method or algorithm being only an abstract concept prescribing how to operate on numbers. No direct technical result is produced by the mathematical method as such.

In contrast:

> if a mathematical method is used in a technical process, that process is carried out on a physical entity (which may be a material object but equally an image stored as an electrical signal) by some technical means implementing the method and provides as its result a certain change in that entity.[38]

The absence of physical change has also been an important factor in the decisions of the Technical Board of Appeal that an invention is non-technical and is therefore unpatentable.[39] That is, if the invention does not lead to a physical change, this is taken as showing that the invention falls within the scope of Article 53(2) and is, therefore, unpatentable. Despite this, it would be untrue to say that the *absence* of physical effect is as important as the *presence* of physical effect in the reasoning of the Technical Board of Appeal. The reason for this seeming illogicality is that when the outcome or result of the invention as interpreted falls within one of the excluded categories, there is no need to inquire into the meaning of 'technical'.[40] This situation arises in those cases where the invention as characterised (that is, the effect) clearly falls within one of the non-patentable, non-technical categories, such as mathematical

---

[37] In the text 'technical' and 'technology' have been used interchangeably.

[38] *Vicom* T208/84 OJ EPO (1987) 14, paragraph 5 (emphasis added). The Board stressed that the original claim would not get patent protection because it did not specify what physical entity was represented by the data.

[39] For example, the absence of effect upon a 'physical' entity was an important factor in the Board's conclusion that a system for automatically generating semantically-related expressions was unpatentable. In particular, the fact that the function/result of the invention was characterised as a purely linguistic/semantic relationship which did not relate to any physical entity led the Board to conclude that the invention was non-technical. 'The effect of this function, namely the resulting information about the existence of semantically related expressions, is a purely linguistic, that is, non-technical result'. T52/85, [1989] 8 EPOR 454, 460, paragraph 5,8 (not to be published in the OJ of the EPO).

[40] This can be seen, for example, in T65/86 where the claims were directed to a method for automatically detecting and correcting contextual homophone errors (that is, when a number of words such as 'affect/effect' are used in an inappropriate context) in a text. An important factor in the conclusion that the invention was unpatentable was that the invention was held to relate only to 'different linguistic expressions, which were purely abstract expressions without any technical significance. The overall effect of the method was thus not technical'. T65/86, 22 June 1989 (to be published in the OJ of the EPO), paragraph 20. On this basis it was distinguished from *Vicom*. See also, T38/86, 14 February 1989 (to be published in the OJ EPO, cited in T42/87, not to be published in the OJ of the EPO).

methods or business methods: categories which are traditionally and, on the whole, uncontroversially regarded as non-technical. In these cases the most important stage of the reasoning process is the act of characterising the invention proper, rather than determining whether this effect is technical or not.

However useful such an analysis may be, it still leaves unanswered the question as to the exact meaning of physical change. The Technical Board of Appeal highlighted this when they said it could not be said that 'any manner of bringing about a change in a physical entity would *ipso facto* qualify as a technical process'.[41] In so doing they shifted attention away from the meaning of technology towards the meaning of physical change and, in turn, the degree of change that is necessary for an invention to be deemed technical. This situation highlights the limits of legal reasoning and is a reminder that one cannot hope to use either technical character or physical change as litmus paper tests for patentability. The reason for this is that no matter how well a subject is analysed, the inherently open-ended nature of interpretation means that we cannot escape the fact that many conclusions depend upon the leap from the abstract idea which characterises much legal thought to the specific questions of the problem in hand. This should not be seen as a fault in the reasoning processes used in patent law so much as an inescapable feature of legal interpretation.

According to the jurisprudence of the Board of Appeal, a physical entity is something which can be described as a material or real object. In addition to its ordinary meanings, 'physical entity' has been extended to include intangible objects. This can be seen in the comment—which clearly reflects the importance of the electronic medium—that 'physical entities' extend to include 'a real thing, that is, an image, even if that thing was represented by an electrical signal'.[42] The intangible nature of the 'physical entity' can also be seen in *Kock & Sterzel* where the fact that the invention controlled an x-ray tube so as to ensure optimum exposure with adequate protection against overloading of the tube was sufficient change for the application to be deemed technical.[43] Perhaps the best example of the way in which the meaning of 'physical entity' has been extended to include intangibles can be seen in T163/85, where it was said that the TV signal was, despite its transient character, a physical reality which could be detected by technical means and therefore could not be considered as an abstract entity'.[44]

While there may be some uncertainty as to the meaning of physical entity in a positive sense, it is clear from the decisions of the Technical Board of Appeal that for an invention to be patentable the change must occur outside the scope of the categories listed in Article 52.[45] That is, if the results of the invention only lead to a change in the nature of, say, information or business methods, then it will not be patentable.[46] This can be seen, for example, in T22/85 where the application was for a system which automatically abstracted documents, stored the abstracts in memory and then retrieved them in response to input

---

[41] T22/85, OJ EPO (1988) 12, paragraph 13.

[42] T22/85, OJ EPO (1990) 12, paragraph 13. The basis for this quote is taken from *Vicom* T208/84 OJ EPO (1987) 14, paragraph 5.

[43] *Kock v Sterzel* T26/86, OJ EPO (1988) 14, paragraph 3. See also T115/85, OJ EPO (1990) 30, where it was held that an invention which automatically gave visual indications about conditions prevailing in an apparatus or system was basically a technical problem.

[44] T163/85, Supplement to OJ EPO (1990) 19. On this basis the invention did not fall within Article 52(2)(d), (3).

[45] See for example T06/83, OJ EPO (1988) 5. An important factor in the conclusion that the data processing unit in question was patentable was that the application did not relate exclusively to 'data', but extended to the co-ordination and control of the internal communications between programs and data files (paragraph 6).

[46] Strictly speaking, this situation is the same as the questions asked as to the meaning of 'technical' discussed earlier. That is, when the effect or result of the invention falls within one of the excluded categories then it is not necessary to inquire as to the meaning of 'physical change' nor the degree of change necessary to show a patentable invention.

queries. The application in this case was similar to the *Vicom* application in that it operated on electrical signals. However unlike the Vicom application—where the change in electrical signals led to further changes in the process—the 'electrical signals processed according to the [T22/85] application [were] not of this kind, but represent (part of) the information content of a document, which could be of any nature'.[47] The telling factor in the Board's decision that the invention fell foul of Article 52 was that the claimed activity did not bring about any change in the thing operated upon (that is the document to be abstracted) but merely derived therefrom new information to be stored.[48]

It seems clear that under the EPC, inventions which include as one of their elements a computer program or mathematical method are *prima facie* patentable, so long as the invention viewed as a whole makes a technical contribution to the art. An ordinary computer program used in a general-purpose computer, however, would in normal circumstances be unpatentable. The reason for this is that while the implementation of the program in the computer transforms mathematical values into electrical signals, the electrical signals amount to no more than a reproduction of information which would not be regarded as a technical effect,[49] that is the change is limited to non-technical subject matter. If however the subject-matter makes a technical contribution to the known art, patentability would not be denied merely on the ground that a computer program is involved in its implementation. Likewise where the subject-matter claimed is concerned only with the internal workings of a known computer, a technical effect must be identified for there to be a patentable invention.[50]

United Kingdom

In distinguishing between inventions which are 'in reality' or 'in truth' patentable from those which are made up solely of excluded subject matter, the courts in the UK have closely followed the approach adopted by the Technical Board of Appeal. That is, despite an absence of any express mention in the 1977 Patents Act, courts in the UK have adopted 'technical character' as the main criterion for determining whether an invention falls within section 1(2) and, in turn, have utilised technical effect as the way of characterising the invention. This was highlighted in the Court of Appeal when Fox LJ said:

> ... it cannot be permissible to patent an item excluded by section 1(2) under the guise of an article which contains that item—that is to say, in the case of a computer program, the patenting of a conventional computer containing that program. Something further is necessary. The nature of that addition is, I think, to be found in the *Vicom* case where it was stated 'Decisive is what technical contribution the invention makes to the known art'. There must, I think, be some technical advance on the prior art in the form of a new result...[51]

While Fox LJ's language at times differed from that of the Technical Board of Appeal,[52] it is

---

[47] T22/85, OJ EPO (1990) 12, paragraph 13.
[48] *Ibid.*
[49] See *Kock & Sterzel* T26/86 (1988) 14; [1988] 2 EPOR 75, paragraph 3.3. If however, the invention provided a technical effect, it would then be patentable.
[50] 'Patentability of Computer Related Inventions' Trilateral Cooperation EPO-JPO-USPTO. Project 12.5 of the EPO, September 1989, at 11, paragraph 13.
[51] *Merrill Lynch Inc.'s Application* (1989) RPC 561, 569 (CA).
[52] For example, Fox LJ said 'Now let it be supposed that claim 1 can be regarded as producing a new result in the form of a technical contribution to the prior art. That result, whatever the technical advance may be, is simply the production of a trading system.' *Merrill Lynch Inc.'s Application* (1989) RPC 561, 569. While the conclusions have been the same, the Technical Board of Appeal would not have used the term 'technical' in such a manner.

clear that the Court of Appeal accepted that the presence of technical character was sufficient to show that an invention did not relate to a disqualified matter. In turn, technical character was to be determined by examining the 'result', 'contribution' or 'effect' made by the invention. These conclusions were recently followed in two decisions in the UK Patents Court concerned with the question of whether computer-related inventions fell within the scope of section 1(2).[53] In these decisions, Aldous J followed the Technical Board of Appeal in using technical character and technical effect to determine whether the inventions in question fell within section 1(2) of the 1977 Patents Act. This can be seen in Aldous J's argument that:

> ... the first task of the court is to construe the claim as that is where the invention is defined. If the claim properly construed is drafted so as to relate to any of the matters disqualified by section 1(2) then the invention is not patentable. If however the claim is drafted to a process or a technique or product and the basis of such process technique or product is a disqualified matter, the court should go on to consider whether the claimed invention is in fact no more than a claim to an invention for a disqualified matter. It is a question of fact to be decided in each case, but if the claimed invention is more than a claim to an invention for a disqualified matter then it qualifies as a patentable invention.
>
> In deciding that question of fact it is always important to consider whether the claimed invention is part of a process which is to be used in providing a technical result. If it is, then the claim cannot be said to be an invention relating to no more than one of the disqualified matters. Similarly, where a claim is directed to a product, it is important to consider whether the product claimed is a new technical product or merely an ordinary product programmed in a different way as in the latter case the claim is in reality to the program and therefore could not relate to a patentable invention.[54]

While few decisions have dealt with the concept of the invention in relation to section 1(2), it seems that the courts in the UK are moving in a similar direction as the Technical Board of Appeal—at least as far as technical character and contribution and effect are concerned.[55]

Meaning of 'technology'

Unlike the use of technical character/technical effect to determine whether an invention falls within section 1(2), it is too early to say whether 'technology' is being defined in the same way in the UK as in the Technical Board of Appeal. The reason for this is that in two of the three decisions concerned with computer-related inventions in the United Kingdom, the invention as characterised clearly fell within the list of non-technical subject-matter. As such,

---

[53] *Norman Henry Gale* unreported (delivered on 22 January 1990 by Aldous J in the Patents Court); *Wang Laboratories Inc.* unreported (delivered on 21 March 1990 by Aldous J in the Patents Court). All references in text refer to the court transcripts.

[54] *Norman Henry Gale*, above Note 53, at 13 to 14. In *Wang Laboratories* Aldous J indicated that the reasoning adopted in *Gale's* case was the same as the Technical Board of Appeal.

[55] The *Merrill Lynch* decisions, both at first instance ((1988) RPC 1) and in the Court of Appeal ((1989) RPC 561) give a good indication of the current law in the UK. Contrary to what some commentators have said (for example see Whitten, 'So are Computer Programs Patentable or Not?' November (1989), CIPA, 44, 52) the author believes the decisions, except for the comments as to the point of novelty approach at first instance, are very much in line with the reasoning and, probably more importantly, the spirit of the Technical Board of Appeal. This is particularly so for the rejection of the invention on the grounds that its effect lay in an excluded category, that is, a method of doing business, a factor which was expressly referred to in *Vicom*.

the question of the meaning of technology did not arise. This can be seen, for example, in the *Merrill Lynch* decision where no indication is given as to the way technology is to be defined. The application in this case was for a 'data processing system for making a trading market in securities'. After outlining the relevant claims, the Court of Appeal simply characterised the invention as a method of doing business which clearly fell within the scope of section 1(2)(c) and was therefore unpatentable.[56] A similar style of reasoning can be seen in the recent *Wang Laboratories* decision.[57] The application in this case was for an expert system comprising a conventional computer operating in the normal way, with an expert system program the knowledge base of which was in the form of hierarchically defined terms and their definitions. For Aldous J the contribution to the art provided by the invention was a computer program which enabled an expert to store his knowledge in a hierarchical form, the purpose of which was to enable advice to be given. Given this characterisation of the invention it was not surprising that Aldous J said that the invention was a mental act and that it was therefore excluded from protection. Aldous J rejected the argument that the invention could be described as having a technical effect because it produced a new machine on the basis that the computer and the program did not combine together to produce a new computer. That is, the computer and the program remained a separate collocation rather than contributing to a different whole. While there was some use of the language of change to a physical entity, as in *Merrill Lynch*, the question of the meaning of technology was not an important issue in the decision.

The only decision where the meaning of technology was confronted directly in the UK was in the *Gale* case.[58] This case differs from many of the other 'computer-related' decisions, however, in that it concentrated not upon the effect of the invention so much as the structure of the subject-matter. The application in question in this case was for a ROM with a particular circuitry. The question before the court was whether this invention related exclusively to a mathematical method, mental act or computer program and was therefore unpatentable, or whether it was a 'genuine' invention. For Aldous J the fact that the program or method forming the basis of the invention altered the structure of the ROM was an important factor in deciding that the invention was patentable. This conclusion was reinforced by the fact that if the ROM was inserted into a computer this would lead to a technical change resulting in a different computer.[59] While there is no clear analysis of the meaning of technology in this decision, it seems that Aldous J, like the Technical Board of Appeal, utilised the language of change to a physical entity to determine whether the application in question fell within section 1(2). It would be premature, however, on the basis of this decision to make any comments as to the way in which 'technology' is being defined in the UK. Further decisions must be awaited to see if the general trend is in favour of the approach of the Technical Board of Appeal.

---

[56] *Merrill Lynch Inc's Application* (1989) RPC 561, 569.
[57] *Wang Laboratories*, see above Note 53. For a general examination of the question of the patentability of artificial intelligence personality in the US see Muse, 'Patented Personality' 4 Computer and High Technology Law Journal (1988) 285.
[58] *Norman Henry Gale*, see above Note 53.
[59] Other important factors in the decision were that the claims related to a new technical product, namely a computer constructed in a particular way. Re-introducing the idea of 'manner of new manufacture' Aldous J also focused on the fact that the claims related to a 'manufactured article'. *Norman Henry Gale*, see above Note 53, at 17.

Part 3

Problems with the new approach in the UK?

In a recent decision of the Technical Board of Appeal it was said that the 'requirement that an invention must have a technical character or in other words, must provide a technical contribution to the art is at the basis of a long-standing legal practice in at least the majority of Contracting States of the EPO'.[60] While the approach adopted by the Technical Board of Appeal may amount to a continuation of the traditional German approach to patentability,[61] it is an approach which is, for the most, alien to UK patent law. Given the alien nature of this way of defining the invention in the UK, it is not surprising that in the recent Patent Court decisions Aldous J expressed some reservations about the approach adopted by the Technical Board of Appeal.[62] The final section of this paper will attempt to answer some of the problems raised by Aldous J and, in turn, attempt to evaluate the nature of this 'new' approach to the patentability of inventions.

Absence of technical character in section 1(2)/Article 52

The first reservation expressed by Aldous J with regard to the approach adopted by the Technical Board of Appeal was that the word 'technical' did not appear in section 1(2) of the 1977 Patents Act or in Article 52 of the EPC.[63] Despite Aldous J's doubts, ample justifications can and have been put forward to support the style of reasoning used by the Technical Board of Appeal. The main basis for the use of 'technical character' by the Technical Board of Appeal stems from an imaginative interpretation of Article 52. The starting point for this interpretation lies, in one sense,[64] with the working group of the EPO and the *Guidelines for Examination* as amended in 1985.[65] The rationale provided by the Technical Board of Appeal can be divided into three parts:

(i) Article 52(2) is made up of a non-exhaustive list of things which are not to be

---

[60] '... Neither from the terms of Article 52 EPC, nor from the legislative history of that Article as appearing from the preparatory documents can it be deduced that these Contracting States would have intended to deviate from their national laws and jurisprudence in this respect. On the contrary, it seems to be borne out by the list of exceptions in Article 52(2)(a) to (d) that they did not wish to do so.' T22/85 OJ EPO (1990) 12, paragraph 3; [1990] EPOR 98, 103.

[61] For example, although not expressly stated in the German Patent Act the German courts long ago added to the patentability requirements the need to show the existence of the technical invention. Indeed these ideas are so strong in German law that it was said recently that it was an undisputed maxim that patents are only granted for technical inventions. Beyer, 'Der Begriff der Information als Grundlage für die Beurteilung des technischen Charakters von programmbezogenen Erfindungen' GRUR (1990) 399.

[62] Interestingly, it has been suggested that one of the reasons why invention was not defined in the EPC was that the non-German patent systems lacked such a requirement and to introduce it would create further problems. Kolle, 'Patentable Inventions in the EPC' (1974) 5 IIC 140, 145 to 146.

[63] *Wang Laboratories*, see above Note 53, at 13.

[64] Much of this approach can be seen in the practice of the German patent system. For example, similar justifications were used by the Bundesgerichthof (German Federal Supreme Court) to explain the use of 'technical' in the Red Dove decision. 'The definition of a patentable invention provided in §1 of the Patent Act, does not include the word "technical". However §17 and §36b(2) of the Patent Act require the "technical" members of the Patent Office and the Bundespatentgericht to be knowledgeable in one branch of "technology". It has been customary in theory and in practice to describe the invention within the meaning of the Patent Act as a teaching of technical content...' *Rote Taube* (1970) 1 IIC 136, 137 to 138.

[65] The EPO Working Group on Computer Programs concluded that the criterion for determining whether any particular subject-matter is excluded from patentability was whether the subject-matter was of a technical character. WG/CP/I/1, part II.

regarded as patentable inventions. Following the working group of the EPO, the Board of Appeal argued that the factors listed in Article 52 are merely declaratory and in turn that they only confirm what could already be deduced from Article 52(1).

(ii) All the categories in Article 52(2) have in common the characteristic that they are non-technical, either because they are abstract (discoveries, scientific theories) or because they are clearly non-technical (aesthetic creations or presentations of information).[66] As Wallace said, this is because, when it is interpreted in its context and in the light of the *travaux préparatoires* relating to the EPC, Article 52(2) excludes from patentability any subject-matter which is not of a 'technical' nature.[67]

(iii) As Article 52(1) and (2) only exclude from protection those inventions which are non-technical, it is a short inductive leap to conclude from this that the term 'invention' relates to inventions of a technical nature.[68] That is, a positive presumption as to the meaning of 'invention' has been abstracted from the negative provisions of Article 52(2).

In addition to the logic of Article 52, a number of other arguments have been put forward to justify the use of 'technical character' in deciding whether an invention falls within the excluded categories. The most prominent arguments have been in relation to Rules 27 and 29 of the Implementing Regulations of the EPC. For example, as the Technical Board of Appeal said recently, Rule 27 tends to imply that an invention within the context of the EPC is made up of technical features and that it requires the technical features to be stated in (at least the characterising part of) the claim(s) of a European Patent application.[69]

The question that arises from this analysis is whether it should now be said that in order to establish patentability, it must be shown that the application relates to a 'technical invention'? On a reading of the decisions outlined above this seems to be the case. This conclusion is reinforced by the decision of the Board of Appeal in *Sternheimer* where it was said that 'it is a fundamental requirement of a European patent that the subject-matter constitute "an invention"'.[70] In the UK, support for this view comes from Mustill LJ who said that it was an essential requirement which 'must be satisfied before a patent can properly

---

[66] 'The exclusion (from patentability) might be arguably generalised to subject-matter which is essentially abstract in character, which is non-physical and therefore is not characterised by technical features in the sense of Rule 29(1) EPC'. T163/85, IPD 12055.

[67] Wallace, 'The Patentability of Software Related Inventions under the European Patent Convention' (1986) Software Law Review 249, 250. Being a multilateral treaty made under international customary law the interpretation of the EPC is governed by the Vienna Convention on the law of Treaties of 25 May 1969 (Articles 31 to 33). The Convention has already been applied in the UK by the House of Lords *Fothergill v Monarch Airlines Ltd* (1980) 3 WLR 209. Some of the factors which the Vienna Convention proposes when interpreting such treaties is that the *travaux préparatoires* and the circumstances in which the treaty was concluded may be taken into consideration (Article 32). The *travaux préparatoires* relating to the EPC indicate that patentable inventions as specified in Article 52 do at any rate need to have a technical character. This is reinforced by the fact that the *Guidelines* speak of the need for the invention to be of a technical character (Part C, Chapter IV, 1 and 2 of the *Guidelines for Examination in the EPO*. See specifically, point 1.2 (ii)).

[68] For a general examination of this see Gall, 'European Patent Office Guidelines 1985 on the protection of inventions relating to computer programs', Computer Law and Practice, September/October (1985) 6.

[69] T22/85, OJ EPO 1–2 (1990) 12, paragraph 4. More specifically the Technical Board of Appeal said that 'Rule 29(1)(b) requires that the characterising portion of a claim shall state the technical features, which in combination with the prior art part it is desired to protect.' *Ibid*. Rules 27 and 29 of the Implementing Regulations of the EPC stipulate that a patentable invention must relate to a technical field (Rule 27(1)(b)), it must be concerned with a technical problem (Rule 27(1)(d)), and that it must be characterised in the claims by means of technical features (Rule 29(1)).

[70] T366/87, 6 July 1989, (not to be published in the OJ of the EPO); [1989] 3 EPOR 131.

be granted ... that the application has made an "invention" '.[71] As with much of the law in relation to section 1(2)/Article 52 it is still too early to determine this point with any certainty. All indications are, however, that from the negative provisions of section 1(2)/Article 52, there is now a positive requirement, in addition to novelty, obviousness and sufficiency of disclosure, that the applicant show the existence of a technical invention.

The meaning of technology

The second problem raised by Aldous J in the UK Patent Court decisions was that he did not understand what the Technical Board of Appeal meant by the term 'technology'. More specifically Aldous J said that the Board of Appeal's focus upon whether an invention made a technical contribution created 'difficulties in that the word "technical" is open to a number of meanings, depending upon its context'.[72] The main reason for Aldous J's criticisms is that unlike German patent law, UK law has never expressly required that the invention be 'technical'. This problem was reinforced by the fact that the Munich Diplomatic Conference on the establishment of the EPC abstained from limiting the concept of the invention by the use of 'technical' as was earlier proposed.[73]

While, strictly speaking, there has never been a requirement in the United Kingdom that an invention be technical, the idea of what is technical has long shaped patent law—most noticeably in relation to the old idea of a 'manner of new manufacture'. In turn while the idea of the technical invention is explicitly alien to the UK patent tradition, the way in which the meaning of technology is determined is not.[74] For when one looks at the reasoning adopted in the UK and by the Technical Board of Appeal, one distinguishing feature has been the shift away from a linguistic or semantic examination of section 1(2)/Article 52 towards a more causal or tangible approach. This can be seen both in the way inventions are characterised in terms of 'effect' and, in turn, the way the 'technical' character of the invention is determined. A linguistic approach is a style of interpretation which focuses primarily on the meaning of particular words, such as the precise meaning of a computer program. In contrast, a causal approach is one that tends to avoid examinations into the meaning of particular words through the introduction of external criteria which show or prove the existence of the object under investigation.[75] With the adoption of 'physical change' as a factor to determine whether the invention is technical there has been a clear move towards the causal approach. This is not to suggest that when courts adopt the causal approach they escape the need to interpret, only that the dependency upon precise words becomes less obvious. With the adoption of this approach to determine what is technical, there is a return to the type of reasoning that characterised pre-EPC law in the UK and in Germany. For example in the *Red Dove* decision in Germany it was said that one of the factors of patentability was the need to show a 'causal, perceivable result'.[76] Likewise, the

---

[71] Mustill LJ *Genentech v Wellcome* (1989) RPC 147, 262 (CA). Mustill LJ based his arguments on the wording of section 1(2), Article 52 and the *Guidelines* (paragraphs 1.1 and 2.2 of ch. IV). Mustill LJ also considered the relationship between this separate requirement and novelty. Query whether this is a return to 'manner of new manufacture', albeit one that is worded differently?

[72] *Wang Laboratories*, see above Note 53, at 12 to 13.

[73] Kolle 'Patentable Inventions in the EPC' (1973) 5 IIC 140, 145.

[74] In any case, Aldous J was of the view that despite the absence of 'technical' in section 1(2), the approach that he adopted in *Gale's Application* was the same as that adopted by the Technical Board of Appeal in T52/85 ([1989] 8 EPOR 454), namely that the court should 'decide as a matter of fact whether the claim relates to an invention for matter excluded by section 1(2) of the Act and should only so hold if the application relates to that matter as such'. *Wang Laboratories*, see above Note 53, at 13.

[75] For example, a law is 'good' if it increases the GNP of a case.

[76] *Red Dove* (1970) 1 IIC 136, 138.

use of such a causal analysis can be seen in the remarks of the Australian High Court in the *NRDC* decision:

> the subject of the relevant claims has as its end result an artificial effect falling squarely within the true concept of what must be produced by a process if it is to be held patentable . . . The effect produced by the appellant's method exhibits the two essential qualities upon which 'product' and 'vendible' seem designed to insist. It is a 'product' because it consists in an artificially created state of affairs, discernable by observing over a period the growth of weeds and crops respectively on sown land on which the method has been put into practice. And the significance is economic; for it provides for a remarkable advantage . . .[77]

In addition to having roots in both patent traditions, there are a number of factors which may have inspired such a response to the question of defining technology: reasons which should provide sufficient justification for those who hunger after them. While the *Guidelines* do not include much detail on the question of defining the invention, they do speak of the invention as having a 'concrete' character. In turn, when deciding whether claims for industrial control of manufacturing processes involved the use of computer programs, the working group of the EPO said they are clearly allowed because they include some 'physical effect'.[78] On a more abstract level, the negative provisions of Article 52 have been of considerable help in determining the boundary between technical and non-technical inventions. As the Technical Board of Appeal said recently, the exclusionary categories in Article 52(2) have in common that they refer to activities which do not aim at any direct technical result, but are rather of an abstract and intellectual character.[79] Using such reasoning it has been argued that a common feature of the examples in Article 52 is that it is not necessary for them to be embodied in a three-dimensional physical form to be communicated nor to be understood, from which it is said that they do not define a physical object.[80]

Is this approach to be welcomed?

Perhaps the most important question to be asked in this context is whether this new approach to the patentability of inventions should be welcomed. For a number of different reasons the author's answer to this question is yes. First, while the focus upon the effect or contribution of an invention seems to exclude the development of patent law in the way that was achieved in the *Merrill Lynch* decision in the United States,[81] the concept of technology is broad enough to allow the courts to interpret and adapt the law accordingly. This flexibility is important because it will not be long before the Board of Appeal and the courts in the UK are presented with skilfully drafted claims for algorithms and computer programs *per se*, as is now happening in the United States. That is, it will not be long before attention is moved

---

[77] *NRDC* [1961] RPC, 134, 146.
[78] WG/CP/I/1, point 9, at 16.
[79] T22/85, OJ EPO 1–2 (1990) 12, paragraph 2.
[80] For a more thorough examination of these arguments see Appleton, 'European Patent Convention: Article 52 and Computer Programs' [1985] EIPR 279.
[81] *Paine, Weber, Jackson, Curtis Inc. v Merrill Lynch, Pierce, Ferner, Smith Inc.* 564 F. Supp. 1358 (D.Del. 1983). The court said that any objection to a claim as a method of doing business was concentrating unduly upon the intended result rather than the means of reaching it. This approach was, in effect, rejected by the Board of Appeal in T42/87, 5 October 1989 (not to be published in the OJ EPO), when it was said: 'schemes, rules and methods for performing mental acts are excluded from patentability by Article 52(2)(c) and (3) EPC and remain so when carried out by, or with the help of, a computer program' (paragraph 4).

away from the question of the patentability of computer-related inventions towards the patentability of computer programs and algorithms *simpliciter*.[82] While the existence of the exclusionary categories will undoubtedly prove problematic, the approach adopted by the Technical Board of Appeal is one which is best suited to deal with the problems associated with such negative provisions. As was highlighted by the decisions following Morton J's judgment in *GEC's Application*[83] however, the degree of flexibility depends very much on the attitude adopted by the court.

The adoption of the abstract concept of the 'technical', combined with the causal or artefact mode of reasoning means that many of the problems associated with linguistic analysis are avoided. One of the major problems with specific linguistic analyses is that they are inevitably dependent upon the current perception of technology and as the technology changes these definitions are often rendered obsolete. Thus by adopting a causal approach, the courts may have avoided the task of having to define a computer program[84] and, more generally, the need to determine how computer programs fit within the software/firmware/hardware distinction. In turn, by adopting an artefact based view of technology, the Technical Board of Appeal is also able to avoid some of the convoluted reasoning often associated with linguistic inquiries.[85] Again such an approach to the definition of the invention provides a flexible system which should be able to adapt easily to changes in subject-matter.

In conclusion the use of the artefact view of technology combined with the focus on the effect or contribution of the invention by the Board of Appeal provides a pragmatic and workable approach to the problem of determining whether an invention falls within one of the excluded categories, or as should perhaps now be said exhibits the necessary requirements of a technical invention. While many of these ideas are alien to UK patent law, given the advantages of the approach of the Board of Appeal, it is hoped that the courts in the UK will continue to follow the lead given by the Technical Board of Appeal in relation to the question of whether an application falls within the scope of section 1(2).

---

[82] See for example Axel von Hellfeld, 'Sind Algorithmen schutzfähig?', GRUR (1989) 471, and more generally Beyer 'Der Begriff der Information als Grundlage für die Beurteilung des technischen Charakters von programmbezogenen Erfindungen' GRUR (1990) 399.

[83] *GEC's Application* (1943) 60 RPC 1.

[84] There are many examples, especially in the United State (where there is still an emphasis on a linguistic analysis) of the difficulties of defining 'software', 'program', and more recently 'algorithm'. As was said in the first edition of 'Software Protection' little headway had been made in the 25-plus years in which the computer industry had been in existence in creating order from the definitional chaos of what exactly software is. 'Software Protection' (1982) 11. For more contemporary examples see Stern, 'Patenting Algorithms in America' Part 1 [1990] 8 EIPR 292, 298. Parformak, 'The Karmarkar Algorithm—"New" patentable subject matter?' (1990) 21 IIC 31, 33. Friedland, 'Computer Software Patentability: The Dilemma of Defining an Algorithm' (1988) *Software Law Journal* 537.

[85] Perhaps one of the best examples of the problems associated with linguistic inquiries can be seen from the reasoning used to distinguish 'treatment' from 'therapy' under the 1949 Patents Act. The chaotic nature of the judicial reasoning in these cases led one commentator to compare these decisions with that which was 'bandied about amongst medieval theologians on the subject of angels dancing on the head of a pin'. Reid, *A Practical Guide to Patent Law* ESC Publishing (1984) 13 to 14.

Patenting Plants Around the World*
[1996] 10 EIPR 531

TIM ROBERTS
Intellectual Property Consultant, Bracknell

Can you patent plants? If so, under what conditions? What is the difference between patenting plants and patenting plant varieties? Is there a need for extra protection for plants over that provided by UPOV's plant variety rights?

This article reviews practice in Europe and the United States, with some comments on positions in other countries; notes the requirements of the World Trade Organization's new Trade-related Intellectual Property provisions (TRIPs); and offers some comments.

It is hoped that the law is correctly stated, though it is often uncertain. This is not legal advice. Do not treat it as such. If you have a problem, you need legal advice based on your exact situation, not on one broadly similar: circumstances alter cases. As to the opinions, these are the author's own and no-one else's: and no guarantee of any kind is offered as to their acceptability or value.

Preamble

Why patents? A patent is a temporary monopoly granted to the introducer of new technology, to encourage him to exploit it. The extent of the monopoly is defined (primarily) by the claims of the patent. If the technology meets a need, people will buy it, and the patentee will profit. If it does not, no harm is done. The patentee is rewarded in proportion to the demand for the invention: this is just, and the reward has the social function of encouraging both invention and investment. As well as the specific benefits of new inventions (transport, drugs, computers, the whole range of things we take for granted that our ancestors would have marvelled at), technical change is important in fuelling economic growth and prosperity.

To justify a monopoly, the invention claimed must be new and inventive (not obvious or trivial). Furthermore the reward is given for a full disclosure of the invention, with full details of how to make and use it. It is also said (in Europe at least) that one can only patent 'inventions' and not 'discoveries'. However, as one who has spent his working life patenting what most would call discoveries, the author finds this rather misleading. A discovery is new knowledge: an invention is a new process or thing. However, a new discovery (unpatentable) often leads directly to a new process or thing (patentable).

For many years it was supposed that patents were only for industrial processes and products: in particular, that living organisms were not patentable. Various grounds were,

---

* *This article is based on a talk given by Tim Roberts to the annual International Congress of ASSINSEL (Association internationale des sélectionneurs—International Association of Plant Breeders) in Amsterdam on 22 to 24 May 1996.*

and are still, put for this: that organisms are 'discoveries' not 'inventions' (in the United States this was known as the 'product of nature' doctrine); that you cannot describe how to make organisms, you can only breed them—and this process cannot be repeated to order; that it is immoral to own life. However, these arguments have wilted under the pressure to protect biological innovations from competition. This need is even greater for biological innovations, because they are so easy to reproduce, in fact they reproduce themselves. Machines that do this have been postulated (von Neumann machines) but not yet achieved. Another spur to change has been the growth of molecular biology, giving the power to change organisms by direct—and partly predictable—interference in their chemistry. This has led to changes different in kind from those attainable by breeding.

There never seems to have been a ban formally recognised on the patenting of life-forms. Pasteur, for example, patented yeasts in the 19th century, obtaining patents in both Europe and the United States. Nevertheless, at the beginning of the present century, plants and animals were not generally regarded as suitable subjects for patents.

The United States

Recognising that there was a gap to be filled, the United States, in the 1930s, introduced a special system of plant patents. Rights were made available for new 'asexually reproduced, non-tuber-propagated' plants (potato growers were against the scheme). It continues to this day, primarily for ornamentals: the patents specifications are typically illustrated in full colour, and make handsome ornaments for the walls of the patent attorney's office. The new plant is claimed 'substantially as described'. However, the economic significance of this method of protection has been rather limited.

Up until the 1970s, there seems to have been an assumption that life was not patentable. This was challenged by the new science of genetic engineering. The first (and for many purposes the master) patent on this was applied for by Cohen and Boyer of the University of Stanford, California, in 1972. In 1980 a test case was taken to the UK Supreme Court. This case[1] related to a genetically modified bacterium for eating oilspills. The court held that there was no objection to patenting living material as such (provided it fulfilled all other requirements for patentability): the court concluded, in a much-quoted phrase, that 'everything under the sun made by the hand of man' was to be protected. Was this to be taken literally? The only material before the court was a micro-organism, and these had been protected before. Did it apply equally to higher organisms, such as plants and animals—or even man?

A case before the US Patent Office[2] settled the Office practice on plants. Hibberd et al. were working on maize cell culture. In April 1986 they applied for a patent on maize mutants, obtained from cell culture, that overproduced the amino-acid tryptophan. Claim 1 read as follows:

> A maize seed having an endogenous free tryptophan content of at least about one-tenth milligram per gram dry seed weight and capable of germination into a plant capable of producing seed having an endogenous free tryptophan content of at least about one-tenth milligram per gram dry seed weight.

The US Patent Office Examiner refused the claim on various grounds, including that the

---

[1] *Diamond v Chakrabarty*, 44 US 303.
[2] *Ex parte Hibberd* 227 USPQ 443, Board of Appeals and Interferences, 1985.

invention was a 'product of nature', and that the US Plant Variety Right law 'pre-empted' the ability to grant patents on plants. It was not argued that this claim describes a desirable objective rather than a specific invention. In any case, the refusal was appealed, and the Patent Office Board of Appeals overturned it: the claim just quoted was allowed, along with 31 others on similar products and processes for making them.

Following this decision—at a rather low level in the US legal system—patents on plants were regularly allowed. It was followed in 1987 by a further decision of the Appeals Board that animals (specifically oysters) could in principle be patented: and finally by a statement of Patent Office practice, that the Office would regard all life forms as patentable, except human beings—these latter it regarded as being unpatentable because of the US constitutional provision against slavery.

Today, patents on plants—similar to *Hibberd et al.*, quoted above—are regularly granted, and are in many respects uncontroversial. There is however some disquiet, both in the industry and outside it, about the form of the claims that is often used. Is it really fair to allow the inventor to define the invention, as Hibberd does, solely in terms of the result to be obtained? The claim is silent about the method used, so it is not limited to cell culture, but would cover genetic modification or indeed crossbreeding or selection of mutants. Worse still, the desired result is a lower limit of amino-acid content, with no maximum. If this method of framing patent claims were extended to other areas, engines, for example, would be no longer defined in terms of structural features, but simply in terms of power-to-weight ratio or fuel consumption: drugs would not be defined by chemical structure, but by effectiveness in curing disease.

Patenting plant varieties

Another trend in US patenting—in no way open to such criticisms—is that of granting patents on plant varieties (this is also done in Australia). Here are the first five claims of a representative patent from a leading US breeder:

> USP 4,812,599
> 1. An inbred corn line designated PHV78.
> 2. A plant or plants of the inbred corn line designated PHV78 of claim 1.
> 3. Pollen of the plant of claim 2.
> 4. Seed or seeds of the inbred corn line designated PHV78 of claim 1.
> 5. An inbred corn line with the phenotypic physiological and morphological characteristics of inbred corn line designated PHV78.

There are a further seven claims: to a method of producing a corn plant using PHV78 as one parent, or as both parents; to F1 hybrid plants of which PHV78 is either parent, or a parent of specified sex; to a method of producing F1 hybrid seed using PHV78 as a parent; and to F1 hybrid corn plants grown from the seed produced.

Hybrids are also claimed: for example, USP 4,731,499 from the same company claims:

> 1. Hybrid seed corn designated 3790.
> 2. A hybrid corn plant and its plant parts produced by the seed of claim 1.
> 3. Corn plants and the seed thereof regenerated from tissue culture of the hybrid corn plant and plant parts of claim 2.

4. A hybrid corn plant with the phenotypic characteristics of the hybrid plant of claim 2.

One or two patentees also include claims to progeny or descendants of the claimed varieties, which might of course be very different from the originals—but such claims are the exception.

Digression—is it appropriate to patent plant varieties?

A stock cartoon shows an inventor waiting outside a door marked 'Patent Office', carrying a wheel, or a better mousetrap. In real life, the door is marked 'Patent Attorney'; and the first instinct of the patent attorney, on being shown the wheel, or the mousetrap, will be to generalise it. What is the novel principle which the inventor's device embodies? In this way, the mousetrap becomes 'Apparatus for catching target fauna comprising fauna-attracting means ... and soon'. Simply to claim a trap baited with a piece of cheese would be anathema to him—even, indeed, grounds for an action in professional negligence, for not properly protecting his client's interests. But no such generalisation is carried out when patents are filed on plant varieties. It is extremely rare to file utility patents which relate specifically to the exact commercial form of the article to be sold: patents on plant varieties are perhaps the only common example. The right requested is closer to that given by a registered design. In some minds, this raises doubts whether there is a patentable invention there to be protected. Where there is, surely it could—and should—be defined more broadly?

What is the effect of patenting plant varieties?

What induces breeders to seek patents on their varieties, instead of—or, in some cases, as well as—protecting them by plant variety rights? For the breeder, there are disadvantages as well as advantages.

The main disadvantage is that US patent law (section 112) requires a full ('enabling') disclosure of the best method ('best mode') of carrying out the invention known to the inventor. Accordingly, the breeder has to make his line available to the public. In other patent fields, this is normally done by verbal description and drawings: but breeding processes are not describably repeatable to order. Thus the breeder may have to put seed of his line in a public depository, whence members of the public may request samples as soon as the patent is granted. This contrasts with PVP, where samples of seed are deposited, but are held in confidence for the full term of the right. Furthermore, to 'enable' a hybrid patent would apparently require depositing both parent lines. Sometimes hybrid seeds are deposited, on the theory that the hybrid can be reproduced from these by tissue culture. The counter-theory is that this does not 'enable' the 'best mode' which clearly is not tissue culture.

Advantages to the patentee are in the greater protection that patents give him. Thus, seed protected by PVP is subject to the 'breeder's privilege'. It may be freely crossed with other lines to produce new genetic combinations which may be refined into new varieties. No such privilege applies under patents. While most patent laws recognise an exemption permitting research into a patented invention, to test and improve it, US law does not. There the exemption is limited to 'philosophical inquiry'—something which in its nature a commercial firm never does.

If you buy a patented pure seed line from a patentee, you receive rights to use it as such seed would normally be used—that is to say, to plant it, harvest the crop and sell it for consumption. You do not get rights to multiply it—that is manufacture, which is reserved to the patentee. You could cross it with a line of your own, and select from the progeny. If you buy on the open market a patented hybrid, you can grow that out and select among the progeny. However, it is not common for patentees to market parent lines. If you obtain the material in some other way—by importing it from abroad where it is not patented, by selecting an offtype from a bag or from a field, by sheer chance (perhaps unlikely) in happening to select an almost identical material from a segregating population, or even by requesting the seed from the public depository where the patentee had placed it—your rights to do anything with it are extremely doubtful. Except in the last case, obtaining the seed from a depository, you are probably already in breach of the patentee's rights. Even with depository seed, it is not clear what you can do with it, other than look at it, and perhaps analyse the tissue (using RFLPs and so on). Probably you can grow it out, and look at the plants produced. Almost certainly you cannot multiply it, even experimentally. Perhaps you can test its combining ability by making test crosses: a patentee might well object to this, and would almost certainly be entitled to object to any subsequent research or development with the crosses so made.

Thus the rights given by a patent to a protected variety go well beyond the corresponding rights available under PVP. There is a serious question whether rights such as these properly fulfil the intention of the US Constitution for patents 'to promote science and the useful arts'. The invention that a plant variety represents is a particular combination of genes. Is it right that a patent on this combination, once granted, should prevent its use, not only for commercial use and profit, but also for research to develop further new and useful combinations? Does not this hold up progress rather than promoting it?

It is also to be noted that patents give breeders stronger rights against farmers than does PVP. Farmers who buy seed may expect to plant it and sell the crop for consumption. They have no right to save and replant—such as they retain under the new US PVP legislation—let alone any right to sell any of the crop for replanting, which would be inducing infringement.

Europe

The situation in Europe is somewhat different. As in the United States, before the last decades of this century, patents were granted for micro-organisms, but not often for other forms of life. Cases where no protection was given include the German *Rote Taube*[3] (Red Dove) where a major consideration was that the breeding process that led to the dove was not reproducible. The current normative law is that of the European Patent Office, to which 15 European countries now adhere: more are applying to join every year. To quote Article 53(b) of the European Patent Convention (EPC):

> European patents shall not be granted in respect of:
>
>> ... (b) plant or animal varieties or essentially biological processes for the production of plants or animals; this provision does not apply to microbiological processes or the products thereof.

What does this mean? It was first considered by the EPO Appeal Board in the *Ciba-Geigy* case (T49/83).[4] Here, the patentees had made an invention relating to a chemical seed coating, and one of the subclaims was to seed coated with the chemical specified. It

---

[3] Bundesgerichtshof, 27 March 1969, BGZH 52 at 74.
[4] *CIBA-GEIGY/Propagating material* [1979–85] EPOR 758.

was objected that such claims claimed plant varieties. The Board found otherwise. They distinguished plant varieties from plants. Exceptions from patentability are to be construed strictly—if the EPC was intended to exempt all plants from patentability, it would say so. Plant varieties are not protectable as such under the EPC because the UPOV system is more suitable for them.

> If plant varieties have been excluded from patent protection because specifically the achievement involved in breeding a new variety is to have its own form of protection, it is perfectly sufficient for *the exclusion to be left restricted*, in conformity with its wording, to cases in which plants are characterised precisely by the genetically determined peculiarities of their natural phenotype. In this respect there is no conflict between areas reserved for national protection of varieties and the field of application of the EPC. On the other hand *innovations which cannot be given the protection afforded to varieties are still patentable if the general prerequisites are met.*[5]

This decision was followed in T19/90 (*Onco-mouse*).[6] This was a case on a mouse to which a gene conferring cancer susceptibility had been transferred, thus having potential for use in more efficient testing of possible cancer cures (also, potentially, cutting down the number of animals used in such tests). The EPO Appeal Board decided that, as with plants, only animal varieties are excluded from protection, not animals as such. The more difficult question, what is an animal variety? was left as an exercise for the Examiner.

What about breeding processes? These are usually excluded as 'essentially biological processes' for the production of plants. Such processes are in principle judged case by case, taking into account the intervention of man in the process. 'The process has to be judged on the basis of the essence of the invention taking into account the totality of human intervention and its impact on the results to be achieved'.[7] The EPO considers crossing and selection to be 'essentially biological', but a step such as cell culture to maintain heterozygous parents can change a 'biological' process into a technical one.[8]

Thus, until recently, patents were regularly being granted in the EPO for transgenic plants. It seemed settled that plants and animals could be claimed in European patents, provided they were not produced by 'conventional breeding'. However, recent litigation in the European Patent Office has thrown this situation into confusion. This litigation is worth reviewing in some detail.

Opposition T356/93[9]

EP 242,236 (Plant Genetic Systems) describes a method of making plants resistant to the herbicide 'Basta', by inserting a transgene. The patent was granted with 44 claims, to processes, vectors, plant cells, plants, seed and so on. In February 1995, the EPO Technical Board of Appeal, in an opposition filed by Greenpeace, revoked six claims to plants and seeds. All other claims—including claims to plant cells—were allowed. The decision appeared to suggest that Article 53(b) EPC prohibited all claims 'embracing' plant or animal varieties.

This seemed to conflict with what had been thought to be the settled law, as set out above. Industry and the patent profession were disturbed, and protests were made to the EPO.

---

[5] *Emphasis added.*
[6] *HARVARD/Onco-mouse* [1990] EPOR 501.
[7] Paterson, *A Concise Guide to European Patents* at 125.
[8] T320/87 *LUBRIZOL/Hybrid plants* [1990] EPOR 173.
[9] *PLANT GENETIC SYSTEMS/Glutamine synthetase inhibitors* [1995] EPOR 357.

Accordingly in September 1995 the President of the EPO, under Article 112 EPC, put the following question to the Enlarged Board of Appeals:

> Does a claim which relates to plants or animals but wherein specific plant or animal varieties are not individually claimed contravene the prohibition on patenting in Article 53(b) EPC, if it embraces plant or animal varieties?

The Enlarged Board of Appeal, in Decision G03/95,[10] issued 27 November 1995, declined to consider this question. In their view, it does not arise from the decision in T356/93. Quoting from Decision G03/95 (Reason 4):

> The file record of [T356/93] shows that the objection to Claim 21 [seeds] ... was put by the opponent in two different ways:
>
> > (1) Claim 21 includes within its scope known plant varieties which have been genetically modified so as to be herbicide-resistant—see the working examples in the description of the patent. Because the claim embraces and thus confers protection upon such known plant varieties, it is not allowable under Article 53(b) EPC.
> >
> > (2) Claim 21 defines plants (whether or not they are 'plant varieties' in the sense of the UPOV Convention before they are genetically transformed) which have been genetically modified so that they are herbicide-resistant. This characteristic of genetic herbicide-resistance is distinctive and stable in succeeding generations of the plants. Thus *the claimed genetic modification itself makes the plants 'plant varieties'* in the sense of the revised UPOV Convention, 1991, and for this reason Claim 21 defines unpatentable subject-matter within the meaning of Article 53(b) EPC.
>
> ... In the view of the Enlarged Board of Appeal, the essential basis for the finding in this Decision [T356/93] ... corresponds to what is summarised above as objection (2) ... [not objection 1]. (Reason 5).[11]

Objection (2) is a new point (say the Enlarged Board). It does not conflict with any of the earlier cases. They only have jurisdiction in cases of conflict, and therefore cannot consider the question put to them. By implication, however, the answer to the question is no: claims in 'embracing' varieties do not necessarily contravene Article 53(b) EPC: T356/93 was wrongly interpreted as meaning that they did.

This decision is disappointing to those who hoped that the Enlarged Board would be able to clarify the meaning of the exclusion of 'varieties' from patentability. This will now await further cases on genetically modified plants before the Technical Appeal Board. At such cases, the following arguments may be expected:

> (1) (*For opponents*) As the Enlarged Board has failed to overrule it, Decision T356/93 stands. Cases with similar facts should be decided the same way. Accordingly, no claims to genetically modified plants can be granted, at least unless the patentee disclaims plant varieties.
>
> (2) (*For patentees*) The Enlarged Board did not approve objection 2 of T356/93. They specifically denied that they had the power to do this: 'objection (2) ... clearly concerns

---

[10]   OJ EPO 1996, 169; see further [1996] 7 EIPR 419.
[11]   *Emphasis added.*

an important point of law, but this point of law is not the subject of the question which the President has referred to the Enlarged Board' (Reason 8, second sentence). The decision in T356/93 stands alone, on its own merits.

However (patentees will argue) these merits are small. The basis of the decision in T356/93 (as explained by the Enlarged Board) is that transforming plant material (of any kind) by insertion of a single gene, stably reproduced, 'itself makes the plants "plant varieties" in the sense of the revised UPOV Convention, 1991'. This statement shows a profound misunderstanding of the nature of a UPOV plant variety. Such a variety *cannot* be characterised by a *single* stable gene. It is characterised by *essentially all* of its genes—at least, of those genes which express and determine plant phenotype. A plant grouping characterised by a single novel gene is a *generic* invention. It is not a plant variety, and cannot be protected as such. Once this is pointed out to a Board, and supported by proper expert evidence, claims to plants and seeds should be obtainable.

It remains to be seen which of these arguments will prevail. Perhaps the controversy will be resolved by the passing of the new Biotechnology Patenting Directive. This was rejected by the European Parliament in March 1995, but is now being presented again in modified form. This tries to make clear (but does it succeed?) that it is only plant and animal varieties 'as such' that may not be patented. While *de jure* the Directive could not alter the law of the European Patent Convention, *de facto* it may be expected to have a considerable influence (if only to encourage patents on plants to be filed by the national route).

Meanwhile it is sad to reflect on the tendency of the EPO to go astray when dealing with plant varieties. The conclusion that plant material containing a single stable gene inevitably constitutes a UPOV plant variety is as strange to plant breeders as the finding in T320/87 (*Lubrizol*) that a hybrid cannot be a variety because it does not reproduce stably. No decision in this area since T49/83 (*Ciba-Geigy*) has thought about the reason behind the exclusion of plant varieties in order to decide how to interpret it. The reason, surely, is that the separate UPOV system of protection was provided for plant varieties, and it was felt that innovations protectable in UPOV were better so protected than by patents. It cannot follow from this that innovations not protectable by UPOV (including generic inventions characterised by a single recombinant gene) should also be denied protection under patents. To re-emphasise what was said in T49/83, 'innovations which cannot be given the protection afforded to varieties are still patentable if the general prerequisites are met'. That is what the European law should be—what many hope it will shortly be proved (or changed) to be.

It may be noted that there is a clear exemption in European law for experimentation on an invention: for example, to test or improve it. Such acts would not become patent infringement until they passed from experimentation into commercial development and preparation to market: and not even then if the material to be marketed was not what was claimed in the patent.

TRIPs

There is not space in this article to deal in detail with the position in patenting plants in all countries in the world. While most developed countries outside the United States and Europe allow patent protection for plants at least as strong as that obtainable in Europe, many developing countries give lesser protection. A number of laws in such countries (for example, the laws in Malaysia, Indonesia and Thailand) are very similar in terms to European law, in excluding protection for plant and animal varieties and biological processes. They are likely to be interpreted, however, to exclude all patents on plants or animals—'variety' will be taken to mean simply type' or 'kind', rather than having the specific meaning of a UPOV variety.

The laws of all countries, however, are coming under powerful external pressures to change. The Uruguay Round of world trade talks extended its scope to cover many new areas, including intellectual property for the first time. The successful conclusion of the talks brought into being a new intellectual property code, known as TRIPs (Trade-related Intellectual Property provisions). All countries who wish to be members of the World Trade Organization, with the trading advantages that this brings, must conform their laws—within specified transition periods, typically five or ten years—to the TRIPs code.

The effect of TRIPs will be considerable. The United States has already made major changes to its law as a consequence—resetting the patent term, taking account of inventive acts in other countries. Europe may also need to make changes, or abandon changes proposed. It is argued, for example, that it would conflict with TRIPs to allow farmers to save patented seed for replanting.

The provisions on patents are far-reaching. In principle, under TRIPs Article 27.1:

> ... patents shall be available for any inventions ... in all fields of technology, provided they are new, involve an inventive step and are capable of industrial application ... patents shall be available and patent rights enjoyable without discrimination as to the place of invention, the field of technology and whether products are imported or locally produced.

This broad principle is subject to exceptions. Article 27.2 allows parties to deny patent protection to inventions to protect *ordre public* or morality. This includes protecting human animal or plant health or avoiding serious damage to the environment. However, protection may only be excluded where it is *necessary to prevent commercial exploitation* of the invention in the territory for such reasons. Moral disapproval by some sections of the community is insufficient.

Specific subject-matter exceptions are set out in Article 27.3. Parties may exclude from patentability:

(a) certain types of treatment of humans or animals;
(b) 'plants and animals other than micro-organisms, and essentially biological processes for the production of plants or animals other than non-biological and microbiological processes. However, *parties shall provide for the protection of plant varieties* either by patents or by an effective *sui generis* system or by any combination thereof'.[12]

Thus TRIPs recognises the importance of plant varieties, and requires members of the WTO to protect them. It does not however prescribe exactly how this is to be done, and almost seems to favour the use of patents. Thus Mexico, for example, to fulfil its WTO obligations (and also as a result of the NAFTA pact) has changed its law to allow patenting, not of all plants, but of plant varieties only (the exact opposite of European law).

What does the term 'effective *sui generis* system' mean? It clearly includes UPOV systems of protection. One theory is that it was intended as a convenient way of making reference to systems of protection based either on UPOV '78 or on UPOV '91. Be that as it may, it has

---

[12] *Emphasis added.*

caused much puzzling among circles who distrust the extension of intellectual property rights to plants. Can a special system be devised which would lack (or minimise) the disadvantages which they detect in conventional systems? Can they construct a system which would reduce dependence on Northern multinationals, preserve biodiversity, implement farmers' rights and the benefit-sharing provisions of the Biodiversity Convention? The hope, and at the same time the difficulty, of devising such a scheme, which could at the same time satisfy the Council of TRIPs that it gave effective protection to breeders, is likely to delay the introduction of rights over varieties in a number of developing countries.

Another factor delaying such introduction is a further term of Article 27.3(b) omitted above. This reads: 'This provision [27.3(b)] shall be reviewed four years after the entry into force of this Agreement'. Northern industrial and professional circles expect this review to lead to the limiting or even removal of 27.3(b), to compel all countries to grant patents on plants and animals. Many developing countries look for the exclusion to be confirmed or widened. The stage is set for a battle royal in 1999.

Conclusion

Plant variety rights give protection for specific individual innovations. Patent rights are needed for generic innovations, such as plants containing transgenes. The patent law of the United States gives breeders complete freedom to patent plants and plant varieties. It may be that the protection offered goes beyond what is necessary, or perhaps even desirable. In Europe, protection may be more balanced: but the picture is obscured by current confusion as to what the law actually is. In countries where neither patents nor plant variety protection are yet available, the World Trade Organization will promote introduction of at least one of these systems: many countries may delay such introduction until its requirements are confirmed.

The Morality of Biotech Patents: Differing Legal Obligations in Europe?

[1997] 6 EIPR 315

RICHARD FORD
Student, Nottingham Law School

There is potentially serious confusion as to the obligations of states concerning the moral problems of patenting the processes and products of biotechnology in Europe. The prolonged wrangling over European Patent Office cases *HARVARD/Onco-mouse*,[1] *PLANT GENETIC SYSTEMS/Glutamine synthetase inhibitors ('PGS')*[2] and *Hormone Relaxin Opposition*[3] may be overshadowed by even greater disputes on the horizon.

Until now, the moral criteria for European patent applications have been contained in Article 53 (a) EPC, and in the implementing national legislation of Contracting States. However, with the arrival of a new version of the draft EU Directive on the legal protection of biotechnological inventions, and of Article 27.2 of the TRIPs Agreement, adopted as part of the 'Final Agreement' of the GATT Uruguay Round, confusion as to the obligations of European states is possible. This article explores the differences between these current provisions, and how such conflicting obligations give rise to the problem of how Member States can comply with them all. Moreover, it seeks to introduce a view that the European Convention on Human Rights ('ECHR') should be the legal basis of a moral examination of the patent application. This is based on the argument that ECHR obligations are binding on subsequent international conventions.[4] If such a view is tenable, it follows that the morality exceptions of the EPC (Art. 53 (a)), of the draft EU Directive (Art. 9) and of the TRIPs agreement (Art. 27.2) must not contain anything that derogates from European Member States' obligations under the ECHR.

Article 27.2 of TRIPs arose from widespread disagreement on the issue of patentability. The United States, Japan, the Nordic countries and Switzerland pressed for no or minimal exceptions to patentable subject-matter, while the EU and a host of developing countries wished to exclude patents for inventions which would be contrary to public policy or health.[5] Article 27.2 in its final compromise form reads:

> Members may exclude from patentability inventions, the prevention within their territory of the commercial exploitation of which is necessary to protect public order or morality,

---

[1] T19/90 [1990] EPOR 501.

[2] T356/93 [1995] EPOR 357.

[3] OJ EPO 1995, 388.

[4] This view is proposed by Professor Deryck Beyleveld and Professor Roger Brownsword at the University of Sheffield, and elaborated in their publication, *Mice, Morality and Patents*, Common Law Institute of Intellectual Property (1993) pp. 68–71.

[5] See Michelle McGrath, 'The Patent Provisions in TRIPs: Protecting Reasonable Remuneration for Services Rendered—Or the Latest Development in Western Colonialism?' [1996] 7 EIPR 401.

including to protect human, animal or plant life or health or to avoid serious prejudice to the environment, provided that such exclusion is not made merely because the exploitation is prohibited by domestic law.

There are distinct differences between this and Article 53 (a) EPC and Article 9 of the draft EU Directive on the legal protection of biotechnologial inventions. Article 53 (a) provides that patents shall not be granted for:

inventions the publication or exploitation of which would be contrary to *ordre public* or morality, provided that the exploitation shall not be deemed to be so merely because it is prohibited by law or regulation in some or all of the Contracting States.

Article 9 of the draft EU Directive splits into two paragraphs. It reads:

(1) Inventions shall be considered unpatentable where exploitation would be contrary to public policy or morality; however, exploitation shall not be deemed to be so contrary merely because it is prohibited by law or regulation.

(2) On the basis of paragraph 1, the following shall be considered unpatentable:
(a) methods of human treatment involving germ line gene therapy
(b) processes for modifying the genetic identity of animals which are likely to cause them suffering or physical handicaps without any substantial benefit to man or animal, and also animals resulting from such processes, wherever the suffering or physical handicaps inflicted on the animals concerned are disproportionate to the objective pursued.

Difference between Article 53 (a) EPC and Article 9 Draft Directive[6]

On first reading, Article 9 does not seem to be radically different from Article 53 (a). In Article 9 (1), the only two real changes from the Article 53 (a) text are the omission of the word 'publication', and the use of the phrase 'public policy' replacing '*ordre public*'. Article 9 (2), however, is a fresh provision intended to provide guidance on the meaning of the new phrase 'public policy'. Instead, it perhaps creates some additional uncertainty to that already experienced in trying to interpret Article 53 (a) EPC. It is recognised that any changes in wording are bound to cause some uncertainty, as the existing precedent established by the EPO under the EPC is substantially thrown away. However, Article 9 (2) in fact adds some new doubt about what is and is not patentable in comparison to Article 53 (a). As a result, if Article 9 of the draft EU Directive is implemented in its current form, this lack of harmonisation with Article 53 (a) could be seen as giving rise to conflicting obligations for States which were members of both the EU and the EPC.

The effect of the first change in Article 9 (1), omitting the word 'publication', is to remove the discretion that the European Patent Office ('EPO') has in looking at the morality of the methods used to create the invention as well as the subsequent use of the invention once a patent has been granted.

The second alteration may appear helpful, because interpreting *ordre public* in the EPC has proved notoriously troublesome. Indeed, guidance as to what this new phrase means is in paragraph 2. However, the relationship between paragraph 1 and paragraph 2 is unclear.

---

[6] Reference has been made to the Opinion of the Sheffield Institute of Biotechnological Law and Ethics ('SIBLE') at the University of Sheffield on the draft proposal for the Directive.

Article 9 (2) is 'on the basis of' Article 9 (1), which is a vague way of defining the relationship between the two, and, in particular, whether Article 9 (2) represents an exhaustive or a non-exhaustive list of examples of activities which will be regarded as being contrary to public policy and morality. It appears that these are examples which the drafters consider unequivocally contrary to public policy or morality. However, this does not preclude further examples from being cited.

Moreover, because the exclusions listed in Article 9 (2) are made 'on the basis of' Article 9 (1), the cost-benefit analysis that the application of Article 9 (2) (b) requires is essentially a calculation of public policy/moral costs and benefits. The 'substantial and proportionate benefit to man or animal' which is needed to justify processes that cause suffering and physical handicaps to animals is a proportionality test based on that in *Onco-mouse*. This failure to provide any further guidance than the case law of the EPO is not in line with the Commission's aim of establishing conformity of practice.

Article 9 (2) contains further provisions which are different from Article 53 (a). Article 9 (2) (a) appears to rule out the specific example of germ line gene therapy for all time as it is considered so contrary to public policy or morality. This inherent presumption that the method should always be regarded as unpatentable is undesirable since, if a scientist, possibly in the relatively near future, developed a method of gene therapy which alleviated some inherited conditions in an individual born with the problem, then the use of this technique would be seen as worse in a moral sense than the introduction of the cure into the germ line cell.

In addition, Recital 21's reference to Article 9 (2) (b), assessing the concept of morality by weighing the benefit of the invention against 'any objections based on the fundamental principles of law', creates interpretative difficulties as to what exactly are 'fundamental principles of law'.

Overall, the provisions of Article 9 of the draft Directive are sufficiently different from those of Article 53 (a) of the EPC for there to be potential confusion as to the obligations of states which are members of both the EU and the EPC. Prima facie, although the EU Directive has no direct impact on the EPC, it would have been preferable to retain the existing 'morality' provisions of the EPC to allow the development of a single body of European law on the point appropriate for all patents. The less the EU and EPC provisions differ, the less the potential for confusion. However, the provisions of TRIPs add complications to the position.

Differences with Article 27.2 TRIPs

There are two main differences between Article 27.2 of TRIPs, and Article 53 (a) of the EPC and Article 9 of the draft EU Directive. First, the exclusion to 'protect human, animal or plant life or health' in Article 27.2 corresponds with the Japanese and the developing countries' suggestions. The exclusion to avoid 'serious prejudice to the environment' is a result of the increasing concern with environmental issues.[7] Although the drafting of this last exclusion is restrictive (non-patentability can only be based on a 'serious' prejudice to the environment), it represents a step which may influence future legislation on the matter.

Although Article 27.2, as a TRIPs provision, takes priority over both Article 9 and Article 53 (a), the fact that there is an element of compulsion in the wording of Article 53 (a) and

---

[7] The EPO Board of Appeal has, however, in its decision on *PGS*, stated that inventions which 'seriously prejudice the environment' would be contrary to 'ordre public': but in the specific case there was not sufficient evidence of this (paragraph 18.7 of its decision).

Article 9 (Members 'shall' exclude) and not in Article 27.2 (Members 'may' exclude), has been seized on, with countries like America unhappy with the international exclusions in TRIPs, pointing out that there is no necessity to apply this test. Article 27.2 thus does not have to be incorporated into national law. However, European Member States wishing to enact legislation to comply with TRIPs will find that, if they do so, Article 9 and Article 53 (a) would not meet their obligations under Article 27.2. Although in the Preamble to the draft Directive it is stated that the Directive is 'compatible' with TRIPs,[8] it seems clear that Article 9 is not in line with Article 27.2.

The problem is quite profound. As members of the EPC, national Member States have an obligation to align their laws in accordance with the EPC. There is a similar obligation for Member States of the EU, by virtue of the Treaty of Rome, to align their laws in accordance with EU directives once implemented. The lack of consistency between Article 9 of the draft Directive and Article 53 (a) of the EPC and resultant problems of state obligations if the draft Directive was implemented have been explored above. Added to this, neither Article 9 nor Article 53 (a) fulfils national Member States' obligations under TRIPs if they chose to implement Article 27.2.

It is thus clear that the situation needs attention. Certainly, Article 9 of the draft EU Directive requires redrafting to be consistent with Article 27.2 of TRIPs. The Commission could, perhaps, produce guidelines (which were not directly effective) based on Article 27.2, which would have the advantage of a degree of flexibility yet recognise the need for a moral criterion. If countries then decided to implement Article 27.2 into their national laws, it would only be Article 53 (a) of the EPC which would be failing to meet the obligations under TRIPs. There might then be a case for amending Article 53 (a).

Obligations under the ECHR?

Beyleveld and Brownsword argue that the moral criteria in European patent applications must be a rights-based approach with the ECHR as its core. Essentially, the argument runs as follows: Contracting States to the EPC did not have a free hand when they were signing up because they were already signatories and bound by the ECHR. This is because a human rights convention, such as the ECHR, is not like any other agreement, in that it accords protected human interests a special status. Respect for human rights prevails therefore in interpreting all subsequent conventions. This would be true even if there was no express morality provision (such as Article 53 (a), Article 9 and Article 27.2) in the subsequent treaties if the treaty presented morally problematic implications (such as (but not exclusively) the ethical questions surrounding biotechnology patenting).

Furthermore, even if there were no morality provision in any of the EPC, the draft EU Directive or TRIPs, it is argued that Contracting States could still not agree to anything which would be contrary to their obligations under the ECHR. This is because there is no need to incorporate the ECHR into national legislation for it to be binding on national law or any treaties to which a state signs up. This is based on the premise that the ECHR has become generally accepted as part of international law. As *some* signatories of TRIPs and Member States of the EU were already signatories of the ECHR, the implication is that *all* the signatories of the subsequent convention were bound by the terms agreed in the first.

Therefore, in questions of patent applications concerning human tissue or processes, for example those involved in the Human Genome Project, the morality 'test' has to be one in line with the human rights afforded by the ECHR. When questions of morality concern

---

[8] Draft Directive, page 10, paragraph 35 of the Preamble.

animals and plants, such as in *Onco-mouse* and *PGS*, then the question turns to an examination under the ECHR as to whether animals and plants have rights under the same principles. The ECHR *has* to be taken into account as the basis of the morality test in all instances.

Patent practitioners are most unlikely to see such a binding connection between the ECHR and subsequent patent conventions or treaties. They view patent law as a technical commercial tool with little or nothing to do with questions of morality. The Examiners at the EPO, and many patent practitioners, have a scientific background and are not sufficiently trained in philosophy or jurisprudence to tackle the moral issues surrounding patent law. At best, they cite the intention of the drafters of the EPC as being to apply a morality test very restrictively, and, at worst, they consider that such issues are best tackled by the national safeguards against immoral exploitation (although these differ widely) outside the domain of patent law.

However, such arguments miss the fundamental point that failure to apply a vigorous moral assessment would be illegal if the ECHR is binding on subsequent international conventions. If such a connection is tenable, then Article 9 of the draft EU Directive and Article 53 (a) of the EPC (and for that matter, any provisions under subsequent international treaties) would have to be interpreted in line with the ECHR, or at least there must be recourse to it in morally problematic patent applications. The ECHR would thus be the basis of the morality test in Europe.

Regarding Article 27.2 of the TRIPs, it might be argued that the ECHR should be confined to the European sphere, and thus would not impinge on treaties such as TRIPs which had non-European states as signatories. However, as is argued below, the ECHR has become an accepted part of international law, so would be applicable to TRIPs. At any rate, the ECHR is based on the UN Declaration of Human Rights. Thus TRIPs should be drafted in line with this, on the same connecting premise.

The real issue in such a view is whether the ECHR, as a human rights convention, is indeed a 'special' convention in that it accords human rights a special protected status. Can a previous treaty impinge its provisions on to subsequent treaties in this way? Articles 30, 31 and 32 of the Vienna Convention on the Law of Treaties 1969, which deals with the interpretation of treaties, provides a useful examination of this view in the area of international law.

Article 30 deals with the relationship between subsequent treaties if their obligations are inconsistent with previous treaties. In this situation, the implied repeal principle operates that it was the intention of the drafters of the second treaty to modify the principles of the first. However, it seems wholly unlikely that the drafters of the subsequent treaties (the EPC, TRIPs) intended to modify the principles of the ECHR. Indeed, it would not be possible to modify a part of the ECHR unless the convention was completely renegotiated—a total withdrawal from the ECHR would have to be undertaken if a state wished to agree to anything in a subsequent treaty that derogated from ECHR principles.

Article 31, dealing with the general rules of interpretation of treaties, may be of greater assistance. Article 31 (3) states (taken with the first part):

> There shall be taken into account, together with the context: ... (c) any relevant rules of international law applicable in the relations between the parties.

A number of questions arise from this:

(1) Can it be said that the ECHR is a generally accepted part of international law? It seems likely that it is, since most provisions, if not all, have become generally accepted in

the international law arena, and human rights considerations have developed very significantly since the ECHR was implemented in the 1950s. It is another thing to say, however, that Member States are bound by the detail of every decision of the European Court of Human Rights, so the extent to which the ECHR is fully accepted is unclear.

(2) Following on from this, does the ECHR create considerations which are applicable to conventions such as the EPC or TRIPs, which patent lawyers would regard as commercial tools? Patent lawyers would argue that the patent system is not a forum for deciding on human rights. To attempt to make a direct and legally enforceable correlation between the concept of morality of patent conventions and the concept of morality of the ECHR is tortuous. The ECHR deals specifically with human rights and there is no reason why this should necessarily form the basis of the interpretation of morality when looking at the patentability of inventions.

Indeed, patent lawyers may argue that every moral question is not necessarily dependent on taking into account the ECHR; one single concept of morality (that based on the ECHR) cannot apply across the board in every legal document or every walk of life. The ECHR only has a bearing on those laws which relate directly to human rights. With regard to the standard of morality, one dogmatic stance is not sensible. An exclusive rights-based approach to morality does not take into account other 'ethical' considerations. For example, economic and social aspects of biotechnology from a utilitarian point of view could be relevant 'ethical' considerations in the commercial environment in which the patent conventions operate. There would be no objection to using the ECHR as a basis for a separate interpretation of these difficult moral problems, not necessarily dependent on an interpretation of the ECHR. However, the test of morality should not *have* to be dependent on it or indeed have to be a rights-based approach at all, as argued by Beyleveld and Brownsword.

These arguments, however, significantly fail to appreciate that the possible rights of humans, animals and plants must, as a matter of principle, be examined in the moral criteria of patent applications. There is *already a requirement* to look at rights in these patent conventions, as they *have* to be interpreted in the light of the ECHR—it is not just a preferred option that a rights-based approach should be used. Other ethical considerations (such as the ethical economic and social circumstances of the biotechnology industry) can be considered in addition, so long as what is decided does not contravene rights derived from the ECHR.

Patent practitioners may, however, also cite the intention of drafters of patent treaties as being that morality exceptions would always be restrictively interpreted. Regarding the EPC, two former Comptrollers of the UK Patent Office,[9] who were involved in the preparatory work, confirm that the intention was always that the morality exceptions would only be invoked where it was virtually 'inconceivable' that the invention could be put to a moral use and the invention was clearly 'abhorrent'.[10] Thus, the test for morality would *not* be based on the ECHR. The relevance of a Contracting State's intentions is dealt with in Article 32, containing supplementary means of interpretation. This reads:

Recourse may be had to supplementary means of interpretation, including the preparatory work of the treaty and the circumstances of its conclusion, in order to confirm

---

[9] Edward Armitage and Ivor Davis. See their argument in *Patents and Morality in Perspective*, Common Law Institute of Intellectual Property (1994), a direct response to *Mice, Morality and Patents*, note 4 above.

[10] The EPO's existing guidelines for Substantive Examination c-IV3.1 state that 'a fair test to apply is to consider whether it is probable that the public in general would regard the invention as so abhorrent that the grant of a patent right would be inconceivable'. The classic example given is that of a letter bomb. These date from the implementation of the EPC.

the meaning resulting from the application of Article 31, or to determine the meaning when the interpretation according to Article 31:

    (a) leaves the meaning ambiguous or obscure; or

    (b) leads to a result which is manifestly absurd or unreasonable.

Thus, when it is unclear what interpretation a provision is to be given (i.e. when to apply the morality 'test'), reference can be had (though there is no compulsion) to the preparatory work of the treaty. Armitage and Davis say that the intention of the drafters involved in the preparatory work was that Article 53 (a) should be applied restrictively. The problem is, however, that they did not specifically contemplate genetic engineering and biotechnology. The position is thus transformed into one where it is necessary to guess at what the intention of the drafters would have been had they envisaged such modern-day scenarios.

(3) The question is, then, given that the intention of the drafters regarding genetic engineering and biotechnology is strictly unknown, does this mean that the rival view of a binding link with the ECHR should prevail? Arguably, yes, particularly since the logical continuation of the view that the ECHR binds Member States in relation to the EPC is that it also binds them in relation to the Vienna Convention. In other words, whatever the Vienna Convention says about interpretative principles must be subject to respect for human rights as required by the ECHR. If this is so, the intentions of the drafters would be superseded in any case. Thus, despite scrutiny, the argument that the moral criteria surrounding the area of European patent applications must be based on the provisions of the ECHR remains viable.

Conclusions

The implications of the points raised here are significant. The obligations of European states regarding the moral criteria for patent applications are conflicting between the EPC, the draft EU Directive on the legal protection of biotechnological inventions and TRIPs. European states wishing to implement TRIPs, in particular, would be unable to reconcile these differing provisions. The scope for litigation against states is huge, given the resulting uncertainty. Moreover, if the ECHR is binding on these subsequent provisions, then there is another question of non-conformity by Member States. European 'Greens', animal welfare supporters and human rights' campaigners, who have raised objections to cases such as *Onco-mouse*, *PGS*, and *Hormone Relaxin* in the past, may now have substantially greater scope to appeal against grants of morally problematic patents.

Novelty under the EPC and the Patents Act 1977*

[1996] 9 EIPR 511

RICHARD DOBLE
London

A Unified View of Merrel Dow and Mobil

The purpose of this comment is to explore the circumstances in which prior use or disclosure of a product or process makes 'matter' form part of 'the state of the art' such that an 'invention' relating to that 'matter' is deprived of novelty—Article 52(2) EPC and the corresponding section 2(2) of the 1977 UK Patents Act.

The EPC (and also the 1977 Act) refer to 'inventions' being 'new' if they do not form 'part of the state of the art' and refer to the 'state of the art' as constituting 'a product, a process, information about either or anything else' that has been 'made available to the public'.

At the outset it should be noted that the Court of Appeal have held[1] that the 1977 Act (and *a fortiori* the EPC):

provided a complete code dealing with the application for and grant of a patent and thus displaced any residual common law element which previously had been preserved by succeeding statutes,

and that:

we should not assume that the new Act is just the old English laws re-written, or that statements of principle or passing observations on individual questions can now be culled from the reported cases and applied without reserve ... This is all the more so given that the source of the Act is a treaty...'[2]

Accordingly it is necessary to consider novelty without being bound by the common law assumptions which have arisen under the earlier cases.

---

* The author acknowledges with thanks the support and assistance of Langner Parry and particularly Iain C. Baillie in the production of an earlier version of this comment.
[1] Purchas LJ in *Genentech Inc.'s Patent* [1989] RPC 198.
[2] *Ibid.*, Mustill LJ, at 258.

Merrell Dow

The Court of Appeal held[3] that a metabolite produced by taking the patented antihistamine terfenadine had been made available to the public by the previous administration of the drug and that a subsequent patent for the previously undiscovered metabolite was invalid. The patentee Merrell Dow had merely discovered the composition of something that had already been made and used and discoveries as such are unpatentable.

Their decision has recently been upheld by the House of Lords[4] but on the ground of anticipation by prior publication rather than by prior use. The defendant's counsel argued that the claim to the metabolite was anticipated by the prior use in clinical trials despite the lack of knowledge it conveyed on the ground that the phrase 'all matter' in section 2(2) of the 1977 Act must include products or processes which conveyed no information about themselves—otherwise why make separate mention of 'information about either'?[5] However this argument was rejected on the ground that section 2(2) is one of the sections of the 1977 Act which was intended to have the same effect as the corresponding provisions of the EPC—and Article 54 EPC requires that *the invention* must have been made available to the public in order to constitute anticipation.

Accordingly it was held that the invention (defined as 'the making of the acid metabolite within the human body by the ingestion of terfenadine'[6]) was not anticipated by the administration of terfenadine during clinical trials.

In this connection Lord Hoffmann stated:

> It is important to note that anticipation by use relies solely upon the fact that volunteers in the clinical trials took terfenadine and therefore made the acid metabolite. There is no suggestion in the Agreed Statement of Facts and Issues that the volunteers were also at liberty to analyse the terfenadine to analyse its composition. If it was open to them to do so, they would have been in the same position as if they had read the terfenadine specification and the arguments for anticipation by use would have been the same as anticipation by disclosure.[7]

Regarding the objection of anticipation by prior publication, Lord Hoffmann considered whether the description was sufficient to make the product part of the state of the art:

> For many purposes obviously not. It would not enable anyone to work the invention in the form of isolating or synthesising the acid metabolite. But for the purpose of working the invention by making the acid metabolite in the body by ingesting terfenadine, I think it plainly was. *It enabled the public to work the invention by making the acid metabolite in their livers.* The fact that they would not have been able to describe the chemical reaction in these terms does not mean that they were not working the invention. *Whether or not a person is working a product invention is an objective fact independent of what he knows or thinks about what he is doing.*[8]

Hence anticipation by prior publication was upheld. He acknowledged that 'the position

[3]   *Merrell Dow v Norton and Penn* [1995] RPC 233.
[4]   SRIS C/82/95; see also [1996] RPC 76 and, for a critique, above at 480.
[5]   *Ibid.*, at 8, final paragraph.
[6]   *Ibid.*, at 5, paragraph 4.
[7]   *Ibid.*, at final paragraph.
[8]   *Ibid.*, at 14 (*emphasis added*).

may be different when the invention is a use for a product; in such a case, a person may only be working the invention when he is using it for the patented purpose' as in the *Mobil* case.[9]

It is interesting to speculate how prior use of terfenadine by members of the public under no constraint regarding analysis would have affected the patentability of the metabolite. It is submitted that a claim to the acid metabolite *simpliciter* would have been anticipated because the invention would have been the product and the product had been made available (albeit with no information about even its existence).[10] Would a claim to the acid metabolite for use in therapy or to a pharmaceutical composition comprising the acid metabolite also be anticipated by such use? Clearly the UK courts would be reluctant to allow such a claim by the patentee of the originating drug because it would have the practical effect of extending the patentee's monopoly on that drug without any corresponding benefit to the public in terms of a new teaching.

It is submitted that the reasoning of the Court of Appeal that the claim to the acid metabolite was not directed to an invention but to a discovery of the way in which a previously disclosed invention works still stands. The objection of anticipation by prior use which was accepted by the Courts of Appeal was only rejected by the House of Lords on the narrow ground that the volunteers in the clinical trials were not free to subject their bodies to analysis. No criticism was made of the lower court's reasoning, which is consistent with numerous decisions of the EPO to the effect that the categories in Article 52(2) (including 'discoveries' and 'scientific theories') which are not to be regarded as inventions are claimed 'as such' (Article 52(3)) and are therefore excluded from patentability if the only distinction over the prior art lies in one of the 'non-invention' categories of Article 52(2). Hence such a claim, being directed to a 'discovery' 'as such' would be excluded from patentability.

The UK and also the corresponding German decisions on anticipation of the metabolite by the Terfenadine patent have been criticised as being inconsistent with the *Friction reducing additive* decision (see below) and with other case law of the EPO by Vossius *et al.*,[11] who compared the occurrence of metabolic products in the liver with the occurrence of undiscovered products in nature—for example, bacteria in the soil. These latter products are held to be unavailable to the public until isolated. However, a distinction can be drawn on the basis that unlike the situation in the *Friction reducing additive* case, the effect of the metabolite would be made apparent by carrying out the teaching of the Terfenadine patent, thereby making the invention available (see paragraph 3.2 of T208/88, below). If the administration of Terfenadine had resulted in a multiplicity of metabolites, of which only a small number were effective, then it is submitted that the discovery of one of these could result in a separate invention which possessed independent novelty.

MOBIL/Friction Reducing Additive[12] and BAYER/Plant Growth Regulating Agent[13]

Both these cases related to the question of anticipation by a prior publication. In the *Friction reducing additive* case, a prior publication disclosed an additive for use as a rust inhibitor and the patentees wished to obtain claims directed to the use of the same compound for reducing friction. The means of realisation were the same in the prior art document and in the claim so that at first sight the only novelty lay in the intention of the user. In the *Plant growth*

---

[9] G02/88 *MOBIL/Friction reducing additive* [1990] EPOR 73; see below.
[10] See Decision T300/86 *RCA/TV receiver* [1994] EPOR 339, below.
[11] [1994] 3 EIPR 130 to 139 at p. 139.
[12] Decision G02/88, Note 9 above.
[13] Decision G06/88 *Bayer/Plant growth regulating agent* [1990] EPOR 257.

regulating agent case, the prior published document described the use of certain compounds for influencing plant growth, whereas the claims submitted by the applicant defined 'use of (certain compounds) for controlling fungi and for preventive fungus control'.[14]

Accordingly the following question was submitted to the Enlarged Board of Appeal:

> (iii) is a claim to the use of a compound for a particular non-medical purpose novel for the purpose of Article 54 EPC, having regard to a prior publication which discloses the use of that compound for different non-medical purpose, so that the only novel feature in the claim is the purpose for which the compound is used?

A similar question was posed in the *Plant growth regulating agent* case. In both cases the Board replied in the affirmative, and applied the Protocol on Article 69 EPC to the interpretation of the 'use' claims in question.

The Board stated:

> ... the claim in question should properly be construed, having regard to the Protocol to Article 69 EPC, as implicitly including the following functional technical feature: that the named compounds, when used in accordance with the described means of realisation, *in fact achieve the effect* (ie. perform the function) of controlling fungus. Such a functional technical feature is a technical feature which qualifies the invention: and the use claim is properly to be considered as a claim containing technical features both to the physical entity (the compound and its nature), as to a physical activity (the means of realisation). In other words, when following the method of interpretation of claims set out in the Protocol, what is required in the context of the claim to the 'use of a compound A for purpose B' is that such a claim should not be interpreted literally, as only including by way of technical features 'the compound' and 'the means of realisation of purpose B'; *it should be interpreted (in appropriate cases) as also including as a technical feature the function of achieving purpose B, because this is the technical result.* Such a method of interpretation, in view of the Enlarged Board, is in accordance with the object and intention of the Protocol to Article 69 EPC.[15]

Similarly, in Decision G06/88, the Board stated:

> Thus with such a claim, where a particular technical effect which underlies such use is described in the patent, having regard to the Protocol, the proper interpretation of the claim will require that a functional feature should be implied into the claim as a technical feature; for example, *that the compound actually achieves the particular effect.*[16]

The Enlarged Board of appeal specifically repudiated the concept of subjective novelty (that is, that novelty could lie in the new intention in the mind of the user) as a basis for their decision.

In Decision T208/88,[17] preceding G06/88, the Board of Appeal stated:

> 3.2 ... if a skilled person unaware of the invention had in fact observed a culture exhibiting an uncharacteristic growth process, he could have sought the cause—had he

---

[14] *Ibid.*, paragraph 7.1.
[15] Note 9 above, paragraph 9 (*emphasis added*).
[16] Note 12 above, paragraph 7 (*emphasis added*).
[17] *BAYER/Plant growth regulation* [1989] EPOR 323.

reflected on the matter at all—among various factors such as the particular properties of the soil, the time or type of cultivation, climate, fertilisation, etc. The public was thus unable—either by reading (1) or by executing its teaching—clearly to identify the essential character of the claimed invention, namely the growth-regulating effect of the compounds (I).

Thus the 'inventions' covered by the use claims did not form part of the 'state of the art' because the technical effect (namely fungus control and friction reduction respectively) was not previously made available in the sense that executing the teaching of the prior document would not lead the skilled person to its cause.

Hence, it is submitted, a 'use of X for purpose Y' invention, being limited to effect Y, is only anticipated by a prior teaching which, when executed, would enable the skilled person to identify X as the cause of Y, the cause being an integral part of the invention. It is clear that an 'invention' must, when the wording of the claim permits, be regarded as an abstract concept including not only the product or process features of the claim but also, in appropriate cases, the technical effect in the sense of the *Mobil* decision.

Before considering the conditions under which disclosure of an 'invention' might make it 'available to the public' it is necessary to consider the provisions of the 1977 Act and the EPC which relate to novelty but without reference to making available to the public.

Unpublished Earlier Applications—Article 54(3) EPC and Section 2(3) of the 1977 Act

Article 54(3) EPC refers to 'the content' of unpublished European patent applications as filed as forming 'state of the art' such as to negate novelty of an invention in a later application. The *ICI/Pyridine herbicides* decision[18] involved a claim to herbicidal pyridine compounds, certain of which were alleged to be disclosed in a co-pending European application which had not been published at the priority date of the claim but which had an earlier priority date and was therefore citable under Article 54(3) EPC.

Two starting compounds required to produce the herbicides disclosed in the cited earlier European patent application were disclosed in the patent literature and in an article in the Journal of Organic Chemistry but there were no specific instructions in the cited earlier European application as to how to prepare the required starting materials.

The Board of Appeal held that the claim was not anticipated because the alleged anticipatory compounds were not effectively disclosed:

It is the view of the Board that a document does not effectively disclose a chemical compound, even though it states the structure and the steps by which it is produced, if the skilled person is unable to find out from the document or from common general knowledge how to obtain the required starting materials or intermediate. Information, which can only be obtained after a comprehensive search is not to be regarded as part of common general knowledge.[19]

Although only the conclusions are stated explicitly, it is suggested that the reasoning was as follows:

---

[18] T206/83 [1986] EPOR 232.
[19] *Ibid.*, paragraph 11.

(1) a previous application must '*specifically disclose*' '*elements of the invention* for which priority is claimed' to confer priority;[20]

(2) an invented compound cannot be specifically disclosed in a document unless publication of that document would make the compound 'available to the public';

(3) a compound cannot be 'made available' if the skilled man cannot *make* the compound, if necessary using his common general knowledge.

The priority provisions of section 5 of the 1977 Act differ somewhat from the corresponding provisions of the EPC but it has been held by the House of Lords[21] that an earlier unpublished patent application cannot be anticipatory if it is non-enabling. It is noted that any publication of the contents of an earlier application can be cited against a later application claiming priority in respect of any invention in the later application which is disentitled to priority.[22]

It is submitted that the overall effect of the above decisions is that the *practical teaching* derivable from the disclosure must be compared with the *invention* (which can in certain cases include the result achieved) in order to determine novelty.

It is now necessary to consider how matter is 'made available to the public' so as to constitute 'state of the art'.

Who Are the Public?

On the basis of Decision T482/89,[23] a single non-confidential sale can constitute anticipation. An independent inventor in his capacity as such is not a member of the public, even if he intends to publish his invention without filing a patent application. This interpretation is consistent with the observations of Purchas LJ in *Genentech's Patent* in which he stated:

> Thus in deciding whether an invention is new within Section 1(1)(a) one must look solely at any matter which has been 'made available' to the public. It is an objective question of fact and has nothing with the subjective qualities or knowledge of anyone.[24]

He also stated:

> The answer to the question: 'What is the public?' would appear in a case such as this to be that community of research workers skilled in the art in general; but not, I would think, merely known to one or two individual research workers pursuing their own experiments in private.

Similarly in the EPO the Technical Board of Appeal held[25] that a report bearing the note 'This report is the property of the RCA Corporation and is loaned to its licensees for their confidential use with the understanding that it will not be distributed or disclosed to third parties or be published in any manner . . .' which was distributed to a large number of major TV manufacturers who were licensees of RCA was not made available to the *public*, which included researchers and other manufacturers, for example. There was no evidence that the

---

[20] Article 88(4) EPC.

[21] *Asahi Kasei Kogyo's Application* [1991] RPC 485.

[22] Decision of the Enlarged Board of Appeal G03/93 *Priority Interval* and *Beloit v Valmet, Intellectual Property Decisions*, July 1995.

[23] *TELEMECANIQUE/Power supply unit* [1993] EPOR 259.

[24] Note 1 above, at 204.

[25] Decision T300/86, Note 10 above.

circuits described in the report had been made available to the public by being incorporated in television sets. Clearly some act of communication is required in order to make an invention available.

How Is an Invention 'Made Available'?

Article 54(2) EPC and section 2(2) of the 1977 UK Patents Act both specify that 'state of the art' may be made available to the public 'by written or oral description, by use or in any other way.' In Decision T877/90 *HOOPER TRADING/T-cell growth factor*[26] it was held that the contents of oral presentations at invitation-only meetings were made available to the public because the invited attenders of the meetings were not subject to any secrecy agreement. There was no evidence that the attenders had disclosed what they had heard prior to the relevant date. The Board held in paragraph 2.1.5 of the Reasons that an oral disclosure is made available to the public 'if, at the relevant date, it was possible for members of the public to gain knowledge of the content of the disclosure and there was no bar of confidentiality restricting the use or dissemination of such knowledge'. This clearly echoes *Humpherson v Syer*[27] that a patent is invalid if some people 'under no obligation of secrecy arising from confidence, or good faith towards the patentee, knew of the invention at the date of the patent'.

In view of the freedom to use the invention given to the licensees in T300/86, which nevertheless did not destroy novelty, it is submitted that a teaching is only 'made available' once *all* fetters of confidentiality on its use or dissemination are removed.

When Is an Invention 'Made Available'?

Decision T381/87 of the Technical Board of Appeal[28] concerned a European patent application which claimed the priority date of 27 November 1981. An article in *Chemical Communications* by the inventors, describing the subject-matter of the patent application, was dispatched by second class mail to subscribers on 25 November 1981 and the Examining Division of the EPO objected that this article was made available to the public on that date.

The Board held that while a document remains in the postbox, and at all times prior to its delivery to the persons to whom it is addressed, it is not 'available to the public'. The Board also held that the patent application had been anticipated in view of the fact that the relevant journal would have been available on 26 November 1981 'to anyone who requested to see it', according to a letter from the librarian of the Royal Society of Chemistry, and indicated that

> It is not necessary as a matter of law that any members of the public would have been aware that the document was available under requests on that day, whether by means of an index in the library or otherwise. It is sufficient if the document was *in fact* available to the public on that day whether or not any member of the public actually knew it was available, and whether or not any member of the public actually asked to see it.

It should be noted that the Board also held that since the article was received by the Royal Society of Chemistry in confidence, and the Society was obliged to keep the contents of the

---

[26] [1993] EPOR 6.
[27] (1887) 4 RPC, at 414, lines 55 to 58.
[28] *RESEARCH CORPORATION/Publication* [1989] EPOR 138.

article secret prior to any publication, the mere receipt of the article, albeit intended for publication, did not deprive the patent application of novelty.

Thus the Board disregarded the intention of the communicator and concentrated instead on the objective situation resulting from his actions, in particular the date of removal of the fetter of confidentiality.

Similarly in Decision T444/88[29] the Board of Appeal held that a disclosure in a Japanese patent file was made available to the public merely by being open to public inspection, even though it was proved that no-one had inspected the file.

It is submitted that these decisions are consistent with Decision G01/92[30] of the Enlarged Board of Appeal of the EPO in which it was held that a product's chemical composition is made available to the public by making the product available to the public, irrespective of whether particular reasons can be identified for carrying out a chemical analysis.

One further EPO decision which should be mentioned is T461/88[31] which concerned a patented control system for a printing press. The control system included a programmed microprocessor and the key features of the invention resided in the program. The control system had been installed in a printing press which had been sold and delivered to a customer before the priority date of the patent. The Board of Appeal, who relied on the fact that it would take several man-years to analyse the microchip, during which time it might be destroyed and in any case would not be used, upheld the patent. They considered that the usefulness of the knowledge gained would be out of proportion to the economic damage incurred. It is doubted whether this decision is correct, bearing in mind that the chip could almost certainly have been analysed within the lifetime of the patent.

Experimental Testing in Public

It is submitted that the purpose for which an article is used in public is irrelevant to the determination of novelty, and that all the features that could lawfully be observed by members of the public are made available to them. This view is at odds with the decision of the British Patents County Court in *Prout v British Gas*.[32] Prout invented a bracket for attaching warning lamps to fencing pillars which was designed to prevent theft and vandalism of the warning lamps. He filed a patent application.

Before the filing date, British Gas manufactured brackets in accordance with the invention and used them in public, in an area notorious for theft and vandalism, to see how secure they were. It was held that the public could see what the invention was, and the judge did not rely in his judgment on there being any necessity to remove the bracket from the post in order to understand how it worked. He referred to a commentary which cited definitions of 'use' in German patent law as it stood prior to the EPC and noted that this defined 'use' was 'going beyond mere trials in public'.[33] Accordingly he held that the public experimental trial did not amount to 'use' which made the invention available to the public.

Even if an experimental trial does not amount to 'use', it should be noted that the EPC and the 1977 Act refer to the state of the art as comprising everything made available to the public 'by use, *or in any other way*' which implicitly includes making available by experimental trial. Thus it is submitted that *Prout v British Gas* was wrongly decided.

---

[29] *JAPAN STYRENE PAPER/Foam particles* [1991] EPOR 94.
[30] *Availability to the public* [1993] EPOR 241.
[31] *HEIDELBERGER DRÜCKMASCHINEN/Microchip* [1993] EPOR 529.
[32] [1992] FSR 478.
[33] *Ibid.*, at 486, middle paragraph.

In *Lux Traffic Controls v Pike Signals Ltd*,[34] one of the two patents at issue included a claim to a traffic light control system which functioned in a defined manner in response to detection of a moving vehicle. The patentees modified two controllers for temporary traffic lights in accordance with the claim and the modified controllers were supplied to contractors for use on public roads before the priority date. The court found that the cabinet of the controller was locked, so that it could not be examined by members of the public.

Finding anticipation, the court held:

> In the case of a written description, what is made available to the public is the description and it is irrelevant whether it is read. In the case of a machine it is that machine which is made available and *it is irrelevant whether it is operated in public* ... Thus what is made available to the public by a machine ... is that which the skilled man would, if asked to describe its construction and operation, write down having carried out an appropriate *test or examination*.[35]

It was held that although the locked controller could not have been examined, it could have been tested and the claimed features discovered. Accordingly, anticipation was found.

Generic Disclosures and Selection Inventions

The general approach taken by the EPO when considering a prior published generic disclosure is to consider whether the skilled man 'would seriously contemplate' working within the sub-range corresponding to the invention.[36] A recording layer was stated in a prior publication to be less than or equal to 3μm in thickness, but preferably 0.1 to 3μm. It was stated in the prior document: 'if the thickness of the recording layer is too small ... a low or insufficient reproduced output is obtained ... Therefore ... the minimum thickness of the recording layer is at least 0.1μm and preferably at least 0.5μm'. It was held that in view of this reasoned statement dissuading the skilled person from utilising the thickness range below 0.1μm, a claim specifying a thickness range of 0.05 to 0.1μm was novel over this disclosure.

According to Decision T279/89,[37] a generic disclosure of a continuous range of values (for example, 0 to 100 mol per cent) does not disclose a claimed sub-range if this is:

(1) sufficiently narrow (for example, 0.02 to 0.2 mol per cent);
(2) sufficiently far removed from the known range illustrated by means of examples (for example, 2 to 13 mol per cent);[38] and
(3) not a mere embodiment of the prior description but another invention.

It is interesting to note the approach taken in item (3), in which the EPO first identifies the *invention* before considering novelty.

In view of the EPO decisions on enabling disclosure, it is submitted that the correct view is that if the prior disclosure enables the product to be made and the product is explicitly disclosed, then no invention can lie in the later preparation of that product, no matter what properties may be discovered.

---

[34] [1993] RPC 107.
[35] *Emphasis added.*
[36] Decision T26/85 *TOSHIBA/Thickness of magnetic layers* [1990] EPOR 267.
[37] *TEXACO/Reaction injection moulded elastomer* [1992] EPOR 294.
[38] Decision T198/84 *HOECHST/Thiochloroformates* [1979–85] EPOR Vol. C 987.

Thus in Decision T958/90,[39] claims to the use of IDA as an additive for improving the performance of NTA as a sequestering agent were held to be anticipated by an earlier disclosure of NTA/IDA mixtures as precursors in a process for obtaining NTA as a sequestering agent. The Board held that an additional reason to do what had already been proposed as a solution to the same technical problem could not be regarded as a new functional technical feature.

However, a list of compounds in a prior document is considered to be a disclosure of each and every one of those compounds so that a later claim to one of those compounds or to a selection from the list lacks novelty, irrespective of any selection advantage. A disclosure of one reactant in conjunction with a group of co-reactants defined by a generic formula is considered not to be a disclosure of a product formed by reacting the reactant with a co-reactant selected from the group[40] and a selection from two lists of starting compounds is considered not to anticipate a product obtained by reacting a particular pair of such compounds, provided that the selected starting compounds are not disclosed in association with each other in the prior document.[41] By the same token, a generic formula having two or more ranges of numbers relating to respective substituents is considered not to anticipate a later formula limited to respective subsets of the disclosed ranges of substituents. However, a disclosed range, for example C_{1-4} alkyl, does disclose the compounds defining the ends of the range, namely, C_1 (methyl) and C_4 (butyl).

Furthermore it has been held that[42] the individual enantiomers (the distinct right- and left-handed molecular structures) of a chiral compound are not anticipated by a disclosure of that compound in racemic form (that is, the normally occurring 50/50 mixture of the enantiomers).

The discrepancy between the treatment of continuous variables and discrete variables was illustrated in Decision T763/89,[43] wherein it was held that a claim to a specified colour photographic material having three layers was not anticipated by a prior art document disclosing a corresponding material having 'at least two' layers. Only two-layer materials were exemplified in the prior art document. It was held that, unlike consecutive numeral *ranges*, numerical values which could only be whole numbers served to characterise objects which were clearly defined. Thus if an earlier document discloses a temperature of 'at least 2°C' a later invention limited to 3°C or greater would be anticipated.

The discrepancy here between the consideration of discrete and continuous variables on the one hand, and continuous variables on the other could lead to odd results.

Conclusion

It is clear that the *invention* must first be identified and that only then can novelty be determined, by comparing it with the *practical teaching* derivable from the earlier disclosure. Accordingly decisions under the 1949 Act such as *Bristol Myers*,[44] in which prior use of unanalysable material destroyed novelty, and *Wheatley's application*,[45] according to which the mere placement of an order was held to be 'use' which anticipated the invention, are submitted to be no longer applicable.

---

[39] *DOW/Sequestering agent* [1994] EPOR 1.
[40] Decision T181/82 *CIBA-GEIGY/Spiro compounds* [1979–85] EPOR Vol. C 684.
[41] Decision T07/86 *DRACO/Xanthines* [1989] EPOR 65.
[42] Decision T296/87 *HOECHST/Enantiomers* [1990] EPOR 337.
[43] *FUJI/Multilayer photographic material* [1994] EPOR 384.
[44] *Bristol Myers (Johnson's) Application* [1973] FSR 43 to 74.
[45] [1985] RPC 91 to 102.

International Exhibitions

[1978] EIPR 29

MARY VITORIA
Barrister, London

Section 2(4) of the Patents Act 1977 provides that if there has been disclosure of an invention due to or in consequence of displaying the invention at an International Exhibition such prior disclosure will not invalidate a subsequent application for a patent provided such application is made within six months of the disclosure. Article 55 (1)(b) of the European Patent Convention makes a similar exception for filing European patent applications.

At first sight this concession is similar to that granted under section 51(2) of the Patents Act 1949 where prior display at an exhibition certified by the Board of Trade was allowed provided such display was followed by an application within six months. Closer examination shows, however, that the concession has been whittled away to virtually nothing.

An 'international exhibition' for the purpose of section 2(4) of the 1977 Act and of Article 55(1)(b) of the EPC is an 'official or officially recognised exhibition falling within the terms of the Convention on International Exhibitions or falling within the terms of any subsequent treaty or convention replacing that convention'.

The Convention on International Exhibitions was signed in 1928 and is set out as an Appendix to the Protocol revising the Convention (Cmnd 5317). It is concerned with exhibitions whose principle purpose is the education of the public. The Convention specifically excludes from its terms

(a) Exhibitions lasting less than three weeks
(b) Fine Arts exhibitions and
(c) Exhibitions of an essentially commercial nature.

Trade fairs are thus specifically excluded. It is likely that only such exhibitions as 'The Festival of Britain 1951' would fall within its terms.

Even those exhibitions which qualify as to subject matter must comply with rigid requirements as to duration (not more than six months) and frequency (e.g. not more than one such exhibition every twenty years in the same country; not more than one such exhibition every ten years in any case) and as to registration with the International Exhibitions Bureau in Paris.

The concessions in section 2(4) and Article 55(1)(b) are worthless for all practical purposes.

Articles 1 to 5 of the Convention are set out below.

Definitions and Objectives

Article 1

(1) An exhibition is a display which, whatever its title, has as its principal purpose the education of the public: it may exhibit the means at man's disposal for meeting the needs of civilisation, or demonstrate the progress achieved in one or more branches of human endeavour, or show prospects for the future.

(2) An exhibition is international when more than one State is invited to take part in it.

(3) Participants in an international exhibition comprise on the one hand exhibitors of States which are officially represented grouped into national sections, on the other hand international organisations or exhibitors from countries which are not officially represented and lastly those who are authorised in accordance with the regulations of the exhibition to carry on some activity, in particular those granted concessions.

Article 2

This Convention applies to all international exhibitions except:

   (a) Exhibitions lasting less than three weeks;
   (b) Fine Arts exhibitions;
   (c) Exhibitions of an essentially commercial nature.

Article 3

(1) Whatever title may be given to an exhibition by its organisers, this Convention recognises a distinction between universal exhibitions and specialised exhibitions.

(2) An exhibition is universal when it displays the methods used and the progress achieved, or to be achieved, in several branches of human endeavour as they are defined in the classification provided for in paragraph 2(a) of Article 30 of this Convention.

(3) An exhibition is specialised when it is devoted to a single branch of human endeavour as defined in the classification.

Duration and Frequency of Exhibitions

Article 4

(1) The duration of an international exhibition shall not exceed six months.

(2) The dates of opening and closing an international exhibition shall be fixed at the time of registration and shall not be changed except in the case of *force majeure* and with the agreement of the International Exhibitions Bureau, herein referred to as 'the Bureau'. In any case the total effective duration shall not exceed six months.

Article 5

(1) The frequency of exhibitions coming within the scope of this Convention shall be regulated in the following manner:

(a) an interval of at least twenty years shall elapse between two universal exhibitions in the same country; an interval of at least five years shall elapse between a universal exhibition and a specialised exhibition in the same country;
(b) in different countries an interval of at least ten years shall elapse between two universal exhibitions;
(c) an interval of at least ten years shall elapse between specialised exhibitions of the same kind in the same country; an interval of at least five years shall elapse between two specialised exhibitions of different kinds in the same country;
(d) in different countries an interval of at least five years shall elapse between two specialised exhibitions of the same kind; an interval of at least two years shall elapse between two specialised exhibitions of different kinds.

(2) Notwithstanding the provisions of paragraph (1) above, in exceptional cases and subject to the conditions envisaged in Article 28(3)(f) below—the Bureau may reduce the intervals specified above in favour of specialised exhibitions and may reduce to not less than seven years the interval between universal exhibitions organised in different countries.

(3) Intervals between registered exhibitions shall run from the actual opening date of such exhibitions.

The Question of Obviousness in the Windsurfers Decision
[1985] 8 EIPR 218

JEANNE-MARIE CLAYDON
Barrister-at-Law, Brussels

It is the purpose of the present article to review the law of patents in relation to obviousness in the light of the recent decision of the Court of Appeal in *Windsurfing International Inc. v Tabur Marine (Great Britain) Ltd.*[1] The case concerns the now famous 'Schweitzer' Windsurfer patent which stands at the base of the windsurfing empire and of the popular watersport to which it has given its name. Although the Schweitzer patent was also found to be anticipated, the present article will deal exclusively with the issue of obviousness.[2] The case raises questions in relation to non-inventiveness which are deserving of further attention:

(1) Is the test of admissibility relating to prior art to be applied in the same way in respect of both anticipation and obviousness?
(2) Is the *interest* of the skilled man in developing a particular piece of prior art a relevant matter for consideration when assessing the obviousness of an invention?

Facts

The case (an action for infringement with a counter-claim for revocation) was heard on appeal from the judgment of Whitford J who at first instance had held the Schweitzer patent invalid on the basis of two instances of prior art, namely:

(1) prior use—consisting of an isolated use by a twelve-year-old boy (Chilvers) of an apparatus similar to the windsurfer off the coast of Hayling Island in 1958, that is, some 12 years before the priority date of the patent;
(2) prior publication—consisting of the publication in 1966 in a UK journal *Practical Hydrofoils* of an article by a Mr Darby (originally published in a US journal *Popular Science Monthly*), describing an apparatus embodying features similar to the windsurfer. The UK journal had a circulation of approximately 600.

It had been argued by the defendants that the Schweitzer patent was invalid for obviousness

---

[1] [1985] RPC 59.

For a general outline of the legal concepts and principles discussed in this article, the reader is referred to *Terrell on the Law of Patents*, 13th ed., paragraphs 5.101 to 5.127. The statutory basis of the test of obviousness discussed in this article is found under section 32(1)(f) of the Patents Act 1949, which is reproduced in Note 5 below

[2] The question of anticipation raised matters of a construction of the patent in suit, rather than issues of general application.

on the basis of both the Chilvers use and the Darby article. While finding for the defendants in respect of their arguments on obviousness based on the Darby article, Whitford J made no finding as to the question of obviousness relating to the Chilvers use. (The Chilvers use was, however, considered to have invalidated the patent on the basis of anticipation.)

The plaintiffs appealed the decision and the defendants put in a respondent's notice on the issue of obviousness and the Chilvers prior use. The Court of Appeal upheld the decision of Whitford J and further held that the Schweitzer patent was obvious having regard to the Chilvers use. In determining the issue of obviousness, Oliver LJ outlined four steps to be followed:[3]

(1) What is the inventive concept embodied in the patent in suit?
(2) What is the common general knowledge in the art in question as held by the normally skilled but unimaginative addressee in the art at the priority date?
(3) What, if any, differences exist between the matter cited as being 'known or used' and the alleged invention?
(4) If viewed without any knowledge of the alleged invention, would those differences constitute steps which would have been obvious to the skilled man or would they require a degree of invention?

(1) Inventive concept

The Court of Appeal held, contrary to the submissions of the appellant, that the inventive concept at the heart of the Schweitzer patent was the so-called 'free-sail concept, viz that the alleged novelty lay in the feature of an unstayed spar, held in place by a universal joint and free to move under the direct control of the user.[4] The appellants had argued that the inventive concept for these purposes was a 'combination' of features namely of (a) the unstayed spar (the so-called 'free sail' concept); (b) the sail attached to the spar along one end; and (c) the connected arcuate booms—all of which combined to form the craft which had given rise to a unique form of watersport.

The restrictive finding of the Court of Appeal as to the nature of the 'inventive concept' is of great significance to the later findings of obviousness, for, in assessing each feature of the windsurfer individually for these purposes and in excluding the particular attachment of the sail to the spar and the use of arcuate booms as concepts already well known in the sailing world—which indeed *individually* they were—the Court arguably failed to take account of the essence of the inventive concept: that of a new type of craft. It is arguable that, owing to the restrictive definition of the inventive concept, the Court was unable to give sufficient weight to the arguments raised in relation to the fourth step in the test of obviousness. It is not the purpose of this article to consider this point in detail but the author would simply question whether, in dealing with an apparatus which, regardless of its commercial success, gives rise to a whole new concept—for example, that of windsurfing—such a restrictive approach can ever do justice to the invention in question.

---

[3] Note 1 above at 73 and 74.
[4] Claim 1 of the patent reads as follows:

    A wind-propelled vehicle comprising body means, an unstayed spar connected to said body means through a joint which will provide universal-type movement of the spar in the absence of support thereof by a user of the vehicle, a sail attached along one edge thereof to the spar, and a pair of arcuate booms, first ends of the booms being connected together and laterally connected on said spar, second ends of the booms being connected together and having means thereon connected to the sail such that said sail is held taut between the booms.

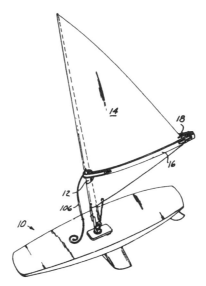

Figure 1   *The Windsurfer in Question*

(2) Common general knowledge of the hypothetical skilled man

It was argued by the respondents that the prior art to be considered in determining the common general knowledge of the notionally skilled man, at the priority date of the patent, should include:

(a) the Chilvers use; and
(b) the Darby article.

While accepting Darby as relevant prior art the appellants challenged the Chilvers use as relevant on the basis that Chilvers was a 'freak' use and was accordingly not a relevant matter for consideration under section 32(1)(f) of the Patents Act 1949.[5] It was argued that section 32(1)(f) had to be construed with reference not to an absolute standard of all possible prior art but to a relative standard based on what was known or would have been known by a person seeking an answer to a preformulated question (to which question the invention in suit provided a solution), viz the 'diligent searcher'.

(3) Differences between the matter cited as being 'known or used' and the alleged invention

It was accepted on the evidence that Darby embodied the free sail concept. This was, of course, the feature taken by the Court of Appeal to represent the inventive concept of the invention. The differences between Darby and the Schweitzer invention were found by the

---

[5] Section 32(1)(f) reads as follows:

... that the invention, so far as claimed in any claim of the complete specification, is obvious and does not involve any inventive step having regard to what was known or used, before the priority date of the claim, in the United Kingdom.

Court, as a matter of evidence, to relate to the type of sail and the technical means of achieving the free movement of the spar, differences which expert evidence suggested were in the nature of obvious improvements.

Again it was held as a matter of evidence that the Chilvers used embodied the free sail concept. The Court of Appeal held that the only real difference between Chilvers apparatus and the Schweitzer windsurfer was in the primitive nature of the boom used by Chilvers which Schweitzer replaced by a new sophisticated version, again, in the view of the experts, an improvement of an obvious nature.

(4) Were those differences obvious improvements to the skilled man?

The appellants acknowledged that once accepted as prior art the Chilvers use rendered the subsequent Schweitzer patent obvious but, as noted under (2) above, suggested that Chilvers should not be considered at all in relation to this question. Regarding Darby, the appellants argued that as a matter of law Whitford J had erred in taking Darby as a starting point for obviousness and automatically applying the evidence to it. In the submission of the appellants, as a matter of law the burden of proof lay upon the respondents to show that Darby was a concept which a skilled man would have recognised as calling for development, and that until this had been done, the question of the obvious nature of the 'improvement' to the article should not be considered. The appellants argued that Darby merely described certain physical features and failed to convey to the skilled man a concept worthy of development. Given, in addition, that the windsurfer was not a solution to an existing problem for which the skilled man had been searching, it was argued by the appellants that no skilled man would have bothered to go on to apply methods of trial and error to improve Darby. This submission was supported by the evidence.

Chilvers Prior Use: Prior Art for the Purposes of Section 32(1)(f)?

The appellants, as stated above, characterised the Chilvers use as a 'freak' use, being the use 'years ago . . . on a comparatively obscure holiday beach, of a primitive plaything put together by an adventurous youth'.[6] The appellants challenged the view that for the purposes of admissibility the test of obviousness takes account of all art, objectively relevant. Referring to the hypothetical skilled man, the appellants argued that his attributes must at least be in the realm of the possible if the test is to have any true significance: to create a skilled man who not only had access to all art but in addition considered all improvements to the same—however obscure—was unrealistic.

In effect the appellants sought to introduce a qualitative dimension to the test of admissibility of prior art for the purposes of obviousness. Support for such an argument was taken from the decision of Lord Reid in *Technograph Printed Circuits Ltd v Mills & Rockley (Electronics) Ltd*[7] who saw a fundamental difference between the tests of admissibility of prior art between section 32(1)(e) of the Patents Act 1949 relating to anticipation and section 32(1)(f) relating to obviousness. Both sections included the expression 'having regard to what was known or used' to denote prior art. According to Lord Reid, as a matter of principle and of law (following *Bristol Myers Co. (Johnson's) Application*[8]), those words under section 32(1)(e) are to be interpreted broadly and objectively as referring to all matter,

---

[6] *Ibid.*, at 76.
[7] [1972] RPC 346.
[8] [1975] RPC 127.

whether or not in reality anyone is ever likely to 'know' of it. The test of anticipation was therefore an objective one to determine whether in fact anything anticipates the invention in issue. By contrast, when considering section 32(1)(f) the purpose of that sub-section dictates a different interpretation, limiting prior art to 'what was or ought to have been known by the diligent searcher'. In Lord Reid's view section 32(1)(f) did not require the same objective test called for by section 32(1)(e) but a more subjective, qualitative assessment of the prior art to correspond to the more subjective/qualitative nature of the test—namely the assessment of whether the invention was obvious. Such a restrictive interpretation was supported by Lord Morris but rejected by Lord Diplock on the basis that the same words used in two sub-paragraphs should be given the same meaning: accordingly the *Bristol Myers* decision was binding on the construction of both sections. The issue was, however, *obiter* to the judgment in *Technograph* and in so far as they felt obliged to deal with the matter the Court of Appeal in *Windsurfers* felt free to follow the views of Lord Diplock: accordingly, the decision in *Bristol Myers* was held to be binding on the construction of both sections.

The author considers that forceful arguments of both law and policy favour Lord Reid's position:

(1) *As a matter of literal interpretation* While accepting the logic of the argument in favour of according the same interpretation to identical expressions used in two sub-sections in the statute, it is equally true that the draftsman could have used only one sub-section for both novelty and obviousness, using the expression 'having regard to what is known or used'. Indeed, that the draftsman chose to deal with prior art in separate sub-sections for novelty and obviousness must raise questions as to his intention. It may be argued that his intention was to apply a separate test of admissibility of prior art under the two sub-sections. This argument gains support from the 'purposive' test, set out below.

(2) *The purposive test* The purposes of section 32(1)(e) and section 32(1)(f) are clearly different, constituting two separate grounds on which a patent may be invalidated. The fact that many challenges to validity raise both grounds should not distort such a difference. Accordingly, while for the purposes of anticipation it is apt that the test for prior art should be dealt with on an objective disinterested view of the evidence, conversely where obviousness is concerned, one is no longer dealing with whether or not the invention has been pre-dated as a matter of fact but whether the notional skilled man would find the invention obvious on the basis of prior art. Under section 32(1)(f) one is faced with a type of 'jury question' which is notoriously difficult to resolve and which admits of, and indeed requires, a more flexible analysis. Thus, it may be argued that as a question of admissibility, there are certain types of art which are not relevant for considerations of obviousness because they are by nature so freak or obscure as to be incapable of consideration as a starting point in the notional skilled man's assessment of obviousness. While there is a danger in such an approach of introducing too great a degree of subjectivity into the inquiry—and consequently a risk of rendering the test for prior art unworkable—it is certainly arguable that bearing in mind the purpose of section 32(1)(f), the words 'having regard to what was known or used' should not include matters which would on any realistic view of affairs not even have come to the attention of the skilled man and so could never have started him off down the road of inquiry.

In the present case, while acknowledging the existence of a difference in purpose between section 32(1)(e) and section 32(1)(f), the Court of Appeal stated that notwithstanding such difference, section 32(1)(f) must 'take into account the same concept as anticipation, namely that it would be wrong to prevent a man from doing something which is merely an obvious extension of what he has been doing or of what was known in the art before the priority date of the patent granted'.[9]

In the author's opinion, such a view imports issues appropriate to the determination of questions under section 32(1)(e) into determination of questions under section 32(1)(f), a step which is not required merely by the repetition of the words 'having regard to what was known or used'.

(3) *Policy* The policy behind the patent system is often stated to be the service of the public interest (rather than the reward of individual merit) through the publication of inventions in consideration of a limited reward to the inventor. In interpreting the Patents Act, it is the view of the author that any interpretation should be tested to see whether or not the public interest is so served. In doing so, it is useful to consider the position on a 'but for' basis: 'But for the Schweitzer patent would the public have had the benefit of the windsurfer craft?' It is the view of the author based on the evidence cited by the Court of Appeal that had Schweitzer not published the patent and had the public been left with the Chilvers use, the windsurfer would not have been produced: such use added nothing, by virtue of its freak and obscure nature, to the sum total of human knowledge. Furthermore, it must be emphasised that what is being considered is not whether 'but for Schweitzer windsurfers would have become as popular as they are' (that is, the commercial success that they have become) but whether the concept was one which was publicly available for development and use.

The Court of Appeal was anxious to state that merely making a commercial success out of an anticipated or obvious idea could not be inventive. This is, of course, correct but should not be confused with the situation where an apparatus which is considered to have no value and consequently to be unworthy of development is developed and improved into a new apparatus which finds widespread commercial success. This is arguably the very essence of inventiveness.

Conclusion

Following *Windsurfers* the position at law appears to be that the test of admissibility for the purposes of anticipation and obviousness under section 32(1)(e) and (f) of the Patents Act 1949 are the same, being based on the decision in *Bristol Myers*. Accordingly, all prior art, however obscure, is relevant not only for the factual inquiry as to whether or not the invention has been anticipated, but also for the more subjective inquiry as to whether or not the notional skilled man would have considered that the earlier instance rendered the invention obvious. While it is clear that such a test is easily applied one might question whether it is so at the expense of realism—and the public interest.

Darby and Obviousness

Is the notional skilled man, faced with the accumulated knowledge of mankind, not only omniscient but also prescient? The author also questions whether, taken to its extreme, the concept of the skilled man applying workshop trial and error to *all* matters, however obscure, however uninteresting, may not be said to endow him with the very imagination and inventive spirit which we are told he does not possess!

---

[9] Note 1 above at 72.

While accepting Darby as relevant prior art the appellants argued that when applying the test of obviousness to such art the Court should take into account the *weight* which the notional skilled man would attach to a given piece of prior art before proceeding to see how close he would have got to the invention in issue by applying workshop trial and error to the prior disclosure.

In this respect, it had been accepted by Whitford J as a matter of evidence at first instance that the Darby article excited no interest in the leisure craft world. The appellants accordingly argued that as Darby aroused no interest it was meaningless to apply the workshop trial and error test as the notional skilled man would have dismissed the article without consideration. It was suggested that in order to succeed the respondents had to show that Darby was art which a skilled man would have recognised as suitable for development and to which he would therefore have applied workshop trial and error methods; that on the facts, the windsurfer did not represent a solution to a problem for which the leisure industry had been searching; and that in the light of the evidence regarding the degree of interest in Darby, the defence had failed to discharge that burden.

At the heart of these points may be seen the argument that inventiveness is very often the ability to imagine a concept. Once that concept has been envisaged the non-inventive man is then able to work towards it. To avoid consideration of the skilled man's perception of the importance of a piece of art (dealt with as a matter of evidence and presumption based on prevailing development trends in the relevant industry) is to assume the ability to perceive a new concept—in other words to assume inventiveness.

This introduces the issue of the dangers of assessment of an invention in hindsight—when it has become an accepted part of life. It is particularly forceful when considered in relation to a product such as the windsurfer which led to the development of a totally novel form of sport. As with many successful ideas, the Schweitzer patent represented a simple concept and yet achieved substantial commercial success: all of which make an *ex post facto* appreciation of its obviousness particularly difficult to avoid. In refusing to consider the matter of interest of the skilled man in its application of the test of obviousness, the Court of Appeal stated that such a concept was not supported in authority and would serve only to obscure the real question which was: 'Whether what is now claimed as inventive would have been obvious, not whether it would have appeared commercially worthwhile to exploit it.'[10]

It is respectfully submitted that the Court, in its concern to exclude commercial success as a basis for a claim of inventiveness, failed to appreciate the significance of considering interest when assessing inventiveness: interest and commercial success are not synonymous concepts. The justification for assessing interest is to be found from the fact that the ability to formulate the question is itself the seed of inventiveness: no one will bother to formulate a question where they have no interest in the answer. Can the means be assumed when the end is not in sight? The Court of Appeal in its judgment held that the ability to formulate a problem was a matter to be dealt with by presumption—in fact, as it would appear, an irrebuttable presumption, as the evidence shows that the skilled man would not have considered the problem to which the windsurfer was a solution. In adopting such a rigid view of the test to be applied it may be argued that, far from refusing to attribute an additional feature to the character of the skilled man, the Court of Appeal may in fact have undermined one of the most fundamental—albeit negative—of his acknowledged features: the lack of imagination. Not only is it arguable that such a finding is contrary to authority but furthermore it would appear to be contrary to policy. Once again, taking the 'but for' test outlined above: 'But for Schweitzer, would the public have been provided with the windsurfer?' Surely

---

[10] *Ibid.*

such a rigid test leaves a gap between the realm of the real world and the realm of what now may appear as an increasingly metaphysical legal world. In applying the test of obviousness without reference to reality, patents without which the public would never have acquired the benefit of an invention may be invalidated. Once again, it is appreciated that assessment of 'interest' may be difficult—yet while it may be grounds for introducing a presumption of interest, it should not require that such presumption be irrebuttable, which is the case where the matter is excluded from judicial consideration.

Conclusion

The *Windsurfer* case presented a set of facts which challenged many hitherto untested assumptions. The evidence showed that the invention embodied a concept disclosed and used before the priority date with additional features which were in the view of the experts merely pedestrian improvements to the prior apparatus. But 'pedestrian' only to the skilled man who (a) had access to all the prior art and (b) could conceive of a final product—viz the windsurfer—as an end to justify the making of improvements to the prior art. The decision of the Court of Appeal in *Windsurfers* has raised once again the question of the suitability of the test of obviousness as a ground for invalidation of a patent. The skilled man may now have passed beyond the realms of reality and in doing so have failed to respond to the needs of the public which he was designed to serve. *Windsurfers* has contributed to the certainty of the law, but has it also tipped the balance in favour of the infringer? It may be that such a test, in encouraging the infringer to devote substantial amounts of time and money to uncover even the obscure and the unlikely in an effort to invalidate a patent and so validate his own exploitation of another's idea, at best endorses a wasteful use of resources and at worst threatens the very benefit which the patent system was designed to achieve.

Delivering the Goods?

[1997] 1 EIPR 21

IAN KARET

Linklaters & Paines

The House of Lords' Decision in Biogen v. Medeva

On October 31, 1996, the House of Lords delivered their opinions in *Biogen v. Medeva*.[1] The case concerned Biogen's patent relating to exploitation of Hepatitis B virus using recombinant DNA (rDNA) technology. The unanimous decision revoking the patent is the first consideration by the House of Lords of a biotechnology invention. The case raises questions of obviousness and sufficiency. In considering obviousness, it is important to identify the 'inventive concept', which should include some express or implied reference to the problem which it required invention to overcome. On sufficiency, the concept of 'enabling disclosure' is central to the law of patents, running as a unifying theme through priority, support for the claims in an application and the attack of insufficiency. While 'lack of fair basis' is no longer an express ground for revocation of a patent,[2] the general principle remains, and patents which do not 'deliver the goods' across the whole width of their claims may still be attacked under UK law. But there is nothing inherently unpatentable about rDNA technology. Biotechnological inventions may be protected, so long as they meet the requirements of the Patents Act 1977.

This was an appeal from the unanimous decision of the Court of Appeal on 27 October 1994[3] which held that Biogen's patent was insufficient, obvious and might well not even relate to an 'invention' at all. Before the House of Lords, the issues were obviousness, support by the priority documents, whether the patent disclosed any 'invention' and sufficiency. As with the decision of the Court of Appeal, the principles the case establishes are important and of broad application. The case will have a particular impact on chemical, biotechnology and pharmaceutical patents.

The main speech was delivered by Lord Hoffmann, with Lord Mustill adding his opinion on whether there was a need for a patent to disclose an 'invention'.[4]

---

[1] *Biogen Inc. v Medeva plc.* The Appellate Committee comprised Lord Goff of Chieveley, Lord Browne-Wilkinson, Lord Mustill, Lord Slynn of Hadley and Lord Hoffmann.

[2] It appeared as s. 32(1) of the Patents Act 1949 but does not appear in the exclusive list of grounds on which a patent may be revoked set out in s. 72(1) of the Patents Act 1977.

[3] [1995] RPC 25 at 68; the judgment of Aldous J in the Patents Court is at 25. See Comment [1995] 1 EIPR 42 at 46.

[4] Mustill LJ was part of the Court of Appeal which gave the first UK appellate decision in a biotechnology case, *Genentech Inc.'s Patent* [1989] RPC 147. The decision is complex and has raised many questions in the field.

The Facts

Biogen Inc. was the proprietor of two European patents relating to Hepatitis B virus (HBV). Both patents derived from an application filed at the European Patent Office ('EPO') on 21 December 1979 which claimed priority from three UK applications, dated 22 and 27 December 1978 and 1 November 1979. The application was divided in the EPO. The broader application EP 0182442 was granted on 11 July 1990. Opposition proceedings culminated before the Technical Board of Appeal on 28 July 1994, where 442 was upheld.[5]

The key claim for this appeal was Claim 1 of 442:

> A recombinant DNA molecule characterised by a DNA sequence coding for a poly-peptide or a fragment thereof displaying HBV antigen specificity, said DNA sequence being operatively linked to an expression control sequence in the recombinant DNA molecule and being expressed to produce a polypeptide displaying HBV antigen speci-ficity when a suitable host cell transformed with said recombinant DNA molecule is cultured, the transformed host cell not producing any human serum proteins and any primate serum proteins other than the polypeptide displaying HBV antigen specificity.

This is a product claim—the molecule is made by rDNA techniques and is expressed to produce HBV proteins. The claim covers both the distinct HBV 'surface' and 'core' proteins and their expression in bacterial, yeast and mammalian host cells. Claim 3 was limited to cover DNA molecules coding for the core antigen; Claim 4 was limited to cover molecules coding for surface antigen.

The patent was based on experimental work done in 1978 by Professor Sir Kenneth Murray of Edinburgh University. In February of that year, Professor Murray and a number of leading molecular biologists formed Biogen to exploit commercially the new and growing rDNA technology.

At that time a fair amount was known about HBV; but the picture was far from clear. In 1970 the infective agent had been identified.[6] The particle was 42nm in diameter and it was named the 'Dane particle' after its discoverer. The Dane particle included a circular molecule of DNA in a protein core which was surrounded by surface proteins. HBV was unusual in that it infected only man and a number of primates. It could not be grown in cell culture, and the usual methods of making vaccines were not available. Also unusual was that the infection was accompanied by an over-production of particles made up only of the surface protein. These were smaller (22nm in diameter) and, because they contained no HBV DNA, non-infective. Preparations of surface antigen taken from patients could be used as a vaccine, because the human immune system reacted to the HBV non-infective surface proteins and was thus primed to counter an infection by the whole virus. However, there were serious concerns about using surface antigen particles collected from infected individuals.

A possible alternative was to make the antigens artificially by chemical synthesis. In 1977 Peterson identified a sequence of nine amino acids at the end of the chain of the surface protein (many surface proteins together made up a surface antigen particle).[7] Another approach was the use of rDNA technology, which allowed the expression of 'foreign' proteins by bacteria. There were two approaches available. The first was to identify that part of the HBV DNA which coded for the surface antigen and to express that. This would have

---

[5] [1995] EPOR 1. See Brian Reid's Comment [1995] 2 EIPR 98–100.
[6] Dane *et al.* (1970) *Lancet* 695–698.
[7] Peterson *et al.* (1977) 74 PNAS USA 1530–1534.

required a complete sequencing of the HBV genome. The second was to express random pieces of the DNA to see what was produced. Professor Murray took the second approach: Biogen carried out a 'shotgun' expression. This involved chopping up HBV DNA at random and cloning and expressing the random segments to see whether DNA coding for any useful proteins had been selected. It was a high-risk strategy in that there was a good chance of failure in any experiment.

In August 1979 Valenzuela published the sequence of the part of the HBV genome coding for the surface protein.[8] This meant that before the EPO application date of 21 December 1979 the sequence of the surface gene was available, and Biogen conceded that it would by that time have been obvious to attempt to express this sequence in bacteria. A method of expressing heterologous eukaryotic proteins in prokaryotic cells was published by Villa-Komaroff in 1978.[9]

In 1979 only bacterial expression systems were available. Later, both yeast and mammalian cells were developed. The claims of 442 covered all expression systems.

Medeva used the sequence information and mammalian host cells to produce their surface antigen particles.

The Need for an 'Invention'

Before the Court of Appeal Medeva argued that 442 did not disclose any invention at all. Hobhouse LJ had agreed that it was difficult to identify any invention: Biogen had in his view simply made a decision to carry out a course of research which seemed unlikely to succeed. He said that a mere commercial decision was not an invention. Lord Hoffmann noted that the Patents Act 1977 ('the Act') laid down conditions which an invention must satisfy in order to be a 'patentable invention'. This scheme might have suggested that logically one should first decide whether the claimed invention could properly be described as an invention at all. Only those things that were 'inventions' would then be examined to see whether they were patentable. Lord Hoffmann thought that this approach would be a mistake and cause unnecessary difficulty. The Act did not define the concept of an invention; nor did Article 52 of the European Patent Convention ('EPC'), which section 1(1) of the Act was intended to reflect. The reason for this was that the question would almost invariably be academic. The condition in section 1(1) of the Act probably contained every element of the concept of an invention in ordinary speech. Section 1(1) provides:

> (1) A patent may be granted only for an invention in respect of which the following conditions are satisfied, that is to say—
> (a) the invention is new;
> (b) it involves an inventive step;
> (c) it is capable of industrial application;
> (d) the grant of a patent is not excluded by subsections (2) and (3) below;
> and references in this Act to a patentable invention should be construed accordingly.

No one had suggested to the House an example of something which satisfied all the conditions (a)–(d) but which could not be described as an 'invention' for the purpose of section 1(1). Section 1(5) of the Act gave the Secretary of State power to vary the list in section 1(1)(d) to exclude matters 'for the purpose of maintaining ... conformity with developments in

---

[8]   Valenzuela *et al.* (1979) 280 *Nature* 815–819.
[9]   Villa-Komaroff *et al.* (1978) 75 PNAS USA 3727–3731.

science and technology'. Accordingly it would normally be convenient to start by deciding in every case whether the four conditions set out in section 1(1) were satisfied, and in virtually every case this would be the end of the inquiry. Lord Hoffmann noted that:

> Judges would therefore be well advised to put on one side their intuitive sense of what constitutes an invention until they have considered the questions of novelty, inventiveness and so forth.

This echoes his comment in *Merrell Dow v Norton* that the lawyer's intuitive response cannot be relied on in patent law.[10] Lord Mustill, however, did not necessarily agree that the question would be 'academic', especially where the claimed product was one already existing in nature. But because the decision did not turn on the point he was happy to let it rest. Lord Mustill's views almost certainly stem from the fact that in *Genentech* the Court of Appeal had to consider a protein that already existed in nature (tissue plasminogen activator) made by rDNA techniques. This seems to cause him genuine concern, but it is submitted that there is no reason why an rDNA product which is not identical to one found in nature should not be patentable if it satisfies the requirements of the Act.

Inventive Step

The House of Lords considered whether what Biogen had done by the first priority date involved an inventive step. Lord Hoffmann said that Aldous J, having heard expert evidence about what people skilled in the art of rDNA technology would have thought and done at the time, decided that the invention was not obvious. Aldous J had followed the procedure suggested by Oliver LJ in *Windsurfing*.[11] That inquiry comprises four steps:

> The first is to identify the inventive concept embodied in the patent in suit. Thereafter, the court has to assume the mantle of the normally skilled but unimaginative addressee in the art at the priority date and impute to him what was, at that date, common general knowledge in the art in question. The third step is to identify what, if any, differences exist between the matter cited as being 'known or used' and the alleged invention. Finally, the court has to ask itself whether, viewed without any knowledge of the alleged invention, those differences constitute steps which would have been obvious to the skilled man or whether they require any degree of invention.

Lord Hoffmann did not explicitly approve this test. However, its adoption and elaboration by the Court of Appeal[12] and its regular use by the Patents Court together with the House of Lords' tacit approval means that it has, implicitly at least, now received approval from UK courts at all levels.

Lord Hoffmann said that in this case much turned on identifying the inventive concept. A proper statement of the inventive concept needed to include some express or implied reference to the problem which it required invention to overcome. Aldous J had formulated it as 'having the idea of making HBV antigens by recombinant DNA technology'. To Lord Hoffmann, that seemed too broad. The idea of making HBV antigens using rDNA technology was shared by many people, just as the idea of flying in a heavier-than-air machine had

---

[10] [1996] RPC 76 at 83 and 87.
[11] *Windsurfing International Inc. v Tabur Marine (Great Britain) Ltd* [1985] RPC 59 at 73–74.
[12] *Mölnlycke AB v Procter & Gamble Ltd* [1994] RPC 49 at 155.

existed for centuries before the Wright brothers. The problem which required invention was to find a way of doing it. For Lord Hoffmann, the inventive concept was 'the notion that Professor Murray's method of achieving the goal ... would work' or 'the idea of trying to express unsequenced eukaryotic DNA in a prokaryotic host'. If the inventive concept was as Aldous J had in fact expressed it, then Lord Hoffmann would have agreed with the Court of Appeal that the concept was obvious.

However, a careful examination of Aldous J's decision showed that he could not have intended the inventive concept to be so broadly stated. Where the application of a legal standard such as negligence or obviousness involved no question of principle but was simply a matter of degree, an appellate court should be very cautious in differing from the judge's evaluation. As Aldous J had had the opportunity of hearing the expert witnesses, his decision should be allowed to stand. It was true that in *Benmax v Austin Motor Co. Ltd*[13] the House of Lords had decided that while the judge's primary findings of fact, particularly if based on an assessment of the credibility of witnesses, should almost always stand, an appellate court would be more ready to differ from the judge's evaluation of those facts by reference to some legal standards such as negligence or obviousness. This was at all times subject to the weight which should be given to the judge's opinion. Here, the type of inventive step was very unusual in that Biogen argued that the inventiveness consisted in attempting something which a skilled person would have thought not worth trying. That might have merited a further investigation by the House, but in view of the other matters to be considered, Lord Hoffmann was prepared to assume, without deciding, that Aldous J had been correct and that what Professor Murray had done was not obvious.

In the Court of Appeal Hobhouse LJ had decided that Biogen's 'shotgun' approach was obvious because the decision to adopt it had been a 'matter of business judgment' and a 'mere commercial decision'. He had also likened Biogen's approach to that of placing a bet. The only question was the odds of success. Lord Hoffmann disagreed. Reference to a commercial decision were irrelevant because there was no reason why such an experimental strategy, although adopted for commercial reasons, should not also involve an inventive step. The analogy of a bet was also not helpful.

Unfortunately, the House did not give an explicit opinion on the correct approach to obviousness. Given the rarity with which patent cases are heard by the House of Lords,[14] a clear statement on inventive step would have been welcome.[15] The UK court still applies more than one test (e.g. the 'obvious to try' test) although the *Windsurfing* approach is now well established. There is, however, a problem with the approach as stated by Oliver LJ. That rests on the definition of 'inventive concept or step'.[16] In trying to determine what the step is, much attention is directed towards what the inventors actually did; it would be better to start with a consideration of the claims and then move on to see how they compare with the state of the art. If they disclose something which is different enough to be a non-obvious invention, the courts should then turn to the question of whether or not the claims are sufficient. Furthermore, a specification may still disclose a valid invention but express poorly the inventive concept. Given that European patents can also be drafted in German and French, more attention may turn to the exact wording of the description at the expense of the claims.

---

[13] [1955] AC 370.
[14] See the list at [1996] 9 EIPR 481–18 times in 25 years and only seven cases under the Act. Christopher Floyd QC has suggested the lack of decisions has prevented the UK courts from influencing the EPO.
[15] For a discussion on inventive step in biotech cases see [1996] 2 EIPR 90–96.
[16] The phrase 'inventive concept' is also quite helpful, because it is used in section 14(5)(d) of the Act, presumably in a different sense.

Priority and Support

Given the House's assumption that the invention was not obvious at its first priority date (22 December 1978—Biogen I) the key question was whether Biogen I supported the invention claimed in 442. Lord Hoffmann said that the concept of 'enabling disclosure' was central to the law of patents. The requirement that a patent application contained an enabling disclosure was a matter of substance and not form. Its absence should therefore be a ground not only for the refusal of an application but also revocation of a patent after grant. In *Asahi*,[17] the House had decided that for a matter to be capable of supporting an invention it must disclose the invention in a way which enabled it to be performed by a person skilled in the art. That principle for founding priority was also one of the requirements of a valid application in section 14 of the Act. Section 14(3) provides that the specification of an application should disclose the invention in a manner which is clear enough and complete enough for the invention to be performed by a person skilled in the art. Furthermore, section 14(5)(c) says that the claims 'must be supported by the description'.

In *Asahi*, Lord Oliver had said that a description would not 'support' the claims for the purpose of section 14(5)(c) unless it contained sufficient material to enable the specification to constitute an enabling disclosure which section 14(3) required. Accordingly, the difficult point raised by the Court of Appeal in *Genentech Inc.'s Patent*,[18] that the failure of an application to comply with section 14(5)(c) was not a ground for revocation, could now be resolved. The substantive effect of section 14 was that the description should, together with the test of the specification, constitute an enabling disclosure. If it did not then it was liable to be revoked under section 72(1)(c) of the Act, and there was 'accordingly no gap or illogicality in the scheme of the Act'.

A long-established principle of UK patent law was that a specification must enable the invention to be performed to the full extent of the monopoly claimed. If the invention disclosed a principle capable of general application then the claims might be in correspondingly general terms. But if the claims included a number of discrete products, then the patent had to enable the invention to be performed in respect of each of them. Thus, said Lord Hoffmann:

> if the patentee has hit upon a new product which has a beneficial effect but cannot demonstrate that there is a common principle by which that effect will be shared by other products in the same class, he will be entitled to a patent for that product but not the class, even though some may subsequently turn out to have the same beneficial effect[19] . . . On the other hand, if he has disclosed a beneficial property which is common to the class, he will be entitled to a patent for all products of that class (assuming them to be new) even though he has not himself made more than one or two of them.

The EPO has asserted this principle in a number of cases. In particular, in *EXXON/Fuel oils*[20] there was a statement of the general principle that 'the extent of the patent monopoly, as defined by the claims, should correspond to the technical contribution to the art in order for it to be supported, or justified'.

The House had therefore to consider whether Biogen I contained an enabling disclosure

---

[17] *Asahi Kasei Kogyo KK's Application* [1991] AC 485, HL.
[18] See note 4 above.
[19] As in *May & Baker Ltd v Boots Pure Drug Co. Ltd* (1950) 67 RPC 23 at 50, HL.
[20] T409/91 OJ EPO 653 at point 3.3.

which supported the claim. Aldous J had concluded that Biogen's method could work for both core and surface antigen and that on that basis the claim was sufficient. In the Court of Appeal, Hobhouse LJ had re-examined the evidence on whether Biogen 1 had enabled the making of surface antigen and concluded that it did not. Lord Hoffmann regretted the decision of the Court of Appeal to revisit evidence on a matter of fact: Aldous J's decision should not have been disturbed.

But Aldous J's finding that the application could 'deliver the goods' across the full width of the claims was not the only issue. The question was whether the claims 'covered other ways in which they might be delivered: ways which owe[d] nothing to the teaching of the patent or any principle which it discussed'.

There was more than one way in which a claim could exceed the 'technical contribution to the art'. First, a claim could cover products the patent did not explain how to make. Secondly, it could claim every way of achieving a result when showing only one way of doing so, when other people could use other ways.

In Lord Hoffmann's view, the claims of 442 went beyond the technical contribution to the art which Professor Murray had made. Claim 1 generalised what Professor Murray had done in two ways. First, there was generalisation as to the results he had achieved. He had made core and surface antigen; but the claim was any recombinant DNA molecule expressing genes of any HBV antigen in any host. Secondly, there was a generalisation of the method used. Biogen had used a standard plasmid (pBR322) and random chunks of DNA. The claim was for any method of making a DNA molecule which would achieve the necessary expression and thus the relevant HBV polypeptide. Lord Hoffmann thought this was good science but not a good patent:

> Professor Murray had won a brilliant Napoleonic victory in cutting through the uncertainties which existed in his day to achieve the desired result. But his success did not in my view establish any new principle which his successors had to follow if they were to achieve the same results.

The technical contribution Biogen made to the art did not deserve the protection which Biogen had claimed for it.

This was in line with both US and UK patent law—just because someone had shown that something could be done, this did not entitle the discoverer to a monopoly over the result itself. An example of an excessive claim was dealt with in the US Supreme Court's decision in *O'Reilly v Morse*.[21] Samuel Morse claimed any use of electricity for 'making or printing intelligible characters, signs or letters, at any distances'. The claim was too broad. Morse discovered one means of achieving the result, not all the ways of achieving it. The position in the United Kingdom was similar: in the case of *British United Shoe Machinery Co. Ltd v Simon Collier Ltd*,[22] Parker J held that the novelty of a method applied to solving a problem did not enable the inventor to make a valid claim for all means of solving the problem where the same or even a different method was applied to solve it.

The metaphor used by one witness was that before the sequence of the HBV genome had been published (some time after Biogen I but before the EPO application date), everyone trying to express HBV antigens had been working in the dark. Professor Murray had invented a way of working with genome in the dark. Biogen did not switch on the light; Valenzuela did that, and once he had made the sequence available, Professor Murray's method was no

---

[21] (1854) 56 US (50 How) 62.
[22] (1908) 26 RPC 21.

longer needed. Medeva used knowledge of the sequence and a mammalian expression system: their work owed nothing to Professor Murray's invention. The excessive breadth of the claim was due to the fact that the results claimed could be produced by different means.

Accordingly, Biogen's first priority document (Biogen I) did not support the invention as claimed in the EPO. The application for 442 was not entitled to the earliest priority date. It had been conceded that the invention was obvious at the application date and so the patent was invalid.

The House of Lords has provided an elegant way of attacking over-broad claims. The question of over-broad claims has been much discussed recently. The UK Patent Office had suggested[23] that lack of support of the claims by the description should be made a ground of revocation in the EPO under Article 84 EPC.[24] That would require a change to the EPC. Lord Hoffmann says that the possibility already exists in UK law. The EPO itself has not interpreted Article 84 as being about 'fair basis'. It prefers the approach to Article 84 taken in *AGREVO/Triazole sulphonamides*[25] that Article 84 was satisfied when 'the technical features stated in the description as being essential features . . . [are] those used to define the invention in the claims . . .'. The EPO then held that Agrevo's patent should not be attacked under Article 84 but that it was invalid for lack of inventive step on the basis that some of the claimed compounds did not work as herbicides. The House of Lords has diverged from the EPO on this point. That is probably because the *Agrevo* decision only works on the basis that the test for inventive step is the problem solution approach, which the UK courts do not apply in the EPO form.

The scheme proposed by Lord Hoffmann should work. Once the question of obviousness is settled the courts can consider lack of support. The decision also raises the possibility of a 'squeeze' argument on fair basis similar to the *Gillette* defence.[26] This would be that if the claim covers the defendant's acts and those acts owe nothing to the plaintiff's work, then the claim must lack support or a fair basis.

Sufficiency

As the House had concluded that the patent was invalid for obviousness, it was not necessary to consider whether it was also invalid for insufficiency. However, Lord Hoffmann said that the reasoning leading to his conclusion on support also led to the conclusion that the patent was insufficient.

But that did not settle the question at what date the specification must be sufficient. The Court of Appeal had thought it was the date of filing the application. Aldous J had said it was the date on which the application was published. In Lord Hoffmann's view the cases under the 1949 Act on which Aldous J had relied were no longer a safe guide. Section 72(1)(c) was intended to ensure two things. First, the public should be able to work the invention after the expiration of the patent monopoly. Secondly, it was also meant to give the court in revocation proceedings a jurisdiction which mirrored that of the UK Patent Office under section 14(3) of the Act or the EPO under Article 83 EPC—to hold a patent invalid on the ground that the extent of the monopoly claimed exceeded the technical contribution to the art made by the invention as specified in the specification. In the UK's

---

[23] See the *CIPA Journal* (September 1996) vol. 25, no. 9, 650–657.
[24] Art. 84 provides: 'The claims shall define the matter for which protection is sought. They shall be clear and concise and be supported by the description.' Art. 100 sets out an exclusive list of the grounds of opposition, which does include Art. 83 (insufficiency of disclosure) but not Art. 84.
[25] T939/92 [1996] 10 EIPR 561–583.
[26] *Gillette Safety Razor Co. v Anglo American Trading Co.* (1913) 30 RPC 465.

1949 Act, this function was performed by another ground for revocation, that the claim was not 'fairly based upon the matter disclosed in the specification'. Decisions of the EPO showed that Articles 83 and 84 EPC should still have effect. In the United Kingdom their equivalents were section 14(3) and (5) and section 72(1)(c) of the Act.

The only logical date at which section 72(1)(c) could be applied was the date of application. It would not be sensible if a patent which ought to have been rejected under section 14(3) was rendered valid by advances in the art between the date of application and the publication of the specification. Section 76(2) provided that an amended application should not disclose matter which extended beyond that previously disclosed. An insufficient application could not be added to, and it was therefore clear that an insufficient application should not become sufficient because of general developments in the state of the art.

The EPO Decision

The result in the House of Lords was contrary to that before the Technical Board of the EPO, which had held 442 to be valid. But given the care which the House of Lords have refused to tackle the *Mobil* case,[27] which many believe to be wrong, it is at first surprising that the House of Lords was prepared to make this finding. Lord Hoffmann noted, as he had in *Merrell Dow*, that decisions of the EPO on questions of law are of 'considerable persuasive authority'. But he thought that the EPO had in the Biogen case directed its attention only to the question of whether the teaching in Biogen I would have enabled the skilled person to achieve expression of core and surface antigen. Nothing was said about whether the claims were too broad because expression could also be achieved without the use of the teaching which it contained or, in the words of the Technical Board in *Genentech I*,[28] 'in a manner which would not have been envisaged without the invention'. The principle was also clearly stated in the *Exxon* case. Lord Hoffmann therefore did not consider the outcome of this appeal to suggest any divergence between the jurisprudence of the House of Lords and the EPO. That reasoning is a key political statement. Yet when it is remembered that it is the very same patent on which the EPO and the House of Lords differ, can Lord Hoffmann be right? In effect the House of Lords behaved as a court of appeal from the EPO—it will be interesting to see what other national European courts think of that.

Conclusions

The House of Lords has undone much of the damage threatened by the Court of Appeal in its decision on this case. In particular, Lord Hoffmann's view that it will be rarely necessary to consider what is an 'invention' is welcome as it will prevent the courts from taking a short cut through questions of novelty and inventive step to hold invalid patents which may seem unattractive. Lord Mustill noted that where a case concerned a compound appearing in nature, as in *Genentech*, it might be necessary to look on the question again.

Attacks on priority will probably increase, particularly where there are intervening publications which may form part of the state of the art.[29] On obviousness the House of Lords has passed up a chance to give clear directions how UK law should develop. The linking

---

[27] *MOBIL/Friction reducing additives*, G02/88 [1990] EPOR 73.
[28] *GENENTECH I/Polypeptide expression* (T292/85) [1989] OJ EPO 275.
[29] See *Beloit Technologies Inc. v Valmer Paper Machinery Inc.* [1995] RPC 705; Jacob J following G03/93 *Priority interval* [1994] EPOR 521.

concept of enabling disclosure is helpful—even though it gives rise to difficulties when considering prior use.[30]

On sufficiency the decision is welcome. The discovery that 'lack of fair basis' has simply been unrecognised as a ground of invalidity should assist greatly in attacks on over-broad claims. It will be interesting to see how attacks on validity, on the basis that compounds do not work, fare before the UK courts. The timing of the date for sufficiency as the date of application is also welcome—the appellate courts should now consider the date at which infringement is assessed.[31]

For those drafting patent claims there are a number of important points. First, claims to a class of compounds may well be insufficient unless all the members of the class display the 'principle'. The presence of a single compound in the claims of a chemical patent which fails to work may invalidate the patent, whether for lack of support or under an EPO-style inventive-step attack.[32] Use of functional claims should therefore probably increase. Secondly, statements of inventive concept are likely to be more specifically and pointedly made, even though it is submitted that is not helpful. Thirdly, there is a new squeeze argument as sufficiency is to be explored by the courts.

The developing rDNA science should welcome the fact that patent protection is available; but there are certainly difficulties ahead in obtaining broad but sustainable protection.

---

[30] See Christopher Floyd QC in note 14 above.
[31] See Hoffmann J's test in *Improver Corp. v Remington Consumer Products Ltd* [1990] FSR 181.
[32] See note 24 above.

Over-broad Patent Claims: An Inventive Step by the EPO

[1996] 10 EIPR 561

IAN KARET
Linklaters & Paines

T939/92 Agrevo/Triazole Sulphonamides

In its decision of 12 December 1995 the Technical Board of Appeal of the European Patent Office (EPO)[1] upheld the decision of the Examining Division refusing Agrevo's patent application EP-A-0246749. The Board of Appeal showed how Article 56 (inventive step) of the European Patent Convention (EPC) can be used successfully to attack over-broad claims.

The Decision

This case concerned triazole herbicides which were active as herbicides in the form: where R_3 was expressed to represent 'optionally substituted phenyl', with certain provisos. They were originally claimed to be biologically active as herbicides.

The Examining Division objected to the definition of the claimed class of compounds using vague terms such as 'substituted', holding that 'substituted' could not be given its ordinary meaning in the context of products which were only claimed because of their biological activity. Since the special meaning of 'substituted' was different in each case it was used in the description, the claims were unclear. AgrEvo appealed.

---

[1] [1996] EPOR 171; Board 3.3.1: A.J. Nuss, Chairman, R.K. Spangenberg and J.A. Stephens-Ofner.

The Board of Appeal held that the claims AgrEvo had submitted during oral proceedings were novel: the Examining Division's objection to the use of the term 'substituted' had fallen away because the claims now covered certain chemical compounds *per se* and not just those having a particular biological activity. As biological activity was no longer an essential technical feature of the claimed subject-matter, it was not a part of the definition of the claimed subject-matter and so the term 'substituted' could have its ordinary technical meaning, that is, 'substituted by absolutely anything'. Accordingly, the claims were clear in the sense of Article 84 EPC.

The Examining Division had also held that claim 1 of the main request was an unreasonable generalisation of the examples contained in the description. The Board of Appeal disagreed. It did not follow from Article 84 EPC[2] that a claim was objectionable simply because it was 'unreasonably broad'. In particular, it did not follow from the requirement that the claims had to be supported by the description, as this simply meant that:

> the technical features stated in the description as being essential features of the described invention must be the same as those used to define the invention in the claims ... or otherwise the claims would not be true definitions but mere descriptions.

The Examining Division had, in the Board's view, wrongly relied on the fact that the skilled person reading the application would not have believed that all the claimed compounds would or could be likely to possess alleged herbicidal activity. As this was not part of the definition of the subject-matter of Claim 1, there was no lack of support by the description for that reason.

But this did not mean that the properties of the claimed subject-matter were irrelevant to the question of patentability. The Board said that this question was strongly linked to that of inventive step under Article 56 EPC. The Board held that it was generally accepted that the extent of a patent monopoly should correspond to and be justified by the patentee's technical contribution to the art.[3] Everything falling within a valid claim had to be inventive. If the claim did not comply with that requirement, then to justify the monopoly it should be amended so as to exclude obvious subject-matter. Accordingly, the notional person skilled in the art should be assumed to act with a specific technical purpose in mind in making the invention. That underlay the consistent approach of the Boards of Appeal in deciding the question of obviousness – they made an objective assessment of the technical results achieved by the claimed subject-matter and compared these with the results obtained accordingly to the state of the art. These results were then taken to be the basis for defining the technical problem which the claimed invention solved and in deciding whether the state of the art suggested that claimed solution.

Considering the large number of compounds AgrEvo had claimed, the Board suggested that it could approach the question in two ways. First, it could assume that the claimed compounds were not meant to be technically useful at all. That meant the technical problem that they 'solved' was merely the provision of new chemical compounds, irrespective of any useful property. In that case all known chemical compounds were equally suitable as a starting point for a structural modification, and no inventive skill needed to be exercised in selecting the compounds chosen in the patent when these were considered against the prior art. Secondly, the Board could assume that the compounds claimed did have some specific

---

[2] Article 84 provides: 'The claims shall define the matter for which protection is sought. They shall be clear and concise and be supported by the description.'

[3] T409/91 *EXXON/Fuel oils* [1994] EPOR 149 and T435/91 *UNILEVER/Hexagonal liquid crystal gel* [1995] EPOR 314.

technical effect. In that case a technical effect which justified the selection of claimed compounds had to be one which could fairly be found in substantially *all* the selected compounds. The assessment of the technical contribution to the art therefore had to take account of the actual technical reason for claiming the new compounds.

AgrEvo itself had chosen the second route and argued that all the claimed compounds had herbicidal activity (the specific technical effect) and the technical problem solved by the patent was thus the provision of new chemical compounds with herbicidal activity. But, in the Board's view, AgrEvo's submission was not supported by the publication. The test results in the description showed that some of the claimed compounds were herbicidally active; but that could not be regarded as sufficient evidence that substantially all the compounds possessed the activity claimed. The Board accepted AgrEvo's own proposition (one commonly made in this field) that a person skilled in the art would not be able to predict herbicidal activity on the basis of a structure alone, as it was known that even small structural modifications might cause major differences in biological activity. The Board concluded that reasonable predictions of relations between chemical, structure and biological activity were, in principle, possible, but there was a limit beyond which no such prediction could validly be made. That limit had to be established on the basis of available facts and evidence submitted for the purpose in each particular case.

The Board was thus not satisfied that substantially all the compounds claimed were likely to be herbicidally active, and as only those compounds which were herbicidally active could provide a solution to the technical problem of providing new herbicidal compounds, it had to be assumed that the claims which covered inactive compounds were simply meant to be claims covering any new chemical compounds. These were, in consequence, not inventive.

Comment

The EPO has moved to attack over-broad patent claims in a new way. In the United Kingdom, the question of how to deal with broad patent claims has been much discussed recently. In the UK Court of Appeal's decision in *Biogen v Medeva*,[4] much of the Court's reasoning appeared driven by a strong feeling that Biogen's claims were unreasonably broad, and the patent was found to be invalid. In contrast, in *Chiron v Murex*,[5] the Court of Appeal said that the old English cases dealing with speculative claims and claims to a 'known desideratum' were not applicable. There is a strong feeling that the UK courts will be receptive to arguments that a claim is not fairly based on the description, even though there is no specific legal ground under which such a claim may be brought.[6] The Board of Appeal decision in this case appears to provide a new way of phrasing an attack on over-broad claims on the grounds that they are not inventive whereas the attack has previously been thought of as a question of sufficiency. It will be interesting to see whether this is carried through in practice in national courts. In the United Kingdom the test for obviousness is that set out in *Mölnlycke v Procter & Gamble*,[7] which does not adopt as its starting point the 'technical problems' to be solved by the invention. Nevertheless, section 3 of the Patents Act 1977 is meant to be interpreted as closely as possible in conformity with the EPC,[8] and there is in

---

[4] [1996] FSR 4 and [1995] 1 EIPR 42.
[5] [1996] FSR 153.
[6] In *Genentech* [1989] RPC 147, the Court of Appeal made clear that section 14(5)(c) of the 1977 Act is not a ground for revocation by the courts.
[7] [1994] RPC 49.
[8] Section 130(7) Patents Act 1977.

theory no reason why the decision should not be applied in England.[9]

While there is no specific attack available against over-broad claims by way of opposition in the EPO or of revocation in the UK courts, the ingenuity of those attacking broad claims will continue the development of the law in this area.

---

[9] See the comments of Lord Jauncey in *Asahi* [1991] RPC 485 at 544 and Lord Hoffmann in *Merrell Dow v Norton* [1996] RPC 1.

Purposive Construction and Inventive Step

[1995] 3 EIPR 147

PAUL COLE
Beresford & Co

The Appeal in PLG Research Ltd and Netlon Ltd v Ardon International Ltd and Others

The present proceedings in the UK Court of Appeal, which were noted in the December issue,[1] related to two patents concerning the production of nets of plastics material by stretching apertured flat plastics sheet. At first instance, they had both been held by Aldous J not to be infringed and to be invalid by reason of obviousness.[2] On appeal his decision was reversed in part; both patents were held to be valid but only one of them was held to be infringed, and then only by the production of a particular group of the defendants' products. Consideration of inventive step focused on whether the selection of a particular starting material in an otherwise known stretching process was a mere workshop variant or involved an inventive insight. On infringement, the court disapproved the view that the *Catnic* test was applicable to patents granted under the 1977 Act and held that the relevant question, which was consistent with cases decided in Germany, was whether the alleged infringement could be derived by a skilled person from the language of the claims when interpreted by reference to the description and drawings. Which test is applicable is uncertain following the subsequent decision of the Patents Court in *Assidoman v Mead* that the remarks of the Court of Appeal in *PLG* were *obiter* and that the court was bound still to apply the *Catnic* test. However, a consistent trend can be discerned from recent decisions that the third *Catnic* question ought to be answered in a way that results in a narrow claim only when this is supported by plausible reasons and does not render the patent worthless.

The Technical Background

The patents in issue related to integral mesh structures of plastics material which were useful in civil engineering.

In the prior art there were two ways of forming a starting material which could subsequently be stretched, and which can be described as the 'strand extruding' and 'flat sheet' processes respectively. Strand extruding processes involve the immediate extrusion of strands with the

---

[1] [1994] 12 EIPR D—318.
[2] See [1993] FSR 197.

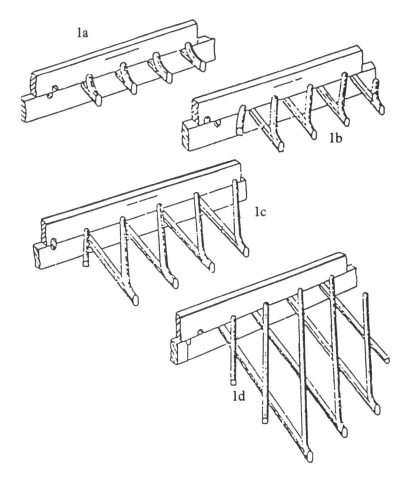

Figure 1 *Typical Strand Extrusion Process*
1a–1d: Extrusion of a biplanar net-like starting material for the Netlon process.

pattern of holes already present, whereas flat sheet processes start from flat extruded sheets, in which strands are created by the subsequent formation of holes.

The main strand extruding processes which were in use were the Netlon process and the Hureau process. The Netlon process was invented by the same Dr F.B. Mercer who was the inventor of the patents in issue, and is described in US-A-2919467. The process is illustrated in Figures 1a to 1d and involves the extrusion of molten plastic through slots in two contra-rotating circular dies, with strands being formed when the slots in the two dies are separated and with junctions being formed when the slots are in register. The extruded tube is expanded over a cylindrical mandrel, cooled, slit open, flattened and stretched to form a net. In the material immediately prior to stretching the strands remained in two separate planes and the material was noticeably asymmetrical, being bumpy on its upper surface and flat on its undersurface where it had been in contract with the mandrel. This so-called 'biplanar' starting material when stretched produced an asymmetrical net in which the strands in the machine direction and those in the transverse direction entered the junctions in different though over-lapping planes. The Hureau process is described in US-A-3252181 and gave rise to an extruded square mesh starting material in which the biplanar structure was also present.

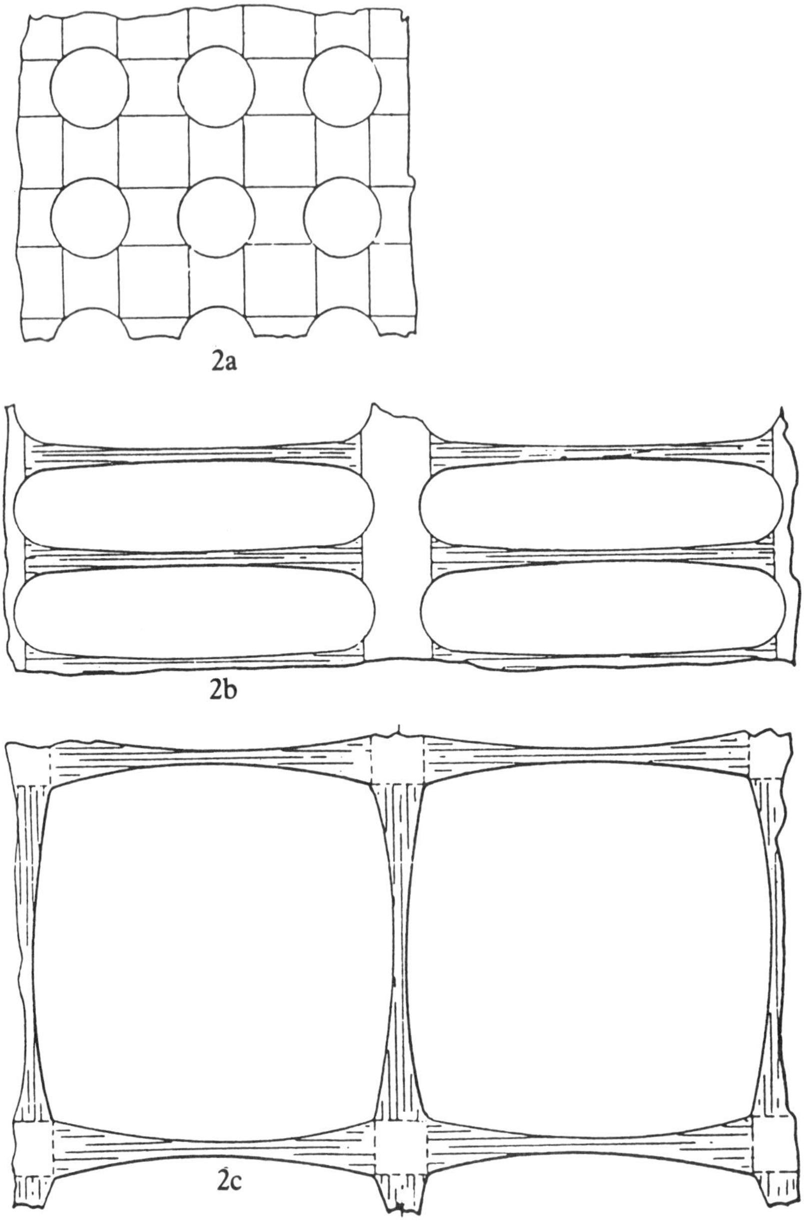

Figure 2   *Typical Flat Sheet Stretching Process*
2a–2c: Biaxial stretching of an apertured flat plastic sheeting according to Wyckoff, GB-A-982036.

Formation of nets by stretching thin flat sheets was described in a number of specifications of which GB-A-982036 (Wyckoff) is typical. In Figures 2a to 2c it can be seen that an apertured flat sheet is stretched in first one direction and then the other to produce a net of inter-connected strands. However, the stretching process is confined to the strands, and the junctions are unaffected by the stretching and consequently not strengthened by the molecular orientation that takes place on stretching.

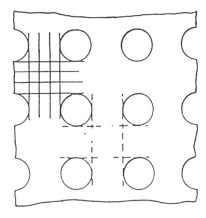

Figure 3 *The Plaintiffs' Starting Material*

In addition to prior patent specifications, the defendants had cited a number of prior used processes.

The two patents in issue identified a problem in all such integral mesh structures which was to provide junctions which were sufficiently strong without containing too much plastics material. The starting material for both patents is illustrated in Figure 3 and was defined in Claim 1 of each of the two patents to be a 'substantially uniplanar' starting material having a thickness of not less than 0.75 mm which had a pattern of holes or depressions whose centres lay on a notional substantially rectangular grid of rows and columns. A first stage of stretching the starting material led to the product shown in Figure 4. The method for producing that structure was claimed in GB-B-2073090 and required:

> stretching the starting material in a direction substantially parallel to the columns to stretch into oriented strands zones between adjacent holes or depressions of each row, the strands being interconnected by a set of substantially parallel bars generally at right angles to the strands, the stretching being effected to such an extent that a notional point which on the starting material lay on the notional straight line which is parallel to

Figure 4 *The Product of the 'Uniax' Patent*

the rows and is tangential to respective holes or depressions moves into the corresponding strand so that, on the mesh structure, the point is substantially spaced from the corresponding notional straight line which is parallel to the rows of mesh openings and is tangential to respective mesh openings, the mid point of the zone of the bar which connects the ends of aligned strands being substantially thicker than the mid-point of either of the strands interconnected by the zone.

A second stage of stretching in which the material of Figure 4 was stretched at right angles to the strands led to the material of Figure 5, whose production method was claimed in GB-B-2035191 (the 'Biax' patent) which required:

stretching the starting material in a direction substantially parallel to the columns and also stretching in a direction substantially parallel to the rows, to form a generally rectangular grid of orientated strands interconnected by orientated junctions each of which has a minimum thickness of not less than 75% of the thickness of the mid point of any of the strands passing into the junction, has a maximum thickness substantially greater than the thickness of any of the strands passing into the junction, and has a central zone which is substantially thicker than orientated zones on two opposite sides thereof, the edge zones of the crotches which extend between respective adjacent pairs of strands passing into the junction between orientated in the direction running around the respective crotch.

Inventive Step

At first instance, Aldous J had held that the two patents were invalid for lack of inventive step. His conclusions are stated as follows:

I have come to the conclusion that the invention of claim 1 of the Biax patent was obvious as of 1978. By that date, biaxial orientation of plastic nets to improve the qualities of the strands appears to have been widely adopted for a variety of nets … Further, the prior uses establish that manufacturers were producing nets having all the features of claim 1, save the starting material … Thus the only step that could have

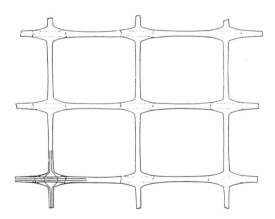

Figure 5   *The Product of the 'Biax' Patent*

been inventive was to start with a flat sheet with punched holes or embossed impressions so that the starting material was substantially uniplanar. Punched flat sheets were suggested in Wyckoff, Kalwaites and Hercules. Use of such a starting material to make the prior uses would have been possible and would, I believe, have been an obvious alternative to a starting material made using the Hureau process. Persons who were not licensed under the Netlon process or Hureau would, I believe, have immediately thought of stretching punched flat sheets ... Similarly the claims alleged to have independent validity in the Uniax patent are also obvious as they cover the first stretching operation of the Biax patent.[3]

The Court of Appeal reversed this finding and held that both patents were valid. It decided the question of obviousness on the basis of the four-part test set out in *Windsurfing v Tabur Marine*.[4] The court pointed out, however, that although the *Windsurfer* case had established that an example of the prior art could not be rejected on the ground of obscurity, there was a danger of making too readily the assumption that the significance of that prior art in relation to the problem dealt with by the patent would necessarily be apparent to the hypothetical skilled person; see the warning given in *Sandoz Ltd (Frei's Application)*,[5] which was repeated in the *Windsurfer* decision. The court observed:

The *Windsurfing* case was a case of what is sometimes called 'workshop variation'. It was not a case like the present of finding a solution to an identified problem. We do not consider it to have thrown any doubt on the many warnings given in previous cases such as *General Tire v Firestone* [1972] RPC 457 at 500–6 against the danger of assessing obviousness in the light of carefully selected pieces of prior art only. There are many cases in which obviousness has been held not to have been established even though the prior art relied on was very close, where the prior art had been selected by the defendants with the benefit of hindsight out of a wide range of other equally plausible starting points. Where the prior art yields many possible starting points for further development, it may not be obvious without hindsight to select a particular one of them for development which leads to the invention claimed. If the patentee has come up with a solution to his problem which is no more than an obvious extension or workshop variation to some piece of prior art, he cannot have a monopoly for his solution whether or not the skilled man would be likely to have known of the prior art in question. On the other hand, if it is found that, even if he had known of it, the skilled man would not have regarded it as the starting point for the solution of the problem with which he was confronted, this will usually demonstrate that his discovery was not an obvious extension or mere workshop variation of the prior art. For the meaning of 'obvious' in this context, it is sufficient to refer to the test formulated by Lord Herschell in *Siddell v Vickers* (1890) 7 RPC 292 at p. 304, i.e. whether what is claimed is: '... so obvious that it would at once occur to anyone acquainted with the subject and desirous of accomplishing the end ...'

In applying the law to the facts of the present case the court stated:

It is important to appreciate that (i) the inventive concept consisted in the selection and combination of a number of features (ii) that there was a multiplicity of possible starting

---

[3] *Ibid.*, at 234 to 235.
[4] [1995] RPC 59.
[5] [1976] RPC 449 at 457.

points in the prior art each of which differed from the patented invention but in a different way, and (iii) the relevant features of the prior art are interdependent, so that changing one of the features invalidates the teaching of the prior art in respect to others.

The problem with which the invention was concerned that was identified by the court was that stated in the specification, namely the production of a junction which was strong enough for heavy duty applications, but at the same time did not contain an excessive amount of plastics material. The court found that there could be an inventive step in Dr Mercer's discovery first that it was possible to produce a junction having the required properties and secondly that his particular recipe did so. It stated:

> The appellants contend that Dr Mercer's insight lay in recognising the importance of obtaining symmetry of orientation in the junctions, and therefore of employing a uniplanar starting material. The Respondents acknowledged that the importance of orientation was not part of the common general knowledge which the skilled addressee would have possessed at the priority date. They pointed out, however, that despite the alleged import-ance of the concept it was nowhere mentioned in the claims, and argued that it could not be the inventive step disclosed by the patents in suit. It was something which the skilled man would need to be taught, and which the patents did not teach him.
>
> But the uniplanarity of the starting material was an essential integer of the claim, and this also was novel at the priority date. It was not part of the common general knowledge. Indeed, the common general knowledge was in the opposite direction: if strong but oriented junctions were required, it was generally thought to be desirable to reduce the degree to which the paths of orientation intersected at the junctions by employing an essentially biplanar starting material . . .
>
> This emphasis on the uniplanarity of the starting material should not detract from the fact that other integers of the alleged invention were also essential, including for example the minimum thickness of the starting material . . . As the evidence showed and the specification itself stated, stretching a flat uniplanar sheet of insufficient thickness sufficiently far into the junctions to produce oriented lateral zones was liable to produce weak junctions with webbed filaments.

In expressing its disagreement with Aldous J that if a skilled man had been requested to produce the same net as the prior uses cited by the defendants, and he was neither a Netlon nor a Hureau licensee, it would have been obvious to start with a punched flat sheet, the court further explained its reasoning as follows:

> Nets made by stretching extruded strand starting materials and nets made by stretching flat sheet starting materials are inherently different; as was well known at the priority date, their paths of orientation during the stretching process were not the same. No doubt a skilled man who was not a Hureau or Netlon licensee and was asked simply to produce a plastics net would use a flat sheet as his starting material. But no one, asked to replicate a product made by stretching a material made of extruded strands, would use a flat sheet as his starting material. If he did so, he might or might not produce a similar product; he might or might not produce a better product; but he knew that he would not produce the same product.
>
> The Judge's error lay in treating the two main methods of forming the starting material as merely workshop variants, like the extent or rate of the stretching operation, either of which could be substituted for the other without affecting the other requirements of

the process. But in truth they were fundamentally different and gave rise to different problems. Stretching starting materials formed of extruded strands produced strong oriented junctions but wasted material at the junctions; they did not result in webbed filaments, but there was a risk of loss of adhesion. Stretching flat sheets avoided the loss of adhesion and (if the stretching was taken into the junctions) wasted less material but tended to produce webbed filaments in the junctions. The two methods of producing plastics nets were essentially different technologies and improvements in one could not necessarily be carried over to the other...

The skilled man, having decided to use a starting material formed from a flat sheet, would never have thought of using any of the cited prior art as a starting point for further development, since it consisted exclusively of products made from a different starting material. There was nothing in the common general knowledge about the stretching of flat sheets which suggested to him that there was any advantage to be gained by using uniplanar starting material; on the contrary the teaching was the other way, since the problem which had been identified by flat sheet stretchers was caused by excessive interference in the paths of orientation, the solution to which was thought to lie in adopting a biplanar starting material. In our judgment it would certainly not be obvious to the skilled man to use a uniplanar starting material, and if he had done so and used a material of insufficient thickness he would not have achieved his object...

Dr Mercer proposed a solution which went against all the prior teaching; he found a means of allowing the paths of orientation to intersect and yet create strong ordered junctions. We cannot hold such a discovery to have been obvious.

The Appropriate Test for Infringement

Interpretation of the claims of a patent in the United Kingdom is governed by section 125 of the Patents Act 1977 which has the same effect in the United Kingdom as Article 69 EPC. Section 125(3) provides that the Protocol on Interpretation of Article 69 shall apply for the purposes of Article 125(1) as it applies to Article 69 EPC. The Protocol reads:

> Article 69 should not be interpreted in the sense that the extent of protection conferred by the European Patent is to be understood as that defined by the strict, literal meaning of the wording used in the claims, the description and drawings being employed only for the purposes of resolving an ambiguity found in the claims. Neither should it be interpreted in the sense that the claims serve only as a guideline and that the actual protection may extend to what, from a consideration of the description and drawings by a person skilled in the art, the patentee had contemplated. On the contrary, it is to be interpreted as defining a position between these extremes which combines a fair protection for the patentee with a reasonable degree of certainty for third parties.

Up to the handing down of the present judgment, there had been a number of decisions of the English Patents Court and Court of Appeal affirming the proposition that the 'purposive construction' approach put forward by Lord Diplock in *Catnic Components Ltd v Hill and Smith Ltd*[6] was in accordance with the Protocol; see *Southco v Dzus*[7] and *Improver Corporation v Remington*.[8] At the trial of the *Improver* case, Hoffmann J, in reaching his decision that the

---

[6] [1982] RPC 183 at 242 to 243.
[7] [1992] RPC 299 (CA).
[8] [1989] RPC 69 (CA) and [1990] FSR 181.

patent in issue was not infringed, stated that, according to Lord Diplock's test, whether or not a particular variant was covered by the claim depended on the answers to the following three questions:

(1) Does the variant have a material effect on the way in which the invention works? If yes, the variant is outside the scope of the claim. If no—
(2) Would this have been obvious at the date of publication of the patent to a reader skilled in the art? If no, the variant is outside the claim. If yes—
(3) Would the reader skilled in the art nevertheless have understood from the language of the claim that the patentee intended that strict compliance with the primary meaning was an essential requirement of the invention? If yes, the variant is outside the claim.

In England, the *Improver* patent had been held not to be infringed, although (according to a statement contained in the Court of Appeal decision) in similar litigation elsewhere in Europe the patent had universally been held to be infringed, and when the case was before the German Oberlandsgericht, the conclusion reached by the English court was expressly rejected, the court commenting that the finding was probably the result of adopting the approach to construction laid down by the *Catnic* decision which was prior to the EPC. PLG submitted that the English law of infringement had been radically altered by the 1977 Act, and that the third *Catnic* question no longer formed any part of the English law of infringement. Instead, favourable answers to the first two *Catnic* questions should be conclusive in favour of the patentee.

The court was unable to accept PLG's proposition that the third *Catnic* question no longer formed any part of the English law of infringement because that question was the only one which raised a question of construction, and because its elimination would be contrary to Article 69 EPC, the Protocol and section 125(1), which made the language of the claim determinative of its scope. The German courts had also made repeated statements to the same effect. In *Improver Corporation and Another v Remington Products Inc.*, the Oberlandsgericht (which had reached the opposite conclusion from Hoffmann J) had stated:

When evaluating the scope of protection of claim 1 of the patent in suit, however, *the argument cannot be limited to identity of effect only* . . . For the purpose of fairly delimiting the actual improvement of the field of technical knowledge achieved by an inventor on the basis of Article 69(1) EPC and the Protocol on Interpretation, the protected invention will only be considered to be used if a person skilled in the art, *on the basis of reflections progressing from the meaning of the patent claims, i.e. the invention described therein* could find out, with the help of his professional knowledge at the priority date, the modified means used with the disputed embodiment as a means being identical in effect for solving the problem underlying the invention.

In the *Ion Analysis* case in 1988 the Düsseldorf Oberlandsgericht had stated:

What is decisive is whether the person skilled in the art, *by studying the invention described in the patent claims*, was able to discover the altered means used in the device attacked . . .

In the *Handle Cord for Battery* case in 1989 the Bundesgerichthof (Federal Supreme Court) stated:

The determination of the scope of protection of a patent under the new Act requires that the meaning of the content of the patent claims, to be determined by interpretation, constitutes not only a point of departure but the decisive basis for the determination of the scope of protection. This must be based on the patent claims ... The fact that the challenged embodiment deviates from the wording of the claim ... does not preclude the inclusion of the challenged embodiment into the scope of the patent at issue from the point of view of equivalency. However, what is missing is the observation that the average person skilled in the art would have been able to discover the embodiment deviating from the wording and literal sense of the patent claim by proceeding from the invention as it is defined in the patent claim.

Based on the above German decisions, the Court of Appeal decisively rejected the *Catnic* test and made the following statement of the present English law:

In applying the Protocol, therefore, the German Courts, no less than ours, insist that the scope of a patent must be determined by its language; and, while the extent of protection goes beyond the literal content of the claim to cover functional equivalents, it does not go beyond functional equivalents which are deducible from the wording of the claim. In determining the extent of protection, they ask whether the variant embodied in the disputed device is one which is deducible by a person skilled in the art from the wording and drawings [*sic*][9] of the claims. This appears to us to be not quite the same as the third *Catnic* question, but to be arguably more in conformity with the requirement of the Protocol that the wording of the patent should be construed so as to afford a fair measure of protection for the patentee.

In the present case the expression to be construed is 'substantially uniplanar'. The word 'substantially' imports a degree of flexibility which precludes an exact and literal construction, and makes it unnecessary to consider whether Lord Diplock's purposive construction was an accurate if proleptic application of the Protocol. It clearly went at least part of the way towards the European position by stretching the claims to cover minor variants which obviously have no material effect on the way the invention works. It does not, however, appear to us to be useful to consider whether it went further and may be taken as indicating the proper approach to construction under the Protocol. Such an exercise merely engenders a sterile debate on the precise meaning of Lord Diplock's words, a matter which should now be left to legal historians. Lord Diplock was expounding the common law approach to the construction of a patent. This has been replaced by the approach laid down in the Protocol. If the two approaches are the same, reference to Lord Diplock's formulation is unnecessary, while if they are different it is dangerous. In future, it is to be hoped that attention will be concentrated on the requirements of the Protocol and the developing European jurisprudence and not on those of the common law before 1977.

'Substantially Uniplanar'

The court was in general agreement with the interpretation adopted by Aldous J, where he stated:

---

[9] It seems tat there is a typographical error in the text here, and that the test that was intended to be put forward was whether the variant embodied in the disputed device was one that could be deduced by a skilled person from the claims as interpreted by the description and drawings. This language is consistent with other parts of the decision and with section 125 of the Act.

Uniplanarity is a physical characteristic which would be judged by the eye. However, the skilled addressee, when deciding whether or not a departure from uniplanarity was insubstantial would judge both the size of the departure and its quality. For instance, a blemish at the edge of a sheet of starting material could be an insubstantial departure, but, if present in the middle of the sheet could be a substantial departure.

What is or is not substantial is a matter of degree and the skilled addressee would understand that many types of starting materials could be used. However, the sort of departures that the patentee considered were insubstantial were those that occurred during the production of flat sheets and the making of holes by punching, embossing or the like ... Clearly the preferred starting material would be a flat sheet made strictly uniplanar.

The particular starting materials used to make the defendant's products had horizontal strands which were substantially flat on one side and rounded on the other, as was characteristic of products made by the Hureau process. Aldous J had held that this departure from uniplanarity was more than contemplated by the patentee, and stated:

Even if it is possible with the aid of photographs and the help of Counsel to steer a line between the alleged infringements and the alleged prior art, I cannot believe that this line is one which would have been drawn by a skilled addressee in 1980. He would read the patent and appreciate that the problem the invention sought to overcome was described by reference to net produced from flat sheets. He would have concluded that the departures from uniplanarity that the patentee was saying were insubstantial were the sort of departures that could occur in manufacture when working or extruding a flat sheet. Thus, using his knowledge of what was available in 1980, he would have been able to decide what was substantially uniplanar. The line sought to be drawn by the plaintiffs appears to me to be a shifting line drawn for convenience of result, rather than through the eyes of a skilled addressee seeking to apply the Protocol in 1980.

PLG had submitted that a starting material was 'substantially uniplanar' if its symmetry about its median plane was sufficient to cause the patterns of orientation in the junctions of the stretched product to be substantially symmetrical about the median plane. In affirming the decision that there was no infringement of the Biax patent, the Court of Appeal stated:

We reject this submission for two reasons. In the first place, symmetry of orientation is nowhere mentioned in the patent. All the integers of the patent, whether of the starting material or of the finished product, are concerned with geometric configuration. In the second place, even if the reference to the patterns of orientation is replaced by a reference to the geometric configuration of the finished product, the definition is circular. The skilled addressee would clearly understand that the degree of uniplanarity in the starting material would dictate the degree of uniplanarity in the finished product. The Appellants, therefore, answer the question: 'How great a departure from uniplanarity may be tolerated in the starting material?' by saying: 'That depends upon the degree of uniplanarity which you are looking for in the finished product'.

However, the court held that there were circumstances special to the Uniax patent which should be taken into account and permitted it to make a finding of infringement of that patent. It stated:

The one qualification which we would make to the Judge's observations is that, in considering the quality of a departure from strict uniplanarity in the starting material, the skilled addressee would apply a functional test. He would appreciate that the patentee had stipulated for a uniplanar starting material because he wanted to stretch it to form a uniplanar product. As Mr Lloyd, the Appellant's expert, said: 'A departure from uniplanarity is substantial if it has a significant effect on the behaviour of the material [during the stretching operation]'. In our view, therefore, not only would the skilled addressee regard a departure from uniplanarity at the edge of a sheet as insubstantial, but so too would he regard a departure from uniplanarity which occurred in a part of the starting material which it was not intended to stretch. He would regard such a departure as immaterial and one which could be disregarded.

The Court of Appeal therefore held that departure from uniplanarity in the transverse bars was something that a skilled person would tolerate for the Uniax patent because these bars constituted a part of the starting material which did not become stretched, and stated:

This does not mean that the expression 'substantially uniplanar' in the Uniax patent bears a substantially different meaning from the meaning it bears in the Biax patent; it means only that the word 'substantially' imports a qualitative as well as a quantitative qualification, and that the skilled man would need to know whether it was intended to stretch the starting material a second time before he could conclude whether the departure from uniplanarity was substantial. We conclude that the starting material of the [defendant's] products was substantially uniplanar within the meaning of that expression in the Uniax patent (though not the similar expression in the Biax patent) and infringed the Uniax patent accordingly.

Comments

In its earlier decision in the *Windsurfer* case, the Court of Appeal rejected the proposition that when considering the question of obviousness it ought to disregard any item of prior art on the ground that the item in question would not have been considered by a skilled person as a starting point for further development. The decision in *Windsurfer* had the advantage of seeming consistency with the EPO Appeal board decisions in T20/81, *SHELL/ Aryloxybenzaldehydes*[10] and T24/81, *BASF/Metal refining*,[11] where the position was taken that the problem to be solved had to be determined on the basis of technical success compared to the closest prior art and that all previously suggested embodiments ought to be taken into consideration which offered a skilled person a suggestion for solving the problem addressed, even where the embodiments were not particularly emphasised in the cited document. However, the *Windsurfer* decision was criticised by Stephen Gratwick QC in an article entitled 'Having regard to what was known or used revisited'[12] in which he argued that later inventions should not be held to lack inventive step over items of prior art which as a matter of historical fact had never had any practical impact and had never stimulated anybody to develop anything. The *Windsurfer* decision was difficult to reconcile with the earlier Court of Appeal decision in *Beecham v Bristol (Amoxycillin)*[13] where the decisive issue was whether

---

[10] OJ (EPO) 6/1982 at 217.
[11] OJ (EPO) 4/1983 at 133.
[12] [1986] LQR 403.
[13] [1980] RPC 261.

or not a prior patent disclosing a group of semi-synthetic penicillins was 'a seminal document'. In a paper by A.W. White and J. Warden, 'The British Approach to Obviousness',[14] it had been argued that it was necessary to look at all possible starting points. It is noteworthy that the present decision distinguishes the *Windsurfer* case and adopts an approach closer to that in the *Amoxycillin* case.

On infringement, it seems that the observations concerning the inapplicability of the *Catnic* test, though of great legal interest, may not have been essential to the decision, and in the later decision of the Patents Court in *Assidoman Multipak Limited v The Mead Corporation*,[15] it was stated that these observations were *obiter*. In that decision Aldous J reviewed at length the historical development of the UK law of infringement and concluded that he ought to continue to apply the *Catnic* test. He stated in relation to UK decisions which ante-date *Catnic*:

> There are numerous reported cases where the courts, having construed a claim of a patent, concluded that it was infringed despite the fact that the alleged infringement did not fall within the literal wording of the claim. That conclusion was based on a finding that the alleged infringement took the 'pith and marrow' of the claim. Thus in those cases the ambit of the monopoly claimed was determined as being wider than the literal meaning of the words of the claim.

In relation to legal developments since *Catnic* he continued:

> In the *Catnic* case, Lord Diplock took the opportunity to restate the law applicable to ascertaining the ambit of the monopoly of a patent, and the rest of their Lordships agreed with his speech. I do not believe that he intended to depart from the principle that had underpinned our law for many years that claims need to be interpreted to give protection to the patentee and at the same time to delimit the invention with sufficient clarity...
>
> It cannot be disputed that 'purposive' construction, as suggested by Lord Diplock in the *Catnic* test fits squarely within the guidelines of the Protocol on interpretation to Article 60. It ascertains the ambit of the invention set out in the claims and does not use the literal meaning of the words nor treat the words purely as a guideline. Its aim is to define a position between the extremes and to give a fair protection to the patentee with a reasonable degree of certainty for third parties. That, of course, has been the aim of the courts in the past and was the reason for invoking the doctrine of 'pith and marrow'. Further, 'purposive construction' provides a structured way to determine the ambit of the invention claimed...
>
> The Court does not approach the task of construction upon the basis of a presumption either that a patentee intended or did not intend to claim or exclude a variant. The court's task is to construe the document and decide what would be apparent to a skilled reader. If that be right, then I believe that 'purposive' construction is a means of navigating between Scylla, the rock of literal construction, and Charybdis, the whirlpool of guided freedom, as required by the Protocol and enables the court to arrive at a similar result to the German courts provided that the facts and submissions are the same...
>
> For myself I would be loathe to discard 14 years of case law unless it is certain that

[14] In John Warden (ed.), *Annual of Industrial Property Law*, 1977, at 447.
[15] Unreported, Aldous J, 13 December 1994.

'purposive' construction is not the correct approach under the Act. If it be right that 'purposive' construction should be left to legal historians, then it is necessary to put forward another means of navigation to enable the court to steer the correct course between Scylla and Charybdis. The middle ground referred to in the Protocol is not clearly defined and every court within the community has adopted a method of interpretation which it believes to be consistent with the Protocol. Recourse can be made to jurisprudence of other signatories to the Convention, but that requires analysis and rationalisation of the views of judges from many countries, not only Germany but also such countries as France, Holland, Denmark and Sweden. There is no European position except that set out in the Protocol.

The Court of Appeal decision in the *PLG* case has made it necessary to decide whether this court is bound to follow the guidance given by Lord Diplock in the *Catnic* case. Having reviewed the authorities in the Court of Appeal, I conclude that the correct approach to construction under the Patents Act 1977 is 'purposive' construction and believe that this court is bound to follow the guidance given by Lord Diplock as developed in the cases to which I have referred. Further, I have been unable to think of any better guidance which hopefully will result in consistent decisions between the courts of this country and those of other parties to the Convention.

It should also be borne in mind that the difference in result in the *Improver* case in the United Kingdom and Germany is at least as likely to have been because of different evidence having been before the court as because of the application of different legal principles, as noted by Aldous J in the *Assidoman* case. In the United Kingdom, expert evidence may be adduced as to the prior state of the art, the meaning of technical terms, the features of the invention which a practical man reading the specification would understand to be essential and novel, and whether any particular variant described within the specification would be understood to be covered by the claims. This evidence is tested in cross-examination. In the *Improver* case, the invention concerned an electrically powered depilatory device in which a helical spring was driven by a motor and had an arcuate hair-engaging portion arranged to define a convex side at which the windings were spread apart to trap the hair and a concave side at which the windings were pressed together to grip the hair. The alleged infringement was a similar device having a synthetic rubber rod which was formed into an arc and had a number of circumferential slits which opened and closed in the manner required by the claim. The question which Hoffmann J decided that he had to consider was (1) whether the expression 'helical spring' meant a particular familiar and readily available engineering component in which a bar or wire of uniform cross-section was wound into a helix, or (2) whether it should be interpreted to mean a class of bendy, slitty rods of which a close-coiled helical spring in the primary sense was a striking and elegant example, but which could also include the defendant's rubber rod. He decided that the rubber rod was not an approximation to a helical spring but was a different thing which could work in the same way only in limited circumstances. He therefore held that the change from a metal spring to a rubber rod was not a minor variant and that a skilled person would have doubted whether the patentee wished to cover a rubber rod because rubber had problems of hysteresis which might be difficult to overcome, the inventors of the patent had done no work on rubber rods, and a rubber rod could not be used in a coiled configuration which was the patentee's preferred embodiment. Hoffmann J therefore decided that a rubber rod was not covered by the claim. If he has asked himself whether a rubber rod could be derived from the language of the claims when interpreted in the light of the description and drawings, it is unlikely that he would have given an affirmative answer unless the claims had already contained a more generalised definition of the hair-gripping element. Indeed, in his judgment in the *Improver* case, Hoffmann J observed that the Düsseldorf Landgericht had treated the claims as a mere guideline rather than adopting the median course required by the Protocol and had differed from the views expressed by the Oberlandesgericht (the Court of Appeal) which during an application for an interlocutory injunction had placed more emphasis on the language of the claims and had held that there was no infringement. It is therefore not clear that the change put forward by the Court of Appeal in *PLG* solves the problem to which it is directed.

It is relevant to consider whether these and other recent decisions do anything to clarify the third part of the *Catnic* test, given the difficulty which the Court of Appeal had experienced in *Daily v Berchet*.[16] In the *Catnic* test, following an affirmative response to the first two Diplock questions, the position is established that the variant in question does not have a material effect on the way in which the invention works and that this fact would have been obvious to a skilled addressee of the specification. The question arises: In these circumstances, when would it be just to deny that the variant is covered by the claim?

An answer which allowed a narrow construction only when supported by plausible reasons was recently put forward by the Court of Appeal in *Glavrabel v British Coal*,[17] which concerned a patent granted under the 1949 Act. The Court of Appeal stated the principles governing the 'purposive construction' of patent claims as follows:

> If possible the meaning of the document must be moulded to conform to the purpose of its author or authors—the purpose being judged from the document as a whole and the surrounding circumstances. To put it another way, there is conflict with the purpose if the Judge is disposed to say to himself: 'He cannot have meant that'. In the *Catnic* case itself, Lord Diplock said (at p. 244): 'No plausible reason has been advanced why any rational patentee should want to place so narrow a limitation on his invention. On the contrary, to do so would be to render his monopoly for practical purposes worthless . . .' This is in my view an example of the purposive method of construction. It is at least allied to, and perhaps an example of, what Lord Reid said in *L. Schuler AG v Wickman Machine Tool Sales Ltd* [1974] AC 235 at p. 251: 'The fact that a particular construction leads to a very unreasonable result must be a relevant consideration. The more unreasonable the result, the more unlikely it is that the parties can have intended it, and if they do intend it the more necessary it is that they should make their intention abundantly clear.'

The same approach was adopted by Aldous J and by the Court of Appeal in *Southco v Dzus*,[18] by the Court of Appeal in *PLG v Ardon* in its decision that uniplanarity was immaterial in a part of the starting material that was not being stretched, and by Aldous J in the *Assidoman* case where he rejected the claim construction put forward by the defendant, *inter alia*, on the ground that if the disputed requirement were essential, then third parties could take the whole benefit of an embodiment illustrated in one of the patent drawings without infringing the relevant claim.

---

[16] [1993] RPC 357, see Cole [1994] 10 EIPR 455.
[17] Unreported, 9 November 1994.
[18] Note 7 above, at 314 and 315.

Section 64 of the UK Patents Act 1977: Right to Continue Use Begun before Priority Date

[1994] 6 EIPR 239

ISABEL DAVIES AND SIMON COHEN
Taylor Joynson Garrett, London

Section 64 Patents Act 1977 gives what is termed a statutory licence to a person who, in good faith, either does an infringing act (as defined in section 60 of the Patents Act) or makes effective and serious preparations to do such an act.

Section 64(1) states:

> where a patent is granted for an invention, a person who in the United Kingdom before the priority date of the invention:
>
> (a) does in good faith an act which would constitute an infringement of the patent if it were in force, or
> (b) makes in good faith effective and serious preparations to do such an act,
>
> has the right to continue to do the act or, as the case may be, to do the act, notwithstanding the grant of the patent; but this right does not extend to granting a licence to another person to do the act.

Section 64(2) confines the statutory licence to the right to continue to do or to do 'that act', namely the act which the person had done or had made effective and serious preparations to do.

Section 64(2) states:

> If the act was done, or the preparations were made, in the course of a business, the person entitled to the right conferred by subsection (1) may—
>
> (a) authorise the doing of that act by any partners of his for the time being in that business, and
> (b) assign that right, or transmit it on death (or in the case of a body corporate on its dissolution), to any person who acquires that part of the business in the course of which the act was done or the preparations were made.

Section 64(3) states:

> where a product is disposed of to another in exercise of the right conferred by subsection (1) or (2), that other and any person claiming through him may deal with the product in the same way as if it had been disposed of by the registered proprietor of the patent.

General

There was no corresponding provision under the 1949 Patents Act, where secret prior use was a ground of invalidity (section 32(1)(1)).[1] With removal of this ground of invalidity in the 1977 Act, the protection for someone who started in good faith carrying out acts which would have constituted patent infringement, had the patent already been granted, is more limited. Whereas, under the old law, the patent was rendered invalid, under the new provisions the prior user himself is given a complete defence to continue the 'infringing' acts, but he must prove that the acts were done in good faith and that either they would have actually constituted an infringement of the patent or, as a minimum, he made effective and serious preparations to do such acts.

It can be readily appreciated that, in contrast with the certainty of the old law, the new law has plenty of areas of ambiguity which can make litigating under section 64 an expensive minefield.

The Choice Between Publicity and Confidentiality

One of these areas of uncertainty is the overlap with section 2(2) of the Act which states:

(1) An invention shall be taken to be new if it does not form part of the state of the art.
(2) The state of the art in the case of an invention shall be taken to comprise all matter (whether a produce, a process, information about either, or anything else) which has at any time before the priority date of that invention been made available to the public (whether in the United Kingdom or elsewhere) by written or oral description, by use or in any other way.

It is settled law that to invalidate a patent a disclosure has to be what has been called an enabling disclosure. That is to say, the disclosure has to be such as to enable the public to make or obtain the invention. It is also settled law that there is no need to prove that anybody actually saw the disclosure provided the relevant disclosure was in public.

However, the invention must have been made available to the public. If this cannot be proved, then the defendant may have to be satisfied with a mere defence rather than invalidating the patent. Inventors may therefore face a dilemma. Should an inventor:

(1) Keep all development work confidential, denying others the technology but not preventing others from applying for patent protection based on their own development work? In this case, if another inventor does obtain patent protection, he risks being sued and must hope that he had done enough before the priority date of the other's patent (albeit not in public) to be entitled to a defence under section 64.
(2) Patent as much as possible as quickly as possible? An expensive option but one which will pay dividends if an invention should become a money-spinner.
(3) Publicise development work and technological advances as quickly as possible to prevent competitors (and consequentially himself) obtaining patent protection for the invention?

Clearly, the choice depends on a number of factors, including the inventor's financial

---

[1] See for example *Wheatley's Application* [1985] RPC 91.

position and aims and the technology involved. Some areas of technology may be perceived as being too short term to justify the patent investment.

What Must Be Proved for a Section 64 Defence?

Another relevant issue is what a defendant must prove for section 64 to apply. A defendant will certainly want to avoid being in a position where not only is he unable to rely on a prior publication to invalidate the patent in suit but he has also not done sufficient for section 64 to apply either. These aspects will be dealt with next.

'Does in good faith an act'

This is not defined in the Act, but as it has wide general usage, it is not difficult to see what the words are aimed at. For example, if information was disclosed in confidence to a defendant and then used in breach of confidence and without consent to carry out acts constituting an infringement, this would doubtless not be good faith.

'An act which would constitute an infringement of the patent if it were in force'

The act must infringe at least one claim of the patent in suit, that is, fall within section 60(1) or (2) of the 1977 Act. These include the situation in which the invention is a product: making, disposing of, offering to dispose of, using and importing the product. Where the invention is a process, infringing acts include: using the process and disposing of, offering to dispose of, using or importing a product made by the process.

Section 60(5) excludes certain acts from constituting infringement, for example, where an act is done privately and for purposes which are not commercial (section 60(5)(a)) or is done for experimental purposes relating to the subject-matter of the invention (section 60(5)(b)).

Therefore, a defendant which has been working the invention privately (non-commercial purposes) before the priority date will not be protected from working the invention for commercial purposes, unless it can be argued that such workings constituted 'effective and serious preparations' to do the infringing act (see further below). He will, of course, be able to continue his non-infringing private activities.

'Effective and serious preparations to do such an act'

If an 'infringing' act has not been done, then the defendant must show 'effective and serious preparations to do such an act'. Again 'effective' and 'serious' are not defined anywhere in the Act although they are also used in section 28 (Restoration of lapsed patents). Turning to the case law, there have only been two cases before the UK courts dealing with section 64 and judicial comment on the ambiguous aspects is unfortunately very limited.

Helitune Ltd v Stewart Hughes Ltd[2]
The patent in suit related to a method of detecting the degree of unbalance of helicopter

---

[2] [1991] FSR 171.

rotor blades using an 'active system' in which light or other radiation was directed up at the blades and was then reflected back from the blades to receivers.

The defendant pleaded a defence under section 64 that it had carried out acts of the type alleged to infringe before the priority date of the patent or alternatively had made effective and serious preparations to do such acts, and was therefore entitled to continue to do the acts alleged to infringe.

Aldous J said:

> I believe that the correct approach is to look first to see what are the acts of the defendant which are alleged to be infringements and which it wishes to continue. Thereafter I must decide whether it carried out those acts in good faith before the priority date or whether it made effective and serious preparations to do so ... At the date of the patent, the defendant had a prototype active tracker which had been fitted on a helicopter ... However, ... the defendant was engaged in developing a passive tracker and was not making preparation to turn the laser tracker into a vendible product or to do anything with it. It was not until August 1984 (after the priority date of the Patent) that the defendant again considered the feasibility of an active tracking device.
>
> At the priority date of the patent, the defendant had not sold an active tracker. It had, however, produced a prototype of an active tracker using a laser with a view to its further development. The position had not been reached where the defendant had decided to sell active trackers, and by the priority date its efforts were concentrated on producing a passive tracker. I do not believe [that at the priority date] *the defendant had reached the stage of making effective and serious preparations to sell an active tracker, and, therefore, section 64 does not give it a defence to the action (emphasis added)*.

Aldous J is saying that the defendant had not gone far enough with its plans to commercialise active trackers: it had no right therefore to sell them now that there was a patent covering this technology. However, only limited guidance is given as to how much the defendant must do to satisfy 'effective and serious preparations'. As Aldous J says in his judgment:

> Section 64(1) relates to acts which constitute an infringement and not to any particular product or process. As I have stated the acts are those covered by a patent as set out in section 60. Thus, provided a person has carried out an infringing act before the priority date, he can continue to carry out that act even though the product or process may be different to some degree. This can be illustrated by considering a person who uses an infringing process. The fact that he alters that process after the priority date does not matter. The section states that the doing of that act, namely using an infringing process, shall not amount to an infringement ...

> ... the [section 64(2)] right is limited to the particular act of infringement done or for which effective and serious preparations had been made. That conclusion can be illustrated by considering a person who had in good faith imported an infringing product. The section enables him to continue to import the product but not to sell it unless the importation amounted to an effective and serious preparation to sell it ...

However, the judge in the subsequent case of *Lubrizol* (see below) casts some doubt on the judgment in *Helitune*.

Lubrizol Corp. and Another v Esso Petroleum Co. Ltd and Others[3]

The patent related to certain additives for oil. The plaintiffs had applied to join the third defendant to the proceedings on the basis that it was a joint tortfeasor with the first two defendants. The particulars of infringement included reliance on sale by the defendant of a lubricating oil additive concentrate under the name ECA 7474, as well as other additives alleged to be infringements.

In their evidence in support of joinder, the plaintiffs relied on documents which showed that the defendant was co-operating in the design, manufacture, testing and marketing of ECA 7474 and sent samples to various potential customers in the United Kingdom and geared up for manufacture of the product in the United Kingdom all before the priority date.

The third defendant therefore argued that if ECA 7474 was within the scope of the claims, then section 64 applied, affording it a complete defence.

Furthermore, it argued that, as a result of Aldous J's decision in *Helitune*, the effect of section 64 is to give it immunity in respect of similar activities conducted in respect of other products, including those other products which are named in the particulars of infringement. The immunity from suit would cover products which did not even come into existence until well after the patent's priority date.

The third defendant said that, in relation to ECA 7474, the plaintiffs relied on evidence which shows that its clients in good faith had marketed, used or kept or had made effective and serious preparations to market, manufacture, use and keep those products in the United Kingdom. It argued that it was therefore bound to have a defence under section 64 and in particular, as a result of the decision of Aldous J in *Helitune*, that it was bound to have a defence not just in relation to ECA 7474 but in relation to all the other products as well.

Hugh Laddie QC, sitting as a deputy judge of the High Court, disagreed:

> It seems to me that this attractive argument does not get [the third defendant] all the way. At its simplest, it can be said as follows. At the end of the day, the court may come to the conclusion that ECA 7474 has never infringed the claims of the patent in suit, although the other products do. Therefore the defence under section 64, even bearing in mind Aldous J's decision in *Helitune*, will give him no protection. Section 64 in those circumstances simply does not come into operation. Perhaps that is sufficient for the purpose of this case.
>
> However, I think it is only right to say that I have some doubts, with great respect to Aldous J, as to whether *Helitune* is correct. The act which the alleged infringer is entitled to continue to conduct by virtue of section 64(2) is the act which he was committing before the priority date. It was not an infringement then. It was an act of commerce. It is that specific act of commerce which he is entitled to continue. I have difficulty in accepting that by, for example, manufacturing product A before the priority date, he was thereby given a right to manufacture any product after the priority date. In my view, section 64 intended to safeguard the existing commercial activity of a person in the United Kingdom which is overtaken by the subsequent grant of a patent. It is not meant to be a charter allowing him to expand into other products and other processes.
>
> As [counsel for the plaintiff] points out, in any event, it may be that at the trial his clients will seek and be allowed to amend the claims so as to exclude ECA 7474, so that even if it is within the scope of the claims now, it will not be at the trial, and that

---

[3] [1992] RPC 281.

amendment will date back to the original grant of the patent. If that is done then, once again, section 64 would have no application.

As can be seen, the ambit of 'effective and serious preparations' is still in a state of flux. It would seem reasonable to state that the defence should be restricted to acts of the same type (as defined in section 60(1)—make, sell, import and so on) unless one can argue that the act itself was effective and serious preparation for another act: if the prior act was an importation, the section enables you to sell but only if you can show that the importation amounted to an effective and serious preparation to sell it. Clearly, this will depend on its facts, but it seems highly arguable that if someone imports a product which is clearly not for their own use, it constitutes effective and serious preparations to sell it (this line of argument was referred to in *Helitune*). But the prior act itself should not be restricted to an identical one (as Mr Laddie seems to be suggesting)—the product or process may be different to some degree, allowing the courts to decide on the merits of the individual case what amount of leeway it should allow.

It may well be that the courts will have to strike a balance between allowing a defendant to continue commercialising its earlier product or process along with routine modifications and improvements to that product or process and allowing the defendant to market a process of product with modifications which result in what is truly a very different product or process. Granted the 20 years' monopoly, an inability to improve a product in line with general developments in the industry might well result in the protection of section 64 being lost for all practical purposes.

Transmission of Section 64 Right

The section makes clear that the right cannot be licensed but can be assigned in certain circumstances: for example, where partners have carried out the relevant acts (prior to the priority date) and then the partnership is incorporated, the company will be able to show that, along with all the assets and in return for shares of the company, the section 64 right has been assigned.

Prior Act Must Be Carried Out in the United Kingdom

The status of section 64 should perhaps be questioned under the provisions of the Treaty of Rome, bearing in mind the recent European Court of Justice decision in *Generics (UK) Ltd and Another v SmithKline & French laboratories Ltd.*[4] This case related to the compulsory licence provisions of the Patents Act 1977.

Section 48 of the 1977 Act provides in essence for the grant of compulsory licences in situations, *inter alia*, where a patent is not being worked in the United Kingdom to the fullest extent that is reasonably practicable or where demand for the patented product in the United Kingdom is being met to a substantial extent by importation. In its judgment in the *SmithKline & French* case, the European Court of Justice held that a policy followed by national authorities which granted compulsory licences on terms which favoured domestic production of the patented product rather than importation from another Member State offended against Article 30 of the Treaty of Rome relating to freedom of movement of goods within the European Community.

---

[4] [1993] RPC 333.

By analogy, there may be an argument that section 64 as well offends Article 30 in that the prior act must have taken place inside the United Kingdom.

The Section 64 Right Around the World

In the United States, no such right is required because priority is based on 'first to invent' rather than 'first to file'. As there are moves afoot to harmonise US law with Europe, the prior use right is a matter which will have to be addressed.

As John Neukom explained in an article in this journal,[5] most countries within the European Community have an express prior use right.

However, the extent of this right varies from country to country. (It is beyond the scope of this article to review development of the right in the other European Patent Convention countries.

Practical Aspects

One of the difficulties likely to arise for a party relying on section 64 in a High Court patent action is in relation to discovery.

Take the following scenario: the year is 1984 and suppose company D is working on a particular area of technology and, unbeknown to it, company P is also working in the same area. Around that time, company P applies for and by 1988 obtains worldwide patent protection. P begins to assert its patent say, in 1992 and sues D for infringement. D relies on section 64.

However, the product which D now markets in the late 1980s is very different from the prototype and first generation products which D worked on before the priority date. There have been many changes in the product and the production process is becoming every more automated.

There will be questions as to whether the pre-priority date work constituted 'effective and serious preparations' for the ultimate product. However, in the meantime, D may be required to give limitless discovery relating to all aspects of each and every production process and each and every product from the first to the current products. Bearing in mind that there is no judicial agreement on how similar the prior act should be to the infringing act, the discovery process is made even more difficult.

Another problem may be the memory of witnesses. A number of years are likely to have elapsed since D's pre-priority date development work. Nevertheless, if D is to mount a persuasive section 64 case, and since the onus of proving its case is on it, detailed evidence of the early work and dealings with third parties will have to be given.

Conclusions

Clearly, further judicial pronouncements are needed to define the extent of the protection to be awarded under section 64. If defendants are to have any real protection in all but limited circumstances (which is surely what Parliament intended), defendants must be given a reasonable amount of leeway to modify and improve that which they were working on before the priority date of another person's patent.

---

[5] [1990] 5 EIPR at 165.

Employees' Inventions:

Inventorship and

Ownership
[1997] 5 EIPR 262

P.A. CHANDLER
Faculty of Law, UWE, Bristol

Greater Glasgow Health Board's Application[1]; Staeng Ltd's Patents[2]

Section 39 of the Patents Act 1977[3] enacted a statutory test for determining the ownership of all employees' inventions.[4] However, as the provisions of the section were skeletal in nature, subsequent interpretation and clarification by the courts and the Patent Office was especially important. Unfortunately, the dearth of reported litigation in this area has meant that a 1985 Patents Court decisions still dominates U.K. thinking.[5] It is therefore with considerable interest that one greets two recently reported decisions in which the provisions of section 39 were applied: *Greater Glasgow Board's Application* in the patents Court and Staeng's *Application* in the Patent Office.

Inventorship

Proof of inventorship is an essential precursor for any employee who wishes to assert ownership of an invention under section 39. Section 7(3) of the PA77 defines an inventor as 'the actual deviser of the invention and "joint inventor" shall be construed accordingly'. Although the PA77 offers little further guidance on the meaning of 'actual deviser', one must assume that the person or persons who contribute the protectable originality in the application (i.e. the inventive step)[6] will be considered the inventor(s).[7]

The issue of inventorship arose specifically in *Staeng's Application*. The facts show that N was an employee of H Ltd, a large company primarily concerned with the manufacture of

---

[1] [1996] RPC 207.
[2] [1996] RPC 183.
[3] Hereinafter referred to as 'PA77'
[4] However, previous common law notions might still prove helpful to the courts. For example, the possibility that senior employees owe a special obligation to further the interests of their employers, contained in section 39(1)(b), owes much to pre-1977 case law, e.g. *Worthington Pumping Engine Co. v Moore* (1903) 20 RPC 41. See also J. Phillips and MJ. Hoolahan, *Employees' Inventions in the United Kingdom* (1982) p.55, and A. Chandler and J Holland, *Information: Protection, Ownership and Rights* (1993), pages 128–29.
[5] *Harris's Patent* [1985] RPC 19.
[6] See, for example, *Homan's Patent* (1889) RPC 104
[7] For this reason, section 36 PA77 provides for the possibility of joint inventorship.

cable markers and heatshrink products for use in the cable industry.[8] He was regularly approached by R, an employee of the applicant, S Ltd, a small specialist company which designed and developed cable harnesses and backshell adaptors. An ongoing business relationship had in fact developed between their two companies, which, subsequent to the making of the invention which formed the basis of the hearing, ended with H Ltd acquiring S Ltd. This acquisition was mutually beneficial: S Ltd designed and arranged for the manufacture of backshell adaptors and H Ltd designed and manufactured the heatshrink sleeves, with these complementary elements being packaged and sold together in kit form by H Ltd. At one of the meetings between N and R, prior to the acquisition, R showed N a backshell adaptor which was being developed and asked if there was an alternative way of holding the cable screen to the adaptor without the use of specialised machinery. N suggested a constant tension spring, a suggestion which proved so successful that it formed the basis of a subsequent patent application by S Ltd. Without N's knowledge R was designated the sole inventor. N now claimed that he should have been named as sole inventor.

The hearing officer recognised that the role performed by N in solving R's problems was far greater than that of R, but concluded that N had failed to discharge the onus of proof required to establish his claim to sole inventorship. Unfortunately, the hearing officer's reasons were extremely terse, to the point of being unhelpful. Having commented on the brief and conflicting arguments by counsel, he stated:

> *It seems clear* on the evidence that [N] did not come up with the idea of using a spring unprompted, and, indeed, that he is unlikely to have done so had [R] not spoken to him about the problem in the first place ... [R] alerted [N] to the notion that the method of attaching cable braids to backshell adaptors which [S Ltd] had been using until then might in some way be improved. *[R] posed the question and [N] came up with a suggested solution.* Tests on that solution far surpassed their expectations.[9]

Thus R was awarded joint inventorship status simply because he 'posed the question' with N, without some 'prompting', would not otherwise have asked himself, owing to his recognised ignorance in matters relating to backshell adaptor construction.

One criticism of this decision is that it fails to take account of section 43(3) of the PA77, which states that a person who merely contributes 'advice or other assistance in the making of the invention' will not be considered to be the inventor or a joint inventor.[10] As R's only recognised contribution was to pose the question, the mere posing of the question must have demonstrated some degree of originality. Indeed, this is a recognisable form of inventiveness. For example, an inventive step may arise from the 'identification of a problem to be solved', even though the solution is obvious once the problem has been posed.[11] In *Re Rider*[12] the Technical Board of Appeal accepted that the 'discovery of a problem until then unrecognised

---

[8] N's official title was 'Product Development Manager'. He was responsible directly to the Managing Director and supervised a group of Product Managers who controlled the technical side of current product development and innovation.

[9] note 2 above, p.190 (*emphasis added*).

[10] The subsection seems to have escaped the attention of everyone involved in the case, even though one can argue that it represents a codification of the nineteenth-century common law position on inventorship. See, for example, *Smith's Patent* (1905) 22 RPC 61. See also *Agawan Woolen Co. v Jordan* (relying on the English authority of *Allen v Rawson* (1841) CB 551, 135 ER 656), where the court stated that if the 'employer has conceived the plan of an invention and is engaged in experiments to perfect it, no suggestions from an employee, not amounting to a new method or arrangement, which, in itself is a complete invention, is sufficient to deprive the employer of the exclusive property in the perfected improvement'.

[11] *European Patents Handbook*, CIPA (2nd ed., 1992) at paragraph 3.5.2.

[12] Decision T02/83 *RIDER/Simethicone tablet* [1979–85] EPOR Vol. C. 715.

may, in certain circumstances, give rise to patentable subject-matter in spite of the fact that the claimed solution is (with hindsight) trivial and in itself obvious'.

However, in *Re Rider* it was crucial that the successful patent applicant had suggested an improvement which contradicted the teachings of the state of the art. In *Staeng*, it is difficult to see how R's formulation of the problem was anything more than a repetition of a known problem which those in backshell adaptor manufacture regularly encountered but had yet to resolve.[13] Certainly, there was no suggestion that the phrasing of the question hinted at the answer. Perhaps the hearing officer assumed that, as N reached the solution so quickly, originality must have lain, at least in part, elsewhere? If so, such a conclusion flies in the face of accepted principle.[14]

Clearly the onus was on N to *prove* sole inventorship. However, given that counsel for S Ltd touched only 'very briefly' on the issue of inventorship, and that R was content to appear as sole inventor on the patent application while admitting that N's contribution represented the whole basis of the invention, perhaps the hearing officer might have shown greater leniency in setting the appropriate standards of proof for N.[15] Certainly, it seems unfortunate that, when recent case law has already placed unnecessary obstacles in the path of employee inventors claiming compensation under sections 40 to 41 of the PA77,[16] further constraints are being imposed on them in so far as they seek to maximise their entitlement by asserting sole inventorship for the purposes of those sections.

Ownership of Invention

Having established inventorship, one must turn to section 39(1) of the PA77. This states that an invention made by an employee will belong to his employer for the purposes of the 1977 Act if:

(a) it was made in the course of the normal duties of the employee ... and the circumstances ... were such that an invention might reasonably be expected to result from the carrying out of his duties; or

(b) the invention was made in the course of the duties of the employee and, at the time of making the invention, because of the nature of his duties and the particular responsibilities arising from the nature of his duties he had a special obligation to further the interests of the employer's undertaking.[17]

Section 39(1)(a) and normal duties

In both *Greater Glasgow* and *Staeng*, attention was drawn first to the respective employees' job descriptions. Clearly, the job description of an employee inventor offers a snap-shot view of the employer's anticipated needs at the time of appointment, offering a basis for for-mulating the duties which the employee will be expected to perform. But, as an employee

---

[13] Certainly, there was no suggestion that the invention had satisfied a long 'unfelt want'. If this had been the case, R might have had an arguable case based on the subsequent success of the invention; see, for example, *Ludlow Jute Co. v Low* (1953) 70 RPC 69 at 73.

[14] See, for example, *Vickers, Sons & Co. Ltd v Siddell* (1890) 7 RPC 292 at 304, and *Riekmann v Thierry* (1897) 14 RPC 105 at 115, HL.

[15] It seems unfortunate that the PA77 does not contain greater discretionary powers in this situation, the benefits of which were clearly exhibited in pre-1977 times by Lord Cranworth in *Re Russell's Patents* (1858) 2 De G & J 130.

[16] See A. Chandler, 'Employee inventions: Outstanding Compensation?' (1992) *Journal of Business Law* 300.

[17] Note that subsection 2 states that 'any other invention shall ... belong to the employee'.

acquires greater experience and develops new skills to meet the challenges of the ever-changing demands of the market and his employer, so his duties will change. The job description is a useful *starting-point* for identifying the employee's actual duties at the time of making the invention, but the reality of the job must also be allowed to intrude. For this reason, the Patents Court in *Harris's Patent* adopted a cautionary approach, preferring to 'lift the veil' and identify the real duties performed by Harris, the employee. Thus, although Harris's job description required him to use his specialist knowledge to deal with problems experienced by customers of his employer, he had no research laboratory or other facilities, never undertook creative design activity and always referred major design problems to another company, S Ltd, licensors of his employee. The court concluded that, as his employers had never taken it on themselves to solve design problems, it could not have been part of Harris's normal duties to provide solutions to these problems.

Do the decisions in *Greater Glasgow* and *Staeng* follow this eminently sensible approach? In particular, what attempts were made to ensure that the link, in practice, between the employees' actual duties and their inventions was sufficiently strong to warrant the use of section 39(1)(a) of the PA77?

Greater Glasgow Health Board's Application

In 1988 M made an invention relating to an optical spacing device for use with an indirect ophthalmoscope. At the time he was employed as a Registrar in the Department of Ophthalmology, by Greater Glasgow's Health Board. His job description stated that his duties included:

- [having] ... clinical responsibilities in the Out-Patient Department and in Casualty and ... duties relating to the ophthalmic and general care of in-patients including ophthalmic surgery.
- [working] ... the standard working week of ten units of medical time (40 hours) and, in addition, the appointee will be available for eleven Class A UMTs (standing by or working at hospital).[18]

There was also an expectation that M would 'participate in undergraduate and postgraduate teaching of Ophthalmology' and that, as his department was active in basic and clinical research, he would be 'expected to avail himself of the facilities provided'.

Following *Harris*, Jacob J was prepared to 'lift the veil' in order to ascertain the precise nature and scope of M's duties. In particular, a letter from M's head of department stated that any 'expectation that [M] would become involved in research and teaching ... was a somewhat informal invitation for him to become involved with the University side of the Institute, thereby making his career more interesting'. This 'expectation' was all the more illusory as M was working 80 hours a week treating patients. Nevertheless, counsel for the Board proffered the following argument: (1) M's duty was to treat patients, focusing on diagnosis and actual treatment; (2) it was his duty to adopt any improved method of diagnosis for the treatment of his patients; so (3) it was M's duty to think of better ways of diagnosing his patients.

His Lordship dismissed this analysis with consummate brevity: 'It leads to the conclusion that it is the duty of this doctor, and probably every other registrar in the country, to devise if he can new ways of diagnosing and treating patients, because his duty is to treat patients'.[19]

---

[18] UMT stands for unit of medical time.
[19] note 1 above, at 223.

The flaw in counsel's argument was thereby exposed. It presupposed that if a doctor made an invention which constituted a better form of treatment, then, as his employer could use this invention, it necessarily belonged to his employer. Jacob J considered this argument unappealing in the extreme. Drawing an analogy with *Stephenson Jordan & Harrison v MacDonald & Evans*,[20] where the Court of Appeal had refused to award the copyright in a lecturer's lecture notes to his employer, Jacob J concluded by paraphrasing the words of Denning LJ: 'M's invention may be "a useful accessory to his contracted work" but it is not "really part" of it'.[21]

In many ways, the logic of the above argument was not dissimilar to that utilised in *Harris's Patent*, where Falconer J had recognised that, if an employee made an invention while applying his mind to problems experienced by his employer, then section 39(1)(a) came into play, always providing that it was part of the employee's duties 'to apply his mind to those problems'.[22] The latter caveat is pivotal. In *Greater Glasgow*, there was no evidence that M's primary duties involved anything other than the hands-on treatment of patients and the performance of associated clinical responsibilities.

Staeng Ltd's Patents

In *Staeng*, the employee's 'objectives' included increasing 'sales by development of markets, by new products to existing customer . . . and ultimately new products to new customers'. N's actual duties, relevant to the issue of making inventions, were:

- To create from discussions with customers, product managers and other . . . personnel, ideas for new products from seeing a need in the market place [and]
- Think of novel uses for existing products.

The original job description also stated that the recognised experience required to perform the functions of the post were twofold: five years experience of marketing/product management ideally in heatshrink/markers business or related industry, and a proven track record of new product development in a managerial role. As for the 'Resources, Equipment' available, the job description simply referred to 'six company cars'. The hearing officer concluded that N's invention fell within his normal duties for the following reasons: (1) the job description assigned to N 'the creative role of using discussions with customers [i.e. R at the time] to generate ideas for new products';[23] (2) N had been described as a joint inventor on at least one previous patent application made by H Ltd; (3) in so far as N's duties centred on performing a marketing role, this role lay 'at the heart of the emergence of the invention in suit, and I dare say that the commonest of motives for applying for a patent in any technical field is, in the final analysis, essentially one of marketing';[24] and (4) backshell connectors lay within the broad field of H Ltd's business.

It is respectfully submitted that each of the above arguments is open to criticism. Point (1) demonstrates the problems of looking at a job description in isolation, especially when one focuses on specific extracts. This danger was highlighted by the Patents Court in *Harris's Application*. If N's role required technical/inventive skills, why were no resources made available to him, apart from the use of six company cars? Why did the job description fail to

---

[20] (1952) 69 RPC 10.
[21] note 1 above at 224, citing Denning LJ, *ibid.*, at 22.
[22] note 5 above, at 35, 37.
[23] note 2 above, at 199.
[24] *ibid.*

specify such skills in describing the necessary type of previous experience?[25] Why did the hearing officer ignore the fact that N's post was described as 'Business Development Manager', and that the technical side of any new product development was controlled by a group of 'Product Managers'?

Point (2) involved conflicting evidence as to why N had been named as a joint inventor on a previous application. Certainly, this prior application had related to heatshrink sleeves with an internal conductive lining partly shrunk on to a cable connector. N had stated that he did not contribute any originality but was added to the patent application for marketing reasons. Ironically, this is exactly why R ended up as the 'sole inventor' for the patent in issue. The hearing officer assumed that evidence of inventive activity by N supported the conclusion that N's duties included the making of inventions. Exactly who has the onus of proof here? It is submitted that the authors of the CIPA *Handbook* are correct in arguing that under section 39 it is the employer who has the onus of establishing ownership.[26] At the very least, as Jacob J hinted at in *Greater Glasgow*, nothing should turn on the onus of proof.[27] If so, to allow such past events to influence the court or tribunal must surely have required clear evidence from N's employer that the subject-matter of that previous patent grant was causally linked to the duties performed by N at the time, and that N's contribution showed sufficient technical originality to warrant his inclusion on the patent application as a joint inventor. Neither point was considered by counsel for the applicant.

Regarding point (3), the overall impression gained from looking at the job description was that of a relatively high-powered marketing manager. H Ltd's ostensible requirements were for an employee with entrepreneurial skills who would sell H's products to customers, identify future product development needs and oversee the ongoing modification of H's range of products in order to meet changing customer demands. The hearing officer circumvented this argument by equating technical with marketing skills for the purposes of applying for a patent application. It is submitted that the motive for seeking patent protection must not be confused with the inventive step which underpins the resultant application. Relevant case law has stressed that the patentee must demonstrate technical inventiveness, not commercial awareness, under section 3 of the PA77.[28]

Finally, point (4) involved a disputed fact which was finally resolved on evidential grounds. To that extent, any criticism of the conclusion would be churlish. Nevertheless, it is interesting to note that the hearing officer, in identifying N's normal duties, was clearly influenced by 'the broad field of [H's] business'.[29] The clear implication was that, if an employee's previous history had included making inventions, then any further invention which fell within his employer's range of business interests would be deemed to have been made within the employee's normal course of duties.

This approach was roundly criticised in *Greater Glasgow* as setting up a presumption that an employer owns all employees' inventions that are *relevant* to his business. More specifically, it contravenes the spirit of section 39(1)(a), which requires that an employer also show that

---

[25] Certainly, there was no evidence that the duty included within the job description to create 'ideas for new products' had an innately technical as opposed to entrepreneurial side (see later).

[26] *CIPA Guide to the Patents Act* (4th ed., 1995) at paragraph 39.07, citing *Harris's Patent* in support of this contention. At present, it would seem that the Comptroller places the onus of proof on the referrer, without differentiating between the use of ss.8, 12, 37 and s.39.

[27] In *Greater Glasgow*, Jacob J stated: 'It would be unfortunate if anything turned on the question of onus of proof because the question of who the applicant was was part of the civilised resolution of the problem between the two parties ... it may make sense in that in relation to any similar dispute the parties agree that nothing shall turn on the onus of proof.'

[28] e.g. *Hallen Co. v Brabantia (UK) Ltd* [1989] RPC 307 at 327, and *Windsurfer International Inc. v Tabur Marine (Great Britain) Ltd* [1985] RPC 59 at 72, 74.

[29] note 2 above at 200.

the circumstances surrounding the invention 'were such that an invention might reasonably be expected to result from the carrying out of [the employee's] duties'. This condition rightly marries the employee's potential for invention with the performance of his duties, not with the much wider business interests of his employer. No doubt, the employer's *apparent* motivations in advertising the job, and his subsequent instructions to and supervision of the employee, are important in determining the question of expectability. However, one must not lose sight of the approach adopted in *Harris*, where Falconer J, referring to the latter condition in subsection (1)(a), commented that it must be 'an invention which achieves, or contributes to achieving, whatever was the aim or object to which *the employee's efforts in carrying out those duties were directed*'.[30]

In this context, recourse might be made to the pre-PA77 decision in *Electrolux Ltd v Hudson*,[31] where the employee's invention was central to the employer's business, but the invention belonged to the employee because it bore no relation to the performance of his duties.[32]

Section 39(1)(b)—special obligations

Where the employee's status within his employer's business creates a special obligation to further the interests of the employer, then the invention will belong to the employer. As yet, there has been no need to define the term 'special obligation', although it will probably follow the tests expounded in *Worthington Pumping Engine Co. v Moor* and *British Syphon Co. Ltd v Homewood*.[33] This obligation might arise where the employee represents the alter ego of his employer or occupies a position very high in the management structure. Thus, apart from exceptional circumstances, middle management will normally be exempt from the strictures of this subsection. For example, in *Harris*, as the employee was merely a departmental manager with no duty to attend board meetings, the court concluded that no special obligation arose.

In *Staeng*, the employee, N, was clearly appointed to the higher echelons of management, but was he sufficiently senior to warrant invoking this 'special obligation'? Interestingly, the hearing officer used the position of Harris as an appropriate comparator. Thus, whereas Harris had no right to attend board meetings, N was 'involved in the sort of meetings and engaged in the sort of discussions that were also the province of directors'. Whereas Harris had no right to hire and fire, or spend any departmental budget, N possessed some limited autonomy, subject to certain approval procedures, applicable even to the managing director. In summary, Harris passed on problems, while N was expected to solve them by identifying the need for new products of the modification of existing ones. The hearing officer concluded that, irrespective of his decision under subsection 1(a), by reason of N's status, his invention belonged to his employer under subsection 1(b). It was clear that the final decision was a difficult one to make, relying on an appropriate sense of balance. As Falconer J said in *Harris's Patent*:

the extent and nature of the 'specific obligation to further the interests of the employer's

---

[30]   note 5 above, p.29 (*emphasis added*).
[31]   [1977] F.S.R. 312. Note that pre-1977 case law required an employer to prove that the employee's invention had been made 'in the course of employment', a term which might be broader than the 'duties' referred to in subsection (1)(a).
[32]   See also *Selz Ltd's Application* (1954) 71 RPC 158, where the employee was awarded ownership of his invention because he had 'never [been] directed to apply his mind for the purposes of devising an invention'.
[33]   (1903) 20 RPC 41; [1956] RPC 225 and 330.

undertaking' will depend upon the status of the employee and the attendant duties and responsibilities of that status. Thus, plainly the position in this regard of a managing director ... will, no doubt, extend across the whole spectrum of the undertaking, [and] will differ from that of, say, a sales manager.[34]

Perhaps in future, bearing in mind that Harris was clearly not the type of employee that Parliament ever intended would be caught by subsection 1(b), the employee in *Staeng* will stand as a more appropriate comparator for determining whether a particular employee has a 'special obligation' to his employer, with those employees falling short of N's position being subject solely to subsection 1(a).

Finally, one should note that even where a special obligation is established, the invention must still arise 'in the course of the duties of the employee'.[35] Such duties will include those contained within subsection (1)(a). They will also include any other duties which the employee has undertaken,[36] provided they are consistent with his position within the business.[37] In short, where a special obligation arises, subsection (1)(b) widens the scope of the employee's duties and dispenses with the requirement that an invention must have been reasonably expected to result from the performance of those duties.

Technically, this was not an issue in *Staeng*, as it had already been found that the invention was made in the course of N's normal duties under subsection 1(a). Nevertheless, the hearing officer, in dealing separately with subsection 1(b), preferred an alternative approach. He implied that, as N had a special obligation, any invention useful to his employer would automatically fall within N's 'duties'. Thus, having established that N knew of the planned acquisition of S Ltd by H Ltd prior to the making of the invention, he said: 'whatever [H]'s earlier interest in backshell adaptors may have been, at that point he would surely have recognised, as a senior ... employee, that an improvement in that field might be of advantage to his employers.'[38]

It is submitted that the drafting of subsection 1(b) intentionally avoids making this automatic connection. The absence of any expectability criterion in subsection (1)(b) does not permit a court to imply a duty to invent into the contracts of all higher management personnel, irrespective of whether they are accountants or technicians.

Conclusion

Clearly, a considerable amount of unreported section 39 ownership disputes have been referred to the Patent Office.[39] Given the litigation costs on appeal, and the meagre resources available to most employee inventors, it is surely in everyone's best interests that the practical 'precedents' set in the Patent Office are clear, predictable and legally watertight. One possible

---

[34] note 5 above, pp.37–38.
[35] This particular condition was not adopted in the pre-1977 decisions of *Worthington Pumping Engine Co. v Moore* and *British Syphon Co. v Homewood*, note 33 above.
[36] Pre-1977 case law suggests that the predictability of defining such duties, and applying them in varying factual situations, appears low. Contrast *Selz Ltd's Application*, note 32 above and *Fine Industrial Commodities Ltd v Powling* (1954) 71 RPC 253.
[37] See *Peart's Patent*, unreported (S.R.I.S./209/87), where the Comptroller held that subsection (1)(b) was potentially applicable even where the employee had maintained an involvement in research and development matters in direct contravention of his employer's explicit prohibition.
[38] note 2 above, at 203.
[39] Those noted in I.P.D. include *Secretary of State for Defence's Application* (S.R.I.S. 0/135/89, I.P.D. 13063), *Stablocel's Application* (S.R.I.S. 0/3/91, I.P.D. 14101), *Travenol Laboratories' Application* (S.R.I.S. 0/45/90, I.P.D. 13141), and *Defence Technology's Application* (S.R.I.S. 0/77/93, I.P.D. 16124).

conclusion to be drawn from the two reported decisions is that we are some way off this position and that a few more commonsense decisions in the Patents Court would be welcome, before the Patent Office 'precedents' become too embedded in concrete.

Breach of Confidence

Prince Albert and the Etchings

[1984] 12 EIPR 344

JEREMY PHILLIPS
(Lecturer-in-Law, Queen Mary College, University of London)

The well-known case of *Prince Albert v Strange*[1] has been the subject of a good deal of analysis, criticism and speculation in the years following its determination in 1849. Indeed, this remarkable piece of litigation contains much which attracts the attention of lawyer and layman alike. This case provided its Victorian commentators with the unique spectacle of the reigning monarch's own Prince Consort instituting proceedings in the Royal Courts of Justice and before judges who had sworn their loyalty to the Queen. It involved a number of legal issues of substantial complexity with regard to the nature of copyright in artistic works, the scope for the legitimate dissemination of unpublished information and the nature of the legal remedies available to the royal plaintiffs. It will be appreciated further that, while the public activity of the royal couple was always a matter of fascination for the public, the defendants' deeds were also well noted, for both defendants were men of some notoriety. The first, William Strange, was a publisher who did not fight shy of controversy,[2] while the second, Jasper Tomsett Judge, was—if one may be permitted the anachronism of employing a term not yet coined in respect of him—an investigative journalist who both nursed a strong sense of injustice and cultivated a flair for initiating the public crusade to rectify it.

In this article an account will be given of the principal legal features of this case, and some suggestions will be put forward by way of explanation of what is perhaps this case's greatest puzzle: why the royal couple, with the avowed intention of protecting the privacy of their domestic pastimes, should have embarked on a course of action which could only make those pastimes the subject of familiar knowledge in every drawing room throughout the land. Precisely what outcome the plaintiffs expected is not plain; but the litigation which ensued was not an occurrence from which any party emerged with particular credit or dignity.

The Facts

It is not, unfortunately, possible to ascertain the exact nature of the events which preceded the issue of the royal writ, nor can one state with conviction their sequence. This is because the various law reports which were subsequently published are not in entire accord as to

---

[1] (1849) 2 De G. & Sm. 652; 1 Mac. & G. 25; 1 H. & Tw. 1; 18 LJ Ch. (NS) 120.
[2] Apart from publishing Judge's scurrilous pamphlets, William Strange was also one of five defendants successfully sued by Charles Dickens in *Dickens v Lee* (1844) 8 Jur. 183. Dickens records, in a letter to Sargeant Talfourd dated 19 March 1844, that Strange sent a man to his house to blackmail him: see *Letters of Charles Dickens*, ed. K. Tillotson, Volume 4, at 77.

what happened[3] and, even if they had been, the affidavits in support of the plaintiffs' claims are in any event contradictory.[4] Nevertheless it is possible to isolate a hard core of what may be described as uncontroversial fact.

It is beyond doubt that Queen Victoria and Prince Albert dabbled in the arts, and that over a period of years they made etchings of a number of drawings, including many drawings which they had themselves executed.[5] Among those artists whose works influenced, or were copied by, the royal couple were names as distinguished as Lucas Cranach the younger,[6] Caracci,[7] the much-admired Sir Edwin Landseer[8] and Sir George Hayter,[9] as well as E. Mansfield.[10] From the copper plates of these etchings a small number of copies were struck, on royal instruction, by a Windsor printer by the name of John Brown.[11] The good copies of the prints thus struck were returned, with the etched plates, to Windsor Castle, but a number of soiled or imperfect prints were retained by one Middleton, a man in Brown's employ. A set of 63[12] different prints made from the royal etchings was later sold by Middleton to the second defendant, Judge, for the then-princely sum of £5.[13]

Once in possession of these works of art, Judge then conceived the notion of making a public exhibition of them. To this end he wrote a descriptive catalogue of the etchings which was—if fulsome in its praise and embarrassing in its patronising comment—at least not apparently intended to give overt offence to the royal artists. The precise contents of the catalogue are no longer known, for only 51 copies were made before the type was broken up,[14] and none of them would seem to be extant. At any rate neither the British library nor Windsor Castle, to which two copies were sent,[15] are in possession of one. It has been implied that the royal etchings were reproduced in the catalogue,[16] but there is no concrete evidence that this was so. The printer of this catalogue was the first defendant, Strange.

The sale of the catalogues was not the only means by which the defendants hoped to achieve a profit; for Judge had planned to offer for sale to the public a choice of facsimile autographs of each of the royal artists.[17] No permission to sell the facsimile autographs was sought or granted, nor indeed was there any legal bar on their unlicensed exploitation, but Judge maintained that he would not have sold them without the royal consent.[18]

---

[3] See D. Tritter. 'A Strange Case of Royalty: the singular "Copyright" Case of *Prince Albert v Strange*', (1983) 4 JMLP 111 at 112.

[4] See J.T. Judge, *The 'Royal Etchings': A Statement of Facts* ..., 1849, at, for example, 12 and 15.

[5] On the royal couple's artistic pursuits see M. Warner, *Queen Victoria's Sketchbook*, 1979, especially at 96 to 100, 144 and 145.

[6] Cranach (1515–1586) carried on the tradition of his famous father's workshop: *Oxford Companion to Art*, 1970, at 289.

[7] The Caracci in question is presumably Agostino (1557–1602), whose anatomical studies were much engraved: *Oxford Companion to Art*, 1970, at 208 and 209.

[8] Landseer (1802–1873) instructed the royal couple in etching; he was a great royal favourite between 1839 and 1866: *Dictionary of National Biography*, Volume XI, at 507.

[9] Hayter (1792–1871) was appointed 'principal painter in ordinary to the Queen' in 1841: *Dictionary of National Biography*, Volume IX, at 304.

[10] No mention is made of Mansfield in the principal works of art reference. He is not to be confused with Edward Mansfield, the Victorian balloonist who fell to his death when his balloon burst at 400 feet.

[11] This John Brown should be distinguished from his better-known namesake, the Queen's personal attendant, who died in 1883. See S. Lee, *Queen Victoria*, 1904 (2nd ed.), at 475 and 476.

[12] (1849) 1 Mac. & G. 25 at 28.

[13] Judge thought this sum extortionate: see Note 4 above at 26 ('... and that, I confess, was twenty times as much as they would have realized at any print-shop in Christendom').

[14] Note 4 above at 46 (Answer of 21 December 1848).

[15] Note 4 above at 6; cf. Tritter, Note 3 above at 113, who maintains that only one catalogue was sent.

[16] Tritter, Note 3 above at 112, indicates that it was illustrated, but the catalogue, which was only 32 pages long (Judge, Note 4 above at 29), was never alleged by the plaintiff to have been so.

[17] Note 4 above at 18 (Information of Prince Albert, 20 October 1848).

[18] Note 4 above at 33, where the royal autographs are described as being 'as plentiful as blackberries'.

Before the proposed exhibition was held, Judge sent copies of his catalogue both to the Queen and to her Consort at Windsor Castle. It is not clear whether these copies were accompanied by a formal request that the works listed in them be exhibited, or that the sale of the remaining copies of the catalogue be permitted. As in the case of facsimile autographs, however, Judge maintained that he did not intend to sell a single copy without the royal consent.[19] To his credit it does not appear, and was not alleged, that he had in fact sold any. But the response from Windsor Castle to the receipt of the catalogues was swift and unambiguous: a writ was issued for the delivery up of all impressions and copies of the etchings, for the prohibition of the exhibition and for the prevention of the publication of any of the etchings.

The Litigation

An *ex parte* injunction was granted on 20 October 1848 by Knight-Bruce V.C., on the assumption that Judge's possession of the prints made from the etchings could only have been obtained by unlawful or surreptitious means, and that Strange's preparation of the catalogue was consequently tainted with the unlawfulness of Judge's unlicensed possession. The defendants' motion to dissolve the injunction was heard on 13 December 1848, again by the Vice-Chancellor; the motion was refused. A subsequent appeal by Strange was heard by Lord Cottenham L.C. on 8 February 1849, the result of which was that the injunction against him was made perpetual.

The Legal Background

Viewed in plain legal terms, the plaintiffs' case would probably present little difficulty if it were instituted today. The royal etchings and the prints made from them would both be protected against the making of unauthorised copies, since etchings and prints fall within the scope of protection given by copyright law to 'artistic works',[20] and even if, as etchings of works drafted by others, some of the etchings could be accounted as copyright infringements, they would probably still be regarded as 'original' works for the purpose of attracting copyright protection.[21] Nevertheless, it is not an infringement of copyright merely to display an artistic work,[22] nor is it an infringement to publicise the existence of such a work by writing about it in a catalogue of other literary work.[23] The display or non-reproductional exploitation of such a work can only be enjoined if it is shown that the act to which the owner of the work objects is a breach of confidence.[24]

In 1848, however, the statutory law of artistic copyright was a good deal less sophisticated than it is today, and prints made from engravings did not enjoy any copyright protection.[25] Indeed, it was conceded by Serjeant Talfourd, on behalf of the Prince Consort, that his client's case did not turn on copyright.[26] Outside of the copyright statutes of the time, the common law provided no real assistance to the plaintiffs' case either; for, although the

---

[19] *Ibid.*, at 29 and 30.
[20] Copyright Act 1956, section 3(1).
[21] See *Warwick Film Co. v Eisinger* [1969] 1 Ch. 508.
[22] Copyright Act 1956, sections 3(5) and 49(2).
[23] *Ibid.*
[24] See for example *Tuck & Sons v Priester* [1887] 19 QB 629.
[25] The Engraving Copyright Acts (8 Geo. 2 c. 13 of 1734 and 7 Geo. 3 c. 38 of 1766) did not protect them, as counsel for the plaintiff conceded.
[26] (1849) 2 De G. & Sm. 652 at 668.

common law regarded the publication of an unpublished work as an actionable wrong if it was done without the author's (or artist's) consent,[27] the production of the catalogue could not be regarded as 'publication' for such an action to succeed, the word 'publication' being understood to mean, for such purposes, the making available of copies of the hitherto unpublished work to the public. The only potential avenue of success left to the plaintiffs was to invoke the jurisdiction of equity to prevent the unfair exploitation of a wrongful act. What was the wrongful act? Not, it seems, the unauthorised retention by Middleton of the soiled or imperfect prints, but the unproven intrusion or spying by Judge on the Royal couple's domestic life.[28] The plaintiffs' successful utilisation of this discretionary jurisdiction of equity paved the way for the later development of the so-called 'equitable tort' of breach of confidence, but it should be noted that the plaintiffs' case in the absence of a clear-cut breach of confidence action, was not easily made out in legal terms. That Prince Albert succeeded was the unfortunate consequence of the Court's acceptance of some tenuous legal inferences and generalisations from existing case law drawn from, *inter alia*, the law of breach of trust.[29]

The trial decision of Knight-Bruce V.C.

The Vice-Chancellor first established that an author enjoys the absolute right at common law of first publication of his work, citing the well-known decision in *Duke of Queensberry v Shebbeare*.[30] That case established that one of the administrators of the Earl of Clarendon's estate enjoyed the right to prevent a publisher from publishing one of two unpublished manuscript copies of the Earl's history of the reign of King James II. It would have been simple for the Vice-Chancellor to hold that this case was of no precedental significance for the instant case, since what was under consideration in it was the publication of an unpublished work, not the publication of critical or descriptive comments on it; but the learned judge chose instead to apply, and indeed extend, the principle which it established. In doing so, he derived support[31] from a proposition expounded, *obiter*, by Yates J. in his dissenting judgment in *Millar v Taylor*:[32]

> Every man has a right to keep his own sentiments, if he pleases. He has certainly a right to judge whether he will make them public or commit them only to the sight of his friends. In that state, the manuscript is, in every sense, his peculiar property; and no man may take it from him, or make any use of it which he has not authorised, without being guilty of a violation of his property.

The interesting feature of this statement is that it draws no distinction between the publication of the tangible, material form of a work and the divulgation of the intangible descriptive or other non-material content embodied in it. Thus 'sentiment' is protected, whether in the form of a copyright work or not. This early enunciation of a right of privacy, which also heralds subsequent developments in the jurisprudence of breach of confidence, would suggest that the protection of unpublished works against unauthorised publication was, by

---

[27] *Duke of Queensberry v Shebbeare* [1758] 2 Eden 329. There was some doubt, however, as to what constituted 'publication' of an artistic work: see T. Scrutton, *The Laws of Copyright*, 1883, paragraph 180.

[28] [1849] 2 De G. & Sm. 652 at 698.

[29] See Tritter, Note 3 above, for a fairly detailed account of the Court's reasoning.

[30] Note 27 above.

[31] (1849) 2 De G. & Sm. 652 at 692 to 693.

[32] (1769) 4 Burr. 2303.

its very nature, more aptly provided by breach of confidence remedies than by the law of copyright.

The appellate decision of Lord Cottenham L.C.

A modern commentator[33] has said of Lord Cottenham's decision:

> A close examination of Cottenham's opinion reveals the curious absence of the word 'copyright', either by reference to common law or statute. Further, there is scant use of precedent that might have lent weight to his decision; there are merely generalised holdings that vaguely incorporate them by reference. His is hardly a shining example of the judicial 'grand manner'.

From this rather unflattering proposition it is difficult to dissent. The Lord Chancellor devoted more of his attention to the facts than to the law, which he regarded as clear and uncontroversial.[34] From a consideration of his appreciation of the affidavits there is no doubt that his personal sympathies lay with the plaintiffs' case and not with the defendants. In particular he was prepared to assume that the prints in question were surreptitiously made and improperly obtained (propositions strenuously denied by Judge), and it was this assumption which rendered the case apt for 'breach of confidence' analysis. In the event, his Lordship found that the plaintiffs were entitled to succeed either on a 'property' (that is, interference with common law copyright) or on a 'breach of trust' theory.[35]

Some unresolved issues

The litigation in *Prince Albert v Strange* could in no sense be said to have produced an exhaustive analysis of the legal issues raised, or of the factual assumptions made and disputed, before the Court. Of these unsettled issues there are four which merit especial attention: the *locus standi* of Prince Albert, the copyright status of the prints of the etchings, their allegedly confidential nature and the alleged bad faith of the defendant Judge.

(1) The 'locus standi' of Prince Albert Relief was sought by the Prince Consort in respect of prints made from etchings made both by himself and by Queen Victoria. While, plainly, he was the appropriate party to seek the prohibition of the dissemination of his own works, it is difficult to see how he could have sued in respect of the threatened disclosure of his wife's works. This matter was raised at first instance by counsel for the first defendant,[36] but it was not dealt with by either of the judges. There was no evidence, nor was there any suggestion, that the Prince enjoyed, either through the status of husband or of agent, the right to sue in his own name to seek redress of proprietary damage suffered by his wife. Counsel for the royal plaintiff did concede: 'A right of property is not claimed in the instrument of mischief, but is the thing which is injured by that instrument',[37] but that is only an implicit rejoinder to the objection.

---

[33] Tritter, Note 3 above, at 120.
[34] (1849) 18 LJ Ch. (NS) 120 at 125.
[35] *Ibid.* at 126.
[36] (1849) 1 Mac. & G. 25 at 32 and 35.
[37] *Ibid.* at 37.

(2) The copyright status of the etchings Not all the etchings were originated entirely through the exercise of the royal intellect. Some were copied from, or influenced by, the works of Landseer, for example, and could arguably be said to have been copyright infringements.[38] While modern copyright jurisprudence[39] admits of a work's being, at the same time, an original work and an infringing one (here an original etching but an infringement of another's drawing), it is by no means clear that such a result could have been reached on the basis of the law as it stood in the 1840's. A further difficulty is that a work which is itself an infringement of another's rights is not a suitable subject for the protection provided by the jurisdiction of equity, which has long required its supplicants to possess 'clean hands' before invoking its jurisdiction.[40] A doctrine of the 'relatively clean hands' variety, which could be argued in favour of the less-than-blameless plaintiff today, was not evolved until relatively recent times.[41]

(3) The confidential nature of the prints The Prince Consort's affidavit averred[42] that the etchings from which the prints were made were kept under lock and key at Windsor Castle, and that they were not made public, although a small number of prints made from them were given as presents to friends of the royal family. The affidavit of Judge, however, indicates[43] that the prints were open to public view in John Brown's printing shop. He states elsewhere[44] that the royal prints had in fact been publicly exhibited, albeit without the permission or consent of the royal artists, in public houses in the Windsor area, and that descriptions of some of the works listed in the catalogue had already been published without any royal objection or threat of reprisal.[45] If there had indeed been public exhibitions of the prints, and their contents were common knowledge to the extent that their descriptions had already been circulated in the press, it is possible that the Court would have been hard pressed to base its decision to grant an injunction on the prevention of unauthorised disclosure, for an injunction cannot prevent what has already happened.

(4) Judge's alleged bad faith Throughout the proceedings Judge maintained that he had obtained the prints openly and honestly, without resorting to any illegal or surreptitious act.[46] The national press,[47] Prince Albert[48] and the local press[49] were, however, prepared to assume the contrary. No evidence was offered which would have established beyond doubt either Judge's *mala fides* or his lack of it which is why, in order to vindicate his reputation, he wrote his remarkable and at times vituperative little pamphlet, *The 'Royal Etchings': a*

---

[38] Drawings were assumed to have been unprotected until the coming into force of the Fine Arts Copyright Act 1862, but T. Scrutton, Note 27 above, argues convincingly that this view was incorrect and that the author of an unpublished work of art had, under the common law, the right to prevent the making of any unauthorised copy of it.

[39] *Warwick Film Co. v Eisinger*, Note 21 above.

[40] On the equitable requirement of 'clean hands' see *Halsbury's Laws of England* (4th ed.), Volume 16, paragraph 1305, and cases cited therein.

[41] *Argyll (Duchess) v Argyll (Duke)* [1967] 1 Ch. 302.

[42] Affidavit sworn at Windsor Castle, 20 October 1848.

[43] See Judge, Note 4, at 42.

[44] *Ibid.* at 28.

[45] *Ibid.* at 24.

[46] See reports cited at Note 1 above.

[47] See for example *The Morning Advertiser*, 15 December 1848; *Atlas*, 28 October 1848; *Douglas Jerrold's Weekly Newspaper*, 4 November 1848; *The Sun*, 6 November 1848; *The Morning Post*, 7 November 1848; *John Bull*, 11 November 1848; *The Literary Gazette*, 28 October 1848.

[48] Affidavit of 20 October 1848.

[49] *The Windsor Express*, 11 November 1848 (leading article).

Statement of Facts.[50] Since the plaintiffs' success apparently depended on the defendants' wrongful acts, it would have been interesting to see how the Court would have proceeded had Judge's behaviour been regarded as entirely honest and legitimate, as he himself suggests it was.

Motivation for the Litigation

It is not clear why the Prince Consort should have been so determined to resort to litigation in order to preserve his privacy, given that the natural consequence of such a course of action was to publicise the very deeds which he sought to enshroud in privacy. His enthusiasm for litigation was so great that he did not first trouble to request the defendants to abandon their venture, prior to the issue of the writs.[51] It may be surmised that the defendants half expected some sort of royal objection to their venture, for no other explanation exists for the fact that they had printed so few catalogues—only 51—while they might have expected to dispose of thousands on the open market.

One persistent rumour had been that the royal couple were anxious to suppress the publication of details of a number of prints which were of an erotic or salacious nature. It should be stated categorically that there is no foundation in fact for this hypothesis. All the etchings made by the royal couple are available for inspection in the Print Room of the Royal Library, Windsor Castle, and it can be seen that their content is singularly lacking in explicit, or indeed implicit, immoral or sexual imagery. Only two of the etchings encompass nudity of the female form ('Pussy. Before going to Bed'[52] and 'various Studies'[53]), and neither was in fact included in the Strange and Judge catalogue; a third etching, 'A Girl Seated, half length, in profile to right',[54] may or may not be topless, a determination which is rendered academic by the fall of her hair.

What may have given rise to that rumour was the publication in the national press of the time[55] of the list of etchings, since it contained references to Goethe's heroine, Mignon. Three prints listed for the defendants' abortive exhibition are 'The Apotheosis of Mignon', treated twice by Queen Victoria,[56] and 'Mignon in her Dramatic Attire',[57] drawn by the Queen but etched by her husband. Mignon appeared in a novel, *The Apprenticeship of Wilhelm Meister*,[58] which was certainly regarded as an immoral work in the mid-19th century.[59] A hauntingly attractive pubescent female, she was rescued by Wilhelm Meister from the depredations of a troupe of itinerant rope-dancers to whom she was bound, and by whom she is sold for the price of her clothes.[60] This heroine becomes passionately attached to her rescuer, for whom she dances the celebrated egg-dance.[61] Both Mignon and Meister are

---

[50] Note 4 above. This work is not listed in the British Museum Catalogue but may be found in the Avon County Library. It is listed in the United States National Union Catalog, from which one may be tempted to infer that the former colonies were the author's preferred market.

[51] The full chronology is set out in Judge, Note 4 above, Chapter 1.

[52] Listed in A.H. Scott-Elliot, 'The Etchings by Queen Victoria and Prince Albert', [1961] 65 *Bulletin of the New York Public Library*, No. 3, at 139 to 153 (referred to below as the 'Scott-Elliot catalogue') as etching no. 56.

[53] Scott-Elliot catalogue, no. 58.

[54] Scott-Elliot catalogue, no. 15; listed in Judge's and Strange's catalogue (referred to below as 'J. & S. catalogue') as etching no. 15.

[55] See *The Times*, 7 November 1848, at 7.

[56] Scott-Elliot catalogue, no. 29 (J. & S. catalogue, no 32); Scott-Elliot catalogue, no. 32 (J. & S. catalogue, no. 35).

[57] Scott-Elliot catalogue, no. 78 (J. & S. catalogue, no. 39).

[58] This novel, the prototype of the German '*Bildungsroman*', was written by Goethe between 1786 and 1830.

[59] G.H. Lewes, *The Life and Works of Goethe*, Volume II, 1855, at 211 and 212.

[60] *The Apprenticeship of Wilhelm Meister*, Volume 1, Book II.

[61] *Ibid.*, Volume II, Book IV.

depicted in situations of a clearly sexual nature,[62] although the author respects the conventions of serious literature then current, exposing his characters' feelings but sparing their actions from the reader's gaze. Despite, or perhaps because of, the somewhat titillating nature of this 19th century Lolita, Mignon became a popular subject for the exercise of a number of distinguished intellects. An opera bearing her name was penned by Ambroise Thomas in 1866;[63] she was reputedly the inspiration for Sir Walter Scott's Fenella in *Peveril of the Peak* (1823);[64] and he song 'Kennst du das Land' was put to music by no lesser musician than Ludwig van Beethoven.[65] Inspection of the royal treatment of the Mignon theme reveals that it was treated with a modesty, indeed with what might today be described as a Victorian prudery, which owes nothing to the sensuous phraseology of Goethe.

Another, more plausible, explanation for Prince Albert's resort to litigation is that he had a particular personal reason for wishing to settle a score with one or both of the defendants. So far as the defendant Strange is concerned, there is no evidence in support of this hypothesis but, with regard to Judge, the hypothesis is quite sustainable; there is no doubt but that Judge regarded himself as the unfortunate object of the enmity of either Prince Albert or, more precisely, his unnamed advisers.[66]

Judge was no stranger to controversy. His career as a pamphleteer commenced in 1825 with the publication of *The Trial of Judge versus Berekeley and others*;[67] from the title of that work it is plain that his career as a litigant had commenced a little earlier. In 1829, turning his attention to religion, he wrote *Popish Treachery; exemplified in the conduct of a Roman Catholic Priest to an Irish Protestant at a Monastery in Brussels*.[68] Thereafter he developed an interest in politics and became a journalist, a sort of extramural court correspondent in Windsor, in 1839. A high Tory himself, he had little patience for Whiggery or for the infiltration (as he saw it) of Whig influence about the Royal Household.[69] Accordingly he wrote a number of court sketches and reports which were not wholly flattering of the court at Windsor, and he was openly critical of the scale of expense which was required for the maintenance of the royal establishment.

Unfortunately, neither the British Library nor the Royal Library at Windsor has any record of three of Judge's publications of this period: *Court Jobbery, A Voice from Windsor* and *A Hand-Book to the New Royal Stables and Riding House at Windsor Castle*.[70] The Royal Library does, however, possess a copy of Judge's more controversial *Sketches of Her Majesty's Household*.[71] Some idea of this book's import can be seen from the review comments of the *Sketches*, which Judge himself cites by way of advertisement of their content. Of this work it was said: 'the exposure—for exposure it really is—is awful';[72] It shows how money is expended by

---

[62] *Ibid.*, Volume II, Book V.

[63] The success of this work (admittedly not performed until 18 years after the litigation under discussion) may be gauged from the fact that, on its 1,000th performance, the composer received the Grand Croix of the Légion d'Honneur.

[64] This work was published in four volumes in 1822, and ran to two further editions in the following year. Thereafter its popularity declined.

[65] The first of Six Songs, Op. 75, written in 1809.

[66] In *The 'Royal Etchings'*, Note 4 above, Judge is careful never to accuse his royal plaintiffs of personal vindictiveness or spite.

[67] This pamphlet, which ran to two editions, is only available at the Cambridge University Library and in the British Library Reference Division.

[68] British Museum Catalogue no. 3938 aaa. 2(3).

[69] Note 4 above, at 62 to 71.

[70] Listed *ibid.* at 75.

[71] Published by Strange in 1848, its title continues: ... *Interspersed with Historical Notes, Political Comments, and Critical Remarks, showing, at one view, the salaries attached to the various appointments, the nature and extent of the duties to be performed, the amount of pensions upon retirement or superannuation, with Descriptive Particulars of Each Department* ...

[72] *The Weekly Dispatch*, 2 April 1848.

royalty as if it were mere dross, instead of the produce of the labour of the over-worked and under-paid million';[73] and 'It is stated that the royal tradesmen have received a hint that it would be palatable to royalty if they would abstain from adding to its circulation by exposing it for sale'.[74] Among the proposals contained in the *Sketches* were suggestions for the dismissal of sinecure-holders, the reduction of the salaries paid to royal officer-holders and the levying of income tax against the Queen. A further unpublished pamphlet, 'The Whigs about the Throne and the Person of the Prince Consort', was circulated to supposedly sympathetic members of the Conservative Government in 1844.[75] Judge was swiftly persuaded that the best interests of the party would be served by his refraining from publication of it, and he was offered £200 for his pains. The pamphlet remained unpublished, but Judge did not accept the 'hush money'.[76]

Judge in Windsor: A Thorn in Albert's Side

No doubt Judge's continued presence at Windsor was an acute embarrassment and annoyance to Her Majesty's advisers, for in September 1840 he was offered a sum of money to leave the town.[77] An attempt was later made to drive him out by buying up all his debts.[78] Judge's response, characteristically, to these intimations that his presence was unwanted was to cling to Windsor like a leech, assuming that events locally must be taking a fairly interesting turn if the town's self-appointed Ombudsman was causing so much anxiety at court. In May 1845 he took the part of an old man who, entrapped by one of the Prince Consort's gamekeepers into buying four pheasants and six accompanying eggs, was convicted by two of the county magistrates and sentenced to a stiff fine or four months' hard labour in Reading Gaol.[79] The 'trial' did not take place in open court but in the magistrates' clerk's private office. Judge sensed a scoop; reports by him appeared in *The Times*, the *Morning Chronicle* and the *Morning Advertiser*, and there was even a debate in the House of Commons.[80]

Encouraged by his success, Judge initiated proceedings against Prince Albert in September of 1845, in connection with the Consort's refusal to pay rates on a property owned by him, Flemish Farm, on the ground that he had no 'beneficial occupation' of it. In fact, the Prince reared cattle there, and grew mangold-wurzels of award-winning stature. The consequence of Judge's initiating proceedings was that the Prince consented to pay all arrears and future rate son the farm.[81] At abut the same time, one of Prince Albert's gamekeepers set a ferocious bloodhound on a poor pregnant woman who gathering dead wood for her fire. The gamekeeper was convicted and fined a small sum of his deed. At the proceedings there was only one reporter, Judge; the others, he claimed, had accepted the bribe offered to all the men of the press to keep away.[82] Finally, in November 1846 Judge took up the case of

---

[73] *Ibid.*, 9 April 1848.

[74] *The Bucks Chronicle*, 8 April 1848.

[75] Note 4 above at 65.

[76] *Ibid.* at 67.

[77] *Ibid.* at 70 and 71.

[78] *Ibid.* at 68.

[79] *Ibid.* at 72; cf. F. Airplay, Note 81 below, at 53: 'Scarcely a week passes but we see accounts of landlord and tenant disputing about the preservation of game, and poachers and keepers about the destruction of it: Prince Albert has been a landlord and a game-preserver during the last twenty years, but I remember no case in which either his name, or that of his agents or gamekeepers, have figured in any game case.'

[80] Note 4 above at 73.

[81] *Ibid.* at 72; cf. F. Airplay (pseud.), *Prince Albert: Why is he Unpopular?* 1857, (2nd ed.), at 57: '. . . yet there is an awful offence of his that entirely cancels all his good behaviour, and that is, his taking all the prizes at the agricultural shows!'

[82] Note 4 above at 72 and 73.

an aged retainer of the Prince Consort. The old man, then in his 74th year, found that his weekly pension of five shillings had been stopped by Prince Albert on the ground that the latter, having lately become liable to pay rates which included the poor rate for the parish, was no longer responsible for the pension, it being the obligation of the parish to keep its poor.[83] Judge's intervention resulted in the restoration of the pension.

From the foregoing it can be seen that, whatever Judge's motives for his actions, the Royal Household in general and Prince Albert in particular would have some justification for a less-than-affectionate attitude towards him. Since the royal family also regarded Judge as a man who had illegally obtained their art works, it is not surprising that resentment against him should have taken the form of a legal reprisal. Whether it was necessary for the Prince Consort to initiate proceedings without first requesting that the catalogue should not be published, and whether it was necessary for him to join Judge's apparently blameless son in the proceedings, it is certainly plain that the Prince was prepared to adopt a course which would be ruinously expensive for the Judge family.

The Discouragement of Royal Thefts

A further motive for embarking on the course of litigation may be ascribed to the desire of the royal family to discourage theft of their artefacts, coupled with the assumption that the prints in Judge's possession had been stolen from Windsor Castle in the first place. The published literature gives no indication that the Castle suffered from thefts, but there is some interesting secondary evidence that this was so, in the form of a newspaper cutting[84] which announces the sale by auction of two engravings by Queen Victoria. According to the cutting, the two works, which were both dated 1840, were stolen from Windsor Castle by a chambermaid and a man-servant when they left the Queen's service. Years later, when the former chambermaid was dying, she asked to see an artist who visited Windsor and whose son-in-law was the late Vicar of Hathersage. The deathbed confession of her theft was reported to the Queen, who presented the engravings to the artist. These two works were purchased at an auction by a Sheffield man in 1939, and the then Librarian at Windsor Castle declined an offer to purchase them from him in 1951.[85] Despite their relative rarity and curiosity value, the royal works of art have not attracted a high commercial value; for in his reply to their owner in Sheffield, the Librarian stated that a set of 50 prints of the royal etchings, auctioned at the Red Cross sales at Christies in 1944, fetched only £50 even though they were contained in a special leather album bearing the cipher and crown of Queen Victoria.[86]

If, then, there were thefts of prints of the royal etchings, and if one notable thorn in the royal side intended exhibiting such prints for gain, it would be quite reasonable for the royal family to have assumed a connection between the two occurrences. As it turns out, Judge was able to offer an explanation of how the prints came into his possession which was full and honest, if not entirely honourable, and his explanation would not have been made public if proceedings against him and his fellow defendant had not been so expeditiously instituted.

In conclusion, it is not clear whether Prince Albert was motivated principally by a desire

---

[83] *Ibid.* at 73.
[84] The source of this cutting is not known. It is recorded in typescript on the reverse of a letter from Mr. P. Graham to the then Librarian of Windsor Castle, Owen Morshead. Their correspondence lies loose inside the front cover of a leather-bound volume, 'Etchings by Her Majesty The Queen Victoria and His Royal Highness The Prince Albert', Volume 1, 1840 and 1841 (there are no further volumes).
[85] Letter of Owen Morshead to P. Graham, *loc. cit.*
[86] The same volume contains some intriguing correspondence with regard to this sale, too.

to avenge himself on Judge or by an anxiety to discourage the theft of royal property by attacking those who would have appeared to him to have been responsible for it. Whatever his motive, however, the Prince Consort's action helped to write a new chapter in intellectual property law and, by so doing, to provide him with a memorial less tangible but far more useful than that which bears his name in Kensington Gardens.

Circumstances Importing an Obligation of Confidence: A Subjective or Objective Test?

[1996] 11 EIPR 632

SIMON CLARK
Theodore Goddard

Carflow Products (UK) Ltd v Linwood Securities (Birmingham) Ltd and Others

The recent judgment of Jacob J in the case of *Carflow Products (UK) Ltd v Linwood Securities (Birmingham) Ltd and Others*[1] considers the circumstances in which a design is disclosed to a third party in confidence, the issue being relevant to the question of whether or not the defendants' design had been published in the United Kingdom prior to the plaintiff's application for registration of its design, which would have resulted in the plaintiff's registration being rendered invalid for want of novelty.

Facts

The plaintiff, Carflow Products, were the proprietors of a locking device to be used on the steering wheel of a car, called the 'Longarm'. The plaintiff's design was registered on 7 August 1992. The defendants designed and manufactured a steering wheel lock device called the 'Toplock'.

The plaintiff sued the defendants for infringement of its registered design, as well as for infringement of copyright and unregistered design right. With respect to the allegations of breach of copyright and design right, the defendants claimed that the design of the toplock had been created independently, and they attacked the novelty of the plaintiff's registered design. In particular, the defendants claimed that a prototype of the toplock had been shown to a Mr Spencer Jones of Argos, the second defendant, in June 1992, namely, two months prior to the plaintiff's application for registration of the Longarm design.

The Preliminary Issues

Since the date of registration of a registered design is the date on which the application is submitted to the Designs Registry,[2] and since publication of the design in the United

---

[1] Patents Court, judgment handed down on 7 March 1996 [1996] FSR 424.
[2] Section 3(5) Registered Designs Act 1949 as substituted by section 272, schedule 3, paragraph 1 Copyright, Designs and Patents Act 1988.

Kingdom before that date jeopardises the registration,[3] it was clear that if the defendants were able to satisfy the court that the Toplock prototype had been shown to Mr Spencer Jones in June 1992, then it must have been an independent design as there would have been no opportunity to copy the plaintiff's design prior to 7 August 1992. Accordingly, the plaintiff's claims for infringement of copyright and unregistered design right would both fail.

Furthermore, if the defendants could satisfy the court that the prototype had been shown to Mr Spencer Jones openly, as opposed to in confidence, and if, as the plaintiff alleged, the design of the Toplock was sufficiently similar to the design of the Longarm to infringe the plaintiff's registered design, then the disclosure of the Toplock prototype at the meeting would amount to prior publication of the plaintiff's design. The defendants would therefore have succeeded in establishing a 'Gillette defence'.[4] Either the design of the Toplock was sufficiently different from that of the Longarm so as not to fall within the scope of the registration of the Longarm design, or the publication of the Toplock design prior to the date of registration of the Longarm design rendered the registration invalid for lack of novelty. Accordingly, the plaintiff's claim for infringement of its registered design would also fail.

It was therefore agreed that the defendants would have a complete answer to the plaintiff's claim if they could satisfy the court on the following two points:

(1) whether the Toplock prototype was offered for sale by Mr Bond, the third defendant and a director of the first defendant, Linwood Securities, to Mr Spencer Jones of Argos, at a meeting in June 1992; and

(2) whether the prototype was shown to Mr Spencer Jones in circumstances whereby he was free in law and equity to use or disclose the same.

The parties agreed to the judge's suggestion that these two points should be tried as preliminary issues.

The Evidence of Mr Bond and Mr Spencer Jones

In order to make out their case on both points, the defendants were reliant on the evidence of Mr Bond and Mr Spencer Jones, being the two parties involved in the meeting on June 1992. Jacob J was impressed by Mr Bond's evidence and found him to be 'a careful and honest witness', and even more so with respect to Mr Spencer Jones who was 'a particularly careful and reliable witness with a high sense of ethics'.

Mr Bond told the court that in September 1991 he became aware of an American steering wheel lock, the 'Lockjaw'—see Figure 1. Mr Bond decided that the design of the Lockjaw could be improved if certain amendments were made to its design, and in particular he felt sure that its marketability would depend on the lock fitting virtually any make of car. This led Mr Bond to collate data relating to the dimensions of a wide range of cars in early 1992.

---

[3] Section 1(4)(b) Registered Designs Act 1949 as substituted by section 265(1) Copyright, Designs and Patents Act 1988.

[4] *Per* Lord Moulton, *Gillette v Anglo-American* (1913) 30 RPC 465 at 480.

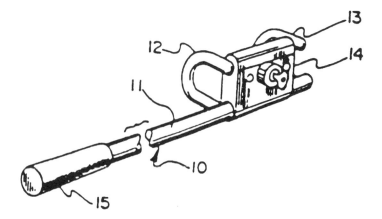

Figure 1   *The US 'Lockjaw' steering wheel lock*

In May 1992, following a nine-month design process, the defendants' final design was completed and two wooden mock-ups of the steering wheel lock were made, one of which was intended to be left with Mr Spencer Jones at the meeting. Mr Spencer Jones worked as a buyer for Argos, and Mr Bond had noticed on previous meetings with Mr Spencer Jones that other people's samples and prototypes had been left lying around and clearly open to view at Argos premises.

Copyright and Design Right Infringement

With respect to the claim for infringement of copyright, Jacob J noted that the plaintiff's counsel did not seek to draw the judge's attention to the alleged similarities between the Toplock and the Longarm when seeking to counter the defendants' allegation that the design of the Toplock had been completed by June 1992. The judge could not find any significant evidence of copying and felt that if the two designs had been very similar to each other, this was an argument which the plaintiff's counsel would have wanted to run. The plaintiff's claim in copyright and design right would therefore fail.

Obligation of Confidence?

Having satisfied himself that the design of the Toplock had been substantially completed by June 1992, Jacob J then went on to consider whether or not the prototype of the Toplock had been disclosed by Mr Bond to Mr Spencer Jones at the meeting under an obligation of confidence. In deciding this question the judge outlined two possible approaches in law:

(1) what did the parties themselves think they were doing by way of imposing or accepting obligations? (the subjective approach); and
(2) what would a reasonable man have thought they were doing? (the objective approach).

Jacob J decided that he preferred to take the subjective approach, stating that, while the subjective unspoken views of the parties would not be taken into account, for example, in relation to the making of a contract, it seemed right to do so in relation to the equitable obligation of confidence.

The subjective approach

Taking the subjective approach, the judge concluded that Mr Bond did not think he was imposing any duty of confidence on Mr Spencer Jones, relying in particular on Mr Bond's evidence that he was prepared to leave a sample of the Toplock with Mr Spencer Jones knowing that it was likely to be left around in Mr Spencer Jones's room where others could see it in much the same way as he had noticed with other samples left at Argos. It was also clear that Mr Bond had in the past expressly imposed obligations of confidence with a number of suppliers by a written document, and was therefore aware of the effect of doing so, yet he had not chosen to do so in this case. Mr Bond had himself stated in evidence that he did not think he was imposing an obligation of confidence on Argos.

With respect to Mr Spencer Jones's evidence, on the one hand he said that it was against his personal ethics and conscience to show a prototype given to him by one manufacturer to another manufacturer, but on the other hand he said that he would have refused to sign an agreement which prevented him from showing the prototype to another manufacturer. The judge concluded that Mr Spencer Jones did not consider that there was any enforceable obligation imposed on him, nor did Mr Spencer Jones consider that the imposition of such an obligation would have been intended by a prospective seller of a proposed new design. Accordingly, the judge concluded that on a subjective basis neither Mr Bond nor Mr Spencer Jones considered that there was an enforceable obligation of confidence being imposed or accepted.

The objective approach

Having decided the matter on a subjective approach, Jacob J then considered whether he would have reached the same conclusion by taking an objective approach, and in doing so he referred to two earlier cases, *Saltman Engineering Co. Ltd and Others v Campbell Engineering Co. Ltd*[5] and *Coco v A.N. Clark (Engineers) Ltd*[6].

The *Saltman* case concerned drawings of tools for the manufacture of leather punches, which had been sent by the plaintiff designer to the defendants for manufacture. The Court of Appeal overturned the decision of the judge at first instance by finding that the drawings had been given to the defendants in confidence for the sole specific purpose of manufacturing tools in accordance with the drawings.

The *Coco* case also involved the disclosure by the designer of drawings together with other information relating to the design of a moped engine to a potential manufacturer. In much the same way as in the present case, the designer had brought the prototype of the engine to the manufacturer's premises and further information was supplied to the manufacturer over the next few months. The parties then fell out and the manufacturer decided to make its own moped. On the hearing of a motion for interlocutory relief, Megarry J found that the documents and information had been communicated in circumstances importing an obligation of confidence (although he did not find the other two elements necessary for a cause of action in breach of confidence to be present).

---

[5] (1948) 65 RPC 20.
[6] [1969] RPC 41.

So, in both these earlier cases the court decided that duties of confidence had been impliedly imposed on the manufacturers when receiving details relating to the designs in question. However, Jacob J sought to distinguish the present case from these earlier authorities on the following basis. He concluded that it would be fair to assume that a reasonable man would be aware that the design of a product may be protected by law in a variety of ways. Therefore, he did not think that on an objective basis the reasonable man would consider that an obligation of confidence had been imposed simply because a prototype of a design was shown to a buyer. Indeed, the judge considered that if manufacturers were put under an obligation of confidence every time they were shown a prototype, knowing (as reasonable men) that the prototype could be the subject of independent legal protection, then manufacturers would be far less willing to look at samples and prototypes in the first place. The position would have been very different, he said, if the subject-matter being disclosed was something more than merely a prototype, and gave the example of the detailed drawings involved in *Saltman* and *Coco*. In the present case the subject-matter of the design was capable of protection by a variety of methods, which were either optional—as in the case of registered design or patents—or automatic— as in the case of copyright and design rights. Jacob J did not consider that the reasonable recipient must assume himself to be under an obligation of confidence in respect of such subject-matter which could have been protected independently. Accordingly, he found that on an objective basis the mere showing of the prototype by Mr Bond to Mr Spencer Jones did not impose an obligation of confidence and therefore the plaintiff's claim for infringement of the registered design would also fail.

Comment

Was Jacob J's decision to prefer the subjective approach to the question of whether a duty of confidence has been imposed a move away from the approach adopted by the court in *Saltman* and *Coco*? In neither of these cases did the court expressly consider which of the two approaches should be adopted. In fact, in *Coco*, Megarry J stated: 'I have not been able to derive any very precise idea of what test is to be applied in determining whether the circumstances import an obligation of confidence', a view which is shared by the current edition of *Copinger*.[7] Megarry J went on to state:

> It seems to me that if the circumstances are such that any reasonable man standing in the shoes of the recipient of the information would have realised that upon reasonable grounds the information was being given to him in confidence, then this should suffice to impose upon him the equitable obligation of confidence. In particular, where information of commercial or industrial value is given on a business-like basis and with some avowed common object in mind, such as joint venture or the manufacture of articles by one party for the other. I would regard the recipient as carrying a heavy burden if he seeks to repel a contention that he was bound by an obligation of confidence.

So, Megarry J seems to have adopted an objective test by considering the view of the reasonable man. In addition, he also called on the services of the officious bystander, and concluded that had the officious bystander asked the parties in *Coco* at the outset: 'Do you not think that you ought to have an express agreement that everything you are discussing is

---

[7] *Copinger and Skone James on Copyright*, Sweet & Maxwell, (13th edn), 1991, at 733.

confidential?' Megarry J concluded that the parties would have 'testily suppressed him with a common "But it obviously is" '.[8]

However, in the earlier case of *Saltman*, it appears that Lord Greene, then Master of the Rolls, tended towards a subjective approach. Since he found that the existence of an obligation of confidence had been 'abundantly proved' he did not consider it necessary to go into any great detail in his judgment, but simply relied on the evidence of the defendant's works manager who admitted that he knew he would not have been entitled to use the drawings sent to him by the plaintiff for any purpose other than to make the tools in accordance with the drawings for the plaintiff.

It is interesting to note that Mr Spencer Jones was not asked directly whether or not he regarded the disclosure to him as confidential, which suggests that the defendants' advisers were not anticipating the subjective approach taken by Jacob J.

Jacob J does make clear in his judgment that the question of whether an obligation of confidence has been imposed will always depend on the circumstances. The facts in the present case differed from the usual situation where the parties to the litigation are the same parties as were involved in the meeting or event at which the confidential matter was revealed. Indeed, both Mr Bond and Mr Spencer Jones were in agreement that the prototype was not presented in confidence; the plaintiff had no involvement in the meeting. It would have been an interesting situation if on an objective basis Jacob J had found that the prototype had been submitted in confidence despite the fact that both parties to the meeting believed that not to have been the case. Furthermore, Jacob J only had to decide on the question of confidence as at a particular date, whereas in both the *Coco* and *Saltman* cases the parties had developed business relationships with respect to the design in question and it was only after a period of months that these relationships broke down. The situation might have been different in the present case had Mr Bond and Mr Spencer Jones proceeded to work together on the development of the Toplock, with the question of confidence falling to be determined in relation to a date several months after their initial June meeting.

Jacob J also appears to have drawn a distinction between the disclosure of a prototype of a design, and the disclosure of detailed drawings of a design. He says that the prototype should not be given additional protection in equity through the importation of a duty of confidence on the recipient, because there are other ways of protecting the rights in the design, whether by registered design, design right, copyright or patent. But would not the same argument apply to the detailed drawings? The information contained in the drawings can be similarly protected under the same intellectual property rights. And where is the line to be drawn with respect to the subject-matter being disclosed? How much additional information would have been required to have been given to Mr Spencer Jones together with the prototype in order for equity to step in?

Furthermore, how much does the reasonable man know about the various ways of protecting designs? Jacob J states that a bystander 'would know, I think it fair to say, that our law provides a variety of ways in which the design of a product may be protected (unregistered design right, registered design, or even patent for an invention)'. If the judge is including the words in brackets as part of the bystander's knowledge, it seems a lot to be asking of the man in the street that he be aware of the difference between registered design and design right, or even that there are two separate forms of protection for designs (not to mention the application of copyright).

The judgment is typical of the commercial and practical approach taken by Jacob J. It is

---

[8] Applying a similar test to that used in relation to implied terms *per* MacKinnon LJ in *Shirlaw v Southern Foundries (1926) Ltd* [1939] 2 KB 206 at 221.

apparent from the judgment that the decision to hear the two points as preliminary issues was as a result of Jacob J's suggestion during the hearing of the summons for directions at which both parties had given fairly lengthy time estimates for the trial. By suggesting the hearing of the preliminary issues, which were effective to dispose of the whole case, considerable cost savings were likely to have been made by both parties, in addition to the matter being resolved many months earlier than the parties would have previously envisaged.

It remains to be seen whether the subjective approach taken by Jacob J will be adopted by the courts in the future. For the time being, the case serves as an added incentive for all designers to ensure that they have imposed the obligation of confidence in writing before they reveal samples and prototypes to buyers of manufacturers, retailers and distributors.

Cork v. McVicar
Confidential Information
and the Public Interest
in disclosure
[1985] 8 EIPR 234

ALLISON COLEMAN
Lecturer-in-Law, University College of Wales

The recent case of *Cork v McVicar*[1] highlights the role of the courts in balancing the public interest in the preservation of the confidentiality of information against the competing public interest in disclosure. This comment reviews *Cork v McVicar* in the light of two other recent cases, *Francome v Mirror Newspapers*[2] and *Lion Laboratories Ltd v Evans*,[3] and the Law Commission proposals on breach of confidence.[4]

Cork v. McVicar: The Facts

Mr Cork, a former detective sergeant in the Metropolitan Police, agreed to supply information about police corruption to John McVicar, who was planning to write a series of articles on that topic. Under the terms of the contract between them, conversations were to be tape recorded, but when Cork wished to supply confidential information off the record, the tape recorder was to be switched off. McVicar agreed to use only legitimately recorded information as the basis for his writings and also to submit manuscripts to Cork for approval prior to publication. Unknown to Cork, McVicar had strapped to his leg a secret tape recorder which he used to record the entire conversations between himself and Cork, including therefore information which was expressed as being confidential and off the record. McVicar then used the information from the secret tape recordings to compile a manuscript which was to be serialised in the *Daily Express* newspaper. Cork had not approved this manuscript. Cork sought an injunction to restrain the disclosure of the confidential information and publication of the articles. The *Daily Express* was joined as a party to the action. They knew of the agreement between Cork and McVicar.

The Decision

Scott J refused to grant the injunction. He said that *prima facie* the equitable remedies of the law would protect information imparted in confidence, but these remedies would not be extended to protect information which disclosed an iniquity or which the public interest

[1] *The Times*, 31 October 1984.
[2] [1984] 2 All ER 408.
[3] [1984] 2 All ER 417.
[4] *Breach of Confidence*, Law Commission Paper No. 110, Cmnd 8388 (1981).

required to be disclosed. That was the position with regard to the material which the *Daily Express* desired to use. They were therefore allowed to publish.

Francome v. Mirror Newspapers

Cork v McVicar may be contrasted with another recent case, *Francome v Mirror Newspapers*.[5] The defendants were also proprietors of a national newspaper. They intended publishing information from unauthorised tape recordings of telephone conversations between the jockey, Johnny Francome, and his wife. These conversations revealed that Francome had breached Jockey Club regulations and possibly committed criminal offences. However, in this case the plaintiffs' action for an injunction succeeded. The Court held that the information imparted in the course of the telephone conversations was confidential. There was no public interest in the disclosure of this information. Confidentiality must be preserved.

The Cases Compared

Although the results in *Cork v McVicar* and *Francome v Mirror Newspapers* conflict, the cases are consistent and are undoubtedly correctly decided. Both involve balancing the public interest in the maintenance of confidences against the public interest in disclosure. Each case must be decided on its facts.

In *Francome* many factors militated against disclosure. The plaintiffs' telephone had been tapped in circumstances constituting a criminal offence under section 5 Wireless Telegraphy Act 1949. The Court held that the plaintiffs had at least an arguable case that this breach of the criminal law gave them private rights against the offenders which they were entitled to protect by an injunction prior to a full trial of the action.[6] No criminal offence had been committed in *Cork v McVicar*.

Public interest requires that disclosure should be to a proper person or authority. In *Initial Services v Putterill*,[7] Lord Denning M.R. said:

> The disclosure must ... be to one who has a proper interest to receive the information. Thus it would be proper to disclose a crime to the police, or a breach of the Restrictive Trade Practices Act to the registrar. There may be cases where the misdeed is of such a character that the public interest may demand, or at least excuse, publication on a broader field, even to the press.[8]

In *Francome*, the Court decided that it was not necessary in the public interest for disclosure to be made in the pages of a national newspaper. In this context a distinction must be drawn between information which is of public interest and information which it is in the public interest to disclose. Furthermore, the courts take into account the commercial interests of certain sections of the press in disclosing alleged confidences and so increasing circulation. Thus, scandal of a confidential nature might be of public interest and in the commercial interest of a newspaper to disclose, but disclosure will not necessarily be in the public interest, or not to a sufficient extent to outweigh the public interest in the maintenance of confidences. In *Francome* the Court held that disclosure to the police or to the Jockey Club

---

[5] Note 2 above.
[6] *Ibid.* at 412.
[7] [1968] 1 QB 396.
[8] *Ibid.* at 405 and 406.

would satisfy the public interest in disclosure. The Court would not allow disclosure through the press prior to a full trial of the action. They did, however, recommend that the full trial be heard as soon as possible. By contrast, in *Cork v McVicar* disclosure to the police might not satisfy the public interest because in this case the information related to alleged police corruption. In this situation a newspaper was held to be an appropriate vehicle for disclosure, for, as Scott J pointed out, a newspaper could provide a means whereby corruption was exposed.

Lion Laboratories Ltd v. Evans

Both *Cork v McVicar* and *Francome v Mirror Newspapers* involved what in this area of the law is described as an iniquity. It was made clear, however, in *Lion Laboratories Ltd v Evans*[9] that there can be a public interest in the disclosure of confidences other than iniquities. Here the information related to inaccuracies in an instrument which was used to test the breath of drivers of motor vehicles who were suspected of driving with a concentration of alcohol above the prescribed limit. The Court held that there was a public interest in the disclosure of this information, as disclosure and publicity might lead to a reappraisal of a device which had the potential for causing a wrongful conviction for a serious offence. Disclosure in the public interest was not limited to cases where the plaintiff had been guilty of a crime or other improper conduct.

The most recent proposals for reform of this area are to be found in the Law Commission Report on breach of confidence.[10] Section 11 of the Draft Bill appended to the Report provides that a defendant should not be liable for breach of confidence if he raises the issue of public interest in disclosure, and the plaintiff is unable to satisfy the court that the public interest relied on by the defendant is outweighed by the public interest in upholding the confidentiality of the information. The public interest in disclosure is not therefore a mere defence, as perhaps it is at present,[11] and the burden of proof is shifted to the plaintiff to show that the balance comes down in his favour. As in the more recent case of *Lion Laboratories*, the Law commission recommend that there may be a public interest in the disclosure of information which does not relate to any crime, fraud or other misconduct.

The Law Commission say that when the court is balancing the competing public interests, they should have regard to all the circumstances of the case. Regrettably, however, they specify that, among other things, the court should consider the manner in which the information was acquired.[12] This undoubtedly relates to the Law Commission's concern for the inadequacy of the present law when dealing with information acquired by reprehensible means. But its inclusion is unfortunate as well as inappropriate. While improper acquisition is not to be encouraged, it should not really affect the assessment of the public interest in disclosure. The two issues are separate. As Stephenson LJ said in *Lion Laboratories*,[13] there may be a public interest in disclosure even if the information has been unlawfully obtained in flagrant breach of confidence and irrespective of the motive of the informer. The improper mode of acquisition did not affect the outcome of *Cork v McVicar*. It should not act as a limiting factor in other cases. The Law Commission proposals should be amended to take this into account.

---

[9] Note 3 above.
[10] Note 4 above. For a detailed analysis of the present law and of the changes proposed by the Law Commission, see Yvonne Cripps, 'The Public Interest Defence to the Action for Breach of Confidence and the Law Commission's Proposals on Disclosure in the Public Interest', [1984] *Oxford Journal of Legal Studies* 361.
[11] See Cripps, Note 10 above.
[12] See also J. Phillips, 'Breach of Confidence; Restraining an Iniquity', [1985] JBL 57 and 58.
[13] Note 3 above at 422.

Remedies

American Cyanamid
Revisited
[1964] 4 EIPR 234

MICHAEL EDENBOROUGH
AND GUY TRITTON
*Barrister, Chambers of Christopher Morcom
QC*

Series 5 Software Ltd v Clarke

In the judgment for *Series 5 Software Ltd v Clarke*,[1] handed down on 19 December 1995 by Laddie J, the learned judge re-examined what should be the correct approach in the exercise of a judge's discretion when considering whether or not to grant an interlocutory injunction.

Facts

The plaintiff was a company involved in the development production and sale of computer software for use in the printing and publishing industry. The first, fourth and fifth defendants had been engaged separately in various capacities by the plaintiff. Their employment was not harmonious and on 25 August 1995 they resigned together. On 24 August, the defendants had removed certain computer equipment as a bargaining tool against their unpaid salaries. The plaintiff applied for, and was granted, an order for interlocutory delivery up, and an injunction to prevent the defendants from contacting any of the customers of the plaintiff, and to prevent the dissemination of its alleged trade secrets. The *ex parte* hearing was before Mr D. Oliver QC sitting as a Deputy Judge of the High Court. In the time between the *ex parte* hearing and the *inter partes* hearing, the material in dispute was returned. There were five rounds of evidence, in which nearly every substantial points was put in conflict, before the matter came before Mr Justice Laddie. The plaintiff's case was that the defendants took not only hardware, but also software, company books and client lists, that the defendants intend to copy the software and that, furthermore, not everything had been returned pursuant to the *ex parte* order. In contrast, the defendants claimed that they only took hardware, that they had not breached any obligation of confidence, nor had they copied any of the software and that, furthermore, they had returned everything. In addition, the defendants claimed that the current proceedings were impeding their attempts to find alternative employment. There were no pleaded allegations of copyright infringement, even though in argument the plaintiff's counsel alleged that its source code had been copied and used by the defendants in the preparation of their own software; however, counsel for the plaintiff indicated that in due course there would be an application to amend the pleadings to include this allegation of copyright infringement.

---

[1] Judgment handed down on 19 December 1995; not yet reported.

At the *inter partes* hearing, at which the plaintiffs sought the continuation of the injunctions obtained *ex parte*, the plaintiff was represented by counsel; the second and third defendants did not appear, while the first, fourth and fifth appeared in person. Counsel for the plaintiff contended that all he had to show was 'at least an arguable case'. However, he admitted that whatever the strict interpretation of *American Cyanamid*,[2] it was known that some courts still paid regard to the relative strength of the parties' cases.

Mr Justice Laddie felt that it was not satisfactory to exercise the court's discretion to grant an interlocutory injunction by paying lip service to the guidance given in *American Cyanamid*. Accordingly, and it would seem without the benefit of substantial argument from counsel, his Lordship embarked on a detailed analysis of the law relating to interlocutory injunctions before and after *American Cyanamid*. He started by saying that:

> It is a matter of common knowledge and frequent comment that there was an apparent sea-change in the court's approach to the grant of [interlocutory] relief in 1975 as a result of the speeches in the House of Lords in *American Cyanamid Co. v Ethicon Ltd* [1975] AC 396. Since then, it has been suggested on a number of occasions that it is now no longer appropriate to consider as a significant factor the apparent strength or weakness of the plaintiff's case as disclosed by the affidavit evidence filed on the application for interlocutory relief.

He then went on to examine the law prior to *American Cyanamid*. Starting with *Hilton v Lord Granville*,[3] moving on through *Kerr on Injunctions* (3rd edition, 1888), *The Yearly Practice of the Supreme Court* (1940 edition) and the case law before 1975, his Lordship concluded that then the relative strength of the parties' cases was a relevant consideration, that there was a growing tendency for the plaintiff to have to show a '*prima facie* case' and that this was an 'essential prelude to the granting of interlocutory relief'.[4] This inflexibility was criticised by Lord Denning in the following terms: 'The remedy by interlocutory injunction is so useful that it should be kept flexible and discretionary. It must not be made the subject of strict rules.'[5] Laddie J concluded this part of his review of the case law by stating:

> In summary, most courts continued to refer to the strong *prima facie* case 'rule' up to the end of 1974, but this was not seen as a mandatory requirement but rather as a particularly significant factor which the courts should take into consideration when exercising the discretion.

1975 in the House of Lords

In 1975, two cases went before the House of Lords on the issue of interlocutory injunctions. The first was *Hoffmann-La Roche v Secretary of State for Trade*,[6] while the second was *American Cyanamid Co. v Ethicon Ltd*. In the course of his speech in the first of these two cases, delivered just before the long vacation, Lord Diplock said:

> To justify the grant of such a remedy the plaintiff must satisfy the court, first, that there

---

[2] *American Cyanamid Co. v Ethicon Ltd* [1975] AC 396.
[3] Cr. & Ph. 283.
[4] *Per* Harman LJ in *Cavendish House (Cheltenham) Ltd v Cavendish-Woodhouse Ltd* [1970] RPC 234, at 235.
[5] *Hubbard v Vosper* [1972] 2 QB 84, at 98.
[6] [1975] AC 295.

is a strong *prima facie* case that he will be entitled to a final order restraining the defendant from doing what he is threatening to do . . .

Thus, Mr Justice Laddie said that the practice before *American Cyanamid* was that the court had to pay regard to the strength or otherwise of the plaintiff's case as revealed by a consideration of all the affidavit evidence.

The judgment in *American Cyanamid* was delivered towards the end of 1975. Lord Diplock was again on the panel. The case was concerned with a complex patent case with sophisticated arguments of patent law, namely ambiguity, construction, inutility, false suggestion, insufficiency and unfair basis being advanced. In the Court of Appeal, the motion lasted for two working weeks while the parties argued questions of polymer chemistry, infringement and validity. At first instance, Graham J had found that the plaintiffs had shown a strong *prima facie* case, but the Court of Appeal upheld an appeal from the defendants by ruling that they were not satisfied that a *prima facie* case of infringement had been made out. On appeal, the House of Lords stated that the Court of Appeal had considered that there was a rule of practice so well-established as to constitute a rule of law that precluded them from granting any interlocutory injunction unless the applicant had satisfied on the balance of probabilities that the defendant had violated the applicant's rights. Leave was given to the House of Lords for it to consider whether or not there existed such a 'rule of law'.

The House of Lords held that there was no such rule and deprecated any attempt to fetter the discretion of the court. Lord Diplock said that the court must be satisfied that the claim is not frivolous or vexatious, that is, that there is a serious question to be tried.

Mr Justice Laddie set out parts of Lord Diplock's judgment where the latter emphasised that one should examine the balance of convenience rather than the strength of the parties' hands. Thus, Lord Diplock said that 'if the extent of the uncompensatable disadvantage to each party would not differ widely, it may not be improper to take into account in tipping the balance the relative strength of each party's case'. This approach suggested that initially the court should examine the relative risk of injustice to each party if the injunction was or was not granted, and then only in a few cases should one examine the merits of the plaintiff's claim. After this case, it became customary for lawyers and judges to say that it was inappropriate on an application for interlocutory relief, save in rare cases, to take into account the apparent strength of the plaintiff's case. However, as Mr Justice Laddie said, that would mean that Lord Diplock performed a *volte face* on this issue in a matter of four months. In his Lordship's view, this was inconceivable.

Accordingly, he said that it was appropriate to consider whether what Lord Diplock said in *Roche* was incompatible with what he said in *American Cyanamid*. After an extensive analysis of Lord Diplock's speech, Laddie J came to the conclusion that Lord Diplock did not intend to exclude consideration of strength in most applications for interlocutory relief, but that the court should not attempt to resolve difficult issues of fact or law on an application for interlocutory relief. If, on the other hand, the court is able to come to a view as to the strength of the parties' cases on credible evidence, then it can do so. To suggest otherwise would be to exclude from consideration an important factor and such exclusion would fly in the face of the flexibility advocated in *American Cyanamid*.

Mr Justice Laddie then stated the following matters which should be borne in mind when a court is considering whether to grant interlocutory relief:

(1) The grant of an interlocutory injunction is a matter of discretion and depends on all the facts of the case.

(2) There are no fixed rules as to when an injunction should or should not be granted. The relief must be kept flexible.

(3) Because of the practice adopted on the hearing of applications for interlocutory relief, the court should rarely attempt to resolve complex issues of disputed fact or law.

(4) Major factors the court can bear in mind are (a) the extent to which damages are likely to be an adequate remedy for each party and the ability of the other party to pay, (b) the balance of convenience, (c) the maintenance of the *status quo*, and (d) any clear view the court may reach as to the relative strength of the parties' cases.

In coming to this conclusion, Mr Justice Laddie stated that the House of Lords in *American Cyanamid* did not suggest that it was changing the basis on which most courts had approached the exercise of discretion in this important area; that the only issue which the House was expressly addressing in *American Cyanamid* was the existence of the inflexible 'rule of law' which had been applied as a mandatory condition by the court of Appeal; and that if the speeches were read in that light, it would mean that there was no significant inconsistency between the *Roche* and *American Cyanamid* decisions. One of the advantages of this approach would be, in the words of Laddie J, that 'it would preserve what was one of the great values of interlocutory proceedings, namely an early, though non-binding, view of the merits from a judge'.

Laddie J then proceeded to apply these principles to the matter before him and, on the basis that the case, even though arguable, was unlikely in his Lordship's opinion to succeed at trial, his Lordship refused the relief sought, save for the delivery up of the items in question, on the grounds that the defendants had claimed to have had already returned it all.

Comment

Mr Justice Laddie's judgment is to be welcomed. There are many cases where a fairly clear view as to the parties' strengths can be formed. However, often courts have felt that they are not permitted to take such a view but rather apply (and often tortuously) the adequacy of damages and balance of convenience principles. In some cases there was clearly an upper hand and often in these cases, judges did pay lip service to the perceived effect of *American Cyanamid*, but in fact actually considered the merits. Mr Justice Laddie's judgment legitimises that practice. It is not intended to bring back the bad old days of weeks-long motions. It is only where a *clear view* on the evidence of the parties' strengths can be formed that it is relevant.

Series 5 was not an intellectual property case. What is the effect of the judgment for IP? In passing-off and trade mark cases, plaintiffs generally seek an interim injunction to safeguard the goodwill associated with their mark or get-up. At an interlocutory stage, except for in the plainest of cases, it is generally difficult to form a clear view as to whether the two marks or get-up are likely to deceive or cause confusion. Judges may form their own view, but the *Neutrogena v Neutralia*[7] case showed that evidence of confusion can make a judge change his mind. In most cases, it is unlikely that a judge will be able to form a 'clear view'. Accordingly, Mr Justice Laddie's judgment will not alter the prior practice in this area. Parties will have to show a serious issue to be tried and then consider the balance of convenience.

In patent and copyright cases, it has been difficult to obtain interlocutory injunctions

---

[7] IPD [1995] 18083.

because normally any loss caused to the plaintiff is capable of being quantified. A patent is normally exploited by means of a licence and therefore a plaintiff can adequately be compensated by the payment of damages by a defendant. Thus, providing the defendant can pay, there is no need for an interlocutory injunction. Where a patentee or copyright owner is concerned about unquantifiable effects of the defendant's activities on the market, *Series 5* will be of assistance if it is clear that the defendant is infringing.

Is *Series 5* an invitation to patentees or copyright owners to seek an interlocutory injunction where there are no grounds for arguing that they cannot be adequately compensated by damages—for instance, where the defendant is of substantial means and the plaintiff has a policy of licensing the protected works? Lord Diplock said in *American Cyanamid*: 'If damages in the measure recoverable at common law would be adequate remedy and the defendant would be in a financial position to pay them, no interlocutory injunction should *normally be granted, however strong the plaintiff's claim appeared to be at that stage*.'[8] Thus, while there is no fetter on the discretion of courts in considering interim injunctive relief, it is the authors' submission that courts as a matter of firm practice should not grant interim relief if it is clear that the plaintiff can and will be compensated by damages. A party is not entitled as of right to obtain interlocutory relief. It is a purely equitable remedy. As Lord Diplock said in *Hoffmann-La Roche v Secretary of State for Trade*, 'an interim injunction is a temporary and *exceptional* remedy'. Thus, the plaintiff either can seek summary judgment if there is no triable issue or must wait until trial for his injunctive relief.

The approach in England should be contrasted with the Dutch approach where patent cases are nearly always brought by way of applications for preliminary relief because patent cases are regarded as urgent by definition owing to the limited duration of patent rights and a perception that effective protection of the patentee demands an early injunction. In the Netherlands, writ, statement of claim and defence are served within a month, accompanied usually by a report from a patent attorney. A hearing will take place within two months from the issue of writ and judgment will be delivered normally within two months from service of the summons. As the action is a preliminary one, the court will decline to grant an injunction if the issues are too complex for a conclusion to be reached before trial. If at trial it is subsequently found that the preliminary injunction should not have been awarded, the defendant is entitled to payment of damages.

Is the English or Dutch approach the better one? The Dutch approach appeals to patentees. It favours the patentee because Dutch courts will grant preliminary injunctions if they form a clear view that there is infringement regardless of whether the patentee can be compensated for the infringement by damages. If judgment at trial goes in favour of the defendant, then the court will order that he be compensated by the patentee. The Dutch approach commends itself in that intellectual property rights are monopoly rights (or, in the case of copyright, a qualified monopoly right) and not rights to money. Accordingly, if one can form a clear view that infringement has occurred (but cannot say that there are no triable issues), then the defendant's product or process should not have been on the market at all. The English approach is in effect to say that unless you can obtain summary judgment, your intellectual property right is transmuted into a right to damages until trial. In effect, the Dutch preliminary procedure is the opposite of the English preliminary procedure. A patentee *will* get an injunction at a preliminary stage if the court is of the clear view that the defendant is infringing, provided the *defendant* can be compensated in damages if successful at trial. In England, the patentee *will not* get an injunction at a preliminary stage if the *plaintiff* can be compensated in damages if successful at trial.

---

[8] *Emphasis added*; this passage, at 408B, was expressly quoted by Mr Justice Laddie.

In most cases, and given a creative lawyer, one can find some argument that damages will not be sufficient. In such cases, Mr Justice Laddie's judgment in *Series 5* is of great assistance. However, in the authors' opinion, there is a need to go further to emphasise the fact that intellectual property is a monopoly and that courts should be permitted to grant interim injunctions where a clear view can be formed that there is infringement, regardless of whether the plaintiff's loss can be quantified in damages. Otherwise, and coupled with the concern of pan-European injunctions being granted by the Dutch courts, patentees and other rights owners may move their litigation to the Netherlands.

Accounting for Profits Gained by Infringement of Copyright: When does it End?*

[1991] 1 EIPR 5

LIONEL BENTLY

Research Fellow, King's College, University of London

An account of profits is one of the two major financial remedies available to a plaintiff whose intellectual property rights have been infringed. However the remedy has not been widely used.[1] It is said to be difficult and unsatisfactory.[2] It is unclear whether it is available for infringement of all intellectual property rights.[3] It is unclear whether it is a requirement that the defendant knows he is infringing the plaintiff's rights. It is unclear whether the remedy is only available where an injunction is granted. It is difficult to assess which profits the defendant is accountable for. It is unclear whether the defendant can claim that some of the profits are attributable to his own efforts. It is unclear whether a plaintiff must always elect between the two remedies of account and damages and, if so, why. These doubts and difficulties have led most plaintiffs to opt for the remedy of damages, and one academic to suggest that the remedy of account be abolished.[4] This is ironic in a period when many commentators are calling for the extension of such a remedy to other areas of law, such as the torts of defamation[5] and invasion of privacy,[6] as well as breach of contract.[7]

This piece examines some of the difficulties encountered in the existing law relating to the grant of an account in the context of copyright law. It then goes on to consider whether these difficulties can be resolved by the adoption of a single theoretical foundation for the remedy.

---

* An earlier draft of this article was delivered at 'Copyright Law and Strategy' at Selfridge Hotel, London on 4 July 1990. The author was at that time a lecturer in law at the University of Keele.

1. Cases are particularly rare in the context of patent law. Blanco White (Jeffs, Jacob, Cornish and Vitoria, *Encyclopaedia of UK and European Patent Law*, Sweet & Maxwell, 1978, with supps, paragraph 10–24, at 1524) remarks that no account seems to have been taken for patent infringement in the 30 years since the Patents Act 1949.

2. *Crosley v Derby Gas-Light Co.* (1838) 3 Myl & Cr 428, 40 ER 992 at 434, 994 per Lord Cottenham LC; *Siddell v Vickers* (1892) 9 RPC 152; *Automatic Coal Gas Retort Co. Ltd v Mayor of Salford* (1897) 14 RPC at 471 per Romer J.

3. There is no specific provision for an account in the context of registered designs under the Registered Designs Act 1949; some doubt also exists as to whether an account is available for breach of confidence where the duty of confidentiality was contractually imposed and damages are available.

4. Patfield, 'The Modern Remedy of Account', (1987), 11 Adel. LR 1.

5. Birks, *Introduction to the Law of Restitution*, Clarendon Press, 1989, at 326 to 328.

6. York, 'Extension of Restitutional Remedies in the Tort Field', (1957) 4 UCLALR 499 at 533 ff.; Vaver, 'What's Mine is Not Yours: Commercial Appropriation of Personality under the Privacy Acts of British Columbia, Manitoba and Saskatchewan', (1981) 15 UBCLR 241 at 318 ff.

7. Farnsworth, 'Your Loss or My Gain? The Dilemma of the Disgorgement Principle in Breach of Contract', (1985) 94 YLJ 1339; Birks, 'Restitutionary Damages for Breach of Contract: *Snepp* and the Fusion of Law and Equity', (1987) LMCLQ 421; Jones, 'The Recovery of Benefits Gained from Breach of Contract', (1983) 99 LQR 442; Goff and Jones, *The Law of Restitution*, Sweet & Maxwell, 1986 (3rd ed.), ch. 36.

The Nature of the Remedy of Account

The remedy of account has two principal characteristics. The first is that it is a restitutionary remedy. It takes away from the defendant anything he has gained and returns to the plaintiff. Thus it resembles the common law action for money had and received. On the other hand, it must be contrasted with damages which are a compensatory remedy, and exemplary damages which are essentially penal.

The second characteristic is that it is an equitable remedy. Before the fusion of Law and Equity, it was available for infringement of purely equitable rights, where it was the only financial remedy available and also where equity acted in its ancillary jurisdiction, for example by granting an injunction in support of a common law right, where damages would be inappropriate. As with all equitable remedies, an account is a discretionary remedy.

The History of the Remedy

Copyright was originally a matter of common law but was extended and placed on a statutory basis by the Statue of Anne 1709. As copyright was a statutory right, one would have expected that the remedies would have been specified in the statute, and this is true today: section 96 of the Copyright Designs and patents Act (CDPA) 1988.[8] Nevertheless, it was not so under many of the early statutes.

The earliest provision for an account is to be found in the Dramatic Literary Property Act 1833, known as the Bulwer Lytton Act. That Act gave the author the sole liberty of representing a production and made an infringer liable to a penalty of not less than forty shillings, or damages for the injury sustained by the plaintiff or 'to the full amount of the benefit or advantage arising from such representation' whichever shall be the greater damages.[9] This provision was extended to cover musical compositions by section 20 of the Literary Copyright Act 1842.[10] However, although it conferred an account, there was nothing which specifically limited its availability to a Court of Equity. It was extended by section 9 of the Fine Arts Copyright Act 1862 to cases of infringement of copyright in paintings, drawings and photographs. The Copyright Act 1911 placed copyright in all types of works on a unified basis and section 6(1) of that Act declared that a copyright owner was entitled to all such remedies by way of injunction or interdict, damages, accounts or otherwise as are or may be conferred by law for the infringement of a right.

Although the remedy of account was not expressly available during the first century of copyright protection, the Courts regularly made use of it. This seems peculiar for two reasons. First, the statutes did specify certain remedies,[11] and hence the remedy of account

---

[8] 'In an action for infringement of copyright all such relief by way of damages, injunctions, accounts or otherwise is available to the plaintiff as is available in respect of the infringement of any other property right.'

[9] G. McFarlane (*Copyright: The Development and Exercise of the Performing Right*, John Offord, 1980) relates that the Dramatic Authors Society always sought the penalty on the basis that it would be very difficult to prove the benefit derived as they were never able to get at the theatre's books to elicit the benefit arising from any performance (at 71).

[10] 5 & 6 Vict. c. 66.

[11] The 1709 Copyright Act conferred the exclusive right to print, reprint and import books and provided specifically for forfeiture of copies and a penalty of one penny for each copy in the infringer's custody, of which a halfpenny was to go to the Crown and a halfpenny to the suer. These rights and remedies were extended to designer, engravers and etchers of print in 1735, although the penalty in that case was five shillings rather than one penny. An action upon the case for damages to be assessed by a jury was provided by the Engraving Act 1777 and became the standard financial remedy for infringement under the 1801 and 1814 Acts and the 1814 Sculpture Act. H. Ransom (*The First Copyright Statute*, Texas University Press, 1956) notes that one of the problems with the Act was that its penalties were judged not to be worth the expense of the risks of a trial at common law.

would appear to have been excluded on the principle *expressio unius est exclusio alterius.* Moreover, it is a long-standing principle of equity that it would not interfere where there existed an adequate remedy at common law, and the remedies available at common law include not only damages, but the possibility of 'waiver of tort' and an action for benefit received by the defendant.

The explanation for equity's intervention derives from the fact that the Court of Equity would become involved in the granting of an injunction, and that the remedy of account was available as incidental to that.[12] If the plaintiff was granted an injunction he had clearly shown his right existed, and it would be unfair (in terms of time and cost) to send him back to the Courts of Law in order to obtain financial recompense. Since equity, prior to Lord Cairn's Act,[13] could not grant damages, an account of profits would be given if a plaintiff wished. The basis for the jurisdiction has been acknowledged widely since. For example, in *Root v Railway Co.*,[14] Matthews J comprehensively reviewed the English and United States case-law concerning the account in patent cases. He remarked that:

> It is the fundamental characteristic and limit of the jurisdiction in equity that it cannot give relief when there is a plain and adequate and complete remedy at law ... When however relief was sought which equity alone could give, as by way of injunction to prevent a continuance of the wrong, in order to avoid multiplicity of suits and do complete justice, the court assumed jurisdiction to award compensation for the past injury, not however, by assessing damages, which was the peculiar office of a jury, but requiring an account of profits, on the ground that if any had been made, it was equitable to require the wrong-doer to refund them, as it would be inequitable that he should make a profit out of his own wrong.[15]

The question of whether the statutory remedies precluded common law remedies was considered in the eleven opinions given by members of the House of Lords in *Donaldson v Becket*.[16] Six of their Lordships urged the House to hold that the Statute of Anne removed the common law right of copyright,[17] and five of those also argued that an author was precluded from every remedy except on the foundations of the said statute and on the terms and conditions prescribed thereby. Baron Eyre agreed that this was so but added that 'there may be a remedy in equity upon the foundation of the statute, independent of the terms and conditions prescribed by the statute'. The opinions were therefore inconclusive, and injunctions and accounts continued to be granted. A rationale for so doing is to be found in *Colburn v Simms*.[18] Here, the plaintiff had waived his right to an account but later sought delivery up of copies of a book published by the defendants which infringed the plaintiff's copyright in 'Spas of England'. Sir James Wigram VC considered the fact that the Statute of Anne created a new right and provided a remedy for invasion of that right. He remarked:

> The cases decided also that, if an Act gives a right or imposes a duty, and does not direct in what manner it shall be enforced, the Courts of Ordinary Jurisdiction must

---

[12] See York, Note 6 above, at 522.

[13] Chancery (Amendment) Act 1858 (21 & 22 Vict. c. 27). Now Supreme Court Act 1981 section 50.

[14] (1881) 105 US 189 at 207.

[15] See also *Tilghman v Proctor* (1888) 125 US 136 at 148; *International Credit Control Ltd v Axelsen* [1974] 1 NZLR 695.

[16] (1774) 4 Burr 2408; 98 ER 257. Abrams ('The Historic Foundation of American Copyright Law: Exploding the Myth of Common Law Copyright', (1983) 29 Wayne LR 1119 esp. at 1156 ff.) explains the confusion between the ruling of the House of Lords and the advisory opinions of the judges.

[17] B. Eyre, Nares J, B. Perrott, Gould J, B. Adams, De Grey LCJ.

[18] (1829) 2 Hare 543, 67 ER 224.

apply the appropriate remedies, and that existing remedies are not taken away by a statute which gives a new one.

The third difficulty—the adequacy of the common law remedy—has not proved important in this country. However, in the United States the question is of some significance in determining whether a defendant is entitled to a jury trial—if the common law remedy is adequate, then a jury trial is available. In *Dairy Queen v Wood*,[19] Black J in the Supreme Court held that the plaintiff must be able to show that accounts at law are of such a complicated nature that only a court of equity could unravel them, and added that because of developments in procedure this would be rare.[20] In England, jury trials are only rarely available in civil actions[21] and are never used in the Chancery Division to which patent and copyright actions are assigned[22] (irrespective of whether the remedy sought is a common law or equitable one). It is therefore unlikely that this issue will ever be raised.

Some Problematic Elements in the Substantive Law

Is an injunction a prerequisite of the remedy of account?

The analysis of the history of the remedy of account illustrates that the remedy was initially only available as ancillary to an injunction. As a result, whenever for some reason an injunction could not be granted an account was not available. In *Parrot v Palmer*[23] Brougham LC considered there to be a general rule 'no injunction, no account'. This was first applied in a copyright action in *Baily v Taylor*[24] by Sir John Leach, where an injunction was refused on the grounds that the piracy was of a small part of the plaintiff's work, and that he had delayed. The Master of the Rolls refused to grant an account, saying that 'if this court do not interfere by injunction, then his remedy as in the case of any other injury to his property, must be at law'.[25] The rule was held to cover patent infringement in *Smith v LSWR*[26] and *Price's Patent*.[27] There, Page Wood VC refused injunctions where patents had expired and hence found himself incapable of granting an order of account. In the latter case he remarked that 'if for any reason an injunction cannot be obtained there can be no right to an account', and added that this was because the latter raised questions of 'great nicety and difficulty'.

The rule is an odd one. An injunction is aimed at preventing future infringement, whereas an account operates with respect to previous wrongs: any infringement after the issue of an injunction would be a contempt, and the infringer would be liable not only to account but also to have his assets sequestered or to be imprisoned. Of course, it will be rare for a plaintiff

---

[19] (1962) 369 US 469.
[20] See Palmer, *The Law of Restitution*, Little Brown & Co., 1978, volume 1, section 1.5, at 28 to 29 and Eichengrin, 'Remedying the Remedy of Account', (1985) 60 Ind. LJ 463 ff.
[21] Supreme Court Act 1981 section 69. The cases are fraud and libel cases, which are to be tried by judge and jury unless too complicated (for example, *Goldsmith v Pressdram Ltd* [1987] 3 All ER 485, *Beta Construction Ltd v Channel Four TV Co. Ltd*, *The Times* 9.11.1989). Under section 6 of the Administration of Justice Act 1933 a jury trial might have been appropriate where the honour and integrity of the claimant was at stake—*Barclays Bank v Cole* (1967) 2 QB 738. All other cases are to be tried by judge alone, unless the court in its discretion orders it to be tried by jury. It might be appropriate, by analogy with defamation cases, to do so where the question concerns the new 'moral right' of an author under Chapter 4 CDPA 1988.
[22] Supreme Court Act 1981 section 61; Schedule 1, paragraph 1(i).
[23] (1834) 3 My & K 632, 40 ER 241 at 640, 244.
[24] (1829) 1 Russ & My 75, 39 ER 28.
[25] *Ibid.* at 75, 29.
[26] (1854) Kay 408; 69 ER 173.
[27] (1858) 4 K & J 727, 70 ER 302.

to seek an account without an injunction. However, the question might arise where, for example, a defendant undertakes not to infringe or is no longer in a position to infringe (so that there is no likelihood of infringement); or where a plaintiff is no longer entitled to an injunction, for example where his rights have expired or been assigned.

The rule does not appear to apply to copyright cases any longer on the basis that specific provision of the remedy has existed since 1911. This argument is not necessarily foolproof. Although Laddie, Prescott and Vitoria[28] nowhere mention the requirement of an injunction, Copinger[29] appears to suggest that an account is still only available as ancillary to an injunction. Furthermore, it should be noted that an injunction has on one occasion been thought necessary in the law of trade marks where a specific statutory provision conferred the remedy of an account. *Colbeam Palmer Ltd and Another v Stock Affiliates Pty Ltd*[30] was a case under the Commonwealth Trade Marks Act 1955–8, which specifically provided that: 'The relief which a court may grant ... includes an injunction ... and ... at the option of the plaintiff, either damages or an account of profits.' Nevertheless, Windeyer J argued that in the normal case an account was only to be granted as ancillary to an injunction.

It is therefore worth considering the exceptions to the general rule that an injunction is a prerequisite of an account.

(1) Accidental Circumstances. One subtlety in the judgment of *Parrott*[31] is the distinction between the denial of an injunction due to 'accidental circumstances' and where 'from the nature of the question, injunction is not competent and could not be prayed'. Thus it was possible for the same laches to disentitle a plaintiff to an injunction, but not to an account (however in this case he was entitled to neither). Applied to its full, this exception would undermine the rule, since an injunction can always be sought for infringement—all the examples just given could be viewed as accidental circumstances.

(2) Partial Infringement. One case where an injunction is inappropriate is where the infringement constitutes only a minor element in the work which the defendant is marketing. In such circumstances in *Mawman v Tegg*,[32] Eldon LC suggested that although an injunction may be inappropriate, the court will in any case order an account.

(3) Changes since the Action Commenced. In *Colbeam Palmer* the High Court of Australia refused to grant an injunction to refrain infringement of a registered trade mark, since it had expired and the plaintiff had assigned the mark. Nevertheless, an account was ordered. Windeyer J acknowledged that as a general rule an account could not be granted without an injunction. However, he made an exception because the circumstances were unusual, since the injunction could have been granted when the action was commenced.

(4) A Recent Development. In *AG v Guardian (No. 2)*[33] the House of Lords awarded an account against the *Sunday Times*, but refused an injunction on the grounds that the information was by that time already in the public domain so that no further damage could be inflicted on the Crown, and that there was no longer anything secret with respect to which the duty of confidence could relate. Their Lordships

---

[28] *The Modern Law of Copyright*, Butterworths, 1980, paragraph 12.28, at 417 to 418.
[29] Skone James, Mummery and Rayner (eds), *Copinger and Skone James on Copyright*, Sweet & Maxwell, 1980 (12th ed.), paragraph 653, at 280.
[30] (1968) 122 CLR 25.
[31] Note 23 above.
[32] (1826) 2 Russ 385, 38 ER 380.
[33] [1988] 3 All ER 545.

did not examine the relationship between injunction and account, though their decision clearly indicates that an account in this context does not depend upon the availability of an injunction.

The case could be used to support any of four possible arguments. First, the *Parrott* argument—an injunction would have been available for the period to which the account applied—it was only 'accidental circumstances' that made the injunction no longer appropriate. Second, it might be argued that the case falls within the *Colbeam Palmer* exception, that an injunction would have been available at the commencement of the action. Third, it might be argued that an injunction is unnecessary where an account is sought for infringement of purely equitable rights. The problem with such an argument is that their Lordships never made it clear if the duty of confidentiality was equitable or legal (for example, as an implied term in Wright's contract). Fourth, it might be argued that the case indicates that the courts will no longer treat an account as dependent on an injunction.

Can an account be ordered against an innocent infringer?

The degree of protection afforded to an innocent infringer of intellectual property rights under both statute and case-law appears both arbitrary and unduly complicated. In the case of infringement of patents, innocence is a complete defence to an action for an account;[34] and in trade mark and passing off cases the complete innocence of the party making the representation may be a reason for limiting the account to the period subsequent to the date at which he becomes aware of the true facts.[35]

However, there is no statutory defence of innocence to copyright infringement (though there is where damages are sought). Section 97(1) states:

> Where in an action for infringement of copyright it is shown that at the time of the infringement the defendant did not know, and had no reason to believe, that copyright subsisted in the work to which the action relates, the plaintiff is not entitled to damages against him, but without prejudice to any other remedy.

The section is in significantly different terms to its equivalent in the 1956 Act. The latter made it quite clear that an account was available against an innocent defendant by use of the word 'entitled'. The new section simply says that the innocence defence is 'without prejudice to any other remedy'. It might, therefore, be open to a court to introduce or develop an innocence defence similar to that mentioned in relation to passing off. It should be borne in mind however that in nearly all circumstances, the defendant will have been aware of the plaintiff's original work. The peculiarity of the fact that innocence is a defence to both pecuniary remedies for patent infringegment, and only to damages for copyright infringement, is heightened by the argument that innocence is a defence to an action for an account, but not for damages, in an action for breach of confidence.[36]

---

[34] Patents Act 1977 section 62(1).
[35] *AG Spalding and Bros v A.W. Gammage Ltd* (1915) 32 RPC 273; *Edward Young & Co. v Stanley Silverwood Holt* (1948) 65 RPC 25.
[36] *Seager v Copydex* [1967] 2 All ER 415.

The requirement of an election

It is the conventional view that a plaintiff must elect between the two remedies of damages and an account, and as a result most plaintiffs in intellectual property action claim 'an injunction, an enquiry as to damages or, at the plaintiff's option, an account of profits'. The requirement of election explains why so few cases on account of profits are brought—given the difficulties with knowing what the rules are and how much the plaintiff will reap from an account (despite the fact that orders for discovery will more than likely have been made at the interlocutory stage), few professionals would advise their clients to risk the election. Yet the requirement of an election is difficult to justify, as we shall see, and it certainly might be worth arguing that the cases are based on a justification which has been long disapproved and ought no longer to be followed.

The requirement derives from the House of Lords decision in a patent infringement case—*Neilson v Betts*.[37] There Lord Westbury remarked that a claim for damages and profits was 'hardly reconcilable, for if you taken an account of profits you condone the infringement'. The case was followed soon after in *De Vitre v Betts*,[38] *Watson v Holliday*[39] and has achieved statutory approval in section 61(2) of the patents Act 1977. It has been extended to all other intellectual property actions,[40] although there is some theoretical doubt in relation to breach of confidence.

The principle on which the requirement of an election was based in *Neilson v Betts* is unsatisfactory. First, the same idea of implied contract which underpinned the doctrine of waiver of tort, was rejected by the House of Lords in *United Australia Ltd v Barclays Bank Ltd*.[41] It seems that it ought, therefore, to be rejected in the context of infringement of intellectual property rights. Second, we have seen such a rejection of the principle in *Codex Corp. v Racal-Milgo*[42] and *Catnic v Evans*.[43] In *Codex* a patentee of moderns had elected to take an account of profits, and the question arose as to whether this meant that subsequent use or sale of the modems was approved. Whitford J held that it was not, and took the view that all that was condoned by the election was that which had taken place up until the time the account was taken.[44] In *Catnic* the plaintiff successfully claimed damages against Hill & Smith Ltd for infringement of his patent by manufacturing and selling patented lintels and then sought an account of profits from Evans to whom the lintels had been sold. Falconer J granted the order.

Furthermore, there are some direct statements suggesting that both an account and damages may be granted. Some such as *Mawman v Tegg*[45] are pre-*Neilson v Betts*. However, most recently, in *AG v Guardian (No. 1)*[46] Lord Ackner suggested, albeit in the context of breach of confidence, that both an account of profits and exemplary damages could be awarded. If that is the case, there seems no reason why an account and compensatory damages might not be available.

---

[37] (1871) LR 5 HL 1 reversing *Hill v Evans*, 4 De G.F. & J. 288, 45 ER 1195.

[38] (1873) LR 6 HL 319.

[39] (1882) 20 Ch.D. 780 at 783.

[40] *Caxton Publishing Co. v Sutherland Publishing Co.* [1939] AC 179 at 198 per Lord Porter (copyright); *My Kinda Town v Soll* [1982] FSR 147 (passing off); *Electrolux v Electrix* (1953) 70 RPC 158 (trade marks); *Van Camp v Auslebrooks* and *Ansell Rubber Co. Pty v Allied Rubber Pty Ltd* [1967] VLR 37, 52 Gowans J (confidential information).

[41] [1941] AC 1.

[42] [1984] FSR 87.

[43] [1983] FSR 401. But note *Van Camp Chocolates Ltd v Auslebrooks Ltd* [1984[1 NZLR 354.

[44] Note 42 above, at 94.

[45] Note 32 above.

[46] [1987] 3 All ER 316 at 364.

The costs of taking an account

Although costs of an action are usually decided at trial and are granted to the successful party, it is normal practice for the court to reserve costs of an inquiry, whether as to damages or accounts, until that process is complete—so as to ensure they are not unreasonably exaggerated.[47] Where no damage or profit is proved by the plaintiff the court will order him to pay costs.[48] Where a defendant offers a sum in settlement, but the plaintiff insists on an inquiry, and that inquiry produces less than the sum offered, the plaintiff will be ordered to pay the costs of the inquiry from the date of the offer.[49] In such circumstances, the plaintiff insists on the account at his own risk, unless he was not given sufficient particulars by the defendant when he made the offer, or the particulars the defendant gave were misleading.[50]

The discretionary nature of the remedy

Although the election between an account and damages is usually at the option of the plaintiff,[51] the remedy of an account, being equitable, is discretionary and the court might therefore withhold the option. This has been done even where the infringement was fraudulent[52] and in many cases it is unclear why the court thought an account unjust.[53]

The position of licensees

Section 101(1) CDPA 1988 grants an exclusive licensee the same rights and remedies in respect of matters occurring after the grant of the licence as if the licensee had been by assignment. These rights and remedies are concurrent with those of the copyright owner. Section 102 deals with the exercise of these rights. In particular section 102(4)(b) declares that 'no account of profits shall be directed if an award of damages has been made, or an account of profits has been directed, in favour of the other of them in respect of infringement', and section 102(4)(c) directs the court to apportion the profits between them as the court considers just.

The Measure of the Account

Two difficult questions arise in relation to calculating the exact sum for which the defendant infringer is to account. The first is to discover what profits the infringer has actually made by infringing; the second is to assess how much of the profit is attributable to the infringement. In *Colbeam Palmer*[54] Windeyer J noted that:

> In modern economic theory the profit of an enterprise is a debatable concept. Consequently the word profit has today varying senses in the vocabulary of economists. For

---

[47] *Slack v Midland Railway* (1880) 16 Ch.D. 81 per Fry J—costs as to inquiry into damages in a nuisance case; *Tate v Thomas* (1921) 1 Ch. 503 per Eve J at 513.
[48] *Tonge v Ward* (1869) 21 LT 480 per Lord Romilly.
[49] *Draper v Trist and Tristbestos Brake Linings Ltd* (1939) 56 RPC 225 per Luxmoore J—a passing off case.
[50] *Fettes v Williams (Birmingham) Ltd* (1908) 25 RPC 511 per Warrington J—a design case.
[51] *Edelsten v Edelsten* (1863) 1 De G.J. & S. 185, 46 ER 72; *Weingarten Bros v Charles Bayer & Co.* (1905) 22 RPC 341—HL.
[52] *Van Zeller v Mason & Cattley* (1908) 25 RPC 37.
[53] *Unic SA v Lyndeau Products* (1964) RPC 37 at 45 to 46 Ungoed Thomas J; *Hodgson v Kynoch* (1898) 15 RPC 465 at 476 per Romer J.
[54] Note 30 above.

law some definition or working rule must be accepted for the case in hand; for as Farwell J said in *Bond v Barrow Haematite Steel Co.*,[55] there is no single definition of the word 'profits' which will fit all cases. Perhaps the only single and simple proposition is Lord Lindley's statement that 'when a person gets out of a concern more than he puts into it the difference is the profit': *In Re Armitage; Armitage v Garnett.*[56] But that is too general to be helpful here.

The case-law gives no clear answer to what is meant by profit in this context. Discussion can be based around four questions: 'gross' and 'net' profits; 'savings' and 'profits'; 'actual' and 'potential' profits; and 'realised' and 'unrealised' profits.

Gross and net profits

The distinction between gross profits and net profits is that the former covers all income with respect to a particular item irrespective of costs, whereas with the latter, costs are taken into account. No cases support an award of gross profits by themselves. There is, however, a divergence between cases which advocate an award of gross profits less costs properly and necessarily incurred;[57] and others awarding simple net profits without investigation of the legitimacy of the costs incurred by the wrong-doer.[58]

Savings and profits

Are savings profits for the purpose of the giving of an account? In most cases it would not matter: clearly the infringer has used the plaintiff's copyright as part of a book which he sells, or has used the plaintiff's trade mark when selling his goods. In such circumstances we are not concerned with what the plaintiff saved by not paying the author, or paying for a licence—that sum is, in many cases, the quantum of damages. Nevertheless, it is possible to envisage scenarios where the only result of infringement is a saving. In *Crosley v Derby Gas-Light Co.*[59] the plaintiff owned a patent for a gas-meter. The defendants, suppliers of gas, distributed the meters free to customers, charging those who used the meters 7s 6d per 1,000 cubic feet, and those who did not 10s for the same amount. By using the meters, 25 per cent of gas was saved. The master awarded the plaintiff £6,000, a sum equivalent to 2s 6d for every 1,000 cubic feet of gas supplied.

The question whether savings are benefit has arisen in other areas of the law of restitution, most notably in the case of *Phillips v Homfray*[60] and where a fiduciary makes a saving by use of trust property or his position. It is fair to conclude, as one leading commentator does,[61] that 'neither Chancery nor the common law courts have as yet evolved a satisfactory basis in principle for attacking savings made'.

---

[55] [1902] 1 Ch. 353 at 366.
[56] [1893] 3 Ch. 337 at 346.
[57] *Caxton v Sutherland.* Note 40 above, at 205 to 206. *AG v Guardian* (No. 2), Note 33 above, may also support such a view.
[58] *Potton v Yorkclose* [1990] FSR 11 at 18.
[59] Note 2 above.
[60] (1883) 24 Ch.D. 439.
[61] Finn, *Fiduciary Obligations*, Law Book Co., 1977, paragraph 282, at 127.

Potential profits

On occasions (such as where a trustee fails to invest trust funds or a mortgagee in possession of the mortgaged property fails to collect a rent on the property) equity requires that an individual account 'on a footing of wilful default'. This means that he must account not only for profits he has made, but also for profits which he would 'but for his wilful default' have received. It does not apply to infringers of intellectual property rights.[62] Thus, if a manufacturer could have sold the infringing goods for a higher price, he only has to account for the profits he has actually made.

Realised and unrealised profits

It is also unclear whether it is only possible to be awarded an account of profits actually realised by an infringer. In most cases the question will not arise—an injunction will have been granted, future sales therefore prohibited and an order of delivery up or destruction of infringing items granted; the account will be taken only with respect to profits made before the injunction, and these profits will be on items that have been sold. However, a situation in which it might be necessary to decide the point is where it is not possible to order delivery up of infringing items—for example, where the infringing item is real property. In the recent case of *Potton v Yorkclose*,[63] the defendants built houses reproducing the plaintiff's architectural designs. As it happened, all the houses had been sold and the profits realised. However, Millet J argued that such a realisation was unnecessary—the account was for profits which had been made, and the profits were made when the houses were built. At that time they were assets of the infringer which were capable of being valued.

The author has commented on the pros and cons of this decision elsewhere.[64] It is attractive because the infringement is the reproduction not the sale; it would be unfortunate if the plaintiff had to wait until all the sales were complete before going to court, and most of all because the defendant benefits whether he sells the property or uses it for occupation. On the other hand, there are problems with granting an account of unrealised profits: in particular, no profit might in fact ever be made by the infringer.

The Problem of Causation

A copyright owner is only entitled to an account of the profits he has made by infringing. It is always important therefore to bear in mind what the infringement consists of; in copyright, a person infringes if he copies, performs, issues copies to the public, broadcasts or adapts the work.[65] It is then necessary to establish the appropriate relationship between the profits and the wrong being considered. It is sometimes said that a defendant must account for the profits made 'by', or 'by reason of', 'by means of',[66] 'in respect of',[67] 'from' or 'derived ... from'[68] the infringement, and sometimes that he must account for the profits 'attributable to'[69] the infringement. This use of the language of causation disguises intractable questions

---

[62] *Potton v Yorkclose*, Note 58 above, at 14.
[63] Note 58 above.
[64] (1990) 9 Copyright World 16; [1990] 12 EIPR 106.
[65] CDPA 1988 section 16. (But note that different methods of infringement apply to different categories of work.)
[66] *Elwood v Christy* (1865) 18 CB (NS) 494, 144 ER 537.
[67] Copyright Act 1956 section 17.
[68] Patents Act 1977 section 61(1)(d).
[69] For example, *United Horse Shoe & Nail Co.* (1888) 13 App. Cas. 401 at 412; *My Kinda Town v Soll*, Note 40 above; *Colbeam Palmer*, Note 30 above, at 42.

of principle and application. In *Crosley v Derby Gas-Light Co.*[70] Lord Cottenham LC noted that: 'To ascertain the profits created by the application of particular means and, for that purpose, to refer a just proportion of the profits made to some only of the agents employed, may involve questions of great nicety.'

There appear to be three elements to the causation problem. The first is the question of what is meant by causation at all. The second is the question of apportioning profits which are attributable to a number of causes. For example, what are the profits attributable to each poem in an anthology of poems, or the 'A' and 'B' sides of a hit single, or the patented starter motor in an otherwise unexceptional car, or to the trade mark attached to a bottle of perfume? The third is the question of what degree of proximity between infringement and profit is necessary for a plaintiff to be able to claim them: for example, can the owner of copyright in a song which is used, without consent, in a television commercial for a coach company, claim the profits made by the company from those travellers who were attracted to it by the advert?

These causation questions have never been subjected to thorough analysis. Hart and Honoré's *Causation and the Law*[71] recognises that in some circumstances a question of causation of benefit can arise,[72] but nowhere attends to the issue of causation of benefits in restitution. Klippert writes: 'Little specific attention has been focused on causation problems in restitution. As an aspect of remoteness, the analysis of causation has been limited traditionally to a discussion of damage rules in contract and tort.'[73]

Causation as a legal concept

It is clear that the concept is not merely a question of fact. In their seminal article, Fuller and Purdue commented on concepts such as causation that 'the process of "measuring" and "determining" them is really a part of the process of creating them'.[74] Legal questions of causation, in relation to causation of profits as much as of loss, are not simply questions of fact, but themselves reflect policy.

There appear to be three possible approaches to causation: the first is to apply a general test of 'fairness' ignoring difficult questions of causation in fact; the second is to take a rigorous view and require proof that the infringer would not have made the profits if he had not infringed—the 'comparison test';[75] the third is to assess what profits an infringer has made in fact by infringing but not to allow argument that the profit would have been made anyway. The choice between them ought in principle to reflect the underlying justification of the grant of an account.

(1) Causation and fairness
Palmer argues that 'perhaps the most useful generalisation is simply that restitution of benefits obtained through tort usually will be limited to benefits that can fairly be regarded as the product of the legally protected interest of the plaintiff which was invaded',[76] and later that 'the court must resort to general principles of fairness'.[77] Certainly it is possible to

---

[70] Note 2 above.
[71] Clarendon Press, 1985, (2nd ed.).
[72] *Ibid.* at 86.
[73] 'Restitutionary Claims for the Appropriation of Property', (1981) 26 McGill LJ 506 at 543.
[74] 'The Reliance Interest in Contract Damages', (1936) 46 YLJ 52.
[75] Klippert, *Unjust Enrichment*, Butterworths, 1983, ch. 7, at 228 ff.
[76] Note 20 above, Volume 1, at 135.
[77] *Ibid.* at 161.

interpret some of the case-law along these lines—in *AG v Guardian (No. 2)*,[78] for example, Lord Brightman thought that the Crown could claim an account of a 'due proportion' of the entirety of the total net profits made by the *Sunday Times*.[79] To talk about fairness in this way, however, seems extremely vague, but is not altogether dissimilar to the approach that has frequently been taken in relation to causation of damage where judges have viewed the question as one of 'common sense'. Nevertheless, such an approach needs to be justified, for it is open to criticism, for example by someone who sees the remedy as based on a principle of unjust enrichment. Klippert, for example, argues that: 'To destroy the causation requirement and award the plaintiff an amount based on profits would be a disguised award of punitive or exemplary damages, which would be outside the cope of unjust enrichment liability.'[80]

(2) 'But for' causation—the 'comparison test'

The second approach to causation is to award only those profits which would not have been gained without infringement—thus it is open for the infringer to argue that he would have made the profit by using an alternative (non-infringing) method. An example of such an approach is *Siddell v Vickers*.[81] In that case the defendants, who had previously forged iron using manual labour, adopted an appliance infringing the plaintiff's patent. The Court of Appeal held that the profit was not the difference between the profit made when using manual labour and when using the infringing machine, but the difference between the profit made when using the infringing machine and what the defendant would have made had he used a different mechanical device available.

The clear difficulty with such an analysis is that it requires consideration of what the defendant's goal was, what alternatives were available, and what alternative the defendant would probably have used. This is obviously a complex inquiry and in many cases it will be impossible to decide satisfactorily on an alternative. The difficulties are reduced when it is accepted that it is for the defendant[82] to show what alternative he would have used.[83] In *Peter Pan v Corsets Silhouette*[84] the Court in effect came to the conclusion that the defendant could not have manufactured bras at all without the use of the confidential information. In *Potton v Yorkclose*, Millet J took the view that the 'comparison test' was only applicable where the infringement was in the 'process' by which the product was made rather than the product itself.[85]

(3) Causation in fact—the 'net profits' test

The third approach is to deny the defendant the right to show that the profit would have been made anyway, and simply to argue that he must account for net profit in fact made.

---

[78] Note 33 above.
[79] For example, *My Kinda Town v Soll*, Note 40 above, where Slade J commented that 'the general intention of the Court in making the order which it has made has been to achieve a *fair* apportionment. What will be required on the inquiry ... will not be mathematical exactness but only a reasonable approximation' (at 159). See also *Watson, Laidlaw & Co. Ltd v Potts, Cassels & Williamson* (1914) 31 RPC 104 per Lord Shaw at 118 commented that assessment is 'to a large extent by the exercise of a sound imagination and the practice of the broad axe'.
[80] Note 73 above.
[81] Note 2 above.
[82] See *Mishawaka Rubber & Woollen Manuf. Co. v SS Kresge Co.* (1942) 316 US 203 and Johnson, 'Remedies in Trade Secret Litigation', (1978) 72 NwULR 1004 at 1016.
[83] Compare Friedman's suggestion of a principle of 'mitigation of gain' relating to profits that the defendant would have made had he not committed the acts for which he is being sued: 'Restitution of Benefits Obtained through the Appropriation of Property or the Commission of a Wrong', (1980) 80 CLR 504 at 553 n. 281.
[84] [1963] RPC 45.
[85] Such a view is criticised by the author in 'Account of Profits for Infringement of Copyright—*Potton v Yorkclose*', [1990] 12 EIPR 106.

For example, on the facts of *Spycatcher*, it seems wrong that it would be open to the *Sunday Times* to argue that they would have sold as many papers (or almost as many) whether the *Spycatcher* extracts were published or not. The obvious retort to any such argument is that they did use Wright's memoirs, and it is too late to argue about what they might have used. Both *Peter Pan* and *Potton v Yorkclose* can be used to support such an approach. In the latter case, Millet J held that it was not open to the defendants to claim that they would have used alternative designs—they were accountable for the net profit they had in fact made from using the plaintiff's designs.

No single approach has been conclusively approved either in the UK, Canada or the united States. It may be that there is in fact little distinction between the fairness approach and the net profits approach, so that we can in fact reduce the choices to two.

Equally, it is possible to argue that the comparison approach and the net profits approach are in fact one and the same—and that cases of 'net profits' are simply cases where the defendant failed to prove that he would have made any of the profit without infringing. The theoretical difference becomes more significant in relation to questions of joint cause. These are usually minimised by application of the 'but for' test. Thus, for example, where a play is used to produce a successful film the questions may be:

(a) What profits did the infringer make? What profits would D have made by using a different play? The difference is the profit due to the infringement.
(b) What profits did D make? To what extent were they attributable to different causes, for example actors, direction, etc.? The award is the appropriate percentage.

Joint causes

Questions of causation of profit take on a greater degree of complexity when the profit is the result of a number of contributory causes: it is necessary to decide what portion of the total profit is attributable to the infringement. If a general approach of fairness has been taken, then this should not cause undue difficulties. However, if either of the other two approaches is deemed appropriate the question of joint cause remains.

The courts have made a distinction between a 'contributory cause of profit' and an 'expense'. For example, in *Potton v Yorkclose* the cost to purchase the land on which the houses were built was an expense, as were the building materials themselves. However, the design of the kitchen was seen as a 'contributory cause' for which apportionment was necessary. Equally, in *Spycatcher*, presumably, the typesetting and paper would be viewed as expenses, the other stories in the paper as 'contributory causes'. In the leading United States case, *Sheldon v Metro Goldwyn Pictures Corp.*,[86] the defendants infringed copyright in the plaintiff's play 'Dishonoured Lady' by producing a motion picture 'Letty Lytton'. The film did not bear the title of the play; it used popular actors, expert producers and directors, and was set against expensive sets. The Court held that it was necessary to apportion the profit, and they found that the testimony of experts was generally helpful. The Second Circuit Court of Appeals and the Supreme Court awarded 20 per cent of the defendant's profit.s

The crucial question is how we are to distinguish between expenses and contributing causes. If a given element has an expense, it may well be viewed as an expense only; if an element does not, then it may be viewed as a contributory cause. Thus, in *Peter Pan* the choice of material for the bras would simply be a matter for expense; in *Sheldon* the status of

---

[86] (1940) 309 US 390.

the actors, presuming they were paid, would not be seen as a contributory cause. In *Potton* the design of the kitchen would be a contributory cause.

On the other hand, it might be that a contributory cause must be something of the same generic nature as the infringed work—that is, only matters of themselves intellectual property are seen as contributing causes. Klippert goes further and sees two distinct lines of cases— some where net profits only are given and others where a percentage of the profits is allowed. 'One possible explanation for drawing the line of demarcation between the two rules is on the predominance of intangibles contributed by the defendant to the ultimate product.'[87] A defendant's own efforts are not generally considered to be contributory causes and are dealt with by the grant of a 'just allowance'.

Once we have distinguished a contributory cause it is necessary to apportion profits—in other words, the profits decide which profits are attributable to it. In *Potton v Yorkclose*, Millet J apportioned profits on the basis of the relative 'costs' of the infringing and non-infringing portions. Other approaches have been taken in the United States—in particular, if the items could be sold separately, the profits can be apportioned in proportion with those selling prices. Alternatively, expert testimony could be taken as to the relative importance of the contributions.[88]

Remoteness of gain

There does not appear, as yet, to be any recognition of a principle of remoteness of gain. That one may be needed is clear from hypothetical examples. If a local pop band makes it big by infringing copyright in a well-known writer's song, the copyright owner may sue for the majority of the profits from that song. Can he not also claim that, as he is responsible for their fame, the song is a cause of their profits from poster sales, guest appearances, etc., and ultimately from all their follow-up hits? Clearly, as we become more distant from the infringement, the mathematics will become more complicated and the plaintiff might well think claiming an account not worthwhile. Ought there not, however, to be a principle of remoteness of gain?[89]

Birks has suggested some principles which a court might adopt in such cases.[90] He classifies gains into 'subtractive receipts' and 'non-subtractive receipts'. He uses the example of A's wrongful use of B's car. If A uses it for his own purposes, that is a subtractive receipt. However, if A hires out the car for £400, that is a non-subtractive receipt. If A then invests that £400 in shares which increase in value and produce a dividend, those increases arc 'second or subsequent non-subtractive receipts'. Second or subsequent indicates receipts on receipts. Birks then goes on to apply his structure.

> It would be unsafe to affirm categorically that the second and subsequent non-subtractive receipts are always too remote, but in general it must be true that they are. For the question which emerges from the cases is whether it is even possible for plaintiffs invariably to get the first non-subtractive receipt or receipts. The basic rule is that they can, but there is an exception of doubtful size and strength.[91]

---

[87] Note 75 above, ch. 7, at 221 to 222.
[88] Klooster, *Patent Accountings: A Phase of Cost Accounting*, Prentice Hall Inc., 1930, ch. lxi.
[89] See especially Birks, 'Restitution and Wrongs', (1982) CLP 53 at 68 to 69.
[90] Note 5 above, at 351 to 355.
[91] *Ibid.* at 353. Note that were a proprietary remedy available gains on gains would be allowed, but only with respect to enrichment surviving. Such a proprietary remedy might be available under CDPA 1988 section 96 which makes available 'all such relief . . . as is available in respect of the infringement of any other property right.' However Goode, 'Ownership and Obligation in Commercial Transactions', (1987) 103 LQR 433, is in favour

Birks's argument therefore suggests that in the example of the pop group the copyright owner could claim only the profits made on the sale of the record; it could not claim profits made by investing those profits. It does not, however, help us to answer the question about profits made on the sale of posters and subsequent records.We can only fit these into the idea of gains on gains by treating them as second receipts obtained from the first receipt, namely the 'fame' of the group.[92]

Just Allowances

A defendant is entitled to deduct the costs of production from the computation of profits, but in general he cannot deduct costs for his own time and effort. However, the case-law reveals that a defendant has, on occasions, been permitted to claim a 'just allowance'. In one copyright case where an account was ordered against a record producer, Goff J held that a liberal allowance should be made for their skill and labour;[93] in a second case concerning a deliberate exploitation of the idea for a book in breach of confidence, Templeman LJ said he did not consider that the court should allow any deduction.[94] More recently, Millet J has suggested that such a grant should be made but that it should not itself amount to a portion of the profit.[95]

The Function of an Account

The difficulties associated with the remedy of account in the context of copyright law also affect the usefulness of the remedy for infringement of other intellectual property rights. There are a number of factors that explain the complexity and uncertainty. A central cause is simply the complexity of modern business relations. Production, marketing and distribution of commodities involves a collective effort in which the act of creation (on which the intellectual property right in question is based) is only one factor. For example, the profit on a book is by no means simply related to the brilliance of the author. As one commentary on the publishing industry has said: "The ultimate sales of the book will be considerably influenced by decisions on, for example, type of jacket, print run, advertising, pre-publication publicity and marketing strategy.'[96] These developments have made the taking of an account a factually complex matter.

A second cause of the difficulties lies in the peculiar historical relationship between the Courts of Law and Courts of Equity—the account arose, as we have noted, in equity as a compensatory measure. The Courts of Law and Equity have long been fused, but the remedy of account has been retained. It clearly can no longer be seen as compensatory (except in the few cases where the plaintiff would have exploited his intellectual property right in the

---

of extending personal liability of a wrong-doing fiduciary to gains on gains without providing for priority by granting a proprietary remedy.

[92] A patent infringer was not required to account for 'goodwill' acquired by infringement in *Byerly v Sun Co.* (1915) 226 Fed. 759. See Klooster, Note 88 above, ch. xxxvii.

[93] *Redwood Music Ltd v Chappell & Co. Ltd* [1982] RPC 109 at 132, applying *Phipps v Boardman* [1964] 1 WLR 993 at 1018 per Wilberforce J as affirmed by the House of Lords in [1967] 2 AC 46.

[94] *Queen Productions v Music Sales* (CA, 1981, unreported but available on *Lexis*).

[95] As it did in the case of *O'Sullivan v Management Agency* [1985] 1 QB 428. But cp. *Guiness v Saunders* [1990] 1 All ER 652 per Lord Templeman at 662 'in exceptional circumstances a court of equity may award remuneration to a trustee' and Lord Goff at 667 to 668 suggesting that no award should be given if it would encourage the forbidden activity.

[96] Coser, Kadushin and Powell, *Books: The Culture and Commerce of Publishing*, University of Chicago Press, 1985, at 6.

same manner and in the same market as the defendant has done). It therefore remains a rule in search of a rationale. The provision of such a justification would be the starting-point for reform and rationalisation of the remedy by the courts.

Damages, implied contract and fiduciaries

A number of theoretical justifications for the remedy can be found in the case-law. Three of these can be dismissed immediately as unsatisfactory. First, it is sometimes suggested that the remedy is compensatory.[97] This is clearly unsatisfactory since damages are available to compensate a plaintiff. A more sophisticated version argues that an account consists of damages 'for the lost opportunity to bargain'.[98] However, it is difficult to agree that 'the amount of the loss can realistically be measured at an amount equal to the defendant's net gain'. Second, it has been argued that the remedy of an account is based upon an implied contract[99] and is analogous to 'waiver of tort'[100] (though the implied contract basis of the waiver of tort doctrine was rejected the very next year).[101] Third, it is said that the infringer, by his wrong-doing, constitutes himself a 'fiduciary', and therefore must account to his principal for profits he has made without his principal's consent.[102] Both of these theories are based on fictions and provide no satisfactory explanation or justification. They beg the questions 'when and why is there an implied contract?' and 'when and why is a person a "fiduciary"?' More convincing justifications are provided by the concepts of 'unjust enrichment', 'property' and 'deterrence'.

Unjust enrichment

In the trade mark case *My Kinda Town v Soll*,[103] Slade J remarked:

> The purpose of ordering an account of profits . . . is to prevent an unjust enrichment of the defendant by compelling him to surrender those profits, or those parts of the profits, actually made by him which were made improperly and nothing beyond this.

The 'principle' of unjust enrichment implies that where a defendant has been unjustly enriched at the expense of the plaintiff, he must give up that benefit to the plaintiff. The

---

[97] *Watson Laidlaw & Co. v Potts, Cassels & Williamson*, Note 79 above, per Lord Kinnear; *Queen Productions v Music Sales*, Note 94 above, 'the court can extract from them sufficient of their ill-gotten gains to compensate the plaintiffs' per Templeman LJ; *Mowry v Whitney*, (1871) 14 Wall 620, 'The profits which are recoverable . . . are in fact compensation . . . They are the measure of his damages. Though called profits, they are really damages' per Strong J; *Sheldon v Metro Goldwyn Corp*, Note 86 above, at 399 per Hughes CJ; and Ashburner, *Principles of Equity*, Butterworths, 1933 (2nd ed.), at 40.

[98] Sharpe and Waddams, 'Damages for Lost Opportunity to Bargain', (1982) OJLS 290.

[99] *Neilson v Betts*, Note 37 above; *Saccharin Corp. Ltd v Chemicals and Drugs Co. Ltd* (1990) RPC 612 at 615 per Lord Alverstone MR; *Van Camp Chocolates v Auslebrooks*, Note 40 above.

[100] *Caxton Publishing Co. v Sutherland Publishing Co.*, Note 40 above, at 199 per Lord Porter.

[101] *United Australia Ltd v Barclays Bank Ltd*, Note 41 above, 'In the ordinary case the plaintiff has never the slightest intention of waiving, excusing or in any kind of way palliating the tort' per Lord Atkin at 28 to 29.

[102] *Hamilton-Brown Shoe v Wolf Bros* (1916) 240 US 251 at 259 per Pitney J; *Electrolux Ltd v Electrix Ltd*, Note 40 above, at 159 per Lloyd Jacob J: 'The principle upon which the court grants an account of profits . . . is this, that where one party owes a duty to another, the person to whom the duty is owed is entitled to recover from the other party every benefit which that other party has received by virtue of his fiduciary position if in fact he has obtained it without the knowledge or the consent of the party to whom he owed the duty.' The theory has, however, been criticised. In the United States Supreme Court, Hughes CJ noted that 'To call the infringer a trustee *maleficio* merely indicates "a mode of approach" and an imperfect analogy by which the wrong-doer will be made to hand over the proceeds of his wrong': *Sheldon v Metro Goldwyn Pictures Corp.*, Note 86 above, at 405.

[103] Note 40 above.

remedy of account requires the defendant to disgorge an 'enrichment' that he has gained by a wrong to the plaintiff and has therefore made 'unjustly' and 'at the expense'[104] of the intellectual property right owner.

Problems exist with such a justification. First, the concept of unjust enrichment has not been unanimously accepted by the English judiciary.[105] Second, advocates of the concept disagree as to whether there is a 'generalised right'[106] to restitution or whether it simply provides a 'rationale' for existing causes of action.[107] If we accept the latter view, it is necessary to explain why a restitutionary remedy should exist for infringement of intellectual property rights, but not for defamation or breach of contract.

Birks provides a threefold classification of cases where a plaintiff can claim 'restitution for wrongs'[108]—cases of deliberate exploitation of wrong-doing, anti-enrichment wrongs, and prophylaxis. It is clear that the availability of an account of profits for infringement of copyright is not dependent upon proof of deliberate infringement, so Birks's first class is of little help. If we utilise the other two cases, it is difficult to see why we are bothering to mediate our analysis through a concept of 'unjust enrichment' at all. They will therefore be considered under the 'property' and 'deterrence' headings.

Property

It is frequently argued that an account of profits is available where there is an infringement of property rights. In *Potten v Yorkclose*,[109] a case on infringement of copyright, Millet J asserted that: 'Unless the plaintiff was entitled to an account of profits there would be no remedy for the unjust enrichment of the defendant as a result of his wrongful use of the plaintiff's property.'

Similarly, in the Australian trade mark case *Colbeam Palmer Ltd v Stock Affiliates Pty Ltd*,[110] Windeyer J based the award squarely on the use of property, and in the American case of *Sammons v Colonial Press*[111] the Court stated that: 'the theory was that it was unconscionable for an infringer to retain a benefit which he had received by the appropriation and use of the plaintiff's property right'.

This theory begs two (related) questions. First, 'what is property?', second, 'why should wrongs to property be treated differently from other wrongs?' The first question is extremely problematic. It is clear that the concept of property is one which changes, and that new objects of property are from time to time added to the list. Pressure to admit new objects to property status is usually part of an attempt to gain better protection for the interest in question. Thus, Friedman argues that contractual rights are property rights, so that restitutionary remedies should be available for breach of contract.[112] Equally Shepherd argues that a fiduciary's liability to account for profits to his principal can be explained on the grounds that the fiduciary holds an 'encumbered power'—a 'property interest'—which

---

[104] Even if he has suffered no loss. See Goff and Jones, Note 7 above, at 25; Birks, Note 5 above.
[105] In *Orakpo v Manson Investments Ltd* [1978] AC 95, Lord Diplock declared that 'there is no general doctrine of unjust enrichment recognised in English law' (at 104).
[106] Goff and Jones, Note 7 above, ch. 1. See generally, S. Hedley ('Unjust Enrichment as the Basis of Restitution—an Overworked Concept', (1985) 5 Leg. Studs. 56) explaining that a principle of 'unjust enrichment' may be adopted in different ways—as a definition of the subject-matter of restitution, as a classification of a part of restitution, as a way to rationalise the law of restitution and as providing a generalised right of restitution.
[107] Birks takes this view (Note 5 above, at 27).
[108] *Ibid.* at 326 ff.
[109] Note 58 above.
[110] Note 30 above.
[111] (1942) 126 F.2d 341, 345.
[112] Note 83 above.

belongs to the principal. These arguments often come dangerously close to circularity.[113]

The second question is, perhaps, slightly more straightforward. According to economic theorists, a property rule protects an entitlement by requiring a person who wishes to remove it from its holder to do so by a voluntary transaction in which the value of the entitlement is agreed upon by the seller.[114] Like an injunction, an account of profits prohibits 'economically efficient conversion' and thus forces market negotiation.

The property justification is easy to apply to patents, copyright and trade marks which are generally accepted to constitute 'property'. In fact, it is implicit in section 96 of the CDPA 1988 that an account is available for infringement of copyright because copyright is a property right. However, difficulties arise with the newer forms of intellectual property such as breach of confidence, misappropriation of personality and unfair competition. It may be that a more flexible concept could be more satisfactorily utilised.

Anti-enrichment wrongs

Such an alternative is suggested by Birks, who argues that one category of wrongs where restitution is available are cases of 'anti-enrichment wrongs'.[115] He contrasts 'anti-enrichment' wrongs, such as conversion of goods with 'anti-harm' wrongs such as defamation. The distinction depends on the 'main purpose' behind the wrong, and Birks admits that there will be difficult cases. He suggests that where the main purpose is unclear because the duty serves mixed policies, as with cases of invasion of privacy, the characterisation of the wrong should depend on the facts of the cases. The facts will, it seems, reveal which one of the policies (underlying the rule) is being applied.

It might be possible to characterise infringement of intellectual property rights as all anti-enrichment wrongs. Such as argument might appeal to the relationship between intellectual property and unfair competition. The idea of unfair competition is a broad one, but one of its central principles is that it is wrong for one person to appropriate the fruits of another's skill, time or labour, and that the law will therefore not permit a person to reap where he has not sown. Intellectual property rights, it can be argued, are specific manifestations of the general principle of unfair competition—each right has a requirement that a certain amount of labour, skill or time has been expended: thus, copyright only exists in 'original literary, artistic, dramatic or musical works' and an invention is only patentable if it is 'new and involves some inventive step'.[116] The famous case of *International News Service v Associated Press*[117] imported into the law of unfair competition the idea of unjust enrichment.[118] This wrong is normally restrained by injunction, but in those cases where it is too late it is easy to see why a legal system would be drawn into ordering the defendant to give up whatever he has reaped.

---

[113] See Windeyer J in *Colbeam Palmer v Stock Affiliates*, Note 30 above.

[114] Calabresi and Melamed, 'Property Rules, Liability Rules and Inalienability: One view of the Cathedral', (1972) 85 HLR 1089. This argument was used by Posner J in a copyright accounting case: *Taylor v Meirick* (1983) 712 F.2d 1112 at 1120.

[115] Note 5 above, at 328 to 332.

[116] See Ricketson, ' "Reaping Without Sowing": Unfair Competition and Intellectual Property Rights in Anglo-Australian Law', (1984) UNSWLJ Special Issue 1.

[117] (1918) 248 US 215.

[118] Callman, 'He Who Reaps Where He Has Not Sown: Unjust Enrichment in the Law of Unfair Competition', (1942) 55 HLR 595, 597.

Deterrence

Birks argues that the basis of one category of 'restitution for wrongs' is 'prophylaxis'—the restitutionary remedy operates to deter wrong doing.[119] The deterrent effect of restitution is a limited one: by removing the possibility of profit, restitution removes any incentive to commit a wrong. The crucial question is when and why we want to deter some wrongs and not others. It may be that the deterrence principle is co-extensive with the property argument: we wish to deter wrongs where we wish to force market negotiations. But a principle of deterrence can clearly go further. For example, we may wish to deter wrong-doing in cases where a party is particularly vulnerable, as in the case of 'fiduciaries'; or where wrong-doing is difficult to detect or prove.

In the context of intellectual property we may have a number of reasons for applying such a principle of deterrence—the intellectual property right owner is often 'vulnerable' and infringements are difficult to detect. Unlike an owner of land or chattels, it will not be immediately apparent that infringement is taking place.[120] Furthermore, an individual intellectual property right owner is particularly vulnerable to mass production of infringing items by big business. It has been argued that 'protection for small firms ... from more muscular organisations during the vital stage of market innovation' is a particularly important function of the patent system.[121]

However, there are a number of problems with the deterrence argument. First, restitution is a poor form of deterrence—a better deterrent might be provided by additional or exemplary damages. Second, it is often said that 'penal measures' are not an appropriate function of the civil law.[122] Third, a simple idea of deterrence assumes a rational decision concerning whether or not to commit a wrong: but an account of profits for infringement is innocent (and possibly unconscious).[123] Fourth, both English and US cases deny that an account is aimed at punishment of an infringer.[124]

These problems are by no means insurmountable. The deterrent effect of exemplary damages differs from that of an account of profits, since the former is more dependent on the whims of the court. As we have seen, an account is a discretionary remedy, but that discretion will rarely be exercised against a plaintiff. The provision of an account is a different sort of deterrent—it provides a smaller penalty than exemplary damages, but that penalty is more likely to be used than exemplary damages. Second, the argument that penal measures are inappropriate in civil cases ignores the difficulties attendant on criminal sanctions in the case of intellectual property. Third, a more sophisticated version of deterrence theory suggests that a deterrent remedy not only deters deliberate infringement but also causes infringers to ascertain whether they are infringing or not.

---

[119] Note 5 above, at 332.

[120] See Accord, 'Trademark Infringement: Accounting of Defendant's Profits in Absence of Direct Competition with Plaintiff', (1966) CLR 983; Hubbard, 'Monetary Recovery under the Copyright, Patent and Trademarks Acts', (1967) 45 Tex. LR 972 to 973.

[121] O'Brien, 'Patents: An Economist's View', ch. 4 in J. Phillips (ed.), *Patents in Perspective*, ESC Publishing, 1984, at 34.

[122] Burrows, *Remedies for Torts and Breach of Contract*, Butterworths, 1987, at 248 to 249; Hedley, 'The Myth of Waiver of Tort', (1984) 100 LQR 653 at 679.

[123] A more sophisticated version might argue that the policy of deterrence is intended not only to deter deliberate infringement but also to make possible infringers check they are not infringing.

[124] 'The purpose of ordering an account of profits in favour of a successful plaintiff in a passing off case is not to inflict punishment on the defendant': per Slade J, *My Kinda Town v Soll*, Note 40 above. See also *Livingstone v Woodworth* (1853) 56 US (15 How) 546 (patent case).

Conclusion

It is clear that a variety of 'purposes' have at various times been attributed to the grant of an account for infringement of intellectual property rights. Sometimes, it has been recognised that the remedy serves a number of purposes. For example, in *AG v Guardian (No. 2)*,[125] Lord Keith attributed the granting of an account of profits to unjust enrichment, deterrence and compensation:

> In cases where the information is of a commercial character an account of profits may provide some compensation to the claimant for loss which he has suffered through the disclosure, but damages are the main remedy for such loss. The remedy is, in my opinion, more satisfactorily to be attributed to the principle that no one should be permitted to gain from his own wrong-doing. Its availability may also, in general, serve a useful purpose in lessening the temptation for recipients of confidential information to misuse it for financial gain.

Attributing several functions to a 'rule', however, leads to difficulties when rationalisation of the rule is proposed. For example, the 'compensation' principle clearly supports the need for an election between the two types of compensation, an account and damages; an 'unjust enrichment' basis allows a plaintiff to claim both an account and damages as long as any overlap is taken into account; a 'deterrence' theory could allow for a situation where a plaintiff claims an account and damages and any overlap is ignored.

The earlier discussion suggests that only two of the possible theories—'property' and 'deterrence'—could provide (by themselves) a satisfactory rationale for the availability of an account. Reform based on either rationale is therefore possible. Neither supports the view that an injunction is a prerequisite to an account, nor that an election is required between an account and damages. Both are compatible with a view that an infringer should not be able to claim a just allowance. The deterrence theory has one major advantage over property theory: the rules of 'causation' could be made much cruder and hence much simpler since there is no difficulty about awarding a plaintiff too much. For this reason (and the sheer difficulty of defining what is 'property' in any sensible way), it is suggested that an account of profits be interpreted as a remedy based upon deterrence.

---

[125] Note 33 above.

Heads of Damage in Passing Off

[1996] 9 EIPR 487

HAZEL CARTY

University of Manchester

The aim of this article is to attempt a review and analysis of the heads of damage in passing off. Despite the enormous volume of passing-off cases reported, McGregor notes: 'little attention has been given to the assessment of damages'.[1]

The majority of passing-off cases involve interlocutory injunctions, with *American Cyanamid Co. v Ethicon Ltd*[2] applying. As the balance of convenience is likely to be the most important issue, no deep analysis of the relevance of the various heads of damage claimed by the plaintiff needs to be undertaken. It is tempting, therefore, for plaintiffs to seek to enlarge the list of heads of damage. Issues raised by plaintiffs, such as potential loss of control or restriction on expansion, may make the award of an injunction more likely, but as such they may not constitute legitimate heads of damage. These extensions focus on injury to commercial magnetism or commercial potential but do not necessarily involve likely damage to goodwill. If the head of damage alleged is not clearly an attack on goodwill, then the court may protect where confusion alone is present or where allegations of loss of distinctiveness/dilution are the real issue. Such concepts of 'damage' are not consistent with the rationale of passing off (see later). The most striking example of an extended concept of damage in the tort occurred in the case of *Taittinger SA v Allbev Ltd*.[3] Here, the prestige worth of the name 'champagne'—and the threat of 'dilution' to that prestige—appeared to be central to the harm alleged by the plaintiffs, and to the decision of the Court of Appeal. What appears to be happening, therefore, is that plaintiffs are, by routinely adding on new heads of damage, attempting to achieve an extension of the tort of passing off. Thus it is apparent that this review is long overdue.

The Ingredients of Passing Off

Passing off is a misrepresentation tort that protects the plaintiff's 'goodwill', his customer connection, the attractive force that brings in custom. The tort can be defined by the so-called classic trinity: misrepresentation, goodwill and damage, a definition that has been reaffirmed in recent years (see *Reckitt & Colman Products v Borden Inc*;[4] *Consorzio del Prosciutto*

---

[1] *McGregor on Damages*, 1988 (15th edn), paragraph 1705.

[2] [1975] RPC 513.

[3] [1993] FSR 641. The implications of this decision, unclear from the start, are even more uncertain owing to the decision of the Court of Appeal in *Harrods Ltd v The Harrodian School*, *The Times*, 3 April 1996. This case is discussed fully later in the article. The author is grateful to John Sissons of Herbert Smith for providing her with a transcript of this decision.

[4] [1990] RPC 341, HL.

di Parma v Marks and Spencer plc;[5] *Harrods Ltd v The Harrodian School Ltd.*[6]

All three ingredients of the tort relate to each other. The misrepresentation, to be relevant to the tort, must relate to the plaintiff's goodwill and harm it in some way. Mere misrepresentation/confusion alone is not sufficient. This was underlined by the Court of Appeal in *Anheuser-Busch Inc. v Budejovicky Budvar PN.*[7] Here, both parties claimed the right to use the name 'Budweiser' for their beer. Although the plaintiff's beer was unavailable to the English public as such—it was supplied to US bases in England—it was known to a substantial number of people in England by reputation alone. Confusion might have arisen, therefore, when the defendant's beer was marketed in the United Kingdom, but no cause of action in passing off arose.[8] No damage to the plaintiff's business arose when in effect he had no business in England. Again, proving financial loss (to the plaintiff) or gain (to the defendant) is not sufficient. The damage that must be shown (as actual or prospective) is damage to the integrity of the plaintiff's goodwill.

The classic trinity applies to all varieties of the tort. Starting with the original case of a misrepresentation made to a third party as to the source of goods—source misrepresentation—the tort has developed to include connection misrepresentation, misrepresentation of the quality of the plaintiff's goods, equivalence misrepresentation and, with the landmark decision of the House of Lords in *Erven Warnik BV v Townend (J) & Sons (Hull) Ltd.*[9] (the *Advocaat* case), product misrepresentation, not harming the plaintiff alone. Most recently it has extended to include inverse passing off, claiming the plaintiff's products or (more likely) the plaintiff's quality as one's own.[10] All these extensions continue to focus ont he classic trinity.

Damage is an essential ingredient of the tort. However, in the typical case of the defendant passing off his goods as the plaintiff's, there is an intrinsic likelihood of damage. As such, the court will easily be persuaded that damage has been proved. Where less typical cases of passing off are involved, the courts should require 'clear and cogent proof' of actual damage or proof that the real likelihood of damage was 'substantial'.[11]

Initially, the tort sought to protect against a defendant misrepresenting that his goods were the goods of the plaintiff. Diversion of trade is the obvious harm posed to the plaintiff. Where less typical cases of passing off are involved they do not present the same automatic consequential diversion of trade. Indeed in *Advocaat*, Lord Diplock accepted that passing off does not require the plaintiff and defendant to be competing traders in the same line of business. As important as an allegation of diversion of trade has become an allegation of injurious association or devaluation of the plaintiff's goodwill. Yet plaintiffs, as will be seen, have added to those two fundamental heads of damage. The validity of these additional heads of damage can only be assessed by relating them to the rationale of the tort.

---

[5] [1991] RPC 351, CA.

[6] Note 3 above.

[7] [1984] FSR 413, CA.

[8] It is important to note, however, that section 56 Trade Marks Act 1994 allows the owner of a well-known foreign trade mark to seek an injunction to prevent a confusing use of a similar mark in the United Kingdom, whether or not he has any goodwill in the United Kingdom.

[9] [1979] AC 731.

[10] *Bristol Conservatories Ltd v Conservatories Custom Built Ltd* [1989] RPC 455, CA. See Carty, 'Inverse Passing Off: a Suitable Addition to Passing Off?' [1993] 10 EIPR 370.

[11] See the analysis in *Stringfellow v McCain* [1984] RPC 501, CA.

The Rationale of Passing Off

Passing off has a more limited scope than an action for unfair competition. It seeks, according to Lord Diplock in *Advocaat*, to protect traders against harm to their property in the goodwill, while serving the public interest in penalising misrepresentations that harm consumer choice. In essence 'deserving' plaintiffs—who have established a customer connection and, therefore, a degree of success for their business—will be protected against misrepresentations affecting that customer connection in some way. At the same time, by strengthening the informational aspect of the trade mark or name (as an indicator of origin or quality) the tort promotes efficient market choices. Thus both private interests and the public interest are served. By demanding that the misrepresentation harm goodwill/customer connection, the tort protects the value of the information given to customers and potential customers.

The link between damage and goodwill is an important limitation on the tort, especially after the *Advocaat* extension to the tort. By these limits, the tort attempts to draw a line between effective and unlawful competition. If simply any damage—in the sense of damage to the plaintiff's competitive edge—could be sufficient, then the tort could develop into allegations of unfair competition. A particular effect of this limit on the tort is that the common law, at least until now, has not accepted that harm to the advertising function of the plaintiff's mark is 'damage' for the purposes of the tort. The tort of passing off protects not the name or mark as such but the effort in establishing the customer connection/goodwill.

> A passing off action is a remedy for the invasion of a right of property not in the mark, name or get up improperly used, but in the business or goodwill likely to be injured by the misrepresentation made by passing off one person's goods as the goods of another.[12]

Heads of Damage in Passing Off

Certain types of harm are commonly pleaded and they all contain varieties within them. An attempt will be made to analyse each head against the rationale of passing off, identified above.

Diversion of trade

The classic case of the defendant passing off his goods as the plaintiff's involves an obvious allegation of diversion of trade. Loss of sales is thus the basic head of damage for passing off. There is no further requirement in such a case to allege that the defendant's goods are inferior, for the defendant should not be allowed 'to cheat the plaintiffs of some of their legitimate trade'.[13]

Such loss may also be involved, of course, in less typical cases of passing off. In *Advocaat*, where the misrepresentation involved product misdescription, the damage was lost sales to the owners of goodwill in the genuine article.[14] Again, in *Bristol Conservatories Ltd v Conservatories Custom Build Ltd*,[15] a case of inverse passing off, with samples of the plaintiffs' work falsely claimed to be the defendant's, the quality misrepresentation was likely to lead to a diversion of sales and thereby harm goodwill.

---

[12] *Star Industrial v Yap Kwee Kor* [1976] FSR 256, PC *per* Lord Diplock.
[13] Lord Herschell, *Reddaway v Banham* [1896] AC 199 at 209.
[14] There was also a potential debasement of the genuine article if the name 'Advocaat' were permitted for use in egg drinks generally and not confined to those that are spirit based.
[15] Note 10 above.

As such the classic trinity is followed: the misrepresentation harms goodwill. The same is true with the next head of damage.

Devaluation of reputation

There is obviously a need to protect the plaintiff's reputation, as goodwill is based on this. This head of damage is useful when an interlocutory injunction is sought, as in such a case the quantification of damages is difficult. As a head of damage, it has two distinct areas.

(1) 'Inferior goods confusion': the plaintiff's inferior goods[16] are passed off as his superior product: this could be summarised as the *Spalding v Gamage* situation. Thus in *Spalding v Gamage*[17] the defendant sold the plaintiffs' substandard stock as their superior line. In order to raise this item of damage, the plaintiff must show distinct categories of his produce: there will be no confusion without separate categories being shown. In *Wilts United Dairies Ltd v Thomas Robinson Sons & Co.*[18] the defendants bought up old stock of the plaintiffs' condensed milk (which had no indication of expiry date) and sold it as their current stock. The Court of Appeal held that they were passing off old milk as fresh milk.

(2) 'Injurious association': the phrase was used by Megarry J in *Unitex Ltd v Union Texturing Co. Ltd.*[19] There the plaintiffs alleged that if there was perceived to be a connection between them and the defendants, their customers would believe that they had entered into competition with them. However, the court held that there was no risk of this on the facts.

There are variations on the theme of injurious association. The most obvious variety occurs when the defendant's misrepresentation is likely to lead to a depreciation of the plaintiff's reputation. If such an allegation is well-founded obviously the 'attractive force that brings in custom' is in jeopardy. Should the defendant who has misrepresented himself or his goods as in some way connected to the plaintiff have a bad or even indifferent reputation, then damage is likely. Thus in *Annabel's v Schock*,[20] a high-class London night-club, Annabel's, successfully restrained the defendant from carrying on the business of an escort agency under the name Annabel's Escort Agency. The public's indifferent estimation of escort agencies in general led to a legitimate concern that the plaintiffs might be 'tarred with the same brush', should the public confuse the two. It is the public's perception that is important: see *Nationwide Estate Agents v Nationwide Building Society*,[21] where the plaintiff showed the risk of injurious association from newspaper reports alleging mortgage fraud against someone alleged to be associated with the defendant. However, there should be some evidence of public perception being less than positive towards the defendant: in *Unitex Ltd v Union Texturing Co.* the Court of Appeal stressed the need for a 'real, tangible risk' of damage.[22]

Probably the most extreme version of 'injurious association' is the allegation that the defendant's misrepresentation may lead to legal liability for the plaintiff or more generally the risk of litigation. This was an item of damage successfully pleaded in *Illustrated Newspapers v Publicity Services*, where the defendant had added advertising material to the plaintiffs' illustrated newspaper.[23] Should objectionable matter have been included in these adver-

---

[16] Although *Spalding v Gamage* concentrates on inferior substitution by a defendant to the plaintiff's products, in fact the ability to complain of substitution goes wider than inferior alternatives. Lord Parker makes this clear in *Spalding v Gamage* itself: 'A cannot without infringing the rights of B, represent goods which are not B's goods of a particular class or quality to be B's goods of that particular class or quality.'

[17] (1915) 32 RPC 273, HL.

[18] [1958] RPC 94, CA.

[19] [1973] RPC 119 (the case went on to the Court of Appeal).

[20] [1972] FSR 261, CA.

[21] [1987] FSR 579.

[22] Note 19 above.

[23] (1938) 55 RPC 172.

tisements, the plaintiffs ran 'a reasonable risk of being exposed to litigation—not successful litigation, but litigation which may none the less be very annoying and possibly cause them considerable expense'.[24] In *Sony KK v Saray Electronics (London) Ltd*,[25] the defendants' misrepresentation of dealership was held to include the misrepresentation that the defendants were empowered to give guarantees on behalf of the plaintiff. An interlocutory injunction was granted.

Obviously the facts may reveal further variations on the theme of injurious association. Thus the plaintiff may allege that an apparent connection with the particular defendant may lead to a loss of goodwill with existing trade connections. This was raised in *Spalding v Gamage*: the fact that the defendant might appear to have been given a discount by the plaintiff might well have caused ill-will with legitimate outlets.

Confusion and loss of control

An allegation that confusion alone is sufficient to constitute damage in the tort of passing off appears to deny the validity of the classic trinity. In addition to the misrepresentation, harm to goodwill has to be shown to constitute the tort. Thus, to complain that the defendant's misrepresentation will lead to a false connection being made by the public between the plaintiff and defendant lacks the necessary further allegation that the effect of the confusion is to damage the plaintiff's goodwill. In *Unitex Ltd v Union Texturing Co. Ltd*[26] there was confusion but no real tangible risk of damage arising from such confusion.

However, there are *dicta* to the effect that mere confusion can be sufficient. Slade LJ, for example, in *Chelsea Man Menswear Ltd v Chelsea Girl Ltd*[27] notes the 'injury which is inherently likely to be suffered by any business' when on frequent occasions it is confused by customers or potential customers with the defendants' business or there is a mis-apprehension that they are connected. However, such cases can perhaps be explained as containing an inherent likelihood of damage. Where there is direct competition such con-fusion seems 'calculated to cause harm' through diversion of trade or injurious association. The courts would be happy to infer a real risk of damage. However, confusion *per se* is not damage, as the Court of Appeal decision in *Budweiser* makes clear. There must be a real tangible risk of harm to the goodwill: this requires specific proof, where there is no direct competition between the parties.

Some plaintiffs have sought to improve their chances of success under this head by further claiming that the false connection involves a 'loss of control' over their own reputation, even where there is no allegation that the defendant's reputation is bad or indifferent.

In *Home Box Office v Channel 5*[28] loss of control was argued by the plaintiffs and Peter Gibson J did not dismiss this proposition as 'unarguable'. Indeed in two earlier cases, *British Legion v British Legion (Street) Ltd*[29] and *Hulton Press Ltd v White Eagle Youth Holiday Camp Ltd*,[30] loss of control appears central to the decision in favour of the plaintiff. In the *British Legion* case there was nothing in the evidence to suggest that the defendant's club was carried on in anything other than a perfectly proper manner. However, it was held that damage was a real possibility 'if evil befalls the defendant and it finds itself . . . in trouble either under the

---

[24] *Ibid.*, at 182.
[25] [1983] FSR 302, CA.
[26] [1973] FSR 181.
[27] [1987] RPC 161, CA. And see Jenkins LJ in *Brestian v Try* [1958] RPC 161, CA.
[28] [1982] FSR 449.
[29] (1931) 48 RPC 555.
[30] (1951) 68 RPC 126.

licensing laws or in financial trouble or in some other way of discredit—even though Farwell J accepted that he was not suggesting that any such problems might occur in practice. In the *White Eagle* case, the publishers of the boy's comic the *Eagle* restrained the defendants from using the name 'White Eagle Youth Holiday Camp' for a children's holiday camp. As the plaintiff was associated with a club to provide holiday camps for children, there was evidence of confusion. However, there was no evidence of the defendants being perceived as disreputable. For Wynn-Parry J the key factor was that 'it would require but one such disaster as an epidemic at a holiday camp like this, or a bad accident' to harm the plaintiff.

As such, on the basis of these cases, it might be difficult to see when a connection misrepresentation would ever require an additional proof of damage: the false connection would always be sufficient. Mere confusion appears to be sufficient. As has been argued above, however, this should not be sufficient on the traditional approach to the tort. Damage to goodwill is a separate ingredient to misrepresentation/confusion.

It may be possible, however, to square these cases with the more traditional analysis of the tort. What might be happening is that the particular facts of such cases reveal at least the potential of a 'real, tangible risk' of harm to the plaintiff. This might be because the plaintiff's business (or the defendant's business) is particularly vulnerable to catastrophe or public concern or there is such a high level of confusion that the defendant's activities pose a risk to the plaintiff in terms of diversion of trade.

Some of the decided cases fall into the 'vulnerable' category. Thus in *Associated Press v Insert Media*[31] the defendant's decision to insert advertising material into the plaintiff's publications without consent posed 'an obvious, appreciable risk of loss of goodwill and reputation by the plaintiff', particularly as the plaintiff enforced high advertising standards for legitimate advertisers.[32] Again, there are obvious hazards[33] in being connected with a holiday camp for children when in fact you have no control over the activities in such a camp.

As far as the high level of confusion is concerned, the additional factor that appears to be present in the British Legion case is the common pool of 'customers'. Diversion of trade appears to be inherent in such a case.

What then of the *Lego* case? In *Lego v Lego M Lemelstrich*[34] the defendants were a long-established Israeli company who used the trade name 'Lego' for their garden equipment (the name having been formed from the names of the company's founders). The plaintiffs, the famous toy building brick company, successfully sought an injunction to prevent the use by the defendants of the name Lego in the United Kingdom. No diversion of trade was alleged; there was no allegation that the defendants' products were inferior or that the plaintiffs had planned to extend into the garden equipment trade. Yet Falconer J accepted the lack of control over the quality of the defendants' products as a reason for the injunction he granted: 'it seems to me that the inability of the plaintiffs to control such use must involve a real risk of injury to their reputation'.

It is submitted that *Lego* is wrong on this point (and, as will be argued, on many more besides!). Loss of control *per se* cannot be sufficient to constitute damage in the tort. The damage has to be damage to goodwill, customer connection. Simply to allege that customers may be confused is not enough. It should be accepted that this head of damage as such does not exist in the tort of passing off.

---

[31] [1991] 1 WLR 571.
[32] Note also, however, that the Court of Appeal found there to be a risk of diversion of trade, given that advertisers might choose the cheaper option of the defendant rather than direct advertising with the plaintiff.
[33] Ranging from hygiene problems to allegations of abuse.
[34] [1983] FSR 155.

Yet, unfortunately, the Court of Appeal in the *Harrods* case appears to accept 'loss of control' as a legitimate head of damage. In *Harrods Ltd v The Harrodian School Ltd*,[35] the well-known Knightsbridge department store sold the site of its former staff club (the Harrodian Club) to the defendant. The defendant opened a preparatory school on this site and called it 'The Harrodian School'. The plaintiffs alleged that this was passing off. They alleged that there was an actionable misrepresentation that the school was connected with the plaintiffs in some way and that damage would ensure, should the school fail or fall short of the standard of excellence set by the plaintiffs in their own trading activities. Millet LJ, while rejecting on the facts that there was a misrepresentation, accepted the reasoning of the *Lego* case that 'the danger in such a case is that the plaintiff loses control over his own reputation'.[36] Sir Michael Kerr (dissenting on the facts), equates a connection misrepresentation with the loss of distinctiveness and loss of control.

Restriction on expansion potential

This item of damage is commonly pleaded by plaintiffs where there is no diversion of trade by the defendant. It should be treated with caution by an court. Although it may be a legitimate item of damage, it runs the danger of circularity. Furthermore, it is frequently argued together with (and mixed up with) loss of control and dilution; see for example *Direct Line Insurance v Lotus Leisure Group Ltd* (1993); *All Weather Sports Activities v All Weather Sports UK* (1987); *Hyper Hyper Ltd v Hyper Active Ltd* (1985).[37]

Merely to allege damage based on the loss of a licensing or expansion opportunity should not be sufficient. Unless the court links this head of damage clearly to the plaintiff's goodwill, it verges on an allegation of misappropriation, rather than passing off. Without establishing existing goodwill to justify protecting future activities, the allegation becomes an attempt to close off markets to others, even before the plaintiff has entered them. This David and Goliath scenario was accepted as a problem by Russell LJ in *Dunhill v Sunoptic SA*: 'a court must always be careful to see that a large, powerful and wealthy corporation does not use its overwhelming financial muscle to the detriment of what would or may ultimately prove to be genuine commercial competition'.[30]

Thus this head of damage has often been rejected. In *Newsweek Inc. v BBC*,[39] the Court of Appeal refused to restrain the BBC from using the plaintiff's magazine title, *Newsweek*, for a current affairs programme, though the plaintiff proposed to move into the English television market. For Lord Denning, the possibility of confusion was too speculative. In *Stringfellow v McCain Foods (GB) Ltd*,[40] the owner of a famous and up-market night club objected to the defendants' using the name Stringfellows for their oven-ready chips[41] and alleged that future licensing potential was thereby prejudiced (he had yet to merchandise the

---

[35] Note 3 above.

[36] It may be that he is happy to accept this head of damage in its own right because he attempts to restrict the scope of connection misrepresentations, relevant to the tort. Thus he contends that to be relevant, the connection must be one by which the plaintiffs would be taken to have made themselves responsible for the quality of the defendant's goods or services (equivalent, in factual terms, to the *British Legion* case). However, it is submitted with respect (and Kerr LJ accepts this wider view) that any connection is sufficient, including sponsorship, where goodwill is at risk. See also Wadlow's review of the relevant case law on this issue: *Passing Off*, 1995 (2nd edn), at 280 to 281.

[37] All unreported, but available on Lexis.

[38] [1979] FSR 337, 368 CA.

[39] [1979] RPC 441.

[40] Note 11 above.

[41] The misrepresentation was made out because of the accompanying advertisement that had a night club theme and appeared modelled on Stringfellows.

name or image). The Court of Appeal refused to indulge in 'pure speculation': there was no evidence that the plaintiff would have been in a position profitably to exploit merchandising the club's image or name nor was it likely that up-market goods would seek to be associated with the name.

Again, this was appreciated in *Lyngstad v Anabas Products Ltd*,[42] the *Abba* case. Here the then famous pop group had yet to merchandise themselves but sought to prevent others using their glamorous image to market their products. They were attempting to close off markets even before they had decided to trade in them. The real concern in such cases is not to protect goodwill—there is none—but to allege that the defendants are 'cashing-in' on the plaintiff's success. As such that is an insufficient allegation for passing off.

However, there may be cases in which the plaintiff can show that his goodwill includes expansion potential. Where future commercial activities are a natural extension of the plaintiff's existing trading activities the court may be prepared to add that to existing goodwill. In *Dunhill v Sunoptic*,[43] the plaintiffs, having originally been producers of tobacco goods, had diversified into luxury items for men. They were able to restrain the defendant from using the name Dunhill for their sunglasses, in part because they were planning to produce sunglasses themselves under their own mark. Indeed, it will be easier to show that an unauthorised use of the plaintiff's trade name and so on involves an attack on his goodwill when the plaintiff's goodwill *includes* licensing or character merchandising. In *Mirage Studios v Counter Feat Clothing*,[44] the *Ninja Turtles* case, the character merchandising industry finally established in England that they have such goodwill. The goodwill in the country is still based on the trading activity, rather than protecting the character itself. For the Vice Chancellor 'there is no reason why a remedy in passing off should be limited to those who market or sell the goods themselves'. The connection misrepresentation, accepted by the court in the *Ninja Turtles* case for the first time, could damage this goodwill.

Applying the orthodox view of goodwill, therefore, the allegation that expansion potential is a head of damages is circular, if the plaintiff has yet to license or if expansion is speculative. Merely to allege the loss of a licensing or expansion opportunity should not be sufficient where there is no actual or likely licensing or merchandising goodwill. Interestingly, in Australia misappropriation of licensing or merchandising potential has been accepted as a head of damage in the tort: *Henderson v Radio Corp. Pty Ltd*;[45] *Hogan v Koala Dundee Pty Ltd* and *Pacific Dunlop v Hogan*[46] make that clear. But this acceptance has involved jettisoning goodwill in the tort, at least in character merchandising cases.

In the *Lego* case, discussed above, another ground for awarding the injunction was the expansion restriction on the plaintiffs, even though they were not licensing their name. The plaintiffs complained that they were deprived of a licensing fee, lost opportunities to license others or develop into those new areas (and, as has already been seen, loss of control of their own reputation). It is surely relevant that Falconer J cited with approval the High Court of Australia's decision in *Henderson v Radio Corp. Pty Ltd*. It is contended that *Lego* is wrongly decided on this point also. Interestingly, HH Judge Baker QC rejected an application for an interlocutory injunction in *Pentagon Stationers Ltd v Pentagon Business Systems Ltd*[47] on the

---

[42] [1977] FSR 62, Oliver J.

[43] Note 38 above.

[44] [1991] FSR 145.

[45] [1969] RPC 218: where the court in effect granted the ballroom dancers a 'publicity right'.

[46] (1988) 83 ALR 187 (Fed. Court of Australia) and (1989) 87 ALR 14 (Fed. Court of Australia) respectively. It was held that the creator of a fictional film character—Crocodile Dundee—could prevent manufacturers 'misappropriating' the value of the character by, in the first case, selling paraphernalia associated with the character and, in the second, by 'spoofing' a scene from the film.

[47] Unreported, 1985.

basis that the plaintiff's case was 'simply that the defendants are trading in an area into which the plaintiffs hope to expand'.

Dilution

The dilution theory 'is based on the fact that the more widely a symbol is used, the less effective it will be for any one user'.[48] The profit potential of the name[49] is diluted by 'over use'. In the United States, dilution actions have been introduced by legislatures in the majority of states. Case law reveals that it is used in both confusion cases (where harm to goodwill is not evident) and in its 'pure' form where the mere use of the plaintiff's trade name is restrained, in the absence of confusion. This latter form of dilution was proposed by Schechter, who introduced the concept of dilution into the American debate over trade mark law in the 1920s.[50] For him, the concept applied to dissimilar goods.

Even on this short description it is apparent that there is no clear definition of dilution from American case law. It is particularly worrying, therefore, that the term 'dilution' has increasingly been alleged in interlocutory passing-off actions. In many ways the allegation of loss of control or loss of expansion potential is a disguised allegation of dilution: dilution, it is submitted, was the real harm being alleged in *Lego*. Indeed, the judge in *Lego*, Falconer J, allowed dilution claims in a series of connection confusion cases in the early 1980s.[51] Dilution was also accepted as a head of damage by Blackburne J in *Dalgety Spillers Foods Ltd v Food Brokers Ltd*.[52] Aldous J accepted 'dilution of goodwill' in *Direct Line Insurance v Lotus Leisure Group Ltd*, while Knox J accepted the plaintiffs' contention in *All Weather Sports Activities Ltd v All Weather Sports (UK) Ltd* that the use of the same name by the defendant would harm the name's 'unique association' with the plaintiff (though he refused to award an injunction). Most significantly, the Court of Appeal in *Taittinger SA v Allbev Ltd* appeared to accept dilution of one form or another as a legitimate head of damage in passing off.

Taittinger involved champagne producers attacking the use of the word 'champagne' in the name of the defendants' non-alcoholic drink, 'Elderflower Champagne'. Although on one level the case could be analysed as a standard claim for product misrepresentation (on the lines of *Advocaat*) with diversion of sales or injurious association alleged, all three members of the court highlighted another aspect of the case: the threat of dilution. Thus Peter Gibson LJ stressed the 'blurring or erosion of the uniqueness that now attaches to the word champagne'. Mann LJ accepted that the plaintiffs' cases was 'that the word champagne has an exclusiveness which is impaired if it is used in relation to a product ... which is neither champagne nor associated with or connected to the businesses which produce champagne'. Finally, Bingham MR continued this theme when he remarked: 'any product which is not champagne but is allowed to describe itself as such must inevitably, in my view, erode the singularity and exclusiveness of the description Champagne [and cause damage] of an insidious but serious kind'.

In reality the complaint of dilution does not fit within the classic analysis of the tort. Dilution is really an allegation that the commercial magnetism of the plaintiff's trade name or mark is threatened. Misappropriation/theft of a trade value is the real issue. Where the

---

[48] Brown, 'Advertising and the Public Interest', 57 Yale LJ at 1191 (1940).

[49] Dilution was argued in relation to a similar get up by the plaintiffs in *Dalgety Spillers Foods Ltd v Food Brokers Ltd*, [1994] FSR 504.

[50] 'The Rational Basis of Trade-Mark Protection' (1927) 40 Har. L. Rev. 813. There is now a Federal Dilution Trademark Act 1995.

[51] Apart from *Lego* all are reported on Lexis: *UBM Group Ltd v Lankester Dibben Steels Ltd* (1981); *Overdrive Ltd v Wells Fargo Bank* (1982); *Hyper Hyper Ltd v Hyper Active Ltd* (1982).

[52] [1994] FSR 504.

alleged dilution arises from confusion, it is not confusion that harms goodwill. There is no goodwill in the name itself: it is the customer connection attached to the name that merits protection. Thus in *Advocaat*, it was not the dilution of the name 'Advocaat' that led to the injunction, but the injurious association and diversion of trade, both long accepted heads of damage. Both focus clearly on goodwill. Of course, with allegations of 'pure dilution' (and arguably some of the *dicta* in *Taittinger* support such a claim) none of the ingredients of the classic trinity are present: there is no misrepresentation and no harm to goodwill.

If dilution is the reason for the injunction in *Taittinger*, then arguably the tort has been refashioned by the back door. It is hard not to conclude that the injunction awarded in that case protected a prestigious name rather than a prestigious source or product. Yet there are powerful arguments, both legal and economic, why persuasive advertising and other equivalent competitive practices should not merit tort protection. For Brown,[53] the economic waste and distortion of consumer choice which emanates from large-scale persuasive advertising indicates the 'dubious social utility' of this area of commerce. And for him, dilution claims involve demanding protection for persuasive values alone.

After *Taittinger* the validity of 'dilution' as head of damage is not clear. In *Harrods Ltd v The Harrodian School*, dilution was raised as a secondary allegation. The judgement of Millett LJ reveals that he is unhappy with the wider implications of the *Taittinger* case. In reply to the plaintiffs' allegation that the defendant was seeking to attract to his school the 'aura of excellence' attached to the name Harrods, he underlines the classic view that the tort protects the trading activity behind the name, not the name itself. He refers to the 'intellectual difficulty' in accepting that the law insists on the presence of both confusion and damage and yet could recognise as sufficient a head of damage which does not depend on confusion.

However, with respect, Millett LJ fails to deal adequately with the effect of the *Taittinger* decision in this area. Thus he only refers to peter Gibson LJ's judgment from that case, even though all members of the Court of Appeal were prepared to highlight the threat to the prestige and distinctiveness of the word 'champagne'. Moreover, he contends that the discussion of dilution in that case refers solely to the threat of 'generification' of a famous name. Yet it is more than arguable that the use of the name 'Elderflower Champagne' for a non-alcoholic drink did not threaten generification (given that it is far removed from sparkling white wine). In essence, the plaintiffs in *Taittinger* were seeking to prevent the use of their name on any other product. By claiming that *Taittinger* was concerned with a generification claim, Millett LJ was able to reject its applicability to the *Harrods* claim (the defendant's actions in no way would lead to the name 'Harrods' becoming a generic term for a retail emporium in the luxury class) without a clear analysis for the future. What is clear, however, from the strong dissenting judgment of Sir Michael Kerr, is that there is a conflict within the Court of Appeal on the issue of dilution. He cites in full the wide *dicta* on dilution from all three members of the Court of Appeal in *Taittinger* and asserts that debasement or dilution of reputation as a result of the defendant's action is a relevant head of damage in the tort of passing off. Plaintiffs will, therefore, continue their quest to establish 'dilution' as a head of damage in the tort.

Moreover, it has to be remembered that the concept of 'dilution' has recently been added to *statutory* trade mark law by the Trade Marks Act 1994. This change mirrors the provisions of the EC Directive on the approximation of trade mark laws (Council Directive 89/104/EEC). 'Pure dilution' has been added to the list of what constitutes infringing acts by section 10(3). The use of a similar sign/mark on dissimilar goods, where the registered mark has a 'reputation' and the use of that mark 'takes unfair advantage of or is detrimental

---

[53] Brown, Note 48 above, at 1190.

to the distinctive character or repute of the trade mark' infringes the registered mark. This is dilution, as defined by Schechter. Moreover, it may be that section 10(2) of the Act could be interpreted as allowing a pure dilution claim, where *similar* goods are involved. The subsection states that management is based on the likelihood of confusion but goes on to state that this includes 'likelihood of association'. The notion of 'likelihood of association' has been acknowledged in the minutes of the EC Council meeting that adopted the new EC trade mark laws to be a concept developed in Benelux case law. In Benelux law association appears to be recognised as distinct from 'confusion', extending the scope of protection into dilution claims. It is likely that plaintiffs will seek to use section 10(2) to pursue dilution claims where similar goods are involved, though in *Wagamama Ltd v City Centre Restaurants plc*[54] Laddie J rejected such a claim, requiring confusion for section 10(2) to apply.

The appearance of 'dilution' in statutory trade mark claims is likely to lead to the growth of similar allegations in passing off claims, as the two causes of action are commonly pleaded together. If dilution is accepted as part of passing off then, as has been shown, the classic trinity will have been rejected and the tort allowed to develop into a wider tort of unfair competition/misappropriation.

There is, however, a species of loss of exclusivity that may be a legitimate head of damage in the tort of passing off: swamping.

Submerging or swamping

Wadlow[55] notes that loss of exclusivity might be a legitimate head of damage where, in an extreme case, the plaintiff's trade name or mark may be swamped or submerged by the subsequent use of that name/mark by a larger defendant. Rather than involving dilution, this involves obliteration of goodwill and is clearly within the tort. An example of this arose in *Falcon Travel Ltd v Owners Abroad Group plc*.[56] There the plaintiffs had operated in Ireland, under the name Falcon Travel. The defendants, a large UK company who traded as Falcon Leisure, opened a Dublin office. The court accepted that the plaintiffs' reputation had been 'submerged' in the defendants' reputation. Here the remedy awarded was interesting: an injunction was denied but the plaintiffs were awarded damages to enable them to mount an advertising campaign to distinguish themselves from the defendants' group of companies.[57]

The Need for Caution

Passing off has many species: the tort has continued to expand. Yet the orthodox view is still that there are key ingredients in the tort that cannot be ignored. Goodwill is still the focal point of the tort; misrepresentations alone are not sufficient.

The continued importance of these ingredients represents a policy to limit the tort. Judges are still reluctant to draw the line between fair and unfair competition and are mindful of 'the basic common law policy of encouraging competition and the fact that the protection of monopolies in names is but a secondary and limiting policy'.[58] Goodwill and damage linked to goodwill mark out the judicial role and ensure that competition is stifled only in predictable cases of excessive competition.

---

[54] [1995] FSR 713.
[55] Wadlow, *The Law of Passing Off*, 1995 (2nd edn), at 173.
[56] Unreported; see [1991] 1 EIPR D-11, HC of Ireland.
[57] And see also *Taylor Bros v Taylor Group* [1988] 2 NZLR 1, NZCA.
[58] Frank J in *Eastern Wine Corp. v Winslow-Warren Ltd* 137 F.2d 955, 959.

All in all, backdoor unprincipled extensions are not acceptable. The gradual extension of the heads of damage requires a clear perception and perhaps reassessment of the rationale of the tort. The commercial bodies pressing for protection against what they perceive to be unfair competition should not be allowed to alter the focus of the tort (from goodwill) in order to gain protection generally for commercial success or magnetism,[59] at least not without clear acknowledgement. As Naresh has noted of passing off: 'the judicial extensions of liability under this head owe more to the manipulation of verbal formulae than to a clarification of its foundations'.[60] The net result, if changes are to be made, must continue to promote competition and not stifle it in favour of the first on the scene or the biggest traders. In particular, the relative worth of 'informational' advertising or its equivalent as against 'persuasive' advertising and sales techniques needs to be explored.

---

[59] Brown, Note 48 above, at 1206: 'In an acquisitive society, the drive for monopoly advantage is a powerful pressure. Unchecked it would no doubt patent the wheel, copyright the alphabet and register the sun and moon as exclusive trade marks.'

[60] Naresh, 'Passing Off, Goodwill and False Advertising: New Wine in Old bottles', 1986 CLJ 97 at 97.

Damages against the Innocent Infringer*
[1994] 4 EIPR 204

ROSHANA KELBRICK
University of South Africa, Pretoria

A recent British decision illustrates the danger of assuming that South African and British intellectual property law and practice always correspond. While the relevant legislation shows substantial similarity, the differing common law origins of the two legal systems can result in different outcomes depending on the jurisdiction in which the matter is determined. In this article, a recent English decision awarding damages against an innocent infringer in respect of both trade mark infringement and passing off will be analysed and compared with the equivalent South African position. The position in other commonwealth jurisdictions is also briefly sketched.

Gillette UK Ltd v Edenwest Ltd is a 1994 decision by the Chancery division of the British High Court.[1] The defendant, Edenwest, who traded as a wholesaler, had bought a large consignment of counterfeit razor cartridges and resold them to retailers in the United Kingdom. The plaintiffs, Gillette, were respectively the registered proprietor of the infringed trade marks and the American holding company. When the plaintiffs discovered the presence of counterfeit cartridges in the United Kingdom and traced the supply source to the defendant, they applied for an injunction and an inquiry into damages. The defendant concede that the plaintiffs were entitled to injunctive relief and this was granted without argument.

The other prayer was for an inquiry as to damages suffered by reason of Edenwest's acts of passing off and infringement, and payment of all sums found due on such inquiry with interest. The defendant opposed the grant of this order, submitting that it was an innocent infringer and, as damages were only recoverable where the defendant was shown to have acted dishonestly, the court could not require it to pay damages in respect of either the passing off or the trade mark infringement. The question of the defendant's innocence, in the sense that it had no knowledge of the infringing nature of the goods, was not disputed by the plaintiffs. However, they submitted that this innocence was irrelevant to their right to damages.

Blackburne J confessed himself startled by the proposition that an innocent infringer was not liable to pay damages 'since it ... seems to me that if the plaintiffs have suffered loss by reason of Edenwest's actions there can be no good reason why they should not recover damages to compensate them for that loss'.[2] The court then proceeded to deal rather

---

* *The author would like to thank the Institute of Advanced Legal Studies, London, for the use of their library facilities while researching this article.*
[1] (1994) RPC 279.
[2] *Ibid.*, at 289.

cursorily with the defendant's submission, Blackburne J stating that he did not propose to deal with all the authorities cited but merely to set out his conclusions and reasoning. The availability of damages in respect of infringement and in respect of passing off was dealt with separately.

Trade Mark Infringement

The liability to pay damages when a trade mark has been innocently infringed was discussed first. Quoting *Kerly* as authority,[3] Blackburne J pronounced it settled law that innocence on the part of an infringer is no defence to a claim for damages, and ordered an inquiry. He stated that he had been referred to only one case, *Slazenger & Sons v Spalding and Bros* where damages against an innocent infringer were denied;[4] that the authorities relied on in this decision were very old; and that it had not been followed in *Henry Heath Ltd v Frederick Gorringe Ltd.*[5] He then referred to three decisions in which an inquiry had been directed without discussion,[6] and suggested that the lack of discussion was doubtless because everyone assumed that the law on the point was well-settled.[7]

Is the court's reliance on *Kerly*'s categorical statement that 'knowledge or absence of knowledge does not affect the right to damages' correct? *Kerly*'s authority is *Spalding & Bros v A. W. Gamage Ltd*[8]—which dealt with passing off, not infringement of a registered mark— and *Henry Heath*—an instance of trade mark infringement where an inquiry as to damages was granted but no reasons for judgment were given. While *Kerly* (12th edition) cites only the above two decisions as authority, previous editions mention two further decisions where *Spalding* was not considered—according to the authors because no decision on the point was necessary.[9] Interestingly, in the first of these, *Hindhaugh & Co v Inch and Son*, a Scottish case dating fro 1923, *Kerly* (4th edition) is cited as authority for the proposition that 'there is well settled English authority against the recovery of damages for the innocent use of a Trade mark by another'.[10] In the light of the paucity of the authority on which *Kerly*'s statements are based, they cannot without further ado be viewed as authoritative on the point. Closer examination would seem appropriate.

As a starting point, it might be helpful to undertake a chronological review of those decisions where damages against innocent infringers of registered trade marks were requested. Although the first three decisions dealt with accounts of profits, not damages, they are mentioned because reference to them is made in later decisions. *Edelsten v Edelsten,*[11] a request for an account of profits, was decided in 1863, before the passage of the first trade mark legislation. The court held that a plaintiff litigating against an innocent infringer 'is not entitled to any account of profits *or compensation . . .*'[12]

This passage was quoted with approval the following year when, on facts very similar to those in *Edenwest*, a request for an account of profits against an innocent infringer was

---

[3] T.A. Blanco-White and R. Jacob, *Kerly's Law of Trade Marks and Trade Names* 1986 (12th edn) ('*Kerly*') at 327 to 328: 'whilst knowledge or absence of knowledge does not affect the right to damages'.
[4] (1910) 1 Ch. 257.
[5] (1924) 51 RPC 457.
[6] *Fialho v Simond & Co Ltd* (1937) 54 RPC 193; *Ravenhead Brick Company Ltd v Ruabon Brick and Terra Cotta Company Ltd* (1937) 54 RPC 341; *Sony Corporation v Anand* (1982) FSR 200.
[7] *Edenwest*, Note 1 above, at 291.
[8] (1915) 32 RPC 273.
[9] 11th edn (1983) at 303 footnote 32; 10th edn (1972), at 344 footnote 30.
[10] (1923) 40 RPC 368 at 371.
[11] (1863) 1 De GJ & S 184, (46 ER 72).
[12] *Ibid.* at 78 (*emphasis added*).

refused.[13] *Ellen v Slack*,[14] decided in 1880 after the adoption of the first trade mark legislation, is a very brief report relying on *Edelsten* for refusal of an account of profits against an innocent infringer. The next decision, *Slazenger* in 1909,[15] states that damages cannot be granted against an innocent infringer. This is the only pre-*Edenwest* decision in which the issue of an innocent trade mark infringer's liability to pay damages has been pertinently considered. In this decision, Neville J held that the principle of *Edelsten* still held true, despite the statutory rights created by trade mark legislation since that decision, and refused to grant an account of profits or inquiry as to damages. He then considered whether the fact that *Edelsten* and *Ellen* dealt with an account of profits, rather than an inquiry as to damages, affected their relevance, and held as follows:

> nowadays, where the right to compensation exists, there is no distinction between an account of profits and an inquiry as to damages, and it rests with the plaintiff to elect whether he will take one form of relief or the other.[16]

He then proceeded to find that, as the defendants were unaware of the plaintiffs' rights, there was no right to compensation but only a right to an injunction. The following year, in *J.J. Horsfield v J. Walkden & Co. Ltd*,[17] an action for trade mark infringement where damages or an account of profits were requested in the alternative, the court held:

> As the law stood under the old Trade Mark Act the cases were quite clear that an innocent infringer was not liable for damages. Since the alteration, under which the registration of a Trade Mark gives the owner of a Trade Mark property in the Trade Mark, it was thought that the law required reconsideration, and it would not be considered to be in accordance with the old decisions; but Mr Justice Neville in the case of *Slazenger v Spalding* held that the new Act of Parliament had not made any difference.[18]

In casu Leigh Clare VC held that the defendants were not innocent infringers and ordered an inquiry, saying that if the defendants could satisfy the registrar that they were innocent infringers up to a certain date, the inquiry could date from that time. By 1923 the Lord Constable of Scotland, when hearing an action for trade mark infringement and damages, stated that 'there is well settled English authority against the recovery of damages for the innocent use of a Trade Mark by another'.[19] However, in the 1924 *Henry Heath* decision the court, without referring to any previous decisions, stated that 'a legal right has been infringed, and *prima facie* the Plaintiffs are entitled to damages, which, of course, the Plaintiffs take at their own risk as to costs'.[20] In this instance the defendants had, in all innocence, published an advertisement using the plaintiff's mark and 'sold at least two hats at that price' (14s 11d)! The next case was a 1926 Chancery decision dealing with trade mark infringement and passing off where an inquiry as to damages had been requested. No authority is given for the statement that, because of the innocence of the second defendant, 'it may be that as

---

[13] *Moet v Couston*, 33 Beav. 578 at 581 (55 ER 493).
[14] 24 Sol. J 290.
[15] Note 4 above, at 261.
[16] *Ibid.*, at 261. While this might be correct in the sense that, after the passage of the Judicature Act in 1875, a plaintiff could elect either form of relief, it cannot be intended to mean that there is no distinction between the effect of the two remedies.
[17] (1911) 28 RPC 175.
[18] *Ibid.*, at 178.
[19] *Hindhaugh*, Note 10 above at 371.
[20] Note 5 above, at 457.

a result of that no claim for damages may be made against him'.[21] In the same year, because of lack of proof of damages, an award of damages was refused against an innocent infringer. Nominal damages were also not awarded.[22] Thereafter, in 1937, inquiries as to damages were granted in two decisions,[23] in neither instance with any consideration by counsel or the court of whether such an order was justified in the light of earlier case law. The last trade mark decision before *Edenwest*, in 1982, granted an inquiry without discussion after the plaintiff's counsel had conceded that there was doubt whether such an order would be granted for innocent passing off.[24]

The finding by the *Edenwest* court that the point is 'settled law' seems justified when only the most recent decisions are considered. However, the chronological review of all the decisions on the point illustrates that this finding was not justified. *Spalding* is cited as authority both by *Kerly* and in those decisions in which an inquiry was granted, but is not authority for the liability of an innocent trade mark infringer, as it deals only with passing off.[25] The issue of innocent trade mark infringement was not canvassed in any of the above decisions, other than *Slazenger*, where it was held that as the defendants did not know of the plaintiffs' rights, there was no right to compensation, but only a right to an injunction.

To summarise the available authority on the grant of damages against an innocent infringer of a registered trade mark: the only case in which the issue was pertinently considered refused to order an inquiry, and has subsequently been quoted with approval; the authority relied on by textbooks and certain decisions is inappropriate as it deals with passing off rather than trade mark infringement; and in three decisions an inquiry was granted without the issue being canvassed. It is submitted that, in the light of the *Slazenger* decision and in the absence of other pertinent authority, the court in *Edenwest* should not have come to its decision without a fuller consideration of the applicable legal principles.

What are these legal principles? Legislation dealing with trade marks, unlike legislation governing other species of intellectual property, has never spelt out all the relief available to a proprietor for the infringement of his registered mark. The first statute which dealt with trade marks provided that registration was necessary for the proprietor to 'be entitled to institute any proceedings to prevent infringement'.[26] The amendment during the following year provided for proceedings to 'prevent or recover damages',[27] and this phrase is found in every subsequent Act up to 1994.[28] It has always been accepted that this was not an exhaustive list of the relief available and that the proprietor of an infringed mark could enforce his rights in the same manner as the holder of any other property right. This has now been statutorily confirmed in the Trade Marks Act of 1994.[29]

The inclusion of the right to recover damages in the various statutes can be interpreted in two ways. First, it can be argued that the fact that statutory provision is made for the recovery of any damages suffered by the proprietor of a registered mark always entitles him to do so, irrespective of the guilt or innocence of the defendant. Viewed in this light, it is understandable why a court will grant damages against an innocent infringer, but refuse an account of profits, for which no statutory provision exists.

---

[21] *Champagne Heidsieck et Cie v Scotto and Bishop* (1926) 43 RPC 101 at 103.
[22] *Société Française Radio-Electrique v West Central Wireless Supplies* (1928) 45 RPC 276 at 280.
[23] *Fialho* and *Ravenhead Brick*, Note 6 above.
[24] *Sony*, Note 6 above, at 201.
[25] For this reason, the decision has been discussed below under passing off and not in the section dealing with trade mark decisions.
[26] Section 1 Trade Mark Registration Act 1875.
[27] Section 1 Trade Marks Registration Amendment Act 1876.
[28] Section 77 Patents, Designs and Trade Marks Act 1883; section 42 Trade Marks Act 1905; section 2 Trade Marks Act 1938.
[29] Section 14(2).

The contrary argument is that to determine the relief available for trade mark infringement, reference to the common law has always been necessary, despite the existence of legislation. The *Edelsten* decision set out the relief available in respect of trade mark infringement prior to the existence of legislation as follows:

> For although it is well founded in reason, and also settled by decision, that if A has acquired property in a trade mark, which is afterwards adopted and used by B in ignorance of A's right, A is entitled to an injunction; yet he is not entitled to any account of profits or compensation, except in respect of any user by B after he became aware of the prior ownership.
>
> At law the proper remedy is by an action on the case for deceit: and proof of fraud on the part of the Defendant is of the essence of the action: but this Court will act on the principle of protecting property alone, and it is not necessary for the injunction to prove fraud in the Defendant.[30]

Historically, therefore, fraud was an essential element of any common law action to recover damages and an inquiry would therefore not be ordered in the absence of fraud.[31] Equitable relief, which did not require proof of fraud, was discretionary, and relief in the form of an account would not be granted for innocent infringement. In terms of *Slazenger* and *Horsfield*, this should still be the position. Viewed on this basis, if the defendant was unaware that he was infringing a registered mark, the court in *Edenwest* should not have granted an inquiry as to damages in respect of the trade mark infringement.

Passing Off

After finding that any inquiry could be granted in respect of trade mark infringement, Blackburne J then turned his attention to the question of whether it was apt in respect of passing off.[32] He once again took *Kerly* as his point of departure. *Kerly* cites *Spalding* as authority for the statement that a plaintiff is entitled to an inquiry even though the defendant was completely innocent, but then points out that there is argument to the contrary, based on the historical requirement that fraud was a necessary ingredient for an action at law to recover damages.[33] The court referred to *Vokes C.G. Ltd v S.J. Evans and Marble Arch Motor Supplies Ltd*,[34] where damages were refused because of the defendants' innocence; quoted *Draper v Trist and Tristbetos Brake Linings Ltd*,[35] where doubts were expressed about the recovery of damages in the absence of fraud or dishonesty; and then mentioned *Marengo v Daily Sketch and Sunday Graphic Ltd*,[36] where the court declined to express a view on this point. Blackburne J, in ordering an inquiry, quoted extensively from *Spalding* to justify his finding that dishonesty on the defendant's part is not necessary before a plaintiff can recover

---

[30] *Edelsten* Note 11 above, at 78.

[31] The statement in *Kerly* (12th edn) at 326 that mere proof of an infringement entitles the plaintiff to damages loses sight of the fact that the common law case cited as authority, *Blofeld v Payne* (1833) 4 B & Ad 410 (110 ER 509), based this finding on the fact that the act of the defendants was a fraud against the plaintiff.

[32] *Edenwest*, Note 1 above, at 291 to 293.

[33] While *Kerly* relies on *Spalding*, Note 8 above, in the 11th and 12th editions, published respectively in 1983 and 1986, strangely enough this decision is not referred to in the 10th edition, published in 1972, in which it is stated: 'A successful plaintiff in a passing-off action is entitled at least to nominal damages, whether the defendant was fraudulent or not. Whether a plaintiff is entitled to claim more than nominal damages—ie is entitled to an inquiry as to damages—against a defendant who innocently passed-off is an open question' (at 447).

[34] (1932) 49 RPC 140.

[35] (1939) 56 RPC 429.

[36] (1948) 65 RPC 242.

damages. The judge mentioned that he had been referred to a number of cases, including *Baume & Co. v Moore A.H. Ltd*[37] and *Fialho*,[38] where inquiries had been ordered notwithstanding the innocence of the defendant.

He was also unpersuaded by Catherine Best's article[39] which argues that damages should not be awarded against innocent defendants. Blackburne J, expressing his own view on the topic, surmised that the difficulty in determining whether damages are due in respect of innocent passing off has its origin in the fact that at common law passing off meant dishonest passing off and proof of dishonesty was required, whereas, in equity, although dishonesty was not an essential element for the court to grant injunctive relief, the court declined to award an account of profits where the passing off was merely innocent. He then criticised it as a little unreal that, in respect of a tort which did not achieve its modern form until the early part of this century, the nature of the relief available should be governed by considerations applicable to the cause of action at an earlier stage of its development.[40]

A study of the various authorities, including those cited by Blackburne J, casts doubts on whether an inquiry was indicated. As mentioned above, while *Kerly* relies on *Spalding* as authority in the most recent two editions, earlier editions, which appeared after *Spalding*, do not refer to this decision and consider the issue an 'open question'.[41] In contrast, Wadlow's interpretation of *Spalding* is that the decision confirmed that at common law a representation must be fraudulently made, while in equity complete innocence of the party making a misrepresentation is a reason for limiting an account of profits to the period after the defendant became aware of the true facts.[42]

Although it is the House of Lords decision in *Spalding* which is cited as authority, it is instructive also to refer to the judgment of the court, *a quo*, which strongly criticised the defendants' behaviour.[43] It is clear that, in the court's opinion, the defendants' behaviour was, if not fraudulent, then at least grossly negligent. A study of the House of Lords decision also casts doubts on *Kerly*'s reliance on it as authority for the proposition that damages may be awarded for innocent passing off. On the facts, the defendants were clearly not completely innocent infringers—Lord Parker in his judgment uses phrases such as 'I find it difficult to imagine that the advertisements were not deliberately framed so as to create this impression'[44] and 'hardly consistent with fair or honest trade'[45] while at no stage where the grant of an inquiry is discussed either by Lord Sumner or by Lord Parmoor is the question of whether damages are appropriate for innocent passing off pertinently raised.[46] Furthermore, the court at no stage used the term 'innocent' to describe the defendants. Finally, that portion of *Spalding*[47] relied on as authority for the principle that damages may be granted against an innocent defendant, is not completely persuasive. The phrase 'it has long been settled that actual passing-off of a defendant's goods for the plaintiff's need not be proved as a condition precedent to relief in Equity either by way of an injunction or of an inquiry as to profits or

---

[37] (1958) RPC 226.

[38] Note 6 above.

[39] C. Best, 'Damages against the innocent infringer in passing off and trade mark infringement' (1985) 1 *Intellectual Property Journal* 201.

[40] *Edenwest*, Note 1 above, 292 to 293.

[41] See Note 33 above, and *Kerly* 1966 (9th edn), at 444 and 1960 (8th edn), at 396.

[42] C. Wadlow, *The Law of Passing-Off*, 1995 (2nd edn), at 49.

[43] *A.G. Spalding & Bros v A.W. Gamage Ltd* (1913) 30 RPC 388 at 397.

[44] *Spalding*, Note 8 above, at 286.

[45] *Ibid.* at 288.

[46] Lord Parmoor briefly considered whether the evidence showed that the defendants' conduct was calculated to deceive or not, but did not decide the matter as he was satisfied that a misrepresentation had been made (*ibid.*, at 290).

[47] *Ibid.*, at 283.

damages' must be seen in the light of what precedes it—Lord Parker, dealing with general principles of passing off, was discussing whether misrepresentation is sufficient or whether actual passing off is required. His citation of *Edelsten* illustrates this. Where he thereafter states that representation need not be fraudulently made, but is treated as an invasion of right giving rise to at least nominal damages, with no citation of authority and in a discussion of general principle, rather than when considering the relief sought by the plaintiffs, his statement must be regarded as *obiter*.

Prior to *Spalding*, damages were not granted in respect of innocent passing off.[48] Even after this decision, the attitude of the courts did not alter immediately. In *Vokes* the defendants were viewed as having 'acted completely innocently'[49] and the court merely stated, without discussion, that the plaintiffs were not entitled to damages. The defendants in the *Draper* decision cannot be viewed as innocent; they had sold the plaintiff their portion of the business previously carried on in partnership with him, together with the goodwill, and then immediately set up business in competition using a name similar to that of the prior partnership.[50] Although the defendants had consented to the order that an inquiry as to damages be held, two of the three judges queried the order, on the basis of the absence of fraudulent intent on the part of the defendants. Goddard LJ doubted seriously 'whether it is the law that damages can be claimed for innocent passing-off',[51] while Clauson LJ queried whether fraud was a necessary element of conduct leading to a judgment for damages.[52] However, as he and Goddard LJ remarked pragmatically, the fact that the parties agreed to the inquiry indicated that they also agreed on the existence of the elements on which damages could be ordered.[53] The *Marengo* decision dealt with 'completely' innocent passing off. The claim for damages had been withdrawn by the time the matter reached the House of Lords, and some of the bench expressly stated that they were not venturing an opinion on whether damages could be awarded where the defendant was innocent.[54] In *Procea Products Ltd v Evans & Sons Ltd*[55] the court considered the *Draper* headnote and interpreted it as meaning that 'it is an open question whether more than nominal damages could be given in an action for passing-off without fraud'.[56] *In casu* only nominal damages were sought, and granted, the court holding that no fraud or dishonesty was involved but nevertheless clearly considering the defendants negligent.[57] Again, as recently as 1982, in *Sony Corporation v Anand*,[58] the court refused to grant an inquiry as to damages in respect of passing off because it doubted whether such an order could be made against an innocent infringer. The two decisions referred to by Blackburne J, where an inquiry was ordered despite the innocence of the defendant, are not persuasive as the issue was considered in neither decision.[59]

This review of the authorities reveals that the question of whether damages could be ordered in respect of innocent passing off was not settled before *Edenwest*—as indeed

---

[48] See *G.H. Gledhill & Sons Ltd v British Perforated Toilet Paper Company* (1911) 28 RPC 429 at 451.
[49] *Vokes*, Note 34 above, at 145.
[50] See the report of the original inquiry as to damages reported at (1939) 56 RPC 225 for the facts.
[51] *Draper*, Note 35 above, at 443.
[52] *Ibid.*, at 441.
[53] *Ibid.*, at 434 and 441.
[54] *Marengo*, Note 36 above, at 247, 251, 252, 254.
[55] (1951) 68 RPC 210.
[56] *Ibid.*, at 220.
[57] *Per* Roxburgh J at 213: 'I entirely acquit him of all dishonest or improper motives; but he knew that that was untrue ... he at any rate would have been bound to have realised, had he thought about it—that 'process' and 'Procea' are words likely to introduce the utmost confusion ... he did not see the danger of the course he was pursuing'.
[58] Note 6 above, at 206.
[59] *Baume* Note 37 above; and *Fialho*, Note 6 above.

conceded by Blackburne J. It is also clear that other courts have found Lord Parker's statements in *Spalding* less persuasive than did Blackburne J.

It is unfortunate that *Edenwest* came before the court in the form of an Order 14 summons, as the facts are not completely clear from the judgment. The court held that the defendant's honesty was not in issue. What is not clear is whether the issue was conceded or was not canvassed, and whether the defendant's behaviour was negligent or completely innocent in the sense that no wrongful conduct whatsoever could be imputed. It is submitted that Blackburne J was correct in holding that dishonest passing off is not a prerequisite for the award of damages.

However, the words 'damages' and 'innocent' require clarification. It is submitted that it is the incorrect use of these terms which has led to discrepancies and confusion as to the award of damages against defendants whom the court has not found to have acted fraudulently. While it has been accepted that nominal damages may be awarded for innocent passing off, an inquiry as to damages presupposes general, not nominal, damages.[60]

A defendant is not necessarily innocent if he is not dishonest. When the decisions discussed above are studied, it becomes clear that some confusion has arisen from careless terminology. Various courts speak of innocence, as opposed to fraud or dishonesty, when a completely innocent defendant is one to whom neither fraud nor negligence can be imputed. In a number of cases, defendants are described as 'innocent' infringers or their actions are described as 'innocent' passing off, in circumstances where this term is used to indicate non-fraudulent, rather than completely innocent, behaviour. The decision in *Edward Young & Co. Ltd v S.S. Holt*[61] is instructive in this regard. Although it deals with an account of profits not an inquiry, the court discusses the meaning of 'innocence' in relation to passing off. To determine the date from which the account should run, the court found it was necessary to decide the date on which the defendant had 'known or could have been in a position to have known' about the plaintiff's mark. Quoting *Spalding*, where Lord Parker remarked that the 'complete innocence' of a party might be a reason for limiting the time from which an account should run, the court said that ' "innocence" is not synonymous with "ignorance". In certain circumstances a man may be ignorant but may not, within the meaning of that phrase, be completely innocent'.[62] Later in the same judgment, the court said that it did not acquit the defendant 'of a certain lack of care which I think he ought to have exercised'.[63] A defendant should therefore not be able to allege that he was innocent if he wilfully or recklessly failed to ascertain whether his actions could cause confusion or deception. This interpretation might explain the grant of an inquiry in *Baume*, where the defendants had clearly been aware of the plaintiff's mark for a considerable period.[64] 'Innocence' also ends once a defendant is made aware of the true position but then continues with his course of action. It is for this reason that, as stated in *Spalding*, at equity an account of profits was ordered from the time the defendants were given notice of proceedings, if they then failed to cease their actions.

The historical position that at common law dishonesty had to be proved, or alternatively at equity a discretion existed for the award of financial recompense, prevented a completely innocent defendant from suffering financial loss. To argue that dishonesty is no longer a requirement, but that damages should still be granted, is to remove all safeguards available to a defendant.

---

[60] *Draper*, Note 35 above, at 443; *Procea*, Note 55 above, at 220.
[61] (1948) 65 RPC 25 at 26.
[62] *Ibid.*
[63] *Ibid.*, at 28.
[64] *Baume*, Note 37 above, at 235.

Although *Kerly* feels that an inquiry may be granted in respect of innocent passing off,[65] Wadlow does not share this view. He submits that although the state of mind of a defendant is irrelevant for the existence of the action, with fraud not a component nor ignorance a defence,[66] innocence is a defence to an account of profits. He argues that it should also be a defence to an inquiry into damages, and that neither remedy should be available to a plaintiff until he has put the defendant on notice, that is, until after the passing off has ceased to be 'innocent'.[67]

The Edenwest Comparison of Trade Mark Infringement and Passing Off

In the final portion of the judgment, Blackburne J, dealing with the distinction between innocent passing off and innocent trade mark infringement, states that he cannot see why damages should not be equally recoverable, as the two wrongs are closely related and may arise from the same act.[68] This view is echoed by Hurdle in her analysis of this judgment: 'Mr Justice Blackburne's decision in *Gillette* is no doubt a sensible one treating trade mark infringement and passing off actions alike and breaking away from 19th century anomalies.'[69]

With respect, the fact that two distinct causes of action may result from a single act is no reason for the relief afforded to correspond—the same act can also give rise to criminal and civil liability. While it is submitted that the correctness of an award for an inquiry against an innocent trade mark infringer is not as clearcut as was assumed in *Edenwest*, such an award can at least be justified by the statutory nature of the right and the statutory provision for this relief.[70] No such justification exists in respect of passing off, and a defendant who was neither dishonest nor negligent should enjoy the 'anomalous' protection of the law which requires either dishonesty or grants the court a discretion in the award of damages.

South Africa

Before discussing the relevance of the *Edenwest* decision in South Africa, some background information is necessary. Roman-Dutch law is the foundation of South African common law and reference is still made to Roman authorities when clarity on a legal point is required. However, the periods of British rule in the country did not leave the legal system unaffected, and all areas of law show, to a greater or lesser extent, influences of English law.

In the field of damages, the existence of liability is largely determined by the substantive law which is Roman-Dutch in origin, while the quantification of damages has been greatly influenced by rules, concepts and terms derived from English law.[71] However, the terminology used to describe different forms of damages does not always correspond to that of English law. Although English terms were frequently used in early decisions, they did not always have the same meaning in South Africa. 'Special' and 'general' damages differ in meaning

---

[65] *Kerly*, Note 3 above, at 430.
[66] Wadlow, Note 42 above, at 200.
[67] *Ibid.*, at 491 to 492.
[68] *Edenwest*, Note 1 above, at 291.
[69] H. Hurdle, 'Has the meaning of 'innocence' been clarified in passing off cases?' 1994 October *Trademark World* 16 at 20.
[70] The justification for an award of damages in respect of trade mark infringement cannot be sought in the allegation that registration serves as notice to the world and that infringement can therefore never be innocent. *Spalding*, Note 8 above, at 261 pertinently states that in the absence of express statutory provision, registration does not serve as notice and no Trade Marks Act contains such a provision.
[71] H.J. Erasmus and J.J. Gauntlett, 'Damages', in W.A. Joubert, LAWSA Vol. 7 at 5.

in this jurisdiction, and although awards of nominal damages were regularly made until the early part of this century, this concept is foreign to Roman-Dutch principles. Such awards have rarely been reported since the 1930s.[72]

The South African equivalent of the English concept 'tort' is the delict. A delict is described as a wrong which can be redressed by civil proceedings. Damages for patrimonial loss suffered by the commission of a delict are recovered by the *actio legis Aquilae* or Aquilian action.[73] In contrast with the English situation where specific torts are recognised, each with their own requirements, all delicts share the same basic requirements, all delicts share the same basic requirements and conversely, if all these requirements are met, the act complained of will be viewed as a delict, despite the fact that it has not previously been recognised as such by the courts.[74] So too, Aquilian liability exists if the essential elements of conduct, wrongfulness, causation, fault and patrimonial loss are present.[75] The fault element, which is the most relevant for this article, can take the form of intention (*dolus*) or negligence (*culpa*). Intention is defined as the direction of the will at causing a particular consequence in the knowledge that it is wrongful, while a person is negligent if his conduct does not conform to the standard of care required by the law, namely, that of the reasonable man.[76]

A strong English influence pervades the field of intellectual property and English legislation has frequently been adopted wholesale in South Africa. However, the adoption of legislation which contains concepts foreign to the South African legal system has led to problems as regards pecuniary remedies. The remedy of an account of profits for trade mark infringement has been rejected by the South African courts.[77] Unlike the English position, where the grant of an inquiry is substantive relief which presupposes that any damages proved will be awarded to the plaintiff, the order of an inquiry in South Africa is interpreted as a procedural aid to investigate what damages can be proved by a plaintiff.[78] If damages are awarded by a South African court and an inquiry is ordered, the order will read that damages are due by the defendant, with a further order than an inquiry be held to determine the quantum thereof.

Bearing the above in mind, the *Edenwest* decision will be assessed in the light of South African legal principles.

The Trade Mark Position

No South African decision has been reported in which the position of an innocent trade mark infringer has been pertinently considered. However, in 1911 the Cape Provincial Division awarded an interdict (injunction) against an innocent infringer, but ordered the applicants to pay the taxed costs after the date on which the respondents offered to abandon use of the mark. Damages were not sought.[79] Again, in 1976, an interdict was awarded against a trade mark infringer although an inference of intentional copying was not made. However, a claim for damages was abandoned at the outset of the trial.[80] This dearth of authority is not surprising bearing in mind that no reported trade mark decision exists in which damages have been awarded for trade mark infringement *per se*.[81] The only deductions

---

[72] *Ibid.*, at 6 to 8.
[73] Hutchinson (ed), *Wille's Principles of South African Law*, 1991 (8th edn) ('*Wille*'), at 645 to 646.
[74] *Dun & Bradstreet (Pty) Ltd v SA Merchants Combined Credit Bureau (Cape) (Pty) Ltd* 1968 1 SA 209 C at 218.
[75] *Wille*, Note 73 above, at 647.
[76] *Ibid.*, at 651 to 652.
[77] *Montres Rolex SA v Kleynhans* 1985 1 SA 58 C at 66.
[78] *Berman Bros (Pty) Ltd v Sodastream Ltd* 1986 3 SA 209 A at 246.
[79] *Apollinaris Co. Ltd v Vasco Natural Mineral Water Co. Ltd* 1911 CPD 234 at 237.
[80] *Adidas Sportschuhfabriken Adi Dassler KG v Harry Walt & Co. (Pty) Ltd* 1976 1 SA 530 T at 540.
[81] C.K. Job, 'The infringement of trade-mark rights', in C. Visser (ed), *The New Law of Trade Marks and Designs*, 1995, at 27.

that can be drawn from these decisions are that innocence is not a defence against the grant of an interdict, and that, where an infringer acted innocently and attempted to rectify the position, the court may indicate its displeasure by a suitable costs order if a plaintiff nevertheless proceeds with litigation.

In the absence of specific judicial authority, the relevant legislation must be considered. Before the implementation of the 1993 Trade Marks Act in South Africa, where for the first time the various remedies available to a successful plaintiff are detailed, legislation was silent on the subject, except to provide that registration was a precondition for the institution of proceedings 'to prevent, or to recover damages for' infringement.[82] In accordance with the first suggested interpretation of the similar absence of stated remedies in British legislation, it could be argued that the statutory provision for the recovery of damages entitles the proprietor of a registered mark to an award of damages, irrespective of the defendant's guilt or innocence. However, when considering the 1963 Act, the South African courts have held that the failure of the legislature to make specific provision for various types of relief 'serves as an indication that the lawmaker never intended to alter the remedies available for infringement under our common law'.[83] At common law, infringement is viewed as a species of delict and the recovery of damage would be by way of an Aquilian action, for which fault, in the form of intent or negligence, is required. This view is strengthened by the South African courts' interpretation of the nature of other forms of statutory damages. Dealing with the award of damages in terms of the Designs Act 57 of 1967, the Appellate Division held that 'The measure of damages is not mentioned in the Act. Since the wrong is a species of delict, the measure will be delictual; ...'[84] Similarly, when considering the award of damages in terms of the Copyright Act 98 of 1978, the court held: '[t]he damages claimable under s 24(1) of the Act are ordinary delictual damages regulated by the common law.'[85] In the light of these decisions it is submitted that it is extremely unlikely, despite the similar legislative provisions, that a South African court will follow the British courts and award damages if infringement has been completely innocent, that is, neither intentional nor negligent. It also seems unlikely that the 1993 Act will be differently interpreted. Section 34(3) provides that, where a trade mark has been infringed 'the court *may* grant ... (c) damages ... (d) in lieu of damages, a reasonable royalty ...'.[86] Even if it could be argued that relief is now founded on some basis other than that of the common law delict, a court will hesitate to exercise the discretion provided by the Act contrary to basic common law principles.

Passing Off

Passing off is classified as a delict in South African law. The South African courts have held that, to obtain an interdict, the applicant need not show fault on the part of the respondent, and therefore neither intent nor negligence need be proved.[87] The reason given by the court is that if a person violates the rights of another, even innocently, the latter is entitled to take steps to prevent him from continuing to do so.[88] However, any action for damages is Aquilian

---

[82] Section 43 Trade Marks Act 62 of 1963; section 124 Trade Marks Act 9 of 1916.
[83] *Montres Rolex SA*, Note 77 above, at 66; see also G.E. Morley, C.E. Webster and G.C. Webster, 'Trade Marks', in W.A. Joubert, LAWSA Vol 29 at 120.
[84] *Omega Africa Plastics (Pty) Ltd v Swisstool Manufacturing Co. (Pty) Ltd* 1978 3 SA 465 A at 471.
[85] *Priority Records (Pty) Ltd v Ban-nab Radio and TV* 1988 2 SA 281 D at 292.
[86] *Emphasis added.*
[87] *Kenitex Africa (Pty) Ltd v Coverite (Pty) Ltd* 1967 3 SA 307 W at 309; *William Grant & Sons Ltd v Cape Wine & Distillers Ltd* 1990 3 SA 897 C at 920.
[88] *Kenitex, ibid.,* at 309.

in nature,[89] and all the requirements of Aquilian liability must be .met.[90] One of these requirements is fault, which can be met by proving either intent or negligence.[91] The South African courts have formulated the test for negligence as follows: 'It was enough for the appellant to prove negligence on the respondent's part ... coupled with objective foresight of a reasonable likelihood of deception or confusion with consequent impairment of the appellant's goodwill ...'.[92] Clearly, an innocent passing off will therefore never found an action for damages in South Africa as complete innocence presupposes the absence of fault in the form of intent or negligence.

Comparison between the Position in England and South Africa

As illustrated above, a claim for damages against an innocent infringer in respect of both trade mark infringement and passing off will be unsuccessful in South Africa. However, it is submitted that the majority of English decisions which are cited as authority for awards of damages against innocent infringers, would be decided in similar fashion in South Africa. This is because the South African legal system considers negligence as sufficient to meet the requirement of fault. In the majority of English decisions, the courts criticised the defendants' behaviour; in South Africa such behaviour would be viewed as negligent and therefore sufficiently blameworthy to justify an award of damages. The South African position is thus that a completely innocent defendant will not be liable for damages. However, a defendant cannot escape an award of damages by alleging that fraud or intention was not proved if his behaviour can be viewed as negligent in the specific circumstances.

Finally the position in other Commonwealth jurisdictions may be considered briefly to see whether *Edenwest* would be followed there.

Australia

Section 65 of the Australian Trade Marks Act of 1955 provides that a court may grant, at the option of the plaintiff, either damages or an account of profits against the infringer of a registered trade mark. The only reported decision which deals pertinently with the issue of innocent trade mark infringement is *Colbeam Palmer Ltd v Stock Affiliates Pty Ltd*.[93] The innocent defendant had, prior to trial, consented to an account of profits to run from the period after he received notice. Confirming that the remedy of accounts was only available after notice, the court held that an inquiry as to damages might be governed by different considerations, but pointed out that cases on the point were conflicting.[94] Textbook authors are also not in agreement. Some hold the view that damages may be awarded even for innocent infringement,[95] but there is also support for the view that only nominal damages may be awarded where a defendant has acted innocently.[96]

The question of whether damages can be awarded when passing off has occurred innocently has also not been pertinently dealt with by an Australian court. In a decision of 1929, the

---

[89] *Geary and Son (Pty) Ltd v Gove* 1964 1 SA 434 A at 440.

[90] *Dun & Bradstreet*, Note 74 above, at 218.

[91] H. Van Heerden and J. Neetling, *Unlawful Competition*, 1995, at 195.

[92] *Link Estates (Pty) Ltd v Rink Estates (Pty) Ltd*, 1979 2 SA 276 E at 281.

[93] 122 CLR 25.

[94] *Ibid.*, at 35.

[95] D.R Shanahan, *Australian Law of Trade Marks and Passing Off*, 1990 (2nd edn), at 359; J. McKeough and A. Stewart, *Intellectual Property in Australia*, 1991, at 35.

[96] S. Ricketson, *The Law of Intellectual Property*, 1984, at 721.

High Court held that ' "fraud" for the purpose mentioned is not necessarily such as would support an action of deceit, but would be constituted by persistence after notice'.[97] Although this statement has been cited subsequently when dealing with claims for damages, it must be remembered that the 'purpose' referred to was the grant of an injunction, not the award of damages. In the 1960 decision of *Henderson v Radio Corporation Pty Ltd*, the High Court held as follows, referring to the period before the defendants became aware of the existence of the plaintiff: 'In respect of distribution before this time the defendant, as an innocent distributor, will not be made liable in damages.'[98] Interestingly *Spalding* is cited as authority for this statement. The subsequent full court decision did not deal with the issue, as it found that the claim for damages had not been established.[99] The full court, when discussing the nature of a passing off action, did however state that fraud was no longer an element of the action and that, after the Judicature Acts, the practice grew of awarding an account of profits or inquiry into damages where fraud was not proved.[100] This finding was based on an article by Morison, but the court omitted Morison's subsequent statement that 'the only question remaining is whether the defendant is liable in damages if he did not know and could not reasonably have known the circumstances which rendered confusion likely ... (T)he authorities at present appear to be opposed to the imposition of liability in such circumstances'.[101] In 1976 appellants before the High Court argued that a damages award could not be sustained because fraud was not sufficiently alleged or proved. The court found it unnecessary to decide the points as it found sufficient fraud in the appellants' persistence in the use of the offending name after notice of the likelihood of deception.[102] The *Henderson* decision was not referred to by the court and is also not referred to by textbook authors. While Shanahan states that substantial damages are not available for innocent passing off, and views it as unclear whether even nominal damages will be awarded,[103] Wadlow's interpretation of the *Turner* and *B.M. Auto Sales* decisions is that a plaintiff may only recover damages arising after notice has been given, if the conduct was originally innocent.[104] Wadlow's interpretation reflects the statutory position of section 68 of the Trade Marks Act, 1955, which provides that, where passing off has arisen from the use of a mark registered by the defendant, a court will not award damages if the defendant was unaware, and had no reasonable means of ascertaining, that the plaintiff's mark was in use, and immediately ceased use on receipt of this information.

Canada

The Canadian Trade Marks Act of 1952 gives the court a wide discretion to grant relief, providing in section 53 that, where any act has been done contrary to the Act, the court 'may make any such order as the circumstances require including provision for relief by way of injunction and the recovery of damages or profits ...'. The position of an innocent infringer of a registered mark has been considered once by a Canadian court. In *J.H. Munro Ltd v T. Eaton Co. Western Ltd* the court held that the plaintiff was only entitled to damages

---

[97] *Turner v General Motors (Australia) Pty Ltd* 42 CLR 352 at 362.
[98] (1969) RPC 218 at 229 (HC).
[99] (1969) RPC 230 at 236 (AC).
[100] *Henderson*, Note 99 above, at 237.
[101] W.L. Morison, 'Unfair competition and passing off', 1956 *Sydney Law Review* 50 at 55. Morison's view is thus that, while fraud is no longer an essential element, a completely innocent infringer will not be held liable for damages.
[102] *B.M. Auto Sales Pty Ltd v Budget Rent A Car System Pty Ltd* 12 ALR 363 at 371.
[103] Shanahan, Note 95 above, at 398; supported by Ricketson, Note 96 above, at 582.
[104] Wadlow, Note 95 above, at 492. His interpretation is shared by McKeough and Stewart, Note 95 above, at 284.

against an innocent infringer after notice, relying on *Slazenger* and *Ellen*.[105] While this would therefore appear to be the position in Canada, Fox criticises this decision and states that the judge misdirected himself, as *Spalding* was settled law on the point both in respect of passing off and trade mark infringement.[106] As Best says in her article, *Spalding* is a passing off case and Fox's criticism is therefore inconsistent.[107] Cairns is less definite than Fox on the position of the innocent infringer, merely stating that authorities on damages are very confused.[108]

No Canadian case on innocent passing off has been reported. Fox states that there is doubt whether more than nominal damages can be recovered, relying on English decisions[109] while Best refers to *dicta* in a Canadian decision to the effect that a court would have only awarded nominal damages if the defendant had been innocent.[110]

Conclusion

The post-*Edenwest* English position of innocent defendants has been assessed against the position in three Commonwealth jurisdictions. In South Africa, the *Edenwest* decision will not be followed. The Australian and Canadian legal systems, unlike South Africa, share the English common law background. However, no court in either of these jurisdictions has pertinently held that an innocent defendant is liable for damages in respect of trade mark infringement or passing off, and *dicta* by the courts seem to indicate that they would be loath to reach such a decision. Textbook writers in these jurisdictions who argue that an innocent defendant is liable for damages at least in respect of infringement rely on the same authority as cited by *Kerly*.

One Australian view is that damages are not available until a defendant is given notice of a plaintiff's rights.[111] In Canada, Best goes a step further by submitting that, despite notice, a defendant should not be liable for damages if he reasonably believes that he is entitled to use the mark concerned.[112] In South Africa, damages will not be awarded unless a defendant acts intentionally or negligently. All these viewpoints, despite their differing origin, have one thing in common: complete innocence on the part of a defendant will protect him against an award of damages in both trade mark and passing off proceedings.

Compliance with intellectual property legislation is of vital importance in the light of burgeoning infringement and counterfeiting worldwide. Existing remedies require strict enforcement to show that interference with intellectual property rights will not be sanctioned. However, such action is necessary against persons who appropriate the fruits of another's labour, not against persons who act in innocence of the rights of another. it is to be regretted if, in the birthplace of equity, other courts follow the *Edenwest* decision and penalise a defendant who has done nothing more than inadvertently choose the wrong mark at the wrong time.

---

[105] (1942) 2 Fox Pat C 204 at 227.
[106] H.G. Fox, *The Canadian Law of Trade Marks and Unfair Competition* 1972 (3rd edn), at 462.
[107] Best, Note 39 above, at 228.
[108] D. Cairns, *The Remedies for Trademark Infringement*, 1988, at 141.
[109] Fox, Note 106 above, at 648.
[110] Best, Note 39 above, at 225.
[111] See Note 104 above.
[112] Best, Note 39 above, at 235.

Index of Authors